Social Psychology in Sport

Sophia Jowett, PhD

David Lavallee, PhD

Loughborough University

Editors

HUMAN KINETICS

Library of Congress Cataloging-in-Publication Data

Jowett, Sophia, 1969-
Social psychology in sport / Sophia Jowett, David Lavallee.
    p. cm.
Includes bibliographical references and index.
ISBN-13: 978-0-7360-5780-6 (hard cover)
ISBN-10: 0-7360-5780-3 (hard cover)
1. Sports--Psychological aspects. 2. Social psychology. I. Lavallee, David, Ph. D. II. Title.
GV706.4.J69 2007
796.01--dc22

                2006008699

ISBN-10: 0-7360-5780-3
ISBN-13: 978-0-7360-5780-6

The Web addresses cited in this text were current as of July 2006, unless otherwise noted.

Acquisitions Editor: Myles Schrag; **Developmental Editor:** Christine M. Drews; **Assistant Editor:** Maureen Eckstein; **Copyeditor:** Alisha Jeddeloh; **Proofreader:** Erin Cler; **Indexer:** Gerry Lynn Messner; **Permission Manager:** Dalene Reeder; **Graphic Designer:** Nancy Rasmus; **Graphic Artist:** Yvonne Griffith; **Photo Manager:** Sarah Ritz; **Cover Designer:** Keith Blomberg; **Photographer (cover):** Warren Little/Getty Images; **Photographer (interior):** © Human Kinetics unless otherwise noted. **Art Manager:** Kelly Hendren; **Illustrator:** Al Wilborn; **Printer:** Sheriden Books

Printed in the United States of America

10 9 8 7 6 5 4 3 2 1

Human Kinetics
Web site: www.HumanKinetics.com
United States: Human Kinetics
P.O. Box 5076
Champaign, IL 61825-5076
800-747-4457
e-mail: humank@hkusa.com

Canada: Human Kinetics
475 Devonshire Road Unit 100
Windsor, ON N8Y 2L5
800-465-7301 (in Canada only)
e-mail: orders@hkcanada.com

Europe: Human Kinetics
107 Bradford Road
Stanningley
Leeds LS28 6AT, United Kingdom
+44 (0) 113 255 5665
e-mail: hk@hkeurope.com

Australia: Human Kinetics
57A Price Avenue
Lower Mitcham, South Australia 5062
08 8277 1555
e-mail: liaw@hkaustralia.com

New Zealand: Human Kinetics
Division of Sports Distributors NZ Ltd.
P.O. Box 300 226 Albany
North Shore City
Auckland
0064 9 448 1207
e-mail: info@humankinetics.co.nz

To our families for their continuous support

contents

foreword

In my first year as a doctoral student at Michigan State University in 1977, I took a course from Dan Gould titled Social Psychology of Sport, and we used a 180-page paperback text by Rainer Martens (1975), *Social Psychology and Physical Activity*. In my previous classes on psychology of motor behavior and sport, we used textbooks that combined topics in motor learning (e.g., attention processes, human perception) and in what eventually became sport psychology (e.g., motivation, social facilitation). Martens' text was a foreshadowing of advancements in the field and has culminated in the need for the present text. Not surprisingly, *Social Psychology in Sport* spans many more topics and pages than the one we used three decades ago.

Martens' book integrated relevant topics in mainstream social psychology with applications to sport settings—such as personality, social facilitation, observational learning, competition processes, social reinforcement, socialization, interpersonal competence, aggression, and attitudes. Shortly after that book was published, the first issue of *Journal of Sport Psychology* arrived in 1979, leading to an influx of studies on these and other topics (e.g., the study of attitudes led to self-conceptions and motivation; the study of social reinforcement led to coaching effectiveness; the study of interpersonal competence led to moral development and peer relationships). When journals such as *Journal of Applied Sport Psychology* and *The Sport Psychologist* were first published in 1987, it was only a matter of time before the knowledge base on social psychology expanded to meet the interest shown in applications to sport, exercise, and other physical activity contexts.

In *Social Psychology in Sport*, editors Jowett and Lavallee present a book that offers a comprehensive and contemporary view of the field, highlighting several key topics in social psychology similar to those of Martens in the 1970s. They define social psychology as the scientific investigation of how feelings, thoughts, and behaviors of individuals are influenced by the actual, imagined, or implied presence of others. By compiling knowledge on state-of-the-art theory and research on social relationships, group processes, environmental influences, and self-perceptions, the contributing authors offer a valuable perspective from which to view

present-day conceptualizations of social psychology of sport in the context of historical approaches. Professors, students, and practitioners alike will benefit from this anthology—one that spans theory, research, and practical implications.

Social Psychology in Sport is divided into five parts. Chapters include theoretical frameworks, empirical research, and practical applications, providing a complete cycle of theory-research-application that other sport psychology books often do not provide. This makes the book an essential resource for appreciating the historical context in which social psychology topics have evolved.

Part I, Relationships in Sport, begins with three chapters on coach–athlete processes that highlight approaches such as social exchange, interdependence, and relational-cultural theories. These perspectives, presented by Jowett, Poczwardowski, and LaVoi, respectively, provide an alternative lens through which to view coaching behaviors, athlete behaviors, and psychosocial outcomes. In chapter 4, Youth Peer Relationships in Sport, Smith shifts focus to group acceptance and friendship processes and explores why such processes are essential research areas in sport contexts.

Part II presents chapters on Coach Leadership and Group Dynamics. In chapter 5 Riemer provides a historical context in which theories in social psychology laid the foundation for the multidimensional model of leadership. In chapter 6 Smith and Smoll emphasize athletes' interpretations of coaching behaviors as mediators of the relationship between leadership and athlete outcomes. In chapter 7 Carron, Eys, and Burke examine leaders' behaviors and teammates' normative beliefs as sources of variation in team cohesiveness. I am pleased to see chapter 8 on social facilitation by Jones, Bray, and Lavallee, as audience effects on athletic performance is a topic from the early days of social psychology research. This topic is relevant today in the understanding of skill performance and the advantages and disadvantages of playing competitions at home and at venues away from home.

Part III, Motivational Climate, is viewed within achievement goal theories. In recent years, considerable work has examined social contextual factors in physical activity settings that enhance or hinder self-perceptions, emotional responses, and motivational processes. The three chapters focus on coaches, parents, and peers in terms of the atmosphere created through expressing achievement beliefs and behaviors to participants. Chapter 9, Coach-Created Motivational Climate (Duda and Balaguer), is compatible with other chapters on coach–athlete relationships, just as chapter 11, Peer-Created Motivational Climate (Ntoumanis, Vazou, and Duda) is compatible with Smith's chapter on youth peer relationships.

Part IV, Key Social and Cognitive Processes in Sport, highlights self-concept, self-efficacy, person perception, and self-presentational processes. In chapter 12 Marsh reviews models of self-conceptions, measurement issues, and self-concept as a predictor and outcome variable. In chapter 13 Beauchamp extends knowledge about predictors and outcomes of individual efficacy to role efficacy and collective efficacy within teams. In chapter 14 Greenlees reviews person perception (i.e., our impressions of others) and provides an intriguing model for understanding processes for forming and modifying such perceptions. In chapter 15 Maddison and Prapavessis explore impression management processes with a focus on self-handicapping strategies. In addition to these important social-cognitive topics, readers will recognize that observational learning, competition, and motivation processes are powerful sources of social influence on cognitions, emotions, and behaviors in sport contexts.

Part V, The Athlete in the Wider Sport Environment, covers a range of topics that mesh well with those in previous chapters. In chapter 16 Rees reviews theory and research on social support processes, including sources, dimensions, and measurement. In chapter 17 Wylleman, De Knop, Verdet, and Cecic-Erpic discuss parental influence in the transitions of elite athletes. In chapter 18 Vallerand and Miquelon write about passion, defined as high-priority goals with emotionally important outcomes. In chapter 19 Kavussanu reviews moral development research. In chapter 20 Si and Lee address how cross-cultural factors such as race, ethnicity, and culture affect thoughts, emotions, and actions in sport settings. Researchers and practitioners must consider variations in cognitions, emotions, motivation, and behaviors within the social contexts in which they occur.

Social Psychology in Sport is a unique book addressing a range of salient topics from theoretical, empirical, and applied perspectives. I enjoyed the historically relevant topics (social facilitation, group dynamics, and peer relationships) as well as the emerging topics (relational efficacy, passion, and cross-cultural issues). Chapters include real-life examples from sport to embellish a conceptual point, strong ideas for inspiring future research, and studies within *and* outside social psychology. As the study of social psychology in sport has become more complex, topics have become more integrated. As such, readers have the option of reading chapters as they are currently ordered or combining chapters to put the puzzle pieces together (coach–athlete relationships and leadership, peer relationships and peer climate, group cohesion and group efficacy). Each chapter stands on its own in covering theory, research, and application, allowing instructors and readers to choose their own paths for pursuing knowledge.

Social Psychology in Sport is an important contribution to the knowledge base on social psychological perspectives in physical activity contexts. It is an essential resource for professors teaching courses, educators doing research, students exploring dissertation topics, and practitioners making the link between research and application. It is simply amazing to compare where we were 30 years ago with Martens' book and where we are today. Jowett and Lavallee are commended for pulling together such a comprehensive book. Its impact will likely be felt in a version of *Social Psychology in Sport* 30 years from now.

Maureen R. Weiss, PhD
Curry School of Education
University of Virginia

preface

The idea for this book came from a realization that social psychology in sport settings has expanded impressively, especially over the last decade, yet no single textbook was available that focused on topics with a social-psychological underpinning. *Social Psychology in Sport* brings together the latest thinking of some of the most active and influential researchers in diverse areas such as social interaction, social relationships, social influences, and social perceptions.

Topics such as motivational climate, coach leadership, and group dynamics have historically attracted the interest of many researchers; on the other hand, topics such as social cognition, social support, and social relationships in sport remain less researched. This book demonstrates that established topics have grown bigger while new topics have grown stronger or have shown great potential to inform our understanding of the social-psychological aspect of sport. It is evident that the study of social issues in sport psychology has grown quickly (and predictably) because scholars have communicated with one another and stepped outside the confines of their own discipline. The growth of this study is extraordinarily lively, and this book aims to fuel more research interest and energy and make a mark in the wider social psychological community.

Bringing together diverse yet interconnected topics from distinct contributors who offer breadth and richness as well as creative new thinking provides a unique opportunity for everyone interested in these topics to learn about the state of scientific study of psychosocial issues in sport. The result is a volume likely to be indispensable to anyone interested in social psychology in sport settings. At the very least, we hope that this volume provides a valuable resource for researchers, students, and practitioners in relevant courses and fields (e.g., social psychology, sport psychology, coaching). At best, we hope that the text provides an impetus for the creation of more courses that focus on psychosocial aspects in sport around the world and the creation of interesting and interdisciplinary social psychology research in sport settings.

What Is Social Psychology?

Social psychology has been defined as the scientific investigation of how the feelings, thoughts, and behaviors of individuals are influenced by the actual, imagined, or implied presence of others. Social psychologists are interested in explaining human social behavior as well as feelings, thoughts, beliefs, attitudes, intentions, and goals. Overt behavior can be objectively measured, while unobservable processes such as thoughts and feelings can be inferred from behavior. Unobservable processes such as thoughts and feelings are crucial because they may affect or directly determine overt behavior. What makes social psychology *social* is that it deals with how people are *influenced* by other people who are physically present or who are imagined or implied to be present.

Social psychology employs scientific methods to construct and test theories in a systematic and organized way. Social psychology contains numerous and rather abstract concepts such as leadership, relationships, motivation, and self-concept that explain social behavior. These concepts are described and explained by theories (sets of interrelated constructs and principles) developed by social psychologists to make better sense of social behavior. Social-psychological theories are developed through the generation of data or from previous theories. Then empirical research is conducted in which data are collected to test the theory. Overall, this book sees social psychology as the scientific study of the way individuals think, feel, and behave in social situations.

Topics of Social Psychology in Sport

Another way to define social psychology in sport is in terms of what sport psychologists or social psychologists study. Thus, social psychology in sport can be defined by the contents of this volume. A look at the table of contents provides a sense of the scope of social psychology in sport settings. As this volume reveals, contemporary sport psychologists study a wide range of topics including social relationships, communication, coach leadership, team cohesion, motivation and motivational climate, self-presentation, person perception, efficacy beliefs, self-concept, audience effects, social support, parenting, morality, and passion in sport. Such social-psychological topics relate with other disciplines and subdisciplines (e.g., cognitive psychology, individual psychology, family psychology, relationship psychology, educational psychology, sociology, social anthropology, language, communication). However, what makes social psychology in the context of sport distinct is a combination of three elements:

- *What* is studied (e.g., theories and hypothesis formation)
- *How* it is studied (e.g., quantitative versus qualitative methods)
- What *level of explanation* is sought (e.g., intrapersonal versus interpersonal and type of data analysis)

Each chapter of this volume contains information relevant to these elements.

Organization of This Volume

The organization of this book offers readers an opportunity to consider one or more topics in isolation should they so choose. Thus, it is not essential to read the text from beginning to end. The chapters are cross-referenced so that, with a few exceptions, chapters or parts of chapters can be read independently in almost any order. Each chapter is devoted to an important social-psychological topic and is presented with the necessary breadth and depth.

Chapters in this volume share five characteristics. First, they provide clear descriptions and definitions of the topic. Second, the majority of the chapters present concise theoretical overviews that focus on the topic of interest alongside a discussion of existing programs of research. Third, the chapters introduce an array of new empirical research ideas and previously unstated or untested theoretical connections. Fourth, the chapters offer a discussion on practical applications of the research conducted thus far and applications that may be generated by future research. Fifth, all chapters conclude with a summary of what has been discussed. Educational features designed to promote pedagogy are also included. For example, each chapter includes learning objectives and discussion questions.

The chapters are organized into five interrelated parts. Part I contains chapters that focus on social relationships and processes between coaches and athletes and between peers (i.e., athletes and athletes). The first two chapters deal with the concept of the coach–athlete relationship, and theoretical and methodological issues are discussed. The issues raised provide food for thought by opening avenues for research that is systematic and scientific. The chapter on coach–athlete communication and conflict brings forth two interpersonal constructs that undergird relationship stability and change processes. The final chapter looks at the role of peer relationships, particularly in youth sport.

Part II contains chapters focusing on coach leadership and group dynamics. In-depth treatments of the role of coach leadership in promoting (or inhibiting) athletes' performance, satisfaction, and self-esteem are provided, along with chapters focusing on team cohesiveness and the mechanisms by which audiences affect sport performers and teams.

Part III takes stock of the preceding chapters and sets out an agenda for understanding coach–athlete interactions as well as athlete–parent interactions and peer dynamics by applying principles of achievement goal theory. The three chapters in this part explain how the motivational climate created by coaches, parents, and peers affects sport performers' cognitive, affective, and behavioral aspects.

In part IV, we turn toward cognitive and personality factors that describe social behavior. The manner in which self-concept, efficacy beliefs, person perception, and self-handicapping affect and are affected by others in the social context of sport provides insight into the complexities and processes of studying social behavior.

Part V, the final part of the book, explores topics that have generated interest in social psychology in sport settings because of their intuitively appealing nature. Social support, parenting, passion, morality, and cultural issues connect, or even elaborate conceptually, the topics previously discussed (e.g., relationships, leadership, motivational climate).

It is with great pleasure that we present *Social Psychology in Sport*, a comprehensive yet very readable volume that is both empirically and practically oriented. This volume has been written specifically for students in upper-undergraduate and graduate courses, as well as researchers interested in the psychosocial aspects of sport. Consequently, we are grateful to any among you who might take the time to throw yourself into *Social Psychology in Sport* and share your reactions with us.

acknowledgments

It is with great appreciation that we thank the following people for playing central roles in the completion of what we thought to be an ambitious project. First we would like to thank the authors of these chapters, who produced thoughtful, relevant, and timely contributions, who not only met our rigid deadlines, but also revised their chapters—often substantially—in light of our suggestions. We are also grateful to Myles Schrag of Human Kinetics, who was always ready to help at each juncture, to share our excitement as new ideas came along, and to serve as a facilitator of this volume coming to fruition. In addition, acknowledgments are extended to Chris Drews for her meticulous work as developmental editor, Dalene Reeder and John Laskowski for their assistance with permissions, Alisha Jeddeloh for her work as copyeditor, as well as Maureen Eckstein (assistant editor), Nancy Rasmus (graphic designer), and Yvonne Griffith (graphic artist). We also would like to thank our colleagues at Loughborough University, Stuart Biddle, Chris Harwood, and Christopher Spray, for their support during the production of this text. Finally, we thank our spouses, Peter Jowett and Ruth Lavallee, for supporting us consistently throughout this most rewarding project.

part I

Relationships in Sport

Relationships form a central part of one's life. The saying "No man is an island" attests to the social character of our being and becoming. Although the expansion of general relationship research over the last 20 years is phenomenal, relationship-specific theory and research as it pertains to the sport context is gathering momentum. This volume begins with four chapters that highlight the interest, progress, and potential associated with this area. Two specific relationship types are addressed: coach–athlete relationships and peer relationships.

In chapter 1, Sophia Jowett and Artur Poczwardowski consider the coach–athlete relationship from a conceptual perspective. Jowett and Poczwardowski highlight the importance of precisely defining the coach–athlete relationship and introduce a taxonomy that describes the relationship in terms of their prizewinning and caring characteristics. An integrated research model that emanates from recent conceptualization of the coach–athlete relationship is offered as a medium for generating systematic, comprehensive, empirically grounded knowledge for coaches, athletes, parents, practitioners, and policy makers. The final sections on future research and practical implications underline the complexities and substance of this topic.

In chapter 2, Sophia Jowett begins by discussing the interdependent nature of coach–athlete relationships as has been viewed through the lenses of asymmetry, power and control, and parent-child relationships. Jowett proposes the application of a theoretical model to fully understand the interdependent nature of coach–athlete relationships. Principles of inter-dependence theory are presented and the notion of interdependence is operationalized through the constructs of closeness, commitment, complementarity, and co-orientation. Future research directions that follow reflect the enormous scope of this theoretical model. She concludes by highlighting practical implications related to the impact of prosocial interactions in repairing dysfunctional coach–athlete relationships.

In chapter 3, Nicole LaVoi focuses on two vital factors that affect the quality of coach–athlete relationships: interpersonal communication and conflict. Definitional and theoretical issues related to communication and conflict are developed and applied to the context of the coach–athlete relationship. LaVoi presents research that addresses these vital factors and reflects on their limited theoretical and empirical breadth and depth. She discusses how effective communication can assist in managing and resolving conflict and proposes relational expertise as a set of skills that has the potential to produce positive outcomes for the athlete and the coach.

In chapter 4, Alan Smith provides a comprehensive review of the theory and research related to peer relationships, particularly those in youth sport. By summarizing conceptual and operational issues of this topic, Smith provides a platform from which the theoretical frameworks of interpersonal theory of psychiatry and attachment theory are proposed to guide empirical endeavors. Smith explains the significance of research on peer relationships in the context of youth sport and discusses the current state of knowledge. He concludes that sport matters to peer relationships and proposes future research directions in this topic.

chapter 1

Understanding the Coach–Athlete Relationship

Sophia Jowett, PhD, and Artur Poczwardowski, PhD

Learning Objectives

On completion of this chapter, the reader should have

1. knowledge of major definitional dimensions in coach–athlete relationships;

2. understanding of the critical link between theory and research and the possibilities for basic and applied research;

3. knowledge of current conceptual models of coach–athlete relationships;

4. familiarity with the application of an integrated conceptual model in accelerating research on coach–athlete relationships;

5. understanding of the importance of a dependable knowledge base for analyzing coach–athlete dyads in sport; and

6. knowledge of problems related to the study of coach–athlete relationships.

© Associated Press

Coaches and athletes often form relationships, alliances, or partnerships through which instruction, guidance, and support are provided to the athlete. In reflecting on athletic success, sport directors and managers, the media, and coaches and athletes themselves have directed public attention to the significance of the coach–athlete relationship. Mutual trust, respect, belief, support, cooperation, communication, and understanding are considered among the most important relationship components that contribute to performance success and satisfaction (e.g., Jowett & Cockerill, 2003; Poczwardowski, Henschen, & Barott, 2002; Wylleman, 2000). In contrast, lack of trust, lack of respect, excessive dominance, and blind obedience as well as verbal, physical, and sexual exploitation are considered to be components that undermine coaches' and athletes' welfare (e.g., Burke, 2001; Jowett, 2003; Nielsen, 2001; Ogilvie, 1995).

Both *performance enhancement* as well as *psychological well-being* lie at the heart of the coach–athlete relationship. Well-being has generally been viewed from either its hedonic characteristics of pleasure attainment as opposed to pain avoidance or from its more subtle eudemonic characteristics of self-realization (e.g., experiencing personal growth and development; see Waterman, 1993). The manner in which either a sole focus on performance enhancement or a combined focus on sport performance and psychological well-being promotes or thwarts coaches' and athletes' development are areas that have been recently explored (e.g., Miller & Kerr, 2002).

In order to develop a sound understanding of what makes coaches and athletes emphasize performance enhancement or psychological well-being in their partnership, scholars should attempt to fully understand the predictive and explanatory functions of the coach–athlete relationship. To that end, the content of the relationship must be described and classified. The aim of this chapter is to explore the possibilities for advancing the study of coach–athlete relationships by building on the existing knowledge. More specifically, the coach–athlete relationship as a psychological concept will be defined as we highlight its pivotal role in athletes' growth and development. Critical issues surrounding research, theory, and practice will be discussed and an overview of recently developed conceptual models will be offered. Finally, the presentation of a research model will provide an opportunity to integrate current thinking on coach–athlete relationships.

Coach–Athlete Relationship Defined

The question "What is a coach–athlete relationship?" is a central issue to both researchers and practitioners in sport psychology. Questions like this help us understand what is involved in a psychosocial phenomenon under investigation. They help us clearly and unambiguously define the *problem* and its boundary conditions. They help us identify the broad spectrum of issues and the processes involved. A definition of the coach–athlete relationship needs to be both sufficiently general in order to contain all facets of the phenomenon but also specific enough to permit rigorous testing and to be of practical use.

In this chapter, the coach–athlete relationship is broadly defined as a situation in which a coach's and an athlete's cognitions, feelings, and behaviors are mutually and causally interrelated (e.g., Jowett & Cockerill, 2002; Jowett, Paull, & Pensgaard, 2005; Poczwardowski, Henschen, & Barott, 2002; see also chapter 2). According to this definition, a relationship is dynamic and therefore may be viewed as a state. Its nature is expected to change over time in response to the dynamic quality of human cognitions, emotions, and behavior shaped through the interaction of the relationship members. In turn, the state in which the content and nature of the relationship resides is determined by the combined interrelating of coaches' and athletes' thoughts, feelings, and behaviors.

For example, a gymnast who is committed and trusts her coach (cognitions and feelings) is likely to respond to the coach's instructions more readily (behavior). In turn, encouraged by the commitment, trust, and responsiveness of the athlete, the coach feels compelled to reciprocate these sentiments by showing a greater interest in the gymnast as an athlete and person. In this example, the relationship outcomes are positive because the coach is in a good position to nurture the athlete's potential. This scenario would be very different, however, if the athlete or the coach were less committed, less trusting, and less cooperative. Consequently, the coach–athlete relationship is characterized by high levels of interdependence that can have positive or negative ramifications depending on how interdependence is experienced (see chapter 2).

Motivations for Initiating and Maintaining a Coach–Athlete Relationship

We would like to argue that the motives for initiating and maintaining a coach–athlete relationship include an attempt to achieve (a) athletic excellence on the part of the athlete and professional excellence on the part of the coach and (b) personal growth on the part of the athlete and coach (see Jowett, 2005; Miller & Kerr, 2002). These motives or objectives shape the quality of the coach–athlete relationship and its outcomes, which might include stability and harmony. For example, consider a coach–athlete dyad that focuses primarily on achieving performance success. In this dyad, a harmonious coach–athlete partnership is based on whether the coach and athlete have reached a level of normative performance success (e.g., a gold medal in world championships). In contrast, another dyad may assess the outcomes of the athletic partnership based on whether it has met the coach's and the athlete's needs for personal growth and development, such as the needs for empathy, confidence, responsibility, and leadership development. This distinction is crucial in understanding how athletes and coaches define the quality of their relationship in terms of effectiveness or success.

Jowett (2005) has stated that coach–athlete relationships can be loosely described on two interrelated dimensions: (1) prizewinning relationships (with two subdimensions, successful and unsuccessful), and (2) helpful, caring relationships (with two subdimensions, effective and ineffective) (see figure 1.1). These characteristics are organized in a 2×2 taxonomy: (1) effective and successful relationships (E-S), (2) effective and unsuccessful relationships (E-U), (3) ineffective and successful relationships (I-S), and (4) ineffective and unsuccessful relationships (I-U). Examples for each category are discussed next.

Effective and Successful (E-S) and Effective and Unsuccessful (E-U) Relationships

A coach–athlete relationship that contains elements of success and effectiveness (E-S) is the ideal athletic relationship because it includes both performance success, as reflected in improving skill or achieving success, and personal growth, as reflected in experiencing a sense of maturity and satisfaction. An example of this type of relationship is Michael Phelps and Bob Bowman. Bowman began coaching Phelps in swimming when Phelps was 11 years old, and at the 2004 Olympic Games in Athens, he helped Phelps at age 19 to become the first American to win eight medals (six of which happened to be gold). Bowman, 39, has reported in the media that their partnership is a close one, and his role as a coach has extended to being a friend, confidant, counselor, and exemplar (Ruane, 2004). This partnership can be described as exceptional because, according to Phelps, his coach knew him better than anyone aside from his mother, and it was his coach who has made him the swimmer he is. Bowman has made Phelps one of the most talked-about swimmers in a generation, carefully crafting the exquisite system that is Phelps' body and mind and overseeing the athlete's development from child to man.

An effective yet unsuccessful (E-U) coach–athlete relationship, on the other hand, will invariably have some positive outcomes for the athlete and the coach in terms of psychological health and well-being, but these outcomes do not extend to performance. These relationships are often found in youth sport programs where the underlying philosophy is (or should be) to be the best that you can be—that is, to partake in sport for the pleasure it provides. Here, the emphasis is on personal growth and development.

Ineffective and Unsuccessful (I-U) and Ineffective and Successful (I-S) Relationships

Ineffective and unsuccessful (I-U) relationships as well as ineffective yet successful (I-S) relationships are psychologically unfavorable because the costs of dissatisfaction, disappointment, frustration, sadness, and loneliness outweigh the rewards even when the relationship is successful. The early stages of these athletic partnerships are often characterized by mutual positive regard, but this relationship quality is not enduring. Negative relational components such as conflict, tension, disagreement, and exploitation change its potentially positive character to a state of disregard, disrespect, and disintegration.

Helpful/caring

		Effective	Ineffective
Prizewinning	Successful	Effective and successful (E-S)	Ineffective and successful (I-S)
	Unsuccessful	Effective and unsuccessful (E-U)	Ineffective and unsuccessful (I-U)

Figure 1.1 The motivational nature of coach–athlete relationships: A 2×2 taxonomy.

Examples of successful yet ineffective relationships are not so difficult to uncover in the sport field. Consider the relationship between football (soccer) coach Alex Ferguson and one of his finest players, David Beckham. This successful but ineffective coach-athlete partnership went through a multiplicity of unpleasant events. Beckham reported in the media that he had grown out of the relationship originally established between him and his coach; he further reported that his coach failed to see him as a man who was strong enough to stand up and handle things (retrieved September 16, 2003, from www.channel4.com/news/2003/04/week_3/24_beck.html). Ultimately, in such situations of conflict there are two routes: either repair the relationship or break it up. The latter was the choice of this dyadic partnership, and they parted each other's company in spring of 2003.

Another vivid example of this type of relationship is that between Renald Knysh and gymnast Olga Korbut. Their partnership started when Korbut was 11. Knysh has been described as a modest, quiet man and a boldly innovative coach. According to Knysh, relations with his athlete were not easy. Korbut had a stubborn streak, and Knysh had to keep convincing her that success only comes with a tremendous amount of hard work. Although Korbut had described her coach as a tough taskmaster who helped her achieve success, in 1999 she accused him of forcing her to have sex with him; Knysh denied the accusation (retrieved September 16, 2003, from http://news.bbc.co.uk/sport1/hi/other_sports/1512051.stm [television broadcast]). Such anecdotes underline the fact that the coach-athlete relationship has a unique nurturing role and any actions that exploit either member undermine the trust that is implicit in the relationship.

The 2×2 taxonomy contains implicit interpersonal properties of the coach-athlete relationship, such as

- affective properties (e.g., trust vs. distrust, respect vs. disrespect, liking vs. disliking),
- cognitive properties (e.g., expecting the relationship to last over time as opposed to terminating shortly), and
- behavioral properties (e.g., dominant vs. submissive, friendly vs. hostile).

The content and quality of affective, cognitive, and behavioral interpersonal properties reflect on the overall quality of the coach-athlete relationship. An important aspect to consider is that although successful coach-athlete relationships may appear to be outstanding and admirable, closer inspection may reveal an adverse interpersonal profile. Athletic success should not be a measure of harmonious, stable, and satisfying relationships because unsuccessful coach-athlete

Should sport *success* be a measure of harmonious, stable, and satisfying coach-athlete relationships?

relationships may prove more valuable than successful relationships when the unsuccessful relationships are effective.

Importance of Studying Coach-Athlete Relationships

The significance of studying the interpersonal dynamics between coaches and their athletes lies to a great extent in its practical applications. The study of the coach-athlete relationship provides ample opportunity to help people manage their interpersonal exchanges more effectively. Problems that confront the sport community such as coach-athlete conflict, parental overinvolvement, lack of support, depression, loneliness, dropout from sport at a young age, aggression, and power struggles are fundamentally interpersonal. These are just a few of the issues that applied researchers could focus on in an attempt to provide valuable guidance. Kenny (1995) stated that "society has an interest in preventing destructive relationships, and we [social scientists] are the people who are best equipped to assist society in this endeavor" (p. 598). The call for more research in this area is motivated by the need for a systematic, comprehensive, and empirically grounded body of knowledge that also contains practical implications for coaches, athletes, parents, practitioners, and policy makers (e.g., sport administrators) in the next decade.

Researchers who focus on this relatively new field should not lose sight of the critical link between theory and research. Hunches based on background knowledge, personal experience, or casual observations that link to theory about social behavior can lead to the formation of theory-bound hypotheses that, in turn, lead to either increasing or decreasing the confidence one can place in the selected theory. Theoretical or conceptual frameworks guide research and establish a dependable and well-organized knowledge base for understanding and analyzing coach–athlete relationships.

Whether one pursues basic research or applied research, theory is important. Basic research refers to studies that examine central mechanisms and processes of coach–athlete relationships. For example, sorting out competing explanations of the effect of closeness on relationship outcomes is an important theoretical issue, but its resolution would add little in the way of intervention benefits over and above the benefits of closeness itself. Although basic research is only minimally concerned with the applied potential of the findings, Reis (2002) has suggested that it does illuminate possibilities of effective application. Applied research, on the other hand, refers to studies that explicitly aim to bring about change in relationships, such as testing the effects of a particular intervention designed to enhance the quality of the coach–athlete relationship, delivering and refining an intervention known to be effective, or identifying the factors that give rise to certain relationship outcomes (e.g., stability and harmony). The value of both basic and applied research lies in the importance of the problem explored and, in turn, in the importance of the answers that exploration of the problem generates.

There is a rich history of interaction between theory and empirical research, though it has been acknowledged that applied research has weaker associations with theory (Bradbury, 2002). Theory and empirical research can fuel each other, complement each other, and even correct each other; thus, theory and empirical research coexist in some useful relation (Muehlhoff & Wood, 2002). To illustrate this with an example, if the aim of research is to improve the coach–athlete relationship by outlining the life cycle or trajectory of the relationship from junior to senior sport, it would be sensible to consult theories that focus on developmental concerns such as relationship evolution, change, or survival. Consulting these theories involves reaching out to domains other than sport sciences (e.g., sport psychology and sociology of sport) to close scientific neighbors such as social anthropology, sociology, communication, organizational psychology, and individual and cognitive psychology (see Poczwardowski, Barott, & Jowett, 2006).

Sport psychology has traditionally examined coach–athlete interpersonal dynamics mainly from a leadership approach (e.g., Chelladurai, 1990; Smoll & Smith, 1989; see also chapters 5 and 6). However,

more recently relationship models and other related approaches have been presented (see Conroy & Coatsworth, 2004, for a representational model of others and self; see Mageau & Vallerand, 2003, for a motivational model of coach–athlete relationships). These attempts place the *relationship* as the focal point of investigation into the interpersonal dynamics of the coach and the athlete. The discussion that follows aims to critically and succinctly outline recent conceptualizations that have explicitly targeted coach–athlete relationships and to propose an integrated model for research on coach–athlete relationships.

Recent Conceptualizations of the Coach–Athlete Relationship

In less than half a decade, sport psychology has enjoyed the development of at least four models in an attempt to delineate the social phenomenon of the coach–athlete relationship by drawing specific assumptions and clarifying what is and is not known about it. The relationship models that will be discussed argue the importance of focusing on the components (i.e., content) of the relationship between the coach and the athlete and on incorporating both the coach and the athlete in any investigation that studies relationship quality and processes. The conceptualizations favor data analyses, interpretations, speculations, and conclusions that consider simultaneously both the coach's and the athlete's perceptions, yielding a more complete picture of the complex dynamics involved. Furthermore, these conceptual models employ diverse methodologies that suit the nature of the problem under study (see Poczwardowski et al., 2006). The conceptual models that will be outlined next include (a) Wylleman (2000); (b) Jowett and colleagues (e.g., Jowett, 2005; Jowett & Ntoumanis, 2004); (c) LaVoi (2004); and (d) Poczwardowski and colleagues (Poczwardowski, 1997; Poczwardowski, Henschen, & Barott, 2002; Poczwardowski, Barott, & Peregoy, 2002).

Wylleman's Conceptual Model

Wylleman's (2000) conceptualization purports that the coach–athlete relationship can be defined based on the *behaviors* coaches and athletes manifest on the sport field. These interpersonal behaviors can be categorized along three dimensions: an acceptance-rejection dimension that describes a positive or negative attitude toward the relationship; a dominance-submission dimension that reflects a strong or weak position in the relationship; and a social-emotional dimension that refers to taking a social or a personal role in the relationship.

While heavily influenced from Kiesler's (1983) seminal work on interpersonal behaviors, according to Wylleman the conceptualization allows one to "operationalize the *complementarity* between individuals within a dyadic relationship" (p. 562). In this sense, athletes' complementary behaviors would attract responses from coaches that are reciprocal for behaviors that reflect the dominance–submission dimension, when, for example, an athlete's submission attracts the coach's dominance and a coach's submission attracts the athlete's dominance. Behaviors may also be correspondent; for example, correspondent behaviors reflecting the acceptance–rejection dimension include an athlete's acceptance attracting acceptance and an athlete's rejection attracting rejection.

The model is intuitively appealing because athletes' and coaches' reciprocation and correspondence of behaviors is likely to occur in the field of play. However, the model does not explain when, how, and why these behaviors are likely to occur. The salience, valence, and implications of interpersonal behaviors perceived and expressed by the coach and the athlete are also unknown. These and other questions await further exploration on conceptual, operational, empirical, and methodological grounds.

Jowett's Conceptual Model

A group of researchers led by Jowett (e.g., Jowett & Chaundy, 2004; Jowett & Clark-Carter, in press; Jowett & Cockerill, 2002, 2003; Jowett & Meek, 2000; Jowett & Ntoumanis, 2004; Jowett & Timson-Katchis, 2005; Olympiou, Jowett, & Duda, 2006) developed and studied an integrated model of the coach–athlete relationship that is influenced by principles from social exchange theory. The integrated model includes established interpersonal psychological constructs, namely, closeness (Berscheid, Snyder, & Omoto, 1989), commitment (Rosenblatt, 1977), complementarity (Kiesler, 1997), and co-orientation (Newcomb, 1953). (In social psychology, these constructs have traditionally been studied independently from one another.) The premise of the 3+1Cs conceptual model (Jowett, 2005; Jowett et al., 2005) is that coaches' and athletes' emotions, thoughts, and behaviors are causally and mutually interdependent. According to the 3+1Cs,

- *closeness* refers to the affective meanings that the athlete and coach ascribe to their relationship (e.g., trust, liking, respect),
- *commitment* is defined as the athlete's and coach's intention to maintain the athletic relationship and therefore maximize its outcomes,

- *complementarity* represents the athlete's and coach's corresponding behaviors of affiliation (e.g., athlete's friendly and responsive attitude is likely to elicit coach's friendly and responsive attitude), and reciprocal behaviors of dominance and submission (e.g., coach instructs and athlete executes), and
- *co-orientation* includes the athlete's and coach's interpersonal perceptions and reflects the degree to which they have established a common ground in their relationship.

The content and significance of closeness, co-orientation, and complementarity in the coach–athlete relationship have been extensively explored in qualitative research designs (see Jowett, 2003; Jowett & Cockerill, 2002; Jowett & Meek, 2000). More recently, all four constructs have attracted quantitative research designs (see Jowett & Chaundy, 2004; Jowett & Clark-Carter, in press; Olympiou et al., 2006). (See chapter 2 for details about the conceptualization and accompanied research.)

LaVoi's Conceptual Model

LaVoi (2004) attempts to depict in sport settings the manner to which the deep human need to belong and to feel close in relationships with others can result in personal gains. Her approach is based on psychological interpretations of relational-cultural theory (see Jordan, Kaplan, Miller, Stiver, & Surrey, 1991; Miller & Stiver, 1997). Evidence from developmental, educational, and social psychology that have used relational-cultural theory as an interpretive framework suggests that interpersonal relationships are formative in acquiring fundamental skills, qualities, and benefits such as language, motor behaviors, self-esteem, and healthy lifestyles. In sharp contrast, deprivations in interpersonal contacts lead to emotional problems and other maladjustments.

The relational-cultural view in sport psychology offers a paradigm shift from traditional theories that view human development as a means for achieving individuation, separation, and independence (LaVoi, 2004). According to the relational-cultural approach, psychological development is facilitated by interdependence, connection, and participation in growth-fostering relationships. When applied to coach–athlete relationships, this approach would focus on athletes achieving potentially higher levels of satisfaction and growth when optimally close or interdependent with their coach and their teammates. According to LaVoi, closeness and interdependence in the context of sport can be studied in terms of four qualities:

- Authenticity (a person's genuine self-expression in the relationship that is respectful of the partner)

- Engagement (commitment and responsiveness)

- Empowerment (being strengthened, encouraged, and inspired to be an active partner in the relationship)

- Ability to deal with difference and conflict (embracing and building on diversity to enhance the relationship)

LaVoi has further suggested a contextual approach that accounts for sociocultural norms and rules and has underlined the importance of studying both relationship members, thus both the coach and athlete are viewed as critical research considerations.

Poczwardowski's Conceptual Model

Poczwardowski and colleagues (Poczwardowski, 1997; Poczwardowski, Henschen, & Barott, 2002; Poczwardowski, Barott, & Peregoy, 2002) proposed a qualitative-interpretive framework to investigate the process and the context of coach–athlete dyads. Poczwardowski's (1997) qualitative investigation of coach–athlete dyads in a gymnastics team centered on interpersonal dynamics in the context of both the athlete and coach as members of a dyadic relationship and as members of a team. Thus, coaches' and athletes' personality traits, interpersonal needs, acts, and activities, as well as interpretation of interpersonal behaviors and meaning attached to the relationship as a whole, were thoroughly examined. Interpersonal variables that emerged from this fieldwork included relationship role, interpersonal interaction, relationship in terms of rewarding outcomes, negotiation, shared meaning, and types of relationships (see Poczwardowski, Barott, & Henschen, 2000, Poczwardowski, Henschen, & Barott, 2002; Poczwardowski, Henschen, & Barott, 1998, 2001).

The results of this study conceptualized the coach–athlete relationship as a recurring pattern of mutual care between the athlete and coach. Relationship-oriented activities and interactions were categorized as instructional or technical, including sport task and goals, and social-psychological or affective, including human needs and emotions. As a result, both sport- and non-sport-related issues within the dyad were postulated to be a subject of an ongoing, interrelated exchange in which behavioral (i.e., actions, interactions) and cognitive-affective (i.e., meaning and care) aspects were incorporated.

Other findings included a strong influence of the context on dyadic relationships. In particular, group dynamics such as formal and informal roles that the coaches and athletes played on the team influenced the dynamics of dyadic coach–athlete relationships. Additionally, the richness of the interview and observational data collected allowed the identification of three phases in the coach–athlete relationship: the (a) prerelationship (or recruiting) phase; (b) the relationship phase consisting of the initial, transition, productive, concluding, and after-eligibility stages; and (c) the postrelationship phase, which may be of two kinds, sentimental or extinct. Importantly, the study provided empirical evidence for the intuitive notion that coaches are influenced in the relationship as well as athletes, growing professionally and maturing personally.

Integrated Research Model

The sport-specific relationship models previously outlined have been offered as rudimentary frameworks to systematically study the interpersonal relationship that coaches and athletes develop in the course of their partnership. The conceptual models presented have derived deductively from well-established psychological theories, including interpersonal theory by Kiesler (1983, 1997), interdependence theory by Kelley and Thibaut (1978), and relational-cultural theory by Jordan and colleagues (1991).

A close inspection of the coach–athlete conceptual models and their main assumptions reveals several similarities. For example, LaVoi's (2004) application of relational-cultural theory to the coach–athlete relationship views closeness and connection as a major relationship quality for personal growth and development. In a similar vein, Jowett et al.'s (e.g., Jowett 2005; Jowett et al., 2005) model includes closeness, while Poczwardowski et al.'s (e.g., Poczwardowski, Henschen, & Barott, 2002) model includes care as one of the main components of coach–athlete relationships. Thus, despite the subtle conceptual differences between these models, both agree that a degree of interdependence (call it closeness, connectedness, or care) is important in the coach–athlete relationship. Furthermore, the conceptualizations put forward by Wylleman (2000), Poczwardowski et al., and Jowett et al. emphasize interpersonal behaviors of both reciprocity (e.g., a coach's friendly attitude attracts the athlete's friendly attitude) and correspondence (e.g., a coach's directive style attracts the athlete's accommodating style). Finally, another similarity can be located in the significance Poczwardowski et al.'s and Jowett et al.'s models place on coaches' and athletes' interpretations of relationship quality through *meanings* (or subjective experience) and through *interpersonal perceptions*.

The study of the coach–athlete relationship requires a clear and unambiguous definition, as proposed earlier in the chapter. We believe that if researchers employ a relationship definition, the study of coach–athlete relationships within sport psychology will benefit from more focused research and a consistent body of knowledge that could be readily accessed by practitioners. Thus, the intent here is to propose an integrated research model that illustrates coach–athlete relationships as part of various social phenomena (e.g., communication, conflict, team cohesion, personality) and to map a pathway for research within the relational context of coach–athlete relationships.

The integrated research model can be seen as layers of a cake (see figure 1.2). The first (top) layer includes antecedent variables such as athletes' and coaches' individual difference variables (e.g., age, gender, experience,

personality), wider social-cultural context (e.g., culturally defined norms, roles, rules, customs, expectations, values), and relationship characteristics (e.g., relationship type, duration).

These three classes of causal conditions are important because they determine the quality of the relationship. It is speculated that these variables are responsible for regularities in the interaction patterns of the coach–athlete relationship and the relationship's quality in general. The capacity to accurately and completely account for the causal antecedents of the coach–athlete relationship is a basic yet important task toward developing a coach–athlete relationship theory.

The second layer of the model delineates the quality (nature or content, features or components) of the

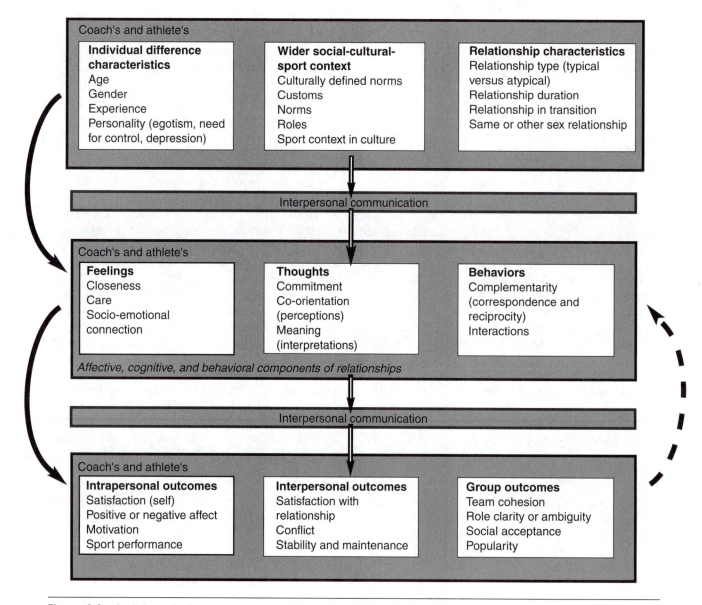

Figure 1.2   An integrated research model of coach–athlete relationships.

coach–athlete relationship. The main components of relationship quality include closeness (care or social-emotional features), commitment (intention to maintain and maximize the effectiveness of the relationship), co-orientation (interpersonal perception and subjective meaning), and complementarity (behavioral interactions that are reciprocal and corresponding).

As can be seen in figure 1.2, the second layer of the model is sandwiched between interpersonal communication. In effect, communication (verbal and nonverbal, intended and unintended, honest and dishonest) is a relational or interpersonal dimension that affects and is affected by the quality of the coach–athlete relationship. As Montgomery and Baxter (1998) have explained, communication can be viewed as the bridge between relationship members. In other words, communication is the process by which the distance between coaches and athletes broadens (coach and athlete become distant), narrows (they become close), and even merges (they become one). In effect, the quality and quantity of communication bring together or tear apart relationship members. Communication becomes the building block toward developing harmonious and stable coach–athlete relationships; in turn, the relationship affects the quality and quantity of communication (see chapter 3). For that reason, communication holds an important place in the model.

The third layer of the relationship model proposes a number of consequent or outcome variables. Three classes of such variables are identified: intrapersonal variables, interpersonal variables, and group-outcome variables. Intrapersonal variables include personal satisfaction (e.g., an athlete's or coach's satisfaction with performance, training, or instruction), sport performance accomplishments (e.g., athletes' personal best, the team's win–loss record), and coach and athlete motivation and burnout. Other intrapersonal outcomes can include an athlete's or a coach's health (e.g., mood, eating disorders). Interpersonal variables include satisfaction with the relationship and interpersonal conflict. Group outcomes involve such variables as athletes' and coaches' perceptions of team cohesion, role clarity, and perceptions of social acceptance or popularity.

The main layers of the model are interrelated. The model postulates that antecedent variables such as coaches' and athletes' gender, age, and experience affect the quality of the relationship, for example, in terms of the level of closeness or commitment experienced. It is also postulated that the central layer of the model, which represents the quality of the coach–athlete relationship, affects consequent variables. Therefore, a coach and an athlete who have formed a relationship based on respect and trust are more likely to experience positive feelings such as satisfaction and happiness as opposed to despair and distress. Finally, the model postulates that the second and third layers are reciprocally related; as such, the quality of the relationship affects and is affected by intrapersonal, interpersonal, and group outcomes.

The proposed integrated research model has the scope to provide an impetus for research that would help us fully understand the predictive and explanatory functions of this crucial relationship in sport. It should help us unearth the processes that regulate interpersonal components such as athletes' and coaches' feelings, thoughts, and behaviors; the role of communication as an antecedent and consequence of relationship quality; and the effects of the fundamental interpersonal components and processes on various outcomes. This endeavor may also shed light on how, when, and what makes coaches and athletes emphasize performance or psychological well-being through their relationship.

Future Research

In order to advance the study of interpersonal relationships in sport and more specifically coach–athlete relationships, attention to several issues in future research is required. Four issues are presented that are critical to advancing our knowledge of coach–athlete relationships: the needs for better samples, including more ethnically and culturally diverse populations; more descriptive research and more interdisciplinary research; causal analyses; and stronger inferences.

Better Samples

Sport psychology research generally employs undergraduate student samples due to convenience and limited resources. However, relationship research that employs undergraduate samples may derive principles that are misspecified. This could be true for coach–athlete relationship research unless we ensure that the phenomenon is elicited in the context (i.e., university sport) in which it is measured. Thus, caution is required, especially because many undergraduate students who participate in university sport or collegiate teams in Europe do not necessarily have formal training and instruction from qualified coaches. For example, athletic teams in Greek universities do not guarantee coaching sessions under the instruction of qualified coaches. The student-athletes themselves are often responsible for a team's organization, training, and competition. Frequency of interactions (how often training and competition take place) and longevity of the athletic relationship (how long the coach and the athlete have known and worked with one another) are also interrelated issues that can affect the representativeness of a sample. These are points that need to be specified in research studies in an attempt to minimize uncertainty about an undergraduate sample's representativeness in relationship research.

Another concern that is worthy of our attention is the relationship experiences of coaches and athletes that come from ethnic minorities and diverse cultures. Ethnic backgrounds of coaches and athletes and the sociocultural nature of the sport context, such as traditionally Western versus Eastern sports, may be thought of as potential moderators (variables that interact with the variables under study so as to modify their impact on the relationship quality). Yet ethnic backgrounds and sociocultural context may be influential in more fully accounting for coach–athlete relationships. Thus, basic and applied research that is designed to cut across cultural, subcultural, contextual, and content complexity is much needed.

More Description

Both basic and applied research involve description. Basic researchers incorporate descriptions in the design of a study in an attempt to pinpoint what to look for, where and when to find it, and how it compares to related concepts and phenomena. Basic researchers use quantitative descriptions (e.g., surveys) and qualitative descriptions (e.g., based on interviews, observations) in identifying problems for basic research. Applied researchers, on the other hand, include rich descriptions from relatively few subjects and many variables. Case studies and the use of interviews for data collection are valuable means for understanding relationships and the meanings that formulate these relationships. In the last decade, research on coach–athlete relationships has employed a qualitative approach to better understand the complex nature of the coach–athlete relational context (see e.g., Jowett & Cockerill, 2003; Poczwardowski, Henschen, & Barott, 2002). As a result, much of what has been proposed in relationship models is extracted from participants in interviews and observations.

The emerging field of interpersonal relationships in sport can be furthered developed if a premature foreclosing of the initial stage of exploration and discovery is avoided (Poczwardowski et al., 2006). As has been argued in this chapter, the coach–athlete relationship is a socially construed phenomenon that we need to understand much better in order to implement scientifically derived knowledge into intervention-based programs and everyday coaching practice. Phenomenological designs, interpretive designs, and other qualitative designs that are sensitive to the relational context should be implemented to provide rich descrip-

tions. Overall, it is expected that the implementation of descriptive (qualitative or quantitative) research will help to ground and inform theoretical work and development.

Causal Analyses

Cause-and-effect relationships are the building blocks of science. Smith (2000) stated that research should be designed to maximize internal validity or "the ability to draw sound conclusions about what actually causes any observed differences in a dependent measure" (p. 17). Greater attention to causation would help advance developmental models of coach–athlete relationship phenomena. Future experimental designs should build on the work conducted on coach leadership (e.g., Barnett, Smoll, & Smith, 1992; Conroy & Coatsworth, 2004). Additionally, the temporal patterning of relationships needs to be incorporated into research, particularly because relationships develop and dissolve and go through various transitional phases (e.g., success and failure, preparative and competitive seasons, injury and recovery periods). To our knowledge, no single study has employed a longitudinal design in order to examine the temporal dimension of coach–athlete relationships. In-depth, longitudinal studies based on multiple methods have the potential to draw our attention to predictive and causal factors that operate within and upon relationships.

Stronger Inferences

Stronger inferences can be achieved by attempting to replicate findings. Replication is integral to science and provides concrete evidence of reliability and validity. Social-psychological phenomena that do not replicate lack credence and often fade from the literature. In addition, to strengthen the inferences that can be drawn from research on coach–athlete relationships, researchers need to eliminate explanations of findings that *contradict* each other and increase explanations that *complement* and support each other. Designing research that aims, for example, to test competing models of coach–athlete relationships against one another should be encouraged because such research can add breadth to theory, research, and potential findings as well as applications.

Finally, the employment of multiple methods in a single approach will help us reduce method-bound results. Method-bound results (related to common method variance) are misspecified; that is, the results reflect instrumentation-related processes rather than the assumed theoretical processes that one sets out to study. Usually such results are overstated associations accompanied by inaccurate interpretations. Consequently, methodological diversity (e.g., combining qualitative and quantitative methods) will go a long way in developing a methodologically sound field of coach–athlete relationships.

Practical Implications

Coaching revolves around the coach–athlete relationship. Thus, coaches need to be able to develop effective relationships with their athletes. Effective relationships are generally characterized by thoughtful and respectful communication about issues related to sport and life more generally. Effective coach–athlete relationships are underlined by stability, appropriateness, trustworthiness, and dependability. Relationships that are characterized by such constructive features make both the coach and the athlete feel like winners. A coach who involves the athlete in the coaching process by negotiating performance goals, discussing attendance at sporting events, communicating expectations related to training and practice, and showing interest in the athlete's academic aspirations or family concerns ultimately may enhance psychological well-being and physical performance.

It is therefore important that coaches and athletes communicate with each other in such a way that meets their commitments, duties, and responsibilities. Coaches and athletes who possess strong interpersonal or communication skills can achieve their interpersonal goals (e.g., to cooperate) and other sought-after goals (e.g., performance goals) in an efficient and appropriate manner. Such skills include communicating nonverbally, rewarding, reinforcing, questioning and reflecting, explaining, listening, leading others, influencing, and self-disclosing. Thus, coach education and university courses in sport sciences should include sufficient information about interpersonal skills in coaching.

As mentioned at the onset of the chapter, one of the most vital reasons for researching coach–athlete relationships is to help the coach and the athlete manage their interpersonal encounters satisfactorily. Research thus far has attempted to provide information about the content of the relationship and its processes. This information is invaluable because it helps make coaches and athletes aware of what their relationship is like and how they can influence their relationship for the best. There is a dearth of research relative to the ways in which relationships between the coach and the athlete can be repaired or improved when conflict is experienced.

The knowledge generated from researching relationship conflict and repair would equip applied sport psychologists to help coach–athlete dyads make unsteady relationships work more satisfactorily by transforming them to steady and harmonious relationships.

Summary

This chapter has addressed critical issues in the conceptualization of and research on coach–athlete relationships. The coach–athlete relationship can be defined as a situation in which a coach's and an athlete's cognitions, feelings, and behaviors are mutually and causally interrelated and change over time. The basic motives for initiating and maintaining relationships can be categorized in a 2×2 taxonomy. A brief outline of conceptual models of coach–athlete relationship led to a proposed integrated research model, which aims to provide an impetus for research that will help develop a strong science of coach–athlete relationships. This model should help researchers understand the processes that regulate interpersonal components, the role of communication in relationship quality, and the influence of interpersonal components and processes on various outcomes. With such a model, the generated scientific knowledge is better organized and makes more apparent what is known and what is not known.

To achieve a dependable body of knowledge and understanding pertaining to the coach–athlete relationship, research must be carefully designed. The critical linkage between theory and research was discussed, and it is imperative that researchers use better samples; provide more thorough description throughout the study process; give greater attention to causation; and make stronger inferences by attempting to replicate findings, eliminate explanations of findings that contradict each other, and increase explanations that complement each other.

The practical implications of studying the coach–athlete relationship are many and include finding methods of establishing positive relationships and repairing unhealthy relationships so that both personal and performance goals can be met. In addition, as Berscheid and Reis (1998) observed, "Knowledge about interpersonal relationships is essential to the further development of social psychology" (p. 196). Indeed, any social psychology in sport settings that emphasizes the individual athlete or coach is naturally tested and stretched by the study of dyadic relationships (e.g., coach–athlete relationships). We hope that this chapter provides a springboard for such testing and expansion.

Discussion Questions

1. What is the importance of studying coach–athlete relationships in sport?

2. Debate the role of effective and successful coach–athlete relationships at different levels of sport performance (e.g., top-level versus grass roots).

3. How do theory and research (basic and applied) contribute to understanding the relationships that coaches and athletes form?

4. Discuss the components of the integrated research model. According to the model, in what ways does relationship quality influence outcome variables through its affective, cognitive, and behavioral components, and how is it influenced by antecedent variables?

5. Which links in the integrated research model (figure 1.2) do you find most compelling, and how have you witnessed these links in sport situations?

6. What problems and concerns need to be taken into account when designing research on coach–athlete relationships?

chapter 2

Interdependence Analysis and the 3+1Cs in the Coach–Athlete Relationship

Sophia Jowett, PhD

Learning Objectives

On completion of this chapter, the reader should have

1. understanding of the essential elements of interdependence theory;

2. knowledge of the relevance of interdependence theory to understanding closeness, commitment, complementarity, and co-orientation (3+1Cs) in the coach–athlete relationship;

3. capacity to use key concepts of interdependence theory to analyze coach–athlete relationships and explain research results and their practical importance;

4. ability to offer future research directions; and

5. insight into practical considerations as they pertain to conflicts of interest between a coach and an athlete.

© Icon Sports Media

The relationship that coaches and athletes develop in the course of their athletic partnership has received a moderate yet rather diverse array of characterizations. For example, Drewe (2002) took a philosophical approach and explained that the coach–athlete relationship is underlined by inequality, asymmetry, and conflict of interest; thus she proposed a type of "utility relationship" that, although "[it] may be a lesser form of human relationship, it will serve the purposes of both coach and athlete seeking their shared sporting goals" (p. 179). In a similar vein, Burke (2001) depicted the relationship as a situation in which a coach's dominance and power over the subordinated athlete is unquestionable. He argued that because exploitation and abuse commonly occur from a position of trust, athletes would benefit from distrusting their coaches. Finally, Tomlinson (1997) adopted a sociocultural view of the coach–athlete relationship, arguing that power and control, especially as they pertain to males coaching female athletes, govern the relationship. Tomlinson viewed female athletes as silent, powerless, dependent pawns of their coaches.

From a psychological perspective, Neale and Tutko (1975) suggested instead that "although the relationship between coach and player changes over time and under different circumstances, basically it is a relationship like that of the parent and child" (p. 143). The relationship thus contains qualities such as trust, care, and responsiveness to the athlete's needs.

However, although the latter one may be an intuitively appealing characterization, the asymmetric power and authority presumably inherent in the parent–child relationship cannot accurately and fully describe the coach–athlete relationship. Thus researchers have intensified their efforts by paying close and systematic attention to the specific content (quality and quantity) of the coach–athlete relationship (see chapter 1 for an overview of four conceptual perspectives on the coach–athlete relationship). These efforts have generated theoretically grounded approaches to the study of coach–athlete relationships that can facilitate our understanding of how such an important and multifaceted relationship affects its members' performance accomplishments and well-being.

The purpose of this chapter is to describe the psychological content of coach–athlete relationships by highlighting the relevance of interdependence theory (Kelley & Thibaut, 1978) to understanding the notion of interdependence in the coach–athlete relationship through the constructs of closeness, commitment, complementarity, and co-orientation, or the 3+1Cs (Jowett, Paull, & Pensgaard, 2005). The chapter is divided into five main sections. The first section presents the essential elements of relationships as described in interdependence theory. The second section presents the interpersonal constructs comprising the 3+1Cs conceptual framework and briefly discusses its measurement and the research conducted thus far. In the third section, the 3+1Cs are viewed as psychological states that represent the coach's and athlete's experience of interdependence. The fourth section discusses future research directions, and the fifth and final section presents practical considerations as they pertain to conflicts of interests between coaches and athletes.

Interdependence Theory: Essential Elements in Dyadic Relationships

Interdependence theory (Kelley & Thibaut, 1978; Thibaut & Kelley, 1959) is a conceptualization of interpersonal relationships that focuses on interpersonal processes (e.g., what is going on in dyadic relationships). Interdependence theory characterizes the relations between individuals in terms of outcome interdependence, or the ways in which relationship members cause one another to experience good versus poor outcomes (see Rusbult, Kumashiro, Coolsen, & Kirchner, 2004).

Interdependence is an inherent element of interdependence theory. It connects relationship members and is the platform from which other social psychological processes take place. In the context of the coach–athlete relationship, interdependence is inevitable and allows the coach and the athlete to fulfil even the most basic roles, duties, and responsibilities (Jowett, 2005). Interdependence is fundamental to the coach–athlete relationship for many reasons. First, interdependence shapes the self. For example, when a young athlete interacts on a regular basis with a coach who is domineering and controlling, she is likely to adopt a submissive attitude and behavior. When a coach experiences a consistent level of performance improvement from an athlete, he is likely to believe that he is a successful coach. Second, interdependence shapes mental events. For example, athletes develop certain perceptions (e.g., "I am competent") that reflect their attempts to understand the meaning of interdependence situations (e.g., "My coach has asked me to try a more difficult routine"); these perceptions help athletes to identify appropriate action in such situations (e.g., "I will give it a try"). From a coaching perspective, coaches are less likely to supply an intensive training session to an athlete when they know from previous interactions that the athlete is not ready to receive such training. Third, interdependence shapes interaction. Interaction demonstrates a coach's and an athlete's needs, thoughts, and motives in relation to one another in the context of the specific interdependence situation (e.g., a training session) in which their interaction transpires.

Interaction between two people can take various forms (Thibaut & Kelley, 1959). For example, during training a coach and an athlete may engage in independent activities (e.g., coach prepares the equipment while the athlete warms up), and when not training they may engage in shared activities (e.g., coach and athlete have lunch together). A coach and an athlete may also exchange information after a training session (e.g., discuss tactics to be employed in tomorrow's competition), and during training they may interact in a manner that has immediate benefit (e.g., the athlete asks the coach for guidance in executing a complicated technique). Consequently, interaction between relationship members is important because it can affect how members influence one another's outcomes (e.g., preferences, choices, decisions) (Thibaut & Kelley, 1959).

Interaction outcomes are another essential element of interdependence theory. According to the theory, outcomes can be defined in terms of rewards and costs. *Rewards* refer to the positive consequences of interaction (e.g., satisfaction, motivation, success), whereas *costs* refer to the negative consequences of interaction (e.g., conflict, power struggles, frustration). Kelley (1979) stated that "the ongoing relationship involves not only the individual production of rewards and costs but also the joint generation of rewards and costs, the latter being consequences that neither person can create independently" (p. 23). Correspondingly, coaches and athletes can yield outcomes for themselves (e.g., personal satisfaction or dissatisfaction) and for their relationship (e.g., a conflicting or successful relationship). Although the theory postulates that people seek to obtain rewards in their relationships and avoid costs, this does not imply that coaches and athletes will pursue self-interest in their relationship. Often coaches and athletes set aside their own preferences and act out of consideration of the other member. This phenomenon is known as *transformation process* (Kelley & Thibaut, 1978, p. 17); its function and character will be discussed later in the chapter.

3+1Cs Conceptualization of the Coach–Athlete Relationship

The coach–athlete relationship has been conceptualized as a situation in which coaches' and athletes' feelings, thoughts, and behaviors are interdependent (Jowett, 2005; Jowett & Meek, 2000a; Jowett, Paull, & Pensgaard, 2005). Coaches' and athletes' interpersonal feelings, thoughts, and behaviors have been operationalized and measured via the constructs of closeness, commitment, and complementarity (e.g., Jowett & Ntoumanis, 2004).

Closeness is reflected in mutual feelings of trust, respect, and the like that result from appraisals of coaches' and athletes' relationship experiences. Closeness characterizes the affective element of the coach–athlete relationship. *Commitment* is represented in coaches' and athletes' long-term orientation toward the relationship. This orientation includes thoughts of attachment and the intention to maintain the athletic relationship. Commitment involves a coach's and an athlete's intention to stay attached to one another while maintaining their relationship over time. Commitment characterizes the cognitive element of the coach–athlete relationship. *Complementarity* is reflected in coaches' and athletes' actions of cooperation. Cooperative interaction includes reciprocal behaviors whereby, for example, the coach instructs while the athlete follows instructions, and corresponding behaviors whereby, for example, both the coach and the athlete manifest a friendly attitude to one another during training sessions. Complementarity characterizes the behavioral element of the dyadic coach–athlete partnership. (See table 2.1.)

In effect, the 3Cs reflect the degree to which coaches and athletes are *interdependent* in terms of closeness, commitment, and complementarity. A coach–athlete dyad is interdependent if a coach and an athlete experience high levels of trust and respect; wish to remain attached and committed to each other in the future; and behave in a responsive, friendly, and easygoing manner. In contrast, a coach–athlete dyad is less interdependent if a coach and an athlete experience lack of mutual respect and trust, lack of interest in maintaining the relationship over time, and/or lack of cooperative interaction in the sport field.

Coaches' and athletes' closeness, commitment, and complementarity can be captured from a direct perspective, a metaperspective, or both (Jowett, 2002, 2005, 2006; Jowett, Paull, & Pensgaard, 2005). The *direct perspective* aims to assess one relationship member's perceptions of closeness, commitment, and complementarity relevant to the other member. For example, an athlete's feelings of closeness in relation to her coach may be very intense (e.g., "I trust my coach," "I respect my coach") or not so intense. The *metaperspective* aims to assess the degree to which one relationship member can accurately infer the other member's closeness, commitment, and complementarity. For instance, an athlete's inference of his coach's closeness may be extremely accurate (e.g., "My coach trusts me," "My coach respects me") or not so accurate.

Table 2.1   The Direct Perspective and Metaperspective of the 3Cs and Their Instrumentations

CART-Qs	3Cs definitions		
	Closeness	*Commitment*	*Complementarity*
	Closeness is reflected in coaches' and athletes' feelings of trust, respect, and interpersonal like resulting from appraisals of their relationship experiences.	Commitment is represented in coaches' and athletes' intention to maintain the athletic relationship where thoughts of attachment form an integrated part.	Complementarity is reflected in coaches' and athletes' cooperation. Cooperative actions include corresponding and reciprocal behaviors.
CART-Q direct perspective[a] (athlete version)	I trust my coach. I respect my coach.	I feel committed to my coach. My sport career with my coach is promising.	When I am coached by my coach, I feel responsive to her efforts. When I am coached by my coach, I am ready to do my best.
CART-Q meta-perspective[a] (athlete version)	My coach trusts me. My coach respects me.	My coach is committed to me. My coach's career with me is promising.	My coach is responsive to my efforts when he coaches me. My coach is ready to do her best when she coaches me.

Note. Coach–Athlete Relationship Questionnaires (CART-Qs) are self-reports that assess the quality of the coach–athlete relationship or the degree to which the coach and the athlete are interdependent. Two versions are available, one for the coach and one for the athlete. Each version contains two types of perspectives: the direct perspective and the metaperspective.

[a]Sample items contained in each subscale for the athlete version.

Table 2.2   Dimensions of Co-Orientation in the Coach–Athlete Relationship

Point of comparison (direct perspective and metaperspective)	Dimensions of co-orientation
Athlete's direct/Athlete's meta & Coach's direct/ Coach's meta A: I respect my coach. / A: My coach respects me. C: I respect my athlete. / C: My athlete respects me.	Assumed similarity
Coach's direct / Athlete's direct C: I like my athlete. / A: I like my coach.	Actual similarity
Coach's direct / Athlete's meta & Athlete's direct / Coach's meta C: I trust my athlete. / A: My coach trusts me. A: I trust my coach. / C: My athlete trusts me.	Empathic understanding

Key: A = athlete; C = coach.

Adapted from S. Jowett, and I.M. Cockerill, 2002, Incompatibility in the coach–athlete relationship. In I.M. Cockerill (Ed.) *Solutions in Sport Psychology* edited by I.M. Cockerill (London: Thomson Learning), 16-31.

The combined study of the direct perspective and metaperspective can uncover three important dimensions of co-orientation in the coach–athlete relationship (see table 2.2): assumed similarity, actual similarity, and empathic understanding. In brief, *assumed similarity* reflects the degree to which a relationship member assumes that how one feels, thinks, and behaves (e.g., "I trust my coach") is shared by the other member (e.g., "My coach trusts me"). *Actual similarity* reflects the degree to which the two relationship members are similar in terms of how they actually feel, think, and behave (e.g., "I trust my coach" and "I trust my athlete"). Finally, *empathic understanding* reflects the degree to which a relationship member understands the other member's feelings, thoughts, and behaviors (e.g., "I trust my athlete" and "My coach trusts me") (e.g., Jowett, 2006).

These dimensions of co-orientation are essential indicators of the quality of the coach–athlete relationship because they facilitate the coordination of relationship members' actions in the accomplishment of common goals, validate one's view of the world, and generally contribute to relationship functioning (see Jowett & Clark-Carter, in press). A coach's and an athlete's level of actual and assumed similarity as well as empathic understanding may provide useful information relevant to their interdependence. For example, if an athlete and a coach are capable of accurately inferring each other's feelings of closeness, one could speculate that this dyad is more interdependent than another dyad that does not have the capacity to accurately infer each other's feelings of closeness. Erroneous inferences may indicate less interdependence in the relationship.

Coach–Athlete Relationship Questionnaires (CART-Qs)

Two instruments have been developed and validated to measure coaches' and athletes' closeness, commitment, and complementarity from a direct perspective (see Jowett, 2005; Jowett & Ntoumanis, 2004) and from a metaperspective (Jowett, 2002, 2005, 2006). Both are called the Coach–Athlete Relationship Questionnaire, or CART-Q. The validation of the direct perspective of the CART-Q included procedures such as testing the content or face validity of the developed items (which were heavily based on the findings of a series of qualitative studies, e.g., Jowett, 2003; Jowett & Meek, 2000b; Jowett & Cockerill, 2003) with a panel of experts, performing a series of exploratory and confirmatory factor analyses of various models of first-order and higher-order factors, and examining the internal reliability of the generated factors.

In the case of the direct perspective, the instrumentation contains 11 items and measures the intensity of a coach's and an athlete's levels of closeness (e.g., "I respect my coach"), commitment (e.g., "I am committed to my coach"), and complementarity (e.g., "When I coach my athlete, I am responsive"). The metaperspective of the CART-Q contains 11 items that correspond to the direct-perspective measure and assesses a coach's and an athlete's judgment of the other's level of closeness (e.g., "My coach respects me"), commitment (e.g., "My athlete is committed to me"), and complementarity (e.g., "My coach is responsive to me"). When both instrumentations are used in applied settings or empirical research, all three dimensions of co-orientation in coach–athlete dyads can be ascertained, supplying an intricate picture of relationship quality and quantity (see tables 2.1 and 2.2) (see also Jowett, 2005).

Research Employing the 3+1Cs Model

Although it is beyond the scope of this chapter to review the quantitative and qualitative research that has been conducted employing the 3+1Cs, a brief account of this research is presented next in order to highlight its emergent features. A series of quantitative research has concentrated on discovering important correlates of the coach–athlete relationship. Specifically, studies have endeavored to examine the links between coach–athlete relationships as defined by the 3+1Cs and variables such as gender and satisfaction (Jowett & Don Carolis, 2003; Jowett & Ntoumanis, 2004), motivational climates (Olympiou, Jowett, & Duda, 2006), coach leadership and team cohesion (Jowett & Chaundy, 2004), and achievement goals (Adie & Jowett, 2006). The co-orientation dimensions of empathic understanding (accuracy) and assumed similarity have also been explored (Jowett & Clark-Carter, in press). This research has begun to develop a body of knowledge by revealing moderating and mediating links as well as important consequent variables of the coach–athlete relationship.

Qualitative research (e.g., Jowett, 2003; Jowett & Cockerill, 2003; Jowett & Frost, in press; Jowett & Meek, 2000a, 2000b; Jowett & Timson-Katchis, 2005; Jowett, Timson-Katchis, & Adams, 2006; Philippe & Seiler, 2006) has concentrated on the mental or subjective experiences of coaches and athletes relevant to their relationship. For example, Jowett and Cockerill (2003) examined the interpersonal relationships of 12 Olympic medalists and found that former athletes viewed their coaches as a close friend or parental figure. The strong affective bond was further evidenced through expressions of trust (e.g., "I trusted his judgment") and respect (e.g., "My respect for him was uppermost"). Moreover, the ability of the coach to be in command while maintaining a bond and affiliation with the athlete was perceived by athletes as an important interpersonal skill (Jowett & Timson-Katchis, 2005).

Another study has shown that effective communication patterns lead to the establishment of relationship rules, corresponding goals, and support systems that maintain and promote the relationship quality (as defined by closeness, commitment, and complementarity) in dual-role relationships where parents assume the role of the coach for their child (Jowett, Timson-Katchis, & Adams, 2005). Overall, qualitative research highlights the content (*what* athletes and coaches think about their relationship) and the process (*how* athletes and coaches think about their relationship) of the coach–athlete relationship as well as the relational context in which coaches' and athletes' experiences, roles, and social behaviors are carried out.

3+1Cs Model and Interdependence Theory

It is proposed that the interdependence a coach and an athlete are likely to experience in their relationship can be represented by closeness, commitment, complementarity, and co-orientation (3+1Cs). Consequently, the 3+1Cs may be able to capture the specific *interdependence structures* in which coaches and athletes cause one another to experience good versus poor outcomes. For example, if a coach and an athlete experience equally high levels of trust and respect for one another (i.e., high levels of closeness), then it is likely that the coach and athlete will cause one another to experience good outcomes (e.g., satisfaction) because they are mutually dependent. In contrast, if a coach attempts to cooperate with the athlete but the athlete is disinterested then this dyad is likely to experience poor outcomes (e.g., dissatisfaction) because there is one-sided dependence.

According to interdependence theory, the *interdependence structure* in dyadic relationships can be defined by examining the main effects and interaction of each relationship member's behaviors, including (a) actor control (a main effect of Ann's actions on Ann's outcomes), (b) partner control (a main effect of John's actions on Ann's outcomes), and (c) joint control (an interaction of John's and Ann's actions on Ann's outcomes). According to Kelley and Thibaut (1978), these components can define four properties of interdependence structure, namely, degree of dependence, mutuality of dependence, basis of dependence, and correspondence of interests. The following discussion explains the four properties of interdependence structures in the coach–athlete relationship and considers the manner to which the 3+1Cs can represent the properties.

Degree of Dependence

Degree of dependence reflects the extent to which a person depends on an interaction partner and thus the degree to which her outcomes are influenced by the partner's actions (table 2.3). If John (athlete) has high control over his outcomes (e.g., performance, satisfaction) and Peter (coach) has little control over John's outcomes, John is more independent. However, if John has little control over his outcomes and Peter has high control over John's outcomes, then John is more dependent on Peter. John is also dependent to the extent that Peter can behave in such a manner as to dictate John's own behavioral choices.

The first section of the chapter revealed that the coach–athlete relationship inevitably contains a degree of dependence. In fact, athletes' dependence is often evidenced in the importance athletes place on specific things their coaches have done for them and with them (i.e., fulfilling important needs) such as the development of effective training programs or displays of care during a difficult period. On the other hand, coaches' dependence on their athletes is, for example, evidenced in their efforts to plan training sessions that benefit the athlete and to provide emotional or informational support when needed. Dependence is a psychologically meaningful feature of interdependence (Rusbult & Arriaga, 2000) and can exert profound effects, both positive and negative, on the coach–athlete relationship.

If one considers that the degree of dependence can range from low to high, then a high degree of dependence could be reflected in an athlete's or coach's levels

Table 2.3   Interdependence Structures in the Coach–Athlete Relationship

Interdependence structures	Definition
Degree of dependence	Extent to which a person depends on an interaction partner and thus the extent to which his outcomes are influenced by the partner's actions (comfort vs. discomfort with dependence, dependence vs. independence.
Mutuality of dependence	Extent to which two people (coach *and* athlete) are mutually rather than separately dependent on one another for generating enjoyable outcomes (comfort vs. discomfort with vulnerability or responsibility attached).
Basis of dependence	Ways in which relationship members influence one another's outcomes, or whether dependence results from partner control vs. joint control (comfort vs. discomfort with submissive vs. dominance attached).
Correspondence of interests	Extent to which members' actions benefit both relationship members similarly or in a corresponding fashion.

of emotional attachment (closeness), loyalty (commitment), and cooperative attitude (complementarity). The implications of dependence are multifaceted. For example, it has been shown that high levels of affective closeness (e.g., like, trust, respect) tend to promote exchanges of information, open channels of communication, and disclosure (e.g., Jowett & Meek, 2000b)

Research has also shown that high levels of commitment promote behaviors that serve to maintain the coach–athlete relationship over time: (a) the tendency to think in terms of "we, us, our" rather than "I, me, mine" (see Jowett & Meek, 2000a); (b) the inclination to perceive the relationship as better than other coach–athlete relationships (e.g., Jowett & Clark-Carter, in press); and (c) the tendency to accommodate rather than retaliate when a relationship member behaves disappointingly (Jowett & Cockerill, 2003; Jowett & Timson-Katchis, 2005). High levels of complementary transactions such as when a coach and athlete have friendly attitudes during training, or when a coach's dominant (directive) behavior is complemented by an athlete's submissive behavior during training, tend to promote a sense of an organized structure in the relationship as well as a friendly and easygoing relationship environment (e.g., Jowett & Meek, 2000a; Jowett & Cockerill, 2003; Jowett & Frost, 2005; Jowett & Timson-Katchis, 2005).

Dependence can also have negative consequences. Consider the following scenario: Jane is dependent on her coach, experiencing high levels of 3Cs; nonetheless, she feels threatened because her coach pays more attention to other athletes in the squad. Jowett (2003) interviewed a single coach–athlete dyad that was experiencing conflict, disagreements, and hurt feelings. Analysis of the interviews revealed that both the coach and the athlete experienced a degree (albeit not high) of closeness, commitment, and complementarity. The athlete expressed that this degree of dependence was not enough to make her feel responsive and committed to the relationship, while the coach felt content with the relationship state. It was found that the degree of dependence was insufficient to influence the athlete's outcomes in a positive way (e.g., achieving further success and improvement), and that the degree of dependence was discomforting or displeasing for the athlete. Thus, it is important to ascertain whether coaches' or athletes' perceptions about the degree of dependence as reflected by the 3Cs trigger comfort or discomfort with dependence versus independence (cf. Rusbult et al., 2004).

Mutuality of Dependence

Mutuality of dependence describes the extent to which two people are mutually rather than separately dependent on one another for generating enjoyable outcomes (table 2.3). Coach–athlete relationships are likely to involve a considerable degree of mutual dependence rather than one-sided dependence. Coaches and athletes develop a give-and-take pattern of interactions in an attempt to provide and receive instruction and support. Such mutually dependent interactions tend to be stable and friendly, yielding positive benefits.

In contrast, interactions with nonmutual dependence involve a power differential (Rusbult et al., 2004). Burke (2001), Neale and Tutko (1975), and others (e.g., Tomlinson, 1997) have suggested that the coach–athlete relationship is characterized by power differentials, or asymmetric power and authority. The athlete, especially the female athlete, is viewed as the low-power member in the coach–athlete relationship. Consequently, the less dependent and more powerful member, the coach, is more likely to exert greater control over issues such as decision making and the allocation of resources, while the dependent relationship member (athlete) is likely to comply with the associated interaction cost (e.g., accommodation, sacrifice, vulnerability). However, stereotyping the coach–athlete relationship in terms of its gendered or role-related power differentials is rather narrow. Consequently, it is argued that the relationship between a coach and an athlete involves a dynamic interplay between mutual and nonmutual dependent interactions.

In terms of the 3Cs, an athlete's and coach's mutual dependent interactions could be reflected in high, medium, or low levels of mutual affective ties of closeness, mutual commitment, and corresponding complementary acts of interactions. The mutuality of dependence for relationship members who experience low levels of the 3Cs could be sufficiently less advantageous in generating beneficial outcomes compared with relationship members who experience high or medium levels of the 3Cs. Moreover, mutually dependent coaches and athletes with high or medium levels of the 3Cs may also be more motivated to take the other's perspective (co-orientation: empathic understanding) and think similarly about their relationship (co-orientation: assumed similarity), while their relationship is indeed similar in terms of how they think, feel, and behave with one another (co-orientation: actual similarity).

Mutual dependence is expected in coach–athlete partnerships where athletes are experienced and coaches are established. In this case, athletes and coaches alike possess experience, knowledge, and skill-based "power" that permits them to establish a relationship on equal terms. Limited findings indicate that when athletes reach high levels of sport performance, they are more active, responsible, and responsive relationship members in terms of participating in decision making and allocation of resources (see e.g., Jowett & Meek, 2000a; Jowett & Cockerill, 2003).

This mutuality may not be achievable, however, if one member in the coach–athlete relationship possesses less experience, knowledge, and skill. Jowett and colleagues (Jowett & Meek, 2000b; Jowett, Timson-Katchis, & Adams, 2005) examined the dynamics of an atypical coach–athlete relationship in which parents made a decision to coach their own children. Findings revealed that the parents and their children were concerned about reaching a performance level where the parents' competence, skills, and expertise would not be sufficient for the developing child. It is not uncommon for athletes to outgrow their coaches' expertise as they move from one performance level to the next. Consequently, in such situations the nonmutual dependence that potentially arises in coaches' and athletes' interactions could be detrimental, particularly for the athlete's development.

According to Rusbult et al. (2004), in situations of nonmutual dependence, two questions need to be asked: Does the dependent relationship member feel comfort or discomfort with the associated vulnerability? Does the powerful relationship member feel comfort or discomfort with the associated responsibility? Thus, an examination of coaches' and athletes' closeness, commitment, complementarity, and co-orientation coupled with an understanding of their level of comfort or discomfort relevant to their vulnerable or responsible position in the relationship can help ascertain the influence of coaches' and athletes' nonmutual dependence on interaction outcomes.

Basis of Dependence

Basis of dependence describes the way in which relationship members influence one another's outcomes, or whether dependence results from partner control (e.g., Mary's actions influence Jane's outcomes) versus joint control (e.g., Mary's and Jane's actions influence Jane's outcomes) (see table 2.3). Joint control, or when both the coach's and the athlete's actions influence each other's outcomes, assumes that there is a degree of coordination between relationship members' actions. For example, when an athlete has been injured, the coach may think, "I will wait to see how the athlete feels today before I determine the intensity of the training session." In contrast, another coach may decide that the athlete should participate in a certain training session despite the injury and if the session is successfully completed he will give the athlete a day off from training. In the latter case, the coach's control involves adaptation in the form of exchange rather than coordination ("I will do this for you if you will do that for me").

The construct of complementarity would be particularly capable to suggest whether the two members exchange actions separately or jointly. Coupled with the construct of co-orientation (empathic understanding), a more intricate picture of the basis of their dependence could be discerned. For example, a discrepancy in accurately inferring each other's behaviors (complementarity) is likely to indicate lack of empathic understanding. If there is lack of empathic understanding on the part of either member, then one could assume that ineptness, laziness, or attractions of competing activities do not allow the coach or athlete to make accurate inferences. These factors can lead a relationship member to become a freeloader, receiving benefits (e.g., satisfaction that the athlete is doing what she is told or an athlete doing what she wants regardless of her coach's instructions) without returning them (cf. Kelley, 1979). The freeloading relationship member is unwilling to make full use of her resources and thus contributes poor individual outcomes to the relationship. Kelley (1979) explained that when relationship members are *not* interdependent or dependent, they are likely to become self-centered (i.e., receiving benefits from the other without returning them).

In Jowett's (2003) qualitative case study, the findings suggested that the coach appeared to possess control (partner control) in that his actions directly influenced the athlete's outcomes. According to the coach's admission, he desired to dominate, control, and lead the athlete and the relationship. However, the athlete reported that her coach's desire to dominate their interactions was not possible or desirable given her maturity, knowledge, and understanding of the context in which she operated. Evidently, the coach and the athlete viewed their dependence from a competing basis in that both desired to dominate. Because the basis of dependence can be experienced as either dominant or submissive (Rusbult et al., 2004), it is important to ascertain whether, for example, coaches' and athletes' perceptions and empathic understanding of complementarity reflect competing or one-sided forms of interaction (e.g., dominance vs. dominance) or coordinated forms of interaction (e.g., dominance vs. submissiveness).

Correspondence of Interests

Correspondence of interests describes the extent to which a coach's and an athlete's actions benefit both relationship members similarly or in a corresponding fashion (see table 2.3). In the coach–athlete relationship, both the coach and the athlete expect similar things. Consequently, what one wants tends to be the same as what the other wants, such as to train hard to achieve performance success, to engage in open channels of communication, and to be honest. These outcomes can be achieved through different behaviors or interactions (e.g., coach directs and athlete performs,

Skill development and performance are outcomes that often underline coaches' and athletes' corresponding interests.

coach sets up the equipment and athlete warms up) and similar behaviors or interactions (e.g., coach and athlete enjoy chatting after training, coach and athlete warm up together).

Interaction is relatively easy when the coach's and the athlete's interests correspond; this implies that they will follow a course of action that will benefit both of them. Each relationship member pursues her own interests, yielding simultaneously beneficial outcomes for one another. Interaction is relatively tricky when there are conflicting interests, yielding outcomes that cast doubt on the relationship members and their intentions to cooperate and be trusted. According to interdependence theory, correspondence of interests ranges from perfectly correspondent (i.e., pure coordination of interaction) to moderately correspondent (i.e., moderate coordination of interaction) to perfectly noncorrespondent (i.e., no coordination of interaction).

Coach–athlete dyads with perfectly noncorrespondent interests may be characterized by a complete lack of closeness, commitment, and complementarity. Dyads with perfectly correspondent interests may record high and corresponding levels of the 3Cs alongside high levels of co-orientation. Dyads with moderate correspondent interests may involve a different combination of high and low 3Cs and co-orientation. In the latter case, a coach and an athlete may feel attached, secure about the future of their relationship, and complementary in their actions, but they may be unable to precisely

understand the other's feelings, thoughts, and behaviors (co-orientation: empathic understanding). Such discrepant perceptions (direct versus meta) could be due to lack of adequate communication between relationship members about their needs, motives, and preferences.

Kelley (1979) stated that moderately correspondent relationships where the pattern is neither correspondent nor noncorrespondent evoke mixtures of cooperative and competitive interests; consequently, they provide a basis for negotiation or bargaining. In the moderately correspondent coach–athlete dyad, the coach and athlete agree about some things and disagree about others; therefore there is room to negotiate by communicating their needs and preferences. Consequently, open channels of communication are a major factor that can lead to correspondence of interests (Kelley, 1979). Communication is considered the building block of coach–athlete relationships (Yambor, 1995; Yukelson, 2001; see also chapter 3 for more information about the role of communication and conflict in the coach–athlete dyad). Negotiation through sincere communication allows the coach and the athlete to know why, what, how, and when the other intends to do something (Jowett, Timson-Katchis & Adams 2005).

The implications of correspondence for the ongoing athletic relationship are various. The degree of correspondence influences the possibilities for harmonious and stable versus discordant and inconsistent relationships (Kelley, 1979). Research findings suggest that many coach–athlete relationships are characterized by moderate correspondence of interests (e.g., Jowett & Cockerill, 2003; Jowett & Timson-Katchis, 2005), signaling that coaches' and athletes' interactions contain a degree of both cooperation and competition. Moderate correspondence of interests can be relatively stormy because relationship members develop somewhat distrustful, competitive, and uncompromising attitudes toward each other; hence, communication and negotiation can help keep these partnerships together. Coach–athlete relationships have also been found to be perfectly correspondent; perfectly correspondent relationships are characterized by easier and smoother interactions and decision-making processes mainly because what one member wants is wholly acceptable to and understood by the other one (e.g., Jowett & Meek, 2000a).

An opportunity for this author to work with an athlete and a coach facing a host of interpersonal issues, including noncorrespondence of interests, occurred while working as sport psychology consultant with the Hellenic Olympic team for the 2004 Olympics. Both coach and athlete expressed unwillingness to work as a unit. Interdependence situations, including training and competition, were characterized by a lack of coordination of interaction. Training sessions were conducted in an antisocial atmosphere of antipathy, antagonism, and anxiousness. For example, the athlete barely talked to the coach and the coach communicated his instructions and feedback largely via the assistant coach. The athlete expressed dislike for the manner in which training was conducted and fear that her coach could deselect her from the team at any time, while the coach often expressed the belief that female athletes are peculiar (i.e., irregular and idiosyncratic) in the manner in which they interact with their coaches compared to their male counterparts, making his job unpredictable. This dyad had difficulty achieving outcomes that could positively benefit both the coach and the athlete simply because they felt they had nothing in common. Their views were so strong that there was no room for bargaining or negotiation by either member. Communication as a means to promote correspondence in this noncorrespondent dyad was not possible because the degree to which the athlete wanted something, the coach did not want it. Although the athlete placed fourth in the finals of the Olympic Games in her sport, this endeavor was viewed by the athlete and others (teammates and sport administrators) as independent from her coach. If the athlete and her coach behaved in a corresponding fashion and had corresponding goals, not only could they have enjoyed the time they had to work together, but they could also have achieved greater performance accomplishments.

Transformation of Motivation

Transformation of motivation refers to the alteration of preferences that occurs in an attempt to promote broader relationship goals. Broader relationship goals depart from merely benefiting self. For example, a coach may evaluate an interaction event (e.g., an athlete's effort during a training session) in relation to the consequences that the event can have for the athlete (i.e., improved skill, technique, performance) as opposed to the consequences that it can have for team selection, performance success, and even for that coach's reputation.

Research supports the idea that this process of transformation takes place in the coach–athlete relationship. Overall, the qualitative case studies colleagues and I have conducted over the years reveal that athletes expect coaches to show sensitivity and be considerate of their needs (e.g., Jowett, 2003; Jowett & Carpenter,

2004; Jowett & Cockerill, 2003; Jowett & Timson-Katchis, 2005). Specifically, a qualitative study revealed that athletes acknowledge their coaches' altruism on behalf of the athlete and the relationship (Jowett & Carpenter, 2004). For example, athletes reported that their coach has "gone out of his way for me," "been a source of help at times where I did not know what to do," and "put up with me and my ways a lot." These quotes suggest that transformation of motivation takes place and permits the development of an effective (and possibly successful) coach–athlete relationship (see chapter 1).

Although it is proposed that coaches and athletes may interact in an altruistic and prosocial way that departs from *immediate self-interest* (e.g., personal success, fame), it is possible that this prosocial transformation simply reflects the pursuit of *long-term self-interest*. Indeed, the nature of the coach–athlete relationship dictates that long-term outcomes (e.g., performance success, team cohesion) can be enjoyed if athletes and coaches cooperate and commit to one another. Such long-term functional values may motivate athletes and coaches to altruistic impulses; thus the existence of an element of self-interest does not exclude sincere altruistic impulses (Rusbult & Arriaga, 2000).

Future Research

Much of the analysis presented thus far aimed to provide an overarching framework in which to understand the interdependence between coaches and athletes. The analysis is built on interdependence theory and the 3+1Cs model and is supported with limited sport-specific empirical evidence that already exists. Thus, there is an enormous scope for research. First, do personal and interpersonal dispositions affect interdependence structure (e.g., athlete's or coach's degree of dependence)? For example, how does one's attachment style (see Bowlby, 1969/1982) or relationship orientation (see Harter, 1999) affect the degree to which an athlete depends on a coach? Specifically, Harter (1999) developed three adult relationship orientations or styles:

- *Self-focused autonomy* defines individuals' lack of interest in thinking about their relationship and the tendency to be occupied with other concerns

- *Other-focused autonomy* defines the tendency of individuals to think about their relationship so much that it can be hard to focus on other concerns

- *Mutuality* defines a balanced approach in which individuals consider their relationship without excluding other concerns

With this framework in mind, the assumption is that coaches' and athletes' chosen relationship orientation shapes their preferences for interdependence or independence. For example, when coaches and athletes adopt a mutuality orientation, it is likely that (a) athletes *or* coaches experience relatively high levels of closeness, commitment, and complementarity; (b) athletes and coaches develop partnerships that are mutually dependent and hence both members experience at least mutually moderate levels of closeness, commitment, and complementarity; (c) coaches and athletes yield good outcomes (e.g., satisfaction, performance accomplishments) for one another; and (d) there are more opportunities to engage in transformation of motivation processes. Thus, an exploration of interdependence structures when coaches or athletes adopt a mutuality, self-focused, or other-focused orientation may shed light on the ways in which they approach and experience specific interdependence situations and each other.

Second, coaches and athletes develop relationship-specific rules to interrelate and solve problems of dependence. What are the norms and rules that govern the coach–athlete relationship? How do norms and rules minimize conflict, disagreements, and antagonism? Jowett and Carpenter's (2004) qualitative study interviewed 15 athletes and 15 coaches to shed some light on the content and impact of rules in the coach–athlete relationship. The findings suggest that (a) coaches and athletes adopt rules that relate to interdependence and equality, (b) rules enhance the relationship's functioning; and (c) when rules are violated coaches and athletes experience discomfort. Although Jowett and Carpenter's study aimed to explore the content of rules and their implications for relationship quality, the ways in which rules affect interdependence structure and outcomes have not been fully explored. Furthermore, it is unknown whether the association between relationship rules and interdependence is moderated by situational variables such as type of sport (team vs. individual sports), level of sport (junior vs. senior), and cultural aspects (Eastern sports vs. Western sports). This information can have practical implications for intervention and relationship-enhancement programs. For example, knowledge relevant to how relationship members negotiate levels of interdependence through relationship rules and norms in specific sports would be invaluable to practitioners who wish to establish a sense of harmony and stability in a coach–athlete dyad while promoting dyad members' personal development and growth.

Other issues that could be explored relate to gender composition in the coach–athlete relationship. If, for example, we consider Tomlinson's (1997) point of view that female athletes are the weaker member in the coach–athlete relationship, then one would expect that the interdependence structure (including transformation process) that transpires for female athletes is different to that of male athletes. Moreover, limited empirical evidence suggests that male coaches should adjust their approach to fit the athlete's gender (e.g., Jowett & Clark-Carter, in press; Gilbert & Trudel, 2004). Similarly, female coaches may need to adjust to their athletes' gender.

Jowett and Clark-Carter (in press) explored interpersonal perceptions of assumed similarity and empathic understanding or accuracy in coach–athlete dyads. Their results indicated that female athletes and their coaches assumed more similarity in terms of commitment than male athletes and their coaches. It was speculated that female athletes perceived that their coaches assumed equal levels of commitment with them in an attempt to enhance their self-concept ("I am worthy of my coach's attention"), and that coaches assumed a similar level of commitment with their female athletes in an attempt to ease the traditional power that coaches possess as authority figures and to promote an atmosphere of mutual dependence. The pursuit of research questions that explore gender composition and interdependence structure would generate valuable theoretical information and may have considerable input for practice and interventions.

Finally, an examination of the temporal patterning of interdependence structures would elicit important information relevant to transitional periods and adaptation. The degree of dependence, mutuality of dependence, and basis of dependence are likely to change over time. How do these structures change, when do they change, and why? What are the implications if both relationship members actively seek to develop high levels of closeness as opposed to one relationship member seeking high levels of closeness? Could athletes' or coaches' maturity (e.g., age, experience), for example, account for changes in interdependence structure over time? Or are athletes' or coaches' level of performance or relationship duration stronger moderators of change? These are just a few of the preliminary empirical questions one can ask when employing the 3+1Cs as a means to examine the basic interdependence structures (degree of dependence, mutuality of dependence, basis of dependence, and correspondence of interests).

Practical Implications

Understanding coach–athlete relationships from an interdependence standpoint can have practical implications in discerning interdependence structures and processes that are *functional* versus *dysfunctional*. This diagnostic element may lead to appropriate interventions and programs for relationship management that benefit coaches, athletes, and their dyadic relationships. This section contains practical information relevant to coach–athlete dyads that face conflicting interests.

Recall the coach–athlete dyad at the Olympic Games in Athens. Both the coach and the athlete experienced conflicting interests. Their interactions were problematic largely because both members wanted to do things their own way. Conflicting situations like these may arise through no fault of either person—it simply happens that their preferences and interests disagree. However, coach–athlete dyads with conflicting interests can (a) engage in antisocial or self-interested behavior, (b) experience hostile thoughts, and (c) attempt to achieve benefits at the other's expense. Overall, such interactions can be antagonistic and cynical. These coach–athlete dyads have an uncertain future that may include further escalation of conflict (hostility and destructiveness) or disengagement from the relationship.

Although these situations are difficult to deal with, practitioners should provide opportunities for both the coach and the athlete to clearly express their goals and motives. The practitioner could provide opportunities in which both relationship members act prosocially rather than antisocially and communicate in ways that are trustworthy and compassionate. This situation calls for more than just open channels of verbal communication. The coach and the athlete must reveal their transformational tendencies and interact in a supportive fashion that allows the expression of feelings, the exchange of clear and reasonable rules, and the achievement of goals. Over time and with both relationship members engaging in effective prosocial interactions, an increase in the coach's and the athlete's mutual trust, respect, appreciation, commitment, and cooperation would be expected. Overall, the practitioner's aim is to help the coach and the athlete interact prosocially and reach a relationship quality or a level of interdependence that yields beneficial outcomes (e.g., satisfaction) for both of them.

Sometimes only one of the two members decides to correct the course of the relationship or align the conflicting interests by cooperating and showing considerateness and warmth. The implications of such a one-sided attempt may be particularly difficult to account for with precision. When the attempt is one-sided, the other member may receive this type of interaction with a degree of suspicion, distrust, and antisocial behavior (e.g., uncooperativeness). According to Rusbult et al. (2004), this incompatible pattern of interaction may lead to exploitation on the part of the less cooperative member, reduced interdependence by both members, or realization by the cooperative member that the full

benefits of interrelating can only be generated if they both act prosocially.

The 3+1Cs and instrumentations could be used to gauge the degree and associations of coaches' and athletes' closeness, commitment, complementarity, and co-orientation over time in dyads that are in the process of managing or resolving their conflicting interests. Thus, when the 3Cs are mutually high, this may indicate that the coach and the athlete have attempted to interact in ways so as to resolve their noncorrespondence and differences. When the 3Cs are mutually low, this may indicate that the coach and the athlete have *not* attempted to interact in ways so as to resolve their noncorrespondence. Finally, when the 3Cs are high for the coach and low for the athlete, it is likely that one relationship member has attempted to resolve the noncorrespondence and differences, but the other relationship member has not responded positively.

Mutual prosocial behavior and interactions that help establish a degree of harmony and stability in the relationship are likely to yield greater dyadic adjustment and longevity. In the coach–athlete relationship, both members need to be able to work together and accommodate each other's motives and preferences if the relationship is to be long enough to yield beneficial outcomes such as performance accomplishments and psychological well-being.

Summary

This chapter aimed to illustrate the ways in which interdependence theory and the 3+1Cs complement each other in explaining the interdependence between coaches and athletes. Interdependence theory characterizes relations between individuals in terms of the ways in which relationship members cause one another to experience good versus poor outcomes. The 3+1Cs conceptual model describes the content and quality of the coach–athlete relationship in terms of closeness, commitment, complementarity, and co-orientation. These constructs are measured with the CART-Questionnaires.

A significant body of quantitative and qualitative research is emerging on the 3+1Cs. Based on interdependence theory, the state of coach–athlete interdependence is represented as closeness, commitment, complementarity, and co-orientation. Although the analysis in this chapter provides an overarching framework in which to understand the interdependence structure and transformation of motivation that occur in the coach–athlete relationship, future research is warranted to confirm the validity of the proposed assumptions and to extend this initial interpretive analysis. By analyzing coach–athlete relationships from an interdependence standpoint, practitioners can discern interdependence structures and processes that are functional or dysfunctional. Diagnosing relationships in this way can lead to appropriate interventions for relationship management that benefit coaches, athletes, and their dyadic relationships.

DISCUSSION QUESTIONS

1. Based on interdependence theory, discuss (a) the manner in which the coach and the athlete are interdependent, and (b) the manner in which both the coach and the athlete control one another's outcomes.

2. Based on the 3+1Cs framework, discuss the conceptualization of the coach–athlete relationship, measures, and research conducted thus far.

3. Discuss briefly the four interdependence structures, using examples that highlight how the state of dependence is subjectively represented and experienced through the constructs of closeness, commitment, complementarity, and co-orientation.

4. What future research directions would generate knowledge relevant to interdependence patterns in coach–athlete relationships? What are the practical ramifications of such research?

5. Describe the three basic patterns of interactions coaches and athletes may engage in when experiencing situations of conflicting interests.

6. How appropriate or necessary is it to study the coach–athlete relationship via the application of relationship theories and models developed to examine relational behavior in other types of relationships? Explain your answer.

chapter 3

Interpersonal Communication and Conflict in the Coach–Athlete Relationship

Nicole M. LaVoi, PhD

Learning Objectives

On completion of this chapter, the reader should have

1. understanding of what is known, as well as what is not known, in the literature on interpersonal processes of communication and conflict in coach–athlete dyad;

2. knowledge of representative theories of interpersonal communication and conflict management as they relate to the coach–athlete relationship; and

3. familiarity with the concept of relational expertise and its relationship to communication and conflict management.

© Icon Sports Media

No written word
nor spoken plea
Can teach our youth
what they should be.
Nor all the books
on all the shelves.
It's what the teachers
are themselves.

Unknown (in Wooden & Jaimeson, 1997)

In a well-publicized event in 1997, National Basketball Association (NBA) basketball player Latrell Sprewell choked his coach, P.J. Carlesimo, because he was angered by the coach's criticism during practice. During the 2004-2005 National Football League (NFL) (American football) season, standout receiver Keyshawn Johnson was released from the Tampa Bay Buccaneers because his disagreements with head coach Jon Gruden had become disruptive to the team. Johnson stated, "I was never Gruden's guy. He never liked me." Johnson's agent, Jerome Stanley, attributed the conflict to a lack of flexibility in Gruden's relational and leadership style, saying "Keyshawn's the type of player who needs to be loved. You understand that when you bring him on your team. Bill Parcells showed him some love. Tony Dungy showed him some love. For some reason, Jon Gruden never did" (ESPN.com, 2004). Both examples illustrate the centrality of interpersonal skills in a coach–athlete relationship.

Communication is a vital interpersonal skill; it is the vehicle for relating with one another and the foundation on which relationships are initiated, maintained, negotiated, and dissolved (Hargie & Tourish, 1997; Montgomery, 1988). Interpersonal communication skills, including the ability to manage conflict, are perhaps taken for granted by coaches and athletes, but there can be no doubt that these processes are fundamental to the success of any coach–athlete relationship. Athletes of all ages and abilities name communication most frequently as a characteristic of a functional and close coach–athlete relationship (LaVoi, 2004; see also chapter 1).

Coaching is much more than teaching Xs and Os. Interventions for relationship enhancement based on empirical evidence are greatly needed. A handful of scholars (e.g., Jowett, Trudel, Gilbert, LaVoi, Poczwardowski) have been laying the groundwork for this endeavor, but the interpersonal aspect of the coach–athlete relationship remains largely underexplored. The aim of this chapter is to provide definitions and theoretical frameworks of interpersonal communication and conflict management that will allow researchers and practitioners to develop knowledge that helps coaches and athletes become relational experts, thus improving the quality of the sport experience.

This chapter first defines interpersonal communication and presents indicative theories; it then turns to defining interpersonal conflict by outlining theoretical frameworks that can be applied to the examination of the origin and management of coach-athlete conflict. Subsequently, the chapter examines the intersection of communication and conflict. The construct of relational expertise will be then forwarded to expand thought and investigation of coaching effectiveness. The chapter concludes with directions for future research and practical implications.

Communication

Communication is *the* vehicle for effective coaching; it transmits competence, knowledge, and skills (Vealey, 2005). Communication is also the vehicle for developing the coach–athlete relationship; it transmits care, concern, respect, and trust. The formation, development, maintenance, and dissolution of the coach–athlete relationship also occur through communication processes. Arguably, communication expertise may be more important to the success of the coach–athlete relationship and the well-being of both parties than the coach's technical expertise. Given this importance, further clarification of different types of communication and the relevance of communication to the coach–athlete relationship is provided in the next section.

Communication Defined

Everything a person does or says can be considered communication. For example, a coach communicates values and philosophy through who is selected for the team, how the team is governed, and how decisions are made, while an athlete's motivation may be nonverbally communicated through effort, persistence, and intensity. Communication occurs through written and spoken words and body language in everyday interactions. Communication is an interpersonal exchange shaped by various factors, including value systems, personal characteristics, tensions, and situational dimensions (e.g., type and level of sport, culture, gender). Definitions, theories, and research pertaining to interpersonal communication and the coach–athlete relationship are the primary focus of this chapter.

Interpersonal Communication

Interpersonal communication is a dynamic, interdependent process between two persons (Gouran, Wiethoff, & Doelger, 1994). Three principles underlie interpersonal communication (DeVito, 1986). First, *communication is inescapable.* It is impossible not to communicate. Even when an athlete does not actively respond to a coach's instruction or a coach remains expressionless on the sidelines after an athlete's error, communication is occurring. Second, *communication is irreversible.* Once a coach rolls his eyes at a poorly executed play and says, "You are the worst point guard this program has ever seen," it can't be taken back. Third, *communication is complex.* It involves the interplay of both individuals' perceptions of self, other, and the relationship.

There are two prevailing definitions of interpersonal communication; one is contextual and the other is developmental. The contextual definition delineates how interpersonal communication differs from other communication contexts (e.g., small group, public or mass communication) and other communication processes (e.g., close proximity, immediate feedback). However, the contextual definition does not take into account the relationship between the interactants.

The developmental definition of interpersonal communication accounts for qualitative differences of communication due to the nature of the relationship. In other words, communication between a coach and her athletic director and the same coach and her athlete are expected to be somewhat different. Differences in communication might also be expected between a coach and incoming recruits versus senior captains. Developmental communication occurs between people who have known each other over an extended period of time and view each other as unique individuals, not just as people who are simply acting out social situations (Gouran et al., 1994). The developmental definition specifies that communication is qualitatively different as the relationship develops (Montgomery, 1988). This definition provides a nuanced framework in which to understand and examine the subtleties and components of interpersonal communication.

Interpersonal communication contains multiple levels of meaning. All communication contains a content component (the *what*) and a relational component (the *how*) (DeVito, 1986). A majority of research pertaining to interpersonal communication in sport is more focused on the content component than the relational component (see e.g., Jowett & Cockerill, 2003; Potrac, Brewer, Jones, Armour, & Hoff, 2000). The *what,* the functional content of the coach–athlete relationship that has been deemed "basic processes" by Poczwardowski, Barott, and Henschen (2002), includes technical, strategical, and tactical skills and stresses interactions that contribute to achieving goals and developing competence. The *how,* the relational element of communication, includes the processes of achieving mutual respect, trust, warmth, understanding, support, empowerment, and shared knowledge of self and other that foster meaningful and satisfying interactions between coach and athlete (Jowett & Cockerill, 2003; LaVoi, 2004). The nuances and

Communication is a process for achieving shared knowledge and mutual understanding.

relational meanings associated with communication are at least as important, if not more important, than the content of communication and consequently exert a powerful metacommunicative influence on a relationship (Montgomery, 1988).

Metacommunication (Bateson, 1972) is a common theoretical framework for examining the *how,* perhaps best described as "the message behind the message." Metacommunication is an act of communication between two individuals that also communicates something about the communication itself, or about the relationship between the two agents, or both (Gouran et al., 1994). Metacommunication includes information such as verbal, nonverbal, contextual, and historical cues of the dyad that tell the receiver how the message should be interpreted.

For example, consider a coach who doesn't give his star tennis player instructional feedback (content) during matches because the coach has confidence in the player; the player wins easily and seems in control of her matches without guidance or interference from the coach. Midseason, though, the player becomes frustrated and begins to lose, feeling that the lack of attention during matches means the coach doesn't care about her matches or believe in her. Metacommunication lies beyond the superficial, discernable, and simple level of interpersonal exchanges and encourages examination of multiple levels of meaning (Montgomery, 1988). Contextual and developmental definitions of interpersonal communication provide a basis for understanding the content and relational components of interpersonal communication in the coach–athlete dyad.

Theoretical Frameworks of Communication

While many theories of interpersonal communication exist, in this chapter two theories, constructivism and dialectics, are presented as potential means to the study of the contextual and developmental aspects of communication in the coach–athlete relationship.

Constructivism

Constructivism (Delia, O'Keefe, & O'Keefe, 1982) is a theory of interpersonal communication that asserts that people make sense of the world through systems of personal constructs derived from socialization. Constructivism focuses on the cognitive processes of the individual (e.g., perception, production, and interpretation of messages) and attempts to account for why individuals' social cognition and communication practices vary in complexity. The development of constructs varies, proceeding from a state of global simplicity to a state of increasing complexity, differentiation, abstraction, and hierarchically organized construct systems (Delia et al., 1982). Research using constructivism demonstrates that individuals who possess cognitively complex construct systems have the ability to perceive and represent the thoughts and inner states of others and subsequently adapt messages to the social and personal needs of the receiver (Waltman, 2002).

Consider a college athlete compared to a 10-year-old athlete. The college athlete exhibits a more complex construct system compared to the child, including perspective-taking skills, when asked to describe a close coach–athlete relationship (LaVoi, 2004); the following quotes illustrate this point.

> I can talk to my coach about all my concerns; I know she cares about my well-being as an athlete and a person. She spends a lot of time working, but I understand that she needs her own time to live her life. She can openly talk to me about her concerns. *(Collegiate female athlete)*

> She is nice, good, she does not yell. *(10-year-old female athlete)*

Moreover, central to the constructivist framework is the idea that constructs are dynamic and change over time depending on experience and context. Thus, the effectiveness of coach–athlete interactions may depend upon the level of cognitive complexity of one, and often both, of the interactants. However, given the implied power asymmetry of the dyad, responsibility of effective communication should fall upon the coach; this idea will be discussed later in the chapter as it pertains to relational expertise. Despite its usefulness, constructivism is a cognitive theory of individual difference that assumes relationship dynamics can be explained by understanding the individuals that comprise the dyad (Baxter, 1988). To explore the complexity of dyadic processes, a relationship-level theory of interpersonal communication may be more informative in unraveling the complexities of two-person relationships.

Relational Dialectics

The second theory of interpersonal communication useful for examining coach–athlete relationships is dialectics (Baxter, 1988). Relationships are based on the dynamic ways people dialogue with one another. Through dialogue, rules, meaning, differences, and common ground are explored. A *dialectic* is the tension between two or more contradictory forces of a system best described by the tug-of-war metaphor (see Vogel-Bauer, 2003). For example, an athlete wants to feel close and connected to her coach because she feels it helps her perform better, but the coach wants to remain a distant expert, focusing solely on improving the athlete's competence. Relational dialectics assumes that no steady state can be achieved, and it examines how a system changes or develops over time as a result of tension between opposing dialectical sources, such as the coach and athlete. Relational dialectics echoes other postmodern theories by acknowledging and capturing the fluid, interdependent, nuanced complexity of relational change as multidirectional, polysemic, and unfinalized (Baxter & Montgomery, 1998).

While relationships contain many dialectics, one in particular holds promise in forwarding research on coach–athlete interpersonal interactions. The autonomy–connection dialectic, regarded as the principal dialectic, is the continuous tension between balancing individual identity with dyadic relational concerns (Baxter, 1988). When figure skater Michelle Kwan split with longtime coach Frank Carroll, she poignantly expressed the autonomy–connection dialectic by saying, "In any relationship, it evolves. When I was younger, the coach was pretty much the skater. You did whatever he said. As I've gotten older, I've gotten more independent and I think for myself. That's the way it should be….You have your differences in the way you should go about things, and that's what Frank and I ran into" (Armour, 2001). Coaches and athletes continuously negotiate the autonomy–connection dialectic (e.g., decision making, feedback, formation of rules, responsibilities) through communicative strategies.

Dialectical theory acknowledges that relationships are embedded in and influenced by multiple contexts of the self, the relationship, and culture. Therefore, relational dialectics offers a useful theoretical framework for developmental and contextual examination of the formation, maintenance, and dissolution of the coach–athlete relationship as well as resultant outcomes.

Research on Coach–Athlete Interpersonal Communication

Communication within sport has typically fallen under the rubrics of leadership, coaching effectiveness, coaching behaviors, and more recently coach–athlete relationships. Summarizing the findings and methods of inquiry in each of these areas is far beyond the scope of this chapter, and comprehensive reviews of proposed models of leadership, coaching effectiveness, and coach education can be found elsewhere (see, e.g., chapters 1, 5, and 6). Despite the attention to coaching behaviors and coach–athlete communication, gaps in the literature exist (Chelladurai & Riemer, 1992; Horn, 2002; Lyle, 2002; Mageau & Vallerand, 2003). Very little information specific to coach–athlete interpersonal communication exists. To this end, the focus turns to recent empirical studies and findings which, while not directly based in constructivist, dialectical, or metacommunicative theoretical frameworks, serve as a platform for future investigation of interpersonal communication in the coach–athlete relationship.

Nonverbal communication and the meaning assigned to it by the coach and athlete is one concrete way to examine metacommunication and dialectics within the dyad. The bulk of research relevant to coach–athlete communication has observed and identified the content level of verbal coach instructions through quantitative description (Portrac, Jones, & Armour, 2002). Despite the attention and necessitation nonverbal communication is given in applied sport psychology and Martens' (1987) assertion that two-thirds of communication is nonverbal, it has received little empirical consideration (Allen & Howe, 1998). Albert Mehrabian suggested the total emotional impact of the expression of feelings is a function of the following formula: Total Impact = .07 verbal + .38 vocal + .55 facial (1968, in DeVito, 1986).

In one of the few studies examining nonverbal communication in sport, negative facial expressions expressed by the coach concurrently with positive feedback had an adverse influence on athlete perception and interpretation of the event; this may be related to negative psychological outcomes for athletes (Crocker, 1990). When verbal and nonverbal communication are incongruent, the receiver of the communication instinctually questions the credibility, sincerity, and honesty of the communicator, and consequently nonverbal communication is given credence (DeVito, 1986). In another study, elite athletes identified a set of appropriate nonverbal communication from coaches (e.g., pat on the back, shaking hands, hugging after good performance, touching related to technical instruction) but did not elaborate on an inappropriate set (Jowett & Carpenter, 2004). Very little is known about how nonverbal communication creates dialectical tension and relates to metacommunication or influences relational outcomes of the coach–athlete relationship.

Empirical evidence pertaining to the relational content of communication or dialectics in the coach–athlete relationship has been limited; the most common unit of analysis has been at the individual level (Poczwardowski, Barott, & Jowett, 2006; Horn, 2002; Jowett & Ntoumanis, 2004; Lyle, 2002). Communication helps form the quality of the relationship, which dictates tangible, *bidirectional* behavioral, emotional, and cognitive consequences (Reis, Capobianco, & Tsai, 2002; see also chapter 2). To date, most communication research in sport contexts assumes that (a) athletes are passive recipients of coach communication, (b) the coach's intended message is successfully received by the athlete, and (c) the coach is unaffected by the interaction. Despite the recognition that communication is a mutual process, few studies have used bidirectional methodologies. Poczwardowski and colleagues (2002) recently used the bidirectional symbolic interactionism framework (Blumer, 1969) and found that coaches are indeed influenced by relationships with their athletes. Through exploring the meanings of both coach and athlete behavior, they illustrated the bidirectionality of the coach–athlete relationship.

Although a number of dialectics exist in the coach–athlete relationship, empirical description and evidence of them are scarce. The self-determination theory (Deci & Ryan, 2000; Ryan & Deci, 2001) provides a framework from which to examine autonomy, part of the autonomy–connection dialectical contradiction. Balancing this tension requires coaches to engage in autonomy-supportive behaviors, encouraging athletes to make choices and solve problems independently while also minimizing criticism, pressure, and control (Deci & Ryan, 1985).

Autonomy-supportive coaches provide choice, rationale for tasks, and opportunities for taking initiative; give noncontrolling feedback; avoid controlling behaviors; prevent ego involvement; and acknowledge feelings and perspectives (Mageau & Vallerand, 2003). Both Jowett and colleagues (see, e.g., chapter 2) and LaVoi (2004) examine connection, the other half of the dialectical contradiction of autonomy and connection, by employing the construct of closeness. However, to gain a more complex picture of the autonomy–connection dialectic and other dialectics, simultaneous investigation of both sides of this and other dialectical contradictions must be undertaken. Very little is known about the origins, processes, strategies, and outcomes of dialectics or conflict in the coach–athlete relationship.

Conflict

Perhaps the common adage "Only two things are certain in life—death and taxes" should be revised to state, "I'm only certain of *three* things in life—death, taxes, and *conflict.*" Conflict may occur within a person (intrapersonal), between two people (interpersonal), between members of a group (intragroup), between groups (intergroup), or between a person and situational factors. Although conflict is an inevitable part of life and relationships, little empirical examination of coach–athlete conflict exists. The aim of this section is to offer theoretical frameworks that will forward research and understanding of interpersonal conflict in the coach–athlete relationship.

Conflict Defined

Many definitions and theoretical frameworks of conflict and conflict management exist. The classical definition of interpersonal conflict falls within the zero-sum, win–lose paradigm, defined as the expressed struggle between at least two interdependent parties who perceive incompatible goals, scarce resources, and interference from others in achieving their goals (Deutcsh, 1973; Wilmot & Hocker, 1998). From this definitional perspective, conflict is rarely constructive organizationally, relationally, or personally (Slack, 1997). Undoubtedly, a more sophisticated view of conflict is defensible, for not all conflict behaviors are inimical and destructive.

Conflict can also be viewed as a constructive, mutually beneficial win–win opportunity (Covey, 1989). Conflict can facilitate understanding and tolerance of difference as both people grow through the process of expressing perspectives and feelings and demonstrate a willingness to respond to the other's unique ways of engaging in the relationship (Heitler, 2001; Jordan, 1997). Conflict can also facilitate learning and increase effectiveness (Rahim, 2002). This relational model of conflict, termed *power-with* (Jordan, Kaplan, Miller, Stiver, & Surrey, 1991), involves the heart and mind; one's success is not achieved at the expense of others and the goal is preserving the relationship. A quote by Dan Zadra (2005), a recognized writer, publisher, and strategic communications consultant, sums it up best: "You don't need to have victims to have a victory." Oftentimes the ways in which coaches communicate with athletes unintentionally destroy confidence, trust, or respect and create conflict within the dyad, which can be counterproductive to optimal performance, development, and experience.

Overall, the definition of interpersonal conflict is similar to the definitional components of communication. Conflict is generally comprised of two dimensions: *content* (task, substantive, issue driven) and *relational*

(affective, emotional) (DeVito, 1986; Rahim, 2002). Research in management and organizational development suggests that moderate levels of content conflict, where individuals disagree about how to solve an issue or task, are beneficial in that they stimulate discussion and debate, which result in higher performance. Relational conflict, on the other hand, impedes optimal performance, loyalty, satisfaction, and commitment in the workplace (see Jehn, 1995, 1997; Jehn, Northcraft, & Neale, 1999). Moreover, relational conflicts impede group performance by causing members to be irritable, negative, resentful, and suspicious (Jehn, 1997).

The majority of interpersonal conflicts are caused by a failure or inability to distinguish between the content and relational levels of communication. In general, content conflicts are much easier to repair than relational conflicts (DeVito, 1986; Rahim, 2002). For example, consider the coach who becomes angry with an athlete who skips practice without asking permission so that she can study for a final exam that is crucial for her acceptance to medical school. Most likely the coach would agree that the athlete's priority should be the exam (content), but the conflict arises because the athlete, by failing to ask permission, metacommunicated a lack of respect, commitment, and responsibility to the team and to the coach (relational).

It is not the presence or frequency of conflict but the mutual process used in negotiating and repairing disconnection that is salient in determining interpersonal and relational outcomes (Collins & Laursen, 1992). Negotiations can be informal and a standard part of role definition, be part of socialization into a sport program, and diffuse misunderstanding (Poczwardowski et al., 2002), or they can be formal and hostile involving contempt, defensiveness, and criticism that indicate a degenerating relationship (Gottman, 1994). This finding is critical because research demonstrates that interdependent dyads show higher levels of conflict than less interdependent dyads (Hartup & Laursen, 1993) and that quality of communication is a critical determinant of whether conflict is functional or dysfunctional in the developmental trajectory of the dyad (Collins & Laursen, 1992).

Interpersonal Conflict and Relationship Development

While empirical evidence exists regarding how positive relational qualities influence development and psychosocial outcomes, less is known about *relational antipathies* (Berscheid, 2001; Hartup, 2001). Relational antipathies are a category of relationships characterized by enmity and animosity (e.g., conflict, avoidance, resentment, anger, rejection). While Jowett and Cockerill (2002) suggest that the coach–athlete relationship can be a source of stress and distraction and that negative closeness (e.g., distrust, incongruent goals, power struggles) compromises relational quality and coach–athlete effectiveness, the assumption that *only* positive relational interaction leads to facilitative developmental and psychosocial outcomes may be faulty.

Conflict episodes and antipathies play a unique role in individual and relational development because people may learn more from negative interpersonal experiences than from positive experiences (Hargie & Tourish, 1997). For example, a coach may learn more from a conflict-ridden relationship with a difficult athlete than from a positive relationship with little conflict. Conflicts help individuals develop conflict resolution skills, self-awareness, and social skills required to get along and pursue team or individual goals despite relational conflict (Hartup, 2001). The following theories may help illuminate ways in which conflict facilitates or destroys personal growth and relationship development.

Representative Theories of Interpersonal Conflict

This section will summarize two interpersonal conflict theories: a competence-based model of interpersonal conflict and the contingency approach to conflict management. Both approaches may be particularly instructive for furthering research within the area of coach–athlete communication.

Competence-Based Model of Interpersonal Conflict

The competence-based model of interpersonal conflict is based on longitudinal research that links interpersonal communication and relationship quality (see Canary & Cupach, 1988; Canary, Cupach, & Serpe, 2001). In the original model (Canary & Cupach, 1988), relational outcomes resulting from a conflict episode are mediated by episode-specific judgments of the partner's communication competence and one's own communication satisfaction. The adapted theoretical model proposed herein (see figure 3.1) expands the original model by suggesting that, in addition to episodic assessments, conflict management strategies mediate relational outcomes as well as intrapersonal outcomes (Canary et al., 2001).

Conflict episodes usually entail the perception of incompatible goals, and thus communication competence becomes salient (Canary et al., 2001). Conflict management strategies include what is done to rectify or manage the conflict and are further explained in the next section (see figure 3.2). Episodic assessments include judgments of communication competence and personal communication satisfaction of the episode. Both in turn influence relational and intrapersonal outcomes. Support for the mediatory role of judgments of competence and communication satisfaction indicate that such judgments filter the influence of conflict behaviors on relationship outcomes such as trust and relational satisfaction (Canary & Cupach, 1988) and

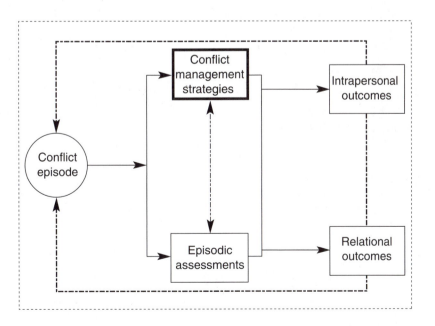

Figure 3.1 Competence-based model of interpersonal conflict.

may influence sport-specific intrapersonal athlete and coach outcomes such as sport enjoyment, confidence, state anxiety, burnout, and self-esteem. Judgments and interpretations of the conflict episode will be shaped by an individual's level of cognitive complexity, thus aligning the competence-based model with a constructivist communication framework.

An example of how the competence-based model of interpersonal conflict applies to a real-life situation ensues. As in many coach–athlete relationships, an athlete and coach experience conflict over playing time. If the athlete perceives that the coach handles the conflict competently by clarifying the athlete's role, explaining exactly what the athlete needs to do to increase playing time, and listening with empathy to the athlete's concerns, the athlete will more likely than not walk away from the conflict with trust and respect for the coach intact as well as feel motivated toward achieving new goals. Alternatively, if the coach handles the athlete's concern over playing time by avoiding the athlete, pacifying him with hollow promises of more playing time, or by telling him not to question the coach's decisions, the athlete will more likely than not walk away frustrated and resentful toward the coach, lack confidence, and feel as if his concerns are not important. The relational and intrapersonal outcomes may vary greatly depending on how a conflict is perceived and judged by the athlete and managed by the coach.

The model also supports developmental analysis by acknowledging the reciprocal nature of conflict tactics and relational properties over time (Canary et al., 2001). The adapted version of the model (see figure 3.1 on page 35) proposes that the meanings attached to partners' communication as well as the conflict management strategies used affect each individual, the relationship, and how subsequent episodes of conflict are negotiated. An assumption could be made that one's level of cognitive complexity and ability to take the perspective of another, as delineated in the constructivist theoretical framework, influence one's ability to successfully manage conflict. This synthetic model, as well as the contingency approach to conflict management theory outlined in the next section, may prove to be useful heuristics for examining coach–athlete relationships; evidence suggests that perceptions of the nature of conflict episodes and the frequency with which they occur vary greatly between coaches and athletes (LaVoi, 2004).

Contingency Approach to Conflict Management

Conflict management refers to strategies employed to accommodate tensions, minimize the dysfunctions of conflict, and enhance learning and effectiveness. Conflict management is distinctly different from conflict

resolution, which implies elimination or termination of conflict (Rahim, 2002). Coaches are continually engaged in conflict management with their athletes, from smoothing out disagreements about playing time to mediating personality differences among athletes to dealing with the fallout of team rule violations. It is safe to assert that on most sport teams a conflict exits between the coach and at least one athlete, or between two or more individuals on the team, at any given time. Successful management (e.g., a win–win strategy) of conflict requires balancing a concern for needs of the self with the needs of the other, or in the case of sport, sometimes the needs of the team.

Rahim and colleagues' theory of the contingency approach to conflict management (Rahim, 2002; Rahim & Bonoma, 1979) is consistent with contemporary management theories that stress there is no one right way to lead, to motivate, or to manage conflict. The contingency approach to conflict management balances concern for self with concern for others. These two dimensions of concern represent individual motivational orientations during conflict, and in combination result in five distinct styles of handling conflict: integrating, obliging, dominating, avoiding, and compromising (see figure 3.2; Rahim & Bonoma, 1979).

A brief summary of each style follows (see Rahim, 2002, for a comprehensive discussion of the styles). *Integrating* involves an active, open exchange of information that seeks alternatives and balances high concern for both self and others. *Compromising* involves both parties giving up something and reflects an intermediate level of concern for both self and others. *Obliging*

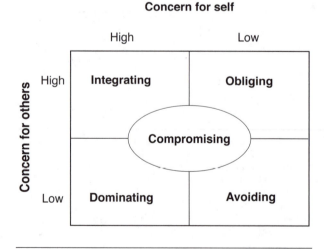

Figure 3.2 The dual-concern model of styles used in managing interpersonal conflict.

emphasizes similarities, attempts to pacify and minimize differences, and is comprised of a low concern for self but a high concern for others. The *dominating* style, comprised of a high concern for self and low concern for others, is the signature of win–lose negotiation where one individual forces her position or will onto others with little regard. *Avoiding* is the most passive style, blending low concern for self and others.

Both the competence-based and contingency-approach frameworks to conflict management hold great usefulness for researchers to help further answer the question of what works in the coach–athlete relationship. A handful of studies thus far have investigated coach–athlete conflict.

Conflict Research in the Coach–Athlete Dyad

A search of the subject indexes of the most recent editions of well-known textbooks in sport psychology fails to yield the term *conflict* (e.g., Singer, Hausenblas, & Janelle, 2001; Weinberg & Gould, 2003; Williams, 2006). As anyone involved in sport knows, it is not because conflict in the coach–athlete dyad does not exist! A small number of studies identify and describe dimensions of negativity and conflict within the coach–athlete relationship (e.g., Greenleaf, Gould, & Dieffenbach, 2001; Jowett, 2003; LaVoi, 2004; Poczwardowski et al., 2002). Jowett (2003) uncovered negative relational aspects of the coach–athlete relationship using the original 3Cs (closeness, co-orientation, and complementarity) model and discovered that a lack of emotional closeness consisted of feeling unattached and distressed, which resulted in isolation, frustration, and anger. Negative co-orientation consisted of disconnection and contention such as unequal needs and disagreements. Noncomplementarity included incompatibility, power struggles, and lack of support. Similar conflict themes stemming from power struggles, favoritism, incompatible goals, lack of character, and failure also emerged between elite coaches and athletes (Jowett & Carpenter, 2004).

Greenleaf et al.'s (2001) interviews of Olympic athletes yielded similar results in that athletes consistently indicated the negative effects of coach–athlete conflict on performance. Particularly, teams and individuals that failed to meet performance expectations cited poor coach–athlete communication and lack of coach–athlete trust as contributing factors to poor performance. Poczwardowski et al. (2002) used a synthesis of theoretical frameworks and methodologies to analyze patterns of activity, care, and interactions, revealing that negative coach–athlete relationships were characterized by mutual dissatisfaction, lack of warmth, less interaction, limited communication, discomfort, hurt feelings, and unfulfilled expectations.

LaVoi (2004) used inductive, grounded analysis to examine open-ended athlete and coach responses pertaining to coach–athlete conflict. Athletes and coaches were asked to respond to the following open-ended question: *If there were conflict or problems between you and your head coach during the season, what were they about? Please describe the sources of conflict or problems below.* Results revealed divergent perceptual patterns of conflict themes and frequency of conflicts between coach and athlete.

On average, only 35% of athletes reported a conflict with a coach, while 100% of coaches reported conflict experiences with athletes. Athletes who reported conflict cited coaching issues (e.g., playing time, strategy, training) and lack of coach warmth (e.g., care, understanding, approachability), whereas coaches cited lack of athlete intrapersonal responsibility (e.g., attitude, work ethic, commitment) and responsibility to the team (e.g., breaking team rules, undermining cohesion) as the most salient sources of conflict. It appears as if both coaches and athletes attribute conflict origins *to the other* in the dyad, which can be problematic if coach awareness and communication expertise are lacking and thus cannot help narrow discrepant perceptions. Communication is a critical skill needed to lessen the frequency, intensity, and duration of coach–athlete conflict. In addition, poor communication is a common origin of conflict. This important and underexplored intersection will be discussed next.

Relationship Between Communication and Conflict

The link between communication and conflict has been recognized by scholars in a variety of disciplines (Roloff, 1987). Communication is the primary means by which needs are satisfied or frustrated. Ideally, communication is a mutual, two-way process, but sometimes it is not, and the dialectical struggles that ensue can be the nexus of conflict. Communication is inextricably linked to interpersonal conflict for the following reasons: (a) Communication behavior, both verbal and nonverbal, often creates conflict; (b) communication reflects conflict; and (c) communication is the vehicle for productive or destructive management of conflict (Heitler, 2001; Wilmot & Hocker, 1998).

A substantial body of research demonstrates strong associations between conflict and relational outcomes such as satisfaction (Canary et al., 2001). Athlete satisfaction has been associated with congruence between the athlete's actual and preferred coach behaviors (Chelladurai, 1984; Riemer & Chelladurai, 1995), but specific attention to actual and preferred dimensions of interpersonal communication, coach–athlete relationship qualities, and conflict management strategies used within the coach–athlete relationship remain underexplored. Mutual communication is often thwarted in sport contexts for a variety of reasons, including lack of coach or athlete communication skills, undesired or nonnegotiated power differentials, and asymmetry in the dyad. Thus it is imperative to identify dimensions of relational expertise that can be learned by coaches and athletes in order to facilitate positive, growth-fostering relationships within sport.

Relational Expertise

Effective communication and management of conflict within the coach–athlete dyad are dimensions of expertise. Expertise is defined as an "ongoing process of the acquisition and consolidation of a set of skills needed for a high level of mastery in one or more domains of life performance" (Sternberg, 1999). In sport, expertise has typically been discussed in terms of psychomotor learning and skill development (Starkes, Helsen, & Jack, 2001). Côté, Salmela, Trudel, Baria, and Russell (1995) stated, "Coaching is an example of a domain in which the tasks and prerequisite knowledge of expertise have never been identified" (p. 3).

Côté, Salmela, and Bloom, in combination and with colleagues (see Bloom, 2002; Côté, Salmela, Trudel, Baria, & Russell, 1995; Côté & Sedgewick, 2003), have made strides in developing knowledge pertaining to coach expertise. This body of research identifies primary (organization, vision, training, competition) and peripheral (coach and athlete characteristics, contextual factors) categories of coach knowledge, demands, and responsibilities that build on the multidimensional model of leadership (Chelladurai & Saleh, 1978, 1980). As emphasized earlier in this chapter, the complexity of cognitive constructs, including perceptions of communication competence within the dyad, influences relational outcomes and subsequent conflict behavior (Canary et al., 2001); thus, expanding dimensions of expertise to include relational expertise is imperative.

Culling from relational-cultural theory (Jordan et al., 1991; Miller, 1976; Miller & Stiver, 1997), the work of Fletcher (1999), and Sternberg's (1998, 1999) emergent concept of expertise, *relational expertise* is the capacity to create good connections and affect the well-being of others in a positive way. Relational expertise requires the abilities to express and experience emotion, participate in the development of others, empower and create strength in others, and embrace the expectation that a relationship can yield mutual growth. Relational expertise also requires a capacity to observe patterns of connection and disconnection, including an awareness of self, other, and the relationship (Jordan, 1995). As with any expertise, relational expertise is best conceptualized as a continuum ranging from relational ineptness to expertise (Starkes, Helsen, & Jack, 2001). Relational expertise is a cultivated strength and a set of skills that has the potential to produce positive consequences for both the athlete and the coach.

The four primary dimensions of relational expertise as they relate to the coach–athlete relationship include *engagement* (the quality of involvement between the coach–athlete including empathy, warmth, and responsiveness); *empowerment* (the experience of feeling strengthened, encouraged, and inspired to take action through connection in a relationship); *authenticity* (the ability to be one's true self in the context of the relationship and be open to influence); and ability to deal with *conflict and difference* (the process of expressing and working through differences in background, perspective, and feeling leading to enlargement of the relationship rather than disconnection) (Jordan, 1997; LaVoi, 2004; Liang et al., 2002; Miller & Stiver, 1997).

Future Research

The following section outlines important future research directions on the interpersonal dimensions of communication and conflict and their intersection within the coach–athlete relationship.

Communication

Future studies should examine both content and relational components of communication within the coach–athlete relationship. Constructivist and dialectical frameworks should be used to investigate communication at both the individual and relationship levels, including a developmental examination of how communication between the coach and athlete changes over time. Future research should examine perceptual accuracy of nonverbal communication and explore the metacommunicative messages sent by coaches (intentionally and unintentionally) and how those messages are perceived by athletes. Communication is the most common theme cited by collegiate coaches and athletes in the development of a close relationship (LaVoi, 2004). Investigation into what athletes and coaches mean by "communication" could be a fruitful next step in understanding interpersonal dimensions of the coach–athlete relationship.

Conflict

Future investigation of conflict in the coach–athlete relationship should focus on the (a) description and origin of conflict (e.g., content or relational); (b) conflict management strategies used by coaches, athletes, and teams to negotiate conflict; (c) frequency, intensity, and duration of conflicts; (d) effectiveness of conflict management strategies; and (e) relational, intrapersonal, and team outcomes of conflict episodes. For example, do the athletes who perceive a compromising (win-win) strategy of conflict management compared to athletes who perceive a dominating (win-lose) strategy vary across relational and intrapersonal variables?

In relationships outside of sport contexts (e.g., married heterosexual couples), it appears that relational properties are relatively stable and do not change as a result of an isolated conflict episode (Canary et al., 2001). Research indicates that continuously high levels of conflict in the family are linked to psychosocial problems (Steinberg, 1990), but parallel knowledge in sport contexts is nonexistent. Future research should use the competence-based model of interpersonal conflict (Canary & Cupach, 1988; Canary et al., 2001) to assess the nature and impact of isolated conflict episodes as well as chronic conflict between coaches and athletes. The model also provides researchers with a means to test antecedents and moderating effects of the conflict episode, such as individual difference variables of both the coach and athlete (e.g., self-construal, trait anxiety), which is consistent with existing models of leadership within sport (Chelladurai & Saleh, 1978, 1980; Côté et al., 1995; Smith, Smoll, & Hunt, 1977). The contingency approach to conflict management (Rahim, 2002; Rahim & Bonoma, 1979) may be useful for expanding knowledge of coach–athlete dialectics and conflict by examining the tensions between the perceived and preferred styles of coach conflict management.

Intersection of Communication and Conflict

Future examination of the intersection of communication and conflict will undoubtedly provide insight into the unique and powerful developmental implications of the coach–athlete relationship. Examining coach–athlete conflict episodes by using relational expertise, the competence-based model, and the contingency approach to managing interpersonal conflicts in combination would yield rich information for researchers and practitioners. How much variance in athlete flourishing, psychosocial outcomes, optimal performance, and sport dropout can be accounted for by athlete perceptions of coach–athlete communication and conflict management? What types of athlete-perceived communication breakdowns (e.g., content: unclear role, lack of feedback; relational: too much criticism, feeling that the coach doesn't care about the athlete) lead to what types of conflicts (e.g., acute or chronic) and relational and intrapersonal outcomes? Do coaches who vary in relational expertise and conflict management styles have varying frequency or intensity of conflict episodes with athletes? Do coaches who vary in relational exper-

tise have shorter career durations and higher rates of burnout than relationally competent coaches?

Given differences in how males and females value, maintain, and experience interpersonal relationships (Crick & Rose, 2000; Cross & Madson, 1997; Reis, Collins, & Berscheid, 2000), future research should consider gender as a moderating variable of interpersonal processes in the coach–athlete relationship. Power and gender are relationship dimensions that transcend context and help further define relationship provisions (Laursen & Bukowski, 1997). In addition, people react to leaders based on gendered expectancies (Eagly, Wood, & Diekman, 2000). Thus, exploration of athletes' gendered expectations and perceptions of coach power and interpersonal behaviors could inform curricular efforts on coaching education and relational expertise as well as gender-specific coaching strategies.

Practical Implications

First and foremost, development and testing of coach–athlete relationship interventions based on empirical evidence is needed. Such programs may include strategies for improving personal awareness of relational competencies, knowledge, and effects of the metacommunication level of interpersonal interactions; perspective taking; empathy; communication skills; conflict management; and dimensions of relational expertise. Creating a good connection between two people is a positive and worthwhile endeavor. Coach effectiveness training (CET) (Smith et al., 1977, see also chapter 6) provides a medium for developing a positive coaching environment. The few interventions targeting athlete social, communication, or relationship skills have effectively improved athlete assertiveness (Connelly & Rotella, 1991) and channels of communication between athletes and their coaches (Dale & Wrisberg, 1996). Empirically and theoretically based interventions are warranted to further uncover the complexity of the coach–athlete relationship in terms of communication mechanisms and processes that help answer the important question of what works in the coach–athlete relationship that simultaneously leads to human flourishing and achievement for both the athlete and the coach.

Summary

This chapter defined the interpersonal processes of communication and conflict, highlighting the role of interpersonal communication and conflict in the quality of the coach–athlete relationship. The contextual definition of communication, or how interpersonal communication differs in different communication contexts and processes, was explained, as was the developmental definition of interpersonal communication, which accounts for qualitative differences of communication due to the nature of a relationship. Interpersonal conflict was defined as being comprised of two dimensions, content and relational.

The discussion further aimed to expand existing knowledge by putting forward theoretical frameworks within the disciplines of communication and organizational conflict that are applicable to the coach–athlete dyad. The competence-based model of interpersonal conflict links interpersonal communication and relationship quality, while the contingency approach to conflict management balances concern for self with concern for others and includes five styles of handling interpersonal conflict. Communication is inextricably linked to interpersonal conflict because communica-

tion, both verbal and nonverbal, often creates conflict, reflects conflict, and is the vehicle for management of conflict. The construct of relational expertise, which includes engagement, empowerment, authenticity, and ability to deal with conflict and difference, is one way to expand investigation of interpersonal dimensions of the coach–athlete relationship.

Future research on the interpersonal dimensions of communication and conflict and their intersection within the coach–athlete relationship should examine both content and relational components of communication within the coach–athlete relationship. As for practical applications, coach–athlete relationship interventions based on empirical evidence should be developed and tested; empirically and theoretically based interventions are necessary to further uncover the complexity of communication in the coach–athlete relationship.

Discussion Questions

1. Define communication and conflict.
2. Describe two theoretical frameworks of communication.
3. Describe two theoretical frameworks of conflict.
4. How are communication and conflict related?
5. What are the dimensions of relational expertise? How can coaches develop relational expertise?
6. What other dimensions that have not been outlined in this chapter might be part of relational expertise?

chapter 4

Youth Peer Relationships in Sport

Alan L. Smith, PhD

Learning Objectives

On completion of this chapter, the reader should have

1. understanding of definitional issues and theoretical perspectives that shape thinking and research on youth peer relationships in sport;

2. appreciation for the significance of peer relationships in youth sport and the significance of youth sport to peer relationships;

3. knowledge of the existing research base on youth peer relationships in sport; and

4. familiarity with promising research questions and practical implications that pertain to peer relationships in sport.

© Icon Sports Media

Sport experiences take place within a social context and are given meaning by interactions with significant others. Indeed, when athletes reminisce about their sport careers, their relationships with coaches, parents, teammates, competitors, spectators, and nonsport peers are as prominently represented as their personal successes and failures. These relationships may be supportive, growth promoting, and of tremendous personal meaning, but they also may be confrontational, growth inhibiting, and disheartening. It is no wonder that sport psychologists have a keen interest in the social relationships of athletes and that *social* psychology in sport settings is a thriving research area.

In this chapter, I will overview the knowledge base on youth peer relationships in sport. While extensive research has targeted coach–athlete relationships (see, e.g., chapter 1) and parent–athlete interactions (see, e.g., chapter 10), much less energy has been expended on the study of peer relationships in sport. This is disappointing in many respects; teammates and fellow competitors are directly and intensely engaged in an athlete's day-to-day sport involvement and they pursue sport from the same social position as the athlete. That is, athletes practice with, compete with (and against), and compare their capabilities to peers who are of relatively equivalent social standing and power. Whereas coaches and parents often have power over the athlete to dictate behavior and access to valued resources, peers share and negotiate power with one another. Peers therefore may play a unique and important role in shaping the quality and meaning of an athlete's sport experience.

This chapter consists of six primary sections. I first address definitional issues, targeting the two constructs of peer relationships that historically have been of greatest interest to researchers: popularity and friendship. Next, I overview two key theoretical perspectives, the interpersonal theory of psychiatry and attachment theory, that have influenced writings on peer relationships. These theoretical perspectives, and most of the literature on peer relationships, emphasize relationships of young people. Corresponding with this state of affairs, the present chapter is delimited to youth peer relationships in sport.

In the third section, I provide justification for examining peer relationships within the sport context. Specifically, the case is made that peer relationships not only matter in sport, but sport matters to peer relationships. This is followed by a section that overviews sport-based research on peer relationships. In the fifth section I share several possible directions for future research and communicate important issues to consider when conducting this work. Finally, I briefly discuss potential practical implications of research on peer relationships in sport.

Peer Relationships Defined

Peer relationships is an umbrella term that often is not directly defined in research articles targeting constructs of peer relationships. Typically it is assumed that the reader knows what a peer is, and most often within research investigations peers are conceptualized as same- or near-age cohorts such as classmates, teammates, or friends. This is sufficient for many research purposes, as interest is often in general age-related developmental phenomena. However, standard definitions of *peer* refer to individuals of equal standing, whether this is a function of age or rank or class. Relative to relationships with adults that are characterized by power imbalance, youth relationships with others roughly the same age are certainly more balanced; therefore it is appropriate to use age as the primary definitional criterion.

In an achievement-focused context such as sport, however, appropriate conceptualizations of peers could include people of similar athletic capabilities, starting status, or experiences regardless of age. For example, consider D.C. United's Freddy Adu, who became the highest paid player in American professional soccer at 14 years of age. Who are his peers? The answer depends on a variety of factors such as the context and the characteristics (e.g., skillfulness) deemed relevant to the research question. Thus, though most investigators examining peer relationships implicitly delimit peers to those of similar ages, certainly it is appropriate to consider alternative conceptualizations of peers when the research question warrants it.

The reader is referred to the first two chapters of this volume for extensive treatment of what constitutes a relationship. Briefly, relationships are characterized by a history of interactions among individuals who are familiar to one another (Rubin, Bukowski, & Parker, 1998). In their extensive review chapter in the fifth edition of the *Handbook of Child Psychology,* Rubin and colleagues place relationships within a hierarchical social complex of interconnected components. That social complex consists of individuals who possess social characteristics and skills, interactions among individuals in the present, historical patterns of interactions among individuals, and expectations for the nature of future interactions among individuals. Furthermore, groups that represent both collections of constituent relationships as well as higher-order properties (e.g., cohesiveness) that are unique to the group as an entity are part of that social complex. Clearly, then, peer relationships can be studied from multiple conceptual vantage points.

The majority of developmental, educational, and sport psychology research targeting youth peer relationships has emphasized either popularity or friendship (for reviews see Berndt & Ladd, 1989; Gifford-Smith & Brownell, 2003; Weiss & Stuntz, 2004). *Popularity* is the experience of being liked or accepted by one's peers, and *friendship* is the experience of a dyadic relationship that is mutual and close (Bukowski & Hoza, 1989). Popularity is a group-level construct that is considered synonymous with the concepts of social acceptance, peer acceptance, and peer status (Weiss & Stuntz, 2004). Underlying dimensions of popularity are the degree to which one is liked or accepted by peers and the degree to which one is rejected or disliked by peers (Bukowski, Hoza, & Boivin, 1993).

In operationalizing popularity, nomination approaches have been used where individuals within a group list those members of the group that they like as well as those that they dislike. Nominations are tallied for each individual, and sociometric status is determined by assessing social impact (the sum of like and dislike nominations) and social preference (the difference between like and dislike nominations). Social impact and social preference are used to categorize individuals, where popular individuals have predominantly positive nominations from peers, rejected individuals have predominantly negative nominations from peers, controversial individuals have many positive and negative nominations, neglected individuals have few positive or negative nominations, and average individuals have moderate numbers of positive and negative nominations. Ratings of liking have also been used to measure popularity, though this strategy introduces challenges when seeking to classify individuals within the categories previously outlined (see Bukowski et al., 1993; Maassen, van der Linden, Goossens, & Bokhorst, 2000). Both approaches to assessing popularity are notably absent in the sport psychology literature; the dominant strategy instead has been to assess individual-level *perceptions* of peer acceptance. Thus, when seeking to understand the psychosocial importance of sport involvement, there has been greater interest in a person's perceptions of popularity than a person's popularity as classified by the group.

Similarly, research efforts examining sport-related friendships have targeted people's perceptions of their relationship with another individual. Conceptually friendship is bilateral in nature, however, and therefore other elements of this construct of peer relationships are of psychosocial relevance. According to Hartup (1996), three distinguishable friendship dimensions should be considered when seeking to understand the developmental significance of friendships. The first involves whether one possesses a reciprocated friendship as well as how one interacts with friends and nonfriends. Assuming one possesses friendships, the second dimension pertains to the characteristics of one's friends. Similarity of friends on various characteristics is highlighted when examining friendship from this standpoint, and therefore factors that may foster similarity (i.e., sociodemographic conditions, social selection, mutual socialization) are of central interest. The third dimension pertains to the quality of friendships as expressed by features such as intimacy, esteem enhancement, and degree of conflict.

Given the breadth of friendship dimensions that can be examined (see Berndt, 2004, for a brief discussion of the historical basis of these dimensions), it is no surprise that a host of techniques have been used by developmental psychologists to operationalize friendship. Nomination procedures (with varying criteria for what constitutes reciprocation on the part of two respondents), questionnaires, interviews, and behavioral observation have been employed with great success (Bukowski & Hoza, 1989; Bukowski et al., 1993; Furman, 1996; Hartup, 1996).

Guiding Theoretical Frameworks

A number of theoretical perspectives exist that explain the nature of social relationships and point to the role of social relationships in shaping psychological and social developmental outcomes (Weiss & Stuntz, 2004). Despite this rich theoretical literature, Furman (1993) argues that little attention has been paid to theory in the study of peer relationships and that the knowledge base would be significantly enhanced by paying greater attention to the proposed links articulated in existing perspectives and by making conscious efforts to advance theory on peer relationships. Greater attention to theory yields more systematic efforts to understand phenomena and ultimately allows more informed practice as we seek to optimize psychosocial outcomes (Brawley, 1993). Two key perspectives that have guided research efforts on peer relationships and that warrant continued and more intensified attention are the interpersonal theory of psychiatry (Sullivan, 1953) and attachment theory (Ainsworth, 1967; Ainsworth, Blehar, Waters, & Wall, 1978; Bowlby, 1973, 1982).

Interpersonal Theory of Psychiatry

Lectures of Harry Stack Sullivan that were published in 1953 have had a strong influence on the study of peer relationships. Sullivan believed that both peer acceptance and friendship are critical to youth development; thus it is not surprising that the literature on peer relationships has largely broken down into work on either popularity and acceptance or friendship as described earlier in this chapter. Sullivan argued that both the larger peer group and specific friends foster developmental growth through *social accommodation*, a broadening of understanding of others and their differences. That is, peers serve to move a person from an egocentric perspective of the self toward an understanding of the self in relation to others.

Sullivan's (1953) perspective is developmental and suggests that the relative importance of peer acceptance and friendship depends on one's stage of development. In what Sullivan referred to as the juvenile era (i.e., early elementary school), peer acceptance is especially salient. Sullivan argued that one's degree of peer acceptance influences perspectives on authority figures (e.g., parents and teachers), views on competition and compromise, development of stereotypic views of others, and perceptions of ostracism. As one moves into preadolescence, no earlier than age 8 1/2 according to Sullivan, the need for interpersonal intimacy is manifested and there is an intensified interest in a same-sex close friend. Close friendships provide the opportunity for validation of worth and help young people better understand and accommodate the needs of others who are of equal social standing, enabling successful romantic relationships to emerge later in development.

Although Sullivan viewed peer acceptance and friendship as making distinct contributions during different stages of development, he also viewed them as having the potential to accommodate for relationship shortcomings in earlier developmental stages. He argued that peer acceptance can temper negative outcomes stemming from family socialization and enable people to develop socially appropriate behaviors. Close friendships can help provide a sense of validation and therefore buffer the deleterious effects of ostracism by the larger peer group. Thus, an important contribution of Sullivan's perspective is the idea that peer acceptance and friendship have distinct developmental functions yet also can serve common developmental functions. It is for this reason that today's researchers advocate including *both* peer acceptance and friendship variables in research designs (e.g., Parker & Asher, 1993; Smith, 1999) rather than examining either peer acceptance or friendship in isolation.

Attachment Theory

Attachment theory (Ainsworth, 1967; Ainsworth et al., 1978; Bowlby, 1973, 1982) suggests that the quality of attachment between infant and caregiver has implications for developmental outcomes in infancy and beyond. When the caregiver is available and appropriately responsive to the infant, the infant forms a secure attachment with the caregiver and effectively uses the caregiver as base from which to explore and learn. Conversely, when an insecure attachment is formed the infant does not effectively use the caregiver to explore his world. The attachment relationship is believed to have implications for later peer relationships by (a) influencing willingness to initiate relationships with peers; (b) providing a behavioral template for responsiveness to others; and (c) influencing the formation of mental representations, referred to as internal working models, of the self and others (Kerns, 1996). Therefore, compared to less securely attached youth, more securely attached young people are expected to more readily engage with peers, more effectively negotiate the give and take of relationships with peers, have more positive views of self, and have more positive expectations for and attributions of their peers' behavior.

Supporting the attachment perspective, a meta-analysis of 63 studies showed a positive, small to moderate effect size between security of child–mother attachment and peer relations, with effect sizes larger in older children and adolescents than in younger children (Schneider, Atkinson, & Tardif, 2001). The effect-size trend likely reflects the increased importance of intimacy in relationships as children develop. This is corroborated in the same meta-analysis by the observation of larger effect sizes in studies targeting close friendship than in studies examining other peer relations. Recent empirical work also supports a link between attachment and friendship in adolescents (e.g., Weimer, Kerns, & Oldenburg, 2004; Zimmermann, 2004).

The interpersonal theory of psychiatry and attachment theory represent only a sampling of the conceptual perspectives that have been used to frame research on peer relationships. Indeed, psychoanalytic, symbolic interactionist, cognitive developmental, social identity, motivational, and other perspectives have also guided work on peer relationships (see Cotterell, 1996; Rubin et al., 1998; Weiss & Stuntz, 2004). The interpersonal theory of psychiatry historically has been the dominant framework in this research, and attachment theory has been of intensified interest in recent efforts. This is no surprise as both perspectives are developmental in nature, hold interpersonal relationships as central to psychosocial adjustment, and specify the interface of multiple relationships in a person's life. However, as Furman (1993) lamented in his discussion of the interpersonal theory of psychiatry, theory has served as a general guide for research on peer relationships, but many of the specific propositions that make theory useful from an explanatory and practical perspective have not been fully explored. Developmental psychology and sport psychology researchers seeking advances in the understanding of peer relationships should benefit greatly from rigorous attention to theoretical detail.

Why Study Peer Relationships in Sport?

In the introductory section I presupposed that peer relationships in sport are important to study because peers are directly involved in most athletes' day-to-day experiences and because the knowledge base on peer relationships in sport is relatively underdeveloped. There are a number of underdeveloped research areas within sport psychology, however, and therefore it is fair to ask why sport psychologists should direct their attention toward this topic. Although a relatively limited research base exists that directly targets peer relationships in the sport context, substantial indirect support exists to suggest that peer relationships matter in sport *and* that sport matters to peer relationships. Examples from the research literature that provide this indirect support are discussed in the following paragraphs, as is research that supports the value of conducting context-specific examinations of peer relationships.

The literatures on sport participation motivation and preferred sources of competence information both support the idea that peer relationships matter in sport. In the late 1970s and through the 1980s, intense research interest was directed toward describing youth sport participation motives. In a review of this research literature, Weiss and Petlichkoff (1989) concluded that the most commonly cited categories of participation motives were fun, competence, fitness, and affiliation. In this literature, affiliation refers both to a sense of connection with a group as well as the opportunity to develop and maintain friendships.

Young people typically cite multiple motives for their sport participation and affiliation is closely linked with enjoyment and competence-related aspects of sport. For example, Scanlan, Stein, and Ravizza (1989) observed in a retrospective study of former elite figure skaters that social opportunities (e.g., to make and have friends) and the expression and recognition of competence are important sources of sport enjoyment. Additionally, a host of conceptual frameworks used to understand motivational processes in sport explicitly specify aspects of social relationships, or perceptions of them, as antecedents of motivation-related outcomes (for a review see Weiss & Ferrer-Caja, 2002).

Research on the sources of information that people use to judge physical competence also suggests that peer relationships in sport are worth further examination (see Horn, 2004; Horn & Amorose, 1998). In this research, youths typically have been presented with a host of potential sources of information about sport competence (e.g., feedback from adults, win–loss record, peer comparison) and asked to rate the importance of each source in helping to gauge their competence. As young people move from childhood to later childhood and early adolescence, an increase is observed in the importance attributed to peer comparison and evaluation in making judgments about competence. Thus, during this developmental period young athletes are especially attuned to their peers. Rates of organized sport participation peak during this period (Ewing & Seefeldt, 1996) and competence perceptions are essential to motivation in achievement contexts (Weiss & Ferrer-Caja, 2002). Therefore, research that provides better understanding of how this intensified attention to peers plays out in the sport context has potential to significantly enhance our understanding of the youth sport experience.

Not only do peers matter in sport, but for several reasons it appears that sport matters to peer relationships. Sport involvement enables young people to interact with peers, to participate in cooperative activity, and to pursue competitive activity in a setting that is engaging and exciting. As children move into and through the elementary school years, social-comparison motivation emerges (see Passer & Wilson, 2002). The sport context is ideal for fulfilling one's interest in social comparison, as the context emphasizes skillfulness and performance capabilities that are relatively transparent when compared to other achievement contexts such as school. In addition, the sport context provides opportunity for youngsters to experience and attempt to accommodate the varied perspectives of others on such issues as the purposes of sport and fairness. Finally, a host of intervention programs grounded in sport and physical education have been successful in creating social and moral developmental changes in young people (Weiss & Smith, 2002b; see also chapter 19), suggesting that the sport context can be shaped to foster positive peer relationships. Figure 4.1 summarizes the interplay of peer relationships and sport.

Beyond asking if peer relationships matter in sport and if sport matters to peer relationships, one must ask if context matters when seeking to understand peer relationships. Can or should findings from existing work in other contexts such as school be extrapolated to the sport domain? If context does not matter, arguably the proverbial wheel need not be reinvented by sport psychology researchers. If context does matter, sport-specific examination of peer relationships is warranted and researchers are well advised to pursue foundational, descriptive work when starting to build a knowledge base. The existing literature certainly would serve as a referent because there are notable similarities of purpose and form across contexts, but fundamental assumptions would be carefully questioned and tested within the sport context before moving to higher-order research questions.

- Affiliation a primary sport participation motive
- Peer comparison a key source of competence information
- Peer evaluation a key source of competence information

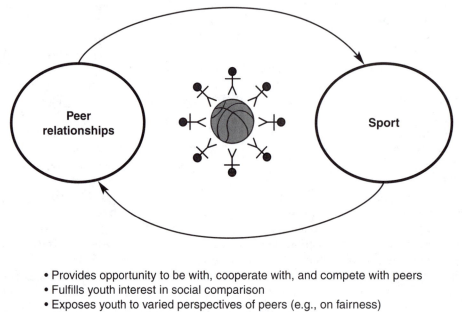

- Provides opportunity to be with, cooperate with, and compete with peers
- Fulfills youth interest in social comparison
- Exposes youth to varied perspectives of peers (e.g., on fairness)
- Can be shaped to foster positive peer relationships

Figure 4.1 Why peer relationships matter in sport and sport matters to peer relationships.

Cross-context research on peer relationships is not extensive; however, the existing literature does suggest that context is an important consideration when seeking to understand peer acceptance and friendship. For example, it is well recognized by those who evaluate social-skills interventions that such interventions are much less effective when taught without consideration of the context where the skills are to be used (see Sheridan, Buhs, & Warnes, 2003). Social competencies that enable one to gain acceptance in the school context may not translate well to other contexts such as sport because norms, expectations, and social cues can differ to a substantial degree.

This idea is supported by a study of friendship expectations held by young people ages 10 to 12 (Zarbatany, Ghesquiere, & Mohr, 1992). The researchers asked participants what behavioral expectations they held for friends when involved in academic activities, sports, games, talking on the phone, and watching television or listening to music. The expectations varied by context. For example, ego reinforcement, preferential treatment, and fair play were especially important in sports and games whereas helping behavior was

expected in academic activities. This pattern might be explained by the degree to which capabilities in these contexts are expressed publicly. Sport competence is readily observed by peers and is highly valued. Helping behavior in this setting may be a reflection of low competence and therefore would be less valued than in school, where one's capabilities are less apparent to the peer group. Alternatively, receiving preferential opportunities to display strengths, ego-reinforcing behaviors, and fair treatment would be expected in sport because these enable positive self-evaluations of competence.

Overall, a good case is made in existing sport psychology literatures for looking closely at peer relationships in sport. Peers are an important draw to young people who participate in sport, peers help young people fulfill their interest in social comparison and judge their capabilities, and interventions have been successful in fostering social and moral development. Furthermore, it seems it is prudent to pay attention to context when studying peer relationships. In the following section I review sport-based research that specifically addresses peer acceptance and popularity, friendship, or both.

Research on Sport-Based Peer Relationships

Although the knowledge base on peer relationships in sport is not extensive, sufficient research has been conducted to provide an outline of how peer relationships matter in sport and how sport matters to peer relationships (see Brustad, Babkes, & Smith, 2001; Smith, 2003; Weiss & Stuntz, 2004). In this section I break down this literature into four general themes. Specifically, I overview work that assesses youth beliefs about sport and acceptance by peers, describes the nature of friendships in sport, examines the link between peer relationships and a host of motivation-related variables in sport, and assesses the association of peer relationships with moral development in sport.

Sport As Social Currency: Youth Beliefs About the Social Value of Sport

Early research on peer relationships in sport was targeted toward understanding youth beliefs about the social currency of sport. That is, do young people believe that being good at sports is a means to peer acceptance and friendship, and is sport competence a more effective means to obtain social acceptance than competence in other activities such as school? The questions were inspired by the emerging sport-related opportunities for American girls promised by federal legislation as well as concerns about the relative priority for young people of such attributes as being athletic and being a good student.

These early research efforts suggest that youths, especially boys, perceive competence in sport as important to their peer relationships (Adler, Kless, & Adler, 1992; Bigelow, Lewko, & Salhani, 1989; Buchanan, Blankenbaker, & Cotten, 1976; Chase & Dummer, 1992; Eitzen, 1975; Feltz, 1978; Kane, 1988; Patrick et al., 1999; Williams & White, 1983). For example, Buchanan et al. asked 4th- through 6th-grade youths about their preferences for making good grades, being good at sports, and being popular. They also had participants nominate peers who were the best students, the best athletes, and the most popular. Though both boys and girls indicated a preference for making good grades over being good at sports, boys felt that being good at sports was most important for popularity. Girls indicated that good grades were more important for popularity than being good at sports, but only by a small margin. The beliefs corresponded well with the peer nominations. Boys categorized as good athletes and girls categorized as student-athletes by the student nominations were those nominated as most popular. These findings are interesting in light of a study on social status of high school girls conducted by Buhrmann and Bratton (1977). They found that athletes received higher status ratings from girls, boys, and teachers than did nonathletes. Furthermore, athletes with greater skill received higher status ratings. Thus, youth perceptions that sport prowess affords social status appear to be grounded in fact.

In a follow-up to the investigation by Buchanan and colleagues, Chase and Dummer (1992) found that boys reported that being good at sports was most important to social status, followed by being handsome, a good student, and wealthy. Girls reported that being pretty was most important to social status, followed by being good at sports, a good student, and wealthy. Their work showed that the importance of physical appearance to popularity increased and the importance of being a good student decreased from the late 1970s to the early 1990s in American children. Girls reported being good at sports as less important to popularity than in the Buchanan et al. study; however, for boys and girls the importance ascribed to sport competence and physical appearance increased as grade level increased. Thus, as children move toward the adolescent years they ascribe progressively more weight to the physical domain as a marker of social status.

Again, youth beliefs about the value of sport to acceptance by peers appear to be grounded in actual acceptance by peers. Evans (cited in Evans & Roberts, 1987) interviewed and observed playground behavior of a group of boys in grades 3 through 6. They found that the most skilled athletes were chosen for teams earlier, played more coveted positions within games, and possessed leadership roles. Playing key roles in games afforded opportunity to further develop physical skills and to acquire and reinforce friendships. Thus, sport ability not only appears germane to acceptance within the larger peer group but also to friendship opportunities.

Though not yet extensively studied, young people appear to see a connection between sport ability and friendship. Over half of the participants in a qualitative investigation of talented (as perceived by themselves and others) adolescents involved in sport and/or the arts expressed that their involvement in these settings provided friendship opportunities (Patrick et al., 1999). Bigelow et al. (1989) assessed expectations of friendships in sport settings held by 9- to 12-year-olds on community sport teams. Participants reported the belief that playing on a sport team is a means to developing friendships and also the belief that low sport ability limits one's friendship options.

In summary, young people believe that sport competence is valuable social currency, enabling both acceptance by the larger peer group and opportunities for friendship. Although few investigations have adopted peer nomination or behavioral observation methods in confirming the accuracy of these beliefs, it appears that perceptions of the social affordances of sport competence have some basis in social reality. Overall, this research suggests that sport matters to peer relationships and that extended analysis of peer relationships in sport is warranted. In the next section I overview work designed to provide a detailed, sport-specific understanding of friendship quality.

Dimensions of Friendship Quality in Sport

As noted earlier in this chapter, constraints on social interactions and expectations for relationships with others can vary by context (Sheridan et al., 2003; Zarbatany et al., 1992). Clearly, then, there is a need for fundamental, sport-specific work that describes the nature of relationships in sport, the expectations young people hold for various relationships in sport, and the meaning of relationships in sport for other context-relevant constructs (e.g., motivation). Much work lies ahead to produce this descriptive database; however, the work thus far has provided a rich understanding of friendship quality in sport.

The developmental significance of friendship stems not only from having friends and from who those friends are, but also from the quality of those friendships (Hartup, 1996). Friendship quality is most often conceptualized as the degree to which friendships offer various provisions or forms of support. Weiss, Smith, and Theeboom (1996) sought to obtain a comprehensive description of friendship quality in sport by interviewing young people aged 8 to 16 years about the positive and negative aspects of, as well as their expectations for, their best friendship in sport. The interview guide asked participants to describe a variety of aspects of their best sport friendship. For example, participants were asked about the differences between their best friend and other peers in sport relative to what they say and do, the positive as well as negative aspects of their friendship, and whether there are differences between a best friend in sport and friends that do not participate in sport. The authors conducted an inductive content analysis of the interview responses. Twelve positive dimensions and four negative dimensions of sport friendship quality were observed, as were several friendship expectations that were largely redundant with the positive friendship-quality dimensions.

The positive dimensions of friendship quality that emerged in the study, the percentage of respondents

citing the dimensions, and the definitions provided by Weiss et al. (1996) for each dimension are as follows: (1) *companionship* (95%), or spending time and doing things together; (2) *pleasant play/association* (89%), or positive valence attached to being together, including enjoying an association with one's best friend; (3) *self-esteem enhancement* (87%), or saying and doing things to boost feelings of self-worth; (4) *help and guidance* (79%), or providing instrumental assistance and tangible support; (5) *prosocial behavior* (76%), or saying and doing things that conform to social convention; (6) *intimacy* (71%), or interactions or mutual feelings of a close personal nature; (7) *loyalty* (71%), or sense of commitment to or being there for each other; (8) *things in common* (63%), or similarity of interests, activities, and values; (9) *attractive personal qualities* (58%), or attractive physical and psychological characteristics; (10) *emotional support* (45%), or feelings or expressions of concern for one another; (11) *absence of conflicts* (39%), or refraining from fights or judgmental attitudes; and (12) *conflict resolution* (16%), or getting over fights.

The negative dimensions of friendship quality were as follows: (1) *conflict* (42%), or negative behaviors that cause disagreement, disrespect, or dissension; (2) *unattractive personal qualities* (37%), or undesirable personality or behavioral characteristics; (3) *betrayal* (16%), or disloyalty or insensitivity; and (4) *inaccessible* (8%), or infrequent opportunity to interact. Analysis of the percentage of respondents citing the dimensions showed relatively few differences by gender and by age (i.e., 8-9 years, 10-12 years, 13-16 years). More females than males referred to emotional support, the two younger groups referred to prosocial behavior and loyalty more than the oldest group, the two older groups referred to attractive personal qualities more than the youngest group, and there was a progressive increase in the percentage of individuals citing intimacy as age increased. Many of the dimensions that emerged were consistent with those found in developmental psychology; however, the underlying themes were specific to sport and therefore this study provides a valuable foundation for research on sport-specific friendship quality.

Weiss and Smith (1999) used these qualitative data to assist in the development of a sport-specific survey instrument designed to tap youth perceptions of friendship quality. After determining that a measure of general friendship quality was not sufficiently valid for use in the sport context, they retained good-performing items from that measure and developed a large set of new items from Weiss et al.'s (1996) qualitative data that represented all of the positive and negative dimensions of friendship quality. Based on item analyses, exploratory factor analyses, and conceptual considerations, the measure was honed to a more parsimonious set of items representing fewer distinct dimensions. A final study tested the refined measure of sport friendship quality. The final measurement model that emerged from this study consisted of six dimensions of friendship quality: self-esteem enhancement and supportiveness, loyalty and intimacy, things in common, companionship and pleasant play, conflict resolution, and conflict. The measure discriminated responses pertaining to one's best versus third best friend and showed good test–retest reliability.

Weiss and Smith (2002a) provided further support for the validity of the measure by confirming the underlying factor structure and showing theoretically consistent relationships between the friendship quality subscales and measures of peer acceptance, enjoyment, and commitment. They also examined age and gender differences in perceptions of friendship quality with a best sport friend. They found that 10- to 13-year-olds perceived significantly higher companionship and pleasant play and significantly lower loyalty and intimacy, things in common, and conflict than 14- to 18-year-olds. Girls reported significantly higher self-esteem enhancement and supportiveness, loyalty and intimacy, and things in common and significantly lower conflict than boys. The gender findings for positive friendship quality were corroborated in a study of young (i.e., ages 9 to 18) athletes with disabilities conducted by Martin and Smith (2002). However, in that study no gender differences emerged in friendship conflict. Overall, significant differences observed by age or gender are consistent with developmental findings. However, in these studies and Weiss et al.'s (1996) qualitative investigation, some differences that would be expected based on the developmental psychology literature did not emerge. This may reflect the relative homogeneity of experiences and expectations within sport across ages and gender when compared to other contexts such as school.

These systematic efforts have provided a foundation for understanding friendship quality in sport. A rich, descriptive account of friendship in sport was provided followed by development of a sport-specific measure of friendship quality. Preliminary work using the measure supports its validity and has provided descriptive information on age and gender differences in perceptions of friendship in sport. These efforts have paved the way for subsequent research exploring associations between friendship quality and other constructs of interest to sport psychologists. Though published work using this particular measurement tool is minimal at present, it is expected that in the future a number of studies exploring the link between perceptions of friendship quality and other psychosocial variables of interest to sport psychologists will appear in the literature.

Peer Relationships and Motivation in Sport

Motivational phenomena are of tremendous interest to sport psychology researchers and there is an emerging literature linking peer relationships with motivation-related constructs. Motivation may be viewed from an outcome vantage, where it is represented by choices individuals make and the effort and persistence with which such choices are pursued, and from an individual difference vantage, where motivation is reflected in the possession of certain motives or dispositions (see Weiss & Ferrer-Caja, 2002). As observed in the literature on youth sport participation motivation discussed earlier and dominant theoretical perspectives on motivation, social factors (e.g., perceptions of social regard), self-perceptions (e.g., of sport competence), and affect (e.g., enjoyment, anxiety) are core motivation-related constructs. These core constructs are known to associate with motivational outcomes as well as individual dispositions, and therefore their links with one another are of great interest. In this section I overview research that examines the association of peer relationship constructs with self-perceptions and affect as well as other motivational indices.

Self-perceptions are views about the self that can range from global (e.g., self-esteem) to domain specific (e.g., perceived physical competence) to behaviorally specific (e.g., self-efficacy) (see Fox, 2002). Weiss and Duncan (1992) examined the association between peer relationships and perceived physical competence in a study of sport-camp participants in grades 3 through 6. The participants completed assessments of perceived peer acceptance and perceived physical competence while teachers rated each participant's actual peer acceptance and physical competence. Higher actual and perceived peer acceptance were associated with higher actual and perceived physical competence. Furthermore, the peer acceptance variables were positively associated with other important motivational variables, namely perceived success, future expectations for success, and stability and personal control attributions for success. Combined with Weiss et al.'s (1996) finding that self-esteem enhancement is a key dimension of friendship quality and literature establishing peer comparison and evaluation as important sources of information on physical competence (see Horn, 2004; Horn & Amorose, 1998), these findings suggest that a meaningful association exists between peer relationships and self-perceptions.

Peer relationships are also linked with both positive and negative affect in sport. Youth sport research on positive affect typically focuses on enjoyment. As noted earlier in this chapter, social affiliation and recognition opportunities are important sources of sport enjoyment

(Scanlan et al., 1989), and pleasant play/association is a frequently cited marker of positive friendship quality (Weiss et al., 1996). Weiss and Smith (2002a) examined the association of friendship quality with enjoyment and commitment in their study of young tennis players. They found that higher perceptions of companionship and pleasant play, conflict resolution, and things in common relative to a best tennis friend were associated with enjoyment of and commitment to tennis. This study suggests that a breadth of friendship qualities can contribute to one's enjoyment of sport.

Friendship conflict was not observed to significantly relate with enjoyment in Weiss and Smith's (2002a) study; however, it is reasonable to hypothesize that friendship conflict may relate with negative affect in sport. In Weiss et al.'s (1996) qualitative investigation of sport friendship quality, 42% of respondents referred to conflict in their best sport friendship. Higher-order themes that comprised this dimension were verbal insults, argumentation, negative competitiveness, and physical aggression that were associated with hurt feelings, frustration, and anger.

The broader peer group also can contribute to negative affect in sport. For example, a sample of 6th-grade girls who were observed and interviewed by Kunesh, Hasbrook, and Lewthwaite (1992) reported receiving more negative treatment by boys in formal, school-based sport activities than while engaged in physical activities at home. This treatment corresponded with the experience of anxiety and embarrassment in the formal, school-based sport setting. Clearly, peer relationships in sport should be examined for their potential negative motivational implications for sport as well as their potential positive motivational implications.

Other motivational indices have been examined relative to peer relationship constructs, such as commitment (Weiss & Smith, 2002a), success expectancies and attributions (Weiss & Duncan, 1992), achievement goal orientations (Escartí, Roberts, Cervelló, & Guzmán, 1999), and sport participation decisions and continuity (e.g., Brown, Frankel, & Fennell, 1989; Coakley & White, 1992). Escartí et al. examined the perceptions held by 14- to 18-year-old tennis and track athletes of the criteria others use to assess their sport success. Perceptions of the criteria used by both sport friends and nonsport friends to judge one's sport success corresponded with one's own goal orientation, suggesting that peers both within and outside of sport may be important motivational agents in the sport context. Furthermore, according to Coakley and White's examination of sport-participation decisions made by British adolescents, type of peer relationship may have meaning for sport involvement depending on gender. They found that female adolescents were more likely than male adolescents to require a friend to accompany them when

pursuing sport. Male adolescents instead were content to find a familiar individual (not necessarily a friend) once they arrived at the sport site. Female adolescents also were more likely than male adolescents to have their participation decisions influenced by a friend of the opposite sex.

Overall, peer relationships in sport are linked with self-perceptions, positive and negative affect, and other constructs that represent sport motivation. Gender appears to be an important moderator of the link between peers and motivation, and both friendships and the larger peer group appear to be motivationally salient. Therefore, both gender and relationship type should be carefully examined as research on peer relationships and motivation progresses.

Peer Relationships and Moral Development in Sport

Sport has long been extolled as a pursuit that builds character, but at the same time it has been criticized as a domain that undermines character. The debate over the character-building versus undermining nature of sport has led to considerable research interest on moral development in sport (see Shields & Bredemeier, 1995; Weiss & Smith, 2002b; see also chapter 19). According to contemporary theory on moral development (e.g., Bandura, 1986; Haan, 1978; Kohlberg, 1969; Piaget, 1965), peers can contribute to moral development by serving as models of and providing reinforcement for moral attitudes and behaviors. They can also influence moral reasoning by discussing or creating moral dilemmas. A few sport-based investigations have explored the link between peers and moral development within these theoretical frameworks, though rarely have peer acceptance and friendship been directly targeted.

Several studies have examined youth beliefs about the degree to which significant others such as coaches, parents, and peers endorse or engage in illegal behavior (e.g., aggression) in sport and how these beliefs associate with youths' own attitudes and behaviors (e.g., Mugno & Feltz, 1985; Smith, 1974; Stephens, 2001; Stuart & Ebbeck, 1995). For example, in adolescent male interscholastic hockey players, Smith found that higher perceptions of nonplaying peers' approval of aggressive behavior in hockey was associated with selection of more violent hockey role models, which in turn was associated with more assault penalties during the playing season. Perceptions of other social agents (i.e., father, mother, coaches/teammates) did not significantly predict selection of role models. Stephens examined female participants in basketball summer camps designed for beginning (grades 4 through 7) and advanced (grades 8 through 12) skill levels. For both groups, perception

Moral attitudes and behaviors can be shaped by teammates.

of a greater number of teammates endorsing injurious behavior and a greater willingness to injure if the coach requested it were associated with greater reported likelihood to aggress. Such work suggests that peers are important agents in shaping young people's attitudes and behaviors in sport and that research specifically targeted at peer relationships and moral development in sport is warranted.

Stuntz and Weiss (2003) recently conducted such an investigation, examining goal orientations and the social context as predictors of physical unsportsmanlike play (e.g., grabbing, elbowing, pushing an opponent). They measured task, ego, friendship, peer acceptance, and coach praise orientations of middle school physical education students and also had the students indicate their intention to use unsportsmanlike play after reading a scenario where the protagonist must decide whether or not to engage in unsportsmanlike play. Social context was manipulated by adding slight alterations to the scenario such that the protagonist's best friend, teammates, or both best friend and teammates condoned the behavior or not. For girls, friendship and peer acceptance goal orientations did not contribute to prediction of intentions to use unsportsmanlike play. For boys, however, higher scores on friendship and peer acceptance goal orientations predicted higher intention to use unsportsmanlike behavior, over and above task and ego orientation. Contrary to expectations, this finding held regardless of the context manipulation. The authors speculated that boys' actual peers may have driven their responses more than the fictional peers in the manipulation and that the different findings by

gender may reflect the study's emphasis on physical aggression versus relational aggression (e.g., ignoring, rumor spreading). In any case, preliminary evidence was provided by this study for the importance of friendship and peer acceptance goal orientations to sportsmanship. Views of success that are grounded in peer relationships therefore may play a role in the degree to which character is promoted or undermined in sport.

Overall, the studies reviewed in this section combined with intervention research described earlier in this chapter (see Weiss & Smith, 2002b) show peers to be intimately connected to moral development. As with the other research strains that were overviewed in this section, however, the research base specifically targeting peer relationships is thin and many questions remain to be answered. This leaves tremendous opportunity for sport psychology researchers. In the next section I provide a number of potentially fruitful directions for future research and highlight several issues worthy of consideration as we seek to extend the knowledge base on peer relationships in sport.

Future Research

Because relatively few direct investigations of peer relationships in sport have been conducted, there is a host of unanswered questions to be addressed by sport psychology researchers. Consider these examples:

- What are the dynamics of peer relationships within sport?

- How do transitions to new teams or competitive levels affect one's peer relationships?
- How are motivation and moral intentions affected when different social agents (e.g., teammates, parents) communicate conflicting viewpoints or expectations about sport behavior?

In this section I share promising directions for future research and discuss several important issues that researchers should consider in the pursuit of these directions.

Clearly, the knowledge base on peer relationships in sport would benefit from developmental research. Taking a developmental perspective involves addressing change over time, seeking to understand such change in quantitative and qualitative terms as well as through consideration of both individual differences and contextual factors (Weiss & Raedeke, 2004). Cross-sectional approaches to understanding development can be adopted where the researcher deliberately selects certain age groups for study or compares age groups that are developmentally distinct. Also, longitudinal approaches can be adopted where study participants are followed over time. Likely because of the demands and challenges of longitudinal research (e.g., longer data collection time frame, subject attrition), such work rarely appears in the sport psychology literature. However, these challenges are well worth facing and can be partially offset by using combined cross-sectional and longitudinal research designs.

Developmental research on peer relationships in sport would be especially fruitful because dominant theoretical perspectives on peer relationships offer testable, developmental hypotheses. Sullivan's (1953) interpersonal theory of psychiatry proposes that peer acceptance and friendship make distinct contributions to psychosocial development and that their salience is a function of one's stage of development. Coupling such theoretical propositions with our understanding of the sport context can lead to interesting research questions. Do friendships become especially important motivational agents in sport as children move into preadolescence, or does the social context of sport (i.e., highly comparative in nature) render peer acceptance most salient across developmental stages?

Attachment theory (Ainsworth, 1967; Ainsworth et al., 1978; Bowlby, 1973, 1982) suggests that early relationships with significant social agents serve as a template for approaching later relationships. Do relationships with significant adults (e.g., parents and coaches) early in a child's sport involvement shape the nature of that child's interactions with and expectations of peers later in her sport career? Is success in negotiating the social transitions associated with entry into organized sport involvement, intensified involvement,

high-level competition, and leaving sport (see Wylleman, De Knop, Ewing, & Cumming, 2000) a function of the security of child–parent attachment? These are just a few examples of the many interesting developmental research questions that could be pursued by sport psychology researchers.

These theoretical perspectives also highlight the importance of the broader social system when seeking to understand peer relationships in sport. To fully understand the role of peers in motivational and moral developmental processes in sport, for example, one must understand the multiple relationships of salience to athletes in the sport setting. Parents, coaches, friends, and the larger peer group may not always communicate the same messages or work in concert to shape attitudes and behaviors in sport. What happens when a coach encourages a child's sport involvement but that child is rejected by teammates? How are attitudes toward aggression shaped and what aggressive behaviors are expressed when an athlete perceives disapproval of aggression by parents but approval by peers? These types of questions have not been systematically explored by researchers, and those studies that do consider multiple social relationships typically examine the relationships in parallel; emphasis is more often placed on the relative contribution each social agent makes to prediction of the criterion variable of interest than on the relevance of the *combination* of relationships in the athletic social system.

The interface of parents and peers in psychosocial development has been discussed by many developmental psychologists (e.g., Parke & O'Neil, 1999; Sullivan, 1953; Youniss, 1980) and certainly is worth understanding in sport. Parents and peers are key socializing agents in the sport context and are of varying psychosocial importance across developmental phases (Brustad & Partridge, 2002). Theory (e.g., Sullivan, 1953) and empirical research (e.g., Gauze, Bukowski, Aquan-Assee, & Sippola, 1996) suggest that the combination of parent–child and peer–child relationships associates with psychosocial outcomes and that poor relationships in one system can be accommodated for by the other system. Examining children in grades 4 through 6, Gauze et al. found that associations between family measures and indices of well-being were stronger in the presence of weak friendships and that the associations between friendship measures and indices of well-being were stronger in the presence of weak family relationships. This suggests that the negative psychosocial implications of poor relationships with one type of social agent can be buffered when good relationships exist with other social agents.

Ullrich-French and Smith (2006) tested this buffering hypothesis in sport by examining young soccer players' (aged 10 to 14 years) perceptions of parent–child relationship quality, friendship quality, and peer acceptance in soccer as predictors of indices of soccer motivation. They found that combinations of social relationships predicted variance in motivational outcomes over and above main effects of social relationships, and they found that two relatively positive social relationships were required to buffer the effects of a relatively less positive relationship on perceived soccer competence and enjoyment. These findings support continued examination of relationship combinations in sport and the inclusion of peer relationship variables in such investigations.

In pursuing future research to better understand peer relationships in sport, there are several items for investigators to consider. These issues have been discussed elsewhere in the chapter and therefore are only briefly touched upon here. First, careful attention to theory in peer relationships research is of utmost importance. To this point much work on peer relationships has been atheoretical or has acknowledged theory as a general backdrop without testing specific theoretical propositions (Furman, 1993). It is through careful attention to theory that we will most rapidly advance our understanding of peer relationships in sport.

Second, researchers should consider the level of analysis employed when selecting peer relationship variables. Most research has emphasized the individual level of analysis, particularly focusing upon perceptions of peer acceptance or friendship. However, as Rubin et al. (1998) have discussed, peer relationships exist within a social complex that not only involves individual-level elements, but also interactive components, historical patterns of interactions, and group-level processes. Thus, the knowledge base on peer relationships in sport will advance as methodological and data-analytic techniques to examine peer relationships at multiple levels of analysis are more broadly employed.

Third, peer relationships and expectations held for such relationships vary by context of peer interaction (Kunesh et al., 1992; Zarbatany et al., 1992). The nature of peer relationships or their meaning may vary as a function of informal versus formal sport involvement, practice versus competitive circumstances, and type of sport, such as team versus individual. Furthermore, peers directly involved as well as peers not involved in an athlete's sport experience may influence beliefs about the social value of sport and sport-based outcomes such as motivation or moral development. The influence of nonsport peers, for example, can range from reinforcing a young athlete's sport involvement by communicating value in his achievements to undermining sport involvement by trivializing it or presenting alternative activities in an attractive light.

Fourth, researchers are advised to consider the negative aspects of peer relationships in sport as well as the positive aspects. For example, conflict, which is omni-present in competitive sport, is an important contributor to development (see Shantz & Hartup, 1992). As observed by Weiss et al. (1996), even relationships with best friends in sport involve features such as conflict and betrayal. Developmental research has established the psychosocial relevance of relational aggression, especially among girls, not only within peer groups but also within friendships (Crick & Nelson, 2002). Exploration of relational forms of aggression within sport warrants attention, as this not only will provide a more complete understanding of peer relationships in sport but also could help sport psychologists understand barriers to the successful implementation of interventions for peer relationships.

Finally, sufficient empirical evidence exists to warrant consideration of age and gender as moderator variables in research on sport-based peer relationships (e.g., Coakley & White, 1992; Weiss & Smith, 2002a). Though differences observed in some sport-based investigations have not been as stark as would be expected from the developmental literature (e.g., Weiss et al., 1996), and though not all future investigations will necessarily target developmental or gender-based hypotheses, researchers should examine their data by these variables when diverse samples are employed.

Practical Implications

As noted throughout this chapter, the knowledge base on peer relationships is underdeveloped. Therefore one must be cautious in forwarding practical implications; much remains to be learned about the nature of peer relationships in sport and how such relationships may or may not be amenable to modifications. Indeed, a critical research direction will be to explore if and how the sport setting can be constructed to meaningfully enhance peer relationships, and if such enhancements in turn foster improved quality of sport experiences. Studies on moral-development interventions suggest that it is possible to shape youth sport settings to promote desired attitudes and behaviors (see Weiss & Smith, 2002b).

Such studies should be consulted as well as intervention work designed to deemphasize aspects of the motivational climate (e.g., excessive normative comparison) that may interfere with peer relationships (see Treasure, 2001). Emerging work on the motivational climate created by peers in sport (see chapter 11) and social goal orientations in sport (Allen, 2003; Stuntz & Weiss, 2003) can further inform research on peer relationship interventions. Clearly, interventions should be dynamic and developmental in nature, and they are likely to be most efficacious when integrated with the myriad elements of the sport social system.

While it is important to be cautious in forwarding practical implications, reasonable suggestions forwarded by Weiss and Stuntz (2004) in their review of the literature on peer relationships in sport include the following: (a) generating cooperative goals in the sport setting, (b) encouraging young people to engage in their own problem solving rather than expecting adults to solve problems for them, (c) enabling young people to engage in shared decision making, (d) designing sport settings for small-group activities and maximal participation, and (e) adopting creative selection of peer leaders (as opposed to relying solely on athletic competence to select leaders). The underlying goals of these strategies are to ensure opportunity for all participants to develop both physical and social skills and to create a proverbial level playing field that directs the attention of young athletes toward inclusion, teamwork, and respect for others. In fulfilling these goals, these strategies have much potential for enhancing individual-level, interactive and dyadic, and group-level features of peer relationships in sport.

Summary

Peer relationships are of tremendous importance to the psychosocial development of young people and therefore should be carefully considered by those interested in the implications of sport involvement for children and adolescents. Several lines of research in sport psychology indicate that peers are salient to the sport experience and that sport experiences matter to peer relationships. Sport psychologists will have a significantly enhanced understanding of the youth sport experience with further theory-based research that specifically targets peer relationship constructs and that addresses dynamic aspects of peer relationships in sport, captures the place of sport-based peer relationships within the larger sport and nonsport social structure, and tests sport-based interventions for peer relationships. This understanding will ultimately allow efficacious practical suggestions to be forwarded to sport professionals and therefore result in more meaningful and positive experiences for young athletes.

Discussion Questions

1. Why are popularity and friendship considered distinct constructs in the literature on peer relationships?

2. According to Hartup (1996), what three distinguishable dimensions must be considered to understand the developmental significance of friendships?

3. How does context matter to peer relationships? What do you believe are salient similarities and differences among social contexts such as sport, school, and music?

4. How do peer relationships link with motivational processes in sport?

5. If you were to conduct a research project on peer relationships in sport, what would be your research question and why? How would you proceed to obtain an answer to that question?

part II

Coach Leadership and Group Dynamics

The need for effective coach leadership is widely recognized. Coaches must have the capacity to interact with their athletes in order to create an interconnected group and to guide the group's progress in such a way that enables the realization of performance and psychosocial goals. However, because athletes and teams do not perform in a vacuum, the impact of an audience on their performance is also important for the achievement of goals. Part II of this volume contains four chapters that investigate three interrelated areas: coach leadership, team cohesion, and audience effects.

In chapter 5, Harold Riemer provides an excellent overview of key leadership theories that have provided the basis for the multidimensional model of coach leadership. The main components and propositions of the model are comprehensibly presented. This presentation includes a relatively new component, namely, transformational leadership; this component is exciting in that it promises to bring conceptual breadth to research on coach leadership. A substantial review of research associated with the various hypotheses of the model is presented. The practical implications highlighted reflect the need for more and better research in this area.

In chapter 6, Ronald Smith and Frank Smoll present a cogent description of the work on the mediational model of coach leadership. The fundamental assumption of the model is that coaches' actual behaviors affect athletes' thoughts and feelings through the athletes' recall and understanding of their coaches' behaviors. The characteristics and processes that influence coaches' behaviors and mediate their effects on athletes are delineated in detail. The model has guided considerable research to date; research findings are discussed and suggestions for further research are put forward. Smith and Smoll conclude by highlighting potential practical implications of current research efforts.

In chapter 7, Albert Carron, Mark Eys, and Shauna Burke consider the nature of cohesion in sport teams and its relationship to team success. Their discussion begins with explaining the multidimensional construct of team cohesion and continues with a methodical presentation of relevant research. The central relationship of team cohesion to team success is presented, followed by potential moderators of the cohesion–performance relationship. Situational, personal, and leadership correlates are addressed. Carron, Eys, and Burke hark back to the potential benefits and problems of cohesion in teams. They summarize the implications of cohesion while making a sound case for more research.

In chapter 8, Marc Jones, Steven Bray, and David Lavallee discuss theories and research that examine the impact of an audience on the psychological and physiological states of sport performers. It is argued that performance often occurs in front of other people who are both attending and evaluating. Jones, Bray, and Lavallee explain the well-known phenomenon of the so-called home advantage and home-field disadvantage. Future research directions include a call for more experimental studies, while the section on practical implications recommends strategies to help athletes cope when performing in front of an audience.

chapter 5

Multidimensional Model of Coach Leadership

Harold A. Riemer, PhD

Learning Objectives

On completion of this chapter, the reader should have

1. appreciation of the theories and leadership research that laid the foundation for the development of the multidimensional model of leadership (MML);

2. understanding of the key constructs presented by the MML;

3. understanding of the key propositions about leadership made by the MML;

4. knowledge of the research results associated with various hypotheses made by the MML;

5. appreciation of concerns associated with the research conducted to date; and

6. capacity to reflect on practical insights that might be drawn from the theory and research behind the MML.

© Sport the Library

Many people in Western societies, athletes and nonathletes alike, perceive a coach's leadership to be one of the most critical components in determining an athlete's or team's performance. In most organizational settings, leadership is thought to be a major factor in determining effectiveness or performance levels (Doherty, 1997; Posner & Brodsky, 1992). In the same way, sport leadership has been assigned great value by participants and spectators alike. Victorious athletes often cite the vital role the coach played in their achievement (e.g., George, 1993), whereas fans may deify coaches who have brought success to an athletic organization (e.g., Woody Hayes at Ohio State University or Clive Woodward, England's former rugby coach).

When athletes or teams are successful, coaches are often considered to have played a major role in those victories. When athletes or teams are not successful, it is generally the coach who is blamed. Every year hundreds of coaches are fired and hired under the belief that if athletes or teams are provided with the appropriate athletic leadership, they will experience success. While for many people there is a direct connection between leadership and performance, most would be unable to articulate what it takes to be an effective leader other than the fact that they win competitions. The purpose of this chapter is to examine the theory and research of coach leadership as it pertains to the multidimensional model of leadership (MML) (Chelladurai, 1978, 1990, 2001).

Historical Perspectives

This section examines important historical contributions to our understanding of leadership in general and the MML in particular. A necessary first step, however, is a basic understanding of how researchers and others have defined leadership over the years.

Definitions of Leadership

Over the last 50 years, hundreds of definitions of leadership have been written. The following is but a small sample:

> The behavior of an individual when he (she) is directing the activities of a group towards a shared goal. (Hemphill & Coons, 1957, p. 7)

> The behavioral process of influencing individuals and groups toward set goals. (Barrow, 1977, p. 232)

> Leadership is a process of social influence in which one person is able to enlist the aid and support of others in the accomplishment of a common task. (Chemers, 1997, p. 1)

Several key concepts are common to most definitions of leadership. First, leadership happens at both an *individual* and *group* or organizational level. Leaders must deal with athletes at an individual level, and they must deal with the collective dynamics of the individuals comprising the team. Second, leadership is a *behavioral process.* Leaders change or direct the behavior of individuals; leadership is concerned with the leader's actions and behavior. Third, leadership is necessarily *interpersonal;* it requires human interaction and therefore the ability to communicate. Finally, leadership is concerned with *achievement;* it is always focused on moving individuals or groups in a specific direction. Leaders must be able to influence others to strive to achieve set objectives or goals.

Clearly, leaders must *do* a great deal. They ensure the group fulfills the requirements of the organizations to which it belongs (e.g., the tennis team, the athletic department, the sport federation), including making certain that organizational goals are reached. Coaches are expected to increase their athletes' performance productivity so that they improve as individuals and a team. In a similar vein, athletic leaders strive to enhance the satisfaction of those they are responsible for, shape organizational objectives, and establish or maintain group and organizational culture.

Key Advances in Leadership Theory

The MML has drawn upon the rich tradition of leadership research associated with the disciplines of management and organizational psychology. To this end, it is important to have a basic understanding of the key advances in these parent disciplines that have contributed to the development of leadership theory in the sporting context.

Early work focused on leadership styles and included the groundbreaking work of Kurt Lewin (Lewin, Lippet, & White, 1939) and work at the Ohio State University (Hemphill, 1950; Halpin & Winer, 1957), the University of Michigan (Kahn, 1951; Katz & Kahn, 1951), and Harvard University (Bales & Slater, 1955). Building on this work, four basic contingency theories formed the foundation for most leadership research: (a) Fiedler's (1967) model of leadership effectiveness, (b) Evans' (1970) and House's (1971; House & Dressler, 1974) path-goal theory of leadership, (c) Osborn and Hunt's (1975) adaptive-reactive theory of leadership, and (d) Yukl's (1971) discrepancy model of leadership.

Two more recent perspectives, transactional leadership theory (also known as exchange leadership) (e.g., Burns, 1978; Bass, 1985) and transformational leadership theory (Bass, 1985), have also made significant contributions to our understanding of leadership. All of these theories examine leadership from one or more of the following perspectives: the *leader,* the *member* (follower, subordinate, athlete), and the *situational context.*

In the late 1930s, Kurt Lewin undertook a research program to examine the relative merits of democratic, autocratic, and laissez-faire leadership styles. He designed an experiment in which he trained graduate students to lead groups of boys in each of the three styles. The results suggested that groups with a democratic style of leadership were most satisfied and operated in the most positive and orderly fashion while those with an autocratic leader were observed to have the greatest levels of aggressive behavior (Lewin et al., 1939). Follow-up work by Lippet and White (1943) suggested that groups with autocratic leadership were most productive, but only when the leader was present.

Between 1945 and 1958, considerable research looked at specific observable behaviors of effective leaders in order to determine what behaviors make a good leader. Work at three different universities (i.e., Ohio State, Michigan, Harvard) using three different research methodologies reached essentially the same conclusion—that there are two basic leadership behaviors or styles. In the first style, the focus of the leader's behavior is on the relationship with the *subordinate* or *follower* (consideration behavior), while in the second style the focus of the leader's behavior is on the *task* (initiating structure). Table 5.1 presents the findings from the three research groups.

Building on this work, Fiedler (1967) assumed that people have a dominant style of leadership that is difficult to change and that this primary leadership style is focused on either accomplishing the group's task or ensuring a good relationship with the employee or follower. He suggested that a leader's effectiveness is a function of whether the particular situation is favorable toward the individual's dominant leadership style. According to Fiedler, the favorableness of a given situation is a function of (a) the nature of the relationship between the leader and member, (b) the power associated with the leader's position in the organization, (c) the clarity of the task goals, (d) the complexity of the task, and (e) the ease of evaluating the outcomes of a leader's decisions. The major contribution of Fiedler's theory was the idea that any leadership style can be effective as long as it is matched with an appropriate situation. Fiedler argued that situations can be changed to better suit the leadership style of the designated leader. For example, a coach often makes changes to how a team is run that better suit her leadership style.

The path-goal theory of leadership (House, 1971) builds on Vroom's (1964) expectancy theory. Expectancy theory suggests that individuals are motivated to engage in a particular behavior because they *expect* it will lead to an outcome they value. House argued that leaders are able to influence all the determinants of motivation proposed by expectancy theory. The critical difference between House's and Fiedler's theories is

Table 5.1   Results of Research Concerning Leadership Behaviors in the 1950s

Construct category	NAME AND DESCRIPTION OF LEADERSHIP BEHAVIOR OR STYLE		
	Ohio State[a]	Michigan[b]	Harvard[c]
Subordinate	*Consideration* • Establishing open communication • Having mutual trust and respect • Using participative decision making • Having interpersonal warmth	*Employee oriented* • Establishing good rapport • Having an open, accepting style • Having concern for problems and feelings of subordinates	*Socioemotional experts* • Focusing on reducing tension • Raising morale • Instigating group participation
Task	*Initiating structure* • Focusing on organizing and structuring group activities • Defining relationships in the group • Directing followers toward group tasks	*Production oriented* • Emphasizing planning • Providing task direction • Ensuring productivity	*Task specialists* • Organizing • Summarizing • Directing

[a]Halpin & Winer (1957)

[b]Kahn (1951); Katz & Kahn (1951)

[c]Bales & Slater (1955)

that House assumed that leaders can and should adapt their leadership style to a given situation. The focus of Fiedler's theory was on the leader, while House's focus was on the subordinate. House believed that the role of the leader was to motivate followers to engage in the organization's tasks by clarifying for the subordinates how the completion of these tasks would result in outcomes that members valued. To quote House, the leader's job is to "increase personal pay-offs to subordinates for work-goal attainment, and making the path to these pay-offs easier to travel by clarifying it, reducing road blocks and pitfalls, and increasing the opportunities for personal satisfaction en route" (p. 324). The major contribution of House's work was the idea that different members require different styles and approaches from the leader.

Osborn and Hunt's (1975) adaptive-reactive theory of leadership focused on how the organization affects its members and leaders. They noted that leaders have to balance the demands of the organizational system with the needs of the individual members. In other words, leaders must *adapt* to the requirements of the organization (e.g., a function of unit size, level of technology, formal structure) and *react* to the needs and desires of the organizational members (e.g., a function of the nature of the task, individual differences).

Yukl's (1971) contributions to the development of leadership theory in sport were threefold. First, he conceptualized consideration behavior, initiating structure, and autocratic–democratic decision making as three independent yet interrelated dimensions of leader behavior. He viewed decision centralization as a single dimension, where a high score indicated a lack of subordinate participation in decision making (i.e., autocratic) and a low score indicated high subordinate influence in decisions (i.e., participative or democratic). More importantly, he argued that scoring high on consideration or initiating structure did not necessarily preclude a high or low score on decision centralization. In Yukl's words, it was possible to have "benevolent autocrats" and "malevolent democrats" (p. 419).

Second, Yukl proposed that a discrepancy model governs the relationship between a leader's behavior and a member's satisfaction with the leader. That is, a person's satisfaction with a leader or coach is a function of the difference between a person's preference for a particular leadership behavior and her actual experience. Yukl hypothesized that a group member's preference for various leader behaviors was determined by the combination of (a) the member's personality, specifically the traits of authoritarianism (see Vroom, 1959) and need for independence (see Trow, 1957; Ross & Zander, 1957), and (b) situational variables (i.e.,

importance of a decision to a member, level of commitment to group goals).

Yukl's third contribution was his explanation of the relationship between leader behaviors and group performance. He suggested that group performance is a function of the interaction of three important variables (referred to as intermediate variables): (a) the members' motivation to engage in the task, (b) the members' task-related skills, and (c) the technical quality of the task decisions. Leader behaviors and situational variables are antecedent to the intermediate variables. Yukl was suggesting that a leader's behavior can only have an indirect effect on group performance, or that performance is mediated by the *intermediate* constructs.

Transactional leadership approaches suggest that leadership is really an exchange relationship between the leader and the follower. As Kuhnert and Lewis (1987) note, "Transactional leaders give followers something they want in exchange for something the leaders want" (p. 649). This exchange could involve something as tangible as economic resources (e.g., an athletic scholarship) or as intangible as emotional resources (e.g., respect for the player). Kuhnert and Lewis refer to the former as *lower-order transactions* and the latter as *higher-order transactions.* Transactional models suggest that the relationship between leaders and followers is one of mutual dependence and, to be effective, leaders must be able to meet the changing and differing expectations that their group members have (Kellerman, 1984). This is a very traditional way of looking at leadership—if a leader does *A* the follower should engage in *B*.

In contrast, transformational leadership (Bass, 1985), also referred to as new leadership (Bryman, 1992), visionary leadership (Sashkin, 1988), and charismatic leadership (Conger, 1989), is a phenomenon where leaders are able to connect with their followers in a unique way that results in extraordinary individual and group performance (Yammarino, Dubinsky, Comer, & Jolson, 1997). Transformational leaders get their followers to take ownership of the organization's (or leader's) vision, pursue the higher-order needs, and perform beyond expectations. Bass (1985) argued that transformational and transactional leadership are two distinct constructs; that is, a leader can exhibit varying degrees of both types of behaviors. As Doherty and Danylchuk (1996) note, "All leaders are transactional to some extent, exchanging rewards for performance, but some leaders are also transformational, going beyond simple leader–subordinate exchange relations" (p. 294).

There has been little discussion of transformational leadership in the literature on coach leadership. However, highly successful coaches are often described in terms that suggest they may be transformational. For example, many athletes talk about a coach getting her players to buy into the team's system or way of doing things. The ability to convince followers to adopt goals, strategies, or tactics as their own is indicative of transformational leaders.

Sport Leadership

The multidimensional model of leadership (MML) (Chelladurai, 1978, 1990, 1993, 2001) is a significant theoretical framework advanced for the study of sport-related leadership and it is the focus of this chapter. The MML and its accompanying measurement tool, the Leadership Scale for Sport (LSS), were an effort by Chelladurai to synthesize, and extend to the sport context, the aforementioned major ideas and research findings concerning leadership from organizational psychology and management. The model's basic premise is that leadership is a complex process in which multiple factors determine effectiveness. It highlights the manner in which the leader, the athlete, and the situation interact to determine the nature of a leader's influence.

Overview of the Multidimensional Model of Leadership (MML)

The MML (figure 5.1) consists of four basic components:

- Leader behaviors
- Antecedents of leader behaviors
- Influence of transformational leadership
- Outcomes of leader behaviors

The model's central hypothesis suggests that a team's performance and the individual athlete's level of satisfaction are a function of the extent to which a leader's actual leadership behavior is *congruent* with the preferred leadership behavior of the athlete and the requirements and constraints placed on leader behavior (arrows 1, 2, and 3). This relationship is generally thought to be positive. That is, the more a leader's actual behavior matches both the athlete's preferred types

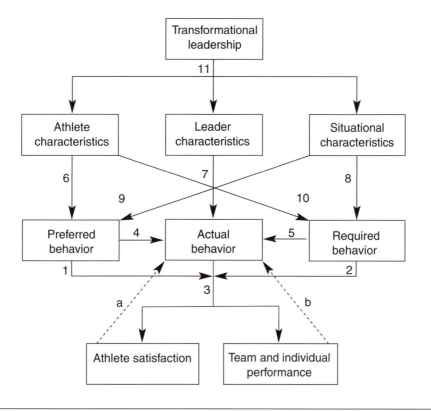

Figure 5.1 Chelladurai's multidimensional model of leadership.

Adapted from P. Chelladurai, 2001, *Managing organization for sport and physical activity: A systems perspective* (Scottsdale, AZ: Holcomb-Hathaway). © P. Chelladurai.

of behaviors and the behaviors required of the leader given the particular situation, the greater the levels of performance and satisfaction are expected to be.

The model also suggests that a leader's actual behavior is influenced by knowledge of the athletes' leadership preferences and by the requirements and constraints of the situation (arrows 4 and 5). For example, a coach who is aware that his starting quarterback prefers to call her own plays (and has the ability to do so) is likely to give more latitude to this player either by letting the player actually call her own plays or allowing more input when developing the week's game plan. Similarly, a coach who receives pressure from an athletic director to decrease the amount of personal contact he has with his female athletes away from the gym is likely to modify that part of his behavior.

Feedback regarding athlete satisfaction and performance also affects the types of actual behavior a coach engages in (arrows a and b). That is, leaders can be flexible and modify their behavior to ensure more favorable outcomes (Chelladurai, 2001). For example, the same coach who allowed his quarterback input into game decisions by letting her call her own plays may revert to a more autocratic approach if he thinks that performance is suffering.

Actual, preferred, and required leadership behaviors are influenced by three categories of antecedents: characteristics of the athletes, of the leader, and of the situation. Preferences for leadership behaviors are believed to be a function of an athlete's individual characteristics (arrow 6) (e.g., abilities, traits, needs) and situational characteristics (e.g., organizational rules, philosophy, culture), to the extent the athlete is aware of such demands and constraints (arrow 9). One athlete with a high need for affiliation may prefer higher levels of social support from the coach, while another with marginal skill levels may prefer a coach to spend a lot of time teaching important skills. From another perspective, an athlete who is aware that the league in which she plays has a fair-play policy governing behavior may allow her preferences to be influenced by this knowledge.

A leader's characteristics play an important antecedent role in determining the type of actual leadership behavior he engages in (arrow 7). These characteristics include abilities, personality, experience, education, and background. For example, a youth sport coach who attends a conference on sport psychology and learns that it is important for players to receive positive feedback may modify her leadership behavior in an effort to increase the feedback she provides to the athletes.

Required leadership behavior is determined by expectations and limitations imposed on the leader by the characteristics of the situation (arrow 8). This includes, for example, organizational and team goals, tasks, and structure; social and cultural norms and values; and regulations imposed by external bodies (e.g., governments, governing bodies, parents associations). In essence, required leadership behavior includes any parameters associated with the team itself, the organizations the team is a part of, and the environment in which the team and organization must function.

Required leader behavior is also influenced by the collective characteristics of the members (arrow 10). General ability level, gender, and age of the group members will have a bearing on behaviors required or expected of the leader. Chelladurai (1993) notes that some athletes lack judgment concerning appropriate leadership behaviors for their situation. In such instances the leader "may be required to decide for the member" (p. 649). For example, 3- and 4-year-old hockey players just learning the sport would not know that it is inappropriate to punish players for losing the game. The coach is expected to take the age and motivations of these children into account when making decisions about leadership behavior.

Finally, transformational leadership behavior (sometimes referred to as charismatic leadership; see, e.g., Yammarino et al., 1997) is presumed to influence not only the characteristics of the leader, but also those of the member and situation (arrow 11). According to Bass (1985; Bass & Aviolo, 1990) and others (Doherty & Danylchuk, 1996; Weese, 1994), the construct of transformational leadership is thought to consist of five dimensions.

• *Charisma* is described as an attribution or character quality that results in subordinates attaching themselves emotionally to the leader and developing a high level of trust in the person, the ideas or vision she stands for, and the leadership she exhibits. Charismatic people are often described as assertive and self-confident.

• *Idealized influence* describes behaviors that actively promote a leader's vision, mission, and beliefs.

• *Inspiration* is a dimension that generates "*emotional identification* with the leader's vision" (Doherty & Danylchuk, 1996, p. 295). Through encouragement and persuasion, the transformational leader will communicate confidence in followers' ability to live up to the high expectations he sets for them.

• *Intellectual stimulation* focuses on cognitions. Transformational leaders create an environment that nurtures proactive, creative, and innovative thinking.

• *Individualized consideration* refers to two things. First, such leaders develop the followers' potential by assigning tasks that best suit their ability and motivation. Second, they provide individualized attention to the subordinate by emphasizing one-on-one relationships and open two-way dialogue.

The component of transformational leadership was recently added to the model (Chelladurai, 2001) and "links the notion of transformational leadership to the elements of transactional leadership within the model" (p. 319). Transformational leaders alter situational characteristics by effecting changes in the organizational values, goals, and traditions through the introduction of a new vision for the organization. Similarly, such leaders affect athlete characteristics by expressing confidence in the member's ability to help the team achieve the new vision and its accompanying goals. Under transformational leadership, members alter their values and aspirations to match those of the organization, and they may gain greater efficacy in their ability to accomplish their tasks.

Bass (1985) and others argue that not all leaders are transformational. As noted previously, at least one of the dimensions of transformational leadership is considered a trait rather than a behavior (i.e., charisma). Moreover, since the construct is measured using an interval scale (Multifactor Leadership Questionnaire; see Bass & Aviolo, 1990), it follows that individuals may exhibit some but not all of the dimensions of a transformational leader, falling on a continuum somewhere between not at all transformational and extremely transformational.

Finally, while the MML suggests that transformational leadership may result in a leader who is more effective, it is not a necessary prerequisite for effective leadership. That is, effectiveness is determined by the interaction or congruence between preferred, actual, and required leadership behaviors. As a construct, transformational leadership plays an indirect role in determining the primary antecedents of these three leadership behaviors. Coaches who are not overly transformational can be very effective in their roles.

Research Associated With the MML

Since the development of the MML, a considerable amount of research has examined some of its primary hypotheses. This section groups and examines that research by major themes. An examination of the impact of various antecedents on athletes' preferences and perceptions of various leadership behavior is presented. The section concludes by looking at the research associated with the relationships of most interest to leadership theorists: how leadership influences outcomes such as performance and satisfaction.

Leadership Preferences

The vast majority of the research associated with the MML has used one particular instrument to operationalize leadership preferences: the Leadership Scale for Sport (LSS) (Chelladurai & Saleh, 1980). It measures five behaviors:

- Training and instruction (i.e., behaviors that improve the athlete's or team's performance through training and instruction from a physical- and skill-development perspective)
- Democratic behavior (i.e., "the extent to which the coach permits participation by the athletes in decision making" p. 41)
- Autocratic behavior (i.e., "the extent to which a coach keeps apart from the athletes and stresses his or her authority in dealing with them" p. 41)
- Social support (i.e., "the extent to which the coach is involved in satisfying the interpersonal needs of the athletes … independent of member performance" p. 41-42)
- Positive feedback (i.e., the extent to which the coach expresses appreciation for athletes' performance and contribution to the team)

Moreover, Chelladurai and Riemer (1998) observed, "Much of the research regarding the multidimensional model of leadership has been descriptive" (p. 237). This is particularly true of the research associated with leadership preferences. Results suggest that the two most preferred forms of leadership behavior are training and instruction and positive feedback. The least preferred leadership behavior is autocratic behavior (cf. Chelladurai, 1993). Much of the research has focused on the relationship between preferred leadership behavior and constructs that the MML would consider antecedents. These constructs are generally characteristics of (a) the individual or athlete or (b) the situation.

Athlete Characteristics

Considerable research has examined the effect of gender (usually operationalized as biological sex) on athletes' preferences for leadership behavior. Drawing on Nieva and Gutek's (1981) hypothesis on sex-role congruency, Schliesman, Beitel, and DeSensi (1994) argued that athletes are subject to gender-role stereotyping and, therefore, differ in their preferences for leadership behavior. Specifically, they hypothesized that male athletes prefer more training and instruction, positive feedback, and autocratic behavior, while female athletes prefer the more people-oriented behaviors of democratic behavior and social support.

Results related to differences in male and female preferences have been mixed. Several authors have reported that males preferred more autocratic behavior than did females (e.g., Chelladurai & Saleh, 1978—physical education students; Terry, 1984—elite Commonwealth Games athletes; Wang, 1997—track and field athletes; Riemer and Toon, 2001—intercollegiate tennis players).

Erle (1981) reported that male intramural and inter-varsity ice hockey players preferred more training and instruction than females (but found no differences relative to autocratic behavior or positive feedback). Riemer and Toon (2001) reported that female athletes preferred more social-support behavior, but Chelladurai and Saleh found that male physical education students preferred more social support. Others have found no sex-based differences (e.g., Terry & Howe, 1984).

The fact that much of the work examining gender and leadership preferences has operationalized gender very simplistically (i.e., biological sex) may account for some of the discrepancies in the reported findings. Differences in leadership preferences may be more associated with socially constructed roles (e.g., masculinity and femininity) than with physiological differences (e.g., male vs. female). If leadership preferences are a function of an athlete's gender role (e.g., Schliesman et al., 1994), then gender role rather than sex should be measured.

Current thinking about gender construction suggests that masculinity and femininity should be seen as two separate constructs rather than anchor points of a single construct. This implies that males and females may exhibit traits and behaviors stereotypically associated with both genders. Moreover, the often vaguely defined constructs of masculinity and femininity have been replaced by the constructs of agency and communion, traits that are considered socially desirable by both sexes and are generally exhibited, at least to some extent, by both. *Agency* refers to characteristics that are instrumental in nature; reflect a strong sense of self; and are manifested by behaviors that assert, protect, and seek to expand the self. Agency behaviors are stereotypically assigned to males. *Communion* refers to those characteristics that are more expressive and focused on others such as selflessness, a concern for others, and the desire to be at one with other organisms—traits stereotypically associated with females (Spence & Helmreich, 1978).

McCreary and Korabik (2000) have noted that individuals may be undersocialized or oversocialized into one of these roles. Undersocialization refers to when an individual fails to develop one of the roles and instead internalizes the opposing set of traits, therefore reflecting a lack of agency or communion. Oversocialization refers to a lack of balance between agency and communion. *Unmitigated communion* (i.e., being overly concerned with others' welfare to the degree that one's own welfare is overlooked) and *unmitigated agency* (i.e., focusing on the self to the exclusion of others) (Helgeson & Lepore, 1997) are constructs used to describe this phenomenon.

If our understanding of the effect of gender-role socialization on leadership preferences is to advance, researchers need to operationalize the construct more precisely. We should be interested in how socialized traits such as communion and agency (and the oversocialized versions, unmitigated communion and agency) affect preferences. Instruments that measure these various constructs have been developed and are available for use (e.g., Spence, Helmreich, & Holahan, 1979; McCreary & Korabik, 2000).

According to Riemer and Toon (2001), some of the varied results in the research on the influence of gender on leadership preferences may be a function of not only the athlete's gender but also the coach's gender. That is, female (or male) athletes may prefer different leadership behaviors from a female coach than they would from a male coach. Riemer and Toon found that males and females with male coaches reported no differences in leadership preferences, but female athletes with a female coach differed significantly from females with male coaches with regard to their leadership preferences. This finding supports the contention that relational demographics (Bauer & Green, 1996) or the composition of the coach–athlete dyad may be an important determinant of a person's preferences for leadership.

Erle (1981) reported that a person's *motivational orientation* influences preferences for leadership behavior. Consistent with theory, individuals who were *task* motivated (i.e., focused on improvement relative to previous performances) preferred more training and instruction behavior, while those who were *affiliation* motivated (i.e., concerned with the maintenance of happy relationships within the group) (Ball & Carron, 1976) and *extrinsically* motivated (i.e., undertaking behaviors to attain an end state separate from the actual behavior) (Vallerand & Ratelle, 2002) preferred more social-support behavior.

Chelladurai and Carron's (1981) research suggested that athletes exhibiting a high need for information and structure in their environment (i.e., cognitive structure) prefer more training and instruction behavior and less autocratic behavior than those who are low on this particular need. They also reported that athletes high on the trait of impulsivity (tendency to be impulsive) preferred more social support than those low on this trait.

Hersey and Blanchard (1969) argued that leaders need to adapt their leadership behaviors to the *maturity* level of their subordinates. They defined maturity as "the capacity to set high but attainable goals, willingness and ability to take responsibility, and education and/or experience of an individual or group" (p. 161). Building on these ideas, Chelladurai and Carron (1978) hypothesized that younger and less athletically mature athletes would prefer high levels of relationship-oriented behaviors and that older and more mature athletes would prefer low levels of such behaviors. Moreover, the importance of task-oriented leadership behaviors (e.g., training and instruction; positive feedback) would increase as one moved from athletic immaturity through midlevel maturity and then decrease in importance again for those who were very mature (i.e., a curvilinear relationship). Maturity has been operationalized using age, experience, and athletic maturity (i.e., competitive level).

Terry and Howe (1984) reported no significant relationship between age and leadership preferences in their sample of intercollegiate and sport-club athletes. However, Serpa (1990) reported that younger female Portugese basketball players (aged 12-15) preferred less autocratic behavior and more social support and democratic behavior than did their older counterparts (aged 17-29). No significant differences between the age groups were found for training and instruction and positive-feedback behaviors. Erle (1981) found that athletes with more experience in their sport indicated a greater preference for positive feedback, while Chelladurai and Carron (1981) observed a greater preference for autocratic behavior and social support among those with more experience. Terry (1984) reported that elite athletes preferred more democratic behavior and social support and less positive feedback than did sport-club athletes. Riemer and Toon (2001) also reported that athletes with more ability (playing at a higher competitive level, i.e., National Collegiate Athletic Association [NCAA] division I vs. division III) preferred less positive feedback than those with less ability.

In their 1983 study, Chelladurai and Carron operationalized athletic maturity using (a) competitive level of play (i.e., high school midget, high school junior, high school senior, and university intercollegiate basketball players), (b) years of experience playing basketball, and (c) age. In all three instances the results were essentially the same. First, a significant linear trend for social-support (relationship-oriented) behavior was found. That is, preferences increased for this behavior as maturity level, experience, and age increased. Second, in the case of training and instruction (i.e., task-oriented leadership), preferences decreased from the high school midget (i.e., 14-15 years of age) group through the high school senior group (i.e., 18-19 years of age), and then increased again among university athletes (i.e., 18-24 years of age). A similar trend was seen when age and experience were the independent variables. Both of these relationships were opposite of those hypothesized by Chelladurai and Carron (1978) and Hersey and Blanchard (1969).

Taken together, the results suggest that preferences for leadership behavior do change as the maturity of the athlete increases. The preference for positive feedback (i.e., task behaviors) seems to decrease and the preference for social support (i.e., relationship behaviors)

increases with maturity. While the results associated with training and instruction were mixed, this type of behavior was generally one of the most preferred across groups.

Situational Characteristics

The nature of a task is believed to influence leadership preferences. Chelladurai (1978), building on House's (1971) theory, proposed that the level of task dependency (i.e., how much success depends on interaction with others) and task variability (i.e., level of variety in the environment in which task performance takes place) would affect leadership preferences. He argued that interdependent- and open-sport athletes would prefer more training and instruction and positive feedback than those involved in independent and closed sports, and that independent-sport athletes would prefer more democratic and social-support behavior and less autocratic behavior.

Research results have been mixed. Chelladurai and Saleh (1978) reported that interdependent- and closed-sport athletes (e.g., rowing, synchronized swimming) preferred the greatest levels of training and instruction. These findings were not consistent with Chelladurai's (and House's) propositions. Consistent with theory, Terry and Howe (1984) and Terry (1984) reported that independent-sport athletes preferred more democratic and less autocratic behavior than did interdependent-sport athletes. Terry (1984) and Kang (2003) also found that athletes in team sports (i.e., greater task dependence) preferred more training and instruction and positive feedback than individual-sport athletes. Kim, Lee, and Lee (1990) and Kang (2003) found that individual-sport athletes (i.e., less task dependence) preferred more democratic behavior than did team-sport athletes. Chelladurai (1993) noted that the general conclusion to be drawn from research in this area was that as task variability and dependence increases, the "need for training and instruction, autocratic behavior, social support, and positive feedback increases" (p. 653).

Riemer and Chelladurai (1995) argued that it was difficult to compare previous results since "they included various sports that differed on the task attributes of dependence and variability (and) . . . also differed in other situational attributes such as organizational size, popularity, and accompanying pressure to perform" (p. 278). To eliminate potentially confounding variables, they examined a single sport, American football, in which playing positions within a team differ in terms of task variability. Riemer and Chelladurai argued that a football team operates as two relatively independent entities and that the offensive players operate in a more closed environment relative to the defensive squad. Their results suggested that players participating in a more open environment (i.e., defensive squad) had greater preferences for democratic, autocratic, and social-support behaviors.

Although the findings related to greater preferences for both democratic and autocratic behavior may seem counterintuitive, it is important to remember that these are two different constructs. As noted previously, in the LSS, democratic behavior refers to participative decision making and autocratic behavior refers to "the extent to which a coach keeps apart from the athletes and stresses his or her authority in dealing with them" (Chelladurai & Saleh, 1980, p. 41). The findings concerning democratic and social-support behavior were consistent with theory in this area.

A second situational characteristic of interest is the influence of culture on leadership preferences. Terry (1984) investigated the preferences of elite athletes participating at the 1983 World University Games and found no differences based on country of origin. However, Terry noted that the majority of athletes participating in the research were from countries that shared similar cultural backgrounds and philosophies of sport (e.g., Canada, Great Britain, and the United States).

Chelladurai, Imamura, Yamaguchi, Oinuma, and Miyauchi (1988) argued that two competing perspectives might explain Terry's results. The first was, indeed, that culture (defined as "attitudes, beliefs, and values of a society"; see Fayerweather, 1959, p. 7) controls and constrains a coach's leadership behaviors. Therefore, if cultures differ significantly, one would also anticipate leadership behaviors to differ. A second explanation builds upon the concept of *convergence* seen in industry. That is, industrialization is thought to impose forces on organizations that, regardless of the type of cultural, political, or economic system they must operate in, the imperative of performance will force them to adapt similar designs and management structures (e.g., Pascale, 1978; Child & Tayeb, 1983). Chelladurai et al. argued that this perspective would suggest that "coaches and athletes from different cultures would have similar behavioral dispositions since they are involved in athletics, which are also governed by performance requirements" (p. 376). To test either of these explanations, it would, however, be necessary to compare two cultures that are "sufficiently different from each other in terms of culture" (p. 376).

To this end, Chelladurai, Malloy, Imamura, and Yamaguchi (1987) compared the leadership preferences of Japanese and Canadian university physical education students. Their results indicated that, overall, Japanese students preferred more supportive leadership. Japanese students who participated in Western sports (i.e., volleyball, basketball) preferred more participative decision making compared to Canadian students, while Japanese students who participated in Eastern sports (i.e., judo, kendo) preferred a more aloof and authoritarian leadership style than Canadian and Japanese

students of Western sport. The authors concluded that culture and sport type affect leadership preferences. Chelladurai (1993) argued that sport type moderates cultural influences. From another perspective, one might also argue that sport type may be influenced by its culture of origin.

Chelladurai et al. (1988) compared preferences of Japanese and Canadian athletes participating in Western sports (e.g., basketball, volleyball, hockey, badminton). Their results indicated that Japanese athletes preferred significantly more social support and autocratic behavior, while Canadian athletes preferred more training and instruction. More recently, Kang (2003) reported that Korean basketball and track and field athletes preferred more autocratic behavior and less training and instruction, positive feedback, and social support than did their American university counterparts.

Taken together, the results suggest that culture is an antecedent of leadership preferences. However, it would also appear from these findings that sport type (i.e., Western sport vs. traditional Eastern sport; team vs. individual sport; levels of task variability and dependence) and the competitive nature of the participants (i.e., students vs. more elite or competitive athletes) affect leadership preferences. This would be consistent with findings reported in the section about athlete characteristics.

Relationship Between Leadership Behaviors and Outcomes

Athletes, athletic administrators, and spectators often use outcomes (i.e., group performance or how satisfied a group is with the leader) to judge a coach's effectiveness. The reader can probably think of many instances where coaches were fired or not asked back (even volunteer coaches) when a team was unhappy with the coach's leadership or the team's performance. A fundamental tenant of the MML is that leadership affects outcomes such as performance and satisfaction, and this section reviews the research that has focused on this particular contention.

Outcomes and Athlete Perceptions of Leadership

Summers (1983) found that athlete satisfaction was positively correlated to perceptions of training and instruction, social support, and positive feedback among lacrosse players. Chelladurai et al. (1988) found perception scores in all five dimensions of the LSS except autocratic behavior were positively related to satisfaction with leadership among Canadian and Japanese university athletes. McMillin (1990) (university soccer players) and Schliesman et al. (1994) (NCAA division I athletes) reported similar results. Dwyer and Fischer's (1990) results also showed a positive relationship

Leadership is a necessary function in a team setting.

between perceptions of positive feedback and training and instruction and satisfaction with the coach, while a negative relationship was reported for autocratic behavior. Weiss and Friedrichs (1986) reported that intercollegiate basketball players' perceptions of positive feedback were the best predictor of team satisfaction, while perceptions of social support and democratic behavior were significant predictors of athlete satisfaction.

With respect to performance, Weiss and Friedrichs (1986) found that perceived social support was the strongest predictor of a team's win–loss record. The greater the perception of social support, the lower the record of performance. Horne and Carron (1985) reported that as perceptions of positive feedback increased, so did athletes' perceptions of their own level of performance. Garland and Barry (1988) defined performance based on playing time (i.e., regulars, substitutes, survivors). While all five dimensions of leadership behavior were found to be significant predictors of performance, autocratic behavior was the best predictor; lower levels of performance were associated with higher perceptions of this behavior. This finding was consistent with Robinson and Carron's (1982) work, which reported that less successful players perceived their coaches as being more autocratic.

Several researchers have compared members of winning and losing teams in an effort to operationalize performance. Gordon (1986) compared players' perceptions of leadership behavior from successful and unsuccessful university soccer teams. Members of the successful teams perceived greater levels of training and instruction, autocratic behavior, social support, and positive feedback. However, Serpa, Pataco, and Santos (1991) reported that members of the first-place team at the 1988 world championships perceived greater levels of autocratic behavior and less positive feedback, social support, and democratic behavior than did players from the last-placed team.

Outcomes and Coaches' Perceptions of Leadership

Lam (1996) (Chinese basketball coaches) and Pizzi (2002) (NCAA division III coaches) reported no relationship between actual leadership as measured by the coach's version of the LSS and performance. Horne and Carron (1985) found that coaches perceived themselves as providing greater levels of all leadership behaviors (except autocratic behavior) than did their athletes.

Leadership-Behavior Congruence and Outcomes

The major hypothesis of the MML is that the relationship between the level of congruence in preferred, actual, and required leadership behaviors and the outcomes of performance and satisfaction is positive in nature. However, before entering a discussion of the research findings associated with this hypothesis, it is necessary to highlight two issues concerning this area of study.

First, the leader's actual behavior has been operationalized as the *average* of the athletes' perceptions of the behavior. Chelladurai and Riemer (1998) highlight two concerns with this particular approach. First, since an athlete's perceptions of the coach's behavior may be influenced by the athlete's own preferences for such behavior and the athlete's affective reactions to the behavior, these perceptions may not reflect reality. Smith, Smoll, and Curtis (1979) and Smoll, Smith, Curtis, and Hunt (1978) have demonstrated that athlete perceptions are not related to actual observations of the same leadership behaviors (see also chapter 6). Therefore, we can expect that a leader's actual behaviors deviate from an athlete's perceptions of those behaviors.

Second, this approach raises the question as to whether a leader treats all athletes on the team in the same manner. The use of the average or mean perception score as the measure of a particular coach's behavior implies that leadership tends to be homogeneous. While there would certainly be instances in which all players are treated the same, particularly in a team setting (e.g., basketball, volleyball), it is likely that there are also instances when a leader reacts differently to individual preferences and needs. Chelladurai (1978) argued that variation relative to social support would exist in team sport settings. Chelladurai and Riemer (1998) noted that using variance of players' perceptions as a measure of homogeneity could help determine whether using the average of players' perceptions would be appropriate; if considerable variance exists, then the use of averages becomes suspect.

The second issue relates to the measurement of congruence. Most research on the MML congruence hypothesis has used discrepancy or difference scores to determine the level of congruence (i.e., the preference score for a given leadership behavior is subtracted from the perception score of that same behavior). Riemer and Chelladurai (1995; Chelladurai and Riemer, 1998) highlighted some potential problems with the use of discrepancy scores, including low reliability, variance restriction, spurious relationships, and lack of discriminant validity. In an effort to overcome some of these concerns, Chelladurai (1993) advocated that researchers "identify and use that set of scores (preferred, perceived, or discrepancy scores) that account for the greatest amount of variance in the dependent variable(s)" (p. 655). Essentially, this would mean entering all the terms into a preliminary regression equation, seeing which variable was the best predictor of the dependent variable of interest, and then using that term as the sole predictor of the outcome variable.

Unfortunately, from a conceptual perspective, this method may not actually evaluate the congruence

hypothesis since some researchers (e.g., Chelladurai et al., 1988) have reported that perceptions of leadership behaviors were actually a better predictor of certain outcomes than discrepancy scores (the variable thought to represent congruence). Another approach is to have athletes estimate what the discrepancy or congruence between actual and perceived behaviors might actually be (Johns, 1981). Although this approach may be worthwhile, it would require the use of an instrument that currently does not exist.

More recently, researchers (e.g., Riemer & Chelladurai 1995; Chelladurai & Riemer, 1998) have advocated the use of regression analysis as a more appropriate method for evaluating the congruence hypothesis given the instruments to measure athletic leadership behavior that are currently available. Cronbach (1958) demonstrated how an interaction term (preference score × perception score) is the equivalent of a discrepancy score, and Berger-Gross (1982; Berger-Gross & Kraut, 1984) showed how using an interaction term overcomes the aforementioned problems associated with discrepancy scores. Using this approach, the hypothesis is tested by entering preferred and perceived scores of a given leadership behavior into a regression equation (i.e., main terms) followed by the interaction of these two terms (i.e., preferred × perceived). The researcher is interested not in the absolute magnitude of the interaction term (i.e., how much actual variance in the dependent variable is accounted for by the interaction), but whether this term significantly increases the amount of variance already accounted for by the main terms in the equation. If the increase is statistically significant, then the congruence hypothesis is supported.

To interpret the nature of the interaction or congruence, the relationships described by the regression equation need to be plotted. This is done by connecting values or scores on the graph as predicted by the equation. The first line, labeled *high preference,* is plotted by calculating and connecting two predicted scores: (a) when preferences for a particular leadership behavior are high and perceptions are high, and (b) when preferences are high but perceptions are low. The second line, labeled *low preference,* is plotted similarly by connecting the points suggested by two predicted scores: (a) when preferences for a particular leadership behavior are low and perceptions are also low, and (b) when preferences are low but perceptions are high.

The values inserted into the regression equation to represent high and low preferences and perceptions are arbitrary, but generally we would use the lowest and highest possible scores suggested by the scale used (in this case the LSS). For the graph itself, the y-axis of the graph is generally defined as the predicted score on the dependent variable (e.g., satisfaction, perfor-

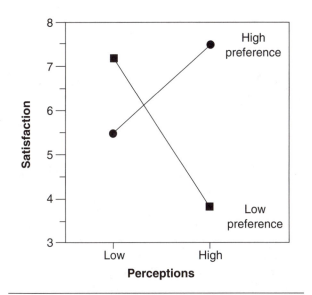

Figure 5.2 Sample graph of the results associated with a regression score.

mance). The x-axis is defined as perception scores and has two values—low and high—and, as noted previously, two separate lines are used to represent low and high preferences. For an example of such a graph, see figure 5.2. An interaction is represented by two lines that appear at two different angles and will intersect at some point. For a more thorough discussion of the challenges concerning the measurement of congruence, see Riemer and Chelladurai (1995) as well as Chelladurai and Riemer (1998).

It is worth mentioning that the research associated with the congruence hypothesis has focused primarily on three different outcomes: athlete satisfaction, athlete performance, and coach–athlete compatibility. However, the majority of the research concerns satisfaction.

Congruence Between Preferred and Actual Leadership

Chelladurai (1984) was interested in the effect of congruence between leadership behavior preferences and perceptions of athletes' satisfaction with individual performance, team performance, leadership, and their overall involvement (all single-item measures). Canadian male university athletes (basketball, wrestling, track and field) participated in the research. Building on Yukl's (1971) discrepancy model, Chelladurai argued that while the relationship between the preference-perception discrepancy and satisfaction might be linear and positive (i.e., athletes more satisfied when perceptions are lower than preferences), linear and negative (i.e., athletes satisfied even when perceptions exceed preferences), or curvilinear and negative (i.e., athletes

most satisfied when perceptions and preferences are the same), the latter seemed most probable. He was interested in determining whether the curvilinear relationship would hold for all dimensions of leadership behavior and across task type (i.e., interdependent, such as basketball; independent and open, such as wrestling; independent and closed, such as track and field).

Using an approach where the congruence hypothesis was evaluated by regressing discrepancy scores on a dependent variable, Chelladurai found that the effects associated with discrepancy scores were most pronounced for satisfaction with leadership. Second, in general only the linear relationship between discrepancy scores and satisfaction was significant; usually, the greater the perceptions relative to preferences for training and instruction, democratic behavior, social support, and positive feedback and the lower the perceptions of autocratic behavior, the higher the satisfaction. Third, a significant curvilinear relationship was only present among independent-sport athletes (i.e., wrestling and track and field).

Horne and Carron (1985) examined the relationship between behavior discrepancy scores and an athlete's perceived level of performance and satisfaction with leadership. They also regressed discrepancy scores on the dependent variables of interest. For the sample of Canadian university athletes, Horne and Carron reported that only the discrepancy scores associated with positive feedback were predictive of athletes' perceptions of their own performance, and discrepancy scores associated with training and instruction, positive feedback, and social support were predictive of athletes' satisfaction with the coach's leadership. They also found that positive feedback and autocratic behavior were best able to discriminate between compatible and incompatible dyads (as measured by the athlete's overall rating of the coach–athlete relationship). When athletes perceived their coach as providing the preferred level of positive feedback and autocratic behavior, the coach–athlete relationship was generally rated as compatible.

Again, using a similar method of analysis (discrepancy scores in regression equation), Schliesman (1987) built on the previous work by examining the relationship between discrepancy scores and general and more specific measures of an athlete's satisfaction with leadership. He reported that in the case of general satisfaction with leadership, perception scores and discrepancy scores of democratic behavior and social support were significantly related. However, the perception scores were slightly stronger predictors of general satisfaction than were the discrepancy scores. In the case of satisfaction with specific leadership behaviors (e.g., satisfaction with leadership and instruction), Schliesman reported a significant linear correlation between the discrepancy scores associated with training and instruction, social support, and positive feedback and their respective measure of satisfaction. It is notable that Schliesman only examined the linear relationships and not the curvilinear relationships between discrepancy scores and satisfaction that Chelladurai (1984) hypothesized would be most probable.

Riemer and Chelladurai (1995) argued that one explanation for the inconsistent results in this line of research was the use of discrepancy scores to operationalize congruency. Therefore, they used the approach discussed at the beginning of this section, using the interaction between preferences and perceptions to evaluate the congruence hypothesis. Their study of NCAA division I American football players found that the hypothesis was only supported in the case of social-support behavior; that is, the interaction term for that particular equation made a significant contribution to the prediction of an athlete's satisfaction with the coach's leadership beyond the contribution made by the preferences or perceptions of that behavior individually. Moreover, consistent with Johns' (1981) proposition, perceptions were found to be better predictors of satisfaction than were preferences in the case of training and instruction and positive feedback.

Riemer and Toon (2001) argued that the manner in which previous research had operationalized the dependent variable of satisfaction may also be a contributing factor to the inconsistent results. All the studies examining the congruence hypothesis had used single-item measures of athlete satisfaction, all with slightly different wording and focal points (e.g., leadership, team performance). One problem with single-item measures is that their reliability and validity cannot be quantitatively established (Zeller & Carmines, 1980). In order to properly evaluate the congruence hypothesis, adequate measures of all the variables involved is necessary. To this end, they used four subscales from Riemer and Chelladurai's (1998) Athlete Satisfaction Scale to measure satisfaction with individual performance, team performance, training and instruction, and personal treatment.

In their sample of male and female NCAA tennis players, the results did not support the hypothesis that satisfaction is dependent on the congruence between preferred and actual behaviors; none of the interaction terms were significant predictors of any dimension of satisfaction. Riemer and Toon noted, "lack of evidence for the congruence hypothesis does not negate it. Its validity might be a function of situational conditions [e.g., task variability, task dependency, team size, etc.] or how actual behavior is operationalized. The absence of a congruence effect might also have resulted from the combination of a relatively small sample size and conservative treatment of the data—an effect was present but not detected" (p. 252).

Congruence Between Required, Actual, and Preferred Leadership

The one underinvestigated aspect of the model is required behavior. This is likely because of difficulties associated with its measurement. Chelladurai (1978) provides us with the only example of an attempt to examine all three aspects of leadership behavior thought to interact to influence performance. He operationalized required behavior as the average of all the subject's preferences for a given sport, arguing that in a mean score the influence of individual differences on preference scores cancel each other out and, therefore, represent the influence of macro variables. His results provided no support for the hypothesis that performance is a function of actual and required behavior. Chelladurai and Riemer (1998) note that this lack of evidence may have been a function of the low number of teams ($n = 10$) that were studied.

Building on the argument advanced in 1978, Chelladurai (1993) suggested that required behavior could also be operationalized as the average of the self-reported behaviors of several successful coaches in a given sport. While some situational contexts may warrant the averaging of preferences or self-reported behaviors (i.e., the situation from team to team is essentially the same), Chelladurai and Riemer (1998) warn that the homogeneity of the situational context cannot be taken for granted. Important antecedent variables (e.g., task variability, culture, maturity, organizational goals) may vary from team to team, even within a context that may appear homogeneous (e.g., intercollegiate sport, professional sport).

Evaluation of the Research to Date

In Chelladurai's (1993) review of sport-related leadership literature, he noted that research results associated with the MML suggest that athletes will be satisfied with the coach's leadership when the athlete emphasizes behaviors that will (a) assist the athlete in accomplishing her task (e.g., training and instruction) and (b) recognize and reward good performance (e.g., positive feedback). This summary is still applicable. Moreover, it is difficult to draw any more specific conclusions regarding the validity of the MML since only segments of the model have been tested. The vast majority of the research has focused on a limited number of situational and member characteristics thought to be antecedent to preferences for leadership behaviors. In addition, only a handful of studies have examined questions concerning the congruence hypothesis, and then only as it relates to leadership preferences and actual behavior. Almost all of these studies have only used satisfaction as an outcome.

Overall, key aspects of the model have not been researched. First, what are the leader's characteristics that influence his actual behaviors? While there have been preliminary investigations in this regard (e.g., Jambor & Zhang, 1997; Gabriel & Brooks, 1986), solid conclusions cannot be drawn. Second, what are the salient antecedents of required leader behavior? Thus far there has been no research seeking to understand these antecedents. Third, what role does transformational leadership play in the model? Fourth, how valid is the congruence hypothesis as it relates to all three elements (preferred, actual, and required) of a coach's leadership? How is performance affected by the congruence of the leadership elements? Finally, what is the nature of the hypothesized feedback loop between the outcomes of performance and satisfaction and a coach's actual behavior?

Another characteristic of most research thus far is simplistic design and analysis. Chelladurai (1993) called for "more comprehensive studies employing more sophisticated procedures" (p. 655). The MML suggests many causal linkages. For example, it hypothesizes that if preferred and actual leadership are congruent, then satisfaction should increase. However, most of the research designs used to evaluate this and other propositions have used designs that Campbell and Stanley (1963) would classify as correlational or ex post facto. The primary concern with such designs is that while they allow for causation to be disconfirmed, they cannot confirm it. Moreover, these designs as a rule are fraught with threats to their internal and external validity, making it difficult to draw hard and fast conclusions from the stated results.

As a first step, researchers must build on previous research and take steps to control for variables known to influence the dependent variables of interest by mechanical (e.g., sample selection) and mathematical (e.g., use of covariants) means. For example, in their examination of the effects of task variability and task dependence on leadership preferences, Riemer and Chelladurai (1995) made an effort to control for other situational attributes (e.g., team size, gender, organizational culture) that might confound the relationship of interest by selecting athletes from a single sport, which provided varying levels of the variables of interest.

Second, leadership research associated with the MML needs to move toward more quasi-experimental and experimental designs. These types of designs are more powerful in helping determine causation. Researchers must thus begin thinking about ways in which the variable of interest (e.g., actual leadership) could be manipulated or seek out instances where it is naturally manipulated. For example, athletes' preferences for autocratic behavior could be measured. Those with high preferences would then randomly be assigned to one of two groups with a leader trained to be either autocratic or unautocratic. The same could be done for those athletes who had low preferences for such behavior. The performance of all four groups could then be assessed on some common athletic task.

While the research associated with the MML to date has provided a solid foundation, it has failed to address many key elements of the model. Moreover, the research has often created more questions than answers. As researchers and students of athletic leadership, we must begin to examine the phenomenon in a more comprehensive, sophisticated, and systematic manner.

Future Research

This chapter has highlighted a number of issues that need to be considered in order to move our understanding of athletic leadership forward. The next section highlights two major concerns: (a) how we measure or operationalize the various constructs of the MML (e.g., satisfaction, leadership behavior, gender, performance), including how we evaluate the dynamic nature of these variables, and (b) the relationship between leadership and other constructs of interest to sport psychologists (e.g., cohesion).

Measurement Instruments

In the foregoing discussion of research related to the MML, I have occasionally alluded to concerns associated with measurement of the model's key constructs. As noted throughout the chapter, the quality of the instruments plays a pivotal role in our ability to fully understand the process of leadership. Although a discussion and critique of the instruments used to operationalize model components are beyond the scope of this chapter, two developments bear mentioning.

First, a multi-item and multidimensional instrument to measure athlete satisfaction has been published. The 56-item Athlete Satisfaction Questionnaire (Riemer and Chelladurai, 1998) measures 15 dimensions of satisfaction. Preliminary evidence suggests that the instrument is a valid and reliable measure of the satisfaction associated with the athletic experience (see Riemer & Chelladurai, 1998, 2001; Riemer & Toon, 2001). Access to this instrument should help standardize findings on outcomes of athlete satisfaction.

Second, Zhang, Jensen, and Mann (1996) have published a revision of the original LSS (Chelladurai & Saleh, 1980). The 60-item Revised Leadership Scale for Sport (RLSS) includes modifications of the original five dimensions of leadership behavior as well as a new dimension, situational consideration. Situational consideration is defined as "coaching behaviors aimed at considering the situation factors; setting up individual goals and clarifying ways to reach the goals; differentiating coaching methods at different stages; and assigning an athlete to the right game position" (Zhang et al., 1996, p. 109-110). Although initial evidence concerning the reliability and validity of the instrument has been mixed (see Zhang et al., 1996; Jambor & Zhang, 1997), the RLSS shows promise; continued evaluation of the psychometric properties of the scale is certainly warranted. Research that compares these properties (e.g., reliability, measurement model fit, predictive validity) for the two instruments (LSS and RLSS) would move our understanding in this area forward.

However, neither the LSS nor the RLSS has incorporated dimensions conceptually aligned with transformational and charismatic leadership. The focus of these instruments is behaviors that are transactional in nature. Moreover, there are questions as to whether five or six leadership behaviors capture all, or even the most salient, elements of leadership. In their work with youth sport leadership, Smith and Smoll have identified 12 leadership behaviors (see chapter 6). Chelladurai and Riemer (1998) have called for a more comprehensive list of dimensions of leader behavior. They suggested that criteria used by Chelladurai and Riemer (1997) might be used to generate a comprehensive list of dimensions. Moreover, qualitative techniques (e.g., focus groups, interviews, case studies) might be employed to generate meaningful categories of leader behavior based on the experiences and insights of players and coaches.

Measurement of Dynamic Constructs

Athletic leadership and the two primary outcomes associated with it—performance and satisfaction—are dynamic rather than static variables; that is, they change over time. Unfortunately, all of the research reviewed in this chapter has been cross-sectional in design: All the measurements were taken at a single point in time. While researchers can ask participants to limit their recall to specific time points, there is no guarantee that this will actually happen. Moreover, these time points (e.g., "Recall your experiences this last month") may be too long for accurate recall—the most recent events are likely to be most salient. From another perspective, situational factors may temporarily alter a coach's normal leadership behaviors. For example, say that one day a coach who generally involves her players in decision making does not because of externally imposed time constraints. Such factors cannot be accounted for using typical single-shot techniques for data collection.

Dynamic variables need to be measured as such. If we are to gain a real understanding of the leadership process, then our research needs to move in the direction of longitudinal or time-series designs. This will provide much richer information about leadership and may also provide insights into the causal nature of leadership and its associated variables. For a more detailed discussion of these measurement challenges, see Chelladurai and Riemer's (1998) review of measurement-related concerns associated with leadership research.

Relationship Between Leadership and Other Social-Psychological Variables

Performance and satisfaction are important outcomes in athletics. Numerous constructs are thought to influence and be influenced by these two constructs. In fact, most of the topics discussed in this text are of interest to coaches and researchers alike because of their hypothesized relationship with performance, and to a lesser extent, satisfaction. Unfortunately, much of the research concerning social-psychological variables in sport is carried out in an isolated, or what Peele (1981) might refer to as reductionist, fashion—the focus is on how one particular construct affects performance. But, as Raymond Cattell has noted, "There are no orthogonal factors in Nature" (quoted in Nesselroade, 1994, p. 150)—everything tends to be related. It is arguable that there would be considerable shared variance, moderating relationships, and mediating relationships among the constructs discussed in this book, including leadership, motivational climate, relationships, and performance and satisfaction. If our understanding of performance is to increase, and if we as a scientific community are to help coaches and athletes increase levels of performance, then it is appropriate for us to begin examining the problem more holistically.

Practical Implications

From a coach's perspective, the body of research related to the MML suggests some important implications for practice. First, coaching leadership does make a difference in performance. Coaching behaviors such as training and instruction and positive feedback play important roles in the level of task-related performance (e.g., Horne & Carron, 1985). Coaches should be encouraged to provide high levels of these two behaviors. Generally speaking, from an athlete's perspective these two behaviors are also the most preferred—athletes understand the close relationship that exists between these leadership behaviors and their own performance.

Second, all athletes are not the same. Some athletes have preferences for certain leadership behaviors while others respond better to other behaviors. Research tells us that some of these differences might be the result of the type of sport, the size of the group, one's personality, or even one's gender. Regardless of why such differences exist, coaches would be well advised to get to know their athletes as a group and as individuals and to adapt their leadership behaviors and styles to the athletes.

Finally, research suggests that an athlete's perceptions of a coach's leadership behaviors explain considerable variation in outcome measures such as satisfaction and performance. The important point for coaches is that an athlete's perception is his view of reality and it may differ from the leader's perception of her own leadership behaviors. Data indicate that coaches tend to perceive higher levels of their own leadership behaviors than athletes do (e.g., Huang, Chen, Chen, & Chiu, 2003; Tsutsumi, 2000). Athletes respond to their own perceptions, not the coach's perception. Coaches need to understand how athletes are interpreting the coach's words and deeds. Only then can a coach hope to respond to the athletes' needs for various leadership behaviors.

Summary

This chapter introduced the theory and research behind the multidimensional model of leadership (MML). This model of leadership draws heavily upon leadership-related literature and the fields of management and organizational psychology. The basic premise of the MML is that leadership is a complex process in which multiple factors determine effectiveness. It highlights the manner in which the leader, the athlete, and the situation interact to determine the nature of a leader's influence. The model's central hypothesis suggests that a team's performance and the individual athlete's level of satisfaction are a function of the extent to which a leader's actual leadership behavior is congruent with the athlete's preferred leadership behavior and the requirements and constraints placed on the leader's behavior.

While some initial work has examined the model's propositions, considerable work is yet to be done. It is difficult to draw specific conclusions regarding the validity of the MML since only segments of the model have been tested. The vast majority of the research has focused on a limited number of situational and member characteristics thought to be antecedent to leadership-behavior preferences; moreover, only a handful of studies have examined questions concerning the congruence hypothesis, and then only as it relates to leadership preferences and actual behavior. Future research needs to become more sophisticated and systematic in its approach. We must reconsider how we measure or operationalize the various constructs of the MML (e.g., satisfaction, leadership behavior, gender, performance) as well as the relationship between leadership and other constructs of interest to sport psychologists, generating data that can be confidently used in practice.

Discussion Questions

1. For coaches, what are some specific implications and applications of early leadership theory from management and organizational psychology literature (e.g., Fiedler, House, Yukl)?

2. Explain the theories that laid the foundation for the MML.

3. Think about the five basic leadership behaviors measured by the LSS. How relevant are they in an athletic context? Are any key leadership behaviors missing?

4. Think about your own experiences as a coach or an athlete. What situational and personal factors might affect the types of leadership behaviors that athletes prefer? What situational and personal factors might determine the types of leadership behaviors that a coach prefers to engage in?

5. From your own experience, what sorts of expectations are thrust upon coaches (i.e., required behavior), and from whom do these expectations come? What sorts of factors might determine which of the expectations are more important?

6. From your own experiences, what is the nature of the relationship between leadership and performance and satisfaction?

chapter 6

Social-Cognitive Approach to Coaching Behaviors

Ronald E. Smith, PhD, and Frank L. Smoll, PhD

Learning Objectives

On completion of this chapter, the reader should have

1. understanding of the manner in which theory, research, and interventions mutually support one another;

2. knowledge of the original mediational model, the measures developed to operationally define its elements, and the ways in which it was expanded to include situational variables and individual difference variables;

3. comprehension of the major findings of the basic and applied research phases;

4. familiarity with the concept of coaching behavioral signatures; and

5. awareness of practical implications of social-cognitive analysis for future research on and interventions for coaching behaviors.

The theoretical model and research program described in this chapter illustrate the application of the social-cognitive perspective within sport psychology (Bandura, 1986; Mischel, Shoda, & Smith, 2004; Smith, 2006). In explaining behavior and its causes, social-cognitive models focus on interactions among situational and personal factors. Personal factors, the environment, and behavior all influence one another in a network of reciprocal causal relations (Bandura, 1986). We present here a theoretical model of leadership behaviors that hypothesizes relations among situational, cognitive, behavioral, and individual difference and personality variables. The supporting research focuses on leadership behaviors in sport—a social environment that is sufficiently circumscribed to permit the use of observational techniques in order to measure overt behaviors, and an environment that is known to influence the personality and social development of participants.

The model of leadership that we advance has been termed a *mediational model* because it involves relations among athletic situations, coaching behaviors, athletes' encoding and recall of coaching behaviors, and athletes' evaluative reactions to the coach (Smoll & Smith, 1984, 1989). The evolution of the mediational model over more than two decades illustrates interactions involving theory, research, and intervention, all of which influence one another (Smith, 1999). Theoretical propositions and measurement techniques derived from social-cognitive theory have inspired basic research on coaching behaviors and their effects on athletes, and these findings have led to elaborations in the original mediational model.

Both the model and the research results provided the conceptual and empirical basis for an intervention program designed to influence coaching behaviors in a positive manner. Applied research on the intervention program, in turn, constituted a means of testing and embellishing the theory from which it was derived. These reciprocal linkages involving theory, research, and intervention are clearly seen in many areas of contemporary sport psychology, and they are the vehicle by which basic and applied science can advance one another.

Leadership Research in Youth Sport Settings

The sport environment offers several advantages as a naturalistic setting for psychological research. First, the range of psychological processes that find expression in that setting is impressive. Learning, perception, atten-

tion, motivation and emotion, developmental processes, memory, problem solving, social interaction, and a wide variety of individual difference factors can all be studied. As reflected in the chapters of this volume, an impressive array of social-psychological phenomena have been the focus of sport psychology research, among them leadership.

Sport provides an inviting setting for studying the behavior of leaders for a number of reasons. First, the sport milieu is sufficiently circumscribed to enable identification of relevant situational variables, and the coach leadership variable is typically confined to this setting. Second, the sport setting elicits a wide range of leadership behaviors that can be reliably measured. Finally, sport evokes high levels of psychological involvement in both coaches and athletes (Feltz, 1978; Gould, 1984; Martens & Gould, 1979; Scanlan, 2002). Consequently, the likelihood of identifying relations between leadership behaviors and athletes' reactions is enhanced. Of particular interest from a developmental perspective is the study of the youth sport environment, for participation occurs during an important period of social and personality development.

In North America, the growth of organized youth sport programs during the past half-century has been dramatic in scope, but not without dispute. Much of the controversy that surrounds youth sport concerns the roles that adults, particularly coaches and parents, play in the process. There is general agreement, as well as empirical evidence, that an important determinant of participation effects lies in the interpersonal dynamics between coach and athlete (Ewing, Seefeldt, & Brown, 1996; Martens, 1997; Smith & Smoll, 2002). Coaches not only occupy an important leadership position in the sport setting, but their influence can extend into other areas of the athlete's life as well. The manner in which coaches structure the sport situation, the goal priorities they establish, the attitudes and values they transmit, and the behaviors they engage in can markedly influence children's psychosocial development.

Because of the important leadership role occupied by youth sport coaches, there are a number of empirical questions worth pursuing. For example, what do coaches do, and how frequently do they engage in such behaviors as encouragement, punishment, instruction, and organization? What psychological dimensions underlie such behaviors? And, finally, how are coaching behaviors related to children's reactions to their sport experiences? Answers to such questions are not only a first step in describing the behavioral ecology of one aspect of the youth sport setting, but they also provide an empirical basis for the development of intervention

Preparation of this chapter and the research reported herein were supported in part by Grants 1066 and 2297 from the William T. Grant Foundation and by Grant MH-24248 from the National Institute of Mental Health.

programs designed to help coaches provide a more positive experience for children in sport.

Initial Mediational Model

In an attempt to answer such questions, we have carried out a program of basic and applied research over several decades. The project was guided by an initially simple three-element model of coach–athlete influences: coaching behaviors → athletes' perception and recall → athletes' evaluative reactions. This model suggests that the effects of a coach's actual behaviors on the athlete's evaluative reactions (attitudes toward the coach, the sport experience, and so on) are not direct; rather, they are mediated by the athlete's recall and the meanings ascribed to the behaviors. In other words, cognitive-affective processes serve as filters between overt coaching behaviors and youngsters' attitudes toward their coach and other aspects of the sport experience. This mediational model required that we measure the targeted variables at three different levels: (1) what coaches actually do; (2) how these behaviors are perceived and recalled by their athletes; and (3) children's attitudinal responses to their coach, teammates, the sport experience, and themselves.

Measurement of Coaching Behaviors

The most frequent criticism of methodology in leadership research has been, with a few notable exceptions (e.g., Bales & Slater, 1955; Komaki, Zlotnick, & Jensen, 1986), its almost exclusive reliance on paper-and-pencil measures. Nearly three decades ago, as we were beginning our program of research, one prominent leadership researcher noted the following (Campbell, 1977):

> We are in very grave danger of transforming the study of leadership to a study of self-report questionnaire behavior, if, indeed, the transformation has not already occurred. The method is too quick, too cheap, and too easy, and there are now many such questionnaire measures that possess no construct validity whatsoever. I submit that when both the independent and dependent variables are based on self-reports by the same person, we have learned absolutely nothing about leadership, no matter what the results turn out to be. (p. 229)

Within the social-cognitive perspective, behavioral assessment in naturalistic and laboratory environments has long been a favored methodological approach. Building on this tradition, we developed a method for measuring actual coaching behaviors. The Coaching Behavior Assessment System (CBAS) permits the direct observation and coding of coaches' leadership behaviors during practices and games (Smith, Smoll, & Hunt, 1977). The behavioral categories of the CBAS were derived from content analyses of numerous audiotaped play-by-play reports of coaches' actions recorded by trained observers during practices and games. Both the measurement approach and some of the categories derive from a social-cognitive orientation (called social learning theory at that time), and the categories incorporate behaviors that have been shown to affect both children and adults in a variety of nonathletic settings (Bales & Slater, 1955; Komaki, 1986; White, 1975).

The 12 CBAS categories, shown in table 6.1, are divided into two major classes of behaviors. *Reactive* (elicited) behaviors are responses to athlete or team behaviors, whereas *spontaneous* (emitted) behaviors are initiated by the coach and are not a response to a discernible preceding event. Reactive behaviors are responses either to desirable performance or to effort, mistakes, and misbehaviors on the part of athletes. The spontaneous class is subdivided into game-related and game-irrelevant behaviors. The system thus involves basic interactions between the situation and the coach's behavior. Use of the CBAS in observing and coding coaching behaviors in a variety of sports indicates that the scoring system is sufficiently comprehensive to incorporate the majority of overt leader behaviors, that high interrater reliability can be obtained, and that individual differences in behavioral patterns can be discerned (e.g., Chaumeton & Duda, 1988; Horn, 1985; Jones, Housman, & Kornspan, 1997; Krane, Eklund, & McDermott, 1991; Smith, Smoll, & Curtis, 1978).

To measure coach and athlete perceptions, we developed paper-and-pencil measures of the corresponding behaviors. Using the same descriptions of the behaviors as those in the CBAS scoring manual, coaches could indicate on 7-point scales how often they engaged in each behavior, and athletes could rate the frequencies of their coaches' behaviors.

Basic Research: Coaching Behaviors and Their Effects on Children

Following development of the CBAS, field studies were conducted to assess relations between coaching behaviors and athlete's reactions to their sport experiences (Curtis, Smith, & Smoll, 1979; Smith & Smoll, 1990; Smith et al., 1978; Smith, Zane, Smoll, & Coppel, 1983). We found that the typical baseball or basketball coach engages in more than 200 codeable actions during an average game. By collecting observational data on four or five occasions, we were able to generate behavioral profiles of up to several thousand responses for each coach over the course of a season. In large-scale

Table 6.1   Response Categories of the Coaching Behavior Assessment System

Response category	Behavioral description
CLASS I: REACTIVE BEHAVIORS	
Responses to desirable performance	
Reinforcement (R)	A positive, rewarding reaction (verbal or nonverbal) to a good play or good effort
Nonreinforcement (NR)	Failure to respond to a good performance
Responses to mistakes	
Mistake-contingent encouragement (EM)	Encouragement given to a player following a mistake
Mistake-contingent technical instruction (TIM)	Instruction on how a player should correct a mistake
Punishment (P)	Negative reaction, verbal or nonverbal, following a mistake
Punitive technical instruction (TIM+P)	Technical instruction following a mistake given in a punitive or hostile manner
Ignoring mistakes (IM)	Failure to respond to a player mistake
Response to misbehavior	
Keeping control (KC)	Reactions intended to restore or maintain order among team members
CLASS II: SPONTANEOUS BEHAVIORS	
Game-related	
General technical instruction (TIG)	Spontaneous instruction in the techniques and strategies of the sport (not following a mistake)
General encouragement (EG)	Spontaneous encouragement (not following a mistake)
Organization (O)	Administrative behavior that sets the stage for play by assigning duties, responsibilities, positions, and so on
Game-irrelevant	
General communication (GC)	Interactions with players unrelated to the game

Adapted from F.L. Smoll and R.E. Smith, 1984, Leadership research in youth sports. In *Psychological foundations of sport*, edited by J.M. Silva and R.S. Weinberg (Champaign, IL: Human Kinetics), 375. By permission of authors.

observational studies, we coded more than 85,000 behaviors of some 80 male coaches in youth sport, then interviewed and administered questionnaires to nearly 1,000 children after the season to measure their recall of their coaches' behaviors and their evaluative reactions to the coach, the sport experience, and themselves.

At the level of overt behavior, three independent behavioral dimensions were identified through factor analysis: supportiveness (reinforcement and mistake-contingent encouragement), instructiveness (general technical instruction and mistake-contingent technical instruction vs. general communication and general encouragement), and punitiveness (punishment and punitive technical instruction vs. organizational behaviors). The first two dimensions correspond closely to the classic leadership styles of relationship orientation

and task orientation emphasized in leadership theories such as Fiedler's (1967) contingency model, situational leadership (Hersey & Blanchard, 1977), and the vertical dyad linkage model of Graen and Schiermann (1978) and identified in other research on leadership behavior (e.g., Stogdill, 1972).

Relations between coaches' scores on these behavioral dimensions and athlete measures provided clear evidence for the crucial role of the coach. The most positive outcomes occurred when children played for coaches who engaged in high levels of reinforcement for both desirable performance and effort and who responded to mistakes with encouragement and technical instruction. Not only did children like these coaches more and have more fun, but they also liked their teammates more. Although only about 3% of the coded behaviors were punitive and critical in nature, they correlated more strongly than any other behavior with children's attitudes. In terms of athlete-perceived behaviors, supportive behaviors were positively related to attitudes toward the coach whereas punitive behaviors were negatively related. At both the behavioral and perceptual level, supportive and punitive behaviors fell on independent dimensions rather than at opposite ends of the same dimension. That is, less supportive behaviors were not necessarily punitive in nature, and vice versa. Instead, supportive behaviors fell on their own dimension, from less to more supportive, and punitive behaviors fell on a different dimension, from more to less punitive.

Notably, the team's win–loss record was essentially unrelated to how well the athletes liked the coach and how much they wanted to play for the coach in the future. However, athletes on winning teams felt that their parents liked the coach more and that the coach liked them more than did athletes on losing teams. Apparently, winning made little difference to the children, but they knew that it was important to the adults. It is worth noting that winning assumed greater importance beyond age 12, although it continued to be a less important attitudinal determinant than coach behaviors.

Another important concern was the degree of accuracy with which coaches perceive their own behaviors. Correlations between CBAS observed behaviors and coaches' ratings of how frequently they performed the behaviors were generally low and nonsignificant. The only actions on their self-report that correlated significantly (around .50) with the observational measures were the punitive behaviors. Overall, we found that children's ratings on the same perceived behavior scales correlated much more highly with CBAS measures than did the coaches' own reports. It thus appears that coaches were, for the most part, blissfully unaware of how they behaved and that athletes were more accurate perceivers of actual coach behaviors. Because behavior change requires an awareness of how one is currently behaving, this finding clearly indicates the need to increase coaches' self-awareness.

Our model suggests that both overt leader behaviors and athletes' perceptions are important; leader effectiveness resides in the behaviors of the leader and the eyes of the beholder. The importance of assessing both observed and perceived behavior was alluded to earlier. Using regresssion analyses to predict athletes' attraction toward the coach, we found that CBAS behaviors independently accounted for 21% of the attitudinal variance. Athlete-perceived behaviors alone accounted for 24%. However, when both observed and perceived behaviors were entered into the regression, the amount of attraction variance rose to 42% (Smoll, Smith, Curtis,

& Hunt, 1978). Clearly, there is not a one-to-one relation between observed and perceived coaching behaviors, and both sets of variables account for independent portions of athlete attitude variance.

Although the rank-order correlation between the CBAS and athlete-perceived behavior was .58, indicating that the frequencies with which the various behaviors occurred was reflected in the athletes' frequency ratings, bivariate correlations within categories revealed only modest agreement. As in the case of the coaches, the strongest observed–perceived relations were found for the punitive behaviors, with correlations of .54 and .37 occurring for the categories of punishment and punitive technical instruction. General communication and mistake-contingent technical instruction also yielded significant positive correlations, but the other behavioral categories were weakly, though positively, correlated.

A recent structural equation modeling test of mediation using the guidelines described by Baron and Kenny (1986) showed that the effects of observed punitive behaviors on athletes' attitudes were strongly mediated by the athletes' perceptions of those behaviors, but the results were more ambiguous for supportive behaviors. Whether a larger sample of observed coaching behaviors (we observed only about one-third of all games and no practices in the baseball studies) would produce larger correlations between observed and athlete-perceived behaviors is a question deserving of empirical attention. What is clear, however, is that perceived behaviors consistently yield stronger relations with outcome measures than do observed coaching behaviors. In other words, athletes appear to respond to the psychological reality produced by their perceptions of the coach's behaviors.

Expanded Mediational Model and Research Implications

Measures derived from the basic three-part mediational model allowed us to study empirical relations between overt leader behaviors, perceived behaviors, and consequences at a rudimentary level. Although the preliminary model did incorporate both overt and athlete-perceived behaviors, it was quite limited in scope, and it required greater elaboration to delineate the characteristics and processes that influence coaching behaviors and mediate their effects on athletes. Of particular importance from a social-cognitive perspective are the roles played by situational factors and individual difference factors in coaches' behaviors and children's reactions to these behaviors. We initially suggested additional variables that might be included in a more comprehensive model (Smoll & Smith, 1984), but we did not specify the role that each of these variables might play in enhancing the explanatory, predictive, and heuristic power of the basic model.

An expanded mediational model is shown in figure 6.1. The model specifies a number of situational and individual difference variables that are expected to influence the core components (coaching behaviors, athlete perception and recall, athlete attitudes) as well as predicted empirical relations among these elements, but it by no means exhausts the list of situational and individual difference variables that might be important. In the hope that this chapter will prove to be a stimulus for future research on coaching behavior, we provide a rationale for the variables, indicate how they might be measured, present preliminary findings where possible, and suggest hypotheses that might be tested in future research.

Coach Individual Difference Variables

In a complex social and interpersonal setting like sport, individual differences are certain to play an important role. For the coach, we assume that behaviors are organized into patterns that reflect particular coaching goals and behavioral intentions. We define a goal as an anticipated positive outcome of an act or sequence of acts. A behavioral intention is a cognitive antecedent of an act and implies a decision to behave in one way as opposed to another (Rise, Thompson, & Verplanken, 2003). For example, an athlete may have the goal of improving her running time by a certain amount. The behavioral intention would be the decision to practice a new and more effective running stride.

Behavioral intention occupies a prominent position in models of interpersonal behavior advanced by Fishbein and Ajzen (1975) and by Triandis (1977).

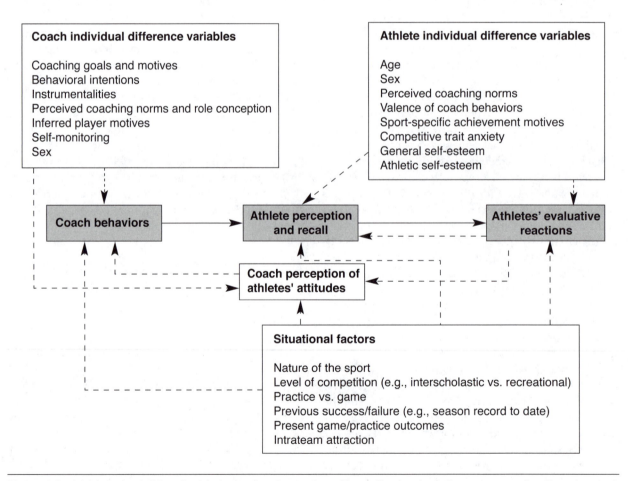

Figure 6.1   Model of adult leadership behaviors in sport and hypothesized relations among situational, cognitive, behavioral, and individual difference variables.

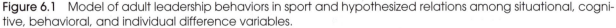

Adapted from F.L. Smoll and R.E. Smith, 1984, Leadership research in youth sports. In *Psychological foundations of sport*, edited by J.M. Silva and R.S. Weinberg (Champaign, IL: Human Kinetics), 383. By permission of authors.

These theorists cite a large body of empirical evidence that, under certain conditions, specific behaviors are highly predictable from behavioral intentions and that behavioral intentions, in turn, are predictable from a number of social, cognitive, and motivational variables. Behavioral intentions seem most highly correlated with overt behaviors when the intentions are couched in specific rather than general terms and when situational conditions facilitate or, at least, do not impede performance of the behavior. The extent to which and conditions under which specific coaching behaviors can be predicted from behavioral intentions should thus be a focus of future research.

Behavioral intentions are assumed to be influenced by cognitive, motivational, and social variables. Cognitive and motivational variables have been combined most successfully in instrumentality (expectancy × value) models of decision making and employee performance (e.g., Edwards, 1962; Vroom, 1964). Empirical evidence indicates that under a wide variety of conditions, instrumentalities (the sum of the products of perceived likelihood of a consequence times the value of the consequence) predict behavior (Bandura, 1986; Mitchell & Biglan, 1971).

To measure instrumentalities, coaches were asked to indicate the extent to which each of the 12 behaviors facilitated the achievement of eight different objectives (e.g., "Developing a winning team," "Developing good qualities in youngsters") that varied in importance to the coach. The proposed model suggests that the predictive usefulness of instrumentalities for behavioral intentions will be highest when the specific coaching behavior is consistently correlated with consequences and when those consequences have high positive or negative valence for the coach. In a preliminary analysis of coaching instrumentalities and behavior (Smith et al., 1978), instrumentalities were found to be related (average correlation = .42) to coaches' self-perceptions of their behavior but unrelated to observed and athlete-perceived behaviors. More extensive investigation of this aspect of the model is clearly warranted, and the role of instrumentalities is unproven at this time.

Social as well as motivational and cognitive variables affect behavioral intentions. One social factor that should influence behavioral intentions of coaches is the role the coach occupies and the perceived norms associated with that role. There is evidence of diversity among amateur coaches in their own role conceptions (Martens & Gould, 1979). Some coaches believe that they are expected to win and that successful coaches are tough on athletes. Others view their role as one of promoting fun, skill development, and personal growth. Such differences would be expected to influence coaching behaviors as well as the attitudes and values that are transmitted to athletes. We would hypothesize, for example, that coaches in the first group would be more punitive, authoritarian, and regimented in their approach and would emphasize the importance of winning more than would coaches in the second group. Thus, individual differences in role and norm conceptions hold heuristic promise for the study of coaching behaviors and have led us to include these variables in our theoretical paradigm.

As adult leaders, coaches not only have their own goals and related instrumentalities, but they also have conceptions of the basic motives of the youngsters who play for them. Coaches' beliefs about why young people try to achieve in sport may influence their expectations of how athletes will respond to specific behaviors on their part and may also affect the manner in which coaches structure the situation and respond to the children, as research on coach-produced motivational climate clearly indicates (see chapter 9).

There is evidence that coaches differ in their perceptions of athletes' sport-related achievement needs. In our initial study (Smith et al., 1978), a forced-choice instrument was developed for assessing coaches' beliefs concerning the relative importance to children of eight different achievement-related goals. Cluster analysis of coaches' responses revealed two main clusters of coaches. The first group of coaches emphasized the importance of intrinsic athletic motives, such as the desire to perfect skills and become a good athlete, whereas the second group ascribed more importance to extrinsic social motives, such as impressing peers and pleasing parents. Additional research is needed to determine how coaches' implicit personality theories influence the interpersonal climate they create and how athletes respond to their behaviors.

A key to behaving effectively involves awareness of one's behavior and its consequences. Individual differences in the self-monitoring of one's behavior may thus affect coaching behaviors in important ways. For example, high self-monitors should be more responsive to situational cues and more flexible in their behaviors. Scales developed to measure individual differences in the tendency to self-monitor behavior and situational cues and adjust behavior accordingly have been developed by Snyder and Gangestad (1986) and by Lennox and Wolfe (1984). There is a clear theoretical basis for the potential role of self-monitoring in our model. Specifically, we noted earlier that, except for the behavioral category of punishment, coach ratings of their behavior correlated poorly with athlete ratings, even when the two sets of ratings are made on identical rating scales. Moreover, the athletes' ratings were more highly correlated with codings of overt behavior than were coaches' self-ratings. Individual differences in coaches' self-monitoring and their relation to self-perceptions and athlete perceptions of coaching behaviors are other important components of the model that deserves future empirical attention.

The expansion of girls' athletic programs has drawn an increasing number of women into coaching roles. Sex thus constitutes a potentially important individual difference variable (Greendorfer, Lewko, & Rosengren, 2002). An examination of possible sex differences in the individual difference variables discussed previously, in coaching behaviors, and in the manner in which children of both sexes respond to those behaviors is an important step in the development of the proposed model. While studies of sex differences in leader behaviors in business settings have frequently failed to find sex differences (e.g., Eagly & Johnson, 1990; Osborn & Vicars, 1976), the youth sport environment provides the opportunity to compare the leadership behaviors of men and women in a different setting.

Athlete Individual Difference Variables

In addition to coach individual difference variables, the model posits a number of athlete individual difference variables that may affect athletes' perceptions of

Coaches play a central role in the sport environment and can provide positive reinforcement to athletes in numerous ways.

coaching behaviors and their responses to them. Our research has demonstrated the importance of age on perception and attitudes. Factor analyses of perceived coaching behaviors indicated that young children (aged 8 and 9) differentiated among coaches primarily on the basis of aversive behaviors, such as punishment and punitive technical instruction. At ages 10 to 12, positive reinforcement and encouragement became the most important bases for differentiation. Adolescents (aged 13-15) differentiated primarily on the basis of amount and quality of technical instruction (Smith et al., 1978). The manner in which age is related to other individual difference variables in the model, such as perceived coaching norms, valence of coaching behaviors, and achievement-related motives, is a worthy topic for future research.

Sex of the child is clearly a variable of major importance in the model. In a preliminary study of elementary school basketball players, striking sex differences were found in athlete perceptions of coaching behaviors and in ratings of their valence (i.e., how much they liked or disliked the behaviors) (Smith & Smoll, 1983). Girls perceived their coaches as giving more frequent reinforcement and encouragement and less punishment and technical instruction than did the boys who rated their male coaches. On their valence ratings, girls expressed greater liking for reinforcement and encouragement and a greater dislike for nonreinforcement, punishment, and punitive technical instruction than did boys. Research on sex differences in other individual difference variables will extend the study of sex roles and sex differences into the youth sport realm.

The effect of normative beliefs is likely to apply to child athletes (followers) as well as to coaches (leaders), and the influence of such beliefs on reactions to the behaviors of others has been demonstrated in many contexts (Myers, 2005). We would thus expect that athletes' notions of how coaches are expected to behave will influence how the athletes react to particular behaviors. For example, one testable hypothesis is that athletes who expect coaches to be tough may respond less negatively to punitive behaviors than those who believe that coaches should be warm and caring. Children's normative beliefs may also vary with the sport. We might hypothesize, for example, that punitive behaviors may be expected and tolerated to a greater degree in a collision sport like rugby or hockey than in a less aggressive sport such as gymnastics. Such beliefs may also interact with those relating to traditional gender roles so that different behaviors may be expected as a function of the coach's gender.

A somewhat related individual difference factor is the valence that athletes attach to various behaviors. For example, some youngsters may value reinforcement more than others, and the positive or negative valence of any coaching behavior can be expected to vary as a function of other individual difference variables, experiential factors, and situational factors. In a similar vein, investigations already have focused on athletes' preferences for different leadership styles and behaviors as a function of athletic maturity (i.e., level of competition) and type of sport (Chelladurai & Carron, 1983; see also chapter 5). Given that behavioral valences occupy an influential role in many theoretical conceptions of interpersonal behavior (e.g., Bandura, 1986; Mischel & Shoda, 1995), they are of interest as dependent variables as well as moderators of attitudinal responses to coaches who engage in certain behavior patterns. As noted earlier, initial research suggests that sex differences exist in this factor.

Competitive sport is an achievement setting, and children's achievement-related motives for trying to perform well seem likely to be an important individual difference component of the model. Research on task and ego-achievement orientations has been a major focus of sport researchers in recent years (see chapter 9; Duda & Hall, 2001; McArdle & Duda, 2002). The literature also indicates that it is important to consider both approach (desire to succeed) and avoidance (fear of failure) motivation for achievement (Elliott & Church, 1997).

In one study of achievement-related motives (Smith et al., 1978), we focused on approach and avoidance motivation and developed a forced-choice ipsative measure of five approach motives (i.e., obtaining self-reinforcement, coach approval, parental approval, peer approval, and winning) and four avoidance motives (i.e., avoiding self-deprecation, parental disapproval, coach disapproval, and peer disapproval). We found that children with low general self-esteem want to impress peers and to avoid self-deprecation, whereas children with high self-esteem are more highly motivated to feel pride in succeeding and to develop their athletic skills. More intensive studies are warranted of achievement-related sport motives and how they relate to other variables in the model.

Many personality variables could conceivably moderate relationships among coaching behaviors, athlete perceptions, and evaluative reactions. Because of their importance on both theoretical and empirical grounds, we have chosen to include three variables—competition anxiety, general self-esteem, and athletic self-esteem.

Competitive trait anxiety is the first of these variables. It is generally recognized that people differ in their predisposition to become anxious under conditions of threat. This general proclivity has been termed *trait anxiety* as distinguished from *state anxiety,* a momentary condition that occurs in the actual situation (Spielberger, 1966). Individuals high in competitive trait anxiety are particularly responsive to sport situations that involve social evaluation. Martens (1977) developed the Sport Competition Anxiety Test (SCAT) to measure this construct, and abundant evidence indicates that SCAT scores are related to the tendency to perceive threat in sport situations and to respond with heightened state anxiety. More recently, a multidimensional trait-anxiety scale, the Sport Anxiety Scale (Smith, Smoll, & Schutz, 1990) was developed to assess the dimensions of somatic anxiety, worry, and concentration disruption.

Although limited information exists concerning how competitive trait anxiety affects perceptions and responses to actual coaching behaviors, several hypotheses are suggested. For example, it is possible that anxious children perceive coaches as less reinforcing and encouraging and as more punitive than they actually are because of greater vigilance to threatening stimuli. Moreover, anxiety would be expected to affect the positive and negative valence attached to coaching behaviors such as reinforcement, encouragement, and criticism.

This hypothesis was tested in a study using the Coaching Behavior Questionnaire, which assesses athletes' perceptions of a variety of coaching behaviors and their perceived effects on performance. In accord with the mediational model, this study revealed that athletes high in performance anxiety tended to evaluate a variety of coaching behaviors more negatively and as damaging to their performance (Williams et al., 2003). Thus, competitive trait anxiety appears to be a potentially important individual difference variable in the model.

General self-esteem, defined as one's evaluation of self-worth, has been shown to play an important role in social perception and adjustment (Wylie, 1978), and it has consistently proved to be an important moderator variable in our previous research. Coaching behaviors are more strongly related to athletes' evaluative responses to supportive and instructive behaviors for children low in self-esteem than for those high in self-esteem (Smith et al., 1978; Smoll, Smith, Barnett, & Everett, 1993). Likewise, children with low self-esteem respond more positively to coaches who are trained to be reinforcing and supportive and less positively to untrained coaches than do children high in self-esteem (Smith, Smoll, & Curtis, 1979). Coppel (1979) reported that self-esteem was related to both athlete perception of coach behaviors and to behavioral valences. Children of both sexes with low self-esteem rated their coaches as less reinforcing and encouraging and as more punitive than did children with high self-esteem who played for the same coaches.

Because of our interest in self-esteem as a moderator variable that might influence responses to coaches' behaviors, we tested a self-enhancement model of self-esteem development (Tesser & Campbell, 1983) against a consistency model (Swann, Griffin, Predmore, & Gaines, 1987). According to the consistency, or self-verification, model, children low in self-esteem should prefer coaches whose lack of supportive behavior serves to confirm their already low opinion of themselves. In contrast, a self-enhancement model would propose that children with low self-esteem are particularly eager to feel better about themselves and would therefore like supportive coaches and dislike nonsupportive ones. Thus, by examining responses of children who vary in self-esteem in relation to coaches whose CBAS behaviors mark them as high or low in supportiveness (reinforcement and mistake-contingent encouragement), we were able to pit these two theories against one another.

As shown in figure 6.2, attraction responses toward the coaches revealed a significant interaction between coach supportiveness and athlete self-esteem (Smith & Smoll, 1990). In agreement with the self-enhancement model, children with low self-esteem were more responsive than other children to variations in supportiveness. Rather than liking the nonsupportive coaches, as the consistency model would predict, these children reacted especially negatively to them, presumably because the coaches frustrated their self-enhancement needs by being nonsupportive. This finding extends a body of results derived from laboratory studies to a naturalistic setting. Collectively, these results suggest that self-enhancement motivation causes people who are low in self-esteem to be especially responsive to variations in supportiveness (Dittes, 1959; Swann, Griffin, Predmore, & Gaines, 1987; Tesser & Campbell, 1983).

A second self-esteem variable included in the model is specific to the sport situation. Athletic self-esteem (also labeled *self-perceived competence*) refers to the individual's evaluation of herself as an athlete. Given that situation-specific individual difference measures are typically more highly related to behavior than are more global measures, it is of interest to examine athletic as well as general self-esteem.

Evidence exists that athletic self-esteem, or perceived competence, influences perception and evaluation of coaching behaviors. Carmichael (2002) found that children high in athletic self-esteem had more positive evaluations of democratic, training, supportive, and positive-feedback behaviors (as measured using Chelladurai's [1984] Leadership Scale for Sports) and reacted more negatively to autocratic behaviors than did children low in perceived competence.

Perceived competence can be influenced by coaching behaviors, since younger children (particularly under age 10) base their self-evaluations in large part on feedback received from adults (Horn & Hasbrook, 1984). Research has also shown that coaches react more favorably to athletes they believe to have high ability than to athletes with low ability, a process that can produce a self-fulfilling prophesy of lowered performance (Horn, 1985; Rejeski, Darracott, & Hutslar, 1979).

Situational Factors Affecting Coaches and Athletes

Although individual difference variables are important, situational factors also influence the manner in which the coach behaves. Comparing the results of our baseball study (Smith et al., 1978) with findings derived from behavioral assessment of youth basketball coaches (Smith et al., 1983) indicates that the nature of the sport may influence behavior patterns. For basketball coaches, the distribution of behaviors across CBAS categories was generally similar to the distribution in baseball, and compared with rates of reinforcement, encouragement, and technical instruction, punitive responses occurred relatively infrequently. However, the factor structure that emerged in the basketball study differed in several respects from that found in the baseball study. The major difference was the placement of the technical instruction categories on the opposite end of a factor that included the supportive behaviors of reinforcement and encouragement. This suggested a dimensional structure involving relationship versus task orientation, whereas the baseball results suggested independent dimensions. Additional research is needed with larger samples of coaches and other

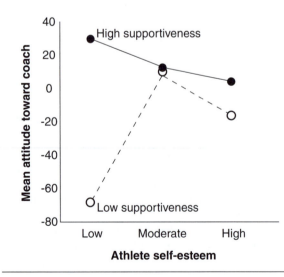

Figure 6.2 Mean evaluations of coaches by athletes as a function of athletes' self-esteem and coaches' supportiveness.

Data from Smith and Smoll 1990.

leaders to determine the extent to which consistent dimensions of adult leadership behaviors occur in different contexts.

As the model in figure 6.1 suggests, other situational factors may affect coaches' behavior or interact with individual difference variables. These include practice settings as opposed to games, level of competition (e.g., recreational as opposed to interscholastic), previous success or failure, present game and practice developments (e.g., being ahead, losing a lead, being behind, making a comeback), and so forth. It should not be difficult to code these kinds of situational factors and to study their effects on behavioral intentions, instrumentalities, and overt behaviors in the sport setting.

Situational factors undoubtedly affect children's perceptions of and reactions to coaching behaviors, just as they influence the behaviors themselves. Under certain circumstances, behavioral valences may change drastically. For example, one testable hypothesis is that athletes respond less negatively to punishment if they attribute poor performance to lack of effort on their part, in other words, if they feel they deserve it. The role of situational factors has not been previously explored, but a clearer specification of important situational factors is critical to the ultimate usefulness of the proposed model.

In addition to one-way causal or moderator relationships, our expanded leadership model allows for reciprocal interactions among relevant variables. For example, significant relations may indicate not only that coaching behaviors affect team performance or morale, but also that the coach's subsequent behaviors are influenced by these outcomes. The model thus indicates directional and bidirectional causal relationships that can serve as the basis for hypotheses concerning the dynamics of coach–athlete situational interactions. Such hypotheses are now amenable to empirical evaluation using structural equation modeling. Although it is virtually impossible to simultaneously study the effects of all the hypothesized causal factors, the model does provide a framework within which direct and interactive influences may be studied.

Development and Evaluation of Coach Effectiveness Training

The data obtained in our initial investigation were basically correlational in nature, although the fact that the behavioral data were collected before the perceptual and attitudinal measures were taken suggests the possibility of causal relations. In order to draw more convincing conclusions regarding causality, we conducted field experiments in which we employed a variety of behavior-change techniques in an attempt to train coaches to relate more effectively to their athletes (Smith et al., 1979). In addition to providing information on the feasibility of training coaches to provide a better athletic experience, the experiment provided additional evidence concerning the validity of the relations established in the correlational studies.

Coach Effectiveness Training constitutes the applied research phase of our program. Using the data obtained in our basic research as an empirical basis for behavioral guidelines, we developed an intervention program to modify coaching behaviors in ways that would enhance the sport experience for young athletes. Social-cognitive theory provided the practical methods that we used to communicate the guidelines to coaches, assist the coaches in applying them, and maintain compliance over time. We named the intervention, presented as a coaching workshop, Coach Effectiveness Training (CET).

CET Principles

The CET workshop emphasizes five key coaching principles and presents behavioral guidelines for implementing each principle (Smith & Smoll, 2002; Smoll & Smith, 2006). The first principle deals with a developmentally oriented philosophy of winning. Coaches are urged to focus on athletes' effort and enjoyment rather than on success as measured by statistics or scoreboards. They are encouraged to emphasize "doing your best," "getting better," and "having fun" as opposed to winning at all costs.

Although this principle was included in our intervention before the emergence of achievement goal theory, it is clearly consistent with a task or mastery motivational climate. It reduces an emphasis on winning in favor of other participation motives (e.g., enjoyment, skill development, affiliation with teammates) and takes into account the inverse relation between enjoyment and competitive anxiety (Scanlan & Lewthwaite, 1984; Scanlan & Passer, 1978, 1979). Moreover, coaches are instructed to help athletes separate feelings of self-worth from game outcomes or win–loss records. Focusing on effort rather than outcome is consistent with Dweck's (1975) highly successful attributional retraining program with low-achieving children. Children who received Dweck's intervention showed improved performance (in a math problem-solving task) and were better able to cope with failure. Within the realm of sport, one might expect this approach to lessen the effects of failure, thereby reducing stress for athletes.

Our second principle emphasizes a positive approach to coaching. In this approach, coach–athlete interactions are characterized by positive reinforcement, encouragement, and sound technical instruction that help create high levels of interpersonal attraction between coaches and athletes. Punitive and hostile responses are strongly discouraged, as they have been shown to create a negative team climate and to promote fear of failure (Scanlan & Lewthwaite, 1984; Scanlan & Passer, 1978). Reinforcement should not be restricted to the learning and performance of sport skills; rather, it should also be used to strengthen desirable responses (e.g., mastery attempts and persistence, teamwork, leadership, sportsmanship).

CET also includes several guidelines for taking a positive approach to technical instruction. For example, when giving instruction, we encourage coaches to emphasize the good things that will happen if athletes perform correctly rather than focusing on the negative things that will happen if they do not. This approach should motivate athletes to make desirable things happen (i.e., develop a positive achievement orientation) rather than building fear of making mistakes.

The third principle is to establish norms that emphasize athletes' obligations to help and support one another. Such norms increase social support and attraction among teammates and thereby enhance cohesion and commitment to the team, and they are most likely to develop when coaches are supportive models themselves and when they reinforce athlete behaviors that promote team unity. We also instruct coaches in how to develop a "we're in this together" group norm. This norm can play an important role in building team cohesion, particularly if the coach frequently reinforces athletes' demonstrations of mutual supportiveness. Such procedures are a positive approach to team building (Smith & Smoll, 1997).

A fourth principle is that compliance with team roles and responsibilities is most effectively achieved by involving athletes in decisions regarding team rules and by reinforcing compliance with rules rather than punishing noncompliance. By setting explicit guidelines that the athletes help formulate and by using positive reinforcement to strengthen desirable responses, coaches can foster self-discipline and prevent athlete misbehavior.

A fifth principle is that coaches should become more aware of their own behavior and its consequences. One of the striking findings from our basic research was that coaches were unaware of how often they behaved in various ways (Smith et al., 1978). Thus, an important goal is to increase coaches' awareness of what they are doing, for change is unlikely to occur without self-awareness. CET coaches are taught two proven behavioral-change techniques, namely, behavioral feedback and self-

monitoring. To obtain feedback, coaches are encouraged to work with their assistants as a team and share descriptions of each others' behaviors. Another feedback procedure involves soliciting input directly from the athletes.

Self-monitoring (observing and recording one's own behavior) is a second behavior-change technique that has potential for increasing coaches' awareness of their own behavioral patterns and encouraging their compliance with the CET guidelines. In CET, coaches are given a brief self-monitoring form that they are encouraged to complete immediately after practices and games (Smoll & Smith, 2005, p. 21). On the form, they indicate approximately what percentage of the time they engaged in the recommended behaviors; for example, coaches are asked, "Approximately what percentage of the times they occurred did you respond to mistakes/errors with encouragement?" Self-monitoring is restricted to desired behaviors so that coaches stay focused on positive behavior-change goals. Coaches are encouraged to engage in self-monitoring on a regular basis in order to achieve optimal results. In research studies, coaches submit their completed self-monitoring forms to the investigators in order to measure compliance with this procedure.

CET Outcome Evaluations

In the first empirical test of CET's effects, 31 Little League Baseball coaches were randomly assigned to an experimental group (training) or to a control group that received no training. The coaches in the experimental group participated in a preseason cognitive-behavioral training program designed to help them relate more effectively to children. During the 2-hour intervention, empirically derived behavioral guidelines were presented and modeled (see Smith et al., 1979). In addition, behavioral feedback and self-monitoring procedures were employed to increase the coaches' self-awareness and encourage them to comply with the coaching guidelines.

To assess the effects of the program, coaches in both groups were observed for an average of four games during the course of the season and an aggregated CBAS behavioral profile was generated for each coach. After the season, 325 youngsters were individually interviewed in their homes to obtain athlete measures. Outcome data indicated that on both observed and athlete-perceived behaviors, the trained coaches differed from the controls in a manner consistent with the coaching guidelines. Trained coaches were also evaluated more positively by their athletes, and a higher level of intrateam attraction was found on their teams despite the fact that they did not differ from the controls in the average win–loss record. Children who played for the trained coaches exhibited a significant increase in self-esteem as compared with scores obtained a year earlier; the children who played for coaches in the control group did not show an increase. In line with the results found in the basic research phase supporting the self-enhancement model (figure 6.2), we also found that athletes who were low in self-esteem reacted most positively to trained (more supportive) coaches, indicating that the program has a salutary effect on the children who are most in need of a positive sport experience.

Subsequent tests of the CET program replicated and extended the results of the first study. Trained coaches were perceived by their athletes as more reinforcing, more encouraging, giving of more technical instruction, and less punitive and controlling than were coaches in the control group. In turn, the athletes who played for the trained coaches indicated that they enjoyed their experience more and liked their coach and teammates more. Such children also demonstrated significant increases in general self-esteem and significant decreases in performance anxiety over the course of the season (Smith, Smoll, & Barnett, 1995; Smoll, Smith, Barnett, & Everett, 1993).

Finally, a study of attrition showed a dropout rate of 26% among children who played for coaches in the control group, a figure that is consistent with previous reports of 30% to 40% annual attrition rates in youth sport programs (Gould, 1987). In contrast, only 5% of the children who played for CET-trained coaches failed to return to the program the next season (Barnett, Smoll, & Smith, 1992). These positive psychosocial outcomes are all the more noteworthy in light of the fact that experimental and control groups have not differed in average win–loss percentages in any of the studies.

Future Research

One important direction for future research is the development of new and better measures of the constructs we are interested in studying. Measurement is an indispensable factor in the success of any research endeavor, and we need advances on a number of fronts. For example, we believe that although the CBAS has been useful in previous research on coaching behaviors, there is a need for fine-tuned behavioral assessment systems. The CBAS categories are quite broad and do not capture behavioral distinctions within categories. For example, the positive reinforcement category includes both verbal and nonverbal positive responses to desirable behaviors. It is quite possible that one of these variations affects athletes more strongly than the other. One of the reasons that behavioral measures of coaching behaviors do not correlate more highly with

athletes' attitudinal responses to the coach is that the categories are too broad to make meaningful distinctions of the type just described.

Another example of the need for better measures is the use of scales developed in adult populations in research with children. We found that one of our own measures, the Sport Anxiety Scale (Smith, Smoll, & Schutz, 1990), developed using samples of high school and college athletes, did not validly measure its target variables of somatic anxiety, worry, and concentration disruption in children when we used it in a CET outcome study on anxiety reduction (Smith, Smoll, & Barnett, 1995). The reading level of the items was simply too high for children to comprehend. We have therefore developed a second-generation scale, the Sport Anxiety Scale-2, written at the 4th-grade level in order to study the multiple components of anxiety in children (Smith, Smoll, Cumming, and Grossband, 2006). This scale is equally valid for adolescents and adults and therefore provides a tool for comparing relations among situation, anxiety, and behavior at different ages and for doing longitudinal studies of sport performance anxiety.

Many questions remain unanswered and invite the attention of future researchers. One intriguing direction relates to the behavioral signatures we have demonstrated in coaches (see Behavioral Signatures of Coaches on page 88). These behavioral signatures provide the basis for the development of what social psychologist Daryl Bem (1983) termed a *triple typology,* that is, a categorization of people, behaviors, and situations that allows accurate statements in the following form: "This type of coach will do these types of behaviors in these types of situations." The next step, then, will be to relate these behavior patterns to other variables, such as athletes' attitudes toward the coach. As an example, suppose we find that some coaches give positive reinforcement more often when their team is winning than when they are losing. Another coach shows the opposite pattern. We might want to know how giving reinforcement in winning versus losing situations affects athletes' liking of the coach.

Another intriguing line of research expands the outcomes studied in evaluations of coach training programs. For example, achievement goal theory (see chapter 9) is a major focus of sport research. As noted, the motivational climate (mastery vs. ego) established by coaches has been shown to have important effects on a range of outcomes, including persistence, performance, anxiety, and the achievement goals adopted by athletes. To this point, however, no one has assessed the effects of coach training on motivational climate and on resultant changes in athletes' achievement goal orientations over the course of a sport season. Also needed is evidence on whether potential changes in achievement goal orientation that occur as the result of sport participation generalize to other achievement domains, such as the classroom. Hopefully, at least some of the readers of this book will become the next generation of sport psychology researchers and provide answers to many of the intriguing questions that remain.

Practical Implications

We conclude the chapter with brief descriptions of current basic and applied research derived from the mediational model within the social-cognitive framework. One line of research focuses on temporally consistent behavior-by-situation interactions that may constitute a stable individual difference factor in coaches. The second line of work involves the development and testing of enhanced intervention programs for coaches and parents inspired by research within another social-cognitive framework, achievement goal theory (Dweck, 1999; Duda & Hall, 2001; Roberts, Treasure, & Kavussanu, 1997).

Behavioral Signatures of Coaches

Person-by-situation interactionism, the notion that personal and situational characteristics interact with one another to cause behavior, is a cornerstone of social-cognitive theory. Behavioral variation takes two forms, the first of which involves differences between people. Some coaches are more supportive or more punitive than others. The other type of variability, less studied in sport psychology but still critical, involves behavioral variation within the same individual across time and situations. For example, one coach may give special attention to the most gifted athletes on the team while paying little attention to the less skilled, whereas another may show the opposite pattern. Although the two coaches are thus similar in their average responsiveness across coach–athlete interactions, the fact that they respond so differently to skilled and unskilled athletes suggests something meaningful and distinctive about them and constitutes a kind of behavioral signature (Shoda & LeeTiernan, 2002).

Relatively stable behavioral signatures have been found in children as they confront particular classes of social situations (Zelli & Dodge, 1999). Do behavioral signatures occur in adult coaches as well as in children? To find out, we reanalyzed the CBAS data collected from 51 youth baseball coaches over 202 complete games in our initial study (Smith et al., 1978). In previous analyses of these data, we aggregated coaches' behaviors in each coding category (e.g., reinforcement, punishment) across all observations and expressed them as percentages of total behaviors (e.g., Smith et al., 1978; Smith & Smoll, 1990). However, during the original data collection, we coded the behaviors during each half-inning and recorded the time and score at the beginning and end of each half-inning. This made it possible to reanalyze the behaviors within three different game situations, namely, leading at the end of the half-inning, being tied, or losing.

For each coach, we randomly divided all of the observed half-innings into two sets (termed time 1 and time 2) so that we could not only determine if coaches differed in their behavior profiles within the three game situations but also how consistent these profiles were by correlating the two sets of situation–behavior data across times 1 and 2 (Smith, Smoll, & Cumming, 2004).

Figure 6.3 presents data for two coaches, showing the relative percentages of supportive, instructional, and punitive behaviors that they exhibited when their teams were winning, tied, or losing. Although the two coaches were very similar in their overall percentages of the three behaviors when summed across the three game-situation categories, their situation–behavior profiles differed in some notable ways. Clearly evident are distinctive "If . . . then" situation–behavior relations, or behavioral signatures that were not evident from their overall percentages of supportive, instructive, and punitive behaviors.

For example, the coaches differed in their pattern of supportive behaviors, with Coach B showing a notable increase in such behavior when the game was tied. He also showed a sharp decline in instructional behaviors when his team was not winning, whereas Coach A did not. Both coaches became more punitive during losing half-innings (whereas some coaches in the data set became more supportive and less punitive when their teams were losing). Moreover, the high-profile stability coefficients indicate that these differences in behavioral patterning occurred consistently in the three classes of situations and were not merely random fluctuations. These behavioral signatures introduce a new way of conceptualizing coaching patterns, and it will be possible to relate them to other variables, such as the athletes' attitudes toward the coach. It may well be that the patterns of behavior in particular situations have equal, or perhaps even greater, importance than average levels of coaching behaviors across situations.

Mastery-Based Coach and Parent Interventions

At the present time, we are evaluating the effects of a training program derived from CET that we have labeled the Mastery Approach to Coaching. Inspired

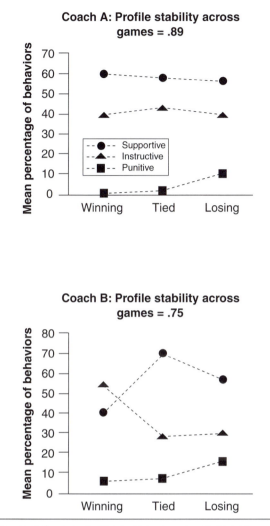

Figure 6.3 Intraindividual behavioral signatures of two youth sport coaches across three game situations, showing situation-specific patterning of supportive, instructive, and punitive behaviors.

From R.E. Smith, F.L. Smoll, and S.P. Cumming, 2004, *Situationally-defined behavioral signatures in youth sport coaches.* Unpublished raw data.

in part by the impressive research outcomes associated with a task or mastery motivational climate (see chapter 9), the revised program builds upon the first principle of CET (see page 85). We have expanded and embellished the CET content on skill development and personal growth versus winning, and we have included specific guidelines for establishing a mastery-oriented motivational climate. We have also developed a parallel intervention, the Mastery Approach to Parenting in Sports, so as to encourage a parent-produced mastery climate. (See chapter 10 for a review of parent-created motivational climate.)

The research program just described illustrates how basic research and applied research can support one another. Basic research on coaching behaviors provided a scientific basis for the development of CET. Testing the effectiveness of the program allowed us to demonstrate the causal implications of the behavior–attitude relations found in the correlational data in the basic research.

Summary

In the original mediational model of coach–athlete influences, coaching behaviors influence athletes' perception and recall, which in turn influence athletes' evaluative reactions. In other words, the effects of a coach's actual behaviors on the athlete's evaluative reactions are mediated by the athlete's recall and the meanings ascribed to the behaviors. This preliminary model was expanded to delineate the characteristics and processes that influence coaching behaviors and mediate their effects on athletes, particularly the roles played by situational and individual difference factors in coaches' behaviors and children's reactions to those behaviors. The research based on a mediational model derived from social-cognitive theory has demonstrated significant and replicable relations between adult leadership behaviors and children's attitudes.

Coach Effectiveness Training (CET) is an intervention program to help coaches enhance the sport experience for young athletes. There are five key CET coaching principles: focus on athletes' effort and enjoyment rather than on statistics or scores; emphasize positive reinforcement, encouragement, and sound technical instruction; establish norms that emphasize athletes' obligations to support one another; involve athletes in decisions regarding team rules and reinforce compliance with rules; and become more aware of one's own behavior as a coach. CET coaches are taught two proven behavioral-change techniques, namely, behavioral feedback and self-monitoring.

In a practical sense, the results obtained from the experimental training program indicate that coaches can be taught to relate more effectively to young athletes. Thus, in addition to guiding our basic research, the conceptual model has fostered a methodology for assessing coaching behaviors, and it has provided an empirical basis for leadership training and for the evaluation of such training.

Discussion Questions

1. How do theory, research, and interventions support one another? How does the theory development and research described in this chapter illustrate these links?

2. Describe the measures of coaching behavior and athlete outcomes that were developed within the context of the mediational model.

3. What were the major findings of the research linking observed and perceived coaching behaviors with children's reactions to their athletic experience? What situational and individual difference variables influenced relations among behavior outcomes?

4. Summarize the five principles underlying Coach Effectiveness Training (CET), and summarize the results observed in the outcome evaluation studies of this intervention.

5. What coaching behaviors would enhance athletes' self-esteem?

6. Describe possible avenues of future research and practical implications of research in coaching behaviors.

chapter 7

Team Cohesion: Nature, Correlates, and Development

Albert V. Carron, EdD, Mark A. Eys, PhD, and Shauna M. Burke, MA

Learning Objectives

On completion of this chapter, the reader should have

1. knowledge regarding the nature of cohesion in sport teams;
2. familiarity with the relationship of task and social cohesion to team success;
3. knowledge regarding the main benefits of higher team cohesion;
4. understanding of the potential negative aspects of too much task and social cohesion; and
5. knowledge of strategies for developing greater team cohesion.

The most deadly of basketball viruses, a disturbing lack of chemistry and complaints about playing time, threaten to sink this stink bomb as one of the all-time American disgraces in Olympic competition.

Mariotti (2004) commenting on the 2004 U.S. men's Olympic basketball team

In 2004, highly underrated teams around the world achieved unexpected success. The quote introducing this chapter provides one example; basketball fans in the United States were dismayed when the latest version of the Dream Team—the heavily favored U.S. Olympic men's basketball team—was defeated by Puerto Rico in the opening round. As another example, soccer aficionados were shocked when Greece defeated home team Portugal to win the Union of European Football Associations (UEFA) football championship. Finally, in 2004 the Los Angeles Lakers were favored to defeat the Detroit Pistons and win the National Basketball Association (NBA) championship, but Detroit prevailed.

A question often posed when underdogs are successful is, why? Not surprisingly, this question received considerable media attention in the case of the three examples just presented. In his analysis of Greece's surprising success, Adam Szreter (2004) noted,

For a tournament in which the big names have so often failed to deliver what they promised, it was fitting that UEFA EURO™ was ultimately won by rank outsiders. Greece's incredible achievement was a triumph of teamwork and camaraderie, and after another never-say-die performance in the final no one can begrudge them their finest hour.

Similarly, Rob Peterson (2004) suggested that Detroit's success over the Lakers resulted from differences in five important factors: speed, health, aggression, intelligent play, and cohesion. Insofar as the latter is concerned, Peterson observed:

When you see the Pistons play, you feel they're playing like a team. Everyone seems in sync, so much so that Detroit can win although they shot .426 in Game 4. When you watch the Lakers play, you feel it's Shaq [Shaquille O'Neil] and Kobe [Kobe Bryant] and no one else.

Cohesion, which is used synonymously in the media with terms such as teamwork, team unity, closeness, and camaraderie, has been defined as "a dynamic process which is reflected in the tendency for a group to stick together and remain united in the pursuit of its instrumental objectives and/or for the satisfaction of member affective needs" (Carron, Brawley, & Widmeyer, 1998, p. 213). Cohesion has been identified by experts in group dynamics as the most important group property (Bollen & Hoyle, 1990; Golembiewski, 1962; Lott & Lott, 1965). The present chapter focuses on some of the reasons why this is the case.

Conceptual Model for Team Cohesion

In order to better understand (and ultimately measure) any theoretical construct such as group cohesion, it is necessary to begin with a clear understanding of that construct's basic nature. Figure 7.1 provides a schematic representation of the conceptual model that Carron, Widmeyer, and Brawley (1985) developed to represent cohesion in sport teams. As figure 7.1 illustrates, Carron et al. proposed that each team member develops and holds perceptions about the team that are related to the group as a totality and to the manner in which the group satisfies personal needs and objectives. These perceptions are labeled as follows:

- Group integration (GI), which reflects the individual's perceptions about the closeness, similarity, and bonding within the group as a whole, as well as the degree of unification of the group
- Individual attractions to the group (ATG), which reflects the individual's perceptions about personal motivations acting to attract and to retain the individual in the group as well as the individual's personal feelings about the group

As figure 7.1 also illustrates, Carron et al. suggested that there are two fundamental foci to a group member's perceptions:

- Task orientation (T), or a general orientation toward achieving the group's objectives (task cohesion)
- Social orientation (S), or a general orientation toward developing and maintaining social relationships and activities within the group (social cohesion)

The result is four manifestations of cohesiveness: group integration-task (GI-T), group integration-social (GI-S), individual attractions to the group-task (ATG-T), and individual attractions to the group-social (ATG-S).

In elaborating their conceptual model, Carron et al. (1998) suggested that a fundamental characteristic of cohesion is *multidimensionality*. That is, cohesion in sport teams is not a unitary construct; it has a number of dimensions. Figure 7.1 reflects this characteristic. A

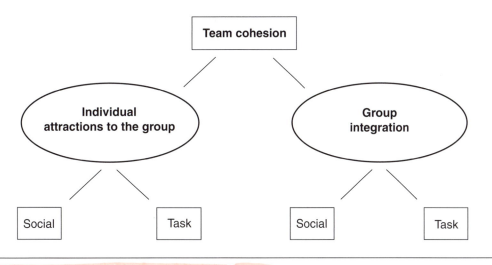

Figure 7.1 A conceptual model for team cohesion in sport.

Adapted, by permission, from A.V. Carron, W.N. Widmeyer, and L.R. Brawley, 1998, "The development of an instrument to assess cohesion in sport teams. The group environment questionnaire," *Journal of Sport Psychology* 7: 244-266.

second fundamental characteristic of cohesion is that it is *dynamic*. This means that it is not a stable, relatively permanent property like a trait. Cohesion in a group changes over time in both its intensity and in its various forms (e.g., task cohesiveness, social cohesiveness) throughout the process of group formation, development, maintenance, and dissolution.

A third fundamental characteristic is that cohesion is *instrumental*. Groups do not stick together solely to stick together—they have a raison d'être. All groups, including sport groups, work groups, families, and so on, form and stay together for a purpose. Even groups that are purely social in nature (and therefore possess a high level of social cohesion) have an instrumental (i.e., task) basis for their formation. Thus, for example, acquaintances that choose to form a social club to develop or maintain better friendships are cohering for instrumental reasons. Finally, cohesion has an *affective* dimension. The social bonding and task unity that develop in groups are pleasing to individual group members. Groups that lose the affective dimension are characterized by conflict and lack of harmony and may even break up.

Relationship of Team Cohesion to Team Success

Considerable research on the team cohesion-team success relationship has been conducted in sport psychology. In 2002, Carron, Colman, Wheeler, and Stevens undertook a meta-analysis of 46 studies that had examined the association between team cohesiveness and team success. An overall moderate to large effect size *(ES)* of .645 was found. The type of cohesiveness

present—task versus social—is irrelevant insofar as team success is concerned. That is, when Carron and his colleagues subdivided the measures according to whether they represented task or social cohesiveness, moderate to large effect sizes *(ES)* for both types were noted (social cohesion *ES* = .702; task cohesion *ES* = .607). As a barometer for interpreting these effect sizes, Cohen (1969, 1992) suggested that effect sizes around .20 are *small* (present but not necessarily evident to the naked eye), effect sizes around .50 are *moderate* (present and evident to informed observers), and effect sizes around .80 are *large* (evident to even casual observers).

There are several potential moderators of the cohesion-performance relationship. As the term suggests, a *moderator* is a factor that modifies the relationship between an independent variable (e.g., cohesion) and a dependent variable (e.g., team success). Once a relationship has been established, researchers are interested in determining whether that relationship holds under all circumstances. In their meta-analysis, Carron and colleagues examined whether gender, level of competition, type of sport, and so on acted as moderator variables in the cohesion-performance relationship.

Gender

The literature on group dynamics is replete with instances where gender has been found to be a moderator of fundamental relationships (see Carron, Hausenblas, & Eys, 2005, for a review). Carron et al. (2002) found that the cohesion-performance relationship is no exception; the association between cohesion and performance is significantly greater in female teams (*ES* = .949) than it is in male teams (*ES* = .556).

Type of Sport

In some of the earliest research on cohesion and performance, negative relationships were found for sports such as bowling (e.g., Landers & Lüschen, 1974). This led some authors (e.g., Carron & Chelladurai, 1981) to propose that cohesion may be important for team success in interactive sports such as volleyball, basketball, and hockey but detrimental to team success in independent sports such as wrestling, tennis, and badminton. This proposal has now been shown to be unwarranted. Carron and his colleagues found that cohesion is equally important for both coactive ($ES = .766$) and interactive ($ES = .657$) teams.

Level of Competition

Carron and colleagues also found that the magnitude of the cohesion–performance relationship varied according to level of competition (i.e., for high school, intercollegiate, and professional teams the ES was .769, .811, and .192, respectively). However, possibly because of the large variability of results in each level or because of the small number of studies at some levels (e.g., professional, high school), these substantial differences were not statistically significant. Thus, the question of whether cohesion is equally important for teams at every level of competition requires further research.

Correlates of Cohesion

Research over the past 20 years has shown that in addition to team performance there are a number of other important group-dynamics constructs associated with team task and social cohesion. For purposes of communication in this chapter, it is convenient to categorize them within the broad categories of situational, personal, and leadership constructs (Carron, Hausenblas, & Eys, 2005). A brief overview of these categories is provided here.

Situational Correlates of Cohesion

Two situational factors related to cohesion are the *level of competition* and the *size* of the team. Insofar as the former is concerned, Granito and Rainey (1988) found that task cohesion was greater in high school versus college American football teams. Also, Gruber and Gray (1982) found that social cohesion was higher in elementary school and junior high school basketball teams than in senior high school teams.

A reasonable generalization is that as a team's size increases, its cohesion decreases (see Carron et al., 2005). Widmeyer, Brawley, and Carron (1990) carried out two studies that demonstrated this generalization. In study 1, a 3-on-3 recreational basketball league was formed consisting of 3, 6, or 9 members. The results showed that task cohesion decreased as roster size increased. In an unusual exception to the generalization, however, social cohesion was highest in the 6-person groups. Widmeyer et al. suggested that in the 3-person teams, the lack of substitutes might not have left sufficient time to develop social relationships. The fact that the 6-person teams had higher social cohesion than the 9-person teams is, of course, consistent with the generalization. In study 2, Widmeyer et al. had individuals compete in volleyball competitions of 3 versus 3, 6 versus 6, and 12 versus 12. As team size increased, there were progressive decreases in the global measure of cohesion.

Personal Correlates of Cohesion

A reasonable generalization is that team cohesion is related to *individual cognitions*. For example, in task-cohesive teams, members are more egalitarian in accepting responsibility for unfavorable results. Brawley, Carron, and Widmeyer (1987) had athletes from a wide cross section of sports use their teammates as a benchmark to estimate degree of personal responsibility for the team's win or loss. The athletes rating their team high in task cohesiveness assumed a level of personal responsibility that was equal to that of the average team member regardless of outcome (i.e., winning or losing). However, those athletes rating their team low in task cohesion showed a self-protective pattern of attribution by accepting less responsibility for the loss than the average team member.

Another reasonable generalization supported by research is that the presence of cohesion is associated with *member behavior.* The interrelationships among sacrifice behavior, team cohesion, and conformity to group norms in sport teams were examined by Prapavessis and Carron (1997) with state-level cricket teams. They found that sacrifice behavior was positively associated with task and social cohesion.

Cohesion represents sticking together. Thus, it's hardly surprising that research has consistently shown a relationship between team cohesion and a wide variety of adherence measures including increased team stability (i.e., lack of dropouts, Robinson & Carron, 1982), reduced absenteeism and lateness (Carron, Widmeyer, & Brawley, 1988), and increased perceptions of the team's ability to handle disruptive events (Brawley, Carron, & Widmeyer, 1988).

Leadership Correlates of Cohesion

Given coaches' substantial role in team development, it should come as no surprise that *coaching behavior is associated with team cohesion* (Jowett & Chaundy, 2004; Kozub, 1993; Lee, Kim, & Lim, 1993; Westre & Weiss, 1991). Specific leader behaviors have varied across studies, but generally higher levels of training and instruction behavior, social-support behavior, and positive feedback from coaches are positively associated with higher levels of task cohesion. A coach's approach to decision making is also related to team cohesion (Brawley, Carron, & Widmeyer, 1993; Jowett & Chaundy, 2004; Kozub, 1993; Lee et al., 1993; Westre & Weiss, 1991). Both a democratic and a delegative decision style have been shown to be positively associated with team task cohesion. However, Jowett and Chaundy (2004) have shown that it is not leader behaviors alone that are important for team cohesion. They found that athletes' perceptions of the coach–athlete relationship (commitment, closeness, complementarity) explained more variance in task and social cohesion than did leader behaviors by themselves.

Benefits and Liabilities of Cohesion

The positive relationship between cohesion and performance highlights an important benefit of maintaining task and social unity on a sport team. However, numerous other benefits exist for teams and their individual members.

Team Benefits of Cohesion

Two team-related correlates of cohesion that have received research attention are collective efficacy and team norms. According to Zaccaro, Blair, Peterson, and Zazanis (1995), collective efficacy represents "a sense of collective competence shared among individuals when allocating, coordinating, and integrating their resources in a successful concerted response to specific situational demands" (p. 309). Zaccaro and colleagues suggested that characteristics of the group itself, such as group cohesion, would influence its sense of collective efficacy. Subsequent studies have supported this contention. For example, Spink (1990) found that perceptions of cohesion were higher for elite and recreational volleyball players who perceived high collective efficacy in their respective teams. Subsequent research (e.g., Kozub & McDonnell, 2000; Paskevich, 1995; Paskevich, Brawley, Dorsch, & Widmeyer, 1995) has produced similar findings, contributing to the sug-

gestion that task cohesion is more strongly related to collective efficacy than is social cohesion.

Group norms are another team-related factor found to be related to cohesion. Norms are standards for behavior that are expected of group members. Norms are important because they inform members about the expectations of the group and integrate those members more closely within the group's structure (Carron, Hausenblas, & Eys, 2005). If members view their team as united concerning task and social aspects (i.e., high cohesion), it is reasonable to expect that they would agree with and conform to standards of behavior that are deemed acceptable for that group.

Research supports this suggestion in a sport environment. For example, Prapavessis and Carron (1997) examined 13 cricket teams and found that perceptions of cohesion were positively related to conformity to group norms. In a lab-based study (Gammage, Carron, & Estabrooks, 2001), subjects read scenarios depicting various combinations of cohesion and norm levels. Participants indicated how much effort the actor in the scenario would likely expend. The situation found to contribute to the best effort by the athlete in the scenario was characterized by high cohesion and a high norm for productivity. Taken in combination, the aforementioned studies highlight both the importance of cohesion to normative behavior as well as the interplay between the two constructs.

Individual Benefits of Cohesion

The benefits that individual athletes accrue from being part of a cohesive team can be classified as cognitive, affective, or behavioral in nature. For example, a cognitive factor shown to be negatively related to cohesion is *role ambiguity*—the lack of clear, consistent information regarding one's role (Kahn, Wolfe, Quinn, Snoek, & Rosenthal, 1964; see also Beauchamp, this volume). Eys and Carron (2001) examined intercollegiate basketball players and found that athletes who believed their team was more task cohesive (group integration–task and individual attractions to the group–task) were likely to perceive less role ambiguity regarding the scope of their responsibilities.

Another example of a cognitive factor related to cohesion is *cognitive state anxiety*. Two studies highlight this relationship. First, Prapavessis and Carron (1996) found that athletes who had higher perceptions of cohesion experienced less cognitive anxiety. Second, Eys, Hardy, Carron, and Beauchamp (2003) extended the Prapavessis and Carron study and found that athletes who interpreted their symptoms of anxiety as facilitative to their performance were also more likely to perceive higher team cohesion.

Terry et al. (2001) provided an example of a positive *affective* relationship with cohesion. Terry et al. examined the relationship between cohesion (as measured by the GEQ; see Carron et al., 1985) and mood (as measured by the Profile of Mood States-C; see Terry, Keohane, & Lane, 1996) for rugby players, rowers, and netball players. Consistently across the samples, higher levels of cohesion were related to lower levels of depression, anger, and tension as well as higher perceptions of vigor.

Finally, there are several examples of the relationship between cohesion and positive behavioral outcomes such as reduced social loafing (McKnight, Williams, & Widmeyer, 1991) and increased effort (Bray & Whaley, 2001; Prapavessis & Carron, 1997). Social loafing refers to a reduction in effort by an individual when working in a group versus when working alone (Carron & Hausenblas, 1998). When McKnight and colleagues compared the performance of swimmers competing in relay teams versus competing individually, they found that social loafing was less common among individuals competing in teams characterized by high team cohesion compared with swimmers in teams with low task cohesion.

From an effort perspective, Prapavessis and Carron (1997) found that athletes who viewed their teams as more cohesive were likely to practice at a work output level closer to their maximum than athletes who viewed their teams as less cohesive. In addition, Bray and Whaley (2001) determined that one of the mediating factors of the cohesion–performance relationship is individual effort. Specifically, they found that more favorable perceptions regarding attractions to social aspects of the group (i.e., the cohesion dimension ATG–S) predicted an increase in effort on the part of the individual that, in turn, led to better performance.

Potential Liabilities of Cohesion

Although cohesion generally is a positive group property, it does have the potential to be negative under some circumstances. Investigation into another individual-level correlate, self-handicapping, highlighted the potential for cohesion to act as a liability to athletes. Self-handicapping represents strategies people use to protect their self-esteem prior to important achievement situations (Jones & Berglas, 1978; see also chapter 15). For example, a pitcher may complain of shoulder pain (real or imagined) to other teammates before pitching in an important baseball game to protect his image in case of failure.

Carron, Prapavessis, and Grove (1994) and Hausenblas and Carron (1996) noted that it would be possible to hypothesize two scenarios when examining the relationship between self-handicapping behavior

and perceptions of cohesion. The first hypothesis, which follows from the perspective that a cohesive team benefits athletes, suggests that greater cohesion should reduce the desire for the individual to engage in self-handicapping. From this viewpoint, individuals on cohesive teams are supported more and there is a diffusion of responsibility if failure occurs; thus, the need to self-handicap and protect one's self-esteem is not as vital.

The contrary hypothesis follows the perspective that members of cohesive groups are more likely to engage in self-handicapping behaviors. The rationale for this hypothesis is that individuals in cohesive groups feel greater attachment to their teammates and thus feel greater pressure to fulfill their responsibilities, which in turn presents a threat to their self-esteem. Overall, both studies examining self-handicapping behaviors in relation to perceptions of cohesion (Carron, Prapavessis, & Grove, 1994; Hausenblas & Carron, 1996) have supported this latter hypothesis (i.e., high cohesion leads to greater self-handicapping).

Prapavessis and Carron (1996) had similar hypotheses when examining cohesion and competitive state anxiety (A-state). They hypothesized that there could be both psychological costs and benefits to being a member of a cohesive team: (a) Being a member of a cohesive group might *reduce* competitive state anxiety because there would be less threat of evaluation due to a higher diffusion of responsibility, or (b) being a member of a cohesive group might *increase* competitive state anxiety because "the pressure to carry out responsibilities and satisfy the expectations of highly valued teammates is maximized" (p. 66). Overall, and contrary to the findings pertaining to self-handicapping, Prapavessis and Carron found that athletes who perceived their teams as more cohesive experienced less competitive state anxiety. Those members also perceived fewer psychological costs of being a member of a cohesive team.

Another interesting avenue of research was taken by Hardy, Eys, and Carron (2005), who asked athletes to indicate whether they felt there were disadvantages to high task and social cohesion on a team and, if so, to identify those disadvantages. They found that 56% of athletes reported potential disadvantages to high social cohesion while 31% reported disadvantages to high task cohesion. Some of the disadvantages to high social cohesion included wasting task-related time, difficulties focusing and committing to task-related goals, problematic communication between friends, and the potential for social isolation of those outside the main group. The disadvantages to high task cohesion included, for example, decreased social relations, communication problems, reduced personal enjoyment, and increased perceived pressures.

These studies on potential liabilities offer an interesting perspective on cohesion, and future research should continue to pursue this question. However, as the majority of researchers, sport psychology practitioners, coaches, and athletes would attest, the benefits of a cohesive team far outweigh any disadvantages that might be present.

Nature of Team Building

As mentioned at the beginning of this chapter, sometimes an underdog team's unexpected success is attributed to the chemistry, or cohesiveness, of the group. Thus, it is essential that athletes and coaches work together to ensure that cohesion is high, which, all other things being equal (e.g., skill, ability, technique), can mean the difference between success and failure (Voight & Callaghan, 2001). Although the benefits of a cohesive group seem rather straightforward, orchestrating a group of individuals—all with different personalities, backgrounds, and personal goals—to work together toward a common goal can be a rather arduous task (Yukelson, 1997). So, what steps can coaches and athletes take to increase perceptions of cohesiveness within their team and in turn increase their team's effectiveness? Recently, sport psychologists have identified numerous team-building strategies to do just that—build more cohesive and effective sport teams. Some of these strategies are highlighted in the following material, but first, a brief discussion of the nature of team building is warranted.

Team building is a dynamic, collaborative, and ongoing process that can positively influence the task-related areas of functioning as well as the interpersonal relationships within a sport group (Stevens, 2002; Yukelson, 1997). In general, two types of team-building programs have been used in sport settings: direct and indirect (Carron et al., 2005; Prapavessis, Carron, & Spink, 1997). In the *direct approach,* the individual responsible for introducing and implementing the team-building intervention works directly with the athletes. Often this person is the coach since most coaches tend to work implicitly or explicitly on the development of a more cohesive, effective team. Occasionally, however, a team-building consultant is brought in to work directly with the team (Carron et al., 2005). In terms of which scenario is superior, it has been suggested that a team-building program may be more effective if a coach implements it rather than a consultant because the athletes will be more invested in the program, thereby increasing the chances that team cohesion and effectiveness will be enhanced (Voight & Callaghan, 2001).

Typically, the implementation of team-building interventions in sport is carried out via an *indirect approach.* In this approach, the consultant serves

Team building can occur through classroom sessions as well as on the field of play.

more of an educational role, working with the coach (rather than directly with the team) in order to identify relevant team-building strategies. The coach then introduces the team-building intervention to the team. This strategy is considered indirect because the information is filtered through the coach before it reaches the athletes (Carron et al., 2005). Again, this type of approach is beneficial in that the coach serves the role of team builder, perhaps increasing the likelihood that the intervention will be successful (Voight & Callaghan, 2001).

Regardless of the approach taken, group effectiveness is most likely to be improved when all athletes are included as active participants in the team-building process (Voight & Callaghan, 2001; Yukelson, 1997). Higher-status members of the team (captains, highly skilled athletes) should also be involved in the development and implementation of the team-building intervention in order to increase the sense of commitment among other team members (Carron & Hausenblas, 1998). In addition, when higher-status athletes make sacrifices for the team (as they would if they sacrificed their own time in the implementation of the team-building program), team cohesiveness is further enhanced (Prapavessis et al., 1996).

Team Building for Cohesion in Sport

At the core of any team-building program is the expectation that the intervention will enhance group effectiveness through the development of a cohesive group (Prapavessis et al., 1996). Stevens (2002) noted that team-building protocols are typically designed to

- set team goals;
- ensure that athletes' roles are understood and accepted;
- ensure that team meetings and practices are efficient;
- ensure that leadership is coherent, effective, and acceptable;
- examine the way in which the team functions (e.g., norms, communication);
- examine the relationships among team members;
- diagnose potential weaknesses and minimize their effects on the team.

The specific strategies developed for sport teams are usually based on one or a combination of the team-building objectives in this list. The following list of team-building strategies is by no means exhaustive,

and these strategies can be employed using either a direct or indirect approach.

Team Performance Profiling

An indispensable component of effective team-building interventions is an assessment of the situation (Yukelson, 1997). One method that is often used to assess a team's primary strengths and weaknesses and to facilitate goal setting is team performance profiling (Butler & Hardy, 1992; Munroe, Terry, & Carron, 2002). With this strategy, athletes collectively identify all the characteristics (physical, mental, tactical) of their sport perceived to be most important for team success. The athletes then rate each of the characteristics in terms of their importance on a scale of 1 (not very important) to 10 (most important), which is the ideal score. Next, the athletes are asked to rate their team's current level for each characteristic on a scale of 1 (could not be any worse) to 10 (could not be any better), which is the current score. Finally, the current score for each characteristic is subtracted from the ideal score, producing the discrepancy score.

Larger discrepancy values indicate that additional attention should be paid to that characteristic, and consequently, group goals should be set in those specific areas (Munroe et al., 2002; Stevens, 2002). Team performance profiling is an extremely beneficial exercise, particularly because it takes into consideration athletes' opinions on areas of concern before the implementation of a team-building program (Carron & Hausenblas, 1998). In addition, with the identification of specific target areas, the stage is set for subsequent team goal setting (Munroe et al., 2002).

Team Goal Setting

Group (or team) goals represent shared perceptions regarding a desirable state of the group (Mills, 1984). Group goals have been shown to be more strongly associated with team success than individual goals (Prapavessis et al., 1996), in addition to providing teams with focus, direction, and motivation (Munroe et al., 2002; Stevens, 2002). Also, group goals contribute to enhanced cohesiveness, particularly if member participation is encouraged (Prapavessis et al., 1996). Thus, when setting group goals, the team should define the target areas in which goals are going to be set. As mentioned, a valuable means of identifying such areas is team performance profiling.

Munroe and colleagues (2002) recommended that the four target areas with the largest discrepancy scores in the team performance profiling exercise should be the foundation for the team's short-term goals. The remainder of the characteristics identified through the performance profiling exercise can then be used to set long-term goals.

Fostering Mutual Respect

A simple yet effective exercise that provides athletes with several reasons why their teammates value and respect them can go a long way in building respect and enhancing cohesion within a team (Munroe et al., 2002). Essentially, athletes write down—confidentially and independently—why each teammate is a valued member of the team. Next, the athletes' comments are collated by the coach or consultant and a single summary sheet containing all of the comments is made up for each athlete. Finally, the summary sheets are distributed to each athlete in a sealed envelope. Munroe and colleagues (2002) suggested that this technique should be used sparingly, that every athlete on the team should be included in the exercise, and that the summary sheets should be distributed the evening before an important competition. In addition to enhancing the self-image and self-belief of each athlete, this exercise may also provide athletes with insight as to how their roles are viewed within the team and why they are deemed important (Munroe et al., 2002). This, in turn, can enhance role clarity and role acceptance, two issues discussed in the following team-building exercise.

Developing Role Clarity and Role Acceptance

An understanding of team and individual roles and behaviors *(role clarity)* and the acceptance of these roles *(role acceptance)* can help athletes function more effectively within a team and can enhance cohesiveness and confidence (Munroe et al., 2002; Prapavessis et al., 1996; Yukelson, 1997). A number of team-building strategies can be used to enhance these role states. In addition to the exercise previously discussed (i.e., fostering mutual respect), a second approach to facilitating role clarity and role acceptance is the use of effective goal-setting programs. Goal setting has been shown to direct attention toward appropriate behaviors, motivate individuals to develop strategies to achieve the goals, and contribute to prolonged effort and increased interest in the activity (Locke, Shaw, Saari, & Latham, 1981), all of which contribute to role clarity and role acceptance.

Another strategy that has been used to enhance the understanding and acceptance of roles involves individual coach–athlete sessions in which the coach clearly outlines what is expected of every athlete on the team (Carron & Widmeyer, 1996; Widmeyer & DuCharme, 1997). Effective, unambiguous communication on the part of the coach is essential to ensuring that athletes understand what is expected of them and feel that their roles are valued and essential to effective team functioning (Stevens, 2002). Athletes can also be asked to clearly define their roles on the team, and group discussions can be scheduled in which athletes can gain insight as to how their roles are perceived by their teammates (Stevens, 2000).

Effective Communication

All team-building interventions should focus on the level and quality of communication among teammates and coaches. Effective communication—which involves effective transmitting and listening skills—has been identified as the most important factor in developing and maintaining effective teamwork (Stevens, 2002; Williams, 1997). Effective communication is not only an essential step in preventing and solving problems within a team, it also increases the likelihood that individual and team goals will be achieved (Orlick, 1986; Yukelson, 1993, 1997). Consequently, team members and coaches should be encouraged to communicate in an open, supportive, and empathetic manner, which is best achieved via regular team meetings in which all team members are encouraged to share information and discuss concerns that affect the team directly (Yukelson, 1997). Regular and effective communication can benefit decision-making processes as well as promote trust, mutual understanding and respect, and support within a team (Orlick, 1986; Yukelson, 1997).

Future Research

Fundamentally, research involves questions. There is no one effective way to ask questions, of course. In the social sciences, one common protocol is to develop questionnaires. One advantage of a psychometrically sound questionnaire is that its reliability and validity are established. To date, few psychometrically sound questionnaires are available that ask questions about the group dynamics of sport teams. Consider, for example, the construct of status congruency—an athlete's perception of the prestige and importance ascribed to her relative to what she believes to be appropriate. Status congruency is well illustrated by constant references from professional athletes about the lack of respect they feel they've received. Problems with status can lead to dissatisfaction, lack of effort, and even withdrawal from the group, yet we have no way to determine the degree to which it is present. A similar void is present in our ability to measure other important group constructs such as role acceptance and group norms (e.g., norm for productivity).

The research findings from the Carron et al. (2002) meta-analysis permit us to reliably conclude that task and social cohesion are related to team success. As Carron et al. pointed out, however,

> One unfortunate byproduct of any meta-analysis . . . is that the results may be assumed to provide the final answer on any issue. . . . Science proceeds in stages from description to explanation to prediction to control. Meta-analyses provide a summary at the descriptive stage. They do not offer insights into questions associated with the "why" or "when" of a relationship—important questions insofar as the cohesion-performance relationship is concerned. (p. 183-184)

Carron and colleagues then suggested that one fruitful avenue for future research would be to identify the "why" factors. Is higher cohesion associated with better performance because it contributes to improved role acceptance or better adherence to team norms for productivity? What is it about the dynamics of women's teams that results in a stronger cohesion–performance relationship than in men's teams? Is a reduced level of cohesion more destructive to women's teams? Are there other factors in men's teams that are more critical to team performance?

Another potential avenue for future research would be the development of a protocol to measure cohesiveness in teams of participants younger than the university level. The Group Environment Questionnaire was developed for teams with members who are at least 18 years old. This means that the items in the questionnaire are only appropriate for athletes at this level of maturity. If cohesion is the most important group variable—as many authors have suggested—some measure of the degree to which it is present in youth sport is necessary.

Finally, minimal attention has been paid to the development of intervention programs to enhance the dynamics of sport teams. As mentioned previously, the stages of research consist of *description* (What is present?), *explanation* (Why is this the case?), *prediction* (What will happen?), and *control/intervention* (How can we?). Overwhelmingly, the research focus in group dynamics has been description and explanation. Coaches and sport psychologists must develop intervention protocols to enhance team cohesion and then evaluate the efficacy of those protocols to better understand what works and why.

Practical Implications

Earlier in this chapter, team-building strategies (e.g., team goal setting, role-clarity and role-acceptance exercises) were discussed. These strategies have been successfully used to enhance the degree of unity present in sport teams. The implications associated with the use of such strategies are substantial considering that team cohesion is positively related to successful team performance (see Carron et al., 2002). Thus, future research aimed at the identification and refinement of additional strategies for fostering a sense of belonging among team members is warranted and could ultimately result in enhanced team performance.

Summary

In this chapter, it was pointed out that cohesion in sport teams is a multidimensional construct composed of individual attractions to the group task and social (GI-T and GI-S) and group integration task and social (ATG-T and ATG-S). It was also shown that teams possessing more cohesion are generally more successful. Individual and team benefits were introduced and potential negative consequences of high cohesion were presented. Although the mere existence of a group or team implies a degree of cohesion (Donnelly, Carron, & Chelladurai, 1978), its level may not be optimal. Identification of team strengths and weaknesses, team goal setting, role clarity and role acceptance, fostering mutual respect, and communication are emphasized by coaches and team leaders (Prapavessis et al., 1996) in an effort to maximize team cohesiveness. Nonetheless, in this chapter we have highlighted specific practical strategies for team building so that a team's cohesiveness and effectiveness can be enhanced as efficiently as possible.

Future research may take several directions. For example, more psychometrically sound questionnaires that ask questions about the group dynamics of sport teams should be developed. In addition, we need to ask *why* it is that task and social cohesion are related to team success. Another potential avenue for future research is the development of a protocol to measure cohesiveness in teams of young participants. Finally, coaches and sport psychologists must develop and evaluate sound intervention protocols to enhance team cohesion.

DISCUSSION QUESTIONS

1. According to the conceptual model of cohesion outlined by Carron, Widmeyer, and Brawley (1985), what are the four manifestations of cohesiveness and how do they differ from one another?

2. What are some potential moderators of the cohesion–performance relationship and how have they been shown to affect this relationship?

3. Cohesion is more strongly related to performance in female teams than in male teams. Why do you think this is the case? Is it a function of the nature of the dynamics of men's teams or women's teams or both?

4. Cohesion is less strongly associated with performance in professional teams than in university teams. Why do you think this is the case? What is it about professional teams that reduces the importance of task or social cohesion for team success?

5. Potential liabilities are associated with high task and high social cohesion. Identify some of these liabilities from your experiences as an athlete. What signs should coaches, sport psychologists, and athletes look for in order to avoid the disadvantages of high cohesion?

6. Team building enhances team cohesion. Identify a team-building strategy that was not presented in the chapter that could be used to increase perceptions of cohesiveness within a team.

chapter 8

All the World's a Stage: Impact of an Audience on Sport Performers

Marc V. Jones, PhD, Steven R. Bray, PhD, and David Lavallee, PhD

Learning Objectives

On completion of this chapter, the reader should have

1. understanding of the impact of an audience on the psychological and physiological states of sport performers;

2. understanding of theories and research that outline how an audience can affect sport performance;

3. knowledge of personality factors that may mediate or moderate the impact of an audience; and

4. knowledge of strategies that can help ensure that an audience has a positive, rather than negative, impact on sport performance.

If, as William Shakespeare said, all the world's a stage and all the men and women merely players, then nowhere is this more apparent than in sport. A total of 1.84 million people attended matches in the 2003 Rugby World Cup; 1.17 million attended matches in the 2004 European Football Championships (soccer); and 3.60 million attended the 2004 Olympic Games in Athens. Many athletes are affected because they have to perform in front of an audience. For example, when discussing the reaction of the home supporters to a frustrating draw, soccer player Jermaine Jenas has said, "The supporters get frustrated, just as the players do, but it's important that they stick behind us and try to remain positive. What they do is often projected onto the pitch. We know they are feeling a bit nervous" ("Jenas urges the fans," 2005, p. 3).

The purpose of this chapter is to review theories and synthesize current research that considers the impact of an audience on sport performance. This will provide a theoretical and empirical basis for strategies to maintain and even enhance performance in the presence of an audience. The chapter begins by providing a historical context for current research developments by reviewing classic research in social facilitation. A broad perspective is then taken by defining what an audience is and outlining why the presence of an audience is important; next, research showing how the mere presence of an audience can affect cognitions and bring about physiological changes is reviewed. Then we consider how the presence of an audience can have negative and positive effects on sport performance by drawing on the extant home-advantage literature. The mechanisms that may account for these effects in addition to potential moderating factors will be considered in detail. Suggestions for future research are then identified and discussed. Finally, the chapter closes with a discussion of implications for practice.

Historical Overview of Theory and Research

The first study on the effects of the presence of others is often credited to Triplett (1898). In this research, Triplett conducted an archival study of professional cycling races based on the official records from the racing board of the League of American Wheelmen and found that times were faster for individuals when they raced against others. He then conducted a follow-up study involving an experiment in which children wound fishing reels, either working alone or alongside a coactor (e.g., one or more persons doing the same task at the same time). Results revealed that children performed significantly faster when in pairs than when alone, and he concluded that this was due to an increase

of energy (termed *dynamogism)* that occurs when in the presence of others.

Following this pioneering research, which documented the phenomenon known as social facilitation, a research literature began to grow that examined the social effects of others on performance. While some of this research confirmed Triplett's findings, some studies revealed that performance could also be impaired by the presence of others. For example, as early as the 1920s researchers found that people working in groups produced greater quantities compared to when working alone, but the quality of their work was not as good (e.g., Allport, 1920). Other researchers have sometimes reported both gains and decrements in performance through coaction or when an audience was watching.

These divergent findings puzzled theorists and researchers until Zajonc (1965) proposed that performance was linked to the performer's arousal state, not simply the presence of others. In his drive theory of social facilitation, Zajonc suggested that facilitating effects occur with tasks that are simple or well learned and decrements in performance occur with tasks that are complex or novel. He interpreted these differences in terms of the Hull-Spence theory of behavior (Spence, 1956) by suggesting that the presence of others can increase an individual's drive arousal and that this state of heightened drive arousal increases the likelihood of the performer's dominant response tendency. In other words, the presence of others increases the tendency to perform dominant responses and at the same time decreases the tendency to perform non-dominant responses. If the dominant response is the most appropriate response in a particular situation, then social facilitation will occur and people will perform better when others are present. If the task calls for a nondominant response, however, then an audience interferes with performance (Forsyth, 1999).

A classic study demonstrating this effect was conducted by Michaels, Blommel, Brocato, Linkous, and Rowe (1982), who overtly observed pool players at a university union. Better players, those who made an average of 71% of their shots when playing alone, increased performance to 80% when a group of four people began watching them. Average pool players, those who made 36% of their shots when playing alone, decreased performance to 25% in front of the four observers.

Over the years, support for Zajonc's (1965, 1980) theory has diminished with evidence that it is not merely the presence of an audience and associated physiological arousal, but also concern with evaluation or conflict between evaluation and presence that may be important (e.g., Cottrell, Wack, Sekerak, & Rittle, 1968). While evaluation apprehension, physiological arousal, and mere presence may be significant contributors to social facilitation, conclusive answers to the *why* questions remain elusive, with different explanations still in competition (Lavallee, Kremer, Moran, & Williams, 2004).

Understanding the impact of others on sport performance is clearly an important endeavor. Sport performance rarely occurs in isolation, and athletes compete against, with, or in front of others. Although the presence of opponents and teammates may substantially affect motor performance (see Strauss, 2002a), in the present chapter we focus exclusively on the effect of audiences on athletes. For the purposes of this chapter, an *audience* is defined as the presence of others who are attending to and evaluating task performance. We choose to focus on the specific effects of an audience because sport performance often occurs in front of an audience. In addition, the sport context allows for the examination of audience characteristics (e.g., size, density) and behaviors (e.g., supportive, hostile) that could mediate and moderate the athlete–performance relationship. In the next section we will discuss how athletes respond to the presence of an audience and whether this response has a positive or negative effect on sport performance.

How Do Athletes Respond to an Audience?

A review of the extant literature indicates that the presence of an audience can have an impact on *cognitive* (e.g., self-concept) and *physiological* (e.g., arousal levels) aspects of the performer.

Impact of an Audience on Athletes' Physiological States

Arousal refers to the degree of activation in the autonomic nervous system (Malmo, 1959) and is thought to increase in the presence of others (e.g., Zajonc, 1965). In a meta-analysis, Mullen, Bryant, and Driskell (1997) found that the presence of an audience was associated with an increase in both self-reported and electrodermal arousal (i.e., changes in the electrical conductance of the skin). Mullen et al. surmised that this increase occurred because of an increase in social monitoring, evaluation apprehension, and attentional conflict. However, individuals merely in the presence of other participants (e.g., people in the same room doing a different task and not monitoring the participant) do not necessarily experience an increase in arousal because they are not likely to be distracted, are not being monitored, and are not concerned about being evaluated.

The presence of coactors is slightly more complicated. The presence of coactors is likely to lead to an increase in arousal because of increased social monitoring, evaluation apprehension, and attentional conflict, but it can also lead to a reduction in arousal because the coactors may provide social support and information on how to behave. Interestingly, the arousal-increasing effects of an audience are weaker when the participants are engaged in an aversive (e.g., unpleasant) task, which indicates that there may be some social-support benefit to having an audience present (Mullen et al., 1997). Accordingly, it may be that audiences in sport settings, particularly those that are vociferous and supportive, do not lead to such substantial increases in arousal because of the social support they provide to some athletes.

Although arousal is likely to be a key factor affecting sport performance, it should not be considered as a unitary response (Hardy, Jones, & Gould, 1996), and in certain situations it may increase activity in one part of the autonomic nervous system (e.g., heart rate) but depress other parts (e.g., skin conductance). In the biopsychosocial model of challenge and threat, Blascovich and Mendes (2000) outlined how an individual may display different physiological responses in the presence of an audience depending on their perception of the situation. When performing in front of an audience (which increases the importance of a performance), if individuals believe that they are able to meet the demands of the situation, then they experience *challenge,* and if they believe that they have insufficient resources to meet the demands of the situation, then they experience *threat.*

In support of this hypothesis, participants who were asked to complete a well-learned task (challenge) or unlearned task (threat) in front of an audience did indeed show different physiological responses (Blascovich, Mendes, Hunter, & Salomon, 1999). An increase in cardiac performance (e.g., cardiac contractile force, cardiac output, beats per minute) and a *decrease* in vascular resistance—(mean arterial pressure / cardiac output) $\times$ 80—was observed when performing a well-learned task (challenge) in front of an audience. This pattern represents the efficient mobilization of energy for coping and is accompanied by the release of epinephrine and norepinephrine, which provide a short burst of energy mobilization (Blascovich et al., 1999).

In contrast, when performing the unlearned task in front of an audience (threat), an increase in some measures of cardiac performance (cardiac contractile force, beats per minute) was observed along with an increase in vascular resistance. This pattern indicates a threat state because the release of epinephrine is inhibited by cortisol and accordingly there is no short

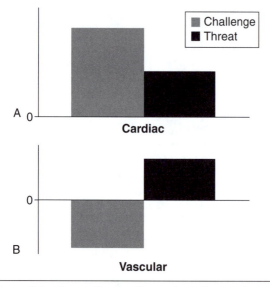

Figure 8.1   Theoretical pattern of cardiac and vascular activity during challenge and threat.

Reprinted, by permission, from J. Blascovich et al., 1999, "Social 'facilitation' challenge and threat," *Journal of Personality and Social Psychology* 77: 68-77.

burst of energy mobilization. Thus, the nature of the changes in arousal resulting from the presence of others may depend on whether an athlete perceives the situation as challenging or threatening. Figure 8.1 outlines the theoretical pattern of cardiac and vascular activity during challenge and threat (Blascovich et al., 1999).

Impact of an Audience on Athletes' Psychological States

Performing in front of an audience may also have a substantial impact on selected cognitive processes. First, behavior in front of an audience may have a greater impact on how people view themselves than the same behavior performed privately. If an individual's recent behavior conflicts with her self-concept, then self-concept can be changed via a process termed *internalization* (Tice, 1992). This effect is more pronounced when the behaviors are performed publicly, such as in front of an audience. For example, missing a series of putts when playing a round of golf in front of an audience may cause a golfer to revise his opinion of himself as a good putter, whereas the same performance done privately will likely have less of an impact on his perception of his putting ability.

People can maintain a favorable self-concept by interpreting events in ways that will enable them to conserve or promote a favorable view of themselves, even if that view is somewhat distorted (Taylor & Brown, 1988). One way this can be done is to make a conscious effort to ignore or block out threatening information as, for example, an athlete making a conscious effort to disregard critical feedback from a coach. However, receiving negative feedback in front of an audience may have a particularly adverse effect on individuals who are prone to avoiding negative information about themselves (termed *repressors*).

Baumeister and Cairns (1992) found that when repressors were presented with negative information (in the form of a fictitious negative personality profile), they spent more time reading the negative information when it was presented publicly than when it was presented privately. It was suggested that the extra time resulted from the repressors worrying about someone else holding negative information about them. Thus, athletes with a tendency to avoid negative information may experience increased worry when negative information is presented publicly (e.g., unfavorable score being read out loud in a tennis match).

Second, the types of attributions made following a performance observed by an audience may differ from those made when performing alone. In a study by Schlenker, Weigold, and Hallam (1990), participants given bogus feedback on a test of social decision making were told whether they were in the 93rd percentile of college students (success condition) or in the 27th percentile (failure condition) and were asked to give feedback on their performance on the test. Not surprisingly, participants claimed to have higher ability after success than after failure.

This effect, however, differed depending on the participants' levels of self-esteem and the nature of the audience they were required to give feedback to. Participants high in self-esteem did not tend to change the perception of their ability after failure, but they did tend to raise the perception of their ability after success, in particular when they perceived a supportive audience. Participants low in self-esteem did not change the perception of their ability after success, but they did lower the rating of their ability, particularly when they failed and perceived a critical audience. These results suggest that athletes high in self-esteem may benefit from performing well at home (in front of a supportive audience) and perceive a greater increase in their ability, whereas athletes low in self-esteem may be negatively affected by playing poorly away from home (in front of a hostile audience) and perceive a reduction in their ability.

It should be clear from the preceding paragraphs that performing in front of an audience affects athletes' physiological and cognitive (psychological) states. The manner to which athletes' physiological and cognitive changes affect their performance is the focus of the discussion that follows.

Positive and Negative Effects of Audiences on Athlete Performance

A host of laboratory studies have shown that performing in front of an audience can affect sport performance. In one of the earliest studies, Laird (1923) found that motor skills decreased among participants when audience members were present. In contrast, Travis (1925) and Dashiell (1930) reported that performance enhancement can occur in audience settings. The impact of the presence of others, such as an audience, in laboratory settings has recently been reviewed by Strauss (2002a), who concluded that the presence of others has a positive impact on simple motor tasks but can inhibit performance on tasks requiring coordination. Accordingly, in the remainder of this section we focus on evidence from a popular and well-known area of sport literature that is believed to be largely determined by audience facilitation effects—the home-field advantage. Because sport is often played in front of large audiences, this literature provides an excellent opportunity to explore how audiences may affect people in a real-world achievement setting.

The Case of Home Advantage

Courneya and Carron (1992) defined *home advantage* as "the term used to describe the consistent finding that home teams in sport competitions win over 50%

of the games played under a balanced home and away schedule" (p. 13). The first formal analysis of the home-advantage phenomenon was carried out by Schwartz and Barsky (1977). Their initial study focused on the major North American sports of baseball, basketball, football, and ice hockey and in each case showed compelling evidence of a home-field advantage. That research stimulated more extensive investigations of home advantage across a variety of sports and time lines.

A synthesis of results from 16 published and unpublished studies representing more than 260 seasons of competition was performed by Courneya and Carron (1992). They concluded that the home advantage is a robust phenomenon; however, the synthesis showed that the magnitude of the home advantage varied significantly across sports. The mean home-winning percentages (%) and effect sizes *(ES)* for decided games (i.e., with tie games excluded from analyses) were as follows: 53.5% *(ES = .07)* for baseball, 57.3% *(ES = .15)* for American football, 61.1% *(ES = .22)* for ice hockey, 64.4 *(ES = .29)* for basketball, and 69.0% *(ES = .38)* for soccer. Nevill and Holder (1999) recently extended Courneya and Carron's review to include 23 additional studies, which showed similar findings.

In an effort to help guide researchers toward an understanding of why teams perform so well when they play at home, Courneya and Carron (1992) devised a framework of game location factors. In that framework, four principle factors were identified: crowd, travel, learning (familiarity), and rules. While a combination of these factors is usually present during sport

Do these fans give their team an advantage?

competition, the facilitative influence of the crowd is generally accepted as the most consistent and powerful factor contributing to home-team performance (Nevill & Holder, 1999). Nonetheless, the literature has produced somewhat equivocal findings when characteristics of the audience have been investigated in relation to the home advantage.

Audience Characteristics and Home Advantage

While it is generally assumed that an audience is present during major sport contests, researchers have honed in on specific characteristics of audiences such as size, density, and behaviors to examine their impact on home-team performance.

Size

One aspect of the audience that has gathered research attention is size. Dowie (1982) assessed the absolute size of the crowd (i.e., number of fans in attendance) in English soccer, but contrary to expectations, found no relationship between crowd size and home advantage. A more recent study involving ice hockey by Agnew and Carron (1994) also showed that crowd size was unrelated to home advantage. In contrast to these findings, Nevill, Newell and Gale (1996) found that absolute crowd size was positively related to the home advantage in English and Scottish soccer. Their results showed that in Premier and Division 1 leagues where crowd sizes were generally large, home teams had better home winning percentages than in two leagues (G.M. Vauxhall League and Scottish Second Division) where crowd sizes were generally small. However, Pollard's (1986) analyses of a much larger dataset showed that home advantage was actually smaller in Division 1 than Division 4, despite a large bias in attendance favoring Division 1. Similarly, Clarke and Norman (1995) found no differences in home advantage across English soccer divisions from 1980 to 1990.

A recent study involving the sport of cricket also indirectly provides evidence against the impact of crowd size. Jones, Bray, and Bolton (2001) found that in English club cricket, although there were seldom crowds larger than 50 spectators, there was a significant home advantage of 57%. Thus, while the crowd itself might be viewed as a potent factor in home advantage, the evidence shows that absolute size does not matter.

Density

Although audience size may have questionable influence on home advantage, researchers have also acknowledged that the size of the crowd is often dictated by the size of the playing venue. Pollard (1986) suggested that crowd density (i.e., the number of

people in the audience relative to the facility's capacity) rather than crowd size might be the telling factor. Yet, Pollard's results showed that crowd density had no association with the home advantage in professional English soccer.

In contrast, Schwartz and Barsky (1977) found that crowd density had a positive effect on home advantage in Major League Baseball. Home-team winning percentages increased significantly from 48% when crowd density was lower (i.e., density of less than 20%) to 57% when crowd density was higher (i.e., more than 40%). Indeed, those authors concluded, "the various findings on audience size [as a proportion of capacity] and team performance . . . leads us to attribute the home advantage to the factor of social support" (p. 656). As mentioned earlier, Agnew and Carron (1994) did not find evidence that crowd size affects home advantage. However, they did find that crowd density was related to game outcomes; as crowd density increased so did the home advantage in North American junior ice hockey.

Audience Behaviors

While size and density are strictly quantitative features of an audience, certain qualities of an audience's behavior are also important when considering audience effects. A study by Greer (1983) found that home-team performances were superior to those of the visiting opponents when crowds behaved normally (i.e., cheering and booing). Despite this evidence that spectator support for the home team (i.e., cheering) is related to greater home-team success, other studies have shown either no effects or a negative effect. Salminen's (1993) study of Finnish soccer, ice hockey, and basketball found that spectator support had neither a positive effect on home-team performance (when cheering was directed at the home team) nor a negative effect on home-team performance (when the crowd cheered for the away team).

Strauss (2002b) reported similar findings in his analysis of crowd behavior in four American football matches from the American Football League. He found no differences between home and away team performances when spectators cheered before the start of a play. Finally, a study by Thirer and Rampey (1979) showed that when audiences behaved normally (e.g., cheering and booing), visiting teams committed more rule violations and were thus penalized to a greater extent. However, when audiences engaged in extreme antisocial behaviors (e.g., fighting, throwing objects onto the playing surface, chanting obscenities), it was the home teams who committed more violations. Thus, despite the completion of some research in this area, there is no clear pattern as to how the behavior of audiences may affect performance.

Presence Versus Absence of an Audience

In one investigation, a unique opportunity to study crowd effects occurred when a measles epidemic resulted in a quarantine that prevented spectators from attending games played by two university basketball teams. Moore and Brylinksy (1993) used this opportunity to compare the performance (total points scored, field-goal percentages, and free-throw percentages) of the two teams in the presence and in the absence of spectators. The results indicated that the performances of both teams improved in the absence of spectators. Both teams showed differences interpreted as moderate to large effect sizes (ES = .45-1.75) for total points and free-throw percentages when playing without an audience. While these results are drawn from only one study, they do raise the question as to whether audiences actually facilitate sport performances. Given that the same teams rarely play with and then without spectators in attendance, further examination of this question in field settings may be elusive.

How Home Audiences Affect Athletes

The research reviewed thus far hinges on a key factor: Although it may vary in size, density, and behavior, there is almost always an audience present during sport competition. Thus, it is rarely the case that audience effects in sport conform to a paradigm of audience versus no audience (with the exception of Moore & Brylinsky, 1993). Rather, audience effects in sport should be interpreted as a social exchange that in many ways depends on the performer's subjective interpretation of the social situation (Wankel, 1984). With this point in mind, our review turns to research that has examined variations in athletes' psychological and behavioral states that correspond to home and away audiences.

Effect of the Home Crowd on Athletes' Psychological States

In an early study of psychological states and home advantage, Jurkovac (1985) reported that collegiate basketball players had higher confidence and motivation when playing at home compared to away. More recently, Bray and Widmeyer (2000) found that female collegiate basketball players had higher levels of team confidence, or collective efficacy, when playing at home, and Bray and Widmeyer (1995) also reported that players were less anxious, more motivated, and better able to concentrate when playing at home. When Bray and Widmeyer (2000) explored factors that players felt contributed to the home advantage, almost all of the factors indicated that support from the home crowd was important

and had a moderate to strong positive effect on their performance. Thus, players seem to interpret the home crowd's presence as a positive influence.

Studies that have focused on sport performers' psychological states before home and away competitions have produced equivocal findings. In some studies, home players' self-confidence, state anxiety, and mood have been found to be more positive before competition (Bray, Jones, & Owen, 2002; Terry, Walrond, & Carron, 1998; Thuot, Kavouras, & Kenefick, 1998). In other studies, there were no differences in psychological states between home and away competitions (Bray & Martin, 2003; Duffy & Hinwood, 1997; Kerr & Vanschaik, 1995; Neave & Wolfson, 2003). In each of these studies, because measures were taken before the start of competitive events, the impact of the audience on the competitors may not have been fully realized. Although some variation in psychological states could be due to anticipation of the audience, it is not clear whether or not this was the case.

The study by Kerr and Vanschaik (1995) examined psychological states of Dutch rugby players after their games were completed. In this case, the athletes had been exposed to the home audience before the measurement of their mood states. However, those data again showed no differences between players' psychological states at home and away.

Audiences Do Not Always Help: The Home-Field Disadvantage

Although the bulk of archival evidence suggests that playing at one's home venue in the presence of supportive spectators has a positive effect on performance, this effect has been questioned under special circumstances. Probably the best-known contradictory evidence to the home advantage was provided by Baumeister and Steinhilber (1984). Those researchers showed that during championship series, baseball and basketball teams that hosted the decisive game of the series had a better chance of losing the game (and the championship title) than winning it.

For example, Major League Baseball results from 1924 to 1982 showed that home teams won only 39% of their decisive championship games, compared with an average home winning percentage of 60% earlier in the season. Baumeister and Steinhilber further analyzed the data from those decisive games and found that visiting teams did not outplay the hosts, but rather the host teams outplayed themselves. Specifically, in basketball home players had lower foul shooting percentages compared to previous games and in baseball home players committed more fielding errors. Although these findings have since been disputed by Schlenker, Phillips, Boniecki, and Schlenker (1995) and then rebutted by Baumeister (1995), a similar set of findings on the home disadvantage has also been reported for archival studies of golf (Wright, Jackson, Christie, McGuire, & Wright, 1991) and ice hockey (Wright, Voyer, Wright, & Roney, 1995).

At the time of Baumeister and Steinhilber's (1984) study, the results were interpreted as being consistent with Baumeister's (1984) concurrent laboratory and fieldwork showing performance decrements in well-learned skills when the participants' attention was focused inward. Baumeister and his colleagues have recently extended this work to examine the nature of audience interaction on performance. In a series of laboratory experiments, Butler and Baumeister (1998) investigated the influence of audience type (i.e., supportive, adversarial, and observation only) on performance of a computer-game task. They found that when participants were challenged with a difficult standard of performance as compared with their own performances on baseline trials, there was a significant decline in performance. Interestingly, however, the performance decline was only detected in the supportive-audience condition; participants who performed in front of neutral and adversarial audiences were unaffected. Perhaps even more interesting, those who performed the task in front of the supportive audience thought that the spectators helped them perform better and rated their own performance higher than participants in the other groups (objective performance feedback was withheld by the experimenters).

More recently, Baumeister's work on audience effects was extended to sport skills. Law, Masters, Bray, Eves, and Bardswell (2003) carried out an experiment similar to Butler and Baumeister's, this time using table tennis. Findings were partially consistent across the investigations; Law et al. found that a supportive audience caused poorer performance. However, there were no differences across the supportive, adversarial, and observation-only conditions in terms of how well participants thought they had performed the task.

Future Research

A review of the research demonstrates that the presence of an audience can affect an individual both physiologically and cognitively. However, controlled laboratory research involving highly skilled athletes is lacking. Accordingly, future research could investigate whether the way in which athletes interpret the difficulty of a task when performing in front of an audience affects the nature of the physiological response or how performing in front of an audience may influence athletes' self-concepts and attributions.

Research from actual sporting contests demonstrates, for the most part, a clear home-field advantage. However,

establishing an empirical link between the audience and players' performances and psychological states has been a challenge. Among the quantitative characteristics of the audience that have been examined, crowd density appears to have received the most support, albeit modest support in most instances. Looking back on these findings, it is instructive to consider earlier work. In their seminal article, Schwartz and Barsky (1977) firmly endorsed the positive effect of the home audience but identified several potential limitations to examining its effects on performance. For example, they noted that in many elite sports, games played before capacity crowds are the norm. Thus, while there is an opportunity for variability in team performance, the crowd is basically a constant for every team. Furthermore, attendance usually declines when teams are performing poorly, meaning performance may affect the audience rather than the other way around.

The work carried out so far on audiences' behaviors has been enlightening. Some studies (e.g., Greer, 1983; Thirer & Rampey, 1979) have incorporated observational analyses of the spectator–performer dynamic in competitive sport. However, there is considerable scope for replication and expansion of this research to further consider how audiences and athletes interact. Future research examining the interaction of audiences and performers is strongly encouraged. Furthermore, few laboratory studies have incorporated audience interaction in a way that resembles sport.

The archival and laboratory research showing performance decrements in the presence of supportive audiences is perplexing. Although the paradox of the individual performing poorly when being encouraged by supporters can be resolved by attentional and self-presentational explanations, it is not clear how those explanations can account for the bulk of evidence showing that athletes generally perform better when playing at home in front of a supportive audience. Indeed, based on current literature we must conclude, albeit counterintuitively, that athletes do not respond positively to performing in front of a supportive audience.

Future research is needed to explore this paradox. One potential avenue of exploration would be to examine how the supportive audience may be perceived differently by the experienced sport performer and the skilled (or at least, trained) laboratory task participant. A second consideration is that laboratory-based research has involved only single participants. Home advantage has been examined to a far lesser degree in individual sports than team sports. Audiences may have a different effect on individual-sport participants when they are the sole target of the audience's attention and there is no diffusion of responsibility as there often is when playing on a team.

Other characteristics of the audience that may affect the responses and performance of individuals have been outlined by Aiello and Douthitt (2001) and are worthy of further research. These include the role of the audience members (e.g., coaches, selectors, scouts) and the quality of relationships that the athlete may have with members of the audience (e.g., family, friends). In addition, the salience of the presence may be an important factor. For example, what role does the absent audience (e.g., TV audience) play? Finally, Aiello and Douthitt suggest that future research should consider how long the presence of an audience may affect an individual. For example, athletes may initially respond negatively to performing in front of a large crowd but become desensitized to those characteristics of the environment as their competition or career progresses.

Although research in this area has led to some contradictory findings, it points sport psychologists, coaches, and athletes toward ways in which it is possible to cope with performing in front of an audience. In the next section we outline these implications for practice.

Practical Implications

In this section we discuss strategies to help athletes cope with the challenges that arise from having to perform in front of an audience. First, we outline how athletes can cope with the increased arousal levels that occur when performing in front of an audience (Blascovich et al., 1999; Mullen et al., 1997). Second, we consider how athletes can maintain focus when performing in front of an audience (Butler & Baumeister, 1998).

Coping With Increased Physiological Arousal

An increase in arousal has a positive impact on performance, particularly on tasks requiring high anaerobic power (Parfitt, Hardy, & Pates, 1995). However, increasing levels of arousal could have a negative impact on fine-motor tasks through increasing muscular tension (Noteboom, Barnholt, & Enoka, 2001; Noteboom, Fleshner, & Enoka, 2001; Parfitt, Jones, & Hardy, 1990). Increased arousal may also result in difficulties with coordination (Oxendine, 1970), affect the movement patterns of athletes by causing them to move less freely (Collins, Jones, Fairweather, Doolan, & Priestley, 2001), and accordingly may predispose athletes to injury (Williams & Andersen, 1998). Increasing arousal may also negatively affect attention (Easterbrook, 1959; Moran, Byrne, & McGlade, 2002).

Physical Relaxation Techniques

One way to control the arousal levels of athletes is to use physical relaxation techniques. Examples of techniques include progressive muscular relaxation, meditation, and breathing control (for guidelines on applying these techniques, see Bull, Albinson, & Shambrook, 1996 and Williams & Harris, 2001). Although there are differences among the techniques, each strategy aims to reduce arousal by slowing the breathing, providing a relaxing focus of attention, and removing tension in the muscles. Research has shown physical relaxation to be effective in reducing arousal levels in a range of sport settings (e.g., Jones, 1993; Maynard, Hemmings, & Warwick-Evans, 1995; Prapavessis, Grove, McNair, & Cable, 1992).

Imagery

Motivational general-arousal (MG-A) imagery, which focuses on feelings such as relaxation, stress, arousal, and anxiety, could be an effective strategy for arousal control in sport competition (Martin, Moritz, & Hall, 1999). Using MG-A imagery, athletes can modify their response to a particular stimulus and change undesirable arousal levels. For example, a soccer player who experiences a debilitating level of arousal when performing in front of a hostile crowd could imagine himself walking out to play, seeing and hearing the crowd, and experiencing an increase in arousal and then imagine controlling the arousal through a breathing strategy, remaining in control, and bringing his arousal level down.

Motivational general-mastery (MG-M) imagery represents effective coping and mastery of challenging situations (Martin et al., 1999) and could also be used to help athletes control arousal levels (Jones, Mace, Bray, MacRae, & Stockbridge, 2002). MG-M imagery may result in a more positive interpretation of the upcoming situation, resulting in higher levels of self-efficacy. For example, a golfer concerned about experiencing a debilitating level of arousal before playing in her first major tournament may imagine coping effectively with being on the first tee and imagine hitting a great drive down the center of the fairway to the delight of onlookers. It is possible that feeling able to cope with a difficult scenario may result in more manageable arousal levels. Indeed, a perception of an ability to cope with a situation is associated with a pattern of arousal that represents the most efficient mobilization of energy for coping (Blascovich et al., 1999).

Maintaining Attentional Focus

Playing in front of an audience can have a negative impact on attentional focus either because an audience can be distracting or because an athlete begins to focus attention inwardly on task-irrelevant thoughts (e.g., Butler & Baumeister, 1998; Law et al., 2003). Because attentional focus can be governed by the subjective importance of cues rather than their location in the visual field (Eysenck, 1992; Hockey & Hamilton, 1983), a person concerned about an audience may focus more on the audience and exacerbate the negative emotional reaction. Losing focus on the task at hand can have a negative impact given the importance of concentration for sport performance (Moran, 1996). Athletes can use several techniques to improve concentration, including self-talk, the use of preshot routines, and desensitization via realistic training scenarios or imagery. The aim of these techniques is to ensure that athletes focus their attention on actions that they can control and are relevant to successful performance.

Key Words

A number of psychologists advocate the use of attentional triggers in order to focus on factors relevant to successful performance (Bull et al., 1996; Butler, 1996; Moran, 2004). Unfortunately, no research has tested whether key words are effective in maintaining and enhancing an appropriate focus of attention (Lavallee et al., 2004). However, athletes do report using key words to maintain focus (Hardy, Gammage, & Hall, 2001), and there is plenty of anecdotal evidence to support their use. For example, tennis player John McEnroe has said,

> Ever since I'd started out, and to this day, I've written down tips to myself—"Keep your head up all through the serve"; "Don't open your body too soon on the backhand." I keep the cards in my tennis bag. Sitting during a changeover, I focus myself by looking at those cards. (McEnroe & Kaplan, 2002, p. 84).

Athletes can use key words in order to remember what to focus on in any given situation. They can use key words before competition, during competition (as John McEnroe did), or before every play (e.g., a golfer using a key word before every shot). Athletes may choose to focus on technical aspects (e.g., "keep your head still"), physical feelings (e.g., "smooth"), emotions ("be excited"), or images ("fight like a cornered animal"). For key words to be effective they should be short, vivid, and positively phrased, with a focus on what to aim for rather than what to avoid (Moran, 2004). In addition to key words, other attentional triggers such as visual (e.g., focusing on a specific point on the court) and physical cues (e.g., taking a deep breath) can be used (Bull et al., 1996). These are often integrated alongside key words into preperformance routines.

Competition Routines

Two types of routines may be effective in enabling athletes to cope with performing in front of an audience: preevent routines and preperformance routines (Lavallee et al., 2004). Preevent routines are sequences of actions that athletes engage in the period before an event. For example, on the morning of an important competition athletes may read through some cards with key words outlining what is important for them, eat the same meal, and give themselves enough time to go through the same physical warm-up routine. A preevent routine may help an athlete cope with performing in front of an audience because it results in the athlete being focused on what needs to be done and facilitates a relaxed and confident frame of mind.

Preperformance routines are sequences of preparatory actions that athletes engage in before they perform a key skill (Moran, 2004). For example, before serving, a tennis player may bounce the ball a set number of times, take a deep breath, and visualize where the serve should go. Preperformance routines are proposed to be effective because they get athletes focused on task-relevant information, they keep the focus on the present, and they prevent the athlete from devoting too much attention to the mechanics of the skill, which can affect automaticity (Moran, 2004). Although studies have not explicitly considered the impact of preperformance routines on attention, there is evidence for their effectiveness in enhancing performance (e.g., Cohn, Rotella, & Lloyd, 1990).

Any preperformance or preevent routine should be short and simple and should involve things that are easy for the athlete to do and are under his or her control (Goldberg, 1998). This distinguishes routines from superstitions because the essence of superstitious behavior is that one's fate is governed by factors outside of one's control, such as an athlete thinking, "I will only play well if I can get changed in a certain corner of the changing room" (Moran, 2004).

Desensitization (Simulation Training)

Athletes may learn to focus attention more appropriately if they are given the opportunity to practice in conditions that mimic the competitive environment. Thus, the more often athletes are able to perform in conditions that approximate the experience in question, the more the athletes may be able to inoculate themselves against the distracting effects of a crowd. Although there is little empirical evidence for the effectiveness of simulation training, it may help athletes by counteracting the tendency for unusual or unexpected stimuli to distract them (Moran, 2004). The closer the training is to the real-life situation, the more beneficial it should be. In terms of dealing with the distracting effects of an audience, athletes could train with crowd noise playing in the background or get teammates and coaches to try to distract them through shouting or cheering their mistakes. Indeed, Tiger Woods' father, Earl Woods, would intentionally cough or drop clubs to train Tiger to block out gallery noises while swinging (Andrisani, 2002). Computer simulations can also help inoculate athletes against distracting crowd effects.

A further consequence of playing in front of an audience is that athletes may be affected by changes in the behavior of officials. Some research has indicated that referees may be influenced by crowd noise to favor the home team (Nevill, Balmer, & Williams, 2002). Accordingly, when playing away from home in front of a hostile crowd, athletes could prepare themselves by engaging in what Bull et al. (1996) call "poor official" training. During practice matches an official or coach can make a few bad calls or favor one particular athlete or team. This enables athletes to become desensitized to bad decisions and gives them an opportunity to practice controlling their emotional reactions and remaining focused.

Summary

The effect of the presence of others on performers has been studied for over 100 years. Early research found that individuals performed better with an audience; however, further research revealed that performance could also be impaired by the presence of others, leading to the theory that performance is linked to the performer's arousal state as well as audience evaluation or conflict between evaluation and presence.

Audiences have the potential to bring about changes in both physiological and cognitive (psychological) states of athletes. Physiologically, an audience can increase arousal; however, there may be some social-support benefit to having an audience present. Cognitively, behavior in front of an audience may have a greater effect on self-concept, or how people view themselves, than the same behavior performed privately. Some studies have shown that performing in front of an audience decreases motor skills, while others have reported that performance enhancement can occur in audience settings. It seems that the presence of others may have a positive impact on simple motor tasks but can inhibit performance on tasks requiring coordination.

The home-field advantage is one example of how audiences may affect individuals. Research on the home advantage reveals that, while the presence of supportive crowds is thought to enhance the performance of the home team and hostile crowds can lead to negative effects on the performance of away teams, in some important games, such as during championships, a supportive audience may have a negative impact on the home team's performance.

Clearly, the presence of an audience affects athletes; however, there are many areas in which further research is needed. For example, controlled laboratory research involving highly skilled athletes is lacking. Another potential direction is establishing an empirical link between the audience and players' performances and psychological states, and there is considerable scope for replication and expansion of current research to further consider how audiences and athletes interact. Finally, the research thus far showing performance decrements in the presence of supportive audiences is perplexing, and future research is needed to explore this paradox.

The effect of the audience on performance has several implications for practice; namely, athletes can use arousal and attention-control strategies to cope when performing in front of an audience. For example, to cope with increased physiological arousal, athletes can use physical relaxation techniques and imagery. To maintain focus, athletes can use key words, competition routines, and desensitization or simulation training.

Discussion Questions

1. Describe how the presence of an audience can bring about changes in cognitive (psychological) and physiological states.

2. Discuss evidence that the presence of an audience can have a positive impact on performance.

3. Under what circumstances might the presence of an audience have a negative impact on sport performance?

4. In what situations have you noticed the impact of an audience on performance, and in what way did it affect performance?

5. Which strategies for coping with performing in front of an audience have you found to be most effective and why?

6. Outline two other strategies that athletes can use to cope with the challenges of playing in front of an audience.

part III

Motivational Climate

There is growing scientific evidence within motivational research indicating the salience of coaches, parents, and peers in creating quality sport involvement in which athletes are happy and active participants. While the home environment shapes the initial constellation of attitudes young athletes develop toward sport, coaches are a powerful influence in consolidating these attitudes, and peers are an agent that can facilitate or debilitate one's experiences. Part III includes three chapters and employs basic tenets from achievement goal theories to address the content, role, and significance of the climate that coaches, parents, and peers create.

In chapter 9, Joan Duda and Isabel Balaguer provide a concise overview of achievement goal theories and outline the importance of the meaning individuals place on engagement in sport and explain the role of demonstrating competence in achievement settings like sport. Two major constructs that reflect the different ways of defining one's competence, namely, a task goal and an ego goal, and their associations with adaptive and maladaptive patterns of achievement are presented. Based on contemporary achievement goal theories, Duda and Balaguer discuss the social-psychological environment created by the coach. They talk about the wide-ranging research that has been conducted in the area and highlight the need for more research employing diverse approaches. The chapter concludes with practical implications that aim to facilitate conditions for sport motivation.

In chapter 10, Sally White discusses the type of atmosphere parents create from which children obtain information about their competence and shape their attitudes about success and failure. White explains how achievement goal theory has influenced the development of a conceptualization and measurement that focus on the parent-created climate in sport. She emphasizes the theoretical significance of considering task and ego goal orientations from a goal-profile approach. Relevant research is discussed and various future research directions are outlined as they pertain to measurement and substantive issues. White concludes by reflecting on personal experiences and the importance of translating findings into practical guidelines to help parents develop an effective motivational climate.

In chapter 11, Nikos Ntoumanis, Spiridoula Vazou, and Joan Duda highlight that the contribution of the social-psychological environment created by peers cannot be underestimated in young athletes' achievement motivation in sport. Ntoumanis and colleagues explain their research endeavors to qualitatively define the content of peer-created climate, develop a measurement tool to quantitatively assess peer-created climate, and examine whether peer-created climate can contribute to the prediction of motivational experiences of young athletes. Peer-created motivational climate remains a relatively new area, and more research is needed to explore the role of peers in sport. Ntoumanis and colleagues put forward interesting research questions and outline practical guidelines for optimizing the peer-created motivational climate.

chapter 9

Coach-Created Motivational Climate

Joan L. Duda, PhD, and Isabel Balaguer, PhD

Learning Objectives

On completion of this chapter, the reader should have

1. understanding of the major constructs and predictions of contemporary achievement goal frameworks;

2. appreciation for the distinctions between a task-involving versus ego-involving climate in sport;

3. knowledge of how perceptions of the motivational climate created by coaches have been measured;

4. familiarity with the major research findings concerning the implications of the coach-created motivational climate;

5. awareness of future research directions regarding the coach-created motivational climate; and

6. appreciation of the practical implications of work on the coach-created motivational climate.

The significance of the coach to the performance, investment, and cognitive and emotional experiences of athletes is readily apparent to anyone who has played or watched competitive sport. In short, it is clear that coaches matter in the real world of sport. In terms of the scientific literature in sport psychology, even a precursory examination points to the salience of the coach with respect to athletes' behaviors, thoughts, and feelings. For example, past research has suggested that the coach can influence athletes' anxiety (e.g., Scanlan & Passer, 1979) as well as their reported enjoyment of sport (e.g., Scanlan & Lewthwaite, 1986) and confidence and perceptions of physical competence (e.g., Horn, 1985; Sinclair & Vealey, 1989). Athletes also list the coach as a reason for dropping out of sport (e.g., Burton & Martens, 1986).

Most would agree that coaches who are considered effective have a number of positive attributes and meet many different responsibilities. At the very least, regardless of the athletes' competitive level or age, a competent coach needs to (1) possess the necessary technical and strategic knowledge regarding how athletes might best execute the skills and techniques fundamental to their sport; (2) be an effective teacher and thus be able to structure optimal practice time, provide clear and informative instruction, and impart performance-enhancing motivational feedback; and (3) create a psychological environment that helps athletes maximize their skills, perform efficaciously in competition, and develop not only as athletes but as people.

With regard to the latter challenges, we can learn much about what effective coaches do by reading autobiographies, biographies, and interviews of accomplished coaches (e.g., Jackson, 1995; Kimiecik & Gould, 1987; Wooden & Jamison, 2005) as well as qualitative research studies of elite coaches' behaviors, knowledge, training approaches, and strategies (e.g., Bloom, Crumpton, & Anderson, 1999; Bloom, Durand-Bush, & Salmela, 1997; Côté, Salmela, & Russell, 1995). Drawing from these studies of elite coaches as well as systematic interviews and observations of youth coaches (e.g., Smith, Smoll, & Hunt, 1977; Smith, Zane, Smoll, & Coppel, 1983; see also chapter 6), we glean that the majority of coach behaviors are instructional in nature and that coaches try to motivate athletes by promoting their inherent desire to learn and improve. Such work also indicates that coaches typically respond to wins and desirable performances with praise and proposals of areas for further improvement. In the case of losing or poor performances, instructional feedback has been found to be the most common response. This literature suggests that relatively limited punitive comments or actions are exhibited by elite coaches.

All of these trends from the anecdotal and scientific literatures are nicely encapsulated in Janssen and Dale's (2002) book summarizing extended discussions with 16 accomplished intercollegiate and professional male and female coaches from a variety of sports. Janssen and Dale refer to the common characteristics of "credible coaches." According to their findings, credible coaches have a broader definition of success than wins and losses. They strive to win in ways that cause athletes to respect and trust them, and they set the stage for their athletes to rebound quickly and effectively following a loss. Credible coaches encourage athletes to become more self-determined and self-regulated rather than blindly compliant or controlled by their coaches. Finally, such coaches, perhaps because they coach with both heart and head, contribute to the development of athletes who are intrinsically motivated, committed, and confident.

Although the work just described provides an overall picture of outstanding coaches, variability in approaches to coaching exists. Such variability holds implications for the motivation, development, and welfare of athletes. In addressing the potential positive or negative effects of the behaviors and attitudes of coaches, the present chapter focuses on the motivation-related features of coach influence and attempts to tie our understanding of coach behavior to contemporary theoretical perspectives regarding motivational processes. Specifically, in considering potential coach influence, we pull from contemporary achievement goal frameworks (Ames, 1992a, 1992b; Dweck, 1986, 1999; Elliot, 1997, 1999; Nicholls, 1984, 1989) that have dominated research on achievement motivation in sport over the past two decades. These frameworks allow us to conceptualize distinctions in and make predictions regarding the effect of the social-psychological environment created by the coach as well as other significant others in the sport domain.

We begin with a brief presentation of the basic tenets of achievement goal frameworks and then distinguish among the three major constructs embedded in this theoretical approach: situationally emphasized achievement goals or the motivational climate, individual differences in goal orientations, and states of goal involvement. Next, we provide a synopsis of a measurement tool designed to tap athletes' perceptions of the motivational climate shaped by their coach. In the following section, we summarize research (correlational and experimental) examining consequences of the perceived coach-created motivational climate.

The chapter then points to some conceptual and measurement concerns pertinent to the study of the motivational climate in sport. Potentially promising research directions regarding perceptions of the coach-created motivational climate are proposed throughout the chapter, but we move next to a brief description of lines of future inquiry we find particularly relevant and exciting. Finally, we conclude by highlighting some of the practical implications of work on the coach-created climate in sport settings.

Basic Tenets and Constructs of Achievement Goal Frameworks

Fundamental to contemporary achievement goal frameworks is the premise that the meaning of individuals' engagement in achievement endeavors (such as competitive sport) influences the motivational patterns exhibited by participants (Ames, 1992a, 1992b; Dweck, 1986, 1999; Elliot, 1997, 1999; Nicholls, 1984, 1989). Achievement goal theory (AGT) also holds that variations in meaning are encapsulated in the achievement goals emphasized in the environment and adopted by those involved (Dweck, 1986; Nicholls, 1984, 1989; Ames, 1992a); that is, what are athletes concerned about when they participate in sport? What do the athletes want to achieve?

According to Nicholls (1984, 1989) and others (e.g., Roberts, 1992, 2001), a hallmark of achievement activities is a focus on demonstrating skill or competence. For example, when an athlete feels as if she has exhibited high competence in her sport, she then feels personally successful at the activity. Achievement goals are assumed to reflect differences in how such demonstrated competence is conceived. That is, what are the criteria underlying the athlete's judgments regarding whether or not she has shown high sport ability?

In the original achievement goal frameworks (Ames, 1992a; Dweck, 1999; Nicholls, 1984), two major goals have been proposed that reflect two different ways of judging one's competence: a task goal and an ego goal. When an athlete is centered on a task goal (e.g., when a basketball player is concerned with increasing his number of rebounds per game), perceptions of competence are self-referenced. Meeting the demands of the task, exerting effort, and improving one's skill level occasion a sense of success in this case. If focused on an ego goal (e.g., in basketball, attempting to get more rebounds than one's teammates), athletes are concerned with demonstrating superior competence. That is, they feel highly competent and successful when they show they are better than others (opponents, teammates) or surpass normative standards in the sport (e.g., breaking someone else's record). The experience of personal improvement and the exertion of high effort will not result in high perceptions of competence if ego goals predominate. Indeed, in this instance, an athlete would feel even more capable and successful if she could exhibit outstanding performance without having to give her best effort.

Fundamental to AGT, as proffered especially by Nicholls (1984, 1989) and Dweck (1986, 1999), are predictions concerning the adaptive and empowering features of an emphasis on task goals. It is assumed that task goals lead to particular motivational processes that help make an athlete's achievement striving more resilient and constructive, regardless of whether the athlete in question perceives his competence to be high or low. Positive achievement behaviors and outcomes, often called an adaptive achievement pattern, include (Duda & Pensgaard, 2002)

- engaging in training (e.g., attending practices even if not mandatory),
- giving one's best effort in training and competitions,
- exhibiting persistence even when things are not going well,
- selecting optimally challenging sport activities and opponents,
- performing up to one's potential on a consistent basis, and
- continually working on improving different facets of one's game.

In addition to being present when task goal orientation is high, such positive behaviors are also expected when ego goals prevail but only when perceived competence is high. If an athlete is focused on demonstrating superiority (i.e., focused on an ego goal) and has questions about his level of ability, a maladaptive achievement pattern is predicted. Such a pattern is reflected when an athlete (Duda & Pensgaard, 2002)

- holds back effort in training or competition,
- experiences performance impairment due to concerns about whether one is good enough,
- chooses sport-related challenges that are much too difficult (so the athlete won't feel bad losing) or too easy (so that success is almost guaranteed), and
- drops out of sport due to diminished commitment and the belief that one does not possess sufficient competence.

Achievement goal frameworks (Dweck, 1999; Nicholls, 1984, 1989) also predict that an athlete who is strongly focused on ego goals as opposed to task goals will come to question the adequacy of her sport competence. Sporting supremacy comes and goes and sometimes, once experienced, never comes back again. Over the course of an athlete's involvement in sport, competitive events and training can present a number of threats to her confidence in her athletic ability, including injuries, performance slumps, and the learning of new techniques or strategies. For athletes who endorse task goals, AGT proposes that their perceptions of competence will be hardier and more resistant to nagging doubts. This is because such an athlete doesn't primarily need to be better than others to feel good about himself or herself.

Central Constructs in Achievement Goal Frameworks

Within contemporary achievement goal frameworks (Ames, 1992a; Dweck, 1999; Nicholls, 1989), there are three major constructs, namely, perceptions of situational goal emphases (or the perceived motivational climate), dispositional goal orientations, and goal involvement. Each of these constructs will now be defined.

Motivational Climate

According to AGT, the social situation created by significant others varies in terms of the achievement goals emphasized. In terms of motivation-related aspects of the social situation surrounding athletes, the focus here

has been on athletes' views of the social-psychological environment rather than on the objective features of the environment. One coach, for example, can be perceived as producing a task-involving atmosphere, making it more likely that athletes will focus on task goals. Another coach might be viewed as generating an ego-involving environment that increases the probability that athletes will emphasize ego goals. Ames (1992a, 1992b) introduced the term *motivational climate* to capture these overriding aspects of the social-psychological environment. Further, Ames proposed that the motivational climate is multidimensional and is comprised of different structures (e.g., the system of evaluation, the type of and basis for recognition, the nature of interactions within and between groups, and the sources of authority).

Goal Orientations

AGT assumes that athletes have varying dispositional goal orientations. That is, as a function of their socialization experiences in sport and perhaps other achievement contexts (such as the classroom), athletes can be characterized by their individual differences in the tendency to emphasize task- or ego-focused criteria for subjective success (Nicholls, 1989). As has been found to be the

© PhotosForMe.com

Coaches create a motivational climate that can influence how athletes feel about themselves and their sport.

case in educational settings (Nicholls, 1989), in the sport domain task and ego orientations tend to be orthogonal or independent (Chi & Duda, 1995; Duda & Whitehead, 1998). This means that there are athletes who are oriented toward both task and ego goals as well as athletes who have one prevailing goal orientation.

Although we would not expect to find such individuals participating at higher competitive levels in sport (Duda, 2001), there are also people who are low in task and ego orientation. It would seem that such individuals are not particularly concerned with demonstrating that they are good in sport, regardless of how that level of competence is judged (i.e., in a self-referenced or other-referenced manner).

Goal Involvement

According to Nicholls (1989) and Dweck (1999), dependent on their goal orientations and the motivational climate operating (Dweck & Leggett, 1988), individuals can interpret achievement activities in terms of a task- or ego-involved goal perspective at any moment of time. That is, during sport engagement, athletes can be in a state of task or ego involvement. At the present time, we do not know whether it is possible for athletes to be strongly task *and* ego involved at *the same time* (see Harwood, Hardy, & Swain, 2000; Treasure et al., 2001), but it is difficult to imagine how two such discrepant ways of thinking and feeling could occur simultaneously (Duda & Whitehead, 1998). Drawing from the work of Nicholls (1984, 1989) specifically, Duda (2001) has argued that the determination of goal involvement states entails more than the assessment of criteria for subjective success (e.g., Williams, 1998) or the focus on personal performance standards, the performance process versus beating others, or competitive outcomes in reference to a competition that is about to commence or is taking place (Gernigon, d'Arripe-Longueville, Delignieres, & Ninot, 2004; Harwood & Swain, 1998; Williams, 1998). Unfortunately, such conceptual questions regarding the most appropriate way to measure task and ego goal states and logistical challenges in assessing goal involvement while athletes are engaged in sport (Duda, 2001) have limited research to date on this central AGT construct.

Measurement of the Coach-Created Motivational Climate

With respect to AGT-based work in sport settings, the majority of research has concentrated on perceptions of the motivational climate created by coaches. In the bulk of these studies, such perceptions have been captured via either version 1 or 2 of the Perceived Motivational Climate in Sport Questionnaire (PMCSQ-1 or PMCSQ-2) (Newton, Duda, & Yin, 2000; Seifriz, Duda, & Chi, 1992; Walling, Duda, & Chi, 1993). The PMCSQ-1 was developed to assess athletes' composite views about the degree to which the climate operating on their team (as reinforced via the coach's perceived attitudes and behaviors) is more or less task and ego involving. The initial pool of items tested in the development of this questionnaire were pulled from Ames and Archer's (1988) Classroom Achievement Goals Questionnaire or generated by the investigators (Seifriz et al., 1992). The validity of the two-dimensional structure of the PMCSQ-1 has been supported in previous sport research (see Duda & Whitehead, 1998, for a review).

With the aim of increasing our understanding of what aspects of the social environment contribute to perceptions of situationally emphasized goals and the effect of these contextual characteristics on athletes' motivation, the PMCSQ-1 was extended and revised to form a multisubscale measure of the perceived coach-created climate—the PMCSQ-2. The measurement model underlying the PMCSQ-2 (Newton et al., 2000) assumes the existence of higher-order task- and ego-involving dimensions undergirded by more specific situational structures. Specifically, via separate subscales, the PMCSQ-2 assesses the following task-involving aspects of the perceived coach-created motivational climate: the views that the coach emphasizes effort and athletes' personal improvement, contributes to all players feeling that they have an important role on the team, and fosters cooperation among team members. An overall score for the degree to which the coach-created atmosphere on the team is deemed task involving is also provided. In terms of the more ego-involving facets of the coach-created environment, athletes' appraisals that their coach typically is punitive in response to mistakes, gives the most attention to the most skilled players, and cultivates rivalry among team members are tapped via separate subscales. The PMCSQ-2 also allows for the calculation of a scale score regarding athletes' overriding assessment of the degree to which the climate is ego involving.

Past work has revealed the task- and ego-climate dimensions of the PMCSQ (1 or 2) to be negatively correlated (i.e., r tends to range from -.3 to -.5). This negative association suggests that the more a coach is perceived to encourage self-referenced competence, cooperation, and exerted effort (i.e., task goal emphasis), the less likely he is viewed as fostering a concern with how able an athlete is when compared with others (i.e., ego goal emphasis).

Research using the PMCSQ-2 has found perceptions of the coach-created motivational climate to be significantly shared or interdependent among team members (e.g., Duda, Newton, & Yin, 1999; Gano-Overway, Guivernau,

Magyar, Waldron, & Ewing, 2005). Similar findings have emerged regarding assessments of the motivational climate operating in physical education classes (Papaioannou, Marsh, & Theodorakis, 2004). This interdependence in perceptions means that, although there might be some degree of variability among team members in terms of how they view the prevailing coach-created climate, players on a particular team tend to be more similar in their perspective compared to players who are members of other teams. Such findings suggest that it is appropriate to aggregate perceptions of the motivational climate at the team level (Gano-Overway et al., 2005) and examine what such team-level perceptions predict.

This work also points to the need to separate group versus individual effects via multilevel analyses when examining the potential effects of the coach-created motivational climate on teams' and athletes' responses (Duda, 2001). In addition, the observed interdependence in perceptions of the coach-created motivational climate holds important practical significance. That is, how might we intervene to help coaches modify the motivational climate if there is little agreement among team members regarding the task- and ego-involving characteristics of that environment (Duda, 2001)?

In addition to the coach-created motivational climate that surrounds an athlete throughout the season, the AGT literature has called for the development of state measures, or measures of situational factors that could influence athletes' goal involvement during a particular training session or competition (Duda & Hall, 2001; Harwood & Swain, 1998). Examples of such state situational factors might include the importance of the particular sport contest (e.g., playing against a key rival), the size and characteristics of the audience watching a competition (e.g., a supportive, demanding, or discouraging home or away crowd), or the expectations and goals expressed in a coach's precompetition exchange with an athlete. Drawing from Vallerand's (2001) hierarchical model of motivation, which assumes that motivational dynamics at the situational level can have a bottom-up effect on motivation-related constructs at the higher, contextual level, it would also be interesting to examine how such state views of the motivational atmosphere can, over time, influence athletes' perceptions of the overriding motivational climate operating on their team.

Research on the Coach-Created Motivational Climate

The testing of the basic assumptions and predictions embedded in AGT (Ames, 1992a; Dweck, 1999; Nicholls, 1989) in sport has primarily examined the correlates of task and ego goal orientations. There have been fewer attempts to determine the implications of the motivational climate created by significant others in the sport setting. With the advent of theory-based and validated measures of athletes' views regarding the motivational climate manifested in sport settings, this line of work has become more popular and should continue to expand.

Correlates of Perceptions of the Coach-Created Motivational Climate

To date, the work conducted on the perceived motivational climate created by the coach has been primarily cross-sectional. In general, the results of studies examining the variables associated with perceptions of the motivational climate have been consonant with the predictions of AGT (Ames, 1992a, 1992b). That is, perceptions of a task-involving environment cultivated by the coach have linked to indices of an adaptive achievement pattern and more positive cognitive and emotional responses among athletes. For example, among sport participants, perceptions of a task-involving climate have been related to

- greater enjoyment, satisfaction, and positive affect (e.g., Boixados, Cruz, Torregrosa, & Valiente, 2004; Carpenter & Morgan, 1999; Ntoumanis & Biddle, 1999; Seifriz et al., 1992; Smith, Balaguer, & Duda, in press; Treasure, 1993; Vazou, Ntoumanis, & Duda, 2005; Walling et al., 1993);

- the belief that effort is an important cause of sport success (e.g., Seifriz et al., 1992; Treasure, 1993);

- self-ratings of performance and improvement (e.g., Balaguer, Duda, Atienza, & Mayo, 2002; Balaguer, Duda, & Crespo, 1999; Pensgaard & Duda, 2004) and objective competitive performance (Pensgaard & Duda, 2004);

- the use of adaptive coping strategies (e.g., problem-solving coping; Kim & Duda, 1998) and a lower propensity to burn out in sport (Duda, Balaguer, Moreno, & Crespo, 2001);

- perceptions that the coach provides positive feedback, training and instruction, and social support (Balaguer, Crespo, & Duda, 1996; Balaguer, Duda, & Mayo, 2002; Gardner, 1998; Smith, Fry, Ethington, & Li, 2005);

- perceived competence (e.g., Boixados, et al., 2004; Reinboth, Duda, & Ntoumanis, 2004);

- higher ratings of the team's degree of task and social cohesion (e.g., Balaguer, Castillo, & Duda, 2003);

- positive peer relationships (Ommundsen, Roberts, Lemyre, & Miller, 2005; Smith et al., in press);

- the view that the purposes of sport include fostering a work ethic and prosocial values (e.g., Ommundsen, Roberts, & Kavussanu, 1998);

- positive moral functioning and stronger sportsmanship values, as reflected in athletes reporting greater respect for the game, rules, and officials; a lower likelihood to exhibit aggression against an opponent; more mature moral reasoning; less endorsement of rough play; and so on (Boixados et al., 2004; Gano-Overway et al., 2005; Guivernau & Duda, 1998; Ommundsen, Roberts, Lemyre, & Treasure, 2003; Miller, Roberts, & Ommundsen, 2005; see also chapter 19); and

- less self-handicapping, or the verbalization of excuses before performance (Kuczka & Treasure, 2005; see also chapter 15).

In contrast, past work has found a perceived ego-involving coach-created environment to correspond to a more maladaptive achievement pattern and more negative cognitive and emotional responses. In particular, perceptions of the ego-involving features of the motivational climate have been related to

- higher anxiety and performance-related worry (e.g., Ntoumanis & Biddle, 1998; Papaioannou & Kouli, 1999; Pensgaard & Roberts, 2002; Walling et al., 1993),

- the belief that ability is an important determinant of sport achievement (e.g., Seifriz et al., 1992),

- dropping out of sport (e.g, Sarrazin, Vallerand, Guillet, Pelletier, & Cury, 2002),

- greater peer conflict (Ommundsen et al., 2005),

- perceiving one's ability in terms of normative or other-referenced criteria (Boixados et al., 2004),

- perceiving one's coach to provide less social support and positive feedback and more punishment-oriented feedback (Balaguer et al., 1996, 2002; Smith et al., 2005),

- greater self-handicapping (Ryska, Yin, & Boyd, 1999), and

- less mature moral reasoning and lower moral functioning (e.g., Kavussanu & Roberts, 1996; Ommundsen et al., 2003).

As is the case in this chapter, when summarizing the variables concomitant to perceptions of the motivational climate, the literature has tended to rely on narrative reviews. This means that little can be definitively said about the direction and strength of the relationship of the perceived task- and ego-involving features of the coach-created climate to athletes' cognitive, emotional, and behavioral responses and which factors moderate these relationships. Only the associations between perceptions of the motivational climate and positive and negative affect have been tested via meta-analytic techniques (Ntoumanis & Biddle, 1999) that allow for the calculation of such effect sizes across research investigations. Unfortunately, the Ntoumanis and Biddle analysis was done a number of years ago and thus was based on a limited number of studies and study participants. Given that much more work examining the perceived motivational climate in sport and other physical activity domains has been conducted in recent years, it seems prudent that we take a more systematic and comprehensive look at its correlates.

Studies have also examined the relationship between the perceived coach-created motivational climate and athletes' reported goal orientations (see Duda, 2001, for a review). Perceptions of the task- and ego-involving motivational climate tend to be low to moderately associated with athletes' reported task orientation and ego orientation. This literature, though, is also almost exclusively comprised of cross-sectional (one point in time) studies. Given this methodological strategy, we cannot decipher whether dispositional goals affect what athletes key in on in their social environments or whether the climate influences how athletes judge their competence and define success in sport (Duda, 2001).

Experimental Studies of the Motivational Climate

Only a few studies have attempted to examine the effect of a task-involving versus ego-involving climate on cognitions, affect, and behavior in laboratory settings (see Duda, 2001, for a review). It is probably more accurate to indicate that such research aimed to manipulate the situationally emphasized goal in terms of the experimental task in question.

For example, in a study of participants riding cycle ergometers, Reinboth and Duda (2006) determined the effects of more task-involving versus more ego-involving goal instructions and feedback on objective performance, perceived exerted effort, and quality of the experience. An important feature of this research was that both conditions entailed objective competition. The general trend in previous attempts to create a more task- versus ego-involving environment in a laboratory setting was to contrast noncompetitive versus competitive conditions (see, e.g., Ames, 1992a). Such tests of the effect of task-focused versus ego-focused situational goals are limited in their relevance to competitive sport. Sport competition typically entails that there is a winner and a loser at the end of the contest.

However, this does not mean that the motivational climate of the competitive event necessarily leads competitors to be exclusively ego involved.

In the Reinboth and Duda (2006) study, an overt competition was established; there was a winner and a loser in terms of distanced covered in two 8-minute competitive trials in both the ego-involving and task-involving conditions. The competitors could see how they and their opponent were doing at all times during the race by viewing monitors. The outcome was manipulated via the continuous addition of 12.5% to the winners' displayed distance while the losers' monitor indicated the actual distance covered.

In the ego-involving condition, emphasis was placed on biking longer than one's opponent and winning the race, and the participants were told that the outcome would be made public (i.e., posted on their school's Web site). At the end of each race, feedback was couched in ego-involving terms (e.g., "You did not bike farther than your opponent. You lost the race."). In the task-involving condition, the participants were requested to try as hard as possible and experience improvement in their performance as they progressed from the first to second race. Although the participants were aware of the outcome, the information that was given to them also considered the process (e.g., pedaling smoothly). Postrace feedback was more task involving. Losers in the ego-involving condition performed less well and reported that they were less satisfied with and interested in the cycling task and exerted less effort than winners in the ego-involving condition and winning and losing participants in the task-involving condition.

The literature on achievement goals also contains a few studies that have aimed to manipulate the motivational climate in the field (Christodoulidis, Papaioannou, & Digelidis, 2001; Morgan and Carpenter, 2002; Theeboom, DeKnop, & Weiss, 1995; Treasure, 1993; Weigand & Burton, 2005). In general, these investigations suggest that it is possible to modify the motivational atmosphere in real-life settings within the physical domain. Moreover, the findings that have emerged from this research are by and large consonant with predictions from AGT.

However, the existent studies of manipulations of the motivational climate have been primarily limited to the physical education context (e.g., Weigand & Burton, 2005) or programs for motor skill development (e.g., Theeboom et al., 1995). Little is known about whether it is possible to modify the coach-created motivational climate in higher-level, organized sport and what the effects of such change might be on athletes' short- and long-term achievement striving. Clearly, this line of work would have great practical significance for understanding and influencing motivation in athletic participants.

Such field experiments would also provide a compelling test of the tenets of AGT in competitive sport.

Motivational Climate, Goal Orientations, and Their Interactive Effects

Early studies based on AGT tended to examine either the implications of individual differences in goal orientations or differences in the perceived motivational climate with respect to athletes' responses. In more recent research, the trend has been to consider both dispositional and situationally emphasized achievement goals as predictors of achievement-related patterns.

Dweck and Leggett (1988) were the first to argue that goal orientations and perceptions of the motivational climate might interact to influence individuals' cognitive, affective, and behavioral responses in achievement settings. A significant goal orientation (person factor, or P) $\times$ motivational climate (situational factor, or S) means that the influence of an athlete's dispositional goal tendencies would depend on the characteristics of the climate (e.g., this athlete would exhibit one achievement pattern if the coach-created environment was high in task-involving features and another if the environment was low in task-involving features).

Some studies have tested for such $P \times S$ interaction effects in sport settings (e.g., Newton & Duda, 1999; Treasure & Roberts, 1998; Gano-Overway et al., 2005). There is also limited research that has pulled from AGT and taken a more comprehensive look at the factors that might interact to affect athletes' thoughts, feelings, and actions in sport; that is, perceptions of ability have been examined in conjunction with dispositional and situationally emphasized achievement goals (e.g., Newton & Duda, 1999). When significant interactions have emerged in this approach, they have generally been aligned with the predictions of AGT (Dweck & Leggett, 1988). However, in most cases, the studies in question have had limited power to detect hypothesized interaction effects (climate $\times$ goal orientation $\times$ perceived ability) (Duda, 2001). This limitation may be due to insufficient sample sizes or limited variability in the predictor variables.

Conceptual Issues and Measurement Challenges

Although there has been impressive advancement in the measurement of key achievement goal constructs in the sport domain such as the perceived coach-created motivational climate (see Duda & Whitehead, 1998, for a review), there is much more work to be done in terms of the refinement of existing measures and the development of new assessment tools. In this section, we will highlight some of the conceptual issues and measurement challenges that should be tackled if we are to progress in our understanding of the nature and implications of the motivational climate in sport settings.

The first two points concern the underpinning facets of task- versus ego-involving sporting environments, as reflected in the item content of existing climate measures. Another matter concerns the assessment and study of the different motivational climates operating in sport that are created by the coach as well as other significant others (e.g., parents, see chapter 10; peers, see chapter 11). We will also highlight attempts to examine the objective, in contrast to the subjective, motivational climate. Finally, we will touch on the implications for motivational-climate assessments of recent work (e.g., see Elliot, 1999) that has extended existing dichotomous models of achievement goals (mainly task and ego goals; e.g., Dweck, 1999; Nicholls, 1984) by considering approach and avoidance aspects of the two achievement goals.

Motivational Climate and Its Underlying Structures

Existing assessments of the perceived motivational climate operating in sport and other physical activity settings are clearly marked by diversity. Although all aim to tap the two major climate dimensions, there are differences among the questionnaires regarding which situational goal structures are addressed (Duda, 2001; Duda & Whitehead, 1998). Most critically in terms of validating measures of the motivational climate, it is important that assessed *subdimensions* of a task-involving versus ego-involving atmosphere are not in actuality theoretically presumed *correlates* of the perceived climate construct. An examination of the existing work on the measurement of the motivational climate has revealed some slippage in the concept (Duda & Whitehead, 1998). For example, worry about performance is hypothesized to be an implication of a highly ego-involving climate (Walling et al., 1993), but subscales tapping such perceptions are included in available assessments of the motivational climate created by parents (see chapter 10) or physical education (Duda & Whitehead, 1998; Papaioannou, 1994).

Pulling from the work of Ames on situational structures underpinning perceptions of the overriding motivational atmosphere (1992a, 1992b) and suggestions made by Nicholls (1989) regarding contextual factors (e.g., interpersonal competition) influencing ego versus task involvement, we would suggest that the motivational climate is "a many-splendored thing." In other words, overall views of whether a motivational climate is more or less task and ego involving are grounded in appraisals of several characteristics of the achievement setting at hand (e.g., How is success defined by the creator of the climate? What aspects of performance are reinforced? How are individuals evaluated in that setting with respect to the emphasized criteria for success? What is the basis of recognition?).

What is not clear or consistent, however, in existing measures of the motivational climate in physical settings, is which of such situational structures should be included or measured (Duda & Whitehead, 1998). We would suggest that such decisions should be based on theoretical as well as empirical reasons. For example, in terms of a theoretical rationale, does it conceptually make sense how each targeted aspect of the climate in a particular questionnaire would contribute to an emphasis on task versus ego goals? From an empirical standpoint, do the questionnaire items tapping what are task-involving in contrast to ego-involving situational structures contribute to athletes' overriding appraisals of the degree to which the motivational climate is task versus ego involving?

Motivational Climates Created by Significant Others

In the sport psychology literature, there have been other approaches to determining perceptions of achievement goals emphasized in the social-psychological environments created by significant others. For example, research has looked at athletes' perceptions of the goal orientations held by their parents (e.g., "My dad or mom thinks I am successful in sport when . . ."; e.g., Duda & Hom, 1993; Ebbeck & Becker, 1994). Findings have indicated that athletes' views of the success criteria used by significant others moderately correlate with their own personal goal orientations. However, athletes' perceptions of the goal orientation of their coach are less associated with perceptions of the coach-created motivational climate (Duda, 2001). We would suggest that these findings make sense. As discussed previously, views regarding the overriding climate are comprised of athletes' appraisal of various aspects of the social environment—for example, as assessed in the PMCSQ-2, the degree to which the coach creates rivalry between team members (ego climate) or makes everyone on the team feel they play an important role (task climate). These views are assumed to make it more or less likely that athletes will focus on task or ego goals. That is, perceptions of the coach-created motivational climate do not specifically center on how coaches personally define sporting success.

Questionnaires have been developed to tap perceptions of the motivational climate in sport-related settings as shaped by parents (see chapter 10; White, 1996; White, Duda, & Hart, 1992) and peers (see chapter 11; Vazou, Ntoumanis, & Duda, 2005). The significant others that influence athletes' goals in and approaches to sport can vary as a function of developmental change, gender, type of sport, and other factors. Not surprisingly, a few studies have aimed at determining the differential importance of the motivational climates created by coaches, parents, and peers on athletes' self-perceptions and interpretations of sport (e.g., Vazou et al., 2006; Weigand, Carr, Petherick, & Taylor, 2001).

At the present time, however, it is not possible to appropriately test the relative significance of the motivational atmospheres created by coaches, parents, and peers on athletes' personal goals and achievement patterns. This is because the current questionnaires that target these divergent motivational climates are not equivalent in terms of the environmental aspects they tap (see Duda & Whitehead, 1998). Consequently, if a study finds the perceived motivational climate shaped by one socializing agent (e.g., parents) to be more pertinent to athletes' cognitive, affective, and behavioral responses than the perceived climate shaped by another, we cannot tell whether these results are due to the differential importance of the significant others in question or cross-instrument variability in the questionnaire content with respect to the situational structures assessed.

Perceived and Objective Coach-Created Motivational Climate

The AGT literature relevant to sport has centered on the nature and significance of the social-psychological environment surrounding athletes. That is, the focus has been the study of the perceived motivational climate operating in sport settings. Primarily pulling from the TARGET taxonomy (Epstein, 1989), in which various features of the motivational climate are presented (see table 9.1 on page 129; more information about the TARGET taxonomy is presented later in the chapter), research has attempted to measure the *objective* climate shaped by physical education teachers (e.g., Morgan, Sproule, Weigand, & Carpenter, 2005; Sluis et al., 1999).

However, there is not yet a validated observational instrument available to tap the objective coach-created motivational climate or what coaches are actually doing that might predispose their athletes to focus on task or ego goals. In interventions designed to modify the motivational atmosphere of sport teams, an assessment of the objective features of the climate could

help coaches become more aware of (and, as a result, potentially self-regulate) their behaviors (Smith et al., 1983; Smith & Smoll, 2005; also see chapter 6). Such a measurement tool would also nicely complement the determination of athletes' perceptions of the coach-created motivational climate when ascertaining the effectiveness of coach training programs.

Multiple Achievement Goals and the Motivational Climate

In recent years, the dichotomous or two-goal models of achievement have been challenged and a multiple-goal approach has been advocated. Researchers such as Elliot (1997, 1999; Elliot & Conroy, 2005; Elliot & McGregor, 2001) have called for a revision of the task–ego goal dichotomy by considering that achievement goals can have an approach and avoidance quality as well. More specifically, Elliot's 2×2 achievement goal framework (Elliot, 1997, 1999) holds that there are four major achievement goals (see figure 9.1 for an example of each goal):

- *Mastery* or *task-approach goals,* which focus on the development of competence and task mastery

- *Mastery* or *task-avoidance goals,* which are concerned with the avoidance of demonstrating self-referenced incompetence

- *Performance* or *ego-approach goals,* which center on the attainment of favorable judgments of normatively defined competence

- *Performance* or *ego-avoidance goals,* which emphasize avoidance of the demonstration of other-referenced incompetence

According to Elliot (1999), the adoption of these achievement goals is dependent on a number of factors, including *personal differences* (e.g., individual perceptions of competence) and *environmental characteristics* (e.g., perceptions of the motivational climate). With respect to environmental factors, there is limited research examining the relationship of the perceived motivational climate to the emphasis placed on the various achievement goals in the physical domain. In physical education settings, a perceived task-involving climate has been positively associated with and a perceived ego-involving climate negatively associated with the endorsement of mastery task-approach goals (Cury, Da Fonseca, Rufo, & Sarrazin, 2002). In contrast, perceptions of an ego-involving climate have been revealed to be a positive predictor of performance ego-approach goals as well as performance ego-avoidance goals.

Building on such work (Cury et al., 2002), we need to know more about the perceived coach-created environ-

Definition of competence

		Intrapersonal/absolute	Normative
Valence	Positive	**Task approach** Example: Goal focus is to improve on one's personal best in the 400m or master a particular dismount in gymnastics.	**Ego approach** Example: Goal focus is to show that one is the best golfer on the team or score the most goals in a soccer match.
	Negative	**Task avoidance** Example: Goal focus for a swimmer is to not swim a worse time than she did in the previous race.	**Ego avoidance** Example: Goal focus for a tennis player is not to do worse score-wise against an opponent played in a previous tennis match.

Figure 9.1 Sport-related examples of multiple goals assumed in Elliot's (1999) 2×2 framework.
Adapted from A.J. Elliot, 1999. "Approach and avoidance motivation and achievement goals," *Educational Psychologist*, 34, 169-189.

ment as a possible antecedent of the emphasis placed on mastery task-avoidance goals. Moreover, the work on the motivational climate in sport has been grounded in a two-goal (task and ego) *approach* model of achievement motivation. It will be interesting to discover whether there are avoidance aspects of the motivational climate that would add to our understanding of goal adoption and ensuing motivational processes in sport settings (Elliot & Conroy, 2005). In other words, would it be theoretically and practically informative to measure the task-approach, task-avoidance, ego-approach, and ego-avoidance features of the motivational atmosphere surrounding athletes?

Future Research

Throughout this chapter, we have proposed some research questions that are worthy of consideration for further study. With reference to what comprises the motivational climate, more work is needed on what situational structures are fundamental to athletes' views about the prevailing motivational climate operating on their teams. Recognizing that there are a number of motivational climates besides the environment shaped by the coach (e.g., the peer-created climate), we need to develop an assessment of the task- and ego-involving features of such environments that can be appropriately referenced in terms of these significant others. In so doing, we can begin to more accurately tease out the effects of these multiple socializing agents on athletes' self-perceptions and responses to the sport experience.

Longitudinal investigations that examine the interplay between goal orientations (task–ego, approach–avoidance) and perceptions of the motivational climate over time are warranted. Such work should contribute to insight into the potentially reciprocal interdependencies between individual differences and situational achievement goals in the athletic setting. Longitudinal methodological strategies are also necessary to discern how daily situational perceptions of the climate in training and competition feed into how athletes appraise the prevailing motivational atmosphere of their team. In addition, more research is needed that determines the effect of the coach-created climate on athletes' achievement striving over time. For example, what might be the influence of task-involving and ego-involving atmospheres on skill development, performance consistency, and continued participation throughout a season and from one season to the next?

A recent research direction has been to examine the implications of the coach-created motivational climate on athletes' cognitions, affective responses, and behaviors that are not strictly related to achievement. Such work increases our awareness of the role of achievement goals in terms of the quantity *and* quality of athletes' motivation (Duda, 2001; Duda & Pensgaard, 2002). Athletes exhibit quantity of motivation when they are performing positively and are actively engaged in sport. The quality of their motivation, however, is reflected in whether they look forward to continuing their sport involvement, work to maximize their skill potential, and strive for personal sporting excellence over time. Other indicators of quality of motivation concern whether athletes' sport participation contributes to their life in positive ways (i.e., enhances their mental, affective, and physical well-being and causes them to experience personal growth) and does not cause them to incur ill-being (e.g., overuse injuries or burnout; Duda, Balaguer, Moreno, & Crespo, 2001).

Exemplifying the potential significance of the coach-created climate on quality of sport engagement, studies have found that achievement goals are predictive of indicators of athletes' mental and physical welfare such as disordered eating attitudes and behaviors, body-image disturbances, performance-enhancing substance use, level of self-esteem and contingency of one's self-worth, and degree of physical exhaustion experienced (e.g., Duda, Benardot, & Kim, 2004; Reinboth & Duda, 2004). To provide further support regarding the significance of the coach-created motivational climate for the well-being of athletes, we need to start examining the relationship of athletes' perceptions regarding this psychological environment to indices of athletes' welfare over time (see Reinboth & Duda, 2006).

Even more compelling evidence will stem from field experiments that manipulate the motivational climate operating on sport teams and examine the effects of such an intervention on the quantity and quality of athletes' engagement. It would also be important for subsequent work on the motivational climate and athletes' welfare (whether correlational or experimental in design) to incorporate physiological and physical measures of well-being (e.g., immune function) along with self-report measures of psychological and emotional health.

Finally, future research might examine the mechanisms by which variations in the coach-created motivational climate may affect the quantity and quality of athletes' motivation and sport experience. For example, integrating another popular contemporary theory of motivation with the achievement goal approach (i.e., self-determination theory; Deci & Ryan, 1985; Ryan & Deci, 2000), we have begun to examine variability in the satisfaction of the needs to feel competent, autonomous, and related to others as mediators of the relationship between the coach-created motivational climate and athlete well-being (Balaguer et al., 2003; Olympiou, Jowett, & Duda, 2005; Reinboth & Duda, 2006; Reinboth, Duda, & Ntoumanis, 2004; Standage, Duda, & Pensgaard, 2005).

Practical Implications

With the aim of providing some clarity and organization to the various situational structures assumed to be pertinent to the created motivational climate, Ames (1992b) brought the TARGET taxonomy to the atten-

tion of sport psychology researchers and practitioners. This taxonomy was developed by Epstein (1989) as a way of summarizing and providing order to the various dimensions of family structure that have been found to influence student motivation. The acronym *TARGET* captures the features of the motivational climate related to task, authority, recognition, grouping, evaluation, and time. These six dimensions of the motivational climate are defined in table 9.1. Also provided are strategies for modifying each of the TARGET environmental components with the aim of fostering a more task-involving climate.

To help ensure that efforts to alter an existing motivational climate are successful, we suggest that coaches be involved in proposing even more specific tactics that bring to life the TARGET conceptualization on a day-to-day basis. We also would like to reemphasize the point that these situational structures are assumed to be interdependent. Thus, modifying one facet of the environment (e.g., how athletes are evaluated) almost assuredly has implications for other aspects of the overriding motivational climate (e.g., how athletes' positive and negative achievement outcomes are recognized). It would seem prudent, and clearly in line with Ames' thinking on the matter (1992a, 1992b), that the overall message given to athletes be as consistent and holistic as possible.

Summary

In this chapter, we gave an overview of the major constructs and assumptions in an achievement goal approach to understanding athletes' cognitive, affective, and behavioral patterns in sport. A major focus was placed on the role that the coach-created motivational climate can play in influencing athletes' interpretation of and responses to the sport experience. Coaches, of course, want to influence their athletes, and indeed this literature suggests that they do. Whether this influence is more positive or negative appears to depend on the degree to which the motivational atmosphere the coach establishes is more or less task-involving and ego-involving.

Some conceptual and methodological issues regarding the assessment of athletes' perceptions of the motivational climate were forwarded for the readers' consideration; there is much more work to be done in terms of the refinement of existing measures of key achievement goal constructs and the development of new assessment tools. The chapter concluded with brief proposals regarding directions for future research and practical implications of the work to date on the coach-created motivational climate. For example, more work is needed to determine what situational structures

Table 9.1 TARGET Structures and Strategies That Enhance Task Involvement

TARGET structure	Strategies
Task: What athletes are asked to learn and what tasks they are given to complete (e.g., training activities, structures of practice conditions)	Provide the athlete with a variety of moderately demanding tasks that emphasize individual challenge and active involvement. Assist athletes in setting self-referenced process and performance goals. Create a developmentally appropriate training environment by individualizing the demands of the task.
Authority: Type and frequency of participation in the decision-making process (e.g., athlete involvement in decisions concerning training, setting and enforcing rules)	Encourage athlete's participation in the decision-making process. Consider the athlete's perspective. Develop opportunities for leadership. Get athletes to take responsibility for their own sport development by teaching self-management and self-monitoring skills.
Recognition: Procedures and practices used to motivate athletes and recognize their progress and achievement (e.g., reasons for recognition, distribution of rewards, opportunities for rewards)	Use private meetings between coach and athlete to focus on individual progress. Recognize individual progress, effort, and improvement. Ensure equal opportunities for rewards to all.
Grouping: How athletes are brought together or kept apart in training and competition	Use flexible and cooperative grouping arrangements. Provide multiple grouping arrangements (i.e., individual, small-group, and large-group activities). Emphasize creative solutions to training problems.
Evaluation: Standards set for athletes' learning and performance and procedures for monitoring and judging attainment of these standards	Develop evaluation criteria based on effort, improvement, persistence, and progress toward individual goals. Involve athletes in self-evaluation. Make evaluation meaningful and consistent.
Timing: Appropriateness of time demands placed on learning and performance (e.g., pace of learning and development, management of time, training schedule)	Recognize that even elite athletes do not train, learn, or develop at the same rate. Provide sufficient time before moving on to the next stage in skill development. Try to spend equal time with all athletes. Assist athletes in establishing training and competition schedules.

Adapted from J. Duda and D. Treasure, 2006, In *Applied sport psychology: Personal growth to peak performance,* edited by J. Williams (New York: McGraw-Hill Companies). With permission from the McGraw-Hill Companies.

are fundamental to athletes' views about the prevailing motivational climate and how the coach-created climate affects athletes' achievement striving over time. Another research direction is the role of achievement goals in terms of athletes' well-being, optimal functioning, and the personal growth they experience via sport participation (Duda, 2001). As for practical implications, the TARGET taxonomy, which includes the features of the motivational climate related to task, authority, recognition, grouping, evaluation, and time, can be used to formulate strategies for engineering a more task-involving climate.

DISCUSSION QUESTIONS

1. Why is it important to examine athletes' goal orientations and their views about the coach-created motivational climate when trying to understand motivational patterns in sport?

2. Provide examples of how a task-involving coach would typically coach. Contrast this with the usual coaching practices of an ego-involving coach.

3. What are some of the challenges of assessing perceptions of the motivational climate in sport settings?

4. Drawing from the literature, what are some of the consequences of creating a task-involving atmosphere in sport? What might be the implications of a highly ego-involving climate on athletes' cognitive, affective, and behavioral responses?

5. What are some directions for future research on the coach-created motivational climate in sport settings?

6. Drawing from the TARGET taxonomy and in reference to your favorite sport, provide specific examples of how a coach could work toward creating a task-involving climate for athletes.

chapter 10

Parent-Created Motivational Climate

Sally A. White, PhD

Learning Objectives

On completion of this chapter, the reader should have

1. knowledge of the key research findings on the role of parents in establishing children's achievement motivation and how parents influence various antecedents and correlates of motivated behavior;

2. understanding of how mothers' and fathers' perceived values and foci of success in physical activity settings have been linked to children's overall achievement motivation patterns; and

3. ability to explain the importance of parents establishing a task-involving climate for maximum positive effect for their children.

AP Photo/Eric Risberg

The study of children's patterns of achievement motivation would not be complete without an examination of the situational factors created by parents. This chapter synthesizes current research on parent-created motivational climate, with a focus on empirical findings from literature on achievement goal theory. In particular, motivation is not viewed as capacity or a personal characteristic but rather as a differentiated individual quality influenced by socialization and environmental forces (Givvin, 2001), and a major relationship during the process of socialization is the parent–child relationship.

In the formative years, parents are significant providers of performance information for children in a wide array of achievement contexts (Eccles & Harold, 1991). It is generally believed that children's fundamental view of themselves as competent and socially acceptable is related to their perception of how they think their parents will react to success and failure (Heyman & Dweck, 1998). Parents who promote sport competence as a function of athletic ability will see one set of responses from their children, and parents who promote physical competence and success as a consequence of personal mastery and the exertion of effort will see another (White, 1998). Thus, evaluation processes, reward structures, and parent expectations play a tremendous role in determining a child's sport motivation. Parent-created motivational climate has tremendous implications for the socialization of children into sport and other achievement contexts (e.g., school), but as yet has limited findings in applying it within various settings.

A review of literature in achievement motivation has been provided elsewhere (see chapter 9). Here, I will identify several areas that are critical to understanding the influence of parent-created motivational climates for children in sport.

Achievement Goal Theory

In the literature on achievement motivation, it has been postulated that whether one is task or ego involved is a context is a function of three factors: (1) the disposition of the individual to demonstrate high and low levels of task or ego orientation or both; (2) the situational differences created by a significant other, such as teacher, parent, coach, peer, or sibling; and (3) the developmental differences established in childhood (Nicholls, 1989). The following discussion will focus on the first factor, highlighting research that used a goal-profiling approach to determine perceptions of parental influence, and on the third factor, describing the ways developmental differences relate to parent-created motivational climates.

As Duda and Balaguer explained in chapter 9, according to achievement goal theory there are two main dispositional goal orientations. In essence, these orientations capture individual differences in the emphasis sport participants place on task- or ego-focused criteria for subjective success. Recent discussion about research on the bipolarity or orthogonality of achievement motivation in physical activity settings makes an interesting distinction. In particular, as goal orientations are not bipolar, each individual has a degree of both goal orientations; this can be thought of as a goal profile (Nicholls, 1989, 1992). Consequently, there are four goal profiles:

- High task orientation and low ego orientation
- High task orientation and high ego orientation
- Low task orientation and high ego orientation
- Low task orientation and low ego orientation.

Several studies have demonstrated the orthogonality of achievement goals as indicated by the zero to low correlations between task and ego orientations (e.g., Fox, Goudas, Biddle, Duda, & Armstrong, 1994; Roberts, Treasure, & Kavussanu, 1996; White, 1998). A goal-profile approach is useful in discerning this orthogonality. Researchers first establish the athlete's goal profile and then analyze the data against the profile. Employing a goal-profile approach in the data analysis, it was indicated that individuals who had a high task orientation and low ego orientation and others who had both high task and high ego orientations were more likely to exhibit one type of motivational pattern. In comparison, individuals who had a high ego and low task orientation exhibited a very different motivational perspective (Fox et al., 1994; Roberts et al., 1996; White, 1998).

Goal profiling has also been used in parent-created climate. For example, White's (1998) investigation used a goal-profile approach to examine the perceptions of the mother- and father-created motivational climate and supported the orthogonality of goal orientations. This study's findings will be discussed later in the chapter. Future research on achievement goal theory would do well to employ a goal-profile approach.

It has been suggested that children up until the age of 9 years hold an undifferentiated conception of ability and tend to view success on achievement tasks as a function of exerting high levels of effort (Nicholls, 1989). As children get older, their conception becomes more differentiated, and by the time they are adolescents they may evoke a highly differentiated conception of ability. An individual who has a highly differentiated conception of ability is likely to have high levels of dispositional ego orientation, whereas the person with an undifferentiated conception of ability tends to be higher in dispositional task orientation (Nicholls, 1989). A burgeoning body of literature in sport and academia has associated adaptive motivational patterns with individuals who have higher levels of task orientation than ego orientation or higher levels of both task and ego orientation, whereas a person high in ego orientation and low in task orientation is more likely to exhibit maladaptive motivational patterns (Duda, 2001; Roberts, 2001; Wigfield & Eccles, 2002; see also chapter 9).

The concept of adaptive and maladaptive behaviors, cognitions, and emotions is discussed at length in chapter 9. To assist the reader in understanding these two divergent patterns when examining the influence of parents in creating motivational contexts, a parent–child interaction model has been created. Figure 10.1 illustrates the relationship between parents' dispositional and situational goals and those of their children, which can lead to the demonstration of either an adaptive or maladaptive motivational pattern.

To test the developmental component of achievement goal theory in the physical education domain, Fry and Duda (1997) completed one of the few quasi-experimental design investigations. Specifically, they discovered that boys and girls were able to differentiate between effort and ability and that their

capability to do so evolved with age. The age range of the children in the investigation was from 5 to 13 years. The researchers watched videotapes of children completing a task involving bean-bag tossing. Results revealed that children who were aged 5 to 9 years were unable to distinguish between effort and ability as being the major determinant of success at the task; they held an undifferentiated conception of ability in the physical domain. However, the older children in the study, between 10 and 13 years of age, were able to discern whether it was effort or ability that led to success; they held a differentiated conception of ability. Through their experiences with achievement tasks and the reaction of significant adults to the result of the child's performance, children learn what is valued, rewarded, and preferred. These experiences are thought to be highly predictive of whether children will be task or ego involved in school and sport and exhibit the corresponding adaptive or maladaptive motivational pattern (e.g., Ames, 1984, 1992).

Overall, achievement goal theorists suggest that goal orientations are a function of both personal and situational factors (e.g., Ames, 1992; Duda, 2001; Roberts, 2001). Dispositional differences are seen as a priori probabilities of internalizing a particular goal

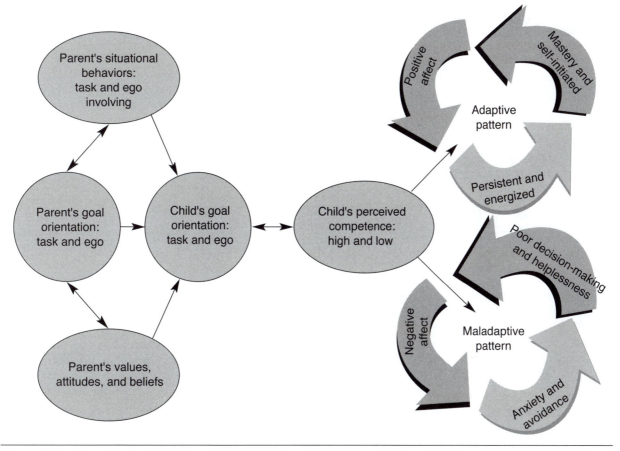

Figure 10.1 The parent–child interaction model.

orientation, and contextual factors are seen as potentially altering those probabilities (Dweck & Leggett, 1988). Consequently, a growing body of research has focused on the relationship between goals and the climate created by significant others. The following sections focus on the role of parents in creating a motivational climate that leads to the adoption of certain motivational patterns.

Parent Motivation in Educational Settings

There is a widely held belief that children pursue goals for a multitude of reasons, and at the heart of research on achievement motivation in school-based settings is an examination of what leads to the adoption of a specific motivational style. In particular, there is evidence to suggest that individuals do not develop goal orientations in a vacuum; instead, specific socialization experiences promote the development of the two goal orientations (e.g., Ames, 1992; Dweck & Leggett, 1988; Maehr, 1984). The role that parents play in creating a motivational climate conducive to the pursuit of achievement goals is very important. Thus, a review of

Parents are important in determining a child's motivation in sport.

the specific mechanisms that associate parental values, attitudes, and beliefs with a child's perceptions of competence is presented next.

Parent–Child Interactions

In one of the first studies to review parent–child interactions, it was determined that children who were granted more opportunities by their parents for self-determination, self-control, and input into the design of the task and who were consistently reinforced for adhering to the rules, developed greater feelings of autonomy, which translated into academic success (Baumrind, 1991). In addition, a relationship has been established between the parent's behavior and a child's academic motivation in the form of intrinsic interest toward learning (Ginsberg & Bronstein, 1993; Hokoda & Fincham, 1995; Rathunde, 1996). Specifically, there is wide acceptance of Ryan's (1993) theory of intrinsic motivation and how parents help establish internal or external controls that children use to motivate themselves to achieve academic success. Overall, a secure parent–child relationship leads to an internally developed set of goals and values, whereas an insecure parent–child relationship fosters detachment, emotional distress, and the use of external control of behavior. A generally accepted hypothesis is that parental socialization processes affect children's motivation to achieve in contexts where competence is being evaluated (Wentzel, 1999), although the ways in which specific parenting practices directly influence the quest of specific goals by children have not been demonstrated.

Children's orientations to academic tasks, therefore, are thought to be grounded in what their parents think of them morally and socially, and these orientations are a direct reflection of how they think that their parents will react to their successes and failures (Heyman & Dweck, 1998; Heyman, Dweck, & Cain, 1992). It has been suggested that the foundations for holding an internal motivation versus an external motivation are laid in the early years during family interactions and that later socialization experiences have little influence (Wentzel, 1999). Moreover, studies with adolescents have determined that perceived social and emotional support from parents is linked to perceived school success, a closer peer relationship, and higher levels of interest in school than for those who did not perceive high levels of parental support (Cauce, Felner, & Primavera, 1982; Connell, Spencer, & Aber, 1994; Felner, Aber, Primavera, & Cauce, 1985; Wentzel, 1998). Consequently, the need to understand how and why children develop the motivational perspectives that they carry into adulthood has been widely viewed as an important line of scientific inquiry in educational psychology, albeit such inquiry is very limited thus far.

Meece (1997) aimed to explore how the home environment influences children's academic motivation. To determine the effect parents have on the intellectual development of their child, a number of family factors have been examined. Certain variables have been shown to be critical, such as parents' responsiveness, discipline style, level of interaction (of mothers) with their children, and organization of the home environment and the availability of daily stimulation to learn via the presence of learning materials. All of these factors have been linked to higher levels of cognitive stimulation in children as well as higher levels of academic motivation in children aged 9 to 13.

In a follow-up study, Gottfried, Fleming, and Gottfried (1998) investigated the role of cognitive stimulation in the home on children's academic intrinsic motivation and found a significant relationship. Specifically, the more social discourse the child had with parents, the more parents encouraged the child to be curious, and the more engagement the child had in extracurricular activities (such as the arts, private lessons, and free play), the higher the child's intrinsic motivation. Consequently, it was determined that the home environment created by parents plays a large role in the development of achievement motivation during the early years.

Influence of Mothers and Fathers

Research has revealed some interesting findings as they specifically pertain to the mother's or the father's influence in developing children's achievement motivation in school settings. In particular, when mothers make positive attributions about their children's performance, have high confidence in their children's abilities, and value school as a place to work hard and succeed, their children tend to have more adaptive motivational perspectives on school (Eccles, Wigfield, Harold, & Blumenfeld, 1993). Likewise, Brody, Flor, and Gibson (1999) determined that mothers who had enhanced perceptions of their parenting efficacy, which includes setting higher educational goals for their children, are more likely to have children who experience greater levels of academic success.

On the other hand, how fathers affect their children's academic motivation is more difficult to identify, as they tend to have less direct involvement in the formative years (Pintrich & Schunk, 1996). A somewhat tangential relationship has been put forward that higher levels of father involvement directly affect the father's relationship with the mother, which is thought to positively influence mother–child interaction (Belsky, 1998; Tamis-LeMonda & Cabrera, 1999). In addition, the higher the socioeconomic status of the father, the more interaction the father is likely to have with the school itself, such as attending parent meetings and events and giving time to the school in the form of volunteer activities. All of these factors have a positive influence on the child's motivation in school (Tamis-LeMonda & Cabrera, 1999). Overall, mothers and fathers appear to contribute to the child's motivation to learn in different ways either directly (mothers) or indirectly (fathers); the general finding is that more parental involvement leads to higher levels of motivation.

From the perspective of achievement goal theory, few studies have specifically examined the effect that a parent-created motivational climate has on the academic success of children; nonetheless, several interesting studies are worth reviewing. In particular, when examining children's conceptions of intelligence, it was indicated that students who perceived their parents to be promoting a process message (e.g., learning, effort, strategies) compared to a trait message (e.g., smart or dumb) had more advanced conceptions of intelligence that have been linked to higher levels of academic success (Dweck & Lennon, 2001).

In another study, it was found that the parents' theory of intelligence predicted the achievement tasks chosen (Smiley, Coulson, & Van Ocker, 2000). Entity intelligence is linked to performance goals, and incremental intelligence is linked to learning goals. Specifically, parents with an incremental theory of intelligence were more likely to encourage their children to pick challenging tasks and not worry about failure. Incremental parents also emphasized effort as the key to task success, whereas entity parents promoted ability and attributed success to the child's talent (Smiley et al., 2000). The study further investigated mother–father differences and determined that entity mothers preferred comparative feedback and incremental fathers had children who were more persistent on tasks (Smiley et al., 2000). Clearly, parents evaluate children on different aspects of their behavior and communicate different types of expectations. This, in turn, leads to the adoption of specific motivational patterns in children (Ames & Archer, 1987).

Children's Perceptions

The expectancy-value model (Eccles, 1993; Eccles, Jacobs, & Harold, 1990) provides an alternative theory to the study of children's values in school and their motivated behaviors, beliefs, and goals (Eccles, 1993; Eccles et al., 1983). According to the model, which was designed to assess adolescents' performance and choices in mathematics, the influence of parents' actual cognitions on children's beliefs occurs through children's perceptions. In particular, the individual's goals and general self-schema are influenced by the perception of the socializers' beliefs and behaviors (Eccles, 1993; Eccles et al., 1983). Moreover, it is one's interpretation of reality rather than reality itself that most directly influences activity choices.

Thus, the influence of reality on achievement-related beliefs is mediated by interpretative systems (e.g., Wigfield & Eccles, 2002). Children's perceptions of the people who interact with them, such as parents, coaches, teachers, and peers, influence children's beliefs, values, and expectations associated with a particular activity (Eccles & Harold, 1991). Ames (1992) has also argued that it is the individual's interpretation of environmental cues, expectations, and rewards that influences a particular goal orientation rather than the actual behavior of significant others. Unfortunately, there has been only one study that has specifically reviewed parental influence using the expectancy-value model (Eccles et al., 1990). The intent was to examine the function of parents in the development of children's ideas about who they are and would like to be and how parents provide children with information that is used to develop a self-schema about specific activities. Overall, gender differences were identified that parallel gender stereotypes, both for the children and for the parents (Eccles et al., 1990). Specifically, parents rate their daughters' ability at sport significantly lower than their sons' at an early age (kindergarten), regardless of actual ability. In addition, boys were given many more opportunities to participate in and practice their sport prowess than girls.

This study was completed more than a decade ago, so it is unclear if these results would be repeated. In fact, as will be discussed in the next section, sport research has indicated that it is the parents' goal orientation that influences the values and beliefs of the child, not the gender of the parent per se (e.g., White, 1996; Roberts, Treasure, & Hall, 1994). Nonetheless, parents still hold strong opinions about suitable activities for young girls and boys that undoubtedly have a tremendous effect upon the self-schema that is established by children and carried into adulthood.

Parent-Created Climate in Sport and Physical Activity Settings

The influence parents are perceived to have in the development of children's achievement motivation is grounded in the contention that goal orientations are developed through socialization experiences in childhood and assumes that parents play a tremendous role in the development of these goal preferences (Nicholls, 1989; Roberts, 2001). Most related to the parent–child interaction research in sport is the expectancy-value model (Eccles & Harold, 1991). The model proposes

that children's goal preferences are related to their perceptions of parent and significant adult preferences rather than the actuality of the situation. Accordingly, it is important to examine the individual's perception of the situation rather than the situation itself. Parent-created motivational climate in physical activity has been studied by employing this basic tenet of the expectancy-value model and modifying items from the Learning and Performance Orientation in Physical Education Classes Questionnaire (LAPOPECQ) (Papaioannou, 1994, 1995) to create an instrument called the Parent-Initiated Motivational Climate Questionnaire (PIMCQ) (White, Duda, & Hart, 1992).

Research Findings Associated With the PIMCQ-2

The majority of research regarding the parent-created motivational climate has been completed by White (1996, 1998) and her colleagues (White & Duda, 1993; White et al., 1992; White, Kavussanu, & Guest, 1998). To assess dimensions and correlates of the perceived situational goal structure initiated by parents when children learn a physical skill, the PIMCQ (White et al., 1992) and a modified version named the PIMCQ-2 (White & Duda, 1993) have been developed. The modifications to the PIMCQ were minor and included adding four items (measuring perceptions of enjoyment) that are repeated for fathers and then mothers. The PIMCQ-2 will be described in detail, followed by results from various studies in which it has been employed.

The PIMCQ-2 has 18 items that are repeated twice to record sport and exercise participants' perceptions of the motivational climate created first by their mother and next by their father. The questionnaire consists of three subscales measuring a learning and enjoyment climate (nine items), a worry-conducive climate (five items), and a success-without-effort climate (four items). When answering the items on the PIMCQ-2, children and young adolescents are asked to think about what their mothers and then fathers think about them when they learn a new sport skill and then indicate their level of agreement with items assessing different dimensions of the mother- and father-initiated motivational climate.

For the mother and father parts of the questionnaire, the stem for each item is "I feel that my mother ..." or "I feel that my father...." For the learning and enjoyment, worry-conducive, and success-without-effort climates, examples of items constituting the individual subscales are "... is most satisfied when I learn something new," "... makes me worried about failing," and "... thinks I should achieve a lot without much effort." The recording of the responses is on a five-point Likert scale anchored by *strongly disagree* (1) and *strongly agree* (5). To calculate a score for the mother and then for the father on the three subscales, the items of each subscale are added and then divided by the number of items.

In exploratory investigations, a three-factor structure of the PIMCQ-2 has been established and two contrasting environments have been identified: a task-involving climate and an ego-involving climate (White & Duda, 1993; White et al., 1992). Specifically, the learning and enjoyment subscale represents a task-involving climate and the two subscales, worry conducive and success without effort, indicate an ego-involving climate. The factor structure was similar for each parent, and in both studies the internal reliabilities for the three subscales have been consistent in exceeding the criteria ($\alpha > .75$) (Cronbach, 1951).

In addition, results of a canonical correlation analysis demonstrated that individuals high in task orientation perceived that both their mother and father valued a climate that focused on learning and enjoyment (task involving), and that this orientation was negatively related to perceptions that success was achieved through the demonstration of low levels of effort (White & Duda, 1993). In contrast, sport participants high in ego orientation perceived mothers and fathers to emphasize a climate where success was related to the exertion of low levels of effort (ego involving).

The PIMCQ-2 has also been used with volleyball players. In particular, it was discovered that female volleyball players' perceptions of the climate initiated by parents was significantly related to their dispositional goal orientation (White, 1996). Employing separate stepwise multiple regression analysis for the two goal orientations revealed that a climate where parents emphasized success without effort predicted ego orientation. Alternatively, it was found that an individual's perception of a climate that focused on learning and enjoyment was a predictor of task orientation. The results from this investigation were critical in that the PIMCQ-2 was able to identify two divergent situational goal structures that are deemed important and are emphasized by parents when children perform physical skills. Moreover, the findings were in the hypothesized direction based upon research examining the motivational climate created by the physical education teacher and classroom teacher (see Ntoumanis & Biddle, 1999, for a review).

In a study designed to examine more than one significant other responsible for the initiation of the motivational climate, the PIMCQ-2 and the Perceived Motivational Climate in Sport Questionnaire-2 (PMCSQ-2) (Newton & Duda, 1993) were used to assess the relationship between goal orientation and perceptions of the motivational climate among young athletes (White et al., 1998). The significant others in the study were physical education teachers, coaches of organized sport teams, and parents. The participants, who were between the ages of 12 to 14, completed five questionnaires on two separate occasions before an organized sport practice.

Overall, results indicated that goal orientations were related differentially to the perceived motivational climate created by significant others (White et al., 1998). Specifically, task orientation was related to perceptions of a task-involving climate created by the coach and both parents. Ego orientation, on the other hand, corresponded to the perception of an ego-involving climate in sport, a success-without-effort climate created by the father, and a worry-conducive climate created by both parents.

An intriguing finding was that goal orientations and perceptions that the physical education teacher created a task- or ego-involving climate were not identified (White et al., 1998). The researchers speculated that physical education teachers appear to be less important socializers than coaches and parents, a hypothesis that makes sense, considering the amount of time athletes spend with their coaches. In addition, parents in the United States tend to transport and watch their children when they play on an organized sport team (Guest & White, 2001). Hence, children participate in sport under the scrutiny of their parents and in a highly supervised adult environment (with a coach). Unfortunately, with the current emphasis on higher academic achievement and testing, physical education classes have been dropped from many U.S. school curriculums in favor of more academic subjects.

The use of a goal-profile approach has been suggested as a more encompassing way to examine individual differences in goal orientations and various antecedents of motivated behavior (e.g., Fox et al., 1994; Roberts et al., 1996). Although a dominant predisposition to be either task or ego oriented has been identified, due to the orthogonal nature of goal orientations it may be possible to be high or low in both. The advantage of a goal-profiling approach was described earlier in this chapter and, to date, only one study has used this approach when examining the parent-created motivational climate. This study looked at dispositional (profile approach) and situationally induced goal perspectives and levels of trait anxiety in a group of adolescents involved in organized sport (White, 1998).

Results indicated that the high-task and low-ego group perceived that both their mother and father endorsed a learning and enjoyment motivational climate. In contrast, the high-ego and low-task group thought that their mother and father valued a climate where success was coupled with low effort, felt that their fathers made them worry about making mistakes, and experienced the highest levels of competitive trait anxiety. For the high-task and high-ego group, it was found that fathers emphasized a climate where success was linked to low levels of exerted effort and mothers were perceived to make the individual worry about making mistakes. However, the high-task and high-ego group also believed that both parents still valued learning and enjoyment in the development of physical skills. Finally, individuals in the low-task and low-ego group perceived that their mothers made them afraid of making mistakes in the learning of skills. More investigations are needed that use a goal-profile approach in the study of goal orientations and certain indices of achievement behaviors, emotions, and cognitions (White, 1998).

Adaption of the PECCS for Parents

An alternative to the PIMCQ-2 in the study of parent–child achievement motivation has been to adapt questionnaires developed for teachers to fit the context for parents. In particular, this has been completed with the Physical Education Class Climate Scale (PECCS) (Biddle et al., 1995). The PECCS is designed to assess children's perceptions of the motivational climate in physical education classes and consists of two subscales that have both exceeded the coefficient alpha criteria of >.75 when measuring internal reliability. The first subscale is focused on perceptions that teachers promote a learning-oriented climate (i.e., the teacher is pleased when a student learns something new) and has four items. The second subscale has three items and measures perceptions that the teacher promotes a performance-oriented climate (i.e., the teacher only pays attention to those who are good at sport).

For the purposes of exploring the influence of the parent-created climate, the PECCS has been altered (i.e., the stem and items altered) to reflect a parental-reaction versus a teacher-promotion focus. When examining children's perceptions of what parents emphasize in a physical education class, it was determined that student perceptions of parental emphasis of learning predicted personal task orientation, effort, and enjoyment in classes (Carr, Weigand, & Hussey, 1999). On the other hand, student perceptions that parents focused on comparison predicted ego orientation and feelings of being under pressure in physical education. These results were in support of those found by most PIMCQ-2 investigations and were in the hypothesized direction.

In a follow-up study adapting the PECCS for use again with parents, Carr and Weigand (2001) examined the influence of five significant others (physical education teacher, father, mother, peer, and sport hero). The study found that task orientation was significantly related to perceptions of a learning climate from mothers,

fathers, peers, and teachers and a mastery orientation from sport heroes. In contrast, perceptions of a comparison-oriented climate from mothers, fathers, peers, and teachers and a performance-oriented climate from sport heroes were identified in children higher in ego orientation than task orientation.

One of the major flaws of this investigation was that the distribution of the questionnaires was not counterbalanced and factor analysis was only performed on the sport-hero questions. Consequently, the results must be treated with caution. In addition, in a review of the various measures of motivational climate, Ntoumanis and Biddle (1999) suggest that in its present form the PECCS is not a very valid measure of the motivational climate in school physical education and so the chance that it can therefore be adapted for parents and be valid is very low. At this point, the PIMCQ-2 appears to be the better instrument.

Related Findings on Parent Achievement Motivation

This section will review research studies that are grounded within a social-cognitive model and focus on parental influence on children's achievement-related behaviors, cognitions, and emotions. However, these studies do not necessarily examine dispositional or situationally induced goals. Several of the studies have been completed using a goal-perspective paradigm, and others come from well-known theories such as Harter's (1978) competence motivation theory and the expectancy-value model (Eccles, 1993).

Parents' Beliefs About Success in School and Physical Activity

It seems intuitive that parents who make certain attributions and hold certain beliefs regarding the importance of effort versus outcome may communicate those beliefs to their children, thereby influencing their children's achievement-related cognitions and subsequent behavior. Indeed, research conducted in academic settings has shown that parental beliefs determine parental actions, which in turn influence children's achievement outcomes.

For example, it was found that parents' beliefs about their children's mathematic and reading abilities were related to parental instruction of mathematics and reading at home (Halle, Kurtz-Cortes, & Mahoney, 1997). Parents' perceptions of children's academic abilities were significantly related to children's achievement within the domains of math and reading. In a related study (Galper, Wigfield, & Seefeldt, 1997), parents' beliefs about how well their children were doing were related to children's beliefs and attitudes toward school. Furthermore, parents' beliefs were a significant predictor of children's reading and mathematic achievement. Based on these findings, one could assume that there is a causal relationship between parental beliefs that are translated into what is valued and children's perceptions about what is important in an achievement domain.

In the sport domain, several different achievement theories have been used to examine children's beliefs about success in sport and how these beliefs relate to their parents' beliefs. In particular, perceived parental beliefs were found to be related to young adults' goal orientations and personal beliefs in a conceptually coherent fashion (White, Kavussanu, Tank, & Wingate, 2004). For instance, the perceived parental belief that effort leads to success in sport was correlated to an athlete's task orientation and personal belief that effort causes sport success. In contrast, the perceived parental belief that superior ability, external factors, and use of deceptive tactics are precursors to success in sport corresponded to an athlete's ego orientation and the same personal beliefs. Clearly, there is a relationship between what parents value and how this translates into the values and beliefs of their children (White et al., 2004).

The psychosocial responses of competitive soccer players and how these pertained to perceptions of parental influence were examined using Harter's (1978) competence motivation theory (Babkes & Weiss, 1999). Regression analyses revealed two interesting findings. First, it was determined that mothers and fathers who were thought to be highly engaged in physical activity gave lots of encouragement for performance success, perceived their children to be competent at sport, and had children with high perceived competence, intrinsic motivation, and enjoyment of physical activity. Second, a gender difference was found for fathers. In particular, those soccer players who perceived their fathers to be highly involved in their sport participation and not pressuring them to perform had the most positive psychosocial responses of all the participants. These findings again supported the notion that parents play a critical role in the socialization of their children in sport and physical activity, and they explained how this notion related to the corresponding expressions of positive affect, cognitions, and behaviors in children.

In the exercise psychology domain, it has been demonstrated that the nature and extent of a child's physical activity are a function of the beliefs and expectations of the parents. Consequently, it is postulated that the major initial socializing influence upon an individual's desire for and likelihood to participate in physical activity is the family, and more likely the parents (Brustad, 1993). Kimiecik, Horn, and Shurin (1996) demonstrated

that perceived parental beliefs explained a significant amount of the variation in children's own beliefs. Specifically, children's perceptions of their parents' task orientation, value of fitness, and fitness competence pertaining to their child corresponded to children's own task orientation and perceived fitness competence.

Taken together, these studies clearly suggest that parents have an important function in socializing children to adopt certain beliefs and cognitions. In addition, they highlight the significance of examining youngsters' *perceptions* of their parents' attitudes, values, and beliefs rather than parents' actual cognitions. Moreover, in an era of higher rates of obesity and early-onset diabetes in children, never before has it been more important for parents to influence children to be physically active and adopt healthy lifestyle behaviors.

Dispositional Goals and Parents

The most frequently used instrument when examining dispositional goals in individuals involved in a range of physical activity settings is the Task- and Ego-Orientation in Sport Questionnaire (TEOSQ) (Duda & Nicholls, 1992). The TEOSQ has high levels of validity and reliability (see Duda & Whitehead, 1998, for a review), and on many occasions the items and stems have been adapted to fit a wide range of environments.

In the case of the TEOSQ modified for parents, it has been found that athletes who are high in task orientation are more likely to believe that their significant parent is task oriented, and athletes high in ego orientation tend to believe that their parents are highly ego oriented (Duda & Hom, 1993; Ebbeck & Becker, 1994; Givvin, 2001). Interestingly, athletes' goal orientations are unrelated to their parents' self-reported goals and instead are related to the athletes' perceptions of their parents' goals (Givvin, 2001). It appears that parents might be giving parent-appropriate responses, and it seems that children pick up on the actual intent instead of the appropriately given cue (i.e., kids are not fooled by the signals that they receive from their parents about what is important and valued). Similarly, if parental messages are unclear, children just insert their own goals in place of their parents' and thus avoid any cognitive dissonance that may occur from a mismatch between the two groups (Givvin, 2001).

A few investigations have used an alternative instrument known as the Perceptions of Success Questionnaire (POSQ; Roberts, Treasure, & Balague, 1998). There are no real differences between this instrument and the TEOSQ, and some argue that they are the same (e.g., Duda & Whitehead, 1998). Parents' achievement goals and how the goals are subsequently interpreted into children's sporting behavior were studied with the POSQ. Counter to the predicted hypothesis that fathers would be more active in sport than mothers, the study discovered that both were highly involved (Roberts et al., 1994).

Also not supporting previous sex stereotype findings (Eccles et al., 1993), there were no parent or child gender differences or gender goal orientation variations. The only significant result was that highly ego-oriented parents emphasized normative standards of success for their children whereas parents who were low in ego orientation viewed cooperating with teammates as the major criteria of success (Roberts et al., 1994). A closer examination of how the gender bias of the parent relates to the gender of the child is warranted in future investigations (White et al., 2004).

The influence of parents in the life of children involved in sport in other cultures has intuitive appeal and needs in-depth examination. In one such study, Spanish adolescents involved in competitive track and field and tennis were asked to complete a modified version of the POSQ that measured perceptions concerning the success criteria of significant others, including a coach, father, mother, sport friend, and nonsport friend (Escartí, Roberts, Cervelló, & Guzmán, 1999). In particular, four more items were added to the POSQ to make a total of 16, with half reflecting a task orientation and half focusing on ego orientation. The new questionnaire was named the Perceptions of Significant Others' Sport Success Criteria Questionnaire (POSOSSCQ) (Escartí et al., 1999).

Two significant results emerged that are critical to the discussion of parents. First, Spanish adolescents high in task and ego orientation perceived their mothers and fathers to have both task- and ego-involving criteria for judging success in athletics; exactly the same was determined for their coach, sport friend, and nonsport friend. Consequently, there was congruence between the individual's perceptions about success and the perceptions of several significant others involved in their sport experience. The second noteworthy result was that high task-oriented and high ego-oriented adolescents believed that sport success was negatively related to ego-involving perceptions of sport success for the coach, mother, father, sport friend, and nonsport friend. The second finding suggests that when a person is high in task orientation as well as high in ego orientation, the high task orientation moderates any negative effects that high ego orientation may have. This is preferred because it means that the person is more likely to display an adaptive versus a maladaptive motivational pattern (Escartí et al., 1999).

The notion of task orientation as adaptive was made by Duda (2001). She suggested that those involved in creating motivational climates should maximize the opportunity to promote task orientation and minimize the emphasis on ego orientation, particularly in children

and young adolescents. This comment has been misconstrued by some to mean that an adaptive motivational perspective (i.e., high task orientation) implies that the person is not competitive and, therefore, achievement goal theory has little validity in the world of competitive sport (e.g., Harwood & Hardy, 1999; Harwood, Hardy, & Swain, 2000).

However, this interpretation is false. The task-oriented person is competitive; surely everyone reads the scorecard or looks at the scoreboard and asks the question, "Did I win?" However, what promotes adaptive versus maladaptive motivational patterns is how being successful was construed and the consequences of that judgment (White, 1998). Specifically, if mastery is at the core of a person's criteria for being successful, then feelings of competence are going to come from performing tasks skillfully and not from the end result of the game alone. Most people want to improve, as they know success is not the process but the product of mastery.

Future Research

It is recommended that future studies focus on adding more dimensions to the PIMCQ-2, creating a conceptual model to explore relationships between certain antecedents and consequences of parents' motivated responses, and then exploring how these responses influence the adoption of motivational patterns in children. In the case of the PIMCQ-2, more stringent measurement analysis is needed. Although the current version has performed well from a statistical perspective in the majority of completed studies, a confirmatory factor analysis is still recommended. It has also been suggested that a third generation of the PIMCQ-2 be designed and should include the expansion of items for both the mastery climate and performance climate subscales (Ntoumanis & Biddle, 1999). The addition of new items and subscales of parental influence would enhance the overall usefulness of this instrument and allow it to be employed with older populations of sport participants.

For example, a dimension might be added that focuses on the degree to which parents involve their son or daughter in the decision making of sport engagement. This new subscale might give sport researchers a better understanding of how empowering children to be responsible for their sport participation leads to the adoption of certain motivational perspectives in physical activity. It would be informative to determine whether children who are highly engaged in their own choice of sport (versus what their parents want them to play) produce adaptive motivational perspectives. Other dimensions to add to the PIMCQ-2 have been suggested, such as parental encouragement, emotional involvement, and the salience of sport to the parents (Ntoumanis & Biddle, 1999).

Once the issue of measurement has been addressed, the next step is to test the causal model showing projected parent–child interactions that was presented earlier in this chapter (see figure 10.1). In reviewing the parent–child interaction model, what needs to be determined is the interplay among certain parent variables, the child's dispositional goals, and how these are mediated by perceptions of competence and then translated into the child's motivational patterns. Specifically, if we review the results of several studies, it will illustrate how the parent–child model might provide parents and educators with more insight into why children exhibit different motivational patterns in the same environment.

Some children have been found to perceive that their parents believe that winning at all costs, taking an illegal advantage over an opponent (i.e., cheating), and being a natural athlete lead to success in sport (White et al., 2004). Moreover, this ego-involving perception is correlated to high levels of ego orientation in the child. Consequently, the assumption is that the child would demonstrate maladaptive motivational patterns in situations where she was not winning or in situations that were very challenging (Duda, 2001; White, 1996).

What was not examined in the White et al. (2004) study was how levels of perceived competence may influence a person's perceptions and how this might mediate the demonstration of subsequent achievement behaviors, cognitions, and emotions. If we examined other study findings, however, we would be able to complete the parent–child interaction model. Specifically, we would hypothesize that the ego-oriented child with perceived ego-involving parental beliefs would exhibit adaptive patterns if he had high levels of perceived competence and maladaptive patterns if he had low perceived competence (e.g., Dweck, 1999; Elliott & Church, 1997). Only future research will reveal the dynamics of the parent–child interaction model when all facets of the model are investigated together.

At the beginning of this chapter it was suggested that due to the orthogonal nature of dispositional goals, individuals are high or low in both task and ego orientation. Moreover, most of the research on achievement goal theory presented in this book has proposed task and ego goals separately. Unfortunately, this does not yield the whole picture as results differ when analysis of goals is done alone compared to profiles of goals in combinations (Fox et al., 1994; Roberts et al., 1996; White, 1998). For example, by now you will have assumed that high levels of ego orientation are linked to negative or maladaptive motivational patterns. This statement is only true, however, when we know the individual's level of

task orientation. Specifically, high levels of ego orientation and high levels of task orientation have indicated adaptive patterns, whereas high ego orientation and low task orientation are related to maladaptive motivational outcomes. Future achievement goal studies would do well to define the distinct goal groups.

Practical Implications

To give the reader some ideas on how to translate the current theoretical, conceptual, and empirical understanding about the influence of parents, I will use a personal situation. Several years ago when consulting for USA Volleyball's Sports Medicine and Performance Commission (SMPC), I engaged in a clinic for juniors and a parent asked me why it was that children from some families seem to belong to every sport club and organized team. The parents were described as always on the move, taking their son to soccer practice in fall, tennis in the winter, baseball in the spring and taking their daughter to volleyball in the fall, basketball in the winter, and golf in the summer.

Assuming that this meant the children were enjoying sport and exhibiting adaptive motivational patterns, I replied that participation has to do with the motivational climate that parents advocate in the home and while on the sidelines watching their children play sport. It's as easy as asking your daughter when she arrives home from a volleyball match if she improved on her past serving or hitting performance. Or, instead did you just ask, "Did you win?" Both of these are natural questions to ask your child, but they send a very different message about what is valued and believed to be salient in her sport experience. In the first instance, the parent is saying that improving in areas of the game is important. In the other comment, the parent is clearly sending the message that winning is the most important thing.

This example shows that two innocent statements by a parent can create a parent–child motivational climate that is either task involving or ego involving. The implications for these two climates have been described throughout this chapter and it has been concluded, that, overall, a task-involving climate is more desirable for children. What tips are there for parents who wish to make sure their children experience a task-involving motivational climate in sport and physical activity settings? Table 10.1 illustrates some fundamental psychological concepts that can be translated into helpful hints for parents when evaluating potential coaches and teams for their children. Deciphering the research findings into meaningful practical examples is critical if we are to communicate the importance of a task-involving climate to parents.

Table 10.1   Choosing a Task-Involving Climate for Children

Situation	Task-involving tip	Achievement motivation rationale
Determine the coach's philosophy and expertise.	Match your personal beliefs about sport participation with those of the coach.	A lack of congruence between adults can lead to conflict and convey mixed goals.
	Check that the practice sessions include creativity and variety to enhance motivation.	Perceptions of adult beliefs should be incorporated into the actual beliefs of the child by creating conditions for them to be translated into action.
How does the coach handle mistakes?	Pick a coach who is focused more on how the game was played rather than if it was won or lost.	Learning strategies that are based on the belief that effort and success covary will assist children in difficult learning situations.
	Encourage your children when they demonstrate high effort and show gains in task mastery.	Recognition of individual progress and improvement will facilitate children's motivation.
What is the role of teammates?	Find a team where all children get to play in the game despite their skill level.	Lack of interteam rivalry will reduce anxiety and increase enjoyment.
		Collaboration and heterogeneity of groups can maximize learning.
How does the coach incorporate the athlete into the decision-making process?	Look for teams where the coach asks athletes for their input and has team discussions.	Lack of input by the child can lead to the development of learned helplessness and total disengagement from sport.
	Allow your children to select the sport they want to engage in, the team they want to play on, and the level of competition.	Learning strategies should encourage children to self-manage and monitor their progress.

Examples extracted from White and Morgan 1996.

Based upon the information in table 10.1, finding the right environment is critical, but so is educating parents. For instance, you might be a coach who has created a task-involving setting and parents keep minimizing its importance. Consequently, teaching the parents how to effectively communicate to their children will be vital. As the coach, you will need to have a discussion with the parents on learning strategies and their salience. These learning strategies should identify how children can overcome difficult situations by employing effort-driven task behaviors, exhibiting positive emotions, and establishing affirming cognitions about one's abilities. The best-known intervention for use in restructuring motivational climates is TARGET (Epstein, 1989), which has been introduced in chapter 9.

Summary

Socialization is the process by which an individual's environment communicates certain values, roles, and expectations. One major contributor to socialization is the influence of parents. Surprisingly, this area has received little attention by sport psychology researchers and yet it has profound implications for children's decisions about engagement in physical activity. In particular, it is believed that children's perceptions and interpretations of the environment are the biggest contributors to their continuance and level of achievement (Wigfield & Eccles, 2002).

In this chapter, important conclusions have been drawn from the findings of studies completed in school-based and physical activity settings. First, how parents respond to their children during and after participation in an achievement context communicates important information about their children's performance and what children will subsequently value in the future. Second, adaptive motivational patterns are discerned when the teacher, coach, or parent is perceived by participants as creating a task-involving motivational climate. Third, the role of perceived competence in mediating the maladaptive motivational pattern of individuals (i.e., those with ego-oriented goals and ego-involving perceptions of the motivational climate) needs to be examined, as this has significant implications for individuals who work with children. Finally, as discussed in the practical implications section of this chapter, learning strategies need to be devised and communicated to parents. These strategies should focus on how children can overcome obstacles by employing effort-driven task behaviors, displaying positive affect, and holding affirming cognitions about the self.

DISCUSSION QUESTIONS

1. How does a goal-profile approach facilitate understanding of how patterns of behaviors, cognitions, and emotions are discerned in athletes?

2. What strategies would you employ to enhance academic attainment in male and female students?

3. Describe the three most significant contributions of the expectancy-value model and of achievement goal theory to the literature on the role of parents in children's school-based learning.

4. What are the five key research findings indicated with the PIMCQ-2?

5. Describe the results of studies identifying maladaptive compared to adaptive motivational patterns in children involved in physical activity.

chapter 11

Peer-Created Motivational Climate

Nikos Ntoumanis, PhD, Spiridoula Vazou, PhD, and Joan L. Duda, PhD

Learning Objectives

On completion of this chapter, the reader should have

1. understanding of the importance of studying perceptions of the peer motivational climate in youth sport;

2. knowledge of how young athletes perceive different facets of the peer motivational climate;

3. capacity to describe the relationship of different dimensions of the peer motivational climate to young athletes' motivational indices;

4. awareness of future research directions that aim to enhance our understanding of the antecedents and consequences of the peer motivational climate; and

5. knowledge of appropriate guidelines for building a task-involving peer motivational climate.

Millions of children and adolescents participate in organized sport programs every year (Weinberg & Gould, 2003). Through sport participation young athletes have the opportunity to interact with and relate to their peers, and it has been shown that peer relationships can contribute to the quality of physical activity experiences of children and adolescents (Smith, 2003). Despite the relevance of peers in shaping athletes' experience of sport, only recently has research examined peers as essential contributors to the overall social environment in youth sport. The link between peer acceptance and perceived athletic competence, sources of competence information, physical self-worth and affect, friendship quality, and moral development are some of the areas that have attracted attention in the youth sport psychology literature (see Smith, 2003; Weiss & Stuntz, 2004). At this juncture, it would be useful to distinguish between friendships and peer relationships. *Friendship* refers to close dyadic relationships, while the concept of *peer relationships* is more generic and refers to interactions among several individuals familiar to one another (Smith, 2003; also see chapter 4).

In this chapter we discuss how peer relationships among team members relate to young athletes' achievement motivation in sport. To date, research on young athletes' motivation has mainly examined their motives for sport participation, their sources and conceptions of ability, and how these relate to different achievement goals (Weiss & Williams, 2004). However, there is a scarcity of research on how peer-held criteria for success and failure are communicated to team members and how these criteria affect young athletes' achievement motivation. It is our position that peers are important contributors to the motivational climate in individual and team sport. We argue that peer use of self-referenced or comparative criteria for judging competence and inferring success and failure can predict young athletes' achievement motivation relatively independent of coach or parent influence.

Achievement Goal Theory and Motivational Climate

A theoretical framework that can enhance our understanding of social-psychological determinants of young athletes' motivation in sport is achievement goal theory. According to this theory (Ames, 1992; Nicholls, 1989; also see chapter 9 for an overview of the basic tenets and constructs), in order to understand the motivation of young athletes it is necessary to study the function and the meaning of their goal-directed actions. Such actions aim to demonstrate competence and to avoid showing incompetence.

Competence can be evaluated in two different ways that reflect two different achievement goal orientations. A *task orientation* is evident when perceptions of competence are self-referenced and are based upon personal improvement and exerting maximum effort. In contrast, an *ego orientation* is evident when competence is normatively referenced and is dependent on outperforming others or achieving success with minimal effort (Nicholls, 1989). Many studies have demonstrated that young people with high task goal orientation report more positive cognitive, affective, and behavioral outcomes in youth sport compared to their peers with high ego goal orientation (for reviews, see Duda, 2001; Duda & Hall, 2001; Duda & Ntoumanis, 2005).

Situational factors, such as the motivational climate created by significant others (e.g., coaches, physical education teachers, parents), are assumed to play a substantial role in the activation and direction of young athletes' achievement behavior (Ames, 1992). According to Ames, the term *motivational climate* refers to students' (or young athletes') perceptions of situational structures and expectations that encourage the development of particular goal orientations by transmitting task- and ego-involving motivational cues. It is common for variations in achievement patterns to be explained by the interplay of individuals' achievement goals and their perceptions of the prevailing motivational climate (e.g., Standage, Duda, & Ntoumanis, 2003b).

Ames (1992) proposed two types of motivational climates: A *task-involving* (or mastery) motivational climate encourages effort and rewards task mastery and individual improvement, while an *ego-involving* (or performance) motivational climate emphasizes normative ability and promotes interindividual comparison. In a task-involving motivational climate, athletes perceive significant others to evaluate performance based on personal skill improvement and to regard errors as part of learning. Past research in sport has found perceptions of a task-involving climate to be associated with positive motivational outcomes, such as enjoyment, performance improvement, and performance satisfaction (e.g., Balaguer, Duda, Atienza, & Mayo, 2002; Seifriz, Duda, & Chi, 1992). On the other hand, in an ego-involving motivational climate, athlete evaluation and recognition are based on normative or comparative criteria for competence. Such an emphasis has been linked to anxiety, maladaptive sources of sport confidence, dysfunctional attributions, and other negative outcomes (e.g., Magyar & Feltz, 2003; Treasure & Roberts, 1998; for a review see Ntoumanis & Biddle, 1999).

The literature so far has focused on adult-created (e.g., coaches, physical education teachers, parents) motivational climate (see chapters 9 and 10). The potential of peers to transmit a task-involving or an ego-involving motivational climate, as well as the nature and dimensions of the peer motivational climate, has not received much attention in the sport psychology literature. It is interesting that both Smith (2003) and Weiss and Williams (2004) highlighted the role of adaptive motivational climates in enhancing the quality of peer relationships; however, both reviews focused on coach-created climate.

To date, only two studies have examined the peer motivational climate. Specifically, Carr and her colleagues (Carr, Weigand, & Hussey, 1999; Carr, Weigand, & Jones, 2000) examined the relative influence of peers, along with parents, teachers, and sporting heroes, on children's achievement patterns in physical education and sport. The results of this research indicated that both adult- and peer-created climates can relate to children's goal orientations, intrinsic motivation, and perceptions of physical competence. In these two studies by Carr and colleagues, the peer motivational climate was measured by rephrasing items from the Physical Education Class Climate Scale (PECCS) (Biddle et al., 1995) and the Parent-Initiated Motivational Climate Questionnaire-2 (PIMCQ-2) (White, 1996). However, by simply rewording questionnaires on adult-created climate, one might not tap the unique aspects of peer influence; thus an attempt has been made to assess the nature and dimensions of the peer motivational climate by interviewing young athletes and developing questionnaire items that specifically tap this type of climate (Vazou, 2004).

Qualitative Investigation of the Peer-Created Motivational Climate

To better understand the nature and dimensions of the peer-created motivational climate in sport, Vazou, Ntoumanis, and Duda (2005) conducted a qualitative study of 30 young British athletes (14 boys and 16 girls) aged 12 to 16, from both individual and team sports. Individual and group in-depth interviews offered considerable insight into how young athletes perceive and manifest a peer motivational climate. Using content analyses, 11 dimensions of peer climate were identified: improvement, equal treatment, relatedness support, cooperation, effort, intrateam competition, intrateam conflict, normative ability, autonomy support, mistakes, and evaluation of competence.

Many of the dimensions of peer climate that emerged in the Vazou et al. (2005) study correspond to identified dimensions of adult-created motivational climate. For example, the Perceived Motivational Climate in Sport Questionnaire-2 (PMCSQ-2) (Newton, Duda, & Yin, 2000; also see chapter 9) taps the degree to which coaches emphasize individual improvement and promote cooperative learning. Nevertheless, new facets of the motivational climate surrounding youth athletes were revealed. These facets result from peer influence and have not previously been tapped by existing coach- or parent-focused motivational climate questionnaires (e.g., intrateam conflict, relatedness support). The dimensions of the peer motivational climate and their definitions are presented in table 11.1.

The *improvement* dimension is the extent to which peers encourage and provide feedback to their teammates to improve their skills. This is an important facet of a task-involving motivational climate. According to Ames and Archer (1988), a focus on self-referent improvement leads to more adaptive beliefs about the causes of success and sustains individual involvement in learning, even when perceived ability is low. The *equal treatment* dimension also reflects a task-involving climate; everyone has an important role and all athletes treat their teammates in a nonpreferential way. As Ames (1992) argued, when everyone is involved in the team decision making, a task-involving climate is perceived and feelings of autonomy are fostered. *Cooperation* is the extent to which young athletes help each other and work together in order to learn new skills. Research on teacher-created climate in the classroom has shown that teacher emphasis on cooperation and group learning is motivationally beneficial and can predict children's involvement in learning (Ames, 1992; Ames & Archer, 1988). The *effort* dimension refers to whether athletes emphasize to their teammates the importance of trying their hardest, clearly an indicator of a task-involving climate.

Intrateam competition is the promotion of interindividual competition and comparison by the peer group. Intrateam competition was conceptualized as a feature of an ego-involving climate (Ames, 1992), as competition should affect athletes' judgment of their normative or comparative ability. Furthermore, some athletes may perceive intrateam competition as an opportunity to validate their sense of self by gaining social status and recognition (Allen, 2003). *Intrateam conflict* refers to negative and unsupportive behaviors (e.g., blaming teammates for poor performance and emphasizing their weaknesses) exhibited by teammates. Such negative behaviors would be expected to undermine interpersonal relationships and induce feelings of lack of social support from peers. The *normative ability* dimension captures the perceived peer emphasis on displaying normative ability and the preference of peers to interact with the most competent teammates.

Table 11.1   Dimensions of Peer Climate

Dimension	Definition
1. Improvement	Encouraging and providing feedback for improvement to teammates
2. Equal treatment	Believing that everyone has an important role on the team and treating teammates in a nonpreferential way
3. Relatedness support	Fostering the feeling of being part of a group and creating a friendly atmosphere on the team
4. Cooperation	Helping each other and working together in order to learn new skills
5. Effort	Emphasizing the importance of exerting effort and trying one's hardest
6. Intrateam competition	Promoting interindividual competition and comparison
7. Intrateam conflict	Exhibiting negative and unsupportive behaviors (e.g., blaming each other for poor performance, laughing at teammates) that are not directly related to competing with others
8. Normative ability	Emphasizing normative ability and interacting only with the most competent teammates
9. Autonomy support	Perceiving that peers allow each other input in decision making and freedom in the way they play or perceiving that their peers act in a controlling manner
10. Mistakes	Worrying about how peers might react if athletes make mistakes; giving positive and negative reactions following athletes' mistakes
11. Evaluation of competence	Using normative or self-referenced criteria to evaluate athletes' competence

Adaped, by permission, from N. Ntoumanis and S. Vazou, 2005, "Peer motivational climate in youth sport: Measurement development and validation," *Journal of Sport and Exercise Psychology* 27: 432-455.

The emphasis upon demonstrating normative ability and normative standards of performance is a defining characteristic of an ego-involving climate (Ames, 1992; Duda & Hall, 2001).

The *relatedness support* and *autonomy support* dimensions are aligned with self-determination theory (Deci & Ryan, 1985), but they are also evident in the grouping and authority structures of a motivational climate (see Ames, 1992). This is because a task-involving motivational climate promotes athlete cooperation (grouping) and encourages individual initiative (authority); therefore, it is an environment that can support relatedness and autonomy. *Relatedness support* is the fostering and facilitation by peers of the feeling of being part of a group as well as the degree to which peers create a friendly atmosphere on the team. The data obtained via the interviews conducted by Vazou et al. (2005) showed that being able to meaningfully connect to their teammates made children less worried about the adequacy of their perceived ability, and work by Ntoumanis and Biddle (1999) and Sarrazin, Guillet, and Cury (2001) has shown that a perceived task-involving motivational climate can support the need for relatedness.

Autonomy support refers to whether athletes feel that their teammates allow them input in decision making and freedom in the way they play. Thus, this dimension includes a number of themes that referred to either the facilitation or the undermining of autonomy. Recent research suggests that a perceived task-involving motivational climate is associated with the satisfaction of the need for autonomy in the physical domain, whereas an ego-involving climate is unrelated or negatively related to the satisfaction of this need (Standage, Duda, & Ntoumanis, 2003a; Sarrazin et al., 2001).

The *mistakes* dimension refers to positive and negative reactions from peers when athletes make mistakes. These positive and negative responses to mistakes could potentially contribute to either a task-involving or an ego-involving motivational climate. That is, deriving from previous work on the coach-created motivational climate (Newton et al., 2000), when mistakes are viewed as part of the learning process and encouragement is provided by teammates, a task-involving peer motivational climate is in operation. In contrast, when peers criticize their fellow athletes and evaluate their ability based on the number of mistakes they make, an ego-involving peer climate is realized.

Last, the *evaluation of competence* dimension refers to whether peers are deemed to use normative or self-referenced criteria to evaluate their teammates' competence. When young athletes are evaluated based on their effort and personal improvement, a task-involving motivational climate is fostered (Ames, 1992). When comparisons based on normative ability are made, on the other hand, an ego-involving climate is manifested. Horn and colleagues (Horn & Weiss, 1991; Horn & Amorose, 1998) have shown that the criteria young people use to assess their competence differ with age; younger children (8-12 years) show greater preference for adult feedback, whereas older children and adolescents (13-16 years) show greater preference for peer comparison and evaluation. Bearing in mind that many of the participants in the Vazou et al. (2005) study were in the latter age group, it is not surprising that some reported a peer emphasis on normative criteria for competence evaluation.

Measurement of the Peer-Created Motivational Climate

Based on the higher-order and lower-order themes derived from the qualitative analysis of Vazou et al. (2005), a new instrument was developed to assess young athletes' perceptions of the peer motivational climate. This questionnaire was named the Peer Motivational Climate in Youth Sport Questionnaire (PeerMCYSQ) and was psychometrically tested in a series of three studies using young British athletes between the ages of 11 and 16 (Ntoumanis & Vazou, 2005). The validation process included pilot testing with a small number of children in order to examine the clarity and age appropriateness of the items, evaluation of the content of the items by a panel of experts, a series of exploratory and confirmatory factor analyses (CFA) of various first-order and higher-order factor models, an examination of the internal reliability of the identified factors, and an assessment of the instrument's test–retest reliability over a 4-week period.

The final version of the PeerMCYSQ includes 21 items representing task-involving and ego-involving higher-order factors, each of which comprises a number of lower-order factors. More specifically, the task-involving factors are improvement, relatedness support, and effort, and the ego-involving factors are intrateam competition and ability and intrateam conflict. The lower-order factors included in the PeerMCYSQ represent a more parsimonious set of the task- and ego-involving dimensions that emerged from Vazou et al.'s (2005) qualitative work. The PeerMCYSQ does not measure all 11 dimensions that emerged from the qualitative analysis

because (a) some of the dimensions were conceptually similar and collapsed together into one factor when subjected to exploratory factor analysis, (b) it would be difficult from a measurement point of view to obtain good model fit indices with an 11-factor model, and (c) we wanted to balance parsimony (i.e., a model with relatively few common factors) with plausibility (i.e., a model with sufficient common factors to account for the correlations among measured variables) (Fabrigar, Wegener, MacCallum, & Strahan, 1999).

We believe that the five factors that emerged from the series of factor analyses are a good representation of the 11 dimensions that emerged from the qualitative work of Vazou et al. (2005). In many cases, the factors combine two dimensions. For example, the improvement factor includes items not only from the improvement dimension but also from the cooperation dimension. In the same way, relatedness support has also items from the equal treatment dimension, and intrateam conflict also captures the "negative reactions" raw data themes of the mistakes dimension. The items of the questionnaire are presented in table 11.2. Participants respond to the stem "On this team, most athletes . . .," and responses are indicated on a 7-point scale ranging from 1 *(strongly disagree)* to 7 *(strongly agree)*.

The psychometric properties of the PeerMCYSQ are promising. In the third study reported by Ntoumanis and Vazou (2005), the five-factor solution had acceptable model fit: scaled $\chi^2(179) = 274.26; p < .001$; robust CFI = .95; robust NNFI = .94; SRMR = .04; and RMSEA = .05. A hypothesized hierarchical version of the PeerMCYSQ with two higher-order factors, underpinned by three and two lower-order factors, respectively (task-involving climate: improvement, relatedness support, effort; ego-involving climate: intrateam competition and ability, intrateam conflict), also had good model fit. Specifically, the fit indices of the hierarchical model were as follows: scaled $\chi^2(184) = 301.15; p < .001$; robust CFI = .94; robust NNFI = .93; SRMR = .04; and RMSEA = .06.

In addition, intraclass correlation coefficients and multilevel CFA were conducted to examine if there were variations in the perceptions of peer climate among teams and whether such variations affect the factorial structure of the PeerMCYSQ at the within- and between-teams levels (Heck, 2001). The results showed that there was some variation in the athletes' perceptions of the five peer climate factors across the different teams, with intraclass correlations ranging from 9% to 19%. The implications of such variations are discussed later in the chapter. Despite these variations, the multilevel CFA showed very good fit for the five-factor model ($\chi^2(358) = 428.82; p < .01$; NNFI = 1.00; CFI = 1.00; SRMR = .03; RMSEA = .02) and its hierarchical version ($\chi^2(368) = 520.31; p < .01$; NNFI

Table 11.2 The Five-Factor PeerMCYSQ

Factor or item	On this team, most athletes . . .
1. Improvement	1. Help each other improve. 3. Offer to help their teammates develop new skills. 6. Work together to improve the skills they don't do well. 10. Teach their teammates new things.
2. Relatedness support	5. Make their teammates feel valued. 13. Make their teammates feel accepted. 18. Care about everyone's opinion.
3. Effort	11. Encourage their teammates to try their hardest. 15. Praise their teammates who try hard. 17. Are pleased when their teammates try hard. 19. Set an example on giving forth maximum effort. 21. Encourage their teammates to keep trying after they make a mistake.
4. Intrateam competition and ability	2. Encourage each other to outplay their teammates. 4. Care more about the opinion of the most able teammates. 8. Try to do better than their teammates. 12. Look pleased when they do better than their teammates. 14. Want to be with the most able teammates.
5. Intrateam conflict	7. Make negative comments that put their teammates down. 9. Criticize their teammates when they make mistakes. 16. Complain when the team doesn't win. 20. Laugh at their teammates when they make mistakes.

Note. The numbers preceding the items indicate the order of each item in the PeerMCYSQ.

= .99; CFI = .99; SRMR = .11; RMSEA = .02), indicating that the PeerMCYSQ has acceptable factor structures at the within- and between-group levels.

Ntoumanis and Vazou (2005) also examined the reliability of the PeerMCYSQ scales. Specifically, the internal consistency of the five peer motivational climate factors was tested using Cronbach's alpha coefficients. These were acceptable for all factors except for the combined intrateam competition and ability factor, whose coefficient was marginally acceptable (improvement α = .77; relatedness support α = .73; effort α = .70; intrateam competition and ability α = .69; intrateam conflict α = .73). A test–retest reliability assessment over a 4-week period showed acceptable levels of stability for all factors (improvement R = .81; relatedness support R = .77; effort R = .82; intrateam competition and ability R = .81; and intrateam conflict R = .74).

Peer-Created Motivational Climate and Indices of Motivation

An important next step in our research was to examine whether the peer motivational climate can contribute to the prediction of important motivational responses.

That is, we were interested to investigate whether, similar to adult-created climates, a task-involving peer motivational climate would be a better predictor of adaptive motivational outcomes associated with sport participation compared with an ego-involving peer climate. We were also interested to examine whether the peer motivational climate can enhance our prediction of these motivational outcomes in youth sport over and above any prediction made by the coach climate. An ancillary purpose of this line of research was to provide information regarding the criterion validity of the PeerMCYSQ.

The following motivational indices were examined by Vazou, Ntoumanis, and Duda (2006): physical self-esteem, enjoyment, competitive trait anxiety, and sport commitment. Participants were 493 British athletes aged 12 to 17, mainly from team sports, who participated in club and school teams. The findings for each dependent variable are presented below and their implications are discussed.

Physical Self-Esteem

Physical self-esteem, that is, individuals' approval or disapproval of their physical self, is an important component of overall self-esteem for many people (Sonstroem, 1997). Perceptions of a task-involving climate are related to higher self-esteem because in such an environment competence criteria are self-referenced and people are not particularly worried about being evaluated (Ames, 1992). In contrast, sustaining high self-esteem in an ego-involving climate is more problematic because in such environments favorable judgments of the self are contingent upon meeting external criteria, such as achieving normative success and superiority. Reinboth and Duda (2004) have provided empirical support for these predictions. In a study of 265 British adolescents, the researchers found that self-esteem was lowest among athletes with low perceived ability in a coach-created high ego-involving climate. In contrast, in a high task-involving climate, levels of self-esteem were high regardless of athletes' perceived ability. Furthermore, contingent self-esteem was positively predicted by an ego-involving climate.

Besides the coach, peers might also influence young athletes' self-esteem. In a sample of 418 adolescents, Smith (1999) found that peer social acceptance was related to higher levels of physical self-esteem. However, one can argue that peer acceptance can be based on both task- and ego-involving criteria. Therefore, research should examine the independent effects of both facets of the peer motivational climate on physical self-esteem. To this end, Vazou et al. (2006) examined whether perceptions of task- and ego-involving peer motivational climates can predict physical self-esteem (as assessed by the physical self-worth subscale of the children's version of the Physical Self-Perception Profile; Whitehead, 1995) with a sample of 12- to 17-year-old athletes (M = 14.08; SD = 1.29). Vazou et al. (2006) also examined whether the perceived peer climate can predict physical self-esteem independent of coach climate (as assessed by the PMCSQ-2) by entering the two climates in different steps of the regression analysis.

The results showed that only a task-involving peer climate was a significant predictor of physical self-esteem (β = .20; p < .001). Thus, athletes who perceived that their peers emphasized personal improvement and effort criteria for success and who felt accepted and supported by their peers had more positive evaluations of their physical self. The nonsignificant independent prediction made by the coach task climate is surprising but could be explained when viewed in conjunction with previous findings, which demonstrate the prominent role of peers as a source of competence information during late childhood and adolescence (Horn & Amorose, 1998).

Enjoyment

Enjoyment has been identified as a key reason for participation in youth sport (Brustad et al., 2001; Weiss & Petlichkoff, 1989), and it has been positively associ-

Enjoyment in youth sport is linked to perceptions of a task-involving peer climate.

ated with perceptions of a task-involving coach motivational climate (e.g., Goudas, 1998; Newton & Duda, 1999). This is probably because in a task-involving climate there is no pressure to outperform others or to demonstrate normative superiority. Furthermore, in a task-involving climate, children acquire reasons for learning and improvement that can increase the quality of their involvement and their intrinsic interest (Ames, 1992).

In relation to our work, Vazou et al.'s (2006) findings indicated that greater enjoyment (measured with the interest–enjoyment subscale of the Intrinsic Motivation Inventory; McAuley, Duncan, & Tammen, 1989) was linked to perceptions that the peer climate was task-involving ($\beta = .32; p < .001$). Perceptions of a coach-created task-involving climate also predicted enjoyment, but to a smaller extent ($\beta = .17; p < .01$). These results suggest that higher enjoyment is more likely when, in addition to the coach, one's peers also transmit task-involving cues. In a related study, Carr et al. (1999) used a sample of 151 young students to examine the relative influence of parents, teachers, and peers on the students' enjoyment of physical education class. The results showed that students' perception of a task-involving climate promoted by peers was the only significant predictor of students' enjoyment and interest in the class. Taken together, the Vazou et al. and Carr et al. studies indicate the importance of assessing the peer climate when examining young people's positive affective experiences in physical activity settings.

Competitive Trait Anxiety

A perceived ego-involving motivational climate that emphasizes normative success and superiority and penalizes athletes for making mistakes is likely to result in negative affective outcomes such as feelings of anxiety. Existing research findings on the coach-created motivational climate support the link between indicators of performance climate and negative affect (Papaioannou & Kouli, 1999; Seifriz et al., 1992; Yoo, 2003).

As far as peer climate is concerned, Carr and colleagues (1999) found that children felt more pressured in physical education classes when they perceived that they would be penalized by their peers for making mistakes. In Vazou et al.'s (2006) study, although a perceived ego-involving peer climate did not predict trait anxiety (measured with the Sport Anxiety Scale; Smith, Smoll, & Schutz, 1990), perceptions of a coach-created ego climate did ($\beta = .24; p < .001$). The nonsignificant finding for ego-involving peer climate is surprising, but it could be attributed to the fact that coaches have the highest authority on a team and are therefore more likely to invoke feelings of doubt and apprehension in athletes. Future studies are needed to further test the

link between the peer motivational climate and negative affect by employing more situation-specific (i.e., state) measures of anxiety, looking at the potential moderator role of perceived competence, and examining other indicators of negative affect (e.g., tension, boredom).

Sport Commitment

Sport commitment refers to the desire and resolve to continue sport participation (Scanlan, Simons, Carpenter, Schmidt, & Keeler, 1993). This variable is a function of both individual and social factors, such as levels of enjoyment, social constraints to continue participation, and social support provided by significant others (Carpenter, 1995). The influence of social support and peer acceptance on individual commitment to sport has received empirical support. For example, Weiss and Smith (2002), using a sample of 191 young male and female tennis athletes, found friendship quality to predict higher tennis commitment and dedication to play in the future.

In our work, we were interested to examine whether the perceived peer and coach motivational climates contribute to the prediction of young people's self-reported sport commitment. Indeed, our study (Vazou et al., 2006) found commitment to be significantly predicted by both the coach ($\beta = .13; p < .01$) and peer ($\beta = .25; p < .001$) task-involving motivational climates, but the prediction of the latter was stronger. A follow-up analysis using the PeerMCYSQ subscales showed that commitment was predicted by the improvement ($\beta = .16; p < .001$) and relatedness support ($\beta = .12; p < .05$) facets of a task-involving peer climate.

These findings make conceptual sense. The emphasis by peers on individual improvement offers more opportunities for young athletes to learn and master skills, and such opportunities serve as antecedents of sport commitment (Scanlan et al., 1993). Furthermore, a sense of relatedness enhances young athletes' perceptions of peer support and acceptance, variables that underlie their commitment and desire to continue sport involvement (Carpenter, 1995; Scanlan et al., 1993).

Age and Gender Differences in Perceptions of the Peer-Created Motivational Climate

The empirical work on peer motivational climate reviewed so far, although scarce, suggests that the peer-oriented environment can predict important indices of motivation in youth sport. However, it is interesting and of practical importance to examine whether perceptions of the peer motivational climate vary as a function of individual or situational factors, such as gender, age, competitive level, sport experience, and type of sport. This issue needs to be investigated so that researchers can build more flexible and effective interventions to promote task-involving climate in youth sport.

Our preliminary work (Vazou et al., 2006) has started addressing this question by looking at gender and age differences in the perceptions of peer climate. The results show significant gender differences, with males scoring higher on perceptions of an ego-involving peer climate and females scoring higher on perceptions of a task-involving peer climate. Similar gender differences have also been found in relation to coach- and parent-created climates (Kavussanu & Roberts, 1996; White, Kavussanu, & Guest, 1998). It is possible that such gender differences in perceptions of the motivational cues transmitted by adults and peers reflect different socialization experiences in sport, with boys being exposed to more ego-involving motivational practices (Lewko & Greendorfer, 1988). Such coaching or parental motivational practices can be internalized and reinforced by the peer group. However, it is also possible that the gender differences partly reflect developmental processes.

This speculation is corroborated by the significant gender–age interaction predicting an ego-involving peer motivational climate. This interaction indicated that among older athletes (14-17 years), males perceived the peer climate to be more ego-involving compared with females. However, in the younger age group (12-13 years), both males and females reported similar perceptions of an ego-involving peer climate. Thus, it seems that gender differences in the perceptions of ego-involving practices of peers are evident only as athletes move from late childhood to adolescence, when the differentiation of ability and effort is assumed to be complete (Nicholls, 1989).

We also examined potential age differences in the peer motivational climate by comparing younger and older athletes (Vazou et al., 2006). Such effects are not so interesting in the presence of a significant age–gender interaction. However, they are briefly presented here for readers who might be interested in these results. Older athletes perceived more intrateam conflict than younger ones. In contrast, younger athletes perceived their peers to be more supportive, but at the same time they also perceived them to use more normatively referenced criteria for competence evaluation and to encourage intrateam competition. These results do not indicate any clear age differences in perceptions of an ego-involving peer climate, as both groups differ in different facets of this climate. Clearly, these results have to be replicated before any firm conclusions can be made.

Between-Group Variations in Perceptions of the Peer-Created Motivational Climate

Using the total sample of athletes reported in the second and third studies of Ntoumanis and Vazou (2005), Vazou (2004) examined whether perceptions of peer climate varied among 41 club and school teams and the factors that might account for such potential variations. Her work showed significant between-team variations, indicating that perceptions of peer climate differ somewhat from team to team (see also Papaioannou, Marsh, & Theodorakis, 2004, for similar findings with regard to the teacher climate in physical education).

Specifically, as far as the task-involving peer climate is concerned, 11.67% of its variance was distributed between teams. Using multilevel modeling, a number of variables at the individual and team levels were found to predict task-involving peer climate and to partly account for its between-teams variability. At the individual level, high task orientation and low ego orientation corresponded to a more task-involving peer climate. At the group level, the success record of the team was a significant positive predictor, with higher perceptions of task-involving peer climate being associated with more successful teams. Moreover, the gender of the coach was a significant predictor, with female coaches being associated with higher levels of a perceived task-involving peer climate. These explanatory variables were able to account for 80.72% of the between-group variance in the perceptions of a task-involving peer climate.

With regard to the ego-involving peer climate, 16.35% of its variance was distributed at the between-group level. Three individual variables were found to partly account for such variation. Specifically, ego goal orientation was a significant predictor, with higher levels of ego orientation being associated with higher levels of ego-involving peer climate. Athlete gender and age were also significant predictors, with boys and older athletes (14-17 years) reporting stronger perceptions of ego-involving climate than girls and younger athletes (12-13 years). At the group level, the success record of the team was the only significant predictor, with higher perceptions of ego-involving peer climate being associated with less successful teams. These explanatory variables accounted for 82.86% of the between-group variance in the perceptions of ego-involving peer climate.

In brief, the evidence reported by Vazou (2004) indicates that although most of the variation in athletes' perceptions of peer climate is idiosyncratic, some variation (11%-16%) can be attributed to their sport grouping. Further research on peer- and adult-created environment is needed using multilevel analysis, because treating athletes as if they are independent of their team ignores the complexity inherent in motivational climate data and can introduce some biases into the statistical analysis (Heck, 2001).

Future Research

The increasing attention dedicated to peer relationships in youth sport over the last few years has resulted in a growing body of knowledge. However, as Brustad and Partridge (2002) have commented, a great deal remains unknown about the role of peers in youth sport. In this chapter, we have argued that we need to know more about the motivational climate created by peers in youth sport and how the different facets of this climate predict important motivational responses. Our work offers preliminary evidence to support the importance of measuring the peer climate in youth sport. However, other questions need to be answered in order to have a more complete understanding of the origins of peer climate, its potentially dynamic nature, how it interrelates with the motivational climate created by adults, and how it affects young athletes' quality and extent of sport involvement.

With regard to the origins of the peer-created motivational climate, an interesting question that arises is how such a climate is created and how it develops over time. The existing research evidence is too limited to offer an answer to this question. We believe that on a newly formed team the coach climate would probably dominate. However, with the passage of time, athletes get to know each other and peer influence starts to shape a particular peer motivational climate.

To some extent, the creation of the peer climate will be the outcome of coach climate. However, peer climate might also develop from other sources, such as the achievement goal dispositions of a few dominant players on the team, the parent-created climate, or the climate promoted by sporting heroes (Carr et al., 2000). Therefore, peers can convey motivational cues that are compatible or incompatible to the cues promoted by the coach. For example, it is possible that even when the coach tries to promote task-involving criteria for recognition and evaluation, the peers might, to some extent, transmit ego-involving criteria to their teammates. In order to fit in, some young athletes will try to conform to the perspective promoted by their peers. After all, adolescence is a period when most young people rebel against adults, challenging their norms and values and paying more emphasis to peer norms (Cobb, 1994).

Our research has shown that the coach- and peer-created motivational climates are interrelated but relatively independent constructs. Specifically, Vazou et al. (2006) showed that the correlation between the two task-involving facets was $r = .49$, similar to the correlation between the ego-involving facets ($r = .45$). Furthermore, in the same study it was shown that the two types of climate can have additive effects on young athletes' motivational indices. Interaction effects between the coach and peer climate were also tested; however, these effects were not significant. Considering the very limited work that has been conducted in this area to date, future research is essential in order to further understand the potential interplay between the coach and peer climates. To this end, longitudinal designs can be instrumental in testing the strength and direction of such relationships over time.

Future investigations might also examine the motivational consequences of being on a team where the prevailing coach- and peer-created motivational climates are contradictory. For example, as a result of media influences, some peers might glorify the demonstration of normative ability and might promote interindividual comparison. Such practices might result in a strong ego-involving peer climate despite the efforts of the coach to transmit task-involving cues. Parents are also significant others who can influence the motivation of young athletes (White et al., 1998; see also White, this volume). Therefore, future research should examine the role of parent-created climate in youth sport in conjunction with the coach- and peer-created climates.

Another interesting avenue for future research is to study whether there are significant within-team variations in the perceptions of peer climate and, if so, what implications these might have for applied work. It is important to examine such within-team variations because interventions to promote a task-involving motivational climate assume that members of the same team are viewing the same "motivational picture," which might not always be the case (see Duda, 2001). Factors such as the size of the team and the type of sport (individual vs. team) might account for such within-team variations and should be considered by future research. For example, it is possible that perceptions of peer climate are more homogeneous in smaller teams and in teams whose members have been together over a number of years.

Furthermore, future qualitative work is needed to examine how young athletes arrive at certain judgments regarding the peer climate on their team. For example, an interesting question to ask is whether perceptions of peer climate on a team are tied to a few young athletes with dominant personalities or whether such perceptions are much broader and encompass the responses of whole team.

In this chapter we showed how the peer-created motivational climate relates to a number of important motivational indices in youth sport. However, our list of such motivational-related responses is by no means exhaustive. In order to further test the contribution of peer climate to young peoples' sport experiences, other outcome variables should be assessed. For example, the relationship of task- and ego-involving motivational climates with moral development and aggression should be investigated. Previous research suggests that positive peer relationships can help athletes develop moral sensitivity, enhance their moral reasoning, and help them act in a prosocial manner (Weiss & Stuntz, 2004). Furthermore, the relationship between peer climate and key consturcts embedded in self-determination theory (Deci & Ryan, 1985) should be examined, in view of previous findings suggesting associations between the climate created by the coach or physical education teacher, psychological need satisfaction (Sarrazin et al., 2001), and self-determined motivation (Ntoumanis, 2001).

Practical Implications

Theoretical knowledge regarding the motivational climate has been increasingly put into practice in a number of intervention studies in physical education and sport (e.g., Papaioannou & Kouli, 1999; Solmon, 1996; Theeboom, DeKnop, & Weiss, 1995). This type of work is important because it provides tangible evidence that teacher- and coach-created climates can be structured in ways that foster student motivation. These intervention studies have manipulated the adult-created motivational climate by promoting task-involving motivational cues and downplaying ego-involving situational goal structures and practices (Treasure, 2001).

Even though we acknowledge the importance of coaches and teachers in determining the quality of young peoples' experiences in sport and physical education, we suggest that future intervention work should also consider how the peer-created motivational climate can be optimized in these settings. This is important considering the research evidence reported in this chapter, which demonstrates that peer influence can predict athletes' achievement-related responses in youth sport independent of the coach climate.

For example, cooperative group learning can be used to enhance athletes' perception of relatedness support from their teammates. When athletes work together to learn or practice skills or when they strive to achieve cooperative goals, they are more likely to feel accepted and related to their peers. Moreover, whenever new athletes are included on a team the coach should give them opportunities to socialize with their teammates and establish friendships. This can be done, for example, by organizing social events outside training or by allocating time during training for the athletes to interact at a social level. The development of such friendships

can foster a task-involving peer climate. This is corroborated by some quotes from Vazou et al.'s (2005) interviews of young athletes: "They make you really good friends so you don't compare yourself to them and how good they are" (13-year-old girl, hockey), and "We are all together, we get on very well, very close, so it's a lot easier for us to give constructive criticism to each other rather than trying to make people feel bad" (16-year-old girl, hockey).

Also, athletes should be encouraged to praise their teammates' improvements and to evaluate them on the basis of self-referenced criteria. Some examples from the interviews of young athletes in the Vazou et al. (2005) study exemplify the importance of peer encouragement and praise: "If I don't win a medal, they [teammates] would still find something positive about my performance, which cheers me up" (15-year-old boy, judo), and "They [teammates] encourage me and I feel more confident to try and improve my weaknesses, and I don't worry about how I am compared to other people" (15-year-old girl, hockey).

Summary

Research examining how peers influence young people's achievement motivation in sport is limited. To this end, research by Vazou and colleagues has examined the nature of the peer-created motivational climate in youth sport and how it relates to important motivational variables. Based on a combination of qualitative and quantitative methodologies, a valid and reliable questionnaire assessing the peer-created climate (PeerMCYSQ) was developed. This questionnaire measures task-involving (improvement, relatedness support, and effort) and ego-involving (intrateam competition and ability and intrateam conflict) facets of the peer climate. Preliminary empirical evidence indicates that a perceived peer-created motivational climate can meaningfully relate to important motivational indices such as physical self-esteem, enjoyment, and commitment.

Research on the peer-created motivational climate is still in its infancy and many questions await exploration. In this chapter, questions regarding the origins of the peer climate, its relationship with the motivational climates created by coaches and parents, and its potential variability within and between teams were discussed, along with avenues for future research. An integrative framework that fosters the task-involving facets of both the adult and peer climates might hold the greatest potential for intervention work in this area. The area of the peer-created motivational climate offers exciting opportunities for researchers interested in youth sport, and we hope that the evidence presented in this chapter will motivate them to join our research journey.

Discussion Questions

1. Describe and give examples of the task-involving and ego-involving dimensions that define the peer-created motivational climate in youth sport, as identified by Vazou et al. (2005).

2. Present the research findings to date regarding the relationship of the peer-created motivational climate to important motivational indices in youth sport. What are the implications of these findings?

3. Identify priorities for future research on the peer-created motivational climate and justify their importance.

4. Discuss possible ways of building a more task-involving peer-created motivational climate on a team. What are some possibilities beyond what was suggested in the chapter?

part IV

Key Social and Cognitive Processes in Sport

Self-concept defines how athletes perceive themselves in the sport context, and self-efficacy and efficacy beliefs determine the extent to which they consider themselves able to competently execute a task independently and with the cooperation of others. People have perceptions about their own and others' abilities as well as views about how they wish to be perceived by others. Part 4 of this volume focuses on these and other concerns and includes self-concept, efficacy beliefs in group and relational contexts, person perception, and self-handicapping as a strategy of self-presentation.

In chapter 12, Herb Marsh provides an account of self-concept where historical, definitional, theoretical, operational, and measurement issues are unraveled. Marsh defines self-concept, explains its role as an outcome and mediating variable in research, and underlines its multidimensional nature. The development and validation of the Self-Description Questionnaire and its variations are addressed and empirical research that involves experimental, cross-sectional, cross-cultural, and longitudinal research designs using these measures is then discussed. Exciting new opportunities for research are outlined, and a section on practical implications highlights the importance of applied research in this area.

In chapter 13, Mark Beauchamp presents a clear and concise treatment of efficacy beliefs. He begins by locating the notion of efficacy beliefs within a broader theoretical framework, namely, social-cognitive theory. Four types of efficacy are presented (role efficacy, collective efficacy, coaching efficacy, and relational efficacy), and explanatory, theoretical, and empirical aspects are addressed. Given the relative recency of efficacy beliefs in sport psychology, the potential for more research is considerable and Beauchamp puts forward interesting directions. The final section on practical implications highlights the idea that efficacy beliefs can be enhanced if one pays attention to the sources that have been found to be related to each type of efficacy.

In chapter 14, Iain Greenlees discusses the notion of person perception as a component of the wider social or interpersonal perception area of study in social psychology. Greenlees uses three perspectives to explain the process by which individuals form impressions of target individuals: schema-driven impression formation, data-driven impression formation, and an integration of the two. The following discussion of research deals with person perception among coaches, athletes, and officials. Research suggestions include a theoretically driven approach to test specific hypotheses from a qualitative and quantitative paradigm. From a practical viewpoint, it is recommended that interventions be developed in order to assist athletes in using their own presentation to project a desired impression to an opponent.

In chapter 15, Ralph Maddison and Harry Prapavessis offer information on a self-presentational strategy known as self-handicapping. Influential research associated with self-handicapping is presented, theoretical developments related to the distinction between behavioral and self-reported self-handicaps are put forward, and associated costs are discussed. Research that addresses the impact of social, personal, and environmental factors on athletes' self-handicapping is also cited. Future research directions include a focus on both substantive and measurement studies of self-handicapping. Practically, this chapter offers two main directions; one focuses on evidence-based intervention and the other focuses on practical guidance for coaches and athletes.

chapter 12

Physical Self-Concept and Sport

Herbert W. Marsh, PhD

Learning Objectives

On completion of this chapter, the reader should have

1. familiarity with multidimensional, hierarchical models of self-concept;

2. knowledge of physical self-concept as an important outcome variable as well as a key to facilitating other desirable outcomes;

3. understanding of a construct approach to validity and the difference between within-network and between-network studies;

4. knowledge of the differences between convergent and discriminant validity; and

5. comprehension of the rationale for the reciprocal effects model of relations between self-concept and performance.

AP Photo/Mark Baker

Seligman and Csikszentmihalyi (2000) and many others (e.g., Vallerand et al., 2003) have argued that a revolution is sweeping psychology, one that emphasizes a positive psychology and focuses on how healthy, normal, and exceptional individuals can get the most from life. A positive self-concept is valued as a desirable outcome in many disciplines of psychology such as sport, exercise, mental and physical health, personality, development, education, and social psychology.

Researchers in sport psychology with a focus on other constructs are often interested in how constructs in their research are related to self-concept because self-concept is frequently posited as a mediating variable that facilitates the attainment of other desired outcomes such as physical skills, health-related physical fitness, physical activity, and exercise adherence (Fox & Corbin, 1989; Marsh, 1997, 2002; Sonstroem, 1978) in nonelite settings, and improved motivation and performance in elite sport. For example, if an intervention or training program unintentionally undermines self-concept, then it is unlikely to have long-lasting effects on the desired outcome. In contrast, if the intervention enhances self-concept as well as the desired outcomes (e.g., performance of fitness), then the effects are likely to be more long-lasting. The rationale behind this expectation is that individuals who perceive themselves to be more effective, confident, and able are individuals who accomplish more than those with less positive self-perceptions ("I believe, therefore I can").

Research on self-concept has a long, controversial history, and it is one of the oldest areas of research in the social sciences. The longest chapter in William James' 1890 textbook, the first introductory psychology textbook, was devoted to self-concept and introduced many issues of current relevance. Despite this rich beginning, advances in theory, research, and measurement of self-concept were slow during the heyday of behaviorism in the middle of the 20th century. Before the 1980s, reviewers typically emphasized the lack of theoretical basis in most studies, the poor quality of measurement instruments used to assess self-concept, methodological shortcomings, and a general lack of consistent findings. Similar observations led Hattie (1992) to describe this period as one of "dustbowl empiricism" in which the predominant research design in self-concept studies was "throw it in and see what happens." In contrast, there have been exciting new developments in self-concept over the last two decades with particular relevance to social psychology in sport.

Critical Issues in Self-Concept Research

Self-concept is defined as how a person perceives himself or herself. It includes feelings of self-confidence, self-worth, self-acceptance, competence, and ability. Self-concept is *not* defined by how other people (e.g., teachers, friends, parents) view a person, although these people can influence self-concept development. Self-concept perceptions are formed through experience with and interpretations of one's environment. Self-concept is also influenced by the evaluations of significant others (e.g., coaches, peers, teachers, parents); experiences of positive and negative reinforcement; and taking responsibility for one's own successes. Self-concept is multidimensional, as it is composed of many different facets. For example, a person can have a good self-concept in mathematics but a poor self-concept in their physical abilities. Self-concept also becomes increasingly multidimensional as a person grows older.

With increasing emphasis on domain-specific measures of self-concept, the distinction between self-concept and self-efficacy becomes blurred. Self-efficacy refers to a more narrowly defined domain than self-concept, but Marsh (1993a; also see Bong & Clark, 1999) noted that this is not an inherent difference—self-concept can be defined in relation to specific domains and self-efficacy can be defined more globally. Instead, Marsh argued that self-efficacy and self-concept responses were likely to differ under the effects of social comparison and frame of reference like those that are the focus of the present investigation. More generally, frame of reference is directly implicated in self-concept measures, as people use the performances of others to establish frames of reference for evaluating their own performances, whereas little emphasis is placed on the criteria, standards, or frames of reference that participants use to evaluate their performances in self-efficacy research.

For example, comparisons with teammates and competitors are likely to influence self-perceptions of oneself as an athlete or a high jumper (self-concept responses), but not, perhaps, of whether one is able to jump 2 meters (self-efficacy response). Bandura (1986) noted that self-esteem and self-concept—but not self-efficacy—are partly determined by "how well one's behavior matches personal standards of worthiness" (p. 410). In support of this theoretical distinction,

Parts of this chapter are based on an invited keynote address at the 10th World Congress on Sport Psychology, Skiathos, Greece, 2001.

Marsh, Walker, and Debus (1991) demonstrated that frames of reference had substantially larger effects on self-concept responses than self-efficacy responses. In support of the importance of this distinction, Marsh (1993a) argued that the self-perceived worthiness of performance expectations in relation to personal and external standards might be central to the motivation and maintenance of performance and the prediction of future performance.

Construct-Validity Approach

Self-concept, like many psychological constructs, suffers in that everybody knows what it is, but few feel compelled to provide a theoretical definition of what they are measuring. Because self-concept is a hypothetical construct, its usefulness must be established by within-network and between-network studies of its construct validity. Within-network studies explore the internal structure of self-concept. They test, for example, the dimensionality of self-concept and may seek to show that the construct has consistent, distinct multidimensional components (e.g., physical, social, academic self-concepts). These studies typically employ empirical techniques such as factor analysis or multitrait–multimethod (MTMM) analysis. Between-network studies attempt to establish a logical, theoretically consistent pattern of relations between measures of self-concept and other constructs. The resolution of at least some within-construct issues should be a logical prerequisite to conducting between-construct research.

A construct-validation approach to the measurement of self-concept in general and of physical self-concept in elite and nonelite sport settings more specifically is clearly consistent with historical trends in sport psychology in which there is general agreement among researchers for the need to develop psychological measures that are specific to sport settings and to evaluate them within a construct-validity framework. More specifically, Gill, Dzewaltowski, and Deeter (1988) concluded that "within sport psychology the most promising work on individual differences involves the development and use of sport-specific constructs and measures" (p. 139-140). They argued for the construction of multidimensional instruments based on theory, followed by item and reliability analysis, exploratory and confirmatory factor analysis, tests of convergent and divergent validity, validation in relation to external criteria, and application in research and practice. Marsh and Craven (1997) argued that much of the failure of early self-concept research stemmed from inadequate attention to the development of psychometrically strong measures implicated in the within-network aspects of construct validity.

Shavelson Model

One cornerstone of the resurgence of self-concept research in the last 25 years is the classic review article by Shavelson, Hubner, and Stanton (1976). This review provided a theoretical blueprint for the development of the many self-concept instruments considered in this chapter (see Marsh & Hattie, 1996, for a more detailed evaluation of the Shavelson model and its influence on subsequent self-concept research). Shavelson et al. noted critical deficiencies in self-concept research, including inadequate definitions of the self-concept construct, a dearth of appropriate measurement instruments, and the lack of rigorous tests of counterinterpretations. They concluded, "It appears that self-concept research has addressed itself to substantive problems before problems of definition, measurement, and interpretation have been resolved" (p. 470).

Shavelson et al. (1976) began by integrating various definitions of self-concept. They identified seven features that were critical to their definition of self-concept. The most important features for present purposes are that self-concept is multifaceted and hierarchically organized with perceptions of personal behavior in specific situations at the base of the hierarchy; inferences about self in broader domains (e.g., social, physical, and academic) at the middle of the hierarchy; and a global, general self-concept at the apex (see figure 12.1). Consistent with a large amount of subsequent research in support of the Shavelson et al. model, Marsh and colleagues (see Marsh & Craven, 1997) argued for the importance of a multidimensional perspective of self-concept in which researchers focus on specific components of self-concept rather than relying on a unidimensional approach that only considers a single global self-concept scale (typically referred to as self-esteem). Fortunately, in sport and exercise research (Fox & Corbin, 1989; Marsh, 1997, 2002; Sonstroem, 1978), there is broad acceptance of this multidimensional perspective in which researchers focus on physical self-concept and particular components of physical self-concept in addition to, or instead of, measures of self-esteem.

Self-Description Questionnaires

When Shavelson et al. (1976) first developed their model, there was only modest support for the hypothesized domains and no instrument was available to differentiate among even the broad academic, social, and physical domains. In order to address these concerns, the Self-Description Questionnaire (SDQ) instruments

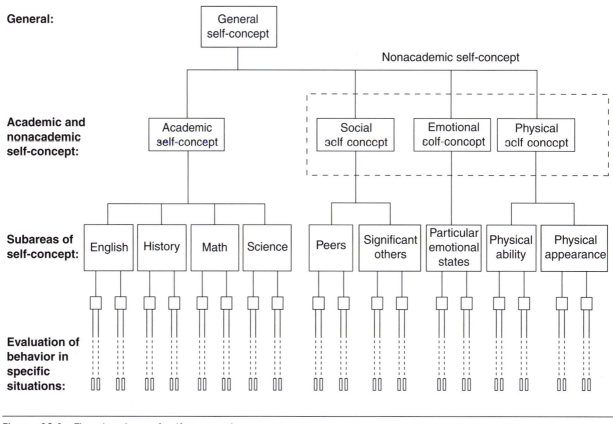

Figure 12.1   The structure of self-concept.

were developed by Marsh and colleagues for preadolescent primary school students (SDQI), adolescent high school students (SDQII), and late adolescents and young adults (SDQIII). (See table 12.1 for a summary of the factors measured by each of the three instruments.) Here the development of the SDQ instruments is reviewed with a particular emphasis on physical self-concept and its relevance to sport psychology.

Marsh developed this set of self-concept instruments with a particular emphasis on a within-network approach to construct validation. In this early SDQ research, Marsh critically evaluated the psychometric properties of the SDQ instruments. SDQ scales were posited on the basis of Shavelson et al.'s (1976) model. Item pools were constructed for each scale, and factor analyses and item analyses were used to select and refine the items used to represent each scale (see table 12.1). The internal consistency of the scales from the three SDQ instruments was good—typically in the .80s and .90s.

The stability of SDQ responses was also good, particularly for older children. For example, the stability of SDQIII scales measured on four occasions varied from

a median of .87 for a 1-month interval to a median of $r = .74$ for intervals of 18 months or longer. Dozens of factor analyses by diverse samples differing in gender, age, country, and language have consistently identified the factors that each SDQ instrument is designed to measure. Marsh (1989; also see Marsh, 1990) summarized factor analyses of more than 12,000 sets of responses from the normative archives of the three SDQ instruments.

In addition to clearly identifying all of the factors that each of the three SDQ instruments is designed to measure, the results indicate that the domains of self-concept are remarkably distinct (median rs among the SDQ scales vary between .1 and .2 for the three SDQ instruments). Hence, the correlations among the different SDQ factors were so low as to call into question the usefulness of a hierarchical or global self-concept measure. These extremely small correlations are also in marked contrast to earlier conclusions that self-concept was unidimensional or that the factors were so highly correlated that they could not be distinguished. In retrospect, it seems that empirical results based on poor measures and, perhaps, misinterpretation of statistical

Table 12.1   Summary of Scales on the Self-Description Questionnaire (SDQ) I, II, and III

Physical ability (SDQI, II, III)	Student perceptions of their skills and interest in sports, games, and physical activities
Physical appearance (SDQI, II, III)	Student perceptions of their physical attractiveness, how their appearance compares with others, and how others think they look
Peer relationships (SDQI only)	Student perceptions of how easily they make friends, their popularity, and whether others want them as a friend
Opposite-sex relationships (SDQII, III)	Student perceptions of their popularity with members of the opposite sex, how easily they make friends with members of the opposite sex, and the quality of their interactions with members of the opposite sex
Same-sex relationships (SDQII, III)	Student perceptions of their popularity with members of the same sex, how easily they make friends with members of the same sex, and the quality of their interactions with members of the same sex
Honesty/trustworthiness (SDQII, III)	Student perceptions of their honesty, reliability, and trustworthiness
Parent relationships (SDQI, II, III)	Student perceptions of how well they get along with their parents, whether they like their parents, and the quality of their interactions with their parents
Spiritual values/religion (SDQIII only)	Student perceptions of themselves as a spiritual or religious person and the importance of spiritual or religious beliefs in how they conduct their life
Emotional stability (SDQII, III)	Student perceptions of themselves as being calm and relaxed, their emotional stability, and how much they worry
Global esteem (SDQI, II, III)	Student perceptions of themselves as effective, capable individuals who have self-confidence and self-respect and are proud and satisfied with the way they are
Read/verbal (SDQI, II, III)	Student perceptions of their ability and interest in reading (for the SDQI); student perceptions of their verbal skills, verbal reasoning ability, and interest in verbal activities (for the SDQII, III)
Math (SDQI, II, III)	Student perceptions of their mathematical skills, mathematical reasoning ability, and interest in mathematics
School (SDQI, II, III)	Student perceptions of their skills, ability, and interest in school subjects in general
Problem solving (SDQIII only)	Student perceptions of their ability to solve problems and think creatively and imaginatively

Note. Consistent with the theoretical model that is the basis of the SDQ instruments, the number and complexity of the SDQ scales increase from the SDQI (preadolescent, primary school), SDQII (adolescent, high school), and SDQIII (late adolescent, young adult).

analyses had led researchers to inappropriate conclusions (see Marsh & Hattie, 1996). This juxtaposition between results based on the SDQ instruments and the historical context from which this research grew provide a dramatic testimonial for the relevance of the construct-validation approach underpinning SDQ research.

Although these results based on the SDQ instruments provided strong support for the Shavelson et al. (1976) model and the multidimensionality of self-concept, they also posed some complications. The strong hierarchical structure posited by Shavelson et al. required self-concepts to be substantially correlated, but the small sizes of correlations actually observed implied that the hierarchical structure of the self-concept responses must be much weaker than anticipated. This eventually led to a revision (see Marsh & Shavelson, 1985) of the original model. Because the revision emphasized the academic components of the model, it is not particularly relevant to the physical focus of this chapter. However, this revision of the model should be viewed as a strength of the research program. In an active research program—particularly in its early stages—theory should be dynamic so that it grows with concurrent developments in measurement, research, and practice. Based on this research, Marsh (1990, 1993a) argued that self-concept researchers and practitioners should measure self-concept at a level of specificity consistent with their particular concerns as well as, perhaps, more general measures of academic self-concept and self-esteem.

This early SDQ research also prompted between-network research, primarily in the academic domains of self-concept (see Marsh, 1990, 1993a; Marsh & Craven, 1997 for overviews of research summarized here). Thus, for example, academic achievement is nearly uncorrelated with general and nonacademic domains of self-concept but is substantially related to academic self-concept. As students grow older, the various domains of self-concept become more differentiated (less correlated) and self-concept becomes more predictable from external criteria and from the evaluations of significant others (teachers, parents, and peers).

In longitudinal panel studies, academic self-concept influenced subsequent school grades beyond the contribution of standardized test scores (e.g., IQ) and previous school grades, suggesting that academic self-concept, as well as being correlated with academic achievement, is causally related to academic achievement. Academic self-concept and in particular self-concepts regarding school subjects are also positively related to other academic outcomes such as time spent on homework, academic course selection, and subsequent university attendance. Because self-concept has such a strong effect on what people choose to pursue, it is not surprising that self-concept is also related to accomplishments that follow from these choices.

Physical Self-Concept Scales on the SDQ

SDQ research provides good support for the construct validity of the scales for physical appearance and physical ability that appear on the SDQI, SDQII, and SDQIII instruments (see table 12.1 on page 163). Consistent with the emphasis on the multidimensional perspective to self-concept research, physical ability and physical appearance are distinct components of self-concept. Although physical ability and physical appearance

self-concepts are modestly related to global esteem and the social components of self-concept, they are nearly unrelated to academic and other components of self-concept. In addition, physical ability and appearance self-concepts are not highly related to each other (rs about .2 for the three SDQ instruments). Because these two components of physical self-concept are so distinct, they should be considered separately rather than incorporated into a single score that would conflate the two components.

One approach to between-construct validation is to demonstrate that physical components of self-concept are substantially related to external criteria logically related to them, whereas nonphysical components of self-concepts are much less correlated to these external criteria. Marsh and Jackson (1986) and Marsh and Peart (1988) provided early support of the convergent and discriminant validity of these SDQ scales of physical ability and appearance. These studies showed that the SDQ physical ability self-concept was significantly related to physical fitness, sport participation, physical activity, and body mass index. In contrast, the SDQ physical appearance self-concept was significantly related only to body mass index. Measures of physical fitness were not significantly related to any of the nonphysical factors on the SDQ instruments—including global self-esteem.

In the known group difference approach, groups known to differ on some characteristics related to physical self-concept are identified. If these groups differ substantially in physical self-concept, then there is support for the validity of physical self-concept. In an application of this approach (Marsh, Perry, Horsely, & Roche, 1995; also see Marsh & Jackson, 1986), elite Australian Institute of Sport (AIS) athletes were compared to a large normative sample of nonathletes on the 13 SDQIII scales. In support of convergent validity, athletes had substantially higher physical ability self-concepts than nonathletes. Whereas athletes were somewhat higher on social self-concepts (same sex, opposite sex, parent) and self-esteem, they did not differ from nonathletes on appearance self-concept.

Consistent with the rationale underlying the known group difference approach, group differences were nonsignificant for academic self-concepts (math, verbal, academic, problem solving) and emotional self-concept, whereas athletes had marginally lower spiritual and honesty self-concepts. In general, differences in favor of athletes compared with nonathletes were large for physical self-concept and smaller or nonsignificant for academic and nonphysical self-concepts. This pattern supports a priori predictions and SDQIII construct validity. The specificity of known group differences to particular components of self-concept shows that self-concept cannot be understood if its multidimensionality is ignored.

Experimental Manipulations: Outward Bound Programs

Following from a multidimensional perspective, Marsh (1997; Marsh & Craven, 1997) argued for a construct-validity approach to self-concept interventions in which the specific dimensions of self-concept most relevant to the intervention should be most affected while less relevant dimensions should be less affected and should serve as a control for response biases. This approach was demonstrated in a series of studies based on the Outward Bound program.

The Outward Bound standard course is a 26-day residential program based on physically and mentally demanding outdoor activities (see Marsh, Richards, & Barnes, 1986a, 1986b). It provides a setting for people to recognize and understand their own weaknesses, strengths, and resources and thus find within themselves the wherewithal to master the difficult and unfamiliar (Marsh et al., 1986a, 1986b). Before the study, the Outward Bound director rated the relevance of the 13 SDQIII scales to the goals of the program. Consistent with the primarily nonacademic goals, (a) gains were significantly larger for the SDQIII scales predicted a priori to be most relevant to the goals of the program, (b) the effect sizes were consistent across 27 different Outward Bound groups run by different instructors at different times and in different locations, and (c) the size and pattern of the gains were maintained over an 18-month follow-up period.

In contrast, the Outward Bound bridging course is a 6-week residential program designed to produce significant gains in the academic domain for underachieving adolescent males through an integrated program of remedial teaching, normal schoolwork, and experiences likely to specifically influence academic self-concept (Marsh & Richards, 1988). Consistent with the primarily academic goals, academic self-concept effects were substantial and significantly larger than nonacademic self-concept effects, and there were also corresponding effects on reading and math achievement.

The juxtaposition of these two interventions and their contrasting predictions demonstrates the importance of a multidimensional perspective of self-concept and a construct-validity approach. In both studies, it was also argued that the inclusion of less relevant self-concept scales provided a test for halo effects and placebo-like biases. Hence, the close match between the intent of the intervention and a pattern of results for multiple dimensions of self-concept

supports the construct validity of interpretations of both the intervention itself and the multidimensional self-concept measures used to evaluate the intervention.

Experimental Manipulations: Competitive Versus Cooperative Interventions

Marsh and Peart (1988) contrasted two physical education programs that manipulated performance feedback given to high school girls who were randomly assigned to one of two experimental groups or to a control group. Participants completed a physical fitness test and a multidimensional self-concept instrument (the SDQII, see table 12.1) before and immediately following a 6-week intervention. Two experimental groups participated in aerobics training programs that provided different feedback and motivational cues to students. The competitive group received social-comparison feedback, which emphasized the relative performances of students and focused on whoever performed best for a particular exercise. The cooperative group received improvement feedback, which emphasized individual progress in relation to the students' previous performances. The cooperative group completed exercises in pairs that required participation between partners, whereas the competitive group completed individual exercises.

Both feedback programs significantly enhanced physical fitness relative to pretest scores and in comparison to the control group; there were no differences between these two experimental groups in terms of fitness gains. The improvement feedback also significantly enhanced self-concept of physical ability, but the social-comparison feedback produced a significant decline in physical self-concept. Apparently, the social-comparison feedback forced participants to compare their own physical accomplishments with the participants who were best at each individual exercise to a much greater degree than had been the case before the intervention or in the control group. Even though girls in the social-comparison condition had substantial gains in actual fitness levels, these gains did not translate into increased physical ability self-concept because of the more demanding standards of comparison forced upon them in the classroom environment.

Critical features in this study were frame-of-reference effects and social-comparison processes. Students in the competitive group knew their fitness had improved. However, they were forced to compare their performances with whoever did best in each exercise. Thus, the frame of reference that they used to evaluate their performances changed even more than their fitness levels. The net effect of the competitive intervention on physical ability self-concept was negative. In highly competitive environments, there are likely to be many losers and few winners, and this is likely to lead to lower levels of self-concept.

The research also demonstrates why it is important to assess physical components of self-concept even when the focus is on skill development or fitness enhancement. Without the inclusion of physical self-concept, the competitive intervention would have been evaluated positively, as it was equivalent to the cooperative intervention in terms of short-term fitness enhancement. The inclusion of the multidimensional self-concept instrument demonstrated that unintended negative effects associated with the competitive intervention would likely undermine any long-term gains associated with the intervention. Short-term gains are more likely to be maintained if there is an increase in self-concept. If interventions inadvertently undermine self-concept, short-term gains are unlikely to be maintained (Marsh & Peart, 1988; also see Marsh, 2002; Marsh & Craven, 1997). More generally, as shown in the academic area, physical self-concept and physical performance are likely to have reciprocal effects. The best way to enhance and maintain development in either one is to enhance both.

Physical Self-Concept and Physical Fitness for Boys and Girls

Although not based on SDQ responses, Marsh (1993c) used data from the Australian Health and Fitness survey to relate academic and physical fitness self-concepts to a diverse set of physical fitness indicators and to academic achievement. Participants (aged 9-15) completed surveys measuring self-perceptions of their physical fitness and academic achievement as well as an extensive battery of field and technical indicators of fitness (see Marsh, 1993c, for a more detailed description of the fitness indicators). Physical fitness self-concept was significantly correlated with 12 diverse, objective indicators of fitness (e.g., 1.6Km run, body mass index, maximal oxygen uptake).

Consistent with a priori predictions, physical fitness and academic self-concepts were distinct and became more distinct with age (low correlations and contrasting relations with physical fitness and academic achievement). Validity coefficients relating physical self-concept to objective measures of fitness increased with age. Although there were gender differences in many of the variables considered, relations between fitness measures and physical self-concept were similar for boys and girls.

Physical Self-Description Questionnaire (PSDQ)

Historically, most self-concept instruments have either ignored physical self-concept completely or have treated physical self-concept as a relatively unidimensional domain incorporating characteristics as diverse as fitness, health, appearance, grooming, sporting competence, body image, sexuality, and physical activity into a single score. While the SDQ instrument contains two separate components of physical self-concept (physical ability and appearance), sport psychology research requires a more differentiated approach to physical self-concept in order to provide outcomes that are specifically related to particular criteria and interventions. Such an approach is also consistent with the Shavelson et al. (1976) hierarchical, multidimensional model of self-concept in which self-concept in a particular domain (physical) is divided into more specific components of self-concept within that domain.

This concern led to the development of the Physical SDQ (PSDQ) instrument. Whereas the intent of the SDQ instruments is to provide a broad array of academic, social, physical, and emotional self-concept factors derived from the Shavelson et al. (1976) model, the intent of the PSDQ is to provide a more detailed evaluation of self-concept in the physical domain. The theoretical basis and design of the PSDQ follow research based on the SDQ instruments. PSDQ scales reflect some SDQ scales (physical ability, physical appearance, and esteem) and parallel physical fitness components identified in a confirmatory factor analysis (CFA) of physical fitness measures (Marsh, 1993b), extending Fleishman's (1964) classic research on the structure of physical fitness. The PSDQ (see table 12.2) consists of nine components of physical self-concept, a global physical scale, and a global self-esteem scale. Each PSDQ item is a simple declarative statement and individuals respond using a 6-point true–false scale (as on the SDQII). The PSDQ is designed for adolescents, but should be appropriate for older participants.

Previous PSDQ research demonstrates (a) good reliability (median coefficient α = .92) across the 11 scales (Marsh, 1996b; Marsh, Richards, Johnson, Roche, & Tremayne, 1994); (b) good test–retest stability over short-term periods (Md r = .83 for 11 PSDQ scales, 3 months) and long-term periods (Md r = .69, 14 months; Marsh, 1996b); (c) a well-defined, replicable factor structure as shown by CFA (Marsh, 1996b; Marsh et al., 1994); (d) a factor structure that is invariant over gender as shown by multiple group CFA (Marsh et al., 1994); (e) convergent and discriminant validity as shown by MTMM studies of responses to three physical self-concept instruments (see Marsh et al., 1994, and

Table 12.2   Summary of the Physical Self-Description Questionnaire (PSDQ) Scales

Scale	Summary
Appearance	Being good looking; having a nice face
Strength	Being strong; having a powerful body or lots of muscles
Condition/endurance	Being able to run a long way without stopping; not tiring easily when exercising hard
Flexibility	Being able to bend and turn one's body easily in different directions
Health	Not getting sick often; getting well quickly
Coordination	Being good at coordinated movements; being able to do physical movements smoothly
Activity	Being physically active; doing lots of physical activities regularly
Body fat	Not being overweight; not being too fat
Sport	Being good at sports; being athletic; having good sport skills
Global physical	Feeling positive about one's physical self
Global esteem	Overall positive feelings about self

subsequent discussion); (f) convergent and discriminant validity as shown by PSDQ relations with external criteria (see Marsh, 1996a; 1997); and (g) applicability for subjects aged 12 to 18 (or older) and for elite athletes and nonathletes (Marsh, Hey, Roche, & Perry, 1997). In summary, the PSDQ is a psychometrically strong instrument that is appropriate for a wide variety of sport and exercise research.

Self-concept is increasingly used as an outcome or a mediating variable in research studies throughout the world. Because many self-concept instruments have been developed in English-speaking countries, it is necessary to systematically evaluate the psychometric properties of responses to these instruments when applied in other countries—particularly when an instrument is translated into a different language. Most PSDQ studies have been based on responses to an English-language version of the instrument completed by Australian high school students, so there was no basis for inferring its cross-cultural validity. With these considerations in mind, Marsh, Tomas, and Asci (2002) used CFA to evaluate the cross-cultural generalizability of the factor structure for the PSDQ in Turkey, Spain, and Australia (also see Marsh, Hau, Sung, & Yu, 2005, a study of a Chinese version of the PSDQ). They found support for the invariance of factor loadings across all three countries, and the median coefficient alpha estimates of reliability for each of the three countries were nearly identical. Hence, these results provide very

good support for the cross-cultural generalizability of the components of physical self-concept assessed by the PSDQ as well as the specific items used to infer each of these constructs.

Multitrait–Multimethod Comparison of Three Physical Self-Concept Instruments

The multitrait–multimethod (MTMM) design is used to test convergent, discriminant, and construct validity (see Marsh, 1988, for a general discussion of MTMM designs and analysis). Reviewers of self-concept measurement (e.g., Byrne, 1984; Hattie, 1992; Marsh, 1990; Shavelson et al., 1976; Wylie, 1979, 1989) emphasize the central role of MTMM analyses in the construct validation of self-concept responses. In this approach, multidimensional self-concept instruments purporting to measure the same or substantially overlapping scales are administered to the same group of respondents. The approach consists of a systematic evaluation of correlations between scales from different instruments that are posited to be matching (the same or similar content) and nonmatching. In this approach, convergent validity is supported by large correlations between matching scales from different instruments. Discriminant validity is supported when convergent validities are larger than other correlations, thus supporting the distinctiveness of the components of self-concept.

MTMM analyses also reveal problems in the scores of the interpretation scale based on the label that is attached to them by their author or other researchers (e.g., Marsh, 1994). Thus, for example, the jingle fallacy (Marsh, 1994) occurs when two scales with the same label are inappropriately assumed to measure the same construct, while the jangle fallacy occurs when two scales with different labels are inappropriately assumed to measure different constructs. Given the prevalence of the MTMM design in self-concept research and, more generally, in most areas of psychological measurement, it is surprising that the technique has not been used more widely in sport and exercise research.

The Marsh et al. (1994) study was the first MTMM study of multidimensional physical self-concept instruments; it revealed some important concerns in the three instruments and it provided a model for other physical self-concept research. In the study, students completed three physical self-concept instruments: the PSDQ, Fox's Physical Self-Perception Profile (PSPP; Fox & Corbin, 1989); and Richard's Physical Self-Concept (PSC; Richards, 1988). Fox's PSPP has five scales (physical condition, physical strength, body attractiveness, sport, physical self-worth) that are widely used. Richard's PSC has seven scales (activity, appearance, health, competence, strength, body build, satisfaction) that are remarkably robust over gender and age (10 through 60). Marsh et al. initially compared the content of items from the 23 scales (11 PSDQ, 5 PSPP, 7 PSC). They predicted which scales from different instruments would be most correlated—the convergent validities. The results supported these predictions in that convergent validities were both consistently large and larger than correlations among nonmatching factors (see table 12.3).

Table 12.3   Correlations Among Scales From Three Physical Self-Concept Instruments

Scales	PSDQ 1	2	3	4	5	6	7	8	9	10	11	PSPP 12	13	14	15	16	PSC 17	18	19	20	21	22	23
PSDQ (MARSH)																							
1 Strength	1																						
2 Body fat	05	1																					
3 Physical activity	56	24	1																				
4 Endurance	56	39	68	1																			
5 Sport	64	36	76	72	1																		
6 Coordination	56	46	70	57	78	1																	
7 Health	21	27	24	18	25	37	1																
8 Appearance	39	45	34	38	50	58	14	1															
9 Flexibility	42	36	51	58	47	62	31	34	1														
10 Global physical	50	60	57	50	65	77	36	64	50	1													
11 Global esteem	47	56	49	50	60	66	58	60	56	74	1												
PSPP (FOX)																							
12 Strength	**86**[a]	20	52	51	62	50	23	39	34	47	47	1											
13 Body	42	**61**[b]	36	46	49	53	14	**68**[b]	37	67	51	65	1										
14 Condition	49	45	**73**[b]	**70**[b]	68	58	20	38	45	60	51	67	71	1									
15 Sport	58	38	69	69	**86**[a]	67	25	47	45	59	55	69	70	89	1								
16 Physical self-worth	54	51	57	60	64	62	24	54	45	**81**[a]	68	73	82	85	86	1							
PSC (RICHARDS)																							
17 Strength	**90**[a]	02	48	43	56	47	16	36	31	42	40	**79**[a]	41	40	51	50	1						
18 Body	46	**68**[b]	46	53	58	60	22	65	44	74	63	46	**81**[a]	60	61	70	46	1					
19 Physical activity	44	23	**66**[b]	53	62	54	36	18	33	37	45	40	22	58	63	48	38	35	1				
20 Physical competence	52	33	57	56	69	**84**[a]	32	57	59	59	62	51	49	50	70	65	59	64	58	1			
21 Health	25	10	25	22	28	37	**83**[a]	18	23	32	42	21	12	20	31	22	15	23	41	41	1		
22 Appearance	34	33	34	29	43	52	18	**88**[a]	25	58	51	33	61	33	41	49	41	64	15	54	21	1	
23 Physical satisfaction	28	38	32	38	41	38	20	33	30	39	38	36	39	41	55	42	31	42	32	44	14	26	1

Note. All coefficients vary between 0 and 1 (decimal points are not presented to conserve space). Scales from different instruments that are predicted to be most highly correlated (i.e., the convergent validities in MTMM analysis) are in bold. Each variable was allowed to load on only the factor that it was designed to measure and all other factor loadings were constrained to be zero (see Marsh et al., 1994, for factor loadings and further analyses).

[a] Convergent validities between scales predicted a priori to be most closely matched.

[b] Convergent validities between scales predicted a priori to be less closely matched.

Based on these results, Marsh et al. (1994) concluded that the PSDQ scales for strength, sport, physical activity, coordination, endurance, health, physical appearance, and global physical were substantially correlated with corresponding scales from the other two instruments. However, PSDQ convergent validities were higher than those involving the other two instruments. The PSDQ scale for body fat was distinct from, but related to, the body scales on the other two instruments. However, the PSDQ scales for flexibility and global esteem were not represented on either of the other two instruments. These results support the convergent and discriminant validity of PSDQ responses. The comparison of responses from the PSDQ, PSPP, and PSC instruments (see Marsh et al., 1994, for more detailed discussion) provided a demanding test of the construct validity of the three physical self-concept instruments. Overall, the results supported the convergent and discriminant validity of responses to the three instruments.

It is also of practical importance to evaluate these results in terms of the relative usefulness of the three physical self-concept instruments. Psychometrically, the PSPP appeared to be the weakest of the three instruments for responses by Australian high school students (as opposed, perhaps, to U.S. university students, for whom the instrument was originally designed). The coefficient alpha estimates of reliability were systematically lower for the PSPP than for either of the other instruments. The CFA analyses consistently demonstrated that the PSPP responses had lower trait factor loadings and more measurement error, and there was also evidence suggesting a systematic method effect apparently associated with the nonstandard response scale used on the PSPP. The very large correlations among the PSPP factors seemed to undermine support for the instrument's ability to differentiate among the factors that it was designed to measure.

Furthermore, two of the PSPP scales seem to combine potentially important components of physical self-concept that are measured with separate scales on the PSDQ (e.g., the PSPP condition scale with the PSDQ scales for physical activity and endurance and, perhaps, the PSPP body with PSDQ scales for body fat and appearance). Also, some participants were apparently confused by the idiosyncratic PSPP response scale. For these reasons, Marsh et al. recommended that the PSPP responses by young adolescents be interpreted cautiously and that these concerns be pursued in a replication of their MTMM study with university students for whom the PSPP was designed and, perhaps, with non-Australian students.

The comparison of the PSDQ and PSC was not so straightforward. The PSDQ is a more comprehensive instrument in that it measures a much broader range of physical self-concept components. This was not, however, the intended purpose of the PSC, which was designed to provide a quick, reliable measure of a few components of physical self-concept that were widely applicable across gender and age. Whereas the psychometric properties of the PSDQ appeared to be slightly stronger than those of the PSC, the differences were not substantial. Hence, the major differences seem to be the brevity of the PSC compared to the comprehensiveness of the PSDQ. (Depending on the age of the subjects, the PSC can be completed in 5 to 10 minutes whereas it takes 10 to 15 minutes to complete the PSDQ.)

In a subsequent cross-cultural replication of this MTMM study, Marsh, Asci, and Tomas-Marco (2002) evaluated support for convergent and discriminant validity of PSDQ responses in relation to PSPP responses by 1,041 Turkish university students. In support of construct-validity interpretations, matching PSDQ and PSPP factors were highly correlated. However, support for the PSPP was undermined by extremely high correlations among several of its factors, apparently due in part to a substantial method effect associated with the idiosyncratic response scale used in the PSPP.

Results based on this study with Turkish university students largely replicated and extended findings by Marsh et al. (1994) with Australian high school students. While the Marsh et al. (2002) study extended evaluation of potential problems associated with the idiosyncratic PSPP response scale, the issue had also been noted in the previous research. Hence, the Marsh et al. (2002) study demonstrates the potential usefulness of cross-cultural research in sport psychology and, coupled with previous research demonstrating support for the construct validity of responses to the PSDQ, the results support continued use of the PSDQ in a wide variety of research and applied settings.

Relations to External Criteria

Marsh (1996a) related PSDQ responses to 23 external validity criteria: subjective measures of body composition (silhouette ratings of actual and ideal body image), objective measures of body composition, physical activity participation, endurance, strength, and flexibility. Each criterion was predicted to be most highly correlated to one of the PSDQ scales (see correlations in bold in table 12.4). In support of convergent validity, every predicted correlation (in bold) was significant. In support of discriminant validity, most predicted correlations were larger than other correlations involving the same criterion. This pattern of relations between PSDQ responses and external validity criteria supports the construct validity of PSDQ responses.

Table 12.4 Relations Between Physical Self-Description Questionnaire (PSDQ) Factors and External Validity Criteria

Body composition											
Body mass	**-.69**	-.19	-.17	-.32	.13	-.29	-.25	-.21	-.00	-.32	-.16
Girths	**-.70**	-.21	-.17	-.34	.14	-.33	-.27	-.23	.01	-.31	-.14
Skinfolds	**-.66**	-.23	-.18	-.41	-.10	-.31	-.29	-.37	.00	-.41	-.17
Body comp	**-.72**	-.23	-.20	-.38	.04	-.32	-.30	-.29	-.01	-.37	-.17
Silhouette ratings											
Actual	**-.66**	-.22	-.17	-.39	-.06	-.40	-.38	-.34	-.07	-.43	-.30
Actual-ideal	**-.76**	-.27	-.20	-.40	-.00	-.36	-.36	-.34	-.01	-.48	-.35
Physical activity participation											
Past partici-pation	.21	.20	**.48**	.42	.27	.32	.27	.40	.20	.35	.34
Present par-ticipation	.12	.26	**.59**	.49	.33	.36	.34	.41	.08	.33	.38
Future desire	.04	.23	**.50**	.32	.24	.30	.35	.38	.09	.26	.26
Future intentions	.03	.15	**.54**	.37	.33	.29	.36	.41	.03	.26	.27
Barriers	-.20	-.30	**-.54**	-.49	-.41	-.45	-.50	-.55	-.17	-.47	-.57
Benefits	-.21	-.03	**.24**	.09	.14	.07	.09	.10	.00	-.06	.00
Commit-ment	-.09	.07	**.27**	.16	.23	.14	.25	.18	.11	.07	.09

Activity levels											
Times/typical	.06	.14	**.55**	.48	.40	.32	.38	.39	.08	.26	.32
Hours/typical	.13	.16	**.37**	.36	.29	.28	.32	.30	.17	.24	.25
Last 7 days	.14	.22	**.36**	.39	.30	.26	.31	.41	.17	.26	.25
Endurance											
1.6Km run	-.51	-.22	-.38	**-.63**	-.35	-.37	-.40	-.54	.06	-.48	-.33
Beep test	.42	.14	.35	**.54**	.25	.34	.35	.48	.02	.44	.34
Dynamic/explosive strength											
Basketball throw	.04	.01	.09	.20	**.40**	.15	.17	.27	.04	.21	.23
Pull-up	.35	.15	.22	.38	**.30**	.30	.29	.32	-.01	.28	.26
50m dash	-.32	-.08	-.20	-.35	**-.23**	-.21	-.23	-.29	.03	-.24	-.19
Long jump	.21	.15	.19	.33	**.38**	.26	.35	.37	.01	.24	.27
Flexibility											
Sit and reach	.11	.05	.15	.12	.01	**.37**	.25	.13	-.13	.07	.08

Note. For a more detailed description of this research and the external validity criteria, see Marsh (1996a), from which this table was derived. See table 12.2 for a summary of the PSDQ factors.

Reprinted, by permission, from H.W. Marsh, 1996a, "Construct validity of Physical Self-Description Questionnaire responses: Relations to external criteria," *Journal of Sport & Exercise Psychology* 18(2): 111-131.

Separation of PSDQ Body Fat and Appearance Scales

As noted by Marsh et al. (1994), the PSDQ instrument differs from other multidimensional self-concept instruments by separating body fat from the more general physical appearance self-concept. There is clear support for the separation of these two scales in that they are only moderately correlated. Here, support for the separation of these two factors is evaluated in relation to external criteria of objective measures of body composition (body mass index, multiple measures of body girths, and skinfold measurements from multiple sites; see table 12.4). Consistent with support for the convergent and discriminant validity of these two PSDQ scales, objective body composition is substantially related to PSDQ (lack of) body fat ($r = -.72$) but is much less correlated with PSDQ physical appearance ($r = -.23$). These results support the need for separate scales for PSDQ body fat and physical appearance. Objective measures of body composition are substantially related to PSDQ body fat and are not substantially related to PSDQ physical appearance.

Discrepancy Theory: Actual and Ideal Body Image

William James (1890-1963) emphasized that "we have the paradox of a man shamed to death because he is only the second pugilist or the second oarsman in the world," leading him to conclude that objective accomplishments are evaluated in relation to internal frames of reference. Following from James and others, discrepancy theory posits self-concept as a function of self-perceived differences between actual accomplishments and ideal standards used to evaluate these accomplishments. Unrealistic expectations can lead to poor self-concepts even when accomplishments are otherwise good. Despite a history of criticism and limited empirical support, this discrepancy model has led to a century of heuristic speculation, empirical research, theoretical debate, and conflicting claims.

Marsh and Roche (1996) devised a new test of discrepancy theory based on a silhouette matching task (SMT). Students selected one of nine silhouettes varying on an ectomorphy–endomorphy continuum to represent their actual body image (actual self; what I actually look like today) and ideal body image (ideal self; what I would ideally like to look like). Actual-self silhouette ratings were substantially correlated ($r = .62$) with objective body composition (BMIs, girths, and skinfolds; see table 12.4). While PSDQ body fat was substantially correlated to actual silhouette ratings ($r = .66$), it was even more highly correlated with actual–ideal discrepancies ($r = .76$). Similar (but smaller) patterns of relations were evident for global physical self-concept

and self-esteem. These results show that ratings of actual self contribute positively to self-concept, but high ideal ratings contribute negatively. More complicated models developed by Marsh and Roche (1996) showed that taking account of the direction as well as the size of the actual–ideal discrepancies resulted in even better predictions of self-concept.

Implicit in discrepancy theory is the untested assumption that actual–ideal discrepancies lead to higher or lower self-concepts. However, causal ordering cannot be adequately evaluated with a single wave of data. Marsh (1999) extended previous research by evaluating structural equation models of longitudinal data in which the same silhouette and self-concept ratings were collected on two occasions. This longitudinal design provided a potentially useful approach to the question of whether previous silhouette ratings have any causal effect on subsequent self-concept beyond the substantial influence of previous self-concept. The critical prediction was that previous silhouette ratings contribute to subsequent self-concept ratings beyond the contribution of previous self-concept ratings. Results of these multiwave–multivariable causal models indicated that previous actual and ideal factors influenced subsequent self-concepts beyond the effects of previous self-concepts. Consistent with cognitive discrepancy models, these results imply that a higher actual self and a lower ideal self lead to higher subsequent self-concepts.

Marsh et al. (2005) recently evaluated results based on the PSDQ and silhouette matching task (SMT) of obese (clinical and nonclinical sample) and nonobese Chinese boys and girls and compared the results with Australian research findings. Gender differences were generally much smaller for Hong Kong students across PSDQ factors and particularly for the SMT ideal body image. Hence, whereas actual–ideal discrepancies were much larger for Australian girls (having ideals much thinner than actual body image) than Australian boys, ideal body images were slightly fatter for Hong Kong girls than boys. Obese children accurately perceived themselves as more obese but had ideal body sizes similar to nonobese children.

Objective and subjective measures of body fat (and corresponding obese–nonobese group differences) for Chinese students were negatively related to many components of physical self-concept but were unrelated to global self-esteem and slightly positively related to health self-concept. Whereas actual–ideal discrepancies were related to all areas of physical self-concept, being too thin relative to personal ideals was almost as detrimental as being too fat for Chinese children. The results reflect Chinese cultural values, in which obesity is more acceptable than in Western culture, and, perhaps, general inadequacies of Chinese health education in relation to obesity.

Elite Athlete and Nonelite Groups

Marsh (1998) tested the appropriateness of the PSDQ instrument for groups of elite and nonelite athletes $(N = 1,514)$ in different settings: elite athletes and nonathletes attending a highly selective sport high school, elite athletes in residence at the Australian Institute of Sport (AIS), and nonathlete high school students attending a school that does not have any particular emphasis on sport. In an application of the known group difference approach, PSDQ responses were predicted to be systematically higher for elite athletes than nonelite groups. Based on social comparison theory, PSDQ responses were also predicted to be higher for nonathletes in the athletically nonselective high school than nonathletes in the athletically selective high school.

Consistent with predictions from the known group difference approach to construct validity, PSDQ responses were much higher for two elite athlete groups (AIS and athletes from sport high school) than for two nonelite groups (nonathlete students from sport high school and nonsport high school). Although males had higher physical self-concepts than females, these gender differences were smaller for elite athletes. Students in a nonsport high school had higher physical self-concepts than nonelite athletes in an athletically selective high school. This is consistent with social comparison theory because the elite athletes provide a demanding frame of reference.

CFA was used to test the invariance of factor loadings for the 11 PSDQ scales in elite and nonelite groups. CFA results demonstrated the 11 PSDQ factors for all four groups and the factor loadings were invariant across the four groups. Factor variances and correlations were invariant across the two elite groups and across the two nonelite groups. As predicted (see Marsh, 1998), PSDQ factors were more distinct (i.e., correlations among PSDQ factors were smaller) for elite athletes than nonathletes, but relations between global self-esteem and the PSDQ scales were no higher for elite athletes than nonelite groups. The results demonstrate the broad appropriateness of the PSDQ.

Elite Athlete Self-Description Questionnaire (EASDQ)

While the PSDQ is suitable for elite athletes, there may be other components of physical self-concept that are particularly relevant for elite athletes. This led to the development of the Elite Athlete Self-Description Questionnaire (EASDQ). In designing the EASDQ, overall performance by elite athletes was hypothesized to be a function of skill level, body suitability, aerobic and anaerobic fitness, mental competence, and overall performance. Based on this theoretical model, Marsh and colleagues (Marsh, Hey, Johnson, & Perry, 1997; Marsh, Hey, Roche, & Perry, 1997) developed the EASDQ to measure these six factors (see table 12.5). For each scale they developed a pool of items that were then evaluated by sport psychology staff at the AIS for their suitability for elite athletes. Pilot studies

Table 12.5 Summary of the Elite Athlete Self-Description (EASDQ) Scales

Scale	Summary
Skills	In my best sport (event) I am a skillful athlete; my technical skills are better than most at my level of competition; I excel because of my skill level.
Body	I excel in my best sport (event) because of the suitability of my body composition, body shape, body structure; having the right body helps me perform well.
Aerobic	In my best sport (event) I am aerobically superior compared to my teammates and competitors; my capacity for endurance makes me a good performer; coaches and my competitors see me as very fit aerobically.
Anaerobic	In my best sport (event) I am anaerobically superior compared to others; my capacity for short bursts of high intensity activity makes me a good performer; coaches and my competitors see me as very fit anaerobically.
Mental competence	I have better mental skills, commitment, discipline, focus, and emotional control than others at my level in my best sport (event).
Overall performance	I am an excellent performer; I perform to my ability level; I give peak performance when necessary; I can pull it all together.

were conducted to select the best items to represent each factor. A compromise between brevity and psychometric soundness was achieved, with acceptable levels of reliability (e.g., all scales having reliability estimates of at least .80) based on short scales (four to six items per scale).

Marsh and colleagues then administered the EASDQ to elite athletes from a selective sport high school (*N* = 349) and from the AIS (*N* = 151). CFAs of EASDQ responses by the total group identified the six a priori factors. Multiple group CFAs of responses by each separate group (AIS and elite high school athletes) supported the factorial invariance of responses across the two groups. Hierarchical CFA provided good support for a single higher-order factor and the invariance of the hierarchical structure across two groups. Results support the appropriateness of the EASDQ for diverse groups of elite athletes. More research is needed, however, to relate EASDQ responses to external validity criteria like those used in PSDQ research and to criteria that are more specific to elite athletes (e.g., actual performance in competition).

Marsh and Perry (2005) administered the Elite Swimmer SDQ (ESSDQ), a swimming version of the EASDQ, to 275 elite swimmers from 30 nations participating at the 1999 Pan Pacific Championships and the fifth World Short Course Championships. After arriving at each championship (but before events took place), swimmers identified their preferred events (up to four) and completed the ESSDQ in relation to each event. Consistent with good psychometric responses found with the EASDQ, coefficient alpha estimates of reliability were at least .90 for all six scales for the total sample as well as for responses by men and by women considered separately. CFAs provided clear support for the a priori six-factor structure for responses to the EASDQ and the factor structure was invariant over different events.

Consistent with the design of the instrument, a higher-order factor model (in which each of the six ESSDQ factors loaded on a single, higher-order factor) provided a good fit to the data. The ESSDQ factor structure (factor loadings, factor correlations, and uniquenesses) was also invariant over gender. Gender was only related to one ESSDQ factor (anaerobic, *r* = .16, favoring women) and no age–gender interactions were significant. Whereas age was significantly related to three scales, none of these age differences was statistically significant after controlling for previous personal best performances that were available for each elite swimmer.

Causal Ordering of Self-Concept and Performance

Do changes in self-concept lead to changes in performance? This is one of the most vexing questions in self-concept research. It has important theoretical and practical implications and has been the focus of considerable research—particularly in educational settings. Byrne (1984) emphasized that much of the interest in the academic self-concept–achievement relation stems from the belief that academic self-concept has motivational properties such that changes in academic self-concept will lead to changes in academic achievement.

Calsyn and Kenny (1977) contrasted self-enhancement and skill development models of this relation. The self-enhancement model posits self-concept as a primary determinant of academic achievement (i.e., self-concept leads to achievement) and would support self-concept interventions explicit or implicit in many educational programs. In contrast, the skill development model implies that academic self-concept emerges principally as a consequence of academic achievement (i.e., achievement leads to self-concept), so the best way to enhance academic self-concept would be to develop stronger academic skills. However, based on more advanced statistical tools, empirical results, and self-concept theory, Marsh and colleagues (1990; Marsh, Byrne, & Yeung, 1999) argued that a more realistic compromise between the models of self-enhancement and skill development was a *reciprocal effects model* in which self-concept affects subsequent achievement *and* achievement affects subsequent self-concept.

A growing body of research (Marsh et al., 1999) supports the reciprocal effects model of relations between academic self-concept and academic achievement. In a recent meta-analysis of relevant research, Valentine, Dubois, and Cooper (2004) also concluded that there was clear support for predictions based on the reciprocal effects model over those derived from self-enhancement and skill development models. Whereas the effect of previous self-concept on subsequent achievement after controlling for the effects of previous achievement was modest, the effect was highly significant overall and positive in 90% of the studies in this meta-analysis.

In support of the multidimensional perspective that is so important to the reciprocal effects model, the effects of previous self-beliefs were significantly stronger when the measure of self-belief was based on a domain-specific measure rather than on global measures such as self-esteem, and when self-concept and achievement measures were matched in terms of domain specificity (e.g., mathematics achievement and math self-concept). Hence, this meta-analysis provides strong support for predictions based on the reciprocal effects model and for the construct validity of the multidimensional perspective of self-concept with its focus on domain-specific measures.

Implicit in the reciprocal effects model is the assumption that processes such as investment of effort, persistence in the face of difficulty, and choice behavior mediate self-concept's influence on subsequent behavior. Thus, for example, a positive self-concept in a specific area may reinforce appropriate decisions about how people spend their time or what activities they pursue that has a subsequent effect on related outcomes. Suggestive of this type of effect is the finding that self-concept in relation to specific school subjects is a better predictor of coursework selection than previous achievement in the different school subjects (Marsh & Yeung, 1997).

Although widely applied in educational research, there are few applications of the reciprocal effects in sport settings with appropriate measures of physical self-concept and physical performance. For this reason, it is useful to summarize briefly the results from recent studies that are apparently the first tests of the generalizability of the reciprocal effects model to the physical domain.

Gymnastics Self-Concept and Achievement

Marsh, Chanal, and Sarrazin (in press) pursued tests of the reciprocal effects, self-enhancement, and skill development models in relation to physical self-concept and performance skills in physical education classes. More specifically, they evaluated predictions about the effects of previous gymnastics self-concept and gymnastics performance skills collected at the start of a gymnastics training program on subsequent self-concept and performance skills collected at the end of the 10-week program. Achievement was based on videotapes of each student's performance on a standardized performance test that was evaluated by three independent expert judges. Interjudge reliability was extremely good, and responses to the gymnastics self-concept instrument by students were also very reliable.

Structural equation models based on responses by 376 adolescents collected at the start and end of the

Gymnastics skill is only one ingredient to good gymnastics performance; a gymnast's self-concept contributes to improving performance.

gymnastics program supported a reciprocal effects model. Even after controlling for the effects of gender and age, the effect of previous gymnastics self-concept on subsequent gymnastics performance (.20) and the effect of previous gymnastics performance on subsequent gymnastics self-concept (.14) were both highly significant. Although there were gender and age effects (girls and older participants had better gymnastics skills while boys had higher self-concepts), multiple group structural equation models indicated that support for the reciprocal effect model was consistent across responses by boys and girls and by younger and older students. In summary, consistent with the reciprocal effects models, gymnastics self-concept and gymnastics performance were both determinants and consequences of each other.

Generalizability to Performances in Elite Swimming

Support for the benefits of a positive self-concept on subsequent performance and achievement, as reviewed by Marsh et al. (1999) and Valentine et al. (2004), is based substantially on the effects of academic self-concept on school performance and achievement. Recent physical education research (Marsh, Chanal, & Sarrazin, in press; Marsh, Papaioannou, & Theodorakis, in press) provides an important extension of this research to a physical context in which the focus is on physical components of self-concept and desirable physical outcomes. Nevertheless, this more recent research into physical self-concept—like most of the research in the Marsh et al. and Valentine et al. reviews—is based on responses by general populations of students in school settings.

Marsh and Perry (2005) extended this research and tested the causal ordering of self-concept and performance of the best swimmers in the world competing at international swimming championships. They measured elite swimming self-concepts of participants in the Pan Pacific Swimming Championships in Australia and the World Short Course Championships in Greece. Top swimmers from 30 countries completed the EASDQ instrument on the first day of these championships before actually competing in any events. Also available for all participants were world rankings and previous personal best performances (PPBs) in each of their events. Following from the reciprocal effects model, it was predicted that elite swimmer self-concept would affect subsequent championship performance even after controlling for the substantial effects of PPBs.

Whereas championship performance was highly related to PPB performance ($r = .90$), structural equation models demonstrated that elite athlete self-concept also contributed significantly to the prediction of subsequent championship performance, explaining approximately 10% of the residual variance after controlling for PPB performance. This is an important contribution, particularly in relation to championship performances of elite swimmers at a level where winning margins are so small. Furthermore, for swimmers who competed in two or more events, these results were replicated by results in the second event. The results show that elite athlete self-concept has an effect on the subsequent championship performances of elite swimmers beyond what can be explained in terms of PPBs.

Future Research

The future of self-concept research in sport psychology is exciting, heuristic, and full of opportunities. Many of these opportunities involve expanding the scope of self-concept research to incorporate new theoretical models, constructs, and applied challenges from other disciplines that are or will be applied in sport and exercise psychology. A few of these include the following themes.

The juxtaposition between specific components of physical self-concept, global physical self-concept, and self-esteem needs further consideration in sport and exercise psychology. The multidimensional perspective of self-concept is widely accepted in sport psychology. However, there are a variety of theoretical models positing that relations between specific components and global components are moderated or mediated by constructs such as importance, salience, relevance, certainty, and ideal standards. These typically are weighted-average models that involve interaction terms (e.g., the positive or negative influence of gymnastics self-concept on global self-esteem varies as a function of the importance a person places on gymnastics). Alternatively, there are discrepancy models in which the effects of self-perceived accomplishments are mediated by internalized or externally imposed standards of performance. Thus, for example, two participants may have similar levels of physical activity but their standards for acceptable or appropriate levels of physical activity may differ substantially.

Much self-concept research has focused on structural aspects of self-concept (e.g., factor structure) while giving insufficient attention to dynamic processes that contribute to the integration of specific components of self-concept that lead to the formation of self-esteem. In contrast, research in social psychology and cognitive psychology has focused more on such dynamic processes but given insufficient attention to measurement issues. Clearly, there is an important opportunity to better integrate these apparently complementary research traditions within a sport and exercise research setting.

There is a critical need to sift through the diverse range of psychological constructs that researchers in sport psychology have incorporated or adapted from other areas of research. There is general awareness that items and constructs from other disciplines have to be translated so that they are appropriate to a sport context. While global and generic constructs may be useful in some settings, constructs that are specific to a sport setting are likely to be more useful. Typically this involves the development of a new item pool, pilot studies to evaluate psychometric properties and select the best items, and research studies in which the usefulness of the measures are tested. This is an ongoing process of refinement, as illustrated in physical self-concept research summarized here.

However, there has also been ongoing debate about the degree of overlap between apparently distinct constructs, particularly those coming from different theoretical frameworks and used by different camps of researchers who typically do not systematically evaluate how their measures of their constructs relate to those used by other researchers. Hence, a stronger focus on construct validation in relation to other constructs should force sport and exercise psychologists to evaluate more carefully the convergent and discriminant validity of their constructs.

At the level of individual items, the observation that items on a given scale all load on a single factor when only one scale is considered provides no evidence that the items will not be more strongly related to different factors when items from a range of constructs are considered in the same factor analysis. At the level of scales, the heuristic label assigned to a particular collection of items is not a sufficient basis for establishing how the scales relate to apparently similar or dissimilar constructs. This concern is clearly not specific to physical self-concept research like that summarized in this chapter, but it clearly calls for more research to more fully define where physical self-concept fits within the ever-increasing set of constructs used in sport and exercise research.

The reciprocal effects model posits that performance accomplishments and specific components of self-concept are reciprocally related and mutually reinforcing. Much of this research has focused on academic outcomes in school settings, but a number of studies summarized here have extended this to sport and exercise settings. Particularly in sport settings where maintenance of short-term gains in performance accomplishment is highly dependent on sustained motivation and persistence, the effects of self-concept in relevant areas are likely to be important. Further tests of the reciprocal effects model in sport and exercise settings represent a vital area of further research with both elite sport participants and the general population.

A major challenge facing health professionals, researchers, and policy makers is how to promote appropriate levels of physical activity, diet, and health-related physical fitness across the life span. Education is clearly important, but apparently it is not sufficient to achieve this goal. Even when people know what is good for them, they often behave in ways inconsistent with this knowledge. Implicit or explicit in much of the research considered here is that specific components of physical self-concept and related psychological constructs are a key to addressing this concern. Hence, the reciprocal effects model posits that physical self-concept and physical activity are reciprocally related and mutually reinforcing such that improvements in either of these constructs lead to gains in the other.

Based on support for a reciprocal effects model of physical self-concept and physical activity, Marsh, Papaioannou, and Theodorakis (in press) argued that widely applied theoretical models such as the theory of planned behavior should be expanded to include specific components of self-concept relevant to the target outcomes, but they also argued that methodological rigor and research design coming from research supporting the reciprocal effects model could contribute to these other research traditions. Hence, there are exciting opportunities to juxtapose constructs, research designs, and theoretical models from different research traditions.

Self-concept research in sport and exercise has incorporated a diverse range of correlational, longitudinal, quasi-experimental, and multimethod research designs, coupled with a growing sophistication of statistical analyses. However, with a few major exceptions, there are relatively few well-designed true experimental designs with participants randomly assigned to experimental and control groups. Although true experimental design and clinical trials are not a panacea for social-psychological research, they are surprisingly underused.

Thus, for example, an experimental test of the reciprocal effects model might be a four-group experimental design in which participants are randomly assigned to physical self-concept enhancement only, physical activity enhancement only, combined physical self-concept and physical activity enhancement, and control groups. In another application, tests of the construct validity could involve a variety of interventions aimed at specific components of physical self-concept (e.g., strength, endurance, flexibility). The construct-validity rationale for predictions would be that each intervention had a significantly larger effect on the matching dimension of physical self-concept, a smaller effect on logically related areas of physical self-concept, and little or no effect on nonphysical areas of self-concept.

Implicit in this proposed direction for future research is the need to incorporate a construct-validation approach in the interpretation of experimental as well as nonexperimental and quasi-experimental research designs. Thus, for example, O'Mara, Marsh, Craven, and Debus (in press) conducted a meta-analysis of self-concept intervention research that incorporated a construct-validity approach. Consistent with this perspective, effect sizes were substantially larger for specific components of self-concept logically related to the intended outcomes of the intervention than for self-esteem and other less relevant components of self-concept. Studies designed to enhance global self-esteem were not very successful compared to studies that focused on more specific components of self-concept that were most relevant to the goals of the intervention.

Practical Implications

The position taken in this chapter is that self-concept is an important outcome variable in its own right as well as a powerful facilitator of other desirable outcomes. Practical implications of this position are that researchers and policy makers need to develop research programs, curricula, and policies that maximize self-concept as well as other desirable outcomes—even if self-concept is not their main focus. If an intervention has unanticipated negative effects on self-concept, then these effects are likely to undermine whatever other effects the program was designed to produce. On the other hand, if the program enhances self-concept, then these positive effects are likely to complement and facilitate other desirable outcomes that are targeted by the program.

In particular, the direction of causality posited in the reciprocal effects model has important practical implications for mentors at all levels (e.g., coaches, trainers, sport psychologists, managers, parents). If the direction of causality is from self-concept to performance (self-enhancement model), then mentors might want to put more effort into enhancing self-concepts rather than focusing on skills and performance outcomes. On the other hand, if the direction of causality is from performance to self-concept (skill development model), then mentors should focus on improving skills and performance as the best way to improve self-concept.

In contrast to these simplistic (either–or) models, the reciprocal effects model implies that self-concept and performance are reciprocally related and mutually reinforcing. Improved self-concepts will lead to better performance, and improved performance will lead to better self-concepts. For example, if mentors enhance self-concepts without improving underlying skills and performance, then the gains in self-concept are likely to be short-lived. However, if mentors improve performances and skills without also fostering self-beliefs in one's capabilities, then the performance gains are also unlikely to be long lasting. Thus, if mentors focus on either performance or self-concept to the exclusion of the other, then both are likely to suffer. Hence, according to the reciprocal effects model, mentors should strive to simultaneously improve both self-concept and performance outcomes.

Summary

Interest in physical self-concept stems from its recognition as a valued outcome, its role as a moderator variable, interest in its relation with other constructs, and methodological and measurement concerns. Theory, measurement, research, and practice are inexorably intertwined; each will suffer if one is ignored. At least initially, an important contribution of the research discussed here is the development of instruments, based on strong empirical and theoretical foundations, for measuring multiple dimensions of physical self-concept. These instruments include the Self-Description Questionnaire (SDQ), which led to the development of the Physical SDQ (PSDQ), a more detailed evaluation of self-concept in the physical domain. While the PSDQ is suitable for elite athletes, other components of physical self-concept not included in the PSDQ are particularly relevant for elite athletes, so the Elite Athlete Self-Description Questionnaire (EASDQ) was developed.

Causal ordering of self-concept and performance is another important research question that was discussed, including a reciprocal effects model in which self-concept affects subsequent achievement *and* achievement affects subsequent self-concept. The research also outlines a construct-validity approach in which an emphasis on good measurement is a critical feature of good research; this approach establishes the usefulness of self-concept by within-network and between-network studies. The construct-validity approach should be useful to other areas of sport psychology and to sport sciences more generally.

The future of self-concept research in sport psychology is full of opportunities, many of which involve expanding the scope of self-concept research to incorporate new theoretical models, constructs, and applied challenges from other disciplines. As for practical implications, the position taken in this chapter is that self-concept is an important outcome variable in its own right as well as a powerful facilitator of other desirable outcomes. Research programs, curricula, and policies should maximize self-concept as well as other desirable outcomes. In particular, the direction of causality posited in the reciprocal effects model has important practical implications for mentors at all levels; mentors should strive to simultaneously improve both self-concept and performance outcomes.

Discussion Questions

1. How does self-esteem fit into a multidimensional, hierarchical model of self-concept? Within such a model, are domain-specific components of self-concept that appear near the base of the hierarchy more or less important than higher-order components at the apex of the hierarchy?

2. In the construct-validity approach, there is a distinction between within-network and between-network research. Describe types of research that would fall at different points along this continuum. Defend (or refute) the argument that the resolution of at least some within-network issues is a logical prerequisite to pursuing between-network issues.

3. In MTMM research, there is a critical distinction between convergent and discriminant validity. Describe the difference between these two aspects of validity and how each is related to the more general concept of construct validity.

4. Assume that interventions for self-concept enhancement led to increases in physical self-concept but also facilitated other desirable outcomes. From this perspective, defend the assumption that it is important to consider physical self-concept in intervention research. On the other hand, defend the assumption that physical self-concept is an important outcome despite research showing that interventions for enhancing physical self-concept led to increases in physical self-concept but did not improve other desirable outcomes.

5. What are the basic predictions of the reciprocal effects model of relations between self-concept and performance, and how have they been tested? What other research designs could be used to test these predictions? What underlying psychological processes might contribute to enhanced performance due to increases in self-concept or enhanced self-concept due to increases in performance?

6. What do you think are the potential moderating factors that affect the influence of self-concept on adherence to competitive sport?

chapter 13

Efficacy Beliefs Within Relational and Group Contexts in Sport

Mark R. Beauchamp, PhD

Learning Objectives

On completion of this chapter, the reader should have

1. understanding of the conceptual bases for different forms of efficacy that may exist within close relationships and groups in sport;

2. knowledge of the sources of different forms of relational and group efficacy as well as the consequences for individuals (athlete, coach), dyads (athlete–athlete, coach–athlete), and groups (teams) in sport;

3. awareness of contemporary efficacy studies focused on relationships and group settings and potential directions for future research; and

4. understanding of theory and recent research to be able to discuss practical implications for athlete, team, and coach functioning.

elf-efficacy refers to an individual's "belief in one's capabilities to organize and execute the courses of action required to produce given attainments" (Bandura, 1997, p. 3), and in sport it has consistently been shown to be an important predictor of positive cognitions (e.g., Kane, Marks, Zaccaro, & Blair, 1996; McAuley, Duncan, & McElroy, 1989), affective responses (e.g., McAuley, Talbot, & Martinez, 1999; Treasure, Monson, & Lox, 1996), and behaviors (e.g., Beauchamp, Bray, & Albinson, 2002; Milne, Hall, & Forwell, 2004). Self-efficacy relates to a person's perceived abilities to perform tasks independently of others. Within most sporting contexts, however, athletes spend a great deal of time training, performing, and working with others (e.g., teammates, coaches), and in such an environment efficacy beliefs should also be considered in relation to the interactive and interdependent tasks athletes perform.

The purpose of this chapter is to review the efficacy literature as it corresponds to behavioral enactment within close relationships (e.g., coach–athlete, athlete-athlete) and group settings in sport. Consistent with Chan (1998) and Moritz and Watson (1998), no distinction is made between the terms *group* and *team* and both are used interchangeably throughout this chapter. Although self-efficacy theory (Bandura, 1977, 1997) provides the theoretical underpinning for efficacy beliefs within relational and group settings, this chapter is not a review of *self*-efficacy research per se. Excellent reviews of the self-efficacy construct have been provided elsewhere (e.g., Feltz, 1992; Feltz & Chase, 1998; Feltz & Lirgg, 2001). This chapter is concerned with those efficacy beliefs that manifest themselves within close relationships and group contexts in sport.

Self-efficacy theory (Bandura, 1977, 1997) exists within the broader theoretical framework provided by social-cognitive theory (Bandura, 1986), in which individuals are considered to be both products and producers of their environment, personality, and actions. Specifically, Bandura (1997) uses the term *triadic reciprocal causation* to describe the functional dependence that occurs among these three factors and reiterates the underlying theme that permeates this book—that athletes, coaches, and teammates influence and are influenced by others within their social environment. Within Bandura's (1986) social-cognitive framework, self-efficacy theory is concerned with how people develop judgments and expectations about their own capabilities and the ability to successfully meet various demands and challenges.

When athletes perform tasks *independently* of others, they invariably develop a set of efficacy beliefs related to the performance of those individual tasks—for example, "I am confident I will hit the ball" or "I believe that I can make this shot." These are termed *self-efficacy beliefs*. Bandura (1986) theorized that these beliefs emanate from past experiences of success or failure, observation of others (vicarious experiences), verbal persuasion, and perceptions of one's physiological state. Although independent enactment does indeed occur in many sporting activities, most sports require interaction of some kind. Even at the individualistic end of the individual–team sport continuum (e.g., golf, track and field, tennis), athletes are required to work with a coach, and in such a setting athletes not only develop beliefs about their own capabilities to perform but also appraise their coaches' abilities to help them achieve their goals (Bandura, 1997). As will be shown later in this chapter, this latter form of efficacy appraisal can influence the way athletes train with their coach and subsequently compete.

When one also considers sports that require effective interaction between athletes (i.e., competing dyads, sport teams), efficacy beliefs can additionally be observed in relation to athletes' interdependent role responsibilities (cf. Bandura, 1999), the capabilities of one's partner to perform specific tasks (cf. Lent and Lopez, 2002), or even the capabilities of a group or team as a whole (cf. Bandura, 2000). In addition, while each of these efficacy appraisals describes cognitions held by the athlete, a growing body of research has also suggested that coaches' efficacy beliefs may have important implications for the learning and performance of their athletes (cf. Feltz, Chase, Moritz, & Sullivan, 1999). This chapter will explore how these disparate forms (see table 13.1) of coach and athlete efficacy manifest themselves within close relational and group contexts in sport, consider how they arise, and examine to what extent they affect both individual and collective functioning.

Role Efficacy Within Sport Teams

Roles refer to sets of expectations about behaviors for a position in a social structure (Biddle & Thomas, 1966; Shaw & Costanzo, 1982; Sherif & Sherif, 1953). They typically involve interdependent behaviors and are a defining feature of teams (Carron & Hausenblas, 1998; Salas, Dickinson, Converse, & Tannenbaum, 1992; Sherif

The author would like to thank Martyn Standage and Ben Jackson for their comments on an earlier draft of this chapter.

Table 13.1 Efficacy Beliefs Within Relational and Group Contexts in Sport

Efficacy construct	Definition	Example
Self-efficacy	A person's confidence in his or her own capabilities to perform independent tasks (Bandura, 1997)	"I had the confidence that I was unstoppable." (Pete Sampras describing his win over Andre Agassi in the 1999 Wimbledon men's singles final. Quoted in Hayward, 2001, p. 61)
Role efficacy	A person's confidence in his or her own capabilities to carry out formal interdependent role responsibilities within a group (Bray et al., 2002)	"Everyone had his role, and I felt great about mine." (Mark Messier commenting on his role within the Stanley Cup–winning Edmonton Oilers hockey team. Quoted in Swift, 1996, p. 60)
Collective efficacy	A group's confidence in their collective capabilities to perform collective tasks (Bandura, 1997)	"We have a lot of confidence in ourselves and each other and we think that's going to show in the next 10 days." (Mario Lemieux commenting on Team Canada's confidence before winning the ice-hockey gold medal at the 2002 Winter Olympics. Quoted in Duhatschek, 2002, p. O6)
Coaching efficacy[a] (type 1)	A coach's confidence in his or her own capabilities to facilitate the learning and development of athletes (Feltz et al., 1999)	"I firmly believe that I'm good enough to do the job. I have every confidence in what I can offer." (Andy Robinson, shortly after being named head coach of the England Rugby Union team. Quoted in Cleary, 2004, p. S2)
Coaching efficacy (type 2)	A coach's confidence in his or her players' abilities to perform given tasks (Chase et al., 1997)	"You're my strongest pairing. I put my trust in you; I expect you to win." (Peter McEvoy's comments on his decision to pair Luke Donald and Paul Casey in the 1999 Walker Cup. Quoted in Mair, 2004, p. S2)
Proxy efficacy	A person's confidence in an intermediary's capabilities, such as a coach or doctor, to function on his or her behalf (Bray et al., 2001)	"He's the driving force behind my ambitions. Much of my confidence and self-belief come from my respect and belief in him." (England Rugby star Jonny Wilkinson describing his relationship with his personal trainer, Steve Black. Quoted in Cleary, 2004, p. S5)
Other-efficacy	A person's belief in his or her partner's capabilities to perform given behaviors (Lent & Lopez, 2002)	"Anybody who has rowed with him will have been blown away by the smoothness of his rhythm and his natural feel for the boat . . . there is nobody I would rather have in my boat." (Two-time Olympic gold medalist James Cracknell commenting on his rowing partner's capabilities—four-time Olympic gold medalist Matthew Pinsent. Quoted in Cracknell, 2004, p. S5)
Relation-inferred self-efficacy (RISE)	An athlete's appraisal of how his or her capabilities are viewed by his or her partner (Lent & Lopez, 2002)	"We've got confidence in each other's golf." (Paul Casey commenting on Luke Donald's confidence in Casey's capabilities prior to the pair winning the 2004 Golf World Cup in Seville. Quoted in Mair, 2004, p. S2)

[a]Within the organizational psychology literature, researchers have used the term *leadership efficacy,* which is analogous to the way in which coaching efficacy has been operationalized in sport (e.g., Hoyt et al., 2003). However, in sport the *leader* may also be someone other than the coach, namely the on-field or on-court leader (e.g., Watson et al., 2001).

& Sherif, 1969). Within sport teams athletes perform both informal as well as formal roles. *Informal roles* develop through intragroup development and interaction (Mabry & Barnes, 1980) and may include the team joker, spokesperson, or social planner. *Formal roles,* on the other hand, relate to responsibilities prescribed to athletes for the specific purpose of meeting the group's performance objectives (Mabry & Barnes, 1980).

In sport, formal roles typically follow positional responsibilities (e.g., striker in soccer), but they can also relate to other prescribed roles (e.g., team captain). In order for sport teams to succeed it is essential for members to be efficacious in the performance of their task-related formal role responsibilities. As Bandura (1999) remarked, "If people are to work together successfully, the members of a group have to perform their roles with a high degree of efficacy" (p. 227). Most of the research in this area has been related to formal or positional roles.

Bray and his colleagues (Beauchamp & Bray, 2001; Bray, Balaguer, & Duda, 2004; Bray & Brawley, 2002; Bray, Brawley, & Carron, 2002) embraced the basic tenets of self-efficacy theory (Bandura, 1997) and sought to examine the construct validity of role-efficacy in sport. Bray et al. (2002) considered role efficacy to represent athletes' confidence in their capabilities to successfully carry out formal interdependent role responsibilities within a group. One of the main purposes of the Bray et al. study was to investigate the conceptual uniqueness of role efficacy. Accordingly, the authors examined role efficacy in relation to both self-efficacy and collective efficacy (a construct that will be returned to later in this chapter). As hypothesized, athletes' efficacy to perform their interdependent role responsibilities was found to be related to, but also distinct from, their confidence to perform independent tasks (i.e., self-efficacy) such as shooting and dribbling. In addition, role efficacy was found to be empirically distinct from collective efficacy.

Several studies have also sought to investigate role efficacy in relation to both potential sources as well as outcomes. One important cognition that has been studied in relation to role efficacy is role ambiguity (Beauchamp & Bray, 2001; Beauchamp, Bray, Eys, & Carron, 2002; Beauchamp, Bray, Fielding, & Eys, 2005; Bray & Brawley, 2002). Role ambiguity relates to the degree to which team members are unclear about their role responsibilities, and it has been theorized to negatively influence a person's ability to successfully carry out his or her role (Kahn, Wolfe, Quinn, Snoek, & Rosenthal, 1964). Role ambiguity is considered diametrically opposite to *role clarity* whereby higher levels of one correspond to lower levels of the other.

From a theoretical perspective, Bandura (1997) suggested that the process through which efficacy cognitions influence behavior involves a conception-matching process whereby "cognitive representations serve as guides for the production of skilled action and as internal standards for making corrective adjustments in the achievement of behavioral proficiency" (p. 373). Unfortunately, however, when this behavior–feedback loop becomes impaired (through insufficient information), one's sense of personal efficacy may be negatively affected (Escartí & Guzmán, 1999; Lindsley, Brass, & Thomas, 1995; Shea & Howell, 2000). This means that if an athlete lacks the requisite information to guide the effective performance of a set of role responsibilities, a lowered sense of role efficacy may result.

Using a sample of youth rugby players, Beauchamp, Bray, Eys, et al. (2002) found support for this proposition. Specifically, they found that when athletes were unclear about their scope of role responsibilities, lower levels of role-related efficacy were more likely. Similar findings have emerged using a wide variety of other interdependent sport team athletes, including those from basketball, water polo, soccer, ice hockey, and field hockey (Beauchamp & Bray, 2001; Bray & Brawley, 2002).

Within self-efficacy theory, the most prominent source of efficacy beliefs is past experiences of mastery (Bandura, 1997). Simply stated, when people experience repeated successes their efficacy to perform the requisite behaviors is bolstered; however, when repeated failure occurs personal efficacy diminishes. Although role efficacy beliefs differ from self-efficacy beliefs in that they involve the performance of interdependent tasks, they are also grounded within the theoretical framework provided by self-efficacy theory (Bandura, 1997) and so conceptually speaking should develop from similar sources.

To test this proposition, Bray et al. (2002) sought to investigate the differential effects of mastery experiences on role efficacy beliefs by comparing the efficacy beliefs of starters and nonstarters (i.e., bench players). Using university basketball players, Bray et al. found that although starters did not differ in their perceived abilities to perform independent tasks (i.e., self-efficacy) such as shooting and dribbling, nonstarters reported significantly lower levels of role efficacy than starters. Bray et al. found that nonstarters reported spending significantly less time performing their interdependent role responsibilities than starters (e.g., less playing time) and suggested that if athletes lack the opportunities to perform their various role responsibilities in practice or competition, they will lack the necessary experiences of successful mastery enactment. Indeed, Bandura (1997) specifically discussed the issue of being benched by remarking, "When you don't play a lot of doubts begin to build in your mind. You wonder how good you are or that you can still do the things you used to do" (p. 398-399).

Although research has yet to investigate whether other sources of efficacy (cf. Bandura, 1997) predict variance in role efficacy, investigations from parallel literatures hold particular promise for understanding potential antecedents of role efficacy in sport. For example, research has consistently found that the modeling (i.e., vicarious experiences) of successful behaviors relates to the efficacious performance of independent tasks (McCullagh & Weiss, 2001). Role models are often regarded as particularly influential with regard to athlete behavior, and it seems likely that successful role modeling (i.e., modeling of interdependent tasks) will also be an important predictor of role efficacy in sport.

A growing body of research has also found the coach to be an important source of an athlete's perceived competence to perform independent tasks (e.g., Vealey, Hayashi, Garner-Holman, & Giacobbi, 1998). Given the significant role of the coach in the development of athletes within interdependent teams (cf. Chelladurai & Reimer, 1998), it seems plausible to suggest that the verbal persuasion inherent within coaching behaviors will also be an important predictor of role efficacy beliefs within sport.

In terms of salient outcomes, performance is perhaps the most extensively researched criterion in relation to efficacy beliefs in sport (cf. Moritz, Feltz, Fahrbach, & Mack, 2000). In line with this, and to further test the predictive utility of role efficacy in sport, a series of studies have sought to examine the relationship between role efficacy and role performance effectiveness (e.g., Beauchamp, Bray, Eys, et al., 2002; Bray and Brawley, 2002; Bray, Balaguer, et al., 2004). In one study, Beauchamp, Bray, Eys, et al. (2002) investigated rugby players' role efficacy beliefs in relation to their performance of offensive and defensive role responsibilities. In line with theory (Bandura, 1997), results revealed that players' efficacy expectations to perform their offensive and defensive responsibilities explained significant variation in coach ratings of role performance effectiveness.

One of the limitations of the Beauchamp et al. study was that relations were examined concurrently. Bray and Brawley (2002) improved on the Beauchamp et al. design and examined the prospective relations between role efficacy and role performance. Over the course of a season, using intercollegiate basketball players, Bray and Brawley found that role efficacy was again related to coach ratings of role performance.

Although role performance represents an important behavioral consequence, research centered on other salient outcomes related to role efficacy is required to understand its broader influence within sport teams. For example, efficacy expectations are theorized to be motivational (cf. Bandura, 1997), and so role efficacy beliefs may also affect team members' effort, persistence, and choice of goals related to role enactment. In addition, given that team members' roles are inextricably linked to achievement of group outcomes, efficacy beliefs related to those roles may also be able to predict group-level outcomes such as team cohesion and team performance (cf. Bandura, 1999).

Future research is clearly needed to investigate the extent to which role efficacy is related to salient cognitive, behavioral, and affective outcomes. However, given that so much sporting behavior occurs within interdependent team settings (Carron & Hausenblas, 1998; Forsyth, 1999) where athletes perform various interdependent role responsibilities, it would seem necessary to understand the extent to which this social cognition affects both athlete and group outcomes in sport.

Collective Efficacy Within Sport Teams

While role efficacy beliefs describe the cognitions a team member has that he or she can perform specific individual role responsibilities, collective efficacy relates to team members' perceptions about the team's collective abilities. Specifically, Bandura (1997) defines collective efficacy as the "group's shared belief in their conjoint capabilities to organize and execute the courses of action required to produce given attainments" (p. 476). Within this definition, four issues are worthy of note.

First, collective efficacy is a *shared perception* that involves a certain degree of consensus. Some researchers have operationalized this aspect of Bandura's definition by using group discussions to derive single agreed-upon group scores (e.g., Gibson, 1999; Gibson, Randel, & Earley, 2000). Unfortunately, such an approach may result in scores that are not representative of *all* group members' beliefs, and indeed Bandura suggests that it is more appropriate to tap into individual team members' perceptions and then aggregate those scores to the team level. This means that although collective efficacy is a group-level construct (cf. Chan, 1998), it represents individual members' beliefs about the group.

Nonetheless, the issue of consensus highlighted by Gibson et al. (2000) is an important one, especially if collective efficacy assessments are to conform to Bandura's definitional point regarding shared beliefs. Typically, researchers conduct initial assessments of within- and between-group variability (e.g., intraclass correlation) to ascertain whether collective efficacy data exhibit "groupness" (cf. Feltz & Chase, 1998; Moritz & Watson, 1998; Prussia & Kinicki, 1996). Once collective efficacy has been shown to reflect a group's shared beliefs and consensus about the group's capabilities has been supported, individual perceptions of the group's capabilities may then be aggregated to the group level.

The second point about Bandura's (1997) definition relates to the fact that it involves beliefs about the group's *conjoint capabilities*. This means that unlike role efficacy, which describes a confidence to perform individual (albeit interdependent) tasks, collective efficacy refers to the enactment of highly integrative tasks that involve the team as a whole. For example, a collective or group task in sport may involve the enactment of a particular integrative system (e.g., full-court press in basketball) or offensive team maneuver (e.g., set-piece play in rugby).

The third point about Bandura's (1997) definition is that it is concerned with the *organization and execution* of courses of action. Zaccaro, Blair, Peterson, and Zazanis (1995) elaborated on this aspect of Bandura's definition by suggesting that collective efficacy involves the "allocation, coordination, and integration" (p. 309) of the group's resources. Implicit within both Bandura's definition and Zaccaro et al.'s suggestion is the notion that collective efficacy involves high levels of interdependence related to multiple collective tasks that combine to result in group execution.

The final point of interest regarding Bandura's (1997) definition relates to the fact that those beliefs are task specific. Other researchers have operationalized similar terms such as *group potency* (Shea & Guzzo, 1987) and *collective self-esteem* (Crocker & Luhtanen, 1990), but in each case these describe general belief systems rather than task-specific cognitions related to a team's capabilities.

Although research on collective efficacy is at a relatively early stage in comparison to the study of self-efficacy, it is probably the most studied form of efficacy involving the performance of tasks within relational or team settings. Given that collective efficacy is grounded within the broader framework provided by self-efficacy theory, Bandura (1997) suggests the sources of collective efficacy are likely to be similar to other forms of efficacy. This means that although the antecedents of collective efficacy may operate at the group level (cf. Chan, 1998), the underlying mechanisms will likely be similar to those that influence both self-efficacy and role efficacy expectations (see figure 13.1).

Previous experiences of success are theorized to be the most powerful source of collective efficacy beliefs (Bandura, 1997). A number of recent studies provide evidence for this theorized relationship (Feltz & Lirgg,

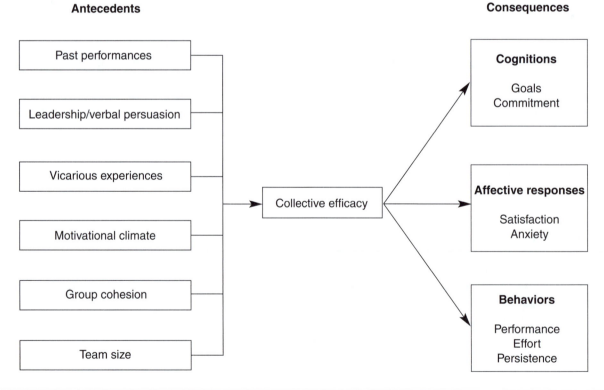

Figure 13.1   Antecedents and consequences of collective efficacy within sport teams.

Adapted from D.L. Feltz and M.A. Chase, 1998, The measurement of self-efficacy and confidence in sport. In *Advances in sport and exercise psychology measurement,* edited by J.L. Duda (Morgantown, WV: Fitness Information Technology Inc.), 66.

1998; Myers, Payment, & Feltz, 2004). In a study with women's ice hockey teams, Myers, Payment, et al. (2004) found that previous performance was predictive of collective efficacy, even after accounting for the effects of previous levels of collective efficacy. The authors used a design whereby the opponent remained constant for two games over a weekend, and so they were able to consider the direction of theorized relations and control for previous levels of the dependent variable, namely collective efficacy.

A growing body of literature has also suggested that leadership behaviors may prove to be an important determinant of collective efficacy beliefs (e.g., Chen & Bliese, 2002; Jung & Sosik, 2002; Watson, Chemers, & Preiser, 2001). Watson et al. (2001) found that teams with more confident leadership, in the form of both appointed and emergent leaders, had greater levels of collective efficacy, and suggested that the findings provided support for Bandura's (1997) theorizing that verbal persuasion from a significant other may positively affect a group's perceptions of competence. Interestingly, Watson and colleagues found that the influence of leadership on collective efficacy diminished over the course of the season (i.e., its influence was greatest at the beginning of the season), and they suggested that collective experiences of success become more influential as subsequent outcomes (success or failure) accumulate.

Recent research by Jung and Sosik (2002) has also found that transformational leadership (cf. Bass & Avolio, 1994; see also chapter 5) is positively related to collective efficacy and that this relationship is mediated by team members' sense of empowerment. Transformational leadership involves behaviors that exert influence by elevating followers' goals and provides members with the confidence to go beyond minimally acceptable expectations (Bass & Avolio, 1994; Avolio, Bass, & Jung, 1999). Although not synonymous constructs, verbal persuasion and empowerment are conceptually very close and both involve processes of persuasion. The construct of transformational leadership has received limited attention within sport or exercise settings (cf. Beauchamp, Welch, & Hulley, in press) but represents a potentially important antecedent of collective efficacy in sport.

Researchers have theorized that vicarious experiences may also be an important source of efficacy beliefs at the group level (Bandura, 1997; Lindsley et al., 1995). If teams see others who are similar to themselves succeed, efficacy beliefs will be fostered, whereas if they see others fail they may question their own capabilities to perform the same tasks. Although researchers have yet to empirically test this proposition in sport, some researchers have sought to investigate the potential influence of *self-modeling* (cf. Dowrick, 1999) at the team level. For example, Halliwell (1990) showed video highlights of successful performances of a professional hockey team with the specific purpose of boosting the team's confidence. Video is often used to provide performance feedback to athletes; however, in order to foster efficacy beliefs through this *collective self-modeling*, coaches would typically eliminate errors and focus on those aspects that reflect efficacious and successful team performance (cf. Dowrick, 1999).

Although mastery enactments, verbal persuasion, and vicarious experiences may prove to be important sources of collective efficacy, a growing body of research suggests that other factors may also be important. These include the motivational climate within the group (Magyar, Feltz, & Simpson, 2004), group cohesion (Paskevich, Brawley, Dorsch, & Widmeyer, 1999), and team size (Watson et al., 2001). In an attempt to examine motivational climates (cf. Ames, 1992) at the team level with rowing crews, Magyar et al. (2004) found that rowers' perceptions of their motivational climate significantly predicted collective efficacy beliefs. Specifically, Magyar et al. found that when athletes perceived the climate in which they trained and performed to be mastery oriented (see chapter 9 for an overview of coach-created motivational climates), higher levels of collective efficacy were reported.

In their conceptualization of collective efficacy, Zaccaro et al. (1995) suggested that the degree to which team cohesion is present may affect the level of collective efficacy within the team. Paskevich et al. (1999) tested this proposition and found that two dimensions of task cohesion (see chapter 7) were positively related to collective efficacy. These dimensions included members' attraction to the group's tasks (ATG-T) as well as the degree to which the group was perceived to be integrated around performing collective task-oriented activities (GI-T). However, Paskevich et al. also recognized that the relationship between collective efficacy and cohesion could be bidirectional. This means that teams may become more efficacious as a result of greater task cohesion, but they may also become more cohesive because of their perceived collective capabilities.

Finally, Watson et al. (2001) tested the proposition provided by Zaccaro et al. (1995) that group size may negatively influence collective efficacy. Zaccaro et al. theorized that coordination difficulties may be more likely as group size increases, thereby making team cohesiveness difficult to maintain. Although Watson et al. did not find support for this proposed relationship at the beginning of the competitive season, it was evident at the end of the season. Watson et al. reasoned that at the beginning of the season teams are yet to be strenuously tested in their ability to coordinate and integrate members' resources, while at the end of the season players have had extensive collective experiences upon which to judge their coordinative and integrative capabilities.

The consequences of collective efficacy can be considered in terms of various behavioral, cognitive, and affective outcomes (see figure 13.1). Although past experiences of success have been examined as an antecedent of collective efficacy, research has also investigated team performance as a behavioral outcome. For example, a series of longitudinal studies with American football and ice-hockey teams by Myers and colleagues found that collective efficacy was predictive of team performance (Myers, Feltz, & Short, 2004), even after controlling for the effects of prior performance (Myers, Payment, & Feltz, 2004). Support for this prospective collective efficacy–team performance relationship has also been found with university (Watson et al., 2001) as well as professional (Heuzé, Raimbault, & Fontayne, 2004) basketball teams.

Experimental research by Bray (2004), in which participants performed a group strength task (i.e., holding a medicine ball aloft), found collective efficacy to be predictive of performance and that group goals mediate this relationship. Bray's findings suggest that groups with higher levels of collective efficacy set higher goals for themselves, and in turn their goals for performance predict eventual performance. In an earlier laboratory study using the same medicine-ball task, Hodges and Carron (1992) demonstrated that collective efficacy is positively related to the effort expended in performing the group task. Hodges and Carron manipulated the levels of collective efficacy within groups by initially providing team members with bogus comparative feedback. They found that when groups perceived themselves to be inefficacious relative to their opponents they exerted less effort in performing the group task.

Research has also demonstrated the potential influence of collective efficacy upon team members' affective states. For example, Greenlees, Nunn, Graydon, and Maynard (1999) examined the relationships between collective efficacy, precompetition anxiety, and positive affect within six Rugby Union teams. Results revealed that collective efficacy was negatively related to members' levels of cognitive state anxiety and positively related to positive affect. Although research on collective efficacy is at a fairly early stage in sport, findings from other domains of psychology suggest that collective efficacy may act as a buffer of stressor–strain relationships (Jex & Bliese, 1999) and may also be related to other salient outcomes, including member satisfaction (Caprara, Barbaranelli, Borgogni, & Steca, 2003) and commitment (Caprara, Barbaranelli, Borgogni, Petitta, & Rubinacci, 2003).

Coaching Efficacy in Sport

An underlying theme of this book is that the coach plays a prominent role in facilitating the development and behaviors of athletes and teams. From an efficacy perspective, research is consistent insofar as coach leadership behaviors may also affect the team's perceived sense of collective competence (see figure 13.1). In light of the central role that coaches play within sport, a growing body of research has sought to investigate the degree to which coaches' efficacy beliefs influence the learning, development, and performance of their athletes (e.g., Feltz et al., 1999; Chase, Lirgg, & Feltz, 1997; Myers, Vargas-Tonsing, & Feltz, 2005).

Two forms of coaching efficacy have received attention, and it is essential to differentiate between the two. One relates to coaches' confidence in their own abilities to facilitate the learning and development of their athletes (cf. Feltz et al., 1999), and the other relates to coaches' confidence in their players' abilities to perform given tasks (cf. Chase et al., 1997). Both describe cognitions held by the coach; however, in the former case the referent is the *coach's* capabilities, whereas in the latter case the referent is the *players'* capabilities. Despite the fact that these two forms of coaching efficacy are conceptually distinct, research has also demonstrated how they are related (Hoyt, Murphy, Halverson, & Watson, 2003), a point that will be addressed later.

Feltz and her colleagues (1999) developed a conceptual model for the former type of coaching efficacy, or coaches' confidence in their own capabilities to affect the learning and development of their players. This conceptual model was based upon theorizing by Bandura (1977) as well as Denham and Michael's (1981) model of teacher efficacy, and it was subsequently operationalized in the form of a Coaching Efficacy Scale (CES) (Feltz et al., 1999). In their conceptual model, Feltz et al. identified four dimensions of coaching efficacy that were theorized to affect outcomes related to the coach, the individual athlete, and the team as a whole. These dimensions included coaches' confidence (a) in their ability to coach during competition and lead their team to successful performance (game-strategy efficacy), (b) in their ability to affect the psychological skills and states of their athletes (motivation efficacy), (c) in their instructional and diagnostic skills (technique efficacy), and (d) in their ability to influence the personal development of their athletes (character-building efficacy).

From a construct-validity perspective, results have supported the factor structure of the CES and provided evidence for the multidimensional conceptualization of coaching efficacy (Feltz et al., 1999; Myers, Wolfe, & Feltz, 2004). Feltz et al. also suggested that in accordance with theory (see Bandura, 1997), coaches' efficacy expectations would be influenced by specific antecedents. In their initial study, Feltz et al. found that coaching efficacy was predicted by coaches' past experiences of mastery and success, coaching experience, athletes' skill levels, and social support from the school and community. Recent research by Myers et al. (2005) found similar results insofar as team ability, social support from the athletes' parents and the community, coaches' career winning percentage, and years of experience as head coach were found to be significant sources of coaching efficacy.

In terms of outcomes related to coaching efficacy, Feltz et al. (1999) found that coaches with higher levels of coaching efficacy provided more praise and encouragement behaviors and fewer instruction and organization behaviors than coaches with low coaching efficacy. Players also reported greater satisfaction with coaches with higher coaching efficacy, and they had better winning percentages than players performing under coaches with low coaching efficacy. Recent research has also found that coaching efficacy is predictive of university coaches' commitment to coaching (Kent & Sullivan, 2003) and is related to the frequency with which coaches employ various behaviors designed to enhance the efficacy of their players (Myers et al., 2005).

Although Feltz et al. (1999) did not examine the relationship between coaching efficacy and player efficacy, they did hypothesize as part of their conceptual model that efficacious coaches would likely have more efficacious and motivated players. A recent laboratory study by Hoyt et al. (2003) lends support to Feltz et al's theorizing in this regard. In their study, Hoyt et al. employed the term *leader efficacy* (i.e., leader's efficacy to lead; Chemers, Watson, & May, 2000) rather than coaching efficacy; however, the two are conceptually similar constructs. They found that leaders' efficacy was significantly related to their confidence in their teams' abilities, which in turn was predictive of followers' perceptions of collective efficacy. This finding suggests that the more the leaders believed their group could perform effectively, the more the followers believed it as well. Hoyt et al. concluded that the process underpinning this relationship may involve the leader communicating expectations to followers and the followers subsequently adopting the leader's views.

As previously mentioned, coaches' confidence in their team's abilities is conceptually distinct from coaches' confidence in their own coaching capabilities. Despite the fact that the Hoyt et al. (2003) laboratory study involved a non-sport task, research in sport by Chase et al. (1997) provides additional evidence for the potential *transference* effects of coaches' efficacy

You *can* do this!

(in their players' capabilities) upon subsequent player behavior. Chase et al. found that coaches' confidence in their team's capabilities was related to two indicators of team performance in basketball, free throws and turnover performance. Although Chase et al. did not test collective efficacy as a mediator of the coach efficacy–team performance relationship as Hoyt et al. did, it seems entirely plausible that when coaches communicate their efficacious expectations to a team the team will in turn become efficacious, resulting in more accomplished performances.

Additional Forms of Relational Efficacy in Sport

The research by both Hoyt et al. (2003) and Chase et al. (1997) highlights the need to ensure that coaches are confident in their players' capabilities. However, an equally interesting question relates to the extent to which athletes' confidence in their coach's capabilities affects the athletes' cognitions and behaviors. Although this question has yet to be examined in sport, recent research on exercise leadership provides some interesting directions for future research. Bandura (1997) described this form of efficacy as *proxy efficacy,* which relates to confidence in an intermediary to function on one's behalf.

Bray and his colleagues (Bray, Gyurcsik, Culos-Reed, Dawson, & Martin, 2001; Bray, Gyurcsik, Martin-Ginis, & Culos-Reed, 2004) recently operationalized Bandura's construct of proxy efficacy and examined exercise participants' confidence in their class leader to help them achieve their goals. In one study focused on exercise participants' adherence, Bray et al. (2001) found that exercisers' confidence in their exercise leader (i.e., proxy efficacy) was related to their self-efficacy expectations and that proxy efficacy was able to explain significant variance in future exercise adherence above and beyond that explained by self-efficacy beliefs alone. Bray et al. (2001) concluded that "proxy efficacy beliefs may play an important role in bolstering exercisers' beliefs about their own abilities to successfully perform the necessary elements of a strenuous aerobic workout within structured group classes" (p. 432). Drawing from the Bray et al. study, it is possible that when athletes are confident in their coach's abilities to help them achieve their goals, this confidence may reinforce their own perceived sense of competence to deal with the demands of competition. Future research that tests this hypothesis in sport seems warranted.

From a similar theoretical perspective, Lent and Lopez (2002) presented a conceptual model for the study of efficacy beliefs within dyadic contexts. They suggested that when people perform within close relationships (e.g., performance dyads), self-efficacy beliefs exist in dynamic interaction with the beliefs people hold about the capabilities of their relationship partners. They referred to this latter form of efficacy as *other-efficacy* and defined this as "an individual's beliefs about his or her significant other's ability to perform particular behaviors" (p. 264). Lent and Lopez theorized that when individuals have an elevated sense of their partners' capabilities, this may affect the level of commitment to their partner, the level of effort expended in activities involving their partner, and various behaviors involving joint performance.

Proxy efficacy as described by Bandura (1997) could be considered a specific type of other-efficacy, albeit one that specifically involves the relinquishment of personal control to the significant other (i.e., proxy agent). However, quite different forms of other-efficacy may also exist in sport, grounded in mutually interdependent dyads that perform together in competition (e.g., tennis doubles, ice-skating dyads, or rowing pairs). These partnerships are prevalent in many sports, yet efficacy beliefs within performing dyads have received limited research attention.

In one study conducted within the sport of equestrian eventing, Beauchamp and Whinton (2005) sought to examine the relationships between riders' confidence in their own capabilities (i.e., self-efficacy), confidence in their horses' capabilities (i.e., other-efficacy), and riding performance. Equestrian eventing provides a unique context in which to study other-efficacy. In this sport, horse and rider are teammates, and it is one of the few Olympic sports where men and women compete on equal terms. As Lent and Lopez (2002) have commented, within the context of dyadic performance enactment "it is advantageous for the performers to possess favorable beliefs both about their own and their co-performer's role capabilities" (p. 276).

In their study, Beauchamp and Whinton found that self-efficacy and other-efficacy were each able to explain unique variance in riding performance. They concluded that one should not only seek to foster athletes' confidence in their own performance capabilities, but also athletes' confidence in the capabilities of their *dyadic partner* (in this case, the horse). Clearly, the Beauchamp and Whinton study involved somewhat atypical dyads. However, the results appear to have implications for other performance dyads involving athlete–athlete relationships (e.g., tennis pairs, ice-skating partnerships). Indeed, Lent and Lopez (2002) suggest that other-efficacy beliefs might be related to additional relational outcomes, and in sport this may include the athlete's choice of partner, motivation to train and compete with that partner, or satisfaction derived from competing with that partner.

While recognizing the potential contribution of other-efficacy, Lent and Lopez (2002) suggested that one should also consider peoples' reflections on how they are viewed by their partners. Specifically, Lent and Lopez described the beliefs a person has about how his or her capabilities are viewed by the significant other as a form of *relation-inferred self-efficacy* (RISE). If, for example, a rookie is paired with a veteran to play in a tennis doubles tournament, the rookie might believe that the veteran is very confident in the rookie's capabilities to play doubles (i.e., high RISE), or conversely he or she may believe that the veteran is completely unconfident in the rookie's capabilities. Depending on how an athlete appraises his or her partner's confidence, these RISE beliefs may affect the way that athlete interacts and performs within that relationship.

In short, Lent and Lopez theorized that RISE beliefs "may complement other-efficacy and self-efficacy in determining relationship satisfaction and persistence outcomes" (p. 268), and they referred to the potential interaction of self-efficacy, other-efficacy, and RISE as a tripartite view of efficacy beliefs within dyadic contexts. Although RISE beliefs have yet to be examined within the sport psychology literature, they would appear to be potentially influential in understanding how any close partnerships are initiated, maintained, and enhanced.

Future Research

The study of efficacy beliefs within relationship and group contexts represents an area of investigation that has enormous potential for future research within sport psychology. Much behavior in sport exists within social contexts that involve numerous influential agents (e.g., coaches, teammates, family, friends). Invariably, people hold a range of efficacy beliefs that correspond to the diverse tasks that involve those agents. Although recent research has begun to articulate, define, and investigate these distinct forms of efficacy, considerable research is still required to understand how each of these forms of efficacy interrelate, how they develop, and what implications they have for individual and collective functioning (vis-à-vis cognition, affect, and behavior).

With regard to interrelations among different forms of efficacy, several lines of inquiry are encouraged. First, research has shown that leadership behaviors are influential in raising followers' collective efficacy beliefs (Hoyt et al., 2003). However, research has yet to ascertain how leadership behaviors affect members' perceptions about their role-related capabilities. Formal roles are typically assigned by the coach to meet the task-specific demands of the group (Mabry & Barnes, 1980), and in line with the transference effects found by Hoyt et al. it seems likely that if coaches and on-field leaders are confident in team members' capabilities, they may in turn feel confident in their abilities to perform their various formal role responsibilities. Thus, it seems likely that coaching efficacy and leadership efficacy will be related to role efficacy in sport.

Second, although Bray et al. (2002) found that role efficacy is related to collective efficacy, research has yet to ascertain the causal direction within this relationship. That is, do athletes feel confident in performing their individual role responsibilities because the team as a whole is confident in performing its collective responsibilities? Or, does the team feel confident in performing its collective responsibilities because individual members are confident in performing their individual role responsibilities?

Although this relationship may be bidirectional, any answer to this question would also have important implications for practice. For example, if collective efficacy was found to be causally antecedent to role efficacy, this would suggest that interventions designed at the group level (development of collective group mastery experiences) may have cross-level effects upon members' role-efficacy beliefs. Alternatively, interventions designed to facilitate role-efficacy (e.g., clarifying members' role responsibilities) may bring about elevated levels of collective efficacy. Interestingly, Zaccaro et al. (1995) specifically discussed this relationship when they suggested that developing role clarity may facilitate collective efficacy within group settings.

Another potential area of interest relates to the possibility that the transference effects found in the Chase et al. (1997) study, whereby a coach's confidence in the team's capabilities affected the team's performance, may also work the other way. That is, how does the team's confidence in the coach's abilities affect the team's sense of collective competence? At the individual level, research by Bray et al. (2001) on proxy efficacy suggests that a person's confidence in a leader's capabilities may bolster that person's own sense of competence. However, it is also possible that the team's confidence in the coach may similarly bolster the team's collective sense of confidence. Numerous anecdotes within professional sport suggest that when a team loses confidence in their coach (i.e., collective proxy efficacy), the organization typically fires the coach under the belief that the coach is unable to meet the group's needs. While this may be the case, it would be interesting to empirically test whether collective proxy efficacy is an additional antecedent of collective efficacy in sport.

Perhaps one of the most important directions for future efficacy research is to conduct intervention-based investigations to determine the extent to which each type of relational and group efficacy described in this chapter can be enhanced. Indeed, within the title of his landmark paper, Bandura (1977) described efficacy theory as a *unifying theory of behavioral change* and theorized that because efficacy beliefs represent social cognitions they should be amenable to change (see also Bandura, 1997). Despite this, coupled with the vast output of efficacy research, surprisingly few studies on efficacy interventions have been conducted in sport.

One interesting exception to this relates to a study by Malete and Feltz (2000), in which they subjected a sample of high school coaches to a coach education program, entitled the Program for Athletic Coaches Education, or PACE (Seefeldt & Brown, 1990). This education program included elements that Malete and Feltz theorized should facilitate coaching efficacy, such as the role of the coach, effective instruction and game strategy, motivating athletes, personal and social skills, positive coaching, and maintaining discipline. Although PACE is a relatively short-term program (i.e., 12 hours of contact time), results of the intervention showed that coaching efficacy significantly increased post-test within the experimental group in comparison to a control group. Given that each form of relational and group efficacy covered in this chapter is grounded within the broader framework of self-efficacy theory (Bandura, 1997), experimental and intervention studies could similarly be employed to determine how these other types of efficacy might be amenable to change.

Finally, the basic tenets of self-efficacy theory suggest that efficacy beliefs should be related to various individual and group outcomes, including motivation, choice of activities, goals, effort, and so forth (cf. Bandura, 1997). Despite the fact that a number of relatively new forms of efficacy are beginning to receive research attention within relational and group contexts in sport (e.g., role efficacy, other-efficacy), much research is still required to ascertain how these cognitions affect various athlete-, team-, and coach-related outcomes.

Practical Implications

From an applied perspective, the results of the efficacy research covered within this chapter suggest a number of considerations for those interested in facilitating behavioral enactment within relational and group settings in sport. One only has to examine the various sources that have been found to be related to each type of efficacy to decipher how that form of efficacy can be enhanced. For example, if a coach is particularly interested in raising the team's collective efficacy (see figure 13.1), he or she could (a) structure practices to ensure that team members are able to draw from successful experiences of performing specific maneuvers, (b) exude confidence in the team's capabilities when communicating with them, (c) develop a mastery-oriented climate rather than a performance-oriented climate, (d)

compile video footage (i.e., a series of highlights) so that the team can see themselves performing specific collective systems or maneuvers effectively (i.e., collective self-modeling), and (e) employ interventions designed to enhance task cohesion (e.g., role-clarity strategies).

The same principles would also apply to facilitating the other forms of efficacy covered in this chapter. For example, if a coach is interested in raising a player's role efficacy, he or she could devise strategies such as ensuring the player is (a) given sufficient experience to perform his or her role responsibilities in practice before being thrown into the cauldron of competition, (b) clear about his or her scope of role responsibilities, and (c) provided with appropriate role models upon which to model the successful execution of specific role responsibilities. Alternatively, if a sport psychology consultant is concerned with enhancing a team captain's leadership efficacy, the consultant could (a) encourage the captain to model leadership behaviors on those of an efficacious leader, or (b) encourage the coach to exude confidence in the captain's leadership capabilities.

The research findings highlighted in this chapter would suggest that efficacy-enhancement interventions can be directed at the coach, the individual athlete, or the team as a whole. Regardless, when developing the intervention one should be acutely aware of the temporal nature of the efficacy cognition being targeted (Bandura, 1997). Efficacy beliefs are likely to change with time, especially as the client (i.e., athlete, coach, team) begins to access different sources of efficacy information, and develops differential levels of success and failure across a range of performance contexts. As Lindsley et al. (1995) remind us, the efficacy–performance relationship is cyclic in nature and can spiral upward or downward. Clearly, this can work in favor of (if the spiral is upward) or against (if the spiral is downward) the client. Practitioners (e.g., coaches, sport psychology consultants) are encouraged to be aware of any efficacy–performance spiral and intervene if necessary, especially if the spiral is downward.

Summary

The overall purpose of this chapter was to provide a comprehensive review of the extant efficacy literature related to behavioral enactment within relational (e.g., coach–athlete, athlete–athlete) and group settings. Each form of relational and group efficacy covered in this chapter is grounded within the broader theoretical framework provided by self-efficacy theory (Bandura, 1977, 1997) and as such is likely to be determined by multiple sources of information. In general, relational and group conceptions of efficacy have been found to be positively related to improved athlete, team, and coach functioning.

Although some of the efficacy constructs covered in this chapter have been the focus of much research attention (e.g., collective efficacy), other forms have only recently begun to be considered, conceptualized, and studied (e.g., other-efficacy, relation-inferred self-efficacy). Given that efficacy beliefs are theorized to be social cognitions amenable to change through the process of intervention (cf. Bandura, 1997), future research is needed to understand the extent to which these beliefs might influence each other (e.g., relations between coaching efficacy and role efficacy) as well as salient individual and collective outcomes in sport.

DISCUSSION QUESTIONS

1. Research conducted on coaching efficacy, proxy efficacy, and other-efficacy suggests that confidence in a significant other may affect an athlete's personal sense of efficacy. To what extent might a parent's confidence in a child's capabilities affect the confidence of that child?

2. What are some of the key sources of collective efficacy beliefs in sport teams? If a coach is interested in developing a team-building intervention to raise the team's collective efficacy, what sort of strategies might be employed? Who should facilitate the intervention (coach or consultant) and why?

3. To date, most of the research conducted on roles within sport psychology has focused on formal roles in sport teams. Drawing from the basic tenets of self-efficacy theory (cf. Bandura, 1997), discuss how team members might develop confidence in their abilities to perform informal role responsibilities (e.g., social coordinator, team confidant). To what extent do you think elevated levels of efficacy to perform informal roles might affect athletes' contributions to their team?

4. If role efficacy is beginning to spiral downward, what strategies might a sport psychology consultant employ to reverse the trend?

5. How might the motivational climate created by a coach affect the collective efficacy of a team?

chapter 14

Person Perception and Sport Performance

Iain Greenlees, PhD

Learning Objectives

On completion of this chapter, the reader should have

1. ability to define person perception;

2. knowledge regarding data-driven and schema-driven explanations of person perception;

3. understanding of the conditions that determine the use of data-driven or schema-driven person perception and ability to apply those principles to sport;

4. knowledge of Warr and Knapper's (1968) model of person perception;

5. familiarity with research that has examined person perception in sport settings; and

6. familiarity with avenues for further research on person perception in sport.

I was walking around the warm-up area. Carl (Lewis) was standing there with his coach and looked at me. I could roughly lip-read what he was saying: 'Effing hell . . . look at that', or something along those lines. It confirmed what I had been thinking earlier on: Carl would not be a problem. He had seen the shape I was in, and that was it.

Linford Christie, former international British sprinter (quoted from Christie, 1996, p. 175)

This quote from Linford Christie illustrates the potential effects of the perception of others in sport. It seems as though the impression Christie formed of Carl Lewis' mental state before the competition enhanced his own mental state. The quote supports anecdotal and experiential evidence from sport performers (e.g., Barnes, 1999; Redgrave & Townsend, 2000) and sport psychologists (e.g., Loehr, 1990; Weinberg, 1988) alike that the way in which athletes perceive opponents can affect the course of sporting interactions. However, only a handful of studies have examined impression formation in sport; therefore, the aim of this chapter is to examine how impressions of others are formed and the potential influence of these impressions in sport settings.

Approaches to Person Perception

Within social psychology, it has long been accepted that the impressions people form of each other are powerful determinants of subsequent social interactions (Fiske, Neuberg, Beattie, & Milberg, 1987), and the process of perceiving those we interact with (person perception) has been the focus of research since the 1950s (Jones, 1996). Within this literature (e.g., Fiske & Neuberg, 1990; Fiske & Taylor, 1991), it is proposed that when perceivers enter social interactions—of which sporting encounters form a distinct subcategory—they actively seek information to understand the demands of the interaction and to predict how it is likely to progress and conclude.

It is proposed that this information enables individuals to experience a sense of control over the interaction and allows them to manipulate their behavior to enhance their chances of achieving their goals for the interaction, whether their goals are to have a pleasant interaction, to gain vital information, or, to take examples from the world of sport, be selected for a team, or defeat an opponent (Fiske & Taylor, 1991). Although many theories have been proposed to explain how people form impressions of target individuals, two broad perspectives have emerged: schema-driven impression formation and data-driven impression formation. These perspectives and a position put forward by Fiske & Neuberg (1990) that integrates these diverse approaches are discussed next.

Schema-Driven Approaches to Person Perception

Schema-driven (or category-driven or expectancy-driven) impression formation is, perhaps, the dominant approach to understanding how people form impressions of others (e.g., Fiske & Neuberg, 1990; Fiske & Taylor, 1991; Jones, 1996). Proponents of schema-driven theories of social cognition (e.g., Fiske & Taylor, 1991) posit that, in order to function effectively, people automatically use cues (e.g., physical appearance, clothing, gender) that are available early on in a social interaction to assign a person to a category (also called a person schema). Person schemas can be defined as cognitive structures that contain a person's knowledge of the attributes of a specific type of person (e.g., judge, delinquent, tennis player) and the relationships among those attributes (Fiske and Taylor, 1991). Schemas include judgments of the characteristics, mental states, and likely goals of that type of person.

For example, the schema for a "good tennis player" may include knowledge of what such players should look like, what clothes they should wear, and what equipment they should use. The schema may also include expectations of how such a person is likely to behave in certain situations. Thus, when a tennis player enters into a match with a new opponent, she will use readily available information (e.g., opponent's ranking, clothing, demeanor) to classify the opponent into a category. Once a category is activated, the perceiver can then fill in the missing gaps (e.g., the opponent's likely tactics, how the match will progress) in her knowledge

This chapter owes much to the assistance and enthusiasm of Richard Buscombe and Matt Rimmer, two of my research students. Their interest in person perception in sport and the ideas and research that they have produced over the last few years have provided a stimulating environment in which to work. Thanks must also go to my current colleagues Terry McMorris and Jan Graydon and former colleagues Tim Holder, Richard Thelwell, Andrew Bradley, Bill Filby, and Mark Bawden for their advice over the last 10 years. Of these, special thanks must go to Tim Holder and Mark Bawden for helping me turn some initial ideas into a program of research.

of the target. This information allows perceivers to manage their behavior and maximize their chances of winning their match (Cohen, 1981).

In addition, it is proposed that schemas have a number of consequences. First, schema theorists propose that activating a schema produces an immediate affective reaction. Such a link between schemas and affect has been supported by research. In work examining ethnic schemas, Dijker (1987) found that use of schemas produced anxiety, irritation, and concern. Thus, it could be proposed that assigning an individual to an "aggressive rugby player" schema may elicit anxiety, fear, or anger. Of course, schema use could also produce positive emotional responses such as relief or joy. Because affective and emotional responses, such as anxiety, have been shown to influence sporting performance (e.g., Lazarus, 2000; Woodman & Hardy, 2003), it can be proposed that such a categorization may have an important impact in sport.

The second major impact of schema use is concerned with the processing of further information. Schema theorists propose that schemas influence the information that individuals attend to and how that information is evaluated and remembered (Fiske & Taylor, 1991). For example, research has shown that schema use causes people to focus more attention on schema-relevant (either schema-consistent or schema-inconsistent) information. Chapman and Chapman (1967, 1969) showed a link between schema use and attention in a study with psychologists. They found that the information that psychologists attended to when examining drawings from patients was influenced by the nature of the mental illnesses that they believed the patients to have: The psychologists focused on information that was consistent with the mental illness of the patient.

However, it has also been found that people will spend more time attending to schema-inconsistent information (Hashtroudi, Mutter, Cole, & Green, 1984). It has been proposed that this is because perceivers need to spend more time trying to understand the inconsistent information and reconcile it with their initial impressions of the target person (Olson, Roese, & Zanna, 1996). For example, an observer may take more notice of the positive sporting behavior of a player who has a reputation of being aggressive or a cheat because that does not match the usual perception of the athlete. Similarly, great athletes' basic errors, such as when Olympic diving champion Greg Louganis hit his head on the springboard during one of his dives, are often remembered with greater clarity than other incidents.

Schemas are also said to influence the encoding and evaluation of information, with individuals interpreting information to confirm the schemas they are using. For instance, Darley and Gross (1983) found that when participants viewed a set of exam results, they evaluated them more positively if they believed that the results had been achieved by a person from a high socioeconomic status than if they believed the results had achieved by someone of low status.

In addition, it is proposed that schemas influence the way in which perceivers attribute the causes of the performances of others. Specifically, perceivers will attempt to attribute the performances of others in such a way as to support the existing schema. Thus, a good performance from someone categorized as a poor player may be attributed to external factors (e.g., good fortune) whereas the same performance from someone categorized as a good performer may be attributed to factors internal to the performer (e.g., skill). Research by Nadler, Fisher, and Streufert (1974) has supported this prediction. These authors found that, in a simulated international negotiation, participants offered aid by a perceived enemy attributed the offer as being more negatively motivated and less altruistic than the same offer from a perceived ally.

It is also proposed that schemas influence the information that people remember about others. Zadney and Gerard (1974) showed participants film footage of a student registering for a university class. When participants believed that the student was a music major they recalled more music-relevant information from the scene (e.g., that the student was carrying a musical score); if led to believe that they were watching a mathematics student, they remembered more mathematical information from the scene. Thus, if a target is assigned to an aggressive schema, perceivers attend to sources of information that will give them more information about the target's aggressiveness, perceive ambiguous acts as being more aggressive than they actually are, and more readily recall instances of aggression from the target. In this sense, the biases in cognition brought about by expectancies result in perceptual confirmation of an individual's initial expectancies or schemas (Snyder, 1984).

The final influence of schemas is on behavior. In a seminal paper, Snyder, Tanke, and Berscheid (1977) demonstrated that male college students led to believe they were having a phone conversation with an attractive female behaved more sociably toward her than those who were led to believe they were having a conversation with a less attractive female. In addition, females were judged to respond more positively to males who believed them to be attractive than to males who believed them to be plain. Therefore, the authors proposed that the social interaction was influenced by preinteraction expectancies and that these expectancies created a self-fulfilling prophecy. Similar results have since been reported in a diverse range of social settings, such as academia, the military, and psychotherapy (for reviews see Snyder, 1984; Miller & Turnbull, 1986).

The influence of initial impressions and expectancies on behavior has also been shown in competitive situations. Langer (1975) found that participants who were competing in a gambling game against an opponent who acted nervously and dressed poorly (the snook condition) betted significantly greater amounts of money against that opponent than participants competing against a well-dressed and confident opponent (the dapper condition). Thus, this research shows that nonverbal behavior may influence the course of competitive encounters.

Theory and research have shown that the early information perceivers receive concerning the people they interact with influences the way in which social interactions develop and conclude. Specifically, this information has been shown to influence the impressions that are formed of others, the expectations of the way others will behave, the processing of interaction-relevant information, and the way in which the perceivers themselves behave. If such processes are operating in sport, it could explain the contention of athletes and sport psychologists that sporting events can be decided before they have even begun. For instance, if, based on the opponent's equipment, clothing, and reputation, a squash player allocated his opponent to an "elite player" schema, then the

following expectations may influence the perceiver's emotions (e.g., anxiety or welcoming the challenge), promote greater attention to and encoding of the target's strengths and good shots during a warm-up, and lead the perceiver to reduce or increase effort or change strategies for the match, all of which influence the outcome of the encounter.

Data-Driven Approaches to Person Perception

The second approach to explaining person perception is the data-driven approach (also referred to as individuating, piecemeal, or attribute-driven processing; Fiske et al., 1987). Theorists who propose this approach argue that the information we receive about others is processed in a systematic and unbiased fashion as it becomes available (Fiske & Taylor, 1991). People form impressions of others by integrating every new piece of information about a target person into their evaluation of the target (Anderson, 1981). As information (e.g., opponent's body size) is received it is evaluated along specific dimensions (e.g., aggressiveness), assigned a weighting according to how predictive it is of the dimension of interest, and integrated into the existing evaluation of the target person. As more information is received and processed, an overall evaluation (through either averaging or adding evaluations) is produced.

Sporting events can be decided before they have even begun.

Therefore, a perceiver's impression is constantly being revised as new sources of information are received (Fiske & Taylor, 1991).

Although this strategy allows for accuracy of person perception due to its systematic nature, it has been suggested that such processing requires considerable attentional resources to be devoted to incoming information and thus results in slower person perception and may hamper performance on secondary tasks (Fiske et al., 1987). Although data-driven theories still propose that person perception results in affective, cognitive, and behavioral responses, it proposes that these are responses to the evaluation of information that is received rather than the categorization of the target person (Fiske et al., 1987). As a consequence, if the data-driven approach to person perception predominates in sport, it would be expected that initial expectancies are amended throughout an encounter and play only a limited role in determining the course and outcome of a sporting encounter.

Continuum Model of Impression Formation

Early research that examined person perception was marked by the debate as to which form of information processing best explains person perception. Schema theorists argued that schema-driven processing predominates because it allows for swifter formation of judgments compared to data-driven approaches. Thus, a sense of prediction and control can be achieved earlier than under data-driven approaches (Fiske et al., 1987). However, proponents of data-driven processing pointed to the need for accuracy in person perception and provided research to support the use of individuating processes (Fiske, Lin, & Neuberg, 1999).

Fiske and Neuberg (1990) challenged the nature of this debate and proposed that people use a range of information-processing strategies dependent on a number of factors. In their continuum model of impression formation, they argued that when people enter into a social interaction, they immediately and automatically seek to categorize the target person into a schema. However, when motivated and in possession of sufficient attentional resources, they seek to apply a more data-driven processing strategy.

These predictions may provide an intriguing debate for sport psychologists interested in person perception in sport. The predictions from Fiske and Neuberg's model would suggest that athletes may be inclined toward data-driven processing. A key determinant of the use of data-driven processing, according to Fiske and Neuberg (1990), is that the target must be of personal relevance (e.g., influencing the achievement of interaction goals) to the perceiver.

This proposal has received support from Pendry and Macrae (1996), who found that when perceivers were motivated to form an accurate perception of a target person, they used data-driven processing strategies. Thus, when a target person may determine whether or not a perceiver will attain his interaction goals, the perceiver will be more inclined to use a data-driven strategy of information processing. As opponents in most sports fulfill this criterion, it can be predicted that data-driven processing is used in sport. This proposition was supported by work by Ruscher and Fiske (1990) and Ruscher, Fiske, Miki, and Van Manen (1991), who found that, in competitive social interactions, information was processed in a more data-driven fashion than when in cooperative social interactions.

However, Fiske and Neuberg (1990) also proposed that the use of data-driven strategies depends on the perceiver having sufficient cognitive resources to attend to the information presented by a target person. They proposed that when a perceiver has limited attentional resources, schema-driven processing will be used. In sport, attentional resources may be restricted in a number of ways. First, the time demands placed on athletes may mean that they do not have sufficient time to process all information systematically. This includes having limited time to make a decision or being confronted with so much information that detailed processing is impossible. Second, Ruscher and Fiske (1990) proposed that the primary focus of athletes is on their own behavior and performance rather than on the information that they can receive from their opponents, which may lead to schema-driven processing.

Third, it can be proposed that attentional resources may be depleted by heightened levels of arousal (Kahneman, 1973), which may promote schema-driven processing (Fiske & Taylor, 1991; Bodenhausen, Macrae, and Sherman, 1999). As sport competition has the power to elicit high levels of arousal, this could also contribute to the use of schema-driven processing in sport. Given that both Ruscher and Fiske's (1990) and Ruscher et al.'s (1991) studies used laboratory-based competitions rather than actual sporting encounters, it could be claimed that arousal levels were not influenced to the extent that they would elicit a change in information processing. Thus, further research is required to examine whether schema- or data-driven processing dominates in sport.

Schematic Model of Person Perception

The term *schema theory* refers to a broad collection of theoretical perspectives on social cognition in the same way that attribution theory encompasses a number of theoretical positions (Fiske & Taylor, 1991). Therefore, research may also benefit from the examination of more specific theories and models of person perception that provide a more comprehensive framework for the study of person perception in sport. One such theoretical model is Warr and Knapper's (1968) schematic model of person perception (see figure 14.1). Rather than concentrating on the extent to which people use either data- or schema-driven processing, as Fiske and Neuberg's (1990) continuum model does, Warr and Knapper's model attempts to provide a fuller description of the determinants and consequences of the impressions that we form of others.

Warr and Knapper proposed that when a person interacts with another person there are three interdependent consequences. First, there is an *attributive response,* which involves the judgments individuals make concerning the characteristics and goals of the people they perceive. Thus, a netball player may make judgments about qualities such as an opponent's size, aggression levels, speed, and experience. Warr and Knapper further proposed that such judgments can be of an episodic or a dispositional nature. Episodic judgments are made about a person at a particular moment in time (e.g., "She's playing aggressively"); because these

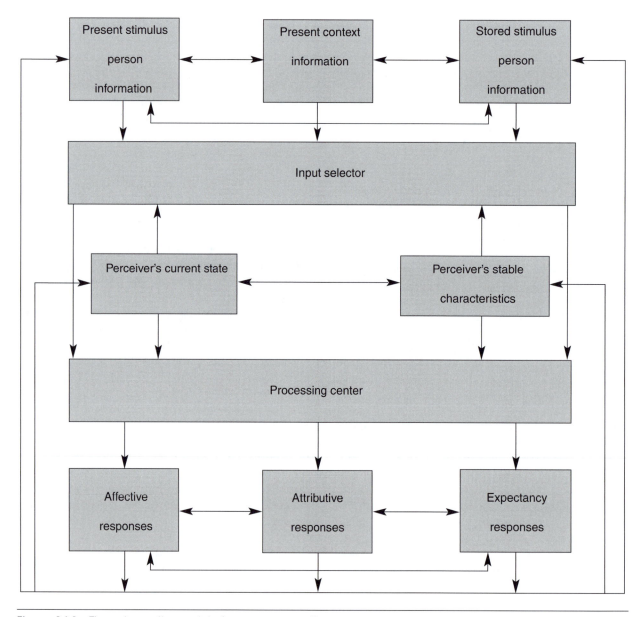

Figure 14.1   The schematic model of person perception.

are judgments of transitory factors, their influence may be confined to the interaction as it occurs. Dispositional judgments are judgments about the enduring characteristics of an individual, such as personality and abilities. These judgments not only influence how a perceiver approaches the immediate interaction with the target person but also how the perceiver approaches future interactions with that individual (Jones, 1996).

The second consequence of person perception proposed by Warr and Knapper is an *affective response* in which the perception of another person elicits a variety of emotional responses such as loathing, fear, or attraction. Thus, the netball player who perceives an opponent to be aggressive, fast, and strong may feel emotions such as anxiety, jealousy, and dislike for that opponent. Finally, Warr and Knapper proposed that person perception produces an *expectancy response*. Specifically, they argued that individuals use the information they receive about others to form expectancies about how people are likely to behave and how interactions with them are likely to progress. Here, the netball player may expect the encounter with an opponent to be physically demanding, potentially one-sided, and ultimately damaging to her chances of impressing spectators.

Thus, attributive and expectancy responses can be said to be akin to schemas whereby an individual infers aspects of a target person's character from the information that is presented (attributive response) and also develops a set of expectancies about how the target person is likely to behave from what they know about that person (expectancy response).

Warr and Knapper (1968) also proposed that three sources of information are used to form an impression of a target person. First, there is information that is already held about another individual, or stored stimulus person information. This may be based on previous encounters or reports from others (e.g., teammates, coaches, the media). Second, there is information that is received directly from the target at the time of the interaction, or present stimulus person information. The amount of information that may be used in this respect is enormous and includes verbal communication, body language, eye contact, and clothing and other possessions (for a review see Knapp, 1978).

Third, the effect of certain information is determined by the context in which the perceiver finds himself, or present context information. That is, information may mean one thing in certain situations and something entirely different in other situations. For instance, when worn at a gymnasium, sport clothing may evoke one set of perceptions about the wearer (e.g., health conscious, active), but when worn to a job interview the clothing may evoke an entirely different set of perceptions (e.g., socially inept, rebellious, unprofessional).

The information that may be garnered from these three sources is clearly huge. Therefore, Warr and Knapper argued that a person only selects a certain amount of information to process. The input selector (see figure 14.1) refers to the part of the mind that chooses which information will be attended to and processed. Accordingly, the input selector's choice of information will be determined by two factors: perceiver's current state and perceiver's stable characteristics. The perceiver's *current state* includes such factors as mood states, arousal levels, and goals for the interaction and the perceiver's *stable characteristics* include factors such as personality, values, and beliefs. It is thus proposed that both an individual's states and traits influence the information he looks for when perceiving another person. For instance, it has been shown that stable characteristics such as gender and experience (Fiske & Taylor, 1991) may influence the information that people seek out. Stable characteristics also include personality factors, such as trait anxiety. Additionally, factors included within perceiver's current states include mood states (Fiske & Taylor, 1991), state anxiety (Eysenck, 1992), and the perceiver's interaction goals (Fiske & Taylor, 1991).

With regard to anxiety, theorists such as Eysenck (1992) and Beck (1976) have proposed that individuals high in trait anxiety will attend to more threatening information. Preliminary support for differences in the attention of anxious and non-anxious individuals in sport settings has been provided by research in visual search patterns. For example, studies by Williams and Elliott (1999) and Janelle, Singer, and Williams (1999) both found that participants with high state anxiety attended to different sources of information than individuals with low anxiety. Williams and Elliott (1999), in a study examining the effects of anxiety on visual search in karate performers, found that heightened anxiety caused the performer to fixate more on the fist and arm (potentially more threatening than the torso or head) of an opponent. Thus, it can be proposed that anxiety may influence the information that people seek out in a sporting environment.

Once information is selected, it is processed at the processing center (see figure 14.1). Information processing includes integrating information, evaluating it, and drawing inferences. According to Warr and Knapper (1968), the perception of information is not solely determined by the information that is taken in but also by the characteristics of the perceiver. Correspondingly, the model predicts that an individual's mood states, arousal and anxiety levels, and interaction goals determine the way in which the individual evaluates information that has been gathered about another person. Similarly, the perception process is influenced by stable characteristics such as personality, beliefs, and values. Again, factors such as trait and state anxiety have been proposed to influence how information is perceived. For instance, Beck (1976) argued that people high in anxiety are more likely to perceive ambiguous information as threatening.

Once a perception is formed and the responses to that perception are experienced, further information about the target person is selected and perceived (Warr & Knapper, 1968). Thus, the model suggests that the responses will contribute to stored stimulus person information (see figure 14.1) and will influence what information is sought out and encoded by the perceiver. In addition, as is evident from the affective response, the impressions that are formed also influence the perceiver's current state and, potentially, the perceiver's stable characteristics. Thus, the model describes a continually evolving process of person perception.

Regardless of the particular theoretical viewpoint adopted by researchers, the study of social cognition is based on the belief that, whether data or schema driven, the impressions that individuals form of the people they interact with will influence the course of social interactions. The question that the remainder of this chapter will examine is the extent to which such assumptions hold true in sport settings.

Research on Person Perception in Sport

Despite anecdotal testimonies from athletes, coaches, and sport psychologists, only a few studies have examined person perception in sport. Nonetheless, within the sport psychology literature, researchers have examined a number of facets of person perception. The purpose of this section is to examine research conducted in three sporting populations: coaches, athletes, and officials.

Person Perception in Coaches

Within coaching, researchers of person perception have focused on the extent to which coaches create self-fulfilling prophecies. Horn and Lox (1993) outlined a four-phase model of this process in sport: (1) The coach forms an impression of an athlete (e.g., her ability, dedication, or scope for improvement), which involves an expectation of how the athlete will respond to coaching (e.g., the athlete will be receptive, make great improvements, and be a key player for the team, or the athlete will not improve whatever the coach does); (2) the coach's expectations influence his behavior toward the athlete (e.g., reinforcement, general encouragement); (3) the manner in which the coach behaves influences the athlete's psychological states, rate of

learning, and, ultimately, the athlete's performances; and (4) the athlete's performance conforms to the expectations of the coach.

The key link within this model is between 1 and 2, the link between impression formation and the future behavior of the perceiver (the coach). In common with schema theorists, Horn and Lox (1993) proposed that a coach's expectations and impressions will influence the way in which she behaves toward an individual. Unfortunately, relatively few researchers have examined the link between coach expectations and behavior in sport. Furthermore, those studies that have been conducted have provided inconsistent and at times contradictory support for the influence of coach expectations on coaching behavior. The authors of early research examined the influence of coach expectations on behavior in youth sports. Rejeski, Darracott, and Hutslar (1979) found that children perceived by their coach to have high ability received more positive reinforcement and less general instruction than children perceived to have lower ability. However, Horn (1984) found no expectancy effects in practice sessions but did find that high-expectancy athletes received less in-game praise and instruction than low-expectancy athletes.

Researchers have also examined the self-fulfilling prophecy in collegiate settings. Sinclair and Vealey (1989) found that the expectations of coaches did not influence the type of feedback that was given to athletes. This has been supported by the work of Solomon, Wiegardt, et al. (1996), who found no expectancy effects of coaches (based on either ethnicity or ability expectations) on their athletes. Moreover, Solomon, Golden, Ciapponi, and Martin (1998) and Solomon and Kosmitzki (1996) found no relationship between coaches' expectations of ability and coaching behavior across the course of a season.

However, some support has been found for the influence of expectations on behaviors. Sinclair and Vealey (1989) and Solomon, Striegel, Eliot, Heon, and Maas (1996) found that high-expectancy athletes received more individual communications and feedback from their coach than low-expectancy athletes in collegiate sport. In addition, Solomon, Golden, et al. (1998) found that the effects of expectations depended on the stage of the season and the nature of the expectation. In the early season they found that athletes perceived to have low potential for improvement received more management feedback than athletes perceived to have high potential for improvement. In late season, they found that athletes perceived to have a high potential for improvement received more instruction than athletes with low potential for improvement. In addition, athletes perceived to be high in ability received more management feedback and overall feedback than athletes perceived to be low in ability, but only at the end of the season. In contrast, Solomon and Kosmitzki (1996) found that expectations for improvement influenced levels of technical instruction and general encouragement, but only in the early part of the season.

Research results in the area of coach expectations are clearly equivocal. Although some influence of expectations has been observed, the results obtained to date should be treated with caution. In addition to the generally low numbers of coaches used in each study (from 3 to 14, with a modal value of 4), the main criticism that can be leveled at the research is lack of experimental control. All of the studies cited were conducted on teams that were already formed, and they distinguished high- and low-expectancy athletes by the coaches' rating of the athletes. Thus, although overall high–low expectancy differences were observed, the differences in coaching behavior could have been due to the different demands of coaching the particular athletes. Researchers examining self-fulfilling prophecies in education overcame this problem by manipulating the expectancies of teachers before they had had contact with the students (e.g., Rosenthal & Jacobsen, 1968). Thus, research of this nature would benefit the examination of self-fulfilling prophecies in sport.

In addition, researchers have not examined the information that coaches use to form impressions of athletes. Although performance is clearly the most useful source of information, it can be argued that coaches may also form impressions of athletes through other sources of information. In line with Warr and Knapper (1968), coaches may use information such as reputation and reports of previous performances to form an impression of, or categorize, an athlete. This, in turn, could lead to schema-driven processing of performance information (e.g., attention to certain aspects of performance, heightened recall of mistakes or good play) that leads to a self-fulfilling prophecy. Researchers thus need to examine how coaches form initial impressions of their athletes and the effects, if any, of these impressions.

Person Perception in Athletes

Researchers have conducted a few studies, albeit limited and with a range of research aims, that have examined person perception among athletes. Sadalla, Linder, and Jenkins (1988) examined the effects of a target person's preference for sport participation on others' perceptions of the target person. Sadalla et al. found differences in the ways in which bowlers, tennis players, golfers, motocross riders, and skiers were perceived on five personality factors (active-daring, cultured, calmness, honesty, and attractiveness). Their results indicated that tennis players and skiers were considered the most attractive people while bowlers

were considered the least attractive. The results also showed that golfers were rated as the calmest and most honest athletes while motocross riders were rated as the least honest.

The finding that athletes from different sports are perceived in different ways by observers has been supported in research conducted by Linder, Farrar, Sadalla, Sheets, and Bartholomew (1992, cited in Prapavessis, Grove, & Eklund, 2004). The results of this study indicated that basketball players were perceived by females as being the most athletic and golfers were rated as the least athletic, and tennis players were perceived as the most attractive athletes. These results show that knowing a person's preferred choice of sport can influence impressions of that person.

In a study of racial stereotyping, Stone, Perry, and Darley (1997) found evidence for perceptual confirmation of a racial stereotype. In a study in the United States, Stone et al. led participants to believe they were hearing a radio commentary on either a white American or black American basketball player. Although all participants heard the same commentary, the two groups perceived the commentary in different ways. Specifically, those individuals led to believe they were hearing a commentary on a black basketball player felt that the commentary showed that the player possessed more athletic ability but displayed less game knowledge and effort than did the individuals led to believe the player was white. This supports the contention that schemas and expectancies may influence the processing and evaluation of information in sport.

Although these studies provide support for the influence of person perception in sport, the research does not address how person perception may influence the course of a sporting encounter between two competitors. To date, only three studies have specifically examined perception processes within a competitive sport setting. Miki, Tsuchiya, and Nishino (1993) examined the influence of expectancies on information processing prior to a simulated golf contest. In this study, participants were either led to believe that they were going to be competing against a good or a weak player, or they received no information about the player. Following this, Miki et al. provided participants with a series of descriptors of the player (e.g., relaxed or unrelaxed, careful or careless, able to concentrate or unable to concentrate) and recorded the time spent by participants processing this information.

The results of the study indicated that participants who held an expectation spent less time attending to and processing the information presented and tended to use the information to confirm their expectancies. These results provide some support for the notion that expectancies (or schemas) may influence what information is attended to and how it is encoded in sport.

Greenlees, Bradley, Holder, and Thelwell (2005) examined the influence of a potential opponent's body language (posture, movement, and eye contact) and clothing (table-tennis-specific vs. general sportswear) on participants' attributive and expectancy responses. Male table-tennis players viewed video footage of four different table-tennis players warming up, each displaying one of four combinations of body language and clothing. Participants viewed (a) one model displaying positive body language (walking with an erect posture with head up and chest forward while maintaining eye contact with the camera for prolonged periods of time) and wearing table-tennis-specific clothing, (b) one model displaying positive body language and wearing general sportswear, (c) one model displaying negative body language (slumped posture and limited eye contact with the camera) and wearing table-tennis-specific clothing, and (d) one model displaying negative body language and wearing general sportswear.

After viewing the models, the participants rated each model on a series of descriptors (attributive responses). Analysis indicated that those models who displayed positive body language were rated as more assertive, aggressive, competitive, experienced, confident, positive, focused, relaxed, and fit than the models who displayed negative body language. Clothing did not influence the participants' perceptions of the models, which suggests that it may not be an important source of information for determining these specific qualities in table tennis.

In addition, Greenlees, Bradley, et al. (2005) asked the participants to indicate their perception of their ability to defeat each of the models they viewed in a hypothetical table-tennis match (expectancy responses). The results indicated that both body language and clothing influenced the participants' perceptions concerning the outcome of a hypothetical table-tennis match with the model. The participants were more confident of defeating models who displayed negative body language and models wearing general sportswear. Because such outcome expectations have been shown to exert an influence on athletic performance (Eyal, Bar-Eli, Tenenbaum, & Pie, 1995; Feltz & Reissinger, 1990; Weinberg, Gould, & Jackson, 1979), it was tentatively concluded that the clothing and body language of an opponent can influence the course and outcomes of social interactions. The results from this study were supportive of predictions derived from Warr and Knapper's (1968) model.

In a second study examining person perception in sport, Greenlees, Buscombe, Thelwell, Holder, and Rimmer (2005) also found support for the influence of body language and clothing on attributive and expectancy responses. The researchers showed participants a video of a male tennis player displaying either positive or negative body language and either tennis-specific or general sportswear. Results indicated that body language exerted a strong influence on episodic judgments (e.g., relaxed, confident, prepared), with the tennis player being rated more positively when he displayed positive body language. No effects of clothing were observed.

In terms of dispositional judgments, Greenlees, Boscombe, et al. (2005) found an interaction effect for clothing and body language. Specifically, they found that when the target was observed displaying positive body language and wearing general sportswear he was rated more positively than when he was observed displaying positive body language and wearing tennis-specific clothing. However, when coupled with negative body language, tennis-specific clothing produced more positive dispositional judgments than general sportswear. These results support the contentions that present stimulus person perception exerts an influence on impression formation and that sources of information interact with each other to produce impressions. Greenlees, Boscombe, et al. also found that body language influenced the outcome expectations of perceivers, although clothing had no effect on these judgments.

As a whole, the results from the two studies just discussed provide initial support for Warr and Knapper's (1968) model in a sporting context. In addition, the findings also indicate that the context within which information is received will influence the manner in which it is perceived. In the table-tennis study, clothing played a more significant role in the perception of an opponent than in the tennis study. This supports the assertion that, rather than having the same effect across all sports, the same information (e.g., smart clothing, the latest equipment) may be perceived differently by athletes from different sports.

Person Perception in Officials

Researchers examining the judging of subjectively scored sports have confirmed the potential influence of pre-event expectancies on information processing and performance evaluation. Scheer and Ansorge (1975) identified a bias favoring gymnasts performing last for their team (a traditional sign of being the strongest performer on the team). This has been supported in a number of studies (e.g., Ansorge, Scheer, Laub, & Howard, 1978; Scheer, 1973; Scheer, Ansorge, & Howard, 1983). Plessner (1999) argued that gymnastics judgments may be guided by schema-driven processing of information in which performing last in a team activates a set of expectations regarding the quality of that performance. Overall, Plessner provided research evidence for such a scoring bias.

However, Plessner (1999) also proposed, in accord with Fiske and Neuberg's continuum model (1990) of information processing, the conditions under which schema-driven processing (the order effect) would occur. First, Plessner proposed that schema-driven processing would occur in fast-paced events (horse, vault, and horizontal bar) where judges had to form judgments in short periods of time (limited processing time available). This was supported by Plessner's findings. The second prediction made by Plessner was that, in situations likely to provoke heightened arousal, expectancy effects would be more likely to be observed. Plessner argued that judging as part of a panel may elicit heightened levels of arousal and so reduce attentional resources needed to undertake data-driven processing. However, the results did not support this prediction and the extent to which the experimental manipulation (judging in the presence of others) affected arousal is unclear.

Plessner (1999) also examined the proposal that expectancies will influence the encoding of individual pieces of information. Plessner's results partially supported this contention, as judges noticed fewer errors if the gymnast appeared last in the order of presentation than if the gymnast appeared first. This research supports the contention that initial impressions of others will influence the processing of information and the evaluation of sporting performances.

More recently, Findlay and Ste-Marie (2004) showed evidence of the influence of expectancies on information processing in figure-skating judges. They showed qualified judges videos of skaters performing a short program. Half of the skaters were known to the judges and were rated as having a good reputation for skating, and half were unknown. The results showed that the overall technical merit scores awarded to the skaters with reputations were better than the scores awarded to unknown skaters, even when there were no differences in the actual performances of the skaters. This result supported the hypothesis that expectancies would influence the evaluation of the overall performance.

However, Findlay and Ste-Marie found no evidence to suggest that expectancies influenced the encoding of individual pieces of information (judgment of specific elements of the routine), as analysis revealed no differences in the identification of errors or in the punishment assigned to separate errors. Despite this, research conducted within sport officiating and judging does indicate that expectancies can influence the evaluation of performances. The findings from this research also provide support for Warr and Knapper's (1968) contention that stored stimulus person information (in this case, reputation from previous encounters) and present context information (via team order) may influence the way in which a person is perceived.

Researchers have also shown the potential influence of impression formation in the refereeing of objectively scored sports. Frank and Gilovich (1988) hypothesized that teams wearing black would be perceived as more aggressive than teams wearing white. Frank and Gilovich showed spectators and referees footage of simulated American football plays and asked the participants to indicate how likely they would be to penalize the defensive team in each of the plays. The videos were filmed so that the same plays were filmed twice, once with the defensive team wearing black and once wearing white. The researchers found that both the spectator group and the referee group perceived the team wearing black to be more "aggressive" and "dirty" when they were wearing black. The results also showed that participants were more likely to penalize the defensive team when they were wearing black than when they were wearing white. Frank and Gilovich argued that this indicated that person perception of sport people and teams could be influenced by cues available before or early on in an encounter.

Jones, Paull, and Erskine (2002) proposed that, in line with comments from professional soccer players and suggestions from schema-driven models of decision making, referees might be more inclined to punish players and teams with aggressive reputations. Jones et al. showed two groups of soccer referees an identical series of video clips showing incidents from games and asked them to report the action they would take if they were refereeing that incident. Before viewing the clips half the referees were told that one of the teams they were viewing had a reputation for aggressive play while the remaining referees received no information. The results indicated that the referees expecting to view an aggressive team perceived more challenges as illegal and dispensed more severe punishments than the referees who did not hold such an expectation. These findings, together with the other research conducted with officials, highlights the potential influence of preinteraction expectancies in sport.

Although the research on person perception in sport settings has examined a diverse range of questions, it does support the notion that people involved in sport (coaches, officials, and athletes) form impressions of other athletes based on initial information. Furthermore, the research suggests that these impressions and expectancies have the potential to influence the course of sporting encounters.

Future Research

It is clear that the research that has been conducted to date is limited in breadth and depth and further research is needed in each of the contexts discussed (i.e., coaching, performing, and officiating). This section highlights potential research areas for further consideration. Given the many gaps that currently exist in the literature, the suggestions will focus on potential research avenues examining person perception among athletes. However, many of the suggestions will be relevant to future research directions in coaching and officiating.

Given the findings from the research conducted to date, it appears that person perception may offer a fruitful avenue of research within sport psychology. Fortunately, the area has a number of theoretical positions to draw upon, and a long tradition of research in this area has seen the development of protocols and paradigms designed to satisfactorily assess person perception in sport (Fiske & Taylor, 1991). What is needed now is a broad and systematic research effort to investigate person perception in sport, focusing on how people form impressions and the effects of those impressions.

The first suggested avenue of research is to extend the examination of hypotheses derived from Warr and Knapper's (1968) model of impression formation. First, researchers may wish to establish what present stimulus person information is used to form impressions in different sports. Currently, research has indicated that clothing style and body language may influence the impressions that people form of their opponents. However, there are many more sources (e.g., equipment, physique, ethnicity) that may determine impression formation and, therefore, researchers need to examine the extent to which these sources are influential in sport.

In an unpublished study, Rimmer, Greenlees, Graydon, and Buscombe (2004) adopted a qualitative approach to studying this issue. They interviewed 12 tennis players (8 males and 4 females) and found that a large range of information was used to form impressions of opponents. Consistent with Warr and Knapper's (1968) model of person personal perception, Rimmer et al. found that participants reported using present stimulus person information, stored stimulus person information, and present context information to form impressions of opponents. In terms of present stimulus person perception, participants reported using cues such as opponents' body size and shape, body language, eye contact, clothing, and equipment. In addition, participants claimed to be influenced by stored stimulus person information in the form of information from previous encounters, information from coaches, information from fellow players, and ranking information. Last, the participants described contextual information in the form of the players that opponents socialized with at the tournament and the level of tournament.

As person perception research in sport is still limited, this qualitative approach may help to formulate hypotheses concerning specific sources of information used by athletes. However, it must be remembered that Fiske and colleagues (e.g., Fiske et al., 1999) have proposed that much impression formation is unconscious. Thus,

people may not be fully aware of the range of cues that they are using and further experimental studies are warranted. In addition, Warr and Knapper (1968) and many other researchers (e.g., Argyle, 1994; Fiske & Taylor, 1991) have suggested that the information that is used to form impressions is specific to context. This claim is supported by the different effects of body language and clothing that have been observed in table tennis (Greenlees, Bradley, et al., 2005) and tennis (Greenlees, Buscombe, et al., 2005).

Research is thus needed in a broad range of sports to examine the information that is used across sports and information that is specific to certain types of sport (e.g., team sports, invasion sports, racket sports). Furthermore, research conducted to date has predominantly been laboratory-based. Future researchers will need to explore the possibilities of more field-based research paradigms.

In addition to examining the determinants of impression formation in sport, research is also needed to examine the effects of these impressions. The work of Greenlees and colleagues has shown a link between the information that an athlete receives and attributive and expectancy responses. In addition to further research examining this link, research is needed to examine the link between impression formation and affective responses. If a link can be established between the information that athletes receive from an opponent's verbal and nonverbal communication and the emotions and anxiety that they experience, it will support the claim that person perception is an important avenue for sport psychology research due to the potential for anxiety and other emotions to influence sporting performances (Lazarus, 2000; Woodman & Hardy, 2003).

Although the work that has been conducted with athletes represents a promising start to the study of person perception in sport, there is still a need to examine the effects of initial impressions and expectancies beyond the initial prematch warm-up. Schema-driven theories of social cognition propose that the expectancies (derived from schema activation) derived from impression formation can influence further information processing (attention, encoding, evaluation, and attribution), affect, and behavior. Although initial research with athletes (Miki et al., 1993; Stone et al., 1997) and with officials (Findlay & Ste-Marie, 2004; Jones et al., 2002; Plessner, 1999) has established that expectancies (derived from knowledge of reputation, team order, ethnicity, and clothing color) can influence information processing, more research is required.

In addition, research is needed to establish a link between athletes', coaches', and officials' expectancies and their behaviors. Fiske and Neuberg's (1990) continuum model proposes that it is by no means certain that expectancies (or schemas) are extensively used in sport.

Therefore research is needed to establish the extent to which schema- and data-driven processing is used and, if used at all, the conditions in which they are used.

Once these fundamental questions have been examined, researchers may wish to investigate those factors that moderate the relationship between the information that is received from a target person and the impressions that are formed of that person. Warr and Knapper's (1968) model predicts that a range of factors (both dispositional and state factors) may moderate this relationship. Factors such as gender, mood (Fiske & Taylor, 1991), and anxiety (Eysenck, 1992) have all been suggested to influence the information that a perceiver attends to and how that information is processed. At present, there are many gaps in the research conducted in sport settings; for instance, researchers have not yet examined impression formation in female athletes or in elite athletes.

Linked to this line of research, there is also a need to examine person perception in different sporting interactions. To date, researchers have focused solely on sporting encounters with a previously unknown opponent. However, interactions of this kind may be rare, if not unheard of, in high-level sport. Thus, research examining person perception with known opponents is warranted. Although Warr and Knapper's (1968) model incorporates knowledge of a performer, it will be interesting to find out what present stimulus person information athletes use to form impressions of opponents they already know, how present stimulus person information and stored stimulus person information are integrated, and the effects of the judgments that are made about an opponent.

Practical Implications

Findings from the research that has been conducted to date provide a number of intriguing avenues for the development of applied interventions aimed at influencing person perception in sport. The first form of potential intervention is to assist performers to use their own presentation to project a desired impression to an opponent. This type of intervention has been suggested in the applied sport psychology literature on numerous occasions (e.g., Bull, Albinson, & Shambrook, 1996; Loehr, 1990; Weinberg, 1988). However, these suggestions have not always been made with a view to changing the impressions formed of an athlete by the opponent; rather, they have been made with a view to changing the cognitions and emotions of the athlete projecting the image and enhancing affect and cognition related to self-presentation (see chapter 15).

In line with this approach, an article by Hackfort and Schlattman (2002) proposed a self-presentation training technique for elite athletes. This training involved the use of video-assisted behavioral training to develop particular forms of emotional self-presentation in athletes. Although no empirical evaluation of the technique was proposed, the authors did argue that the technique might be effective in provoking desired reactions in opponents or in intimidating opponents. Thus, in the future researchers may seek to examine the extent to which athletes can be trained to exhibit appropriate nonverbal communication and the extent to which it may influence their opponents.

The second potential intervention approach is to change the way in which athletes perceive their opponents to ensure that athletes form accurate and realistic data-driven impressions. Work on stereotyping (a form of schema-driven processing) has proposed that people can be encouraged to form more data-driven impressions by making them aware of their stereotypical thinking, providing evidence that refutes stereotypical beliefs, and asking them to consciously attend to the information that is available (Fiske & Taylor, 1991).

However, Macrae (2000) has argued that stereotypical or schema-driven thinking may be extremely difficult to overcome through such methods. Indeed, Macrae pointed to research showing that attempts to consciously suppress schema-driven thinking could lead, through ironic mental processes, to increases in stereotypical thinking and discriminatory behavior (Macrae, Bodenhausen, Milne, and Jetten, 1994; Wyer, Sherman, & Stroessner, 1998). However, as these studies examined perceptions of broader social groups (i.e., based on race), it remains to be seen whether suppression is effective in reducing schema-driven processing and behavior in sport settings. Should researchers establish that schema-driven processing can be detrimental to sporting performance, the exploration of suppression strategies would then be warranted.

Summary

Although still in its infancy, research examining person perception in sport has provided support for its potential to enhance our understanding of the psychology of sport, coaching, and officiating. At present, a research base is building to support the claim that individuals form impressions of the people they compete against (or coach or judge) and that these impressions may influence cognitions (e.g., outcome expectations, evaluations of an opponent's performance) that in turn may influence the course of a sporting interaction. However, many questions concerning person perception in sport remain unanswered and many avenues of research remain unexplored. This chapter therefore finishes with a call for a comprehensive and sustained research effort in the area of person perception in sport.

Discussion Questions

1. What sources of information do you use to form impressions of others in (a) social interactions in general and (b) your sport of choice?

2. What are the potential effects of impression formation in sport?

3. To what extent have schema-driven strategies of information processing been shown to be used by coaches, athletes, and officials?

4. Under what conditions will coaches, athletes, and officials use schema-driven information processing?

5. What factors do you think influence (a) the information that coaches, athletes, and officials attend to and (b) the way in which coaches, athletes, and officials perceive the information that they receive?

6. What processing strategy dominates in your sport—a schema-driven or data-driven strategy? Justify your answer.

chapter 15

Self-Handicapping in Sport: A Self-Presentation Strategy

Ralph Maddison, PhD, and Harry Prapavessis, PhD

Learning Objectives

On completion of this chapter, the reader should have

1. understanding of what self-presentation is and why it might occur;

2. familiarity with benefits and costs of self-presentation strategies;

3. understanding of self-handicapping and the two broad types of strategies used;

4. knowledge of the situations in which self-handicapping might take place;

5. understanding of the relationship between self-handicapping and cognitions, emotions, and behavior in competitive situations; and

6. insight into the effect of group processes on self-handicapping.

How we are viewed by others in our environment has numerous implications for the way in which we are perceived, treated, and evaluated. Sport represents an environment in which presentation of one's self in a favorable manner can have positive implications for an individual. Various strategies have been suggested that can be employed to create a favorable impression. It is this notion of self-presentational concern that will form the basis for this chapter. This chapter will illustrate that when people are concerned about the impressions others form of them, they may adopt a particular strategy such as self-handicapping to create a favorable impression.

To this end, this chapter reviews the self-handicapping and sport literature and is divided into four main sections. The first section focuses on self-presentation (impression management) and explains what it is and why it occurs. It also discusses self-handicapping, a self-presentation strategy, by explaining what it is, factors known to influence it, and costs associated with it. The second section reviews the self-handicapping and sport literature. The third section provides an overview of future research with an emphasis on methodological concerns and avenues of research, and the fourth section presents practical implications and recommendations for coaches.

Self-Presentation

Self-presentation, or impression management, is not a new concept, and interest in this domain has been evident since the 1950s. For example, in 1959 Goffman presented his thoughts about impression management, a process by which people manage their overt behaviors in order to manipulate the impressions others form of them. Taking a different approach, Heider (1958) articulated a framework for thinking about the manner in which people perceive and attempt to make sense of behavior.

Current definitions refer to self-presentation as a process by which people attempt to control the impressions that others form of them (Leary, 1992; Leary & Kowalski, 1990). It is an essential part of interpersonal behavior, as one's image can influence how one is evaluated and treated by others (Leary & Kowalski, 1990), which in turn can influence one's social life, employment, and romantic involvement (Leary, Tchividjian, & Kraxberger, 1994). Ultimately, these impressions can even influence how people see themselves (Leary et al., 1994).

The concept of self-presentation often evokes images of shrewd concealment; however, self-presentation is neither Machiavellian nor manipulative. Rather, it is a natural and necessary component of human interpersonal behavior. There are few social situations in which

people can afford to disregard the self-presentational implications of their behavior (Goffman, 1959). Each person's response to another is based on the individual's impressions of the other's personality, abilities, motives, and other attributes. Thus, one's outcomes in life depend at least in part on conveying impressions that lead others to respond in desired ways. Even when people are not consciously trying to create a particular impression, they nevertheless monitor the reactions of others, often at an unconscious or preattentive level, and adjust their behavior when they believe they are making undesired impressions (see Leary & Kowalski, 1990, for a review).

The fact that people monitor and try to control how they are being perceived and evaluated does not necessarily mean that the impressions they try to create are deceptive. Although people do sometimes try to convey images of themselves that are different (usually better) than how they see themselves, most self-presentations are reasonably consistent with the individual's own self-concept (Leary & Kowalski, 1990). Rather than involving conscious dissimulation, self-presentation usually entails a selective presentation of those aspects of oneself that will create a desired impression on specific people within a particular social encounter and a selective omission of information that will create undesired impressions.

A two-component model of self-presentation has been proposed by Leary and Kowalski (1990) to better understand the complexity of self-presentational variables. The first component of the model refers to possible motives for self-presentation, such as maintenance of self-esteem, achievement of social and material outcomes, and development of a particular identity. The second component refers to impression construction and includes all behavioral attempts to create impressions in the minds of others. Self-handicapping is a strategy that fits well within this self-presentation paradigm.

Self-Handicapping As a Form of Self-Presentation

The term *self-handicapping* was coined by Berglas and Jones (1978) to describe the process of proactively avoiding threats to one's self-esteem via "any action or choice of performance setting that enhances the opportunity to externalise (excuse) failure and to internalise (reasonably accept credit) success" (p. 406).

In their original work, Berglas and Jones (1978) predicted that subjects would self-handicap by electing to use a performance-inhibiting drug (Pandocrin) rather than a performance-enhancing drug (Actavil) when anticipating a retest on an intelligence test for which they received noncontingent success feedback. Specifically, noncontingent evaluative feedback involves any form of feedback that is either out of kilter with actual performance or otherwise prevents people from adequately diagnosing the cause of their performance outcome. Conversely, contingent success is in line with performance and allows people to adequately assess the performance outcome.

In Berglas and Jones' first experiment, participants in a contingent-success group worked on soluble problems and participants in a noncontingent-success group worked on insoluble problems. Results revealed that male participants in the noncontingent-success group selected Pandocrin more often than did those in the contingent-success condition. In a second experiment, participants received either success feedback or no feedback following soluble and insoluble problems. Again, males in the noncontingent-success conditions selected Pandocrin more often than those in the contingent-success condition. Participants in the groups with no feedback and contingent success did not reliably differ.

Since the original work by Jones and Berglas, a theoretical distinction has been made between behavioral and self-reported self-handicaps (Leary & Shepperd, 1986; Snyder, 1990). Behavioral handicaps refer to deliberate, overt acts that make success at a task more difficult such as ingesting drugs or alcohol, withholding effort (Rhodewalt, Saltzman, & Wittmer, 1984; Harris & Snyder, 1986; Tice & Baumeister, 1990), actively assisting competitors, and choosing to perform in suboptimal conditions (Ferrari & Tice, 2000; Shepperd & Arkin, 1989, 1991). Self-reported handicaps are verbal claims of being injured, ill (Smith, Snyder, & Perkins, 1983), socially anxious, in a bad mood, or a victim of traumatic life events (Snyder, Augelli, Ingram, & Smith, 1985; Smith,

Snyder, & Handelsman, 1982). It is worth highlighting that gender differences appear to be more evident in behavioral self-handicaps than claimed self-handicaps (Hirt, McCrea, & Kimble, 2000). Specifically, men self-handicap more when they are self-focused but women do not behaviorally self-handicap under self- or other-focused conditions.

The underlying motives to self-handicap have been described as self-protective (Berglas & Jones, 1978) and self-presentational (Leary & Kowalski, 1990). Berglas and Jones suggested that people self-handicap in order to protect self-esteem, whereas Leary and Kowalski argued that the prime motive for self-handicapping is to preserve or enhance self-concept. Self-handicapping strategies permit people to capitalize on the attributional principles of augmentation and discountation (Kelly, 1971). That is, proactive handicaps allow individuals to augment the role of personal factors such as ability if performance is good and discount the importance of personal factors if performance is bad. Hence, the handicap helps people take advantage of personal attributes to either weaken or strengthen the link between them and performance outcomes, thereby insulating them to some degree from the self-relevant implications of failure (Leary & Kowalski, 1990).

From an empirical standpoint, studies of attributions made for one's own performance in the presence of potential handicaps provide consistent support for discounting (i.e., self-protection) following failure and occasional support for augmentation (i.e., self-enhancement) following success (Levesque, Lowe, & Mendenhall, 2001). For example, in a study

Self-handicapping strategies include using the excuse of an injury or putting forth low effort to avoid looking bad if performance is poor.

of reactions to good and bad performances in a university exam, Feick and Rhodewalt (1997) found that claimed handicaps were associated with discounting of ability attributions among failing students and also with augmenting of ability attributions among students who were more successful. On the other hand, Rhodewalt, Morf, Hazlett, and Fairfield (1991) found that, while self-protection was a general post-failure response among those claiming handicaps, self-enhancement was restricted to individuals with high self-esteem who claimed handicaps. Tice (1991, 1993) also argued that self-enhancement via the generation of preperformance impediments is most characteristic of individuals with high self-esteem.

The dispositional tendency to use claimed or behavioral self-handicapping strategies before performance appears to differ among individuals (Rhodewalt, 1990). The Self-Handicapping Scale (SHS), originally developed by Jones and Rhodewalt (1982), has been the principal instrument for assessing these dispositional tendencies to self-handicap. The original SHS is a 25-item self-report questionnaire that requires respondents to rate their agreement (on 6-point scales) with statements reflecting the use of self-handicapping behaviors as lack of effort ("I would do better if I tried harder"), illness ("I suppose I feel 'under the weather' more often than most people"), or procrastination ("I tend to put things off to the last minute") in conjunction with evaluative performances. The scale also includes items designed to assess concerns about achievement.

Due to concern about the SHS factor structure, Rhodewalt (1990) reanalyzed the scale and found that only 14 items loaded significantly (greater than .40) on one of two scale factors—excuse making and diminished effort. The subscale for excuse making assesses the tendency to make excuses before evaluative performances (i.e., claimed self-handicapping), whereas the subscale for diminished effort taps a person's willingness to withhold effort in achievement settings (i.e., behavioral self-handicapping). The most widely used version of the SHS has been the 14-item version.

Construct validity for the SHS has been demonstrated by theoretically relevant relationships to a variety of measures, which include perceived stress level, objective and subjective indices of underachievement, level of intended effort, and performance on tasks thought to be difficult (Deppe & Harackiewicz, 1996; McCrea & Hirt, 2001; Rhodewalt, 1990; Rhodewalt & Fairfield, 1991). Moreover, SHS scores have been found to have positive relationships with self-consciousness, neuroticism, ego-oriented goals, other-directedness, and social anxiety (Knee & Zuckerman, 1998; Rhodewalt, 1990, 1994; Ross, Canada, & Rausch, 2002; Strube, 1986). In addition, negative associations between scores on the SHS have been found with autonomy, conscientiousness, self-esteem, and task-orientated achievement goals (Knee & Zuckerman, 1998; Rhodewalt, 1990, 1994; Ross et al., 2002).

Costs of Self-Handicapping

Using self-handicapping strategies to influence the impressions others form is not without cost (Self, 1990; Sanna & Mark, 1995; Crant, 1996). As mentioned earlier, Kelly's (1971) attribution principle suggests that people will derive benefits from impression management (e.g., Bailis, 2001); however, they still run the risk of failure and possibly losing face if they are found out. It is also possible that in avoiding evaluation of ability through self-handicapping, individuals may never actually know how much they can accomplish.

Effective self-handicapping serves to convince both the actor and the observer that the actor is in control and a good person (Higgins & Snyder, 1990). Negative consequences will thus result from employing a handicap if it gives the impression that the actor either lacks control or is not so good. According to Snyder (1990), the believability of the handicap to both the actor and the observer is crucial to the impressions of goodness and control (Martin & Brawley, 1999).

In a recent review of the literature on self-presentation in sport, Prapavessis, Grove, and Eklund (2004) present a conceptual model that emphasizes the "potential advantages and disadvantages of excuses, their credibility, and the need for effective excuses to address such components of responsibility as intentionality, control, and obligation" (p. 22). The model proposes that other aspects of the handicap require consideration to fully understand the self-presentational consequences of self-handicapping strategies. Specifically, the impression will be influenced by whether the audience perceives the extent to which the handicap was unintentionally versus intentionally evoked, a result of situational factors versus dispositional factors, non-controllable versus personally controllable, and socially desirable. Further work is required to fully explore the tenets of this model.

Although the benefits of self-handicapping have been examined in the physical domain (e.g., Bailis, 2001; Deppe & Harackiewicz, 1996), the associated costs have not. Research evidence from nonsporting environments does exist and has shown that peers who viewed others using self-handicapping strategies considered them to be less confident and less motivated than those who did not self-handicap (Luginbuhl & Palmer, 1991). Moreover, Rhodewalt, Sanbonmatsu, Tschanz, Feick, and Waller (1995) provided evidence that participants evaluated objectively equivalent performances less favorably if they came from a self-handicapper than if they came from a non-self-handicapper.

Self-Handicapping in Sport

Sport presents an ideal environment in which to examine self-handicapping: Self-handicapping is most likely to occur in situations that are public, are important to the individual's self-concept, and in which the individual is evaluated against high standards or relative to another person's performance (Berglas & Jones, 1978; Self, 1990). These conditions are inherent in sport competition where an athlete's self-concept can be strongly influenced by self-evaluations and public evaluations of the athlete's physical abilities (cf. Vallerand, Pelletier, & Gagne, 1991), thus creating a situation where self-handicapping is predicted to occur (Rhodewalt et al., 1984). In their seminal paper, Jones and Berglas (1978) noted the strong potential for self-handicapping among athletes when they stated that "self-handicappers are legion in the sports world, from the tennis player who externalises a bad shot by adjusting his racket strings, to the avid golfer who systematically avoids taking lessons or even practicing on the driving range" (p. 201).

Insofar as self-handicapping in sport is concerned, research studies have documented the types of self-handicapping behaviors used by athletes (Rhodewalt, et al., 1984); the nature of impediments reported by athletes (Carron, Prapavessis, & Grove, 1994); the role of team cohesion in self-handicapping (Carron et al., 1994; Hausenblas & Carron, 1996); the relationship between self-handicapping and self-esteem (Prapavessis & Grove, 1998; Cooley, 2004); the relationships among self-handicapping, goal orientation, and team climate (Ryska, Yin, and Boyd, 1999); and the effects of self-handicapping on competitive anxiety (Ryska, Yin, & Cooley, 1998), mood (Prapavessis & Grove, 1994), and coping strategies (Prapavessis, Grove, Maddison, & Zillmann, 2003).

Most recently, self-handicapping in performance situations has been examined using experimental studies that have tried to determine whether feelings of uncertainty with respect to not doing well (contingent negative reinforcement) or feelings of uncertainty with respect to why one is doing well (noncontingent positive reinforcement) elicit more self-handicaps (Cooley, 2004). The remainder of this section will provide a more comprehensive review of this literature.

Presence of Others

In one of the earliest studies to examine self-handicapping in competitive situations, Gould, Brounstein, and Sigall (1977) had participants take part in a laboratory competition in which they were led to believe that another person had either won or lost a previous contest. Participants then rated the degree to which ability had contributed to that person's outcome. Findings from this study suggested that participants expressed higher opinions of the opponent's ability when they expected to compete against the opponent in the near future. These results were interpreted to be a self-presentation strategy designed to help participants save face in the event of a negative outcome in the upcoming competition. Later studies have shown that when people expect their performances to be compared with those of others, particularly under competitive conditions, self-handicapping and other-enhancement strategies are most likely to occur (Hirt, McCrea, & Kimble, 2000; Shepperd & Arkin, 1991; Thill & Curry, 2000).

Frequently Cited Impediments

In an attempt to determine the nature of self-reported impediments (self-handicaps), Carron, Prapavessis, and Grove (1994) adopted an alternative, open-ended approach in which male athletes from a variety of team sports were asked to list events that had disrupted their preparation for competition during the past week. The athletes cited 170 perceived obstacles, which were then classified into 11 higher-order categories. Since then, various researchers have adopted a similar approach to the assessment of self-handicapping (Hausenblas & Carron, 1996; Prapavessis & Grove, 1998; Ryska, Yin, & Boyd, 1999; Ryska, Yin, & Cooley, 1998). The findings suggest that the most frequently cited impediments are school activities and related commitments or obligations; physical states, injuries, or illnesses; sport-related problems or disruptions; and commitments to family and friends (see Prapavessis et al., 2004, for a review). Within the sporting environment, most research studies have used the impediment approach to examine the self-handicapping phenomenon.

Practice and Effort Withdrawal

Rhodewalt, Saltzman, and Wittmer (1984) were the first researchers to use the SHS to examine the dispositional tendency to self-handicap. Two related studies were performed that investigated the use of behavioral self-handicaps among competitive swimmers and golfers. In the first study, athletes completed the SHS the day before each of 11 swim meets throughout the competitive season. Participants also responded anonymously to questions about their practice, health, seeing the trainer or doctor, eating and sleeping, and course load for the week before the meet. In addition, the coach, who was blinded to the study purpose, evaluated swimmers' practice efforts and attitudes and evaluated their performances after swim meets. Swimmers' attendance at training sessions was also recorded on a weekly basis.

Results showed that both high self-handicappers (HSH) and low self-handicappers (LSH) increased in the number of sessions attended and effort before an important event. However, before an important event, low self-handicappers had significantly greater attendance and effort compared to those in the HSH group. In a second study, Rhodewalt et al. (1984) found that those in the LSH group increased the amount of practice before an important golf event, whereas those in the HSH group did not. Both subgroups increased their reporting of illness and injuries prior to important events.

Reducing the amount of practice effort before competition among those with high self-handicapping tendencies has been supported by others (Bailis, 2001; Deppe & Harackiewicz, 1996). Although not specifically a sporting situation, the Deppe and Harackiewicz study had males who were identified as low and high self-handicappers play pinball in either a competitive or noncompetitive situation. Feedback was given to all players after the initial practice sessions. Players were then offered time to practice on a computerized reaction-time device (which allegedly would help them perform better) before participating a pinball contest.

Results suggested that there was a general tendency for those with high SHS scores to practice less than those with low SHS scores, and the amount of time spent practicing before the contest influenced task involvement and enjoyment. Specifically, high self-handicappers felt more competent and enjoyed the game more when they spent less time practicing before the contest and low self-handicappers felt more competent and enjoyed the game more when they spent more time practicing before the contest. The pattern of results with respect to direction and level of enjoyment is consistent with the self-presentational view of why self-handicapping occurs (see Prapavessis et al., 2004).

This pattern of reduced practice and greater enjoyment of the task was also found by Bailis (2001) in a sample of wrestlers and swimmers with a high dispositional tendency to self-handicap. In a recent review of self-presentation in sport, Prapavessis et al. (2004) commented that "the behavioral self-handicapping strategy of reduced practice effort may be beneficial for competitors with strong self-handicapping tendencies because it offers them and the audience a viable alternative to personal ability as an explanation for negative outcomes and thereby gives them breathing room" (p. 25).

More recently, Cooley (2004) found that young people did not withhold effort when given the opportunity to practice a performance task (overarm throwing) in the presence of performance uncertainty. Cooley noted that the use of behavior as a means of self-handicapping is problematic in young people, suggesting this population may not have the cognitive sophistication to use effort withdrawal as a means of self-handicapping to deal with threatening situations.

However, he also suggested that the potential cost to the individual of withholding effort may simply be too great.

Goal Orientation and Motivational Climate

The correlates of individual differences in self-handicapping tendencies have been the focus of much sport-related research on this phenomenon. It has been suggested that the situational environment in which the individual operates may influence the extent to which he or she chooses to self-handicap. With this proposition in mind, Ryska et al. (1999) examined the relationships among situational self-handicapping, athlete goal orientation, and team motivational climate. In their study, teenage soccer players completed the SHS and recorded situational self-handicaps as well as measures of team motivational climate, achievement goal orientation, and perceived competence.

Results highlighted a negative relationship between SHS scores and task orientation and a negative relationship between SHS scores and perceived competence; that is, higher self-handicappers were lower in task orientation and perceived competence. Results also showed that athletes low in competence and high in ego involvement were more prone to self-handicap as a protection from threat of competition. The situational variable of team climate was also the best predictor of actual self-handicapping behavior. This evidence suggests that an athlete's motivational goals and perceptions of team motivational climate are relevant when discussing the tendency to adopt self-handicapping strategies.

Similar findings have been offered by Ommundsen (2001), who reported that the tendency to self-handicap was explained by a lower task goal orientation in a sample of physical education students. Thill and Curry (2000) offered further support for the goal orientation–self-handicapping relationship. In a study using a sample of golfers, achievement goals were manipulated during the learning of a golf task and the use of self-handicapping strategies was assessed. Results revealed that an increase in the reported frequency of self-handicapping was associated with a learning environment that emphasized competition and other-referenced standards of performance, while a decrease in the reported frequency of self-handicapping was associated with a learning environment that emphasized self-referenced standards.

Kuczka and Treasure (2002) have suggested that the interaction between a person's perception of motivational climate and perceived ability may be an important determinant of self-handicapping behavior. In their study, male and female competitive golfers completed measures of perceived ability, self-handicapping, and perceived motivation climate in sport as well as an assessment of event importance the day before competition. Regression analyses revealed that perceptions of an ego-involving motivational climate, task-involving climate, and perceived ability were all significant predictors of self-handicapping. Positive relations between situational self-handicapping and perceptions of ego-involving motivational climates were found, as were negative relations between task-involving climates and self-handicapping.

Stressful Performance Situations

A series of four studies (Prapavessis et al., 2003) examined relationships between self-handicapping tendencies and reactions to two different stressful performance situations: performance slumps and emotional reactions to competition. The first two studies demonstrated that self-handicapping tendencies were related to general and specific emotion-coping strategies when dealing with a performance slump. Results of the second two studies showed that the tendency to self-handicap was related to precompetitive anxiety. Other studies of competitive anxiety and mood states have shown that individual differences in self-handicapping tendencies are positively correlated with cognitive anxiety, somatic anxiety, tension, and confusion but at the same time are negatively correlated with vigor and esteem-related affect (Prapavessis & Grove, 1994; Ryska et al., 1998).

Snyder (1990) has suggested that the very nature of presenting an impediment (handicap) before an important event weakens the causal link between the individual and the potentially poor performance. Therefore, it is possible that self-handicapping may provide a buffer to stressful competitive situations, which results in lowered levels of competitive anxiety. In a study to examine this proposition, Ryska et al. (1998) found that both trait and situational self-handicapping were associated with greater cognitive and somatic anxiety. Furthermore, the buffering effect of situational self-handicapping was not present among those with high trait anxiety.

Self-Esteem

The relationship of self-esteem with self-handicapping has been examined extensively and in a variety of settings (e.g., Harris & Snyder, 1986; Tice, 1991; Tice & Baumeister, 1990). Tice (1991) has suggested that people with high and low self-esteem self-handicap for different reasons; people with high self-esteem do so to enhance success, whereas those with low self-esteem do so to protect themselves from the threatening implications of failure. Newman and Wada (1997) have provided research

evidence that self-esteem instability can motivate self-handicapping to enhance and protect self-esteem.

The moderating effects of self-esteem on self-handicapping have been examined within the sporting domain (Martin & Brawley, 1996). Results showed that although the tendency to self-handicap was related to both general and physical self-esteem, only physical self-esteem discriminated athletes' self-handicap for self-enhancing versus self-protective or self-preservational motives, which suggested a domain-specific phenomenon. According to the authors, the findings support the idea that athletes with high and low physical self-esteem are motivated by different self-presentation goals.

Prapavessis and Grove (1998) have examined the mediating effects of self-esteem on the relationship between trait self-handicapping and impediments to competitive performance (potential handicaps). In male competitive golfers, self-esteem served as a negative mediator between trait self-handicapping and potential handicaps. Their findings suggest that golfers with a dispositional tendency to handicap use more impediments before competition because they have low self-esteem.

As previously highlighted, people self-handicap to protect their self-esteem and sense of competence. These self-effacing tactics are used by threatened individuals as a way of coping with situations in which the outcome is uncertain. Snyder (1990) suggested that this performance uncertainty is a critical element of self-handicapping. Jones and Berglas (1978) have argued that self-handicapping results from noncontingent positive reinforcement rather than negative expectancy.

A number of experimental studies have examined these hypotheses (e.g., Berglas & Jones, 1978; Higgins & Harris, 1988; Hobden & Pliner, 1995; Kolditz & Arkin, 1982). In general, these studies have adopted an experimental paradigm in which some form of contingent and noncontingent success or failure feedback is given in association to some performance task. Within this paradigm, participants typically complete a task before receiving contingent or noncontingent feedback. The opportunity to self-handicap (ingesting alcohol, taking drugs, withholding effort) is provided before participants complete the task a second time. Results have generally found that people who experience noncontingent success after an evaluative test have a greater tendency to self-handicap.

Until now, neither Jones and Berglas' (1978) nor Snyder's (1990) hypotheses have been investigated in the physical domain. However, Cooley (2004) recently addressed this gap, performing a series of experimental studies using a throwing task. Cooley investigated self-handicapping within the context of young people's responses to an evaluative threat to self-concept. Results showed that school-aged children self-handicapped more following noncontingent failure feedback compared with those who received noncontingent success feedback or those in a nonevaluative condition. A similar study revealed age-related differences in which a link between self-handicapping and noncontingent failure feedback was demonstrated with older children (13 years old) but not with younger ones (10 years old) (Cooley, 2004).

In two other studies, Cooley (2004) found that young people between the ages of 13 and 16 who determined success by using other-referenced standards rather than internal-referenced standards were most likely to self-handicap. In addition, self-handicapping and ego orientation were related when performance uncertainty was associated with noncontingent failure feedback. In a final study, low self-esteem was shown to be related to self-handicapping. Domain-specific measures of self-esteem and task-specific self-efficacy were related to self-handicapping under a condition of noncontingent failure feedback.

Cooley's results underpin the complex relationship between self-esteem and self-handicapping in that when performance concerns are linked to failure, younger individuals who have high regard for self-judgments related to physical activity but also have low efficacy beliefs for completing a task have greater self-handicapping tendencies. Collectively, these findings in the physical activity domain are contrary to those reported in other settings because noncontingent failure feedback consistently resulted in greater self-handicapping. Cooley's findings support the suggestion that young people use more self-reported handicaps in situations where there is some form of evaluative threat to their self-concept.

Group Cohesion

Although self-handicapping behavior is an individual dispositional strategy, it is proposed that group influence could affect self-handicapping in two ways: (a) The tendency to use self-handicapping strategies might be predicted to be lower in more cohesive groups because the environment is supportive, responsibilities for negative outcomes are shared, and threats to self-esteem are reduced, or (b) they might be higher in cohesive groups because members feel greater responsibility to the group (Carron, Burke, & Prapavessis, 2004).

The effect of the group on self-handicapping has been examined by Carron and colleagues (Carron et al., 1994; Hausenblas & Carron, 1996). In the first of these two studies, Carron et al. found that group cohesion moderated the degree to which athletes reported impediments (handicaps) to their prepara-

tion for important performance events. Specifically, a negative relationship was found, suggesting that when the perception of social cohesion was higher, *high* trait self-handicappers claimed more excuses (handicaps) compared to *low* trait self-handicappers. In the Hausenblas and Carron (1996) study, cohesion again served to moderate the relationship between trait self-handicapping and the claiming of impediments. Results showed that both male and females athletes low on the trait of self-handicapping rated the severity of disruptions they experienced as low regardless of cohesion levels. However, similar to Carron et al. (1994), athletes high on the trait of self-handicapping rated the severity of disruptions as high when cohesion was high and low when cohesion was low.

The authors suggested possible mechanisms to support these results. The first was that high trait self-handicappers might feel secure enough in a cohesive group to actually report potential impediments (excuses). Alternatively, a more cohesive group may exert more pressure on group members and therefore high trait self-handicappers may proactively set out impediments to protect self-esteem in the event of an unsuccessful performance. Ryska et al. (1999) have also found evidence to support the influence of the group on self-handicapping behavior. In their study, soccer players on teams where the prevalent emphasis was on outcomes (e.g., winning) rather than on mastery (e.g., skill development) were more likely to self-handicap.

Future Research

Examination of the self-handicapping phenomenon in sport has increased dramatically over the past 10 years, and many important concerns relating to self-handicapping have been addressed. However, as with all research endeavors, certain areas require further empirical scrutiny.

Methodological Concerns

The predominant approach to the assessment of self-handicapping in sport has been the open-ended impediment approach in which participants are asked to list recent events that interfered with their competition preparation and to indicate the extent of disruption caused by each event (Carron et al., 1994). These disruption ratings (e.g., Carron et al., 1994; Ryska et al., 1998, 1999), or the number of impediments listed (e.g., Prapavessis & Grove, 1998) are used as an index of situational self-handicapping.

One of the major criticisms of this approach is that researchers don't know whether the impediments are real or fabricated. It is entirely possible that the impediment was indeed an obstacle rather than a fictional self-presentational strategy. For example, an athlete who lists a car accident during the precompetition period as affecting performance may actually have suffered this incident and of course is not self-handicapping. The issue of claimed versus actual impediments is a legitimate concern, and investigators who use the impediment approach or disruption ratings as indices of self-handicapping run the risk of introducing noise into their data by unintentionally mixing the two (Prapavessis et al., 2004).

One of the prerequisites of self-handicapping is the situational importance of the upcoming event from a self-presentational or self-concept perspective (Rhodewalt et al., 1984; Self, 1990; Shepperd & Arkin, 1989), and event importance is typically assessed in studies of self-handicapping in sport. Some have used these ratings as a manipulation check (e.g., Martin & Brawley, 2002) and others have used them to screen out participants with low importance ratings before analyses (e.g., Carron et al., 1994; Hausenblas & Carron, 1996; Prapavessis & Grove, 1998).

It is not clear how using importance ratings to screen participants might affect the data. One of the reasons for invoking handicaps is to reduce negative affect before performance (Snyder, 1990), but reductions in the perceived importance of the task could accomplish this same end (Martens, Vealy, & Burton, 1990). When deciding which participants to retain for data analyses, researchers might do well to consider other measures together with importance ratings. Low perceived-importance ratings alone may not necessarily indicate the absence of a desire or need to self-handicap (Prapavessis et al., 2004).

Another methodological consideration is the measurement of the dispositional tendency to self-handicap. Although the SHS (Jones & Rhodewalt, 1982) is the instrument most commonly used for this purpose in sport, its psychometric properties have often been poor. Specifically, the internal consistency of the diminished effort factor (i.e., behavioral handicap) has been found to be unacceptably low (Hausenblas & Carron, 1996; Martin & Brawley, 1999; Prapavessis & Grove, 1998). In addition, examination of the SHS factor structure across various sport samples (Martin & Brawley, 1999) revealed it to be unstable. These authors and others (Hausenblas & Carron, 1996) have suggested that the SHS is not reliable for identifying the trait of self-handicapping in a sport setting and that a sport-specific questionnaire is needed. Martens (1977) has suggested that "sport psychologists need to develop sport-specific constructs and instruments to measure these constructs in order to better understand human behavior in sport contexts" (p. iv). Researchers must do more than simply reword items on the SHS to reflect a sport-specific context because rewording has failed to resolve these psychometric concerns (Martin & Brawley, 1999).

Shields, Paskevich, and Brawley (2003) have examined the issue of specificity and have developed a theoretically driven measure, the Self-Handicapping Exercise Questionnaire (SHEQ), to assess the frequency of self-handicapping in the exercise context. Findings from model-testing studies revealed three unique and stable factors addressing self-handicapping claims about making exercise a routine, training in an exercise facility, and healthy physical functioning.

To address the psychometric concerns of the original SHS as well as the scale's lack of specificity in sport, we have made significant inroads into developing a domain-specific scale (Maddison, Prapavessis, & Fletcher, in preparation). The starting point for generating items for this scale was the higher-order categories presented by Carron, Prapavessis, and Grove (1994) and the anticipatory and active strategies used by both Midgley, Arunkumar, and Urdan (1996) and Shields et al. (2003). Both claimed and behavioral forms of self-handicapping have been included to form the basis of the subscales for excuse making and withholding effort. In table 15.1, we present sample items from this instrument to emphasize sport-specific self-presentational behavior. There is no doubt that our measure of self-handicapping tendencies reflects the types of strategies athletes might use for self-protection or self-enhancement.

Avenues of Research

Further research should be directed toward understanding whether a relationship between self-handicapping and performance exists. For example, one might suspect that symptom-reported handicaps (e.g., illness, discomfort) would not be as detrimental to performance as behavioral self-handicaps (e.g., alcohol consumption, reduced effort). Moreover, reduced or withheld effort before competition should be detrimental to performance. At present, we are unaware of any literature showing that self-handicaps lower the probability of performance success.

Researchers might also consider investigating the antecedent conditions that are associated with claimed and behavioral self-handicaps in the sporting domain. As previously highlighted, Cooley (2004) performed a series of experiments exploring this issue in the physical domain with young children; however, greater understanding is required before these findings can be generalized to adults. Indeed, there is a dearth of experimental studies investigating the conditions in which self-handicapping is hypothesized to exist. Such experimental work with athletes might also lay the groundwork for subsequent fieldwork.

Table 15.1   Self-Handicapping in Sport Questionnaire (SHSQ) Sample Items

1 Disagree very much	2 Disagree pretty much	3 Disagree a little	4 Agree a little	5 Agree pretty much	6 Agree very much

I tend to make excuses because	1	2	3	4	5	6
1. I am always carrying niggling injuries.	○	○	○	○	○	○
2. The competition was so badly organized.	○	○	○	○	○	○
3. I never have enough time to devote to my sport.	○	○	○	○	○	○
4. I spend too much time going out with my friends.	○	○	○	○	○	○
5. I can't cope with stress.	○	○	○	○	○	○
6. My coach and I argue.	○	○	○	○	○	○

I tend to withhold effort because	1	2	3	4	5	6
1. I am physically tired.	○	○	○	○	○	○
2. There is no point in trying to win when the competition is poorly organized.	○	○	○	○	○	○
3. Family and friends commitments affect how often I could train.	○	○	○	○	○	○
4. The amount of time it takes to travel to work makes training difficult.	○	○	○	○	○	○
5. I could not be bothered because of stress.	○	○	○	○	○	○
6. It is pointless trying to win when you disagree with your teammates.	○	○	○	○	○	○

From R. Maddison, H. Prapavessis, and R. Fletcher, 2006, *Scale development of a sport specific Self-Handicapping Scale.*

Although the effect of group influence on self-handicapping has been examined (Carron et al., 1994; Hausenblas & Carron, 1996; Ryska et al., 1999), to our knowledge self-handicapping has not been explored in two-person relationships or interactions (coach–athlete, athlete–parent, and athlete–athlete relationships). The relationships formed between, for example, coaches and athletes, might present self-handicapping effects that differ from those currently understood.

Further research is required to fully explore the costs of self-handicapping in team or group situations.

Based on the suggestions of Carron et al. (1994), it is plausible that individuals in a cohesive group who self-handicap might be viewed neutrally or at least not too negatively; hence the costs of handicapping would be low. Alternatively, the cohesive group may take an extremely negative view of an individual; hence the cost of handicapping would be high.

The behavioral self-handicapping strategy of reduced practice effort also warrants further examination. The reduced-practice phenomenon is extremely well documented in the experimental literature (e.g.,

Ferrari & Tice, 2000; Harris & Snyder, 1986; Hirt, Deppe, & Gordon, 1991; Thompson & Richardson, 2001; Tice & Baumeister, 1990), and it has also been observed in field studies of swimmers, golfers, and wrestlers (Bailis, 2001; Rhodewalt et al., 1984). In addition, factors that affect the amount and quality of practice are relevant to those interested in coaching, skill development, and performance improvement.

Nevertheless, this topic has received minimal empirical attention by sport researchers interested in self-handicapping. Prapavessis et al. (2004) stated, "Effort reduction is . . . the aspect of self-handicapping that is most closely linked to changes in practice behavior. . . . self-report methodologies used in most of the sport-based studies appear to tap into claimed self-handicaps more readily than behavioral self-handicaps. An adequate analysis of behavioral self-presentation strategies like reduced practice requires a more labor-intensive approach to assessment that includes observer ratings of practice quality and/or direct observation of time-on-task" (p. 27).

Practical Implications

Certain practical implications of future research outcomes warrant consideration. First, better understanding of the antecedents to self-handicapping can help athletes develop appropriate strategies and avoid the need to self-handicap. By having a clear understanding of motivational and team climate, researchers might be able to develop interventions that help coaches foster appropriate motivational perspectives and levels of group cohesion. The development of an improved measure of trait self-handicapping will enhance the understanding of this phenomenon in sport, which in turn might help athletes identify their own disposition to handicap.

Here, we offer some advice with respect to self-handicapping in sport. First, coaches should not necessarily focus on trying to keep athletes from self-handicapping. Rather, a more fruitful approach might be to better understand the underlying motives and possible causes of self-handicapping. It is also important for coaches to be aware that continued withholding effort as a self-handicapping strategy may be detrimental to performance. Thus, gaining insight into the use of this behavioral strategy might be beneficial. For example, athletes who self-handicap before an important event may anticipate an unsuccessful performance or feel their self-esteem is under threat. A coach might look at strategies to minimize the perceived threat of the impending event, such as having the athlete focus on the process of the performance rather than the outcome.

Trainers or coaches of team sports might also be cognizant of the effects of the group on individuals who tend to make excuses. An awareness of how the group views individuals who self-handicap might assist the coach when dealing with team dynamics. For example, a coach who believes that an individual self-handicaps (withholds effort) in a cohesive group might consider reevaluating the group's goals as well as the individual's goals so that congruency is assured between the two, thereby reducing the individual's need for handicapping.

Summary

This chapter has provided an overview of the literature on self-presentation in sport, with a particular focus on self-handicapping. Because sport and competition offer an ideal environment in which to examine the nature and correlates of self-handicapping, research interest in the sporting domain has been particularly strong. While an open-ended impediment approach has been predominantly used in the assessment of self-handicapping in sport, these impediments are not necessarily synonymous with claimed self-handicaps.

Research that has examined individual differences in self-handicapping tendencies, assessed through the Self-Handicapping Scale (SHS), has shown that SHS scores are related to self-esteem, precompetitive anxiety, coping, concerns about impression management, mood states, coping, achievement goal orientation, cohesion, and reduced practice effort. Due to psychometric concerns with the SHS, research is needed to develop a sport-specific measure of self-handicapping tendencies that better reflects the types of strategies athletes might use for self-protection and self-enhancement. Directions for future research were presented with a focus on methodological concerns and further research avenues such as reduced practice effort. Finally, practical tips for coaches were suggested; for example, coaches might consider focusing on possible causes of self-handicapping and the effects of the group on self-handicapping.

DISCUSSION QUESTIONS

1. Explain the term *self-presentation* (e.g., impression management).

2. Give a definition of self-handicapping and present the two broad components of self-handicapping as presented in the Self-Handicapping Scale (SHS).

3. Describe the effect of group cohesion on self-handicapping. Give possible reasons for your answer.

4. What types of self-handicapping in sport have you witnessed? What do you think led the athletes to use those strategies?

part V

The Athlete in the Wider Sport Environment

Within the world of sport, there are numerous social-cognitive and cultural factors that can influence dyadic relationships and group dynamics. Some of these factors have become more prominent within the sport psychology literature in recent years. Supportive social networks, for example, have been found to play a crucial role in the lives of athletes across their careers. The influence of factors such as passion and morality on behavior in sport settings is also important, as well as the degree to which these behaviors and expressions are a function of culture. The final part of this volume includes five chapters that focus on the athlete and environment: social support, the role of parents during different stages of an athlete's career, passion in sport, morality, and cross-cultural concerns.

In chapter 16, Tim Rees focuses on social support and its implications in sporting contexts. Social support is defined, and the stress-buffering and main effects models, which identify the conditions under which different kinds of social support influence outcomes, are reviewed. Both the positive and negative aspects of social support are highlighted for researchers and practitioners.

In chapter 17, Paul Wylleman, Paul De Knop, Marie-Christine Verdet, and Saša Cecič-Erpič consider the roles played by parents throughout the career of an elite athlete. These authors take a life-span perspective on transitions faced by athletes at sport, individual, psychosocial, and academic or vocational levels, and they present a developmental model that guides an overview of research on parental involvement across these levels. The chapter concludes with suggestions for future research as well as strategies that can help ensure that parental involvement during and after the athletic career has a positive impact on the development of athletes.

In chapter 18, Robert Vallerand and Paule Miquelon consider the concept of passion, which they refer to as a strong inclination toward an activity that people like, that they find important, and in which they invest time and energy. The chapter focuses on the applicability of passion within sport, and key research findings are woven throughout their review of the relevant theories. Future research directions on passion in sport are presented, along with practical implications for developing passion for sport.

In chapter 19, Maria Kavussanu offers a review of theories of morality as they apply to sport. Research based on these theories is then considered, with a focus on the effects of sport type, social context, motivation, and gender on moral behavior. The unanswered questions associated with morality in sport, such as whether certain aspects of sport participation are related to the processes involved in moral thought and action, are the focus of the section on future research. The chapter concludes with recommended implications for practice based on existing knowledge.

In chapter 20, Gangyan Si and Hing-chu Lee consider cultural contexts in understanding human psychological processes. The developments of cross-cultural research in sport psychology are reviewed, with a focus on relevant theories, methods, and implications for practice. A three-step framework is proposed for researchers interested in designing cross-cultural research within the context of sport.

chapter 16

Influence of Social Support on Athletes

Tim Rees, PhD

Learning Objectives

On completion of this chapter, the reader should have

1. understanding of social support and its implications for sport;
2. understanding of the two principal models that explain how social support may affect outcomes in sport;
3. understanding of the differences between structural and functional elements of social support;
4. familiarity with optimal matching of social support with stressors;
5. appreciation for the negative side of social support; and
6. awareness of avenues for future research on social support in sport.

© Sport the Library

I think it would be difficult if you were just totally on your own and never had anyone really helping you out and giving you support, basically. I think it's a big difference . . . I can't see how you can totally do it on your own . . . You do need encouragement and advice, and, good times, bad times, you need people to help you out. I think it's pretty hard to do it without them.

Davis Cup tennis player (Rees & Hardy, 2000, p. 342)

Comments such as this one from a British tennis player are not universal among those involved with sport. As noted by Hardy, Jones, and Gould (1996), the prevailing attitude is that some athletes feel they must "go it alone" (p. 234) in their pursuit of success and not seek out social support in times of need. The recommendation from the sport psychology literature is that athletes should be encouraged to be proactive in harnessing social support from those around them (e.g., Gould, Jackson, & Finch, 1993; Hardy & Crace, 1991; Richman, Hardy, Rosenfeld, & Callanan, 1989; Rosenfeld & Richman, 1997). In part, this recommendation is based upon evidence that low social support is associated with increased vulnerability to injury and increased risk of burnout while high social support is associated with better coping with stress and better performance.

What Is Social Support?

Two definitions of social support are often used: "Knowing that one is loved and that others will do all they can when a problem arises" (Sarason, Sarason, & Pierce, 1990, p. 119), and "an exchange of resources between at least two individuals perceived by the provider or the recipient to be intended to enhance the well-being of the recipient" (Shumaker & Brownell, 1984, p. 13). Neither of these definitions encompasses a full understanding of social support, and there is little consensus on an exact definition of this construct. As Veiel and Baumann (1992a) noted, "If asked, almost every researcher in the field will present a more or less precise definition of support, but, more than likely, it will be different from that of his or her colleagues" (p. 3).

Various terms have been used to describe social support, including social network size, social integration, quantity and quality of relationships, social resources, satisfaction with support, perceived and received support, and structural and functional elements of support (for reviews, see Cohen, 1988; Cohen, Underwood, &

Gottlieb, 2000; Heitzmann & Kaplan, 1988; Sarason, Sarason, & Pierce, 1990a; Veiel & Baumann, 1992c). Various approaches to the study of social support have been used (see Cohen, Gottlieb, & Underwood, 2000), including the sociological tradition, the cognitive tradition and the stress-buffering hypothesis, the interpersonal process tradition, and the intervention tradition.

Lakey and Cohen (2000) outlined three key theoretical perspectives in research on social support: (a) the stress and coping perspective, (b) the social constructionist perspective, and (c) the relationship perspective. Such diversity leads to difficulty in stating simply what should constitute social support, what should be measured, how it should be measured, and how social support should affect outcomes.

It appears that social support involves a complex combination of multiple processes. In sport, this means that the existence of a caring and supportive network, including family, friends, teammates, coaches, managers, fitness trainers, physiotherapists, and psychologists, should have a positive effect on an athlete's cognitions, emotions, and behaviors. The athlete should also be helped by the perception that others are available to provide help and support in times of need and by the actual receipt of help and support. The quality and type of social support an athlete perceives or receives could presumably affect such things as performance level, resistance to dropping out, enjoyment, and ability to cope with and recover from injury.

Awareness of social support became more explicit in the general psychology research of the 1970s. Subsequently, social support has been the most frequently studied psychosocial resource and has been noted alongside stress and coping as one of the three most important constructs in mental health research (Cohen, Underwood, & Gottlieb, 2000; Heitzmann & Kaplan, 1988; Sarason et al., 1990a; Thoits, 1995; Veiel & Baumann, 1992a). Relationships have also been observed between physiological processes (Uchino, Cacioppo, & Kiecolt-Glaser, 1996), and physical disease and mortality (Cohen, 1988). Despite this research base, varied definitions, a plethora of measures, and a proliferation of atheoretical research led to comments that the literature on social support was typified by work demonstrating a "conceptual agnosticism" (Veiel & Baumann, 1992b, p. 317). It was Veiel and Baumann's view that there had been an enthusiastic acceptance of simple research paradigms that did not deal with intricate mechanisms or processes:

As tends to happen when ideas and concepts turn into scientific paradigms, the support paradigm has ceased to be seen as needing justification, and support measures are now routinely included in assessment batteries for no other reason than to "cover" it. (p. 1-2)

Today, despite social support remaining "more a promising concept than an established, fleshed-out fact" (Reis & Collins, 2000, p. 182), there is sufficiently developed theory upon which to base empirical investigations.

Principal Theoretical Frameworks

Two principal models that identify the conditions under which social support influences outcomes have evolved: the stress-buffering model and the main effect model (see Cohen & Wills, 1985). The stress-buffering model proposes that support is related to outcomes only for those persons under stress. The main effect model, also known as the direct effect model, proposes that social resources have a beneficial effect regardless of whether individuals are under stress.

Main Effects

The main effect model proposes that increases in social support are associated with increases in positive outcomes. For example, being part of a supportive social network might lead to increased positive affect, which might in turn lead to a greater likelihood of experiencing flow states, represented by experiences of peak performance and peak experience (cf. Cohen, 1988; Rees, Ingledew, & Hardy, 1999). *Structural elements* of social support (e.g., Cohen & Syme, 1985) are most commonly associated with main effects and refer to social-network characteristics such as the following:

- Social integration—the extent to which the athlete participates in a broad range of social relationships and activities
- Network size—the number of friends, family, and sport-related personnel (e.g., coaches, trainers, teammates) supporting the athlete

- Frequency of social contact—how often the athlete is in contact with each person in her social network

Research on structural elements of social support notes that integration in a supportive social network may positively influence cognitions, emotions, and behaviors through interactions that are not explicitly intended to give help or support. Belonging to a supportive network can lead to positive outcomes such as improved self-concept, feelings of self-worth, and personal control. It may also lead to the adoption of behavioral patterns that lead to positive outcomes in sport. The main effect model is shown in the first part of figure 16.1, with social support having a possible direct effect on performance.

Stress Buffering

The stress-buffering model suggests that high levels of social support protect one from the harmful effects of stress but that level of social support is relatively unimportant for those not experiencing stress. For example, given the extensive literature on stress and performance in sport (Woodman & Hardy, 2001), it would seem reasonable to examine whether support buffers the effect of stress upon performance. This is shown in the second part of figure 16.1. *Functional elements* of social support (e.g., Cohen & Syme, 1985) are most commonly associated with stress-buffering effects. Functional support refers to types of social support that protect people from the negative effects of specific stressors. Esteem and informational support are examples of functional support an athlete may receive; for example, a coach might provide esteem support by bolstering a team's confidence. The same coach might also provide informational support by giving technical and tactical input.

Functional social support may be divided into perceived and received support. *Perceived support* is the perception of available support, and *received support*

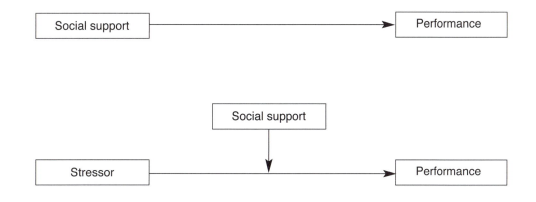

Figure 16.1 Main and stress-buffering effects of social support.

is the actual receipt of social support, often referred to as enacted support (Dunkel-Schetter & Bennett, 1990; Helgeson, 1993; Wethington & Kessler, 1986). Although empirically perceived support has been most consistently linked with the stress-buffering hypothesis (Cohen, 1988; Cohen, Gottlieb, & Underwood, 2000; Cohen & Wills, 1985; Wills & Shinar, 2000), theoretically both perceived and received support should aid stress buffering (Lakey & Cohen, 2000).

The notion of stress buffering is tied to models of the stress process, appraisal, and coping (e.g., Cox, 1978; Lazarus, 1966; Lazarus & Folkman, 1984); stress arises when a person appraises a demand as threatening or otherwise and does not have an appropriate coping response. The protective (stress-buffering) influence of social support might operate via a number of mechanisms, for example, by leading to benign appraisal of the stressful events, by a direct transfer of resources (e.g., giving financial aid), or by promoting better coping behaviors (Cohen, Gottlieb, & Underwood, 2000; Cohen & Wills, 1985; Lakey & Cohen, 2000; Wills & Shinar, 2000).

A key concern for stress buffering is the need for a match between specific types of social support and stressors (Cutrona & Russell, 1990). Carefully matched social support–stressor combinations that produce significant results in empirical studies will aid understanding of the types of social support that protect people from the harmful effects of specific stressors (Cutrona & Russell, 1990; Lakey & Cohen, 2000; Wills & Shinar, 2000); conversely, matched social support–stressor combinations that produce nonsignificant interactions will aid understanding of which types of social support do not help or when support is not useful (cf. Dakof & Taylor, 1990; Rook, 1992). For example, if research were to find that athletes facing pressure to beat tough opponents achieve the most stress reduction and performance benefits from encouragement from coaches rather than technical advice, this knowledge would be extremely useful.

Theoretically, structural forms of social support, such as social integration, are most commonly associated with main effects, and functional forms of social support (perceived and received support) are most commonly associated with stress-buffering effects. Empirically, however, there are examples of main effects of perceived support, and even stress-buffering effects of social integration. The most common procedure for testing stress-buffering effects of functional social support is moderated hierarchical regression analysis (Cohen & Wills, 1985; Jaccard, Turrisi, & Wan, 1990), in which there are tests for both main and interactive (stress-buffering) effects. Here, main effects of perceived support might occur because the security provided by the perception that others are available in times of need leads to positive affective and cognitive states.

Social Support in Sport

Despite encouragement for athletes to use social support (e.g., Gould et al., 1993; Hardy & Crace, 1991; Richman et al., 1989; Rosenfeld & Richman, 1997) and recommendations for research (e.g., Hardy & Jones, 1994; Sarason et al., 1990), there has been comparatively little research on social support. The following examples give insight into research on social support in sport to date.

Seeking social support has been considered a coping strategy for dealing with competitive stress (Crocker, 1992) and slumps in performance (Madden, Kirkby, & McDonald, 1989). Social support has figured in the burnout literature. Gould, Tuffey, Udry, and Loehr (1996) found that as the competitive nature of tennis increased, players' support diminished, leading to a decreased ability to combat stress. In studies of coach leadership (for a review, see Chelladurai, 1993; see also chapter 5), players' perceptions of the supportive behaviors of their coach have been found to have an effect on players' satisfaction with the coach's leadership. Social support has also been empirically linked to group cohesion. Westre and Weiss (1991) found that players who considered their coaches to provide high levels of social support also perceived their teams to have higher levels of task cohesion.

Where research has been most prevalent is in relation to sport injury, including the study of social support and injury vulnerability, etiology of injury, recovery from injury, and subsequent return to fully competitive sport (for reviews, see Bianco & Eklund, 2001; Brewer, 2001; Hardy, Burke, & Crace, 1999; Udry, 1996; Williams, 2001). There is also recent work documenting the role of social support for those coping with a spinal-cord injury suffered through sport (Rees, Smith, & Sparkes, 2003).

A crucial area is performance. Sarason et al. (1990) convincingly argued that social support might directly affect sport performance. For example, they suggested that a performer might pull out of a batting slump simply due to the knowledge that a coach would be available to provide technical support. Until recently (Rees & Hardy, 2004; Rees, Hardy, & Freeman, in press; Rees et al., 1999), however, there has been little empirical evidence to support such a link, although Weiss and Friedrichs (1986) did find that the dimension of social support in the Leadership Scale for Sports (LSS) (Chelladurai & Saleh, 1978, 1980) was negatively associated with win–loss percentage. The studies of Rees and colleagues found main (direct) and stress-buffering (interactive) effects of social support upon processes underpinning performance, with main effects accounting for as much as 20% of the variance in performance. As one of the aims of sport is high-level performance, this is notable, suggesting a great potential for social support in sport psychology research.

© Sport the Library

England soccer players support each other during a penalty shoot-out.

Dimensions of Social Support

An important question surrounds the functional dimensionality of social support. Is social support about a general sense of being supported, or could it be broken down into more specific functional elements, such as emotional support, informational advice, and tangible aid? Although there is wider agreement that social support should be viewed as a multidimensional construct, diversity exists over how many dimensions comprise social support (Cutrona & Russell, 1990).

The belief of some that social support is a general sense of being loved and cared for is bolstered by concerns regarding the psychometric properties of the majority of functional measures, which frequently contain overly high correlations among dimensions (e.g., B.R. Sarason, Sarason, & Pierce, 1990b; Sarason, Shearin, Pierce, & Sarason, 1987). It has been demonstrated in confirmatory factor analysis with the Interpersonal Support Evaluation List (ISEL) (Cohen, Mermelstein, Kamarck, & Hoberman, 1985) that such correlations may be accounted for by the introduction of a higher-order factor (Brookings & Bolton, 1988).

At a conceptual level, there is still evidence that support should be broken down into dimensional components. For example, Cohen (1992) noted that "having someone who would loan you money may be useful in the face of a temporary job loss, but useless in the face of the death of a friend" (p. 112), and in sport, Rees and colleagues (Rees & Hardy, 2004; Rees et al., 1999) have found differential relationships among different support dimensions and performance components. For example, with high levels of esteem support, participants experience greater levels of flow. With high levels of tangible support, participants experience greater levels of flow and feel less flat, sluggish, and mentally tired.

Measurement Issues

In summarizing the state of research on social support at that time, House and Kahn (1985) wrote, "Measurement in this area is still in a fairly primitive state" (p. 102). Some years later, Vaux (1992) expressed concerns regarding the psychometric properties of measures of social support and the plethora of different measures, which have made synthesis of findings difficult. Underpinning all these points is the difficulty of measuring a construct that has no clear definition.

Despite the association of social support with tennis performance found by Rees et al. (1999), their findings were tempered by questions regarding the applied relevance to sport of the instrument they used to measure social support. Rees and colleagues used the ISEL (Cohen et al., 1985), a measure of perceived functional social support with a confirmed factor structure (Brookings & Bolton, 1988). The basic concern in using the ISEL in a sport setting is content validity; the questions posed by the ISEL relate to general support and do not account for the specific support issues that might be relevant to high-level athletes. Although it is undoubtedly necessary for a measure of social support to have structural validity, taking a measure directly from general psychology may not help in understanding the specific experiences of athletes.

In sport, there is a need to look at the support transactions an athlete might experience with family, friends, teammates, coaches, managers, fitness trainers, physiotherapists, and psychologists in dealing with the stresses and strains of high-level sport. The structure of one multidimensional measure of social support, the Social Support Survey (SSS) (Richman, Rosenfeld, & Hardy, 1993), may be used to generate this sort of information. In sport psychology, Richman et al.'s model of social support is increasingly used as a framework for researching social support, particularly in relation to sport injury (Bianco & Eklund, 2001; Brewer, 2001; Hardy et al., 1999), and the SSS is based upon this model.

Despite some validation work with college athletes (see Richman et al., 1993), Rees, Hardy, Ingledew, and Evans (2000) raised concerns about the content and structural validity of the SSS. For example, Rees et al. questioned the assumption that it is meaningful and appropriate to consider the SSS as comprising eight separate dimensions of social support, despite previous conceptualizations regarding the construct as unidimensional or comprising just three, four, or five dimensions (see Cutrona & Russell, 1990; Heitzmann & Kaplan, 1988; Vaux, 1992). Confirmatory factor analyses of the SSS (Rees et al., 2000) also revealed that the items on the scales might be ambiguous indicators of the latent constructs, leading to difficulties in pinpointing the eight dimensions in the SSS with certainty.

In light of concerns over the content validity, structural validity, and applied relevance to sport of many measures of social support, Rees and Hardy (2000) conducted interviews with high-level athletes about their social support. Through this process, four dimensions of sport-relevant social support were generated: emotional, esteem, informational, and tangible support. Rees and Hardy used the definitions of Cutrona and Russell (1990) to reflect the nature of the social support found in their study. Thus, in their simplest forms,

- *emotional support* refers to being there for comfort and security, leading to a person feeling loved and cared for;
- *esteem support* refers to bolstering a person's sense of competence or self-esteem;
- *informational support* refers to providing advice or guidance; and
- *tangible support* refers to providing concrete instrumental assistance.

Subsequently, these four dimensions of support have been used to frame research on spinal-cord injury (Rees et al., 2003) and the main and stress-buffering effects of social support on sport performance (Rees & Hardy, 2004; Rees et al., in press).

Providers of Social Support

As Bianco (2001) noted in the context of injury, various network members tend to engage in the provision of various types of social support. Unfortunately, these people do not always provide their support well (Lehman, Ellard, & Wortman, 1986), and people may differ in their expertise in providing specific types of support (Rosenfeld & Richman, 1997). In relation to sport injury and spinal-cord injury, Rees et al. (2003) and Johnston and Carroll (1998) noted that informational support, whether beneficial or negatively received, was generally provided by medical personnel or others with a similar injury.

Participants have been shown to have preferences regarding who provides them with specific types of support (Dakof & Taylor, 1990; Warwick, Joseph, Cordle, & Ashworth, 2004), and differences have been noted between providers and recipients regarding what they see as useful (Coriell & Cohen, 1995). So, although the quality of support should depend upon its functional effectiveness and how well it is matched to stressors, one might need to consider more closely the providers of support. There may, then, be an interaction between the best-suited provider of support and the quality of the provision. Research has indicated that individuals' appraisals of others' supportiveness may reflect a unique matching (interaction) between the individual and the person providing the support (Lakey, McCabe, Fisicaro, & Drew, 1996).

Negative Aspects of Social Support

Despite the sport psychology literature encouraging the use of social support, not all support is beneficial. For example, Gould et al. (1996) found that, although friends were important for maintaining motivation, pressure from others, especially parents, played a major role in the burnout of junior tennis players. Udry, Gould, Bridges, and Tuffey (1997) demonstrated in a sport-injury setting how athletes tended to view their social support as more negative than positive. In particular, they noted examples of inappropriate or insufficient rehabilitation guidance, lack of sensitivity to the injury, and lack of concern. Both Dakof and Taylor (1990) and Rees et al. (2003) noted similar results, with participants listing unhelpful actions by physicians as the following: expressed little concern, empathy, or affection; provided insufficient information; and provided technically incompetent medical care.

This touches upon issues related to the term *non-support* (e.g., Rook, 1992; Harris, 1992) and the discrepancies observed between the perceptions of supporters and the supported on what is useful. Such discrepancies have been demonstrated with students taking exams (Coriell & Cohen, 1995), cancer patients (Dakof & Taylor, 1990), the bereaved (Lehman et al., 1986), and sufferers of headaches and irritable bowel syndrome (Martin, Davis, Baron, Suls, & Blanchard, 1994).

Future Research

Understanding how social support affects outcomes in sport is important for research in sport psychology. Research should move beyond mere description of social networks and simple correlational designs to well-designed studies that test specific hypotheses related to the main and stress-buffering effects of social support on various outcomes in sport. In this regard, the measurement of social support is a key concern, and researchers should consider the psychometric properties and content relevance of the measures they use.

As an example, before testing main effect and stress-buffering models, Rees and colleagues (Rees & Hardy, 2004; Rees et al., in press) constructed and refined their measurement of four sport-relevant dimensions of social support (emotional, esteem, informational, and tangible support), the purpose of which was to ensure context-specific and accurate measurement of social support, not to develop and validate a scale. This followed two recommendations from the social support literature: measures of social support should be relevant to the situational context; and researchers should write new items to capture the specific support needs of the target population (Bianco & Eklund, 2001; House & Kahn, 1985; Wills & Shinar, 2000). This is akin to the measurement strategy of self-efficacy research (Bandura, 1997), for which it has been noted that a "one measure fits all" approach has only limited explanatory and predictive value.

Specification of models might be guided by the optimal matching hypothesis, whereby specific types of social support are carefully matched to the demands elicited by specific stressors (Cutrona & Russell, 1990; Lakey & Cohen, 2000; Wills & Shinar, 2000). In this regard, three strategies might be employed. First, consider the relative controllability of the stressors (Cutrona & Russell, 1990): Uncontrollable stressors, such as sustaining an injury, lead to a need for social support that fosters emotion-focused forms of coping (e.g., emotional support). Controllable stressors, such as technical problems in training, lead to a need for social support that fosters problem-focused coping (e.g., informational support). Second, pay close attention to the content of the items on the support scales in relation to the stressors. Third, as recommended by Wills and Shinar (2000), make use of previous knowledge of the target population.

Within such studies, researchers should attempt to examine the differential impact of specific dimensions of social support. Studies should also examine the differential impact of perceived and received support within the same study and should further explore the mechanisms by which stress buffering occurs. For example, both perceived and received support might play specific roles at several points along the causal chain, linking stressors to outcomes in sport through appraisal and coping mechanisms (see figure 16.2).

Given the differential expertise of support providers and the negative aspects of social support, research might also focus on the interaction between the person being supported and the person providing the support and the consequences of this interaction. This might involve exploration of poorly matched, inappropriate, or negatively received support. It might also involve exploration of the effects of supportive interactions on the support providers.

This chapter's discussion of models and measures may appear to have ignored qualitative research on social support in sport. Regardless of method, however, researchers should carefully consider the type of social support they wish to focus on (e.g., social integration, perceived support, received support) as well as the

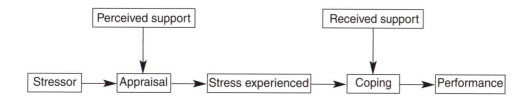

Figure 16.2 Potential effects of perceived and received support and appraisal and coping mechanisms on performance.

model of social support they use to frame their research. Future qualitative research might then also shed light on the pressing concerns for social support in sport, using alternative forms of analysis and representation (Sparkes, 2002).

Practical Implications

The literature on social support has important implications for athletes and for all those involved with them. Important others can play a crucial role in the athlete's life, and the consequences of being isolated from support can be damaging. Therefore, the oft-hailed ideal of going it alone in pursuit of success rather than seeking out social support in times of need is outmoded and limiting. Athletes should be encouraged to be proactive in their use of social support, and along with all those in their support network, they should be helped to understand that such action is not a sign of weakness (Hardy et al., 1996).

Such comments might lead important others to the conclusion that they should actively provide support. Herein lies a complex issue in that unskilled others are often poor providers of support, basing their understanding of what the person needs solely on intuition. For example, Lehman et al. (1986) noted that people can provide unhelpful support by trying, among other things, to minimize the importance of an event, avoid open communication about the event, criticize attempts at coping, encourage quicker coping, and give inappropriate advice. Understanding the need to match the correct support to the needs arising from stressors (Cutrona & Russell, 1990) would be important for family, friends, teammates, coaches, managers, fitness trainers, physiotherapists, and psychologists.

In their study of tennis players, Rees and Hardy (2004) found that informational support (in the form of technical advice) did not buffer the negative effects of technical problems in training upon performance, but tangible support did. It was tangible support in the form of someone to plan, organize, and set training sessions that helped. So, although many coaches might naturally offer informational support when approached about technical problems, such support might not always be beneficial for alleviating this particular stressor.

Interventions might, therefore, focus on helping providers improve the quality and aptness of their support. Interventions might also focus on helping athletes fully understand how they can maximize the available support in their network and to learn the skills

necessary to be proactive in using this resource. The concept of matching support with stressors implies that performers might be taught to recognize their needs and to understand that specific problems and stressors require specific types of support.

As Richman et al. (1989) noted, social support might be best considered "within a proactive model, one requiring the athlete to assume the responsibility for recognizing support needs and taking action to satisfy them" (p. 158) As applied practitioners, sport psychologists could then help provide a context for empowering individuals to purposefully develop and nurture their social support. Certainly, intervention work in social support is different from most other types of applied practice in that the benefits of social support are not received from direct contact with the practitioner (except in the case of the athlete needing psychological support); the beneficial effects are realized through the performers' subsequent interaction with their social environment (Gottlieb, 1992).

Summary

Although there is no simple definition of social support, it appears that athletes may benefit from being part of a supportive social network, from perceiving that support is available to them, and from receiving support from others. There are two principal models of social support: the main effect model and the stress-buffering model. Key issues are the distinctions between structural and functional elements of support, the distinctions between perceived and received support, and the matching of social support with stressors. Consideration should also be paid to the dimensions of support, measurement of support, providers of support, and negative aspects of support.

Future theory-driven research is warranted in which researchers carefully consider the models and methods they choose to frame their research. In applied settings, important others can play a crucial role in the life of athletes, and athletes and their family, friends, teammates, coaches, managers, fitness trainers, physiotherapists, psychologists, and others should be aware of the need to carefully match social support to the needs arising from stressors. Given that social support has been shown to account for as much as 20% of the variance in performance over and above the effects of stress (Rees et al., in press), social support should become a key variable in future research in sport psychology.

DISCUSSION QUESTIONS

1. What, in general, does social support encompass?

2. What are the two principal models that explain effects of social support on outcomes? Which model do you think offers the best explanation of these effects? Why?

3. What are the differences between structural and functional elements of social support?

4. What does optimal matching (Cutrona & Russell, 1990) refer to? Do you think this is an important consideration for sport psychologists to be aware of?

5. What are some of the future research issues for social support in sport? How do you envisage research progressing? What are some potential links between social support and other variables in sport psychology?

chapter 17

Parenting and Career Transitions of Elite Athletes

Paul Wylleman, PhD, Paul De Knop, PhD, Marie-Christine Verdet, PhD, and Saša Cecič-Erpič, PhD

Learning Objectives

On completion of this chapter, the reader should have

1. understanding of the life-span perspective on the athletic and the postathletic career;
2. understanding of multistage research into the development of talented and elite performers;
3. knowledge of the roles played by parents during the initiation, development, mastery, and discontinuation stages; and
4. knowledge of strategies that can help ensure that parental involvement during and after the athletic career has a positive influence on the athlete's development.

© Sport the Library

Within research studies, the role of parents has generally been situated during the early period of children's sport involvement (Weiss & Williams, 2004), but research into the development of talented and expert performers has begun to uncover the importance of parental involvement during the latter periods in athletes' sport careers as well. As Wylleman, De Knop, Ewing, and Cumming (2000) stated in conclusion to their review of parental involvement in elite youth sport, "Not only the way in which young athletes start out participating in competitive sport, but also the way in which their athletic careers will develop, will be influenced by their parents." (p. 158).

In view of their relevance throughout the sport career, this chapter takes a developmental perspective on parental roles and influence. In particular, this chapter will present a life-span model that considers the developmental events talented athletes face during as well as following their sport career. Second, research on how parental involvement evolves during the different stages in a child's athletic and postathletic career will be reviewed. Finally, directions for future research on the roles of parents and practical implications for interventions with parents will be discussed.

Life-Span Perspective on the Athletic Career

During the past four decades research into the career development of talented athletes has evolved into a growing topic of study in sport psychology (Wylleman, Lavallee, & Theeboom, 2004). Initiated during the 1960s and 1970s, the focus was originally on the career end as a singular event and included anecdotal evidence of the effects of retirement from high-level competitive and professional sport (e.g., Haerle, 1975; Hallden, 1965; Mihovilovic, 1968). As researchers shifted their perspective on athletic career termination to a transitional process-oriented approach, other transitions (e.g., young athletes' transition into high-level competitive sport) occurring throughout the athletic career also became topics of study (e.g., Donnelly, 1993; Hellstedt, 1990; Stevenson, 1990). In this way research as well as conceptualizations from the fields of career transitions (e.g., Lavallee, Gordon, & Grove, 1997; Stambulova, 1994; Wylleman, De Knop, Menkehorst, Theeboom, & Annerel, 1993), youth sport (e.g., Greendorfer, Lewko, & Rosengren, 1996; Hellstedt, 1987; Power & Woolger, 1994; Scanlan & Lewthwaite, 1986), and talent and expert development (e.g., Bloom, 1985; Côté, 1999; Csikszentmihalyi, Rathunde, & Whalen, 1993; Van Rossum & Van der Loo, 1997) became linked to a career-development perspective.

Building upon this career-development approach, a holistic life-span approach of the sport and post-sport career of elite athletes was recently proposed by Wylleman and Lavallee (2004). Acknowledging the strong concurrent, interactive, and reciprocal nature of transitions in the athletic career and in other domains of athletes' lives (e.g., academic, psychosocial, and professional transitions), they considered the dynamic interplay of key variables at various developmental periods. First, an athletic career is described in terms of succeeding normative stages. Athletes progress in their athletic development when they cope successfully with the tasks and challenges of each career stage as well as with the demands of the transition from one stage into another. Second, as athletes develop in sport, they also need to cope with the challenges of the stages and transitions in other domains. Concurrent to their athletic career, athletes also develop in psychological, psychosocial, and academic or vocational levels.

Using research data on the career development of active as well as former talented athletes, professional and elite athletes, and Olympians, Wylleman and Lavallee (2004) proposed a life-span model (see figure 17.1), which includes the normative stages and transitions faced by athletes at athletic, individual, psychosocial, and academic or vocational levels.

The top layer represents the stages and transitions athletes face in their athletic development and includes four stages that are tentatively linked to approximated ages: (a) the initiation stage, during which the young athlete is introduced into organized competitive sport (6-7 years of age); (b) the development stage, during which the athlete is recognized as talented and which entails an intensification of training and participation in competitions (12-13 years of age); (c) the mastery stage, which reflects the athlete's participation at the highest competitive level (18-19 years of age); and (d) the discontinuation stage, which describes the elite athlete's transition out of competitive sport (28-30 years of age). Although these stages are normative in nature, major differences may occur between sports; for example, at age 18 to 19, the mastery stage among female gymnasts may be coming to an end (Kerr & Dacyshyn, 2000), while for male rowers the mastery stage may actually be starting (Wylleman et al., 1993).

The second layer represents the developmental stages and transitions occurring at the psychological level and is based on different conceptual frameworks for psychological development, such as Erikson's (1963) developmental stages, Piaget's (1971) stages of cognitive development, and Havighurst's (1973) developmental tasks over the life span. The stages of psychological development include childhood, adolescence, and adulthood.

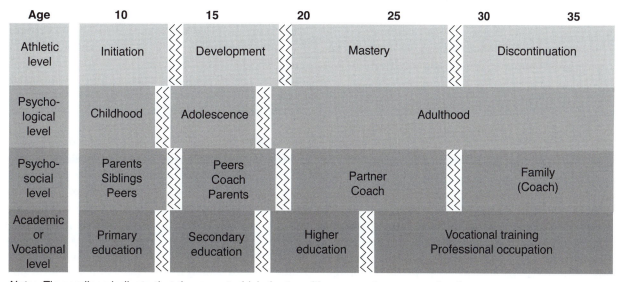

Note: Zig zag lines indicate that the age at which the transition occurs is an approximation.

Figure 17.1 A developmental perspective on transitions athletes face at the athletic, individual, psychosocial, and academic or vocational levels.

Reprinted, by permission, from P. Wylleman and D. Lavallee, 2004, A developmental perspective on transitions faced by athletes. In *Developmental sport and exercise psychology: A lifespan perspective,* edited by M.R. Weiss (Morganstown, WV: Fitness Information Technology).

The third layer represents the changes that can occur in athletes' psychosocial context relative to their athletic involvement and that have been identified in earlier research (e.g., Rees & Hardy, 2000; Rice, 1998). It situates those people whom athletes perceive as being the most significant during the particular stages. These changing contexts include the athletic triangle (athlete–parents, athlete–coach, and coach–parents relationships) (e.g., Carlson, 1988; Hellstedt, 1987, 1990; Scanlan, 1988; Smith & Smoll, 1996; Wylleman, 2000; Wylleman, De Knop, Sloore, Vanden Auweele, & Ewing, 2003), the athlete's relationships within the athletic family (e.g., Hellstedt, 1995), peer relationships (e.g., Smith, 2003; Weiss, Smith, & Theeboom, 1996; Weiss & Stuntz, 2004), marital or lifetime-partner relationships (e.g., Coppel, 1995; Jowett & Meek, 2000), and other interpersonal relationships significant to athletes.

Finally, as most countries have compulsory education up until the age of 16 or 17, athletes are confronted with a major overlap between their academic and athletic development (De Knop, Wylleman, Van Hoecke, & Bollaert, 1999). For example, the normative transitions in the sport life cycle of an elite basketball player in the United States will run parallel to transitions between academic levels—from youth sport to high school junior varsity to high school varsity to college to, finally, professional sport (Petitpas, Champagne, Chartrand, Danish, & Murphy, 1997). In nonprofessional sport, Beamish (1992) found that 6 in 10 Canadian Olympians were students at the time of participating in the Olym-

pic Games, whereas during the 2000 Olympic Games in Sydney, 1 Belgian athlete in 10 was a current or recently graduated university student-athlete.

The final layer therefore reflects academic stages and transitions, including the transitions into primary education (elementary school), secondary education (high school), and higher education (college or university). However, as vocational training and the development of a professional occupation may also have a strong influence on a talented athlete's sport career (Bussmann & Alfermann, 1994; Greendorfer & Blinde, 1985; Koukouris, 1991; Petitpas, Brewer, & Van Raalte, 1996; Wylleman et al., 1993), the final stage in this fourth layer represents vocational training or a professional occupation.

As can be seen, this life-span model situates the role of parents primarily during the initiation and development stages of the sport career. But to what extent are parents involved in the other career stages? Do parents play a role during the mastery stage, when athletes perform at their highest level of achievement? What kind of involvement do parents have as athletes retire from competitive sport and start their postathletic career?

In the next sections, this life-span model will be used as a guide to an overview of research on parental involvement throughout as well as after the athletic career. To set the scene, the first section will focus on multistage research, namely, studies that provide empirical data on the role of parents during different athletic career stages. The second section will then take a stage-by-stage perspective on parental involvement and describe parents' influence during each of the four athletic career stages identified in the life-span model (i.e., initiation, development, mastery, discontinuation).

Multistage Perspective on Parental Involvement

While limited in number, several studies have embraced a multistage perspective and provide insight into parental involvement in the development of talented and elite athletes. These studies originate from research on talented and expert performers in different domains of expertise (including the sport domain), on the development of and the transitions in the elite athletic career, and on the psychological characteristics of elite and Olympic athletes.

Talented and Expert Performers

Two of the major studies relevant to the sport domain that have investigated the development of talented and expert performers in different domains of expertise have been conducted by Bloom (1985) and Csikszentmihalyi, Rathunde, and Whalen (1993).

The research by Bloom (1985) and colleagues focused on the developmental events that occur in the lives of exceptionally talented artists, musicians, mathematicians, scientists, and athletes, including Olympic swimmers and professional tennis players. An integrative analysis of the home environments of these talented athletes revealed that the route of talent development consisted not only of three fairly similar stages of learning and development, but also that parents played an influential role in each of these stages.

During the early years (ages 4-12) or initiation stage, parents introduced their child to a variety of sports with an emphasis on playfulness, fun, and family involvement in athletic activity. While parents may have provided early instruction, they tried to ensure a coaching or instructional program that exposed their child to a higher skill level. Parents were supportive of the nurturing atmosphere created by the coach and did not attempt to undermine the process-oriented training (e.g., by pushing their children to achieve more competitive results before they came to love the activity in itself). This stage ended with parents taking their children to entry-level competitions where the emphasis was still on fun rather than on winning.

During the second stage (ages 13-18)—the middle years or development stage—the emphasis was found to shift from fun and playfulness to the development of sport specialization and higher levels of training and competition. Parents remained supportive of their children, who participated in a more intense, demanding, and outcome-oriented training environment. Parents accepted the prerequisite sacrifices and adjustments required of them (e.g., increased financial support, transport), and sometimes focused the family on the child's athletic activities, ensuring their presence at practice and competitions.

Finally, during the later years (ages 19-late 20s) or the perfection stage, where the athlete went on to national or even international competitions, athletes were found to develop an independency from their family while still considering the family of origin as an emotional support system and refuge from the ups and downs of athletic life. Although parents played a less immediate role in the training environment, they often still provided social and financial support for their more independent children. Bloom's work was innovative, as it clearly identified the different stages that occur in talent development and outlined the role parents play in each stage of the learning process and the development of their gifted children.

In their study, Csikszentmihalyi and colleagues (1993) investigated talented adolescents in different fields of expertise. These researchers concluded that talent development involved not only the learning of habits conducive to talent development, but also the acquisition of a mature personality during the teenage years and support from caring adults (e.g., parents). Specifically with regard to parental involvement, Csikszentmihalyi and colleagues suggested the notion of the *complex family,* which refers to the finding that families of talented youngsters were found to be both integrated (i.e., they were stable in their sense of support to their children) and differentiated (i.e., they encouraged each of their children to seek out new challenges and opportunities).

Talented adolescents of this type of family were perceived to feel happier at home, to invest more time and energy in school activities, and to be more energetic and determined. The researchers noted that, while talented youngsters did not exclusively develop in these types of families, these family characteristics increased the adolescents' chances to develop their talents. Csikszentmihalyi and colleagues added new and significant insights by confirming the role of parental involvement as well as by identifying the structure and characteristics of talented adolescents' families.

Development and Career of Elite Athletes

Alongside the research on talented and expert performers in different domains of expertise, other research has focused on the development and career of talented and elite athletes. A first line of research consists of studies conducted by national sport governing bodies on the development of their talented and elite athletes. For example, in its survey of 816 Olympians who competed from 1984 to 1998, the United States Olympic Committee (Gibbons, 2002) reported that while one athlete in three was introduced to sport via family activities, parents had but a moderate influence in directing and motivating their children to participate in their sport as well as in motivating them to pursue excellence. In both cases friends and private or commercial clubs played a more important role than did parents. Nevertheless, the athletic family was still perceived by the Olympians to be the most important social factor (together with coaches) affecting their *long-term* performance progression.

In a similar vein, the Australian National Athlete Development Survey surveyed 673 advanced, preelite, elite, and Olympic competitors on their lifetime sporting development (Australian Sports Commission, 2003). Regarding parental involvement, it was found that 15% of athletes' parents competed themselves at the preelite sporting level, and 5% even competed at the elite sporting level. Furthermore, parents were reported to demonstrate a positive empathy for sport, to be instrumental in the initial encouragement of the athlete's sporting participation, and to provide ongoing support at all levels of competition.

More particularly, it was shown that for one athlete in two, parents were instrumental in their child beginning her first sport ever played; for one athlete in three, parents were important in their child's start with his current sport; and for one athlete in three the parents were first to notice that their child possessed outstanding talent. Encouragement from the family was therefore one of the four most important factors perceived to contribute to progress at the basic competition level. Parental behaviors included, among others, financial support, transportation, presence at practice and competition, and emotional support. Athletes perceived their parents to remain positive and to provide active support throughout the entire athletic career.

The importance of a supportive family was also identified in a number of other studies. For example, in New Zealand, the Talent Identification and Development Taskforce (2003) found that immense support and lack of pressure to succeed from their family was not only an attribute common to elite athletes, but also (together with the support provided by friends and coaches) one of three key success factors common to most successful Olympians.

In a study on the perceived supporting and inhibiting factors in the careers of 15- to 52-year-old Irish (developmental to world-class) athletes, Duffy, Lyons, Moran, Warrington, and MacManus (2001) found that 4 athletes in 10 were introduced to sport by a family member, of which the father was most frequently cited. Parents were also perceived by athletes as the second most important factor of support (just behind coaches) not only contributing to their past development, but also contributing to their possible success in the future. This perceived importance of parental support was strongest for developmental athletes, followed closely by international and junior athletes and then world-class athletes.

Finally, in their survey of 140 elite athletes on the influence of the social and sport-related environment on athletes' development to elite level, De Knop, De Bosscher, and Leblicq (2004) found that parental involvement was fairly intensive during the athletes' sport career, assisting their children an average of 11.3 hours per week in their athletic activities. Nevertheless, 1 athlete in 10 also reported some kind of support lacking from parents (e.g., financial support, knowledge of elite-level sport, confidence in the athlete's ability to combine an athletic and an academic career).

A second line of research investigated the stages and transitions in the elite athletic career with which athletes need to cope successfully in order to progress during as well as after their sport career (for an overview, see Wylleman, Lavallee, & Theeboom, 2004). For example, in a retrospective study with 44 former Olympians, Wylleman and colleagues (1993) showed that parental involvement during the sport career was focused not only on creating a daily lifestyle that allowed their children to train daily, but also on a mentality to progress (e.g., perseverance, will to succeed) and thus transition into the next career stage. These former Olympians also recognized the support of their parents and their family of origin during and after their transition out of elite sport (e.g., by assisting them in finding a job, by motivating them to reenter higher education, by providing financial support).

During her investigations into the career transitions faced by Russian athletes, Stambulova (1994, 1995) found that parental involvement was related to athletes' satisfaction with their sport career. Those who were satisfied had experienced great support and appreciation from family, while those who were less satisfied found that their dissatisfaction was often reinforced by family disappointment or by a lack of parental recognition.

The possible role of parents in athletes' progress to the next athletic career stage was also examined by Würth, Lee, and Alfermann (2004). In studying parental involvement across the different career stages of 193 athletes from 10 to 20 years old, Würth et al. found that athletes (and parents) perceived parental involvement to decrease from the initiation into the development stage but then remain stable across the later career stages. Moreover, those athletes who achieved athletic success and moved into the next career stage reported that their parents showed much more directive behavior than those athletes who remained in the same stage of athletic development.

Wylleman, De Knop, and Van Kerckhoven (2000) studied the role of parents during different athletic stages. The study involved 10 highly talented swimmers at 20 years of age. These athletes perceived their parents' role to evolve from an active, participation-inducing role (advocating the need for hard work so as to develop their athletic abilities) during their childhood to an emotional, supportive role (underlining the need for discipline and motivation in order to enhance athletic achievements) during adolescence. Furthermore, during young adulthood, swimmers perceived their parents to acknowledge their need for more freedom and personal space and felt that if they were to decide to discontinue their athletic career, their parents would support their decision.

Finally, in a retrospective study, Cecič-Erpič, Wylleman, and Zupančič (2004) investigated 85 former elite athletes ranging in age from 21 to 44 years old on the quality of the career-termination process and found that the quality of parental involvement during an athlete's career could in itself become antecedent to a transitional moment. In other words, while parental support during an important life event was perceived as indicating a positive transition, the severe illness or injury of one parent or the deterioration of relationships with parents was perceived as a possible precursor to a negative transition.

In a third line of research, the perspective of deliberate play and practice is used to look at the development of expert performers in sport. This approach emphasizes that talent development is the result of deliberate practice—a process that is not only under the constraints of motivation, effort, and resources, but that is also affected by the family environment (Durand-Bush & Salmela, 2002).

Based on qualitative data from a retrospective study with four 18-year-old national-level athletes, four siblings, and seven parents, Côté (1999) described the role parents played during three stages of sport development. During the sampling years (ages 6-13), when the young athlete becomes interested in sport, parents assumed a leadership role and allowed their children to get involved in a wide range of enjoyable sporting activities. During the specializing years (ages 13-15), which are characterized by a gradual focus on one or two specific sport activities and a shift toward more sport-specific skill development, parents became committed supporters, without, however, putting pressure on their children regarding the type of sport in which to specialize. During the investment years (ages 15-18), when athletes become committed to achieving elite performance in one sport, parents' roles as follower and supporter became more apparent as they made sacrifices in their family life to allow their child to have optimal training conditions while also responding to the various demands put on their children by fostering an optimal learning environment rather than creating new demands or pressure.

In a similar vein, Durand-Bush and colleagues (Durand-Bush & Salmela, 2002; Durand-Bush, Salmela, & Thompson, 2004) examined the factors that contributed to the development and maintenance of 10 Olympic or world champions aged 19 to 36 years. Results confirmed that parents were very supportive throughout the athletic career, although they did not remain as actively involved in the latter stages of the athletes' development. These findings elaborated Côté's (1999) three-stage model with a fourth stage of development, namely, the maintenance years, when athletes reach the pinnacle of their sport and continue to train and compete in order to maintain and continue improving their performance. During this time the family functions as an emotional support system.

Psychological and Psychosocial Characteristics of Elite Athletes

A third perspective shedding light on the role of parents in elite athletes' sport careers includes research into the psychological characteristics of world- and Olympic-level athletes. Gould, Dieffenbach, and Moffett (2002), who interviewed 10 Olympic champions and 10 significant others (including parents and siblings), found that the development of psychological talent in these athletes was influenced by family dynamics. The influence of family dynamics included keeping success in perspective, objectively evaluating performance, having an overall understanding of the sport, intentionally teaching psychological skills and characteristics, modeling, and using motivational techniques. Moreover, the family also emphasized expectations and standards, hard work and discipline, the importance of following through, and the attitude that hard work pays off. At the same time, the family did not place undue pressure on the athlete but provided instead unconditional support and love.

In an earlier study, Gould and colleagues (Gould, Guinan, Greenleaf, Medbery, & Peterson, 1999) also revealed the importance of on-site parental involvement during a major competition. More particularly, they found that Olympic teams that met or exceeded performance expectations at the 1996 Olympic Games in Atlanta cited family support more often than those teams that failed to meet performance expectations. More specifically, a good structure of communication between the athletes and their families during the Games and education of the families on how to be a resource for the athletes helped athletes to enjoy their family's support.

Stages of Parental Involvement

As shown in the life-span model, athletic development can be described in terms of four major stages, namely, the initiation, development, mastery, and discontinuation stages. In this section, after each stage has been introduced in terms of its specific characteristics, parental involvement in the athletic development of their children will be considered using empirical data from studies involving talented and elite athletes (some of which have already been described in the previous section).

Initiation Stage

In this stage, which generally starts between ages 6 and 9 (e.g., Australian Sports Commission, 2003; Gibbons, 2002, Wylleman et al., 1993), children are introduced to the demands of organized sport (e.g., scheduled training sessions, coaches, team members, officials). As children still participate in an average of two or three different sports (Gibbons, 2002), it should not be surprising that Olympic athletes have been found to start in their Olympic discipline only at the ages of 14 to 15

(Wylleman et al., 1993). Children participate in sport an average of 6 to 8 hours per week, averaging a training duration of up to 6.1 months per season (Australian Sports Commission, 2003; Gibbons, 2002).

Research into sport socialization (Greendorfer, 1992) and youth sport participation (e.g., Brustad, Babkes, & Smith, 2001; Weiss & Williams, 2004) underlines the important role played by parents. This importance is a function of the large proportion of time young athletes spend in the family, the varied parental roles (e.g., chauffeur, financier, spectator, coach), and the possibilities for parents to provide immediate and specific feedback in and outside of the athletic arena (Fredericks & Eccles, 2004). Parental influence during this period of life (i.e., childhood) has thus been found to have a greater and more lasting effect on children's sport involvement than in other periods of development (e.g., adolescence) (Greendorfer, 1977).

Parents can influence children's perceptions of their ability and sport involvement through their own beliefs and values (Fredericks & Eccles, 2004). Côté (1999) found that elite athletes' parents encouraged all of their children to try different sports for enjoyment rather than for any other specific aim. Parents tried to provide their children with opportunities to have fun and develop basic motor skills. Baxter-Jones and Maffulli (2003) interviewed 282 elite 8- to 17-year-old athletes in gymnastics, soccer, swimming, and tennis and their parents on how the athletes were introduced to their

Parental influence during childhood can have a great and lasting effect on sport involvement.

sport and how they were encouraged to progress to intensive systematic training. Results showed that while parents largely influenced their children's introduction into their sport (with variations in function of type of sport: 70% in swimming, 57% in tennis, 53% in soccer, and 42% in gymnastics), coaches and sport clubs generally influenced how these young athletes progressed to a higher level of training.

Durand-Bush et al. (2004) also found that most parents of elite athletes were very sport-minded and pushed their children into participating in different sport activities, generally in those sports they themselves had practiced. This kind of positive parental pushing was described by the athletes interviewed in Gould and colleagues' (2002) study as "pushing me enough so it still came from the heart," "the times I really needed the motivation, they were right there giving it to me," and ". . . a good balance between enough discipline and enough good humor that it worked out well" (p. 197).

In studying psychosocial factors, Holt and Morley (2004) found that parental involvement was strongly related to providing emotional support (e.g., showing interest, instilling confidence); informational support (e.g., providing advice and guidance, being a practice partner); and, to a lesser extent, tangible support (e.g., money, transportation). This mix of support (i.e., driving, watching practices and games) was also important to 20 Canadian hockey players ranging in age from 6 to 15 years old (Robertson-Wilson & Côté, 2002). Furthermore, in a study with young male wrestlers it was shown that emotional support in the form of high parental satisfaction with performance, low parent pressure, and positive perception of parent involvement contributed to the athletes' enjoyment in wrestling (Scanlan & Lewthwaite, 1986). The role of positive parenting was also shown in basketball (Brustad, 1988); swimming (Power & Woolger, 1994); and soccer, volleyball, and American football (Stein, Raedeke, & Glenn, 1999).

Gould and colleagues (2002), on the other hand, found that there were athletes who had one parent who was not positively supportive, pressuring and pushing and even providing love depending on how the athlete performed. These researchers underlined, however, that even in these cases, the positive parent always exhibited unconditional love and support that offset many of the other parent's negative behaviors.

Donnelly (1993) reported that 65% of athletes experienced family problems, including missing a large part of family life, parental pressure, guilt about family time and attention received in comparison to siblings (including sibling rivalries and jealousies), constant parental presence at practices and competition at an age when independence was sought, and lack of financial or emotional support. Donnelly reported not only

a general impression of greater child–parent problems than the norm, but also that, as parents attempt to help their children achieve their full potential, "they often find that they are powerless in the high performance sport system" (p. 102).

Parental expectations are specifically relevant when the child starts to compete. In a retrospective study with 147 athletes, Stambulova (2004) found that the age at which this first competition took place varied among sport disciplines (between 9 years of age for swimmers and 13 years of age for wrestlers) and that the perceived parental demands as well as the athlete's own perceptions of parental expectations played a crucial role in making this important transition.

Parents may also provide early instruction before locating a coaching or instructional program that will expose their child to a higher skill level (e.g., Durand-Bush et al., 2004; Fredericks & Eccles, 2004). Parents often get involved in the organization of the sport by providing training, by managing youth teams, or by becoming the principle coach to their child. For example, Wylleman and De Knop (1998) found that due to a perceived or actual lack of qualified coaches, 67% of parents started their coaching relationship with their child during the initiation stage of the child's swimming or track and field career. Parents chose to coach their own children due to a lack of coaches in the sport club (53.2%) or because they were already coaching in the sport club (46.8%).

In one of the few other studies available on the dual role of parent-coach, Weiss and Fretwell (2003) studied the relationship of six parent soccer coaches with their sons (under 12 years old). While the soccer players perceived the benefits of being coached by their father (e.g., technical instruction, insider information, special attention, quality time), pressure of expectations, conflict, lack of empathy, and unfair behaviors were also prominent interaction features. From the parents' point of view, social interactions, taking pride in their son's achievements, and the opportunity to teach skills and values were among the positive aspects. Inability to separate the parent–son relationship role from the coach–player role, higher expectations for and pressure on their son, and paying greater attention to their son were some examples of differential treatment.

Finally, parental involvement is not only related to athletic activities. For example, by using a family systems model, Hellstedt (1995) elaborated on the role of parents within the context of the athlete's family. He suggested that during the initiation stage parents should, among other things, maintain permeable boundaries to allow for nonathletic individual and family experiences and demonstrate family values of hard work and goal attainment by parental example and role modeling rather than verbal persuasion.

Furthermore, it was shown that securing the child's possibilities to continue participation in competitive sport in combination with school activities is also an important role for parents. In particular, the academic transition—when young athletes reach their final year in primary school and prepare to go to secondary education—has been linked to the occurrence of attrition in competitive youth sport: As children change educational levels, they also generally disperse to different schools, thus breaking up the friendship networks that were a primary source of initiation of sport participation (Wylleman, Verdet, Lévèque, De Knop, & Huts, 2004). It was advocated that parents help their children find other incentives and goals that may enhance their participation motivation in competitive sport.

Development Stage

This stage in the athletic career begins as young athletes are identified as talented and capable of achieving high-level athletic achievements. It generally starts between ages 14 and 15 (Wylleman et al., 1993). As athletes become more dedicated to their sport, their amount of training—averages of 12 to 19 hours of practice per week and 9.4 months of training per season (Australian Sports Commission, 2003; Gibbons, 2002)—and level of specialization increase. Young athletes need to cope with new training loads, higher frequency of training sessions, more specialized technical and tactical training, an increased need to prepare physically and psychologically for competitions, an increased equality in competitors' athletic abilities at competitions, and higher expectations from significant others to show athletic proficiency, as well as the growing demands of their athletic career and their education, other leisure interests, and psychosocial development (Wylleman, De Knop, Ewing, & Cumming, 2000).

Parental influence remains important, as was shown, for example, by Hellstedt (1990), who studied the parent–athlete relationships of 12- and 13-year-old elite ski racers as they made the transition into the development stage of their ski career. These young athletes found their parents to have a strong influence on their sport career via, for example, parental coaching and support to continue in the sport. Furthermore, parents kept showing interest in their child's sport involvement by being present as spectators or even by coaching their child.

This type of parental coaching involvement was also confirmed by Ewing, Hedstrom, and Wiesner (2004), who interviewed parents of regionally ranked 12- to 15-year-old tennis players on their involvement in their children's tennis careers. Parents consistently reported direct involvement with their children's development as competitive tennis players, even though each

child had a coach from one of the local clubs. This involvement may also be actively sought by the young athletes themselves. For example, when interviewing 29 national-level players on the contingencies that influenced their decision to specialize in their sport, Stevenson (1990) found that many of them consulted with some of their significant others, including their parents, before making their decision.

During this stage the emphasis shifts from fun and playfulness to the development of sport specialization and commitment to higher levels of training and competition (see Bloom, 1985), so parents try to develop in their children a commitment to the sport and to the role demands of being a committed athlete (Hellstedt, 1995). In a study with 20-year-old talented swimmers and their parents, Wylleman, De Knop, and Van Kerckhoven (2000) found that swimmers perceived retrospectively that during their adolescence, their parents advocated the need for hard work to develop their athletic abilities. This finding corroborated Côté's (1999) suggestion that, during the development stage, parents should help their children develop a strong work ethic by instructing them about the virtues of hard work and by rewarding hard work with positive reinforcement.

The need for parental support has been shown to be present among young talented athletes. For example, Verdet and colleagues (Verdet et al., 2001; Verdet et al., 2003), who studied the quality of the relationships in the athletic triangle as perceived by 13- to 18-year-old high-level competitors, found that athletes not only had an open attitude toward their parents, they also expressed a clear need for emotional support from their parents. Furthermore, results revealed that these young athletes felt their parents provided them with this type of support.

The link between this type of positive parental behavior and children's athletic development has also been investigated. In a follow-up study in which 8- to 21-year-old athletes and their parents were studied over a 2-year period, Würth et al. (2004) found that athletes who made a successful transition from one athletic career stage to another felt that they received more sport-related advice and emotional support from their parents compared with those athletes who did not make the transition.

These findings corroborated research among successful Swedish elite tennis players who, in comparison to those players who did not make it to the international level, perceived that they not only enjoyed parental support but also that they were not pressured by their parents to achieve (Carlson, 1988). In a 5-year follow-up study of 14- to 18-year-old track and field champions, it was found that athletes who had become successful (i.e., regularly participated in competition, regularly improved performance, selected for national team) as well as those who had dropped out cited their parents as an important influence. For those who had been successful, parents were a major source of support, while for the dropouts, parents were perceived to be unsupportive, indifferent, showing low expectations, or lacking faith in their children's competence (Vanden Auweele, De Martelaer, Rzewnicki, De Knop, & Wylleman, 2004). Finally, in a study of highly skilled 15- to 22-year-old soccer players, Van Yperen (1995) showed that parental support had a buffering effect on the negative feelings of young players when their soccer performances were judged by the coach to be below average.

Parental support is also required due to the nature of competitive sport. For example, Durand-Bush and colleagues (2004) reported that because parents recognized that their children required a higher level of training, they respected and supported their child's decisions to participate more in training and competitions. In fact, athletes' families have been found to adapt family life to revolve around the young athlete. In examining the central role played by the family in the development of children's sport talent, Kay (2000) interviewed 20 families from three sports (swimming, tennis, and rowing). Results showed that, in addition to providing essential financial resources, a family's ability to accommodate the activity patterns required by the sport is critical to children's participation.

As was shown by Durand-Bush and Salmela (2002), parental involvement and family life may remain focused on the young athlete even when the need to provide transportation changes as the athletes acquire their own driving licenses or when the need for financial support decreases as athletes enter university on an athletic scholarship. These two points may mark a cultural difference between North American and European athletes: Not only is the system of athletic scholarships rarely available in European higher education (De Knop et al., 1999), but the age for driving in Europe varies from 16 to 18. This may explain why European athletes are still heavily reliant on their parents when going into the mastery stage or into higher education.

Parental involvement has also been found to change as young athletes progress in sporting achievements. A study on talented athletes' perceptions of the quality of the relationships within their athletic triangle (i.e., athlete–parents, athlete–coach, and coach–parents) (Wylleman et al., 2003) showed that athletes competing at the international level perceived themselves to solicit significantly less support from their parents compared with those athletes who still competed at the national level. A transition specific to sporting progress that occurs during the development stage is the transition into junior-level, junior league, or even professional sport at the ages of 16 to 18. At this level,

young athletes participate in more competitions on a more regular basis, generally with a strong national or even international overtone.

As athletes move away from home, parental roles and athletes' perceptions of parental involvement also may change. For example, Robertson-Wilson and Côté's (2002) study on parental support behaviors among 20 Canadian hockey players showed that the frequency of parental involvement changed after the age of 16; parents traveled less regularly (on a weekly or even biweekly basis) to games as their sons drove alone or with friends to games. A similar reduction in parental involvement was found in a study on the perceptions of 24 football (soccer) players, between the ages of 16 and 19, during their transition into professional football (Rea, 2003). As these players moved away from home into a professional football academy of one of four Premiership and Division 1 clubs, they reported their interactions with their parents to decrease and thus also the direct involvement of their parents. All players reported homesickness as a major concern of this transition and were reported to call their parents repeatedly, to go home, or to even have their family come to visit during the season.

Parental involvement also relates to parent–coach interactions. Although parent–coach conflicts have been reported (e.g., Monsaas, 1985), this is not always the case, as was shown in a study in which 71 coaches and 140 parents perceived themselves to have a good relationship when coaches worked with the athletes toward a higher level of athletic achievement (Vanden Auweele, Van Mele, & Wylleman, 1994). Furthermore, in Wylleman et al.'s (2003) study on the quality of the interpersonal relationships within the athletic triangle, the athletes perceived the frequency of parent–coach interactions to decrease as they made the transition into international competitions. It was argued that this decrease reflected the fact that as athletes matured they gained more and more responsibility for their own sport involvement.

As in the initiation stage, parents are found to coach their own children during the development stage. Notwithstanding the limited amount of research available, some studies have revealed that during this stage in the athletic career, parent-coaches generally relinquish their active coaching role in favor of another coach (Durand-Bush et al., 2004). This can result in young athletes perceiving less parental pressure, but it also can result in a shift of the source of this pressure from parents to the coach (Hellstedt, 1990).

Research has also shown, however, that parents may actually become a coach to their children during this stage. In their study on parent-coaches in swimming and track and field, Wylleman and De Knop (1998) found that one parent-coach in five started coaching their child during the development stage specifically due to a perceived lack of a viable alternative. On the one hand, receiving training outside of regular sessions, a stronger parental interest in their children's sport career, and a lack of conflicts between parents and coach were perceived by athletes as the most positive effects of being coached by their parent; on the other hand, athletes found the difficulty of separating the parent and the coach roles at home and being permanently scrutinized by the parent-coach as two of the more distinct disadvantages.

The parent-coaches themselves perceived that they were not only more strict and demanding with their own children than with the other athletes, at the same time they were trying to keep a positive relationship with their child. The researchers also reported that athletes perceived their other noncoaching parent as trying to buffer the negative effects of the parent-coach's behaviors.

Finally, during this stage, parental involvement is relevant with regard to talented athletes' involvement in secondary education. Due to compulsory school attendance, talented athletes' opportunities to attend training sessions may be restricted, or the athletes may need private tutoring due to increased absenteeism from participating in training camps and competitions (De Knop et al., 1999). Consequently, parents have been found to play a crucial role in enabling their children to combine secondary education and elite sport—sometimes by fighting battles with school administrators over timetables, changing tests and exams, and allowing the child-athlete to stay at home from school during regular school days to study for tests or to complete required assignments that were neglected due to athletic activities (Donnelly, 1993).

Several European countries have awarded a prominent role to secondary education in the development of talented athletes by creating a specific educational system that promotes a combination of school and high-level competitive sport. For example, talented young Flemish athletes are given the opportunity to complete their secondary education in one of nine "topsport" schools, which include 20 hours per week of academic courses and 12 hours of high-level training by specialized coaches. Parental involvement was also found to remain important in this particular system. More specifically, athletes (90.1%), coaches (77.5%), teachers (80.8%), and medical and physiotherapy staff (53.8%) judged parents' roles to consist of providing emotional and financial support (Wylleman, 2001).

Mastery Stage

The mastery athletic stage, during which athletes are required to perform at their highest level in a consistent way for as long as possible (Wylleman et al., 2004), generally starts when the talented athlete moves from the junior category into the senior category. As the amount of practice averages 19 to 22 hours per week (Australian Sports Commission, 2003; Gibbons, 2002), athletes may need to work toward attaining professional status, thus spending a period of their life almost exclusively focusing on training and competition. While the average tenure in professional baseball, American football, basketball, and ice hockey in the United States is between 4 and 7 years (Leonard, 1996), the mastery stage of Olympic athletes spans 10 to 15 years on average (Conzelmann, Gabler, & Nagel, 2001; Wylleman et al., 1993).

During this athletic stage, the family is reported to remain a support system and an emotional refuge from the stress of competition (Bloom, 1985). Durand-Bush et al. (2004) found that when asked who had played an important role during the mastery stage of their career, several athletes referred to their families. While parents were less involved at this stage, their emotional support and love remained high in the best as well in the worst of times. In another study, Durand-Bush and Salmela (2002) reported that for one athlete, the parents were actually the only people who the athlete could rely on after having experienced setbacks at the Olympics. In his study on the psychosocial characteristics of elite adolescent athletes, Holt (2001) also showed that for the under-20 Canadian national soccer team, players perceived the support offered by their parents as important for their success in general and for the transition into the senior level in particular. For example, a study with athletes in lifesaving revealed that family and financial support were perceived as the two most important resources for coping with the transition from the junior to senior level (Rimbaut, 2004).

Sometimes parents may be more actively involved than one would expect at this stage. For example, when questioned about the roles parents had played during the preceding 12 months, members of different national squads of the Netherlands (judo, speed skating, swimming, table tennis) listed financial assistance, household organization, transportation, presence at games, and moral support as important parental roles (Van Rossum, 1995). In their study on social support in high-level sport, Rees and Hardy (2000) found that 10 international competitors aged 18 to 27 received emotional support (e.g., help with being dropped, just being there), esteem support (e.g., help with pulling out of slumps), and tangible support (e.g., reducing worries about practical matters such as finances) from their parents. Rees and Hardy (2000) also reported that athletes sometimes perceived this type of parental involvement less positively, as athletes found themselves put off by the presence of their parents.

Parental involvement is not always similar for both parents. For example, in their study on 265 talented athletes, Wylleman and colleagues (Wylleman et al., 2003;

Wylleman, Vanden Auweele, De Knop, Sloore, & De Martelaer, 1995) found that, compared with the developmental stage, athletes perceived the quality of their interactions with both parents to have changed during the mastery stage. In particular, athletes expected less emotional support from their mother and more emotional support from their fathers. It was hypothesized that this differentiation was related to the fathers' surging interest in the athletic achievements of their children as they reached a higher level of athletic proficiency—an interest that made athletes shift their attention away from their mothers, who in general had been involved since their initiation into organized sport.

As the mastery stage runs parallel to the developmental stage of adulthood, parents are faced with the task of launching their children into the real world so that they can establish independent living apart from the family and develop partner relationships that may lead to the formation of the adult child's own family (Hellstedt, 1995). The intense parental involvement and the (possible) dependence upon the family during the previous stage, however, may not only delay the onset of athletes' individuation and independence, but may also affect the parents. For example, Monsaas (1985) reported that parents sometimes missed traveling with their children to competitions and thus felt somewhat left out during this stage. Nevertheless, it is worth nothing that 13% of the parents of competitive swimmers and track and field athletes developed or maintained a coaching relationship with their adult child during the mastery stage (Wylleman & De Knop, 1998).

Finally, during this stage parental involvement can be linked to athletes' efforts in combining athletic training and academic pursuits in higher education or a vocational career. The importance awarded to higher education as a crucial step toward a professional occupation is reflected in parents of talented athletes: One parent in two of young athletes who ended their secondary education emphasized that they expected their talented child to continue into higher education. Furthermore, parents have been shown to gently pressure their children into continued formal education on the way to a professional future (Koukouris, 1991). The transition into the job market is often accompanied by an athlete's increased efforts to secure greater financial and personal security. This is necessary for those athletes who cannot rely on income via their athletic achievements. Here again, parents may be called upon for financial and logistical support.

Discontinuation Stage

While usually linked to the end of a multistage athletic career, discontinuation can actually occur sooner and cut short previous stages. For example, due to lack of enjoyment a young athlete may drop out during the initiation stage, a career-ending injury may cut short a talented athlete's career during the development stage, or a talented athlete may favor an academic career over an athletic career when the mastery stage starts. On the other hand, anticipated athletic retirement may occur between the ages of 20 (e.g., female gymnasts) and 40 (e.g., male rowers). In a prospective study with 561 athletes, North and Lavallee (2004) found that, while athletes intended on average to retire at the age of 34, retirement could already occur at 25 years, followed by peaks around the ages of 30, 35, and 40.

Sport psychologists have conducted extensive research into the career-ending process and the post-athletic career (see Lavallee & Wylleman, 2000). Important aspects of this process include adjusting to a new life following the sport career in which they are suddenly like everyone else (Lavallee et al., 1997), missing the sport atmosphere and competition (Kerr & Dacyshyn, 2000; Stambulova, 2000), coping with the changes in subjective well-being (Stephan, Bilard, Ninot, & Delignières, 2003), and adapting to a new social status and professional responsibilities (Wylleman et al., 1993). In contrast to the empirical data on how former elite athletes cope with the career-ending process, very few research findings are available on the role of parents in the discontinuation stage. However, significant others, which may include parents, have been found to play a role in the discontinuation process.

In their retrospective qualitative study of track and field athletes, Carpenter and Kieran (1997) reported that athletes found it difficult to leave competitive sport because of the pressure applied by significant others. This is to some extent linked to the age at which athletes discontinue their athletic career. For example, Bona (1998) reported case studies on the perceptions of two 18-year-olds on the changes that occurred in their social network after retiring from elite sport. Analysis showed that these former athletes perceived the role played by their family to increase significantly during the discontinuation stage compared with the roles played by coaches and athletic peers.

With regard to adult athletes, a retrospective study on the retirement experiences of eight Olympians confirmed the importance of the support, efforts, and understanding of their parents and family of origin (Carron, 2004). These former Olympic athletes described their parents' behavior during the discontinuation process as level-headed, down-to-earth pride. This study corroborated with the findings from Wylleman and colleagues' (1993) study in which 44 former Olympians acknowledged the support of their parents and their family of origin during and after their transition out of elite sport, for example, by assisting them in finding or reintegrating in a full-time job, by motivating them to reenter higher education, or by providing financial support.

Independent of age group, research clearly reflects the importance of social support during this stage. From their study on the retirement experiences of 19- to 31-year-old elite athletes, Seiler, Schmid, and Schilling (1998) concluded that social support was one of three factors relevant to a successful retirement. Specifically, parents not only showed understanding of the problems these former athletes faced, but also provided emotional support that enhanced the athletes' self-esteem. Furthermore, the effect of this type of support was linked to the intensity with which it was provided (even if it was only provided by one person) rather than to the size of the social network. It was also shown that, after their athletic career ended, former Olympians significantly increased the amount of time spent with their family (Wylleman, De Knop, & Sillen, 1998).

The active role that the family of origin can play has also been suggested by Hellstedt (1995), who stated that parents of retiring athletes should assist their children in coping with the transition from competitive athletics. For adolescent former athletes this may entail moving back in with their parents after having lived away from home (e.g., in a training center) for several years (Wylleman, De Knop, & Van Kerckhoven, 2000). This may not always run smoothly, however, as these former athletes may need to rekindle their interactions with their parents (and siblings) before fitting back in at home (Bona, 1998).

Taking into account the average age category during which athletic retirement may occur, which is 25 to 35 years (North & Lavallee, 2004; Wylleman & Lavallee, 2004), it is not unlikely that retired athletes may already be or may plan to become parents themselves. Wylleman et al. (1998) found that among 13 former Olympians, 4 athletes had become parents during the mastery stage and 2 started a family after ending their athletic career. North and Lavallee (2004) found that almost 1 athlete in 10 planned to start their own family after retirement. Hellstedt (1995) argues that for adult former athletes, parental support may also consist of helping their children in setting up their own family.

A final aspect that parental involvement may be related to consists of the integration of former elite athletes into academia or the job market. Although sport governing bodies such as the International Olympic Committee emphasize that elite athletes need to be provided with opportunities to develop a vocational career (Olympic News, 1994), only a few well-structured and efficient programs have been found to run (Wylleman & Parker, 2004). This has led many former elite athletes to turn to their parents and family of origin for financial and logistical support (Wylleman et al., 1993). In fact, this lack of social provisions for former elite athletes has caused athletes to terminate their sport career earlier than required in order to obtain vocational training or find a job in order to earn a living (Bussmann & Alfermann, 1994).

Finally, former athletes who have started a professional occupation after ending their athletic career may be confronted with the process of occupational delay (Naul, 1994): Because most athletes have been busy with the development of their athletic career, few will have had the opportunity to participate in summer jobs or vocational or in-service training. In consequence, these athletes may lack the relevant professional skills, experience, and networking necessary for vocational success and thus must start at the bottom of the ladder. This may once again lead former elite athletes to turn to their family of origin for support.

Future Research

As was acknowledged earlier, there is a limited amount of research on parental involvement throughout and following an athlete's sport career. This could be due to the fact that, as stated by Hellstedt (1995), research on family influences is complex, and it is often difficult to explore "the intricacies of the family processes that exist in athlete families" (p. 119). Nevertheless, current research into, for example, the quality of interpersonal relationships within the athletic triangle of talented and elite athletes (e.g., Verdet et al., 2001; Wylleman et al., 2003) shows that it is possible to map the important dimensions of parental involvement—not only as perceived by the adults, but also by the young athletes themselves.

Notwithstanding the possible complexity, several avenues for further research can be advanced. First, in order to capture stage-related differences, researchers should, whenever possible, take a life-span developmental perspective on parental involvement. This would allow for more empirical data on parenting practices and parents' role in talent development. Furthermore, this approach may direct researchers' attention not only to those athletic career stages where little empirical data on parental involvement is available (i.e., mastery, discontinuation), but also to the role parents play in the development of their talented children in the nonathletic stages (i.e., psychological, psychosocial, academic or vocational). In this way, parenting dimensions would be examined not only within the athletic context but rather within the larger social context in which talented athletes develop (Fredericks & Eccles, 2004). Wylleman and Lavallee's (2004) model (see figure 17.1 on page 235) may assist researchers in taking a life-span perspective in developmental research.

Second, future studies should focus on the intricacies of the athlete families. The work by Csikszentmihalyi and colleagues (1993) on the complex family and the family systems approach as translated by Hellstedt (1995) to the athletic family both offer excellent starting points to look into, for example, the role of family status (e.g., parental involvement in single versus two-parent families) or of parental sport experience.

Third, researchers should invest in the continued development of specific measures of parental behavior. The Sport Interpersonal Relationships Questionnaires (SIRQ) (Verdet et al., 2001; Verdet et al., 2003; Wylleman et al., 2003) and the Parental Involvement in Sport Questionnaire (PISQ) (Würth et al., 2004) can be considered as initial responses to the need to measure and conceptualize the constructs of parent involvement, encouragement, and support in the athletic context.

In line with Wylleman's (2000) guidelines for research into interpersonal relationships, a methodology should be used that captures the different elements relevant to interpersonal relationships, including the interpersonal perceptions of both athlete and parents, the bidirectionality of the constituting relationships (e.g., how athletes perceive their behavior toward their parents and how they perceive their parents to behave toward them), the parent–coach relationship (including the relationship as perceived by the athletes), and the causal associations between parental involvement and talented athletes' development. Furthermore, as was shown that the involvement of mothers and fathers may vary during specific career stages (Wylleman et al., 2003), researchers should compare paternal as well as maternal roles in talent development.

Finally, as advocated by Wylleman (2000), parental involvement should be investigated in intervention studies. Such a field-based intervention study in high-level sport was conducted by Harwood and Swain (2002) in order to investigate the effects of a season-long player, parent, and coach intervention program on the goal orientations of three junior tennis players. Parents participated not only in educational sessions but also in task-involving roles related to creating an optimal motivational climate, learning a simple match analysis and charting strategy in order to provide useful performance-related feedback to their children, and leading a postmatch discussion session with the players. The researchers reported positive directional changes in all tennis players.

In conclusion, questions that beckon for new or more in-depth research include the following:

- In what way do parental behavior and practices in nonathletic domains (e.g., academics) influence their child's involvement in the athletic setting?

- How do the constitution of the athletic family (e.g., single versus two-parent families) and family interaction patterns play a role in the development of the gifted young athlete?

- What kind of parental support is relevant to adult elite athletes?

- What roles do parents play during the discontinuation stage?

- How do former elite athletes interact with their own talented children?

- What type of research instrument allows for a developmental approach to the study of parenting in talent development?

- What kind of interventions can be conducted by sport federations in order to educate parents and optimize their roles within the setting of competitions?

Practical Implications

Optimizing parental involvement in the development of talented, elite, and retired athletes can be considered on two levels. First, at the individual level, instruments and strategies should be developed to help parents understand what influence they have in the development of their athletic children and how they can enhance this development at athletic and nonathletic levels (psychological, psychosocial, academic or vocational). Second, as parents have been reported to play a pivotal role in the ongoing support provided to their children at all levels of competition (Australian Sports Commission, 2003), it is important for sport governing bodies to understand and to involve parents in the development of talented and elite athletes. Researchers should therefore also focus on how sport clubs as well as national sport governing bodies can help optimize parental involvement during and after the athletic career.

At the local level, sport clubs have been developing parental guidelines, while other initiatives have come from private sport-related organizations (e.g., American Sport Education Program, 1994; Marriott & Nilsson, 2003), experts and academic centers of excellence (e.g., De Knop, Wylleman, Theeboom, De Martelaer, Van Puymbroeck, & Wittock, 1994; Rotella & Bunker, 1987), and national sport governing bodies (e.g., Howie, 2004). As an example of the latter, a book was developed by the English Football Association as an official guide to the roles of the football (soccer) parent. The book includes a step-by-step guide to the development of young football players as well as parental roles, code of conduct, and safety guidelines.

Summary

Using a life-span developmental model, parental involvement is situated within the psychosocial development of talented and elite athletes. This model provides the basis for a more in-depth review of the roles parents have been found to play during the athletic career. Multistage studies on talented and elite athletes highlight the roles parents play throughout different athletic career stages. Empirical data on parental involvement during each of the four career stages (initiation, development, mastery, and discontinuation) reveal that parental involvement optimal to talent development includes providing different types of support (e.g., emotional, financial, logistical) and avoiding specific interpersonal behaviors (e.g., pressure, disappointment, lack of parental recognition). Research also shows that parental behaviors are specific to each of the four career stages.

Suggestions for future research include capturing the stage-related differences by using a life-span developmental perspective on parental involvement; unlocking the intricacies of the athlete family; continuing to develop specific measures of parental behavior; and conducting field-based intervention studies on parental involvement in the development of talented, elite, and retired elite athletes. Finally, implications for practice include assisting parents as well as sport governing bodies in optimizing the roles played by parents.

DISCUSSION QUESTIONS

1. Describe the life-span developmental model, focusing on how parental involvement is situated within athletes' development at the psychosocial level.
2. Discuss the major findings on parental involvement resulting from multistage studies.
3. List and explain the roles parents have been found to play during each of the four career stages.
4. List the proposals outlined in this chapter and formulate your own proposals for further research into parental involvement in the development of talented, elite, and former elite athletes.
5. Outline a strategy that (a) a sport club and (b) a national sport governing body can use to optimize the roles of parents in the development of talented, elite, and former elite athletes.

chapter 18

Passion for Sport in Athletes

Robert J. Vallerand, PhD, and Paule Miquelon, PhD

Learning Objectives

On completion of this chapter, the reader should have

1. understanding of the new conceptualization on passion (Vallerand et al., 2003) and its applicability to the realm of sport;

2. knowledge of research that provides empirical support for our conceptualization of passion;

3. appreciation of future research directions on passion in sport; and

4. knowledge of practical implications for developing passion in athletes.

nn and Ruth play basketball just about every day. They love the game, value it, and spend lots of time and energy on it. For them, basketball is more than a game: It's part of who they are. They are basketball players and have developed a passion for the game. This passion for basketball has led them to practice hard for several years, enabling them to achieve excellence in their sport. However, while both are passionate toward basketball, they are different in some ways. For instance, while Ann takes basketball seriously, she nevertheless smiles and experiences enjoyment when playing the game. When basketball is over at the end of the day, she can turn the page and devote herself to other activities and interests. As a result, Ann is happy while playing basketball and just as happy when doing something else.

On the other hand, when Ruth plays ball, she doesn't smile. According to her, basketball is too serious for her to smile while playing. Performing well is almost a matter of life and death for Ruth, and she often feels low after a bad performance. Furthermore, she talks and thinks about basketball all the time, even at the expense of her enjoyment in other activities. Thus, while Ruth and Ann are equally good players, Ann is happier both while playing basketball and in her life in general. As we'll see in this chapter, Ann and Ruth illustrate just one example of how passion may influence athletes' participation in sport.

Theory and Research on Passion

While the concept of passion has generated much interest from philosophers (see Rony, 1990, for a review), it has received little attention in psychology. Those psychologists who have looked at passion have underscored its motivational aspect. For instance, Frijda, Mesquita, Sonnemans, and Van Goozen (1991) posit that "passions are defined as high-priority goals with emotionally important outcomes" (p. 218). Frijda et al. suggest that people will spend large amounts of time and effort in order to reach their important goals. Other psychologists have looked at romantic passion (Hatfield & Sprecher, 1986; Sternberg, 1986). However, this type of passion is different from passion toward activities and will not be discussed herein.

Still other researchers have focused on concepts that appear similar in nature such as positive and negative dependence (Glasser, 1976), running addiction (e.g., Morgan, 1979; Sachs, 1981), exercise dependence, and obligatory running (for a review see Hausenblas & Symons Downs, 2002). However, it is not clear from such work how the concepts of sport and positive dependence, obligatory running, and addiction can be adaptive, leading to positive outcomes and processes. Furthermore, such concepts have not been fully presented in a coherent theoretical formulation (Hausenblas & Symons Downs, 2002).

Finally, others have discussed the concept of commitment (e.g., Carmac & Martens, 1979) in sport. However, although people who are heavily committed to a given sport can be passionate, it is also possible for such people not to be passionate toward their sport because they may not necessarily love or even like the sport. For instance, one person may be highly committed to jogging not because he loves it but because he desperately needs to lose weight. Thus, the concept of commitment is not equivalent to that of passion. In sum, it would appear that no theoretical conceptualization exists to explain the positive and negative effects that may result from having a passion toward activities.

Dualistic Approach to Passion

We propose a new conceptualization of passion toward activities. According to this position (Vallerand et al., 2003; Vallerand & Houlfort, 2003), passion refers to a strong inclination toward an activity that people like, that they find important, and in which they invest time and energy. For instance, a basketball player who loves her sport, values it greatly, and invests a lot of time in it by practicing often after regular practice hours would be considered passionate toward basketball. Past research has indeed shown that activity valuation (e.g., Deci, Eghrari, Patrick, & Leone, 1994), time and energy expenditure (Emmons, 1999), and liking for the task (Csikszentmihalyi, Rathunde, & Whalen, 1993) are all associated with strong investment in activities.

Certain activities are so self-defining that they become central features of one's identity. We posit that such is the case for passionate activities. They become part of one's identity because of an innate tendency toward higher-order organization that takes place through the organismic integration process (Deci & Ryan, 2000). In this process the self becomes more complex over time through the internalization of elements from the environment, among other things. We posit that representations of activities that people like and engage in on a regular basis will be incorporated in the person's identity to the extent that it is highly valued (Aron, Aron, & Smolan, 1992; Csikszentmihalyi

This research program was supported by a grant from the Social Sciences Humanities Research Council of Canada (SSHRC) to the first author and an SSHRC fellowship to the second author.

et al., 1993), thereby leading to a passion toward that specific activity. This passion becomes a central feature of a person's identity and serves to define the person. Those who have a passion for playing basketball or soccer, for example, do not simply engage in these activities. They are basketball players or soccer players. Passionate activities are part of who they are.

We further posit that passion can be of two forms: obsessive or harmonious. *Obsessive passion* refers to a motivational force that pushes a person toward an activity. Thus, although people with an obsessive passion toward their sport activity like the sport, they nevertheless feel compelled to engage in it due to an internal force that is controlling them. People who are obsessively passionate toward their sport feel that they cannot help but engage in it. The passion must run its course. It is as if the passionate activity controls them. People with an obsessive passion toward their sport cannot envision their life without it; they may even come to be emotionally dependent upon it. Because activity engagement is out of the person's control, it eventually comes to take disproportionate space in the person's identity, and conflicts arise between participation in the sport activity and other aspects of the person's life. The passionate golfer who can't help but play 18 holes on both days of the weekend and in so doing neglects his family is bound to experience conflict between the passionate activity (golf) and other aspects of his life, including his family.

On the other hand, *harmonious passion* refers to a motivational force that leads a person to engage in the activity willingly and engenders a sense of volition and personal endorsement about pursuing the activity. People with a harmonious passion don't feel compelled to do the activity; rather, they choose to do so. It is as if they have control over the activity that they love. Thus, athletes report that they enjoy a variety of positive experiences while playing their sport, that their activity is in harmony with other aspects of their life, and that it reflects things that they like about themselves. With this type of passion, the activity does not occupy most of the person's identity and it is in harmony with other aspects of the person's life. People with a harmonious passion who arrange their schedule in such a way that they play their golf game during the week or on only one day of the weekend are less likely to experience conflict between the passionate activity and their other activities and family life.

Athletes with harmonious passion like, value, and invest a tremendous amount of time and effort while enjoying most aspects of their sport.

Development of Passion

In his book, *The Values of the Game*, former senator of New Jersey and former NBA player for the New York Knicks Bill Bradley makes the following observation: "I'm not sure exactly when my interest [toward basketball] turned to passion . . ." (Bradley, 2000, p. 1). This quote makes at least two points. First, interest and passion are not synonymous, as we will see in the next section. Second, it begs the question, What psychological processes are involved in such a transformation from interest to passion?

We believe that an activity becomes passionate through a three-step process (figure 18.1). The first step involves activity selection. Research reveals that the social environment, especially parents, adults, and peers when it comes to children, plays a major role in activity selection (e.g., Kenyon & McPherson, 1973). We will not elaborate on this aspect as it is beyond the scope of this chapter.

Once the activity has been selected and the person has started to engage in it, two processes are crucial: valuation of the activity and internalization of the representation of the activity in one's core aspect of the self (identity). Most forms of physical activity and sport have the potential to become either a harmonious or an obsessive passion because they involve at least some elements of interest. To the extent that such interest is not fleeting and that the activity is highly valued, a passion toward the activity will develop. Thus, personal valuation of the activity is the second step in the sequence leading to passion development.

Research has indeed shown that when the object of interest is highly valued and meaningful, people are inclined to internalize the valued object, making it part of themselves (Aron et al., 1992; Deci et al., 1994). However, if the person doesn't enjoy that given activity, the internalization will not turn into a passion. At best it may become an integrated regulation. Deci and Ryan (1985, 2000) propose that values and regulations related to activities that are *not* interesting can also be internalized in the self. When the internalization is autonomous in nature and is coherent with other aspects of the self, the regulation is integrated. Integrated regulation entails that the activity can be engaged in out of a high level of choice and feelings of volitional involvement and can lead to adaptive cognitive, affective, and behavioral outcomes. However, the activity still remains relatively less interesting and not as profoundly part of the person's identity. Thus, the phenomenological experience should not be as powerful as that originating from passion.

How people internalize the highly valued and enjoyable sport activity in their identity determines the type of passion that will develop. This represents the last step in the development of passion. Past research has shown that values and regulations concerning *uninteresting* activities can be internalized in a controlled or autonomous fashion (Deci & Ryan, 2000; Sheldon, 2002). We believe that such internalization also takes place with respect to the representations of interesting activities. A controlled internalization is hypothesized to lead to obsessive passion. This type of internalization involves internalizing the activity into one's identity because one feels pressured to do so or because some contingencies are attached to the activity, such as feelings of social acceptance or self-esteem. When the activity is internalized in a controlled fashion, the activity is then part of the person's identity but has not been willingly integrated in it. Thus, although people like the activity, they feel compelled to engage in it due to the obsessive nature of their passion toward the activity.

Second, the activity may also be internalized in one's identity in an autonomous way. This kind of internalization leads to the other type of passion, harmonious passion. Autonomous internalization occurs when people have freely accepted an activity as important for them without any contingencies attached to it. The resulting passion leads them to engage in the activity out of choice and not from internal pressure. This internalization is hypothesized to produce a motivational force to engage in the activity willingly and with little conflict with other activities.

To answer Bill Bradley's question, we propose that when an interesting activity such as basketball becomes highly valued, interest toward the activity will turn into a passion as the activity is internalized into the person's identity. The type of passion that ensues is determined by the type of internalization that takes place, with a controlled internalization of the sport representation leading to an obsessive passion and an autonomous internalization leading to a harmonious passion.

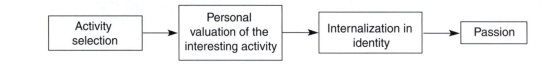

Figure 18.1   Development of passion.

An important question becomes, What are the determinants of the internalization process? In accord with previous research on motivation (e.g., Deci & Ryan, 2000; Vallerand, 1997; for reviews of such research in sport, see Vallerand, 2001; Vallerand & Rousseau, 2001), it is proposed that the internalization process can be influenced by at least two major factors. The first factor concerns the *social conditions* under which the person engages in the activity. Self-determination theory (Deci & Ryan, 1985, 2000) posits that people have three fundamental human needs: competence, autonomy, and relatedness. As Deci and Ryan (1994) have suggested, "People are inherently motivated to feel connected to others within a social milieu, to function effectively in that milieu, and to feel a sense of personal initiative while doing so" (p. 7). These needs have been found not only to facilitate people's engagement in interesting activities, but also to promote the internalization of regulations and values about noninteresting activities.

We posit that to the extent that the social environment promotes people's needs for competence, relatedness, and especially autonomy, and to the extent that a given interesting activity is highly valued by the person, then an autonomous internalization process will occur for that activity. Such internalization is likely to occur when an autonomy-supportive context has been created where people feel some sense of participation, ownership, or voice regarding decisions and behaviors. Thus, individuals who engage in the sport that they love and value in an autonomy-supportive context (e.g., Grolnick & Ryan, 1989) where there is room for choices and personal involvement should be more likely to internalize their sport in an autonomous fashion and consequently to develop a harmonious passion. Conversely, individuals who engage in a sport that they love and value within a controlling context where they feel coerced to behave in specific ways are likely to develop an obsessive passion toward that sport.

A second determinant of the internalization process pertains to one's personality. One aspect of personality that appears important is internalization style (e.g., Vallerand, 1997), which is the tendency for individuals to internalize values, regulations, and activities in either an autonomous or a controlled way. Thus, to the extent that a person values a sport activity and finds it interesting, having an autonomous internalization style should lead the person to develop a harmonious passion toward sport. However, given the same level of interest and valuation toward sport, a controlled internalization style should lead the person to develop an obsessive passion toward sport. Personality is expected to become a progressively important determinant of the internalization process as people get older and their personality becomes more crystallized.

Passion and Intrinsic and Extrinsic Motivation

At this point, a discussion on the distinction between passion on the one hand and intrinsic and extrinsic motivation on the other is in order. Intrinsic motivation entails engaging in an activity out of pleasure and enjoyment; thus, it shares the aspect of liking an activity with the concept of passion. However, intrinsically motivated activities are typically not internalized in the person's identity (Deci & Ryan, 1985, 2000). Intrinsic motivation naturally emerges from the person–task interaction in the short term (Koestner & Losier, 2002) and as such it doesn't lead to the internalization of the activity. As Bradley suggested, one can be interested in an activity without being passionate about it. We propose that only when the activity is both interesting and part of one's identity can this motivational force be considered a passion.

On the other hand, extrinsic motivation entails engaging in an activity not out of pleasure but in order to obtain something outside the activity. Thus, the relative lack of liking for the activity is a fundamental difference between extrinsic motivation and passion. Although some forms of extrinsic motivation entail some internalization (e.g., introjected, identified, and integrated regulation), such forms of regulation pertain to an activity that one does not like. In addition, because it is extrinsic in nature, such internalization is unlikely to characterize the person's identity in an important way. Overall, it appears that while both passion and intrinsic and extrinsic motivation are motivational concepts, they represent different constructs.

In sum, two types of passion are proposed: harmonious passion and obsessive passion. These are hypothesized to differ as to how the activity representation has been internalized in the person's identity. Because it originates from an autonomous internalization of the passionate activity in one's identity, harmonious passion is expected to lead to adaptive outcomes. However, obsessive passion is expected to lead to less adaptive or even maladaptive outcomes because it results from a controlled form of internalization where the activity controls the person. Finally, both forms of passion differ from intrinsic and extrinsic motivation. We now turn to recent research on passion that has tested some of these hypotheses.

Research on Passion in Sport

Over the past few years we've conducted a series of studies on the concept of passion. These studies deal with a variety of activities, settings, and outcomes. In this section, we briefly present the results of some of these studies. For obvious reasons, we focus on those studies conducted in the field of sport and physical activity.

Development of the Passion Scale

In a first study (Vallerand et al., 2003, study 1) we sought to develop the Passion Scale and to test the validity of our definition of passion. Participants *(n = 525)* completed the Passion Scale with respect to an activity that they liked, that they valued, and in which they invested time and energy. Interestingly, more than 60% of college students indicated that their passionate activity dealt with either sport or physical activity. Participants engaged in these activities an average of 8.5 hours per week and had been engaging in them for almost 6 years. Thus, clearly these activities were meaningful. The Passion Scale consists of two subscales of seven items each: the obsessive passion subscale (e.g., "I almost have an

obsessive feeling toward this activity") and the harmonious passion subscale (e.g., "This activity is in harmony with other activities in my life"). Results from exploratory and confirmatory factor analyses and reliability analyses provided strong support for the scale validity and reliability. Table 18.1 presents the Passion Scale.

We then proceeded to correlate the Passion Scale with other constructs in order to test our definition of passion. It was found that both harmonious and obsessive passion correlated positively with perceptions of the task as being valued, as being part of one's identity (e.g., Aron et al., 1992), and as being a passion. (All correlations conducted were partial correlations because the two passion subscales were significantly correlated between themselves.) Finally, only obsessive passion was found to positively and significantly correlate with conflict with other life activities. Thus, results from this first study provided support for our definition of passion and the validity of the Passion Scale.

Table 18.1   The Passion Scale

HARMONIOUS PASSION	
1. My activity allows me to live a variety of experiences.	
2. The new things that I discover within the confines of my activity allow me to appreciate it even more.	
3. My activity reflects the qualities I like about myself.	
4. My activity is in harmony with the other activities in my life.	
5. My activity is a passion that I still manage to control.	
6. My activity allows me to live memorable experiences.	
7. I am completely taken with my activity.	
OBSESSIVE PASSION	
8. I cannot live without my activity.	
9. The urge is so strong, I can't help myself from doing my activity.	
10. I have difficulty imagining my life without my activity.	
11. I am emotionally dependent on my activity.	
12. I have a tough time controlling my need to do my activity.	
13. I have almost an obsessive feeling for my activity.	
14. My mood depends on me being able to do my activity.	

Note. One can adapt the scale for any activity by changing the name of the desired activity (such as basketball, football, and so on).

This scale has been translated from French. No cross-cultural validation has taken place in English at this point. The scale is only presented for illustrative purposes.

From R.J. Vallerand et al., 2003. "Les passions de l'âme: On obsessive and harmonious Passion," *Journal of Personality and Social Psychology* 85: 756-767.

Passion and Affective Outcomes

While emotions can be influenced by several factors (see Vallerand & Blanchard, 2000), it is posited that passion also plays an important role in affective outcomes. Specifically, harmonious passion should lead to more positive affect and less negative affect than obsessive passion during task engagement. This is because the autonomous internalization of an activity that people like should lead them to engage in the task in a more flexible manner; to experience less conflict, allowing better focus and a more profound task engagement; and consequently to experience more positive affective outcomes. Such is not the case for obsessive passion because controlled internalization nurtures an internal compulsion to engage in the activity, leading to conflict as well as a more rigid form of task engagement that should prevent task enjoyment and eventually positive affect.

Results from the Vallerand et al. study (2003, study 1) supported these hypotheses. Harmonious passion was positively related to task focus, feelings of flow (feelings of being totally immersed in an activity; Csikszentmihalyi et al., 1993), and positive affect, but was negatively related to negative affect (shame). On the other hand, obsessive passion was unrelated to positive affect and positively related to shame but not to anxiety. These findings were also replicated in the Mageau, Vallerand, Rousseau, Ratelle, and Provencher (2005) study on gambling.

What about the emotions that follow task engagement? Our conceptualization proposes that harmonious passion should contribute to the experience of positive affect while minimizing the experience of negative affect after task engagement. This is because with harmonious passion, people are in control of the activity; they typically engage in the activity when it is appropriate to do so and therefore experience little conflict with other life activities. On the other hand, with obsessive passion the activity controls the individual because of the internal pressure to engage in it. Such an internal compulsion should lead people to engage in the activity even when they should not, to experience conflict between the passionate activity and other tasks, and eventually to experience negative emotions once engagement in the passionate activity is terminated. For instance, a person could feel guilty for playing baseball on a Sunday while he was supposed to go away for the day with the family. These hypotheses were upheld in recent studies where people participated in gambling (Mageau et al., 2005) and various activities (Vallerand et al., 2003, study 1).

Finally, because with obsessive passion the activity controls the person, she is likely to experience negative affective states when prevented from engaging in the activity. Indeed, because of the internal pressure (or push) one feels to engage in the activity, one cannot disengage from thoughts about the activity. Thus, an athlete may not be able to concentrate on other activities when prevented from engaging in her obsessively passionate activity because the obsessive passion pulls her back to it. Consequently, the athlete feels frustrated from not being able to engage in the passionate activity as well as from not being able to experience pleasure in nonpassionate activities. Such should not be the case with harmonious passion, however, because the athlete has an autonomous relationship with the activity and has control over it.

Results from the Vallerand et al. study (2003, study 1) revealed that when a person was prevented from engaging in the activity, obsessive passion was positively related to both negative affect (e.g., guilt, anxiety) and cognition (e.g., ruminations about the activity), and harmonious passion was unrelated to these negative states. The same findings were replicated in a study on gambling (Ratelle, Vallerand, Mageau, Rousseau, & Provencher, 2004) where being obsessively passionate about gambling predicted ruminative thoughts and feelings of psychological dependence on the activity. Harmonious passion was unrelated to these negative thoughts and feelings.

Results from Vallerand et al. (2003, study 1) showed that the two forms of passion were differentially related to affect toward the activity. But how generalizable and long lasting are these affective experiences? Furthermore, is it possible to predict changes in general positive affect and negative affect over time? A study involving intercollegiate American football players (Vallerand et al., 2003, study 2) explored these questions by assessing the role of passion in predicting changes in general positive and negative affect over the course of a football season. Harmonious passion was expected to be associated with increased positive affect while being unrelated to general negative affect over the course of the season. On the other hand, obsessive passion was expected to be unrelated to general positive affect while being related to increased negative affect. Results from multiple regression analyses supported the hypotheses.

Passion and Persistence

Another important outcome of passion is persistence in an activity. Because the activity is dear to the heart of those who engage in it (after all, it is part of their identity), people are likely to devote considerable time and energy to the activity and to persist in it for a rather long period of time. Sport represents a good example of such activities, as people may engage in their sport for several years and sometimes for a lifetime. However, there seem to be some differences in the persistence associated with the two types of passion. With harmonious passion, the person is in control of the activity; as such, the person decides when to engage in the activity and is even able to drop out of the activity if it becomes negative for the person. Thus, behavioral engagement and persistence are flexible. Such is not the case with obsessive passion. Because the activity has taken control of the person, obsessive passion would be expected to lead to persistence. However, such persistence can be rigid because it takes place not only in the absence of positive emotional experience, but even when important costs are accrued.

The hypothesis that obsessive passion leads people to persist when personal costs are accrued was supported in the football study mentioned previously (Vallerand et al., 2003, study 2). In that study, we also looked at changes in the intentions to play the following season. Only obsessive passion was found to be significantly related to this variable, positively predicting *increases* in intentions to play next season. These findings thus reveal a paradox: Obsessive passion is associated with intentions to play even more next season despite being associated with increased general negative affect over the course of the season.

We believe that these findings fit in well with our position on obsessive passion inducing a form of rigid persistence in the activity. It would appear that such a form of rigid persistence may lead athletes to persist no matter what, without asking themselves if they are making the best decision. If obsessive passion is conducive to rigid persistence, then it may be expected to lead to self-defeating behavior. Such should not be the case for harmonious passion because it entails a more flexible type of persistence where people may disengage from the activity if important costs are experienced. We have tested this hypothesis in two studies.

The first study (Vallerand et al., 2003, study 3) pertained to cycling. Cycling in the spring, summer, and fall can be a lot of fun and can promote health. However, the reality in the winter is drastically different, at least in the Canadian province of Quebec. The roads are icy and full of snow and they make cycling a hazardous affair that may lead to falls and injuries. Clearly, it would be advisable not to cycle under such conditions. If our hypothesis on the rigidity of obsessive passion is correct, then obsessive passion should lead to winter cycling, and if we are correct with respect to the flexibility of harmonious passion, then the latter should not lead to cycling in winter when conditions are dangerous. The purpose of this study was to test this hypothesis.

Cyclists (*n* = 59) completed the Passion Scale with respect to cycling in August. Six months later, they were contacted again through e-mail to determine who was still cycling in the dead of winter (February). Results showed that only 30% of participants were still cycling in winter. It was found that those cyclists had reported higher levels of obsessive passion 6 months earlier than those who did not cycle in the winter. No differences were found with respect to harmonious passion. Thus, through its rigid motivational pattern, obsessive passion may lead people to engage in activities when they should not (such as cycling in subzero temperatures on icy roads).

The second study (Vallerand et al., 2003, study 4) involved pathological gambling. It was found that people with severe gambling problems who ask the Montreal Casino to bar them from entering display significantly higher levels of obsessive passion than regular gamblers who play at least twice a week. No difference existed on harmonious passion. Other research on gambling has supported the role of obsessive passion in gambling problems (Ratelle et al., 2004; Rousseau, Vallerand, Ratelle, Mageau, & Provencher, 2002). Overall, these findings reveal that obsessive, but not harmonious, passion is implicated in self-defeating forms of behavioral persistence.

Passion and Subjective Well-Being

Research reveals that sport engagement may positively contribute to subjective well-being (Bouchard, Shephard, & Stephens, 1994). Based on the Vallerand et al. study (2003, study 2) showing that harmonious passion increases general positive affect but obsessive passion increases general negative affect, we believed that similar relations may exist with subjective well-being. Our research in this area has used structural equation modeling and path analysis to look at the psychological processes that may mediate the effects of passion on subjective well-being. We propose that engaging in a passionate activity leads to the cumulative experience of positive affect, which leads to increases in subjective well-being. Research by Frederickson and Joiner (2002) has actually shown the existence of a spiral where positive affect leads to higher levels of subjective well-being and higher levels of subjective well-being lead to subsequent experiences of positive affect, and we believe that experiencing a harmonious passion toward a sport or physical activity can trigger this spiral.

Two studies conducted with elderly individuals by Rousseau and Vallerand (2005, studies 1 and 2) provided support for this hypothesis. Study 2 in particular is pertinent as it dealt with passion toward physical activity. At time 1, participants completed the Passion Scale with respect to physical activity and they completed measures of subjective well-being. At time 2, immediately following an exercise bout, they completed measures of positive and negative affect. Finally, at time 3, they completed measures of subjective well-being again. A path analysis was performed. Results revealed that harmonious passion positively predicted positive affect, which led to increases in subjective well-being from time 1 to time 3. On the other hand, obsessive passion was unrelated to positive affect but positively predicted negative affect. The latter did not predict subjective well-being. These findings strongly support the suggestion that positive affect contributes to subjective well-being.

Another explanation of the positive effect of harmonious passion on subjective well-being originates from self-determination theory (SDT) (Deci & Ryan, 1985, 2000) and focuses on the satisfaction of core human needs. Deci and Ryan suggest that all human beings have to satisfy three fundamental psychological needs in order to achieve psychological adjustment and personal growth: autonomy, competence, and relatedness. Much research in a variety of areas with numerous populations has demonstrated the benefits of autonomy, competence, and relatedness satisfaction and the negative consequences of having these needs thwarted (Koestner, Losier, Vallerand, & Carducci, 1996; Ryan, 1995; Vallerand, Fortier, & Guay, 1997; Vallerand & Reid, 1984, 1988).

Because with harmonious passion the activity is internalized in a person's identity in an autonomous fashion, the activity should be in harmony with other aspects of the self. Consequently, engagement in the sport activity should enhance the coherence of the entire self-system, not simply the sport dimension, and lead to the facilitation of the three human needs. However, with obsessive passion the activity is internalized in a controlled fashion. Controlled internalization reflects a lack of coherence with one's core values and sense of self and has been found to cause conflict with other aspects of the self (Sheldon & Kasser, 1995). Thus, obsessive passion may hinder the growth of the self-system and hinder satisfaction of the needs of competence, autonomy, and relatedness.

Based on this reasoning, harmonious passion should facilitate the satisfaction of the three human needs. In turn, fulfillment of those needs should pave the way to subjective well-being. The reverse hypothesis can be made with respect to obsessive passion. Results of a prospective study conducted in the realm of work provided support for this basic model (Houlfort, Koestner, Vallerand, & Blanchard, 2005, study 2).

In sum, preliminary evidence reveals that harmonious passion may positively contribute to subjective well-being through its influence on positive affect and the satisfaction of the needs for competence, autonomy, and relatedness. Obsessive passion, on the other hand, does not contribute to subjective well-being and may even detract from it. Research is needed in order to replicate these findings in sport settings.

Passion and Performance

Research on expert performance reveals that high-level performers, including athletes, spend considerable time on deliberate practice (i.e., engagement in an activity with clear goals of improving on certain task components) in order to reach excellence in their chosen field of expertise (Ericsson & Charness, 1994; Starkes, Deakin, Allard, Hodges, & Hayes, 1996). What is the underlying motivation that leads athletes to spend so much time on their activity in order to become top-level performers? We believe that passion is one key determinant of experts' involvement in their activity. Indeed, in order to engage in the activity for long hours, one must love the activity and have the desire to pursue engagement, especially when times are rough. Thus, the two types of passion (harmonious and obsessive) should lead to engagement in deliberate practice that in turn should lead to improved sport performance.

This model was tested in a study with basketball players (Vallerand, Mageau et al., 2006, study 1). Male and female basketball players completed scales assessing their passion as well as deliberate practice (based on Ericsson & Charness, 1994). Coaches rated athletes' performance on a global scale of 0 to 100 where 60% was defined as the passing grade. A structural equation modeling analysis provided support for the basic model. Results are presented in figure 18.2. As can be seen, both harmonious passion (.36) and obsessive passion (.50) led to engagement in deliberate practice (.35), which led to objective performance (that is, the rating that the coaches gave).

These findings were replicated in a prospective design with dramatic arts performers (Vallerand, Salvy et al., in press, study 1). Also of interest is the study's finding that harmonious passion toward dramatic arts was positively and significantly related to subjective well-being, while obsessive passion was unrelated to it. It thus appears that both types of passion positively contribute to deliberate practice and performance at least in the short term. However, it might very well be that obsessive passion leads to some sense of suffering (e.g., lower levels of subjective well-being) than harmonious passion in the process of pursuing high performance levels.

The two performance studies just discussed established a direct relationship between passion and deliberate practice and an indirect relationship between passion and performance (through deliberate practice). We conducted an additional study (Vallerand, Salvy et al., in press, study 2) in order to examine the psychological processes through which passion directly contributes

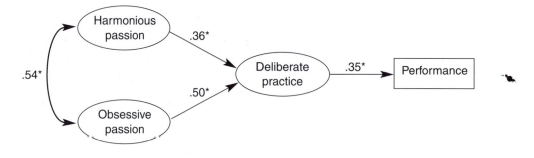

Figure 18.2 Passion and performance in basketball (Vallerand, Mageau et al., 2006, study 1): Results of the structural equation modeling analyses. The measurement model is not presented for purposes of clarity.

Reprinted from R.J. Vallerand, G.A. Mageau, and M.-A. Demers, 2005. *On passion and performance in sport* (Montreal, Canada: University of Quebec at Montreal). Unpublished manuscript. By permission of R.J. Vallerand.

to deliberate practice and indirectly contributes to performance. In line with Elliot (1997), we proposed that achievement goals should be important mediators between passion and deliberate practice. Elliot and colleagues (Elliot & Church, 1997; Elliot & Harackiewicz, 1996), as discussed in chapter 9, delineated three types of achievement goals: mastery goals (focusing on the development of competence and task mastery), performance-approach goals (focusing on the attainment of personal competence relative to others), and performance-avoidance goals (focusing on avoiding incompetence relative to others).

Passion has been found to relate to affective and cognitive investment in an activity, thereby implying that the individual is committed to engaging in that activity in a competent manner. Harmonious passion, being an autonomous form of regulation, is predicted to be positively related to mastery goals but not to performance goals of either type. On the other hand, obsessive passion, being a more pressured, internally controlling form of regulation, is likely to compel individuals to seek any and all forms of success at the activity and may even evoke concerns about doing poorly. As such, obsessive passion should be positively related to mastery, performance-approach, and even performance-avoidance goals. Finally, in line with our previous findings it was hypothesized that harmonious passion is positively related to subjective well-being.

A study with water-polo and synchronized swimmers was conducted to test the model (Vallerand, Mageau et al., in press, study 2). At time 1, athletes completed the Passion Scale, the Goals Scale, and scales assessing subjective well-being. At time 2, they completed the Deliberate Practice Scale. Finally, at time 3, coaches assessed athletes' performance over the entire season. Results of a path analysis yielded support for the proposed model. Specifically, harmonious passion was found to lead only to mastery goals, which in turn led to deliberate practice,

which positively predicted objective performance. On the other hand, obsessive passion was positively related to all three goals. While performance-approach goals did not predict any variables in the model, performance-avoidance goals negatively predicted performance. Finally, harmonious passion was positively associated with subjective well-being and obsessive passion was unrelated to it. This basic model was replicated in another study involving students with a passion toward studying psychology as their future profession (Vallerand, Salvy et al., in press, study 2).

In sum, it appears that harmonious passion not only contributes to subjective well-being but also to objective indices of performance. Such effect seems to take place through mastery goals, which lead to deliberate practice, which in turn leads to performance. The role of obsessive passion in performance is rather complex as it positively predicts mastery goals, which lead to performance through deliberate practice, but also performance-avoidance goals, which may negatively influence performance. Because of the preliminary status of the present findings, additional research on this issue in sport is warranted.

Development of Passion in Sport

Our conceptualization posits that once interest in an activity begins, passion results from two basic psychological processes: valuation of the activity (the extent to which an activity is deemed important and meaningful for someone) and the internalization of the activity in one's identity (refer to figure 18.1). This valuation process will ensure that the activity is internalized in the person's identity. However, the type of passion that will develop depends on how the activity is internalized. To the extent that the internalization process takes place in an autonomous fashion, then a harmonious passion will develop; if the internalization is carried out in a controlled fashion, an obsessive passion will develop. It is further proposed that the type of internalization process that will take place depends on two major factors: personality and social factors.

The role of social factors in the development of passion was explored in a study on children's passion toward music (Mageau, Vallerand, Koestner, & Charest, 2006, study 3). This study found that increases in children's passion toward music over 6 months were positively predicted by their own values attached to music as well as by adult behavior toward them within the context of music. Specifically, to the extent that children valued music, controlling behavior from the parents and music teachers who coerced children to engage in it led to the development of an obsessive passion toward music. On the other hand, music valuation by children coupled with autonomy-supportive adult behavior where children were allowed freedom with respect to their engagement and practice of music led to increases in harmonious passion. In light of the numerous benefits such research would provide, it would appear important to replicate this research within the confines of sport and physical activity.

Personality also plays a role in the development of passion. For example, as mentioned, a person's internalization style can influence the internalization process (e.g., Guay, Mageau, & Vallerand, 2003). The Global Motivation Scale (Guay et al., 2003) assesses such a tendency. Given a similar high level of activity valuation, people with a tendency to internalize activities in an autonomous way should develop a harmonious passion and those with a controlled internalization style should develop an obsessive passion. Research by Vallerand, Rousseau, Grouzet, Dumais, and Grenier (in press, study 3) conducted with athletes of aquatic sports (water polo and synchronized swimming) supported this hypothesis. Results from a path analysis showed that valuation of the sport activity coupled with an autonomous internalization style predicted harmonious passion, while valuation of the activity coupled with a controlled internalization style led to an obsessive passion. Furthermore, harmonious passion was found to lead to subjective well-being over time while obsessive passion was unrelated to it. Thus, personality factors play an important role in the type of passion that develops, and in turn passion can lead to important outcomes.

Future Research

Thus far we have reviewed several studies, including some in sport, that provide strong support for the proposed approach on passion. While the research conducted to date is indeed encouraging, additional research is necessary in order to better understand the concept of passion and its influence on sport participants. Following, we present certain directions for future research that pertain specifically to sport.

Concept of Passion in Sport

One area where research is needed is a better understanding of the concept of passion. Among other things, we need to empirically demonstrate the link between the two types of passion and the concept of athletic identity (Brewer, Van Raalte, & Linder, 1993). Because it is hypothesized that with passion, sport is internalized in the person's identity, a moderate to strong positive relationship would be expected between athletic identity on the one hand and harmonious and obsessive passion on the other.

We also need to study the distinction between passion and other concepts in sport such as commitment (Carmac & Martens, 1979) and exercise dependence (e.g., Hausenblas & Symons Downs, 2002). As mentioned in the introduction, we believe that although related, these three concepts are distinct. In keeping with our theory, the relationship between passion and commitment should be only moderate in magnitude because committed people may not necessarily love the activity. Furthermore, the two types of passion should relate differently to sport and exercise dependence. Because obsessive passion entails a rigid persistence, it should be moderately and positively related to sport and exercise dependence. However, this should not be the case for harmonious passion because of the flexible activity engagement it promotes.

Also of great importance is the need to conduct such research in a variety of sport and physical activities. Hausenblas and Symons Downs (2002) made it clear that a major limitation of the research on exercise dependence is that most studies thus far (at least 50%) have dealt with running. It is believed that the concept of passion applies to most if not all sport activities, and future research should test this hypothesis.

Finally, it might be instructive to assess the relations between compulsivity (e.g., Squires & Kagan, 1985) and the two types of passion. People high on the dimension of compulsivity experience internal pressure to engage in an activity in order to relieve anxiety. While the distinction between compulsivity and harmonious passion is straightforward, such is not the case with obsessive passion. At first glance, there seems to be a similarity between the two constructs. However, an important difference is that people with a compulsivity disorder don't like the behavior they engage in repeatedly. People with a compulsivity disorder would gladly stop engaging in the compulsive behavior if they could, as they hate washing hands for a whole day, for example, whereas athletes with an obsessive passion love their sport and do not want to stop doing it. Thus, while obsessive passion and compulsivity may seem similar, important differences exist. However, an empirical test of this hypothesis would provide additional clarity to the concept of passion in sport.

Stages of Passion

Another interesting issue is the potential existence of stages of passion. Is there some form of universal sequence such that initially the passion toward a given activity is, let's say, obsessive, and then later on becomes more harmonious? We don't have any direct empirical evidence on this question so far. Preliminary evidence seems to indicate that such is not the case. Vallerand et al. (2003, study 1) didn't find any relationship between length of involvement and the two types of passion. However, these findings are limited in scope as the design used was not longitudinal.

What is needed is to follow people from their beginnings in a given sport up to their decision to become heavily involved in that sport. It is possible that a sequence exists, but changes may take place quickly, perhaps in the first month of involvement in the activity. Furthermore, the type of activity might influence the passion that develops. For instance, in the Vallerand et al. (2003) study just cited, it was found that team-sport participants displayed higher levels of harmonious passion than individual-sport participants. No differences were found on obsessive passion. The generalizability of these findings, however, needs to be ascertained.

Finally, perceptions of competence and progress in the activity may moderate the development of the passion sequence. We need to assess whether athletes who perceive themselves as competent and who expect a bright future in their sport might maintain or develop an obsessive passion for their sport, while those who foresee a more limited future might move from an initial obsessive passion to a more harmonious passion or even a loss of passion for the activity.

Passion and Conflict

Our conceptualization of passion posits that obsessive passion toward an activity should lead to conflict with other life activities while harmonious passion should not. Results from Vallerand et al. (2003, study 1) provided preliminary evidence for this hypothesis. We believe that this basic hypothesis has important implications for people engaged passionately in sport, as athletes with a predominantly obsessive passion toward sport would seem to experience much more conflict with a variety of life activities than those with a predominantly harmonious passion. Such life activities could include school or work, self-expanding leisure pursuits, friend-

ships, intimate relationships, and family life. Although we have not conducted a study on all of these themes, a recent study with adults (Séguin-Lévesque, Laliberté, Pelletier, Vallerand, & Blanchard, 2003) has shown that obsessive passion for the Internet was positively related to conflict with one's spouse and harmonious passion was negatively related to it.

Based on this hypothesis, it might even be predicted that passion greatly affects the quality of the relationship between athletes and coaches as well as relationships among athletes. Future research on the role of passion in the development of conflict in athletes' lives would appear fruitful.

Health and Dropping Out of Sport

It seems that the present conceptualization of passion should lead to important insights into why people drop out of sport. First, passionate athletes should pursue sport engagement much more than nonpassionate athletes. Second, the proposed conceptualization posits that both harmonious and obsessive passion can lead to high levels of persistence, especially when activity engagement leads to positive benefits. However, a major difference is expected when persistence in sport leads to negative outcomes. Under aversive conditions (e.g., playing tennis for the high school team leads a student to have poor grades and jeopardizes entry in college), harmonious passion is hypothesized to lead to disengagement and obsessive passion to lead to continued engagement. Research reported earlier on cyclists and gamblers supports this hypothesis (Vallerand et al., 2003, studies 3 and 4). Thus, obsessively passionate athletes should be less likely to drop out of sport than harmoniously passionate athletes. Future research is needed in order to test this interesting hypothesis.

These hypotheses may also have implications for athletes' physical and mental health. As indicated, obsessively passionate athletes should be less likely to drop out than those who are predominantly harmonious about their sport, especially if the conditions under which they participate are not positive. While such persistence from obsessively passionate athletes may appear profitable, high-level persistence at any cost may be associated with physical and emotional health problems, especially under aversive conditions (Koeske & Kelly, 1995; Raedeke, Granzyk, & Warren, 2000). Therefore, the high-level persistence of obsessively passionate athletes may come at a high cost, possibly leading to injuries, burnout, and decreased subjective well-being. Preliminary research on this issue indicates that dancers who have an obsessive passion for dance experience higher levels of chronic injuries than those with a harmonious passion (Rip, Fortin, & Vallerand, 2006). Additional research is needed to explore the link between passion and other health issues.

Retirement From Sport and Subjective Well-Being

Passion may have important long-term effects. One interesting question deals with retirement from sport. Do harmoniously passionate athletes adjust better psychologically after retirement than obsessive athletes? Based on our conceptualization of passion, we would answer affirmatively. First, harmonious passion allows athletes to fully immerse themselves in the activity and to experience flow (see Vallerand et al., 2003, study 1). Such positive involvement should allow athletes to experience feelings of competence, autonomy, and relatedness, or, in other words, to be more fulfilled during their athletic career. Having fulfilled these needs, they are ready to move on to other things after their career in sport ends.

A second explanation is that because harmonious passion is characterized by a flexible persistence toward the activity (Vallerand et al., 2003), it should be relatively easy for harmoniously passionate athletes to move on to something else after retirement. On the other hand, athletes with an obsessive passion should have difficulty adjusting to retirement because they have negated their own needs during their working career. They should therefore have a tough time being in tune with those needs after retirement. Furthermore, because obsessive passion is characterized by a rigid persistence toward the activity, athletes with an obsessive passion should have a difficult time letting go of their sport and should not adjust well after retirement.

A recent study (Houlfort et al., 2006) addressed these questions within the work domain. Workers who had recently retired were asked retrospectively to rate their level of passion toward their work and satisfaction of their psychological needs (competence, autonomy, and relatedness) as a worker. They were also asked to assess their current subjective well-being following retirement. Results from the path analysis confirmed our hypotheses. Harmonious passion facilitated need satisfaction while obsessive passion thwarted the satisfaction of the basic psychological needs in the workplace. In turn, need satisfaction at work was positively associated with enhanced subjective well-being following retirement. Obsessive passion was also found to be directly and negatively related to subjective well-being following retirement. Research is needed to replicate these findings in the realm of sport. In addition, in light of the decision of several athletes such as basketball player Michael Jordan and hockey player Mario Lemieux to come out of retirement, additional research is needed in order to determine if passion is at play in such a decision to return to the game.

Long-Term Sport Performance

Another research concern pertains to long-term performance. In our review of research on passion, we have shown that both types of passion facilitate performance by influencing deliberate practice and achievement goals (Vallerand, Salvy et al., in press; Vallerand, Mageau, et al., 2006). However, such research was limited in scope, spanning 6 months at most. What about athletes who train to reach the Olympics or professional levels? It may take up to 10 years to attain such levels (Ericsson & Charness, 1994). What type of passion may benefit the athlete the most?

Our research on persistence (e.g., Vallerand et al., 2003, studies 3 and 4) suggests that athletes with an obsessive passion should persist more, especially if conditions are difficult. Given similar levels of time involvement and quality of deliberate practice, increased persistence in sport should be conducive to higher levels of performance. Thus, it might be predicted that obsessive passion is conducive to higher levels of performance in the long run.

However, much research has also demonstrated that obsessive passion is either unrelated (Vallerand, Salvy et al., in press, study 1) or negatively related (Vallerand, Salvy et al., in press, study 2; Vallerand, Mageau et al., 2006, study 2) to subjective well-being while harmonious passion has been consistently and positively associated to subjective well-being (Vallerand et al., 2003, study 2; Vallerand, Salvy et al., in press, studies 1 and 2; Vallerand, Mageau et al., 2006, study 2). Thus, the high performance level obtained by obsessive passionate athletes may come at a high cost. Low subjective well-being levels could even lead athletes with a predominantly obsessive passion to eventually cease sport participation. Such should not be the case for harmoniously passionate athletes. Thus, because harmonious passion leads to engagement in deliberate practice (which is conducive to performance) and facilitates high levels of subjective well-being in the process, it may lead athletes to persist more in sport and eventually reach the highest performance levels. Future research is needed to test these competing hypotheses on the long-term effects of passion on sport performance.

Practical Implications

Research reviewed in this chapter reveals that harmonious passion typically promotes adaptive sport outcomes and that obsessive passion is either unrelated to adaptive consequences or is positively associated with maladaptive ones. Thus, it would seem appropriate to propose ways of facilitating athletes' harmonious passion. As indicated earlier, once children have selected a sport or physical activity that they like and wish to invest a lot of time in, two elements will determine the type of passion that results: activity valuation and internalization of the activity in one's identity.

The social environment is crucial in these two elements. Passion depends largely on the extent to which an activity is valued and meaningful for the athlete, so it would seem that parents, physical educators, and coaches should take a step back and let children take responsibility for their sport involvement. If young athletes have decided to get involved in a specific sport, it probably means something to them. Strong, overt, and controlling statements to the effect that "Sport is a matter of life and death" or "Winning is everything" may only put undue pressure on children and eventually either undermine the development of passion altogether or lead to obsessive passion. Noncontrolling and supportive parents, physical educators, and coaches who serve as models (e.g., Bandura, 1986) may provide the necessary impetus to lead young athletes to invest further in the sport activity and value it even more.

The broader social environment can also influence the internalization process. We have previously mentioned that how people internalize the highly valued and enjoyable sport activity in their identity will determine the type of passion that develops. It is proposed that a harmonious passion will develop if the internalization process takes place in an autonomous fashion while an obsessive passion will develop if the internalization process takes place in a controlled fashion.

What should be done to promote the internalization of the sport activity in an autonomous fashion? Once again, an important factor that can influence the internalization process is the extent to which the social environment (e.g., parents, friends, and especially coaches) promotes individuals' needs for autonomy, competence, and relatedness (Deci & Ryan, 2000). This can be done by providing athletes with experiences in which they

- get a meaningful rationale of why their sport activity is important (so they can understand its importance for themselves), feel they have opportunities to make choices, and are encouraged to accept more responsibility for their sport activity;
- feel that they have control over their sport activity; and

- have a sense of being positively related to the person who is helping them on the road toward progress in their sport activity (Deci et al., 1994; Deci & Ryan, 2000; Ryan & Deci, 2000).

For example, athletes who have recently developed a passion toward swimming would be more likely to develop a harmonious passion if their coach explains to them why it is important to have a daily practice; gives them opportunities for choosing among different practice regimens (so that they feel autonomous); provides them with positive feedback on their swimming performance (so that they feel competent) in addition to corrective feedback (so that such feelings of competence are based on solid ground and they know how to improve); and displays a genuine, warm, and caring attitude toward them (so that they feel related to their coach). Inversely, chances are that these same athletes would develop an obsessive passion toward swimming if their coach were to pressure or coerce them to practice their sport to the extent that athletes feel that this sport is important to them.

In sum, the present position on passion suggests that the social environment plays a major role in determining the type of passion that will develop and the outcomes that follow such development. It is hoped that adults and parents who mean well will heed the call and nurture children's burgeoning harmonious passion and associated well-being.

Summary

Sport is a significant part of many people's lives. In this chapter, we have proposed a new conceptualization of passion that gives us a better understanding of the psychological forces that lead athletes and other sport participants (e.g., coaches and officials) to sustain intense engagement in sport and experience different types of outcomes. Specifically, we have shown the applicability of our conceptualization of passion to the realm of sport and proposed the existence of two types of passion: harmonious passion and obsessive passion. The Passion Scale has been developed and validated to assess passion in sport.

We propose that harmonious passion typically leads to adaptive outcomes and obsessive passion leads mainly to maladaptive outcomes. Passion is developed via a three-step process, beginning with activity selection. This is followed by valuation of the activity and finally by internalization of the activity in one's identity in either autonomous or controlled ways. Finally, future research should help us better understand and apply the processes through which passion may affect participants' engagement in sport.

Discussion Questions

1. Is passion needed for top sport performance to take place? If so, which type of passion is more likely to produce high performance levels?

2. Which type of passion is more likely to contribute to positive psychological adjustment and why?

3. Which type of passion should coaches and parents try to foster in young athletes, Olympic athletes, and professional or senior athletes? Why?

4. How can harmonious passion be best achieved? How can obsessive passion be achieved?

5. Take the Passion Scale yourself (see table 18.1). Which type of passion is predominant toward your favorite activity, harmonious or obsessive passion? How do you think you developed that type of passion?

6. If a person has an obsessive passion toward a sport, do you think it is possible for that person to develop characteristics of harmonious passion? What measures might help obsessively passionate athletes find balance in their lives?

chapter 19

Morality in Sport

Maria Kavussanu, PhD

Learning Objectives

On completion of this chapter, the reader should have

1. knowledge of theories of morality, which have spawned considerable research in the sport domain;

2. understanding of important empirical studies on morality in sport, especially research examining the effects of sport type, social context, motivation, and gender;

3. ability to provide directions for future research; and

4. familiarity with potential implications for practice based on the current literature.

Imagine you are playing in a critical basketball game. You and a player from the opposing team are running after a loose ball at half-court. You come into contact with the other player, but she manages to get the ball and is going for a fast break. Your only opportunity to stop her from making the basket is to fake an injury, hoping that the referees will stop the play. In another instance during the same game, you and the star player of the other team, who has mildly injured her wrist but is still playing, are jumping for a rebound. You know that you could hit the other player's hand and take her out of the game without being caught by the referee. Finally, just before the end of the game, when your team is leading by a point, a player from the opposing team is going for a fast break, and you are the sole defender. Because of your position, the only way to stop the player from making the basket may result in an injury.

Faking an injury, intentionally hurting an opposing player to take him out of the game, and risking injury to an opposing player are all behaviors encountered in many team sports because these sports involve physical contact and therefore have the inherent potential for injury. Other behaviors, such as using illegal substances to improve performance and arranging to severely injure a contestant, cut across both individual and team sports. Such acts have been exemplified in the past by world-class athletes like sprinters Ben Johnson and Dwain Chambers in the first case and ice-skater Tonya Harding in the second. In contrast, behaviors such as not seizing the opportunity to score in order to allow an injured opponent to receive medical treatment, which has been demonstrated by the soccer player Paolo di Canio, or the typical practice of calling your own penalty shots in golf are shining examples of admirable social conduct.

What factors influence whether sport participants will engage in behaviors that have positive consequences for others at the expense of their own interest? Why do some athletes refuse to engage in behaviors that will give them a competitive edge but are detrimental to other athletes? Research on morality in sport searches for answers to these questions and is the focus of this chapter.

Morality in sport has been the subject of systematic empirical investigation in the last two decades (see Shields & Bredemeier, 2001; Weiss & Smith, 2002). Research has examined various aspects of morality, including moral reasoning in response to dilemmas set in sport and daily life (Bredemeier & Shields, 1986a, 1986b); moral intention (Vallerand, Deshaies, Cuerrier, Pelletier, & Mongeau, 1992); moral functioning as reflected in moral judgment, intention, and behavior (Kavussanu & Roberts, 2001); judgments about the legitimacy of injurious acts (Bredemeier, 1985; Duda, Olson, & Templin, 1991); and sportsmanship orientations

(Vallerand, Briere, Blanchard, & Provencher, 1997). (In this text, the term *sportsmanship* is used synonymously with what is often called *sportspersonship*.) Moreoever, Bredemeier and Shields (1984) have suggested that aggression, defined as the initiation of an attack with the intent to injure, is an issue of contextual morality; thus, aggressive tendencies and behaviors have also been examined under the umbrella of moral variables (Bredemeier, 1994; Stephens & Bredemeier, 1996).

Theories of Morality

Various theories have been proposed to explain moral development and behavior. The most prominent ones are structural developmental theories and social learning theories. To date, a great deal of the empirical research conducted in sport has been driven by structural-developmental theories. Lawrence Kohlberg (1969, 1971, 1984) and Norma Haan (1978, 1983) are theorists who belong to this tradition; their ideas are briefly discussed because they have spawned the vast majority of research on sport morality. Next, James Rest's (1983, 1984) model of morality is presented. Finally, Shields and Bredemeier's (1995) work is briefly reviewed because it applies Rest's model to the sport domain.

Lawrence Kohlberg

Kohlberg (1969, 1971, 1984) has assumed a structural-developmental approach to the study of moral development. Structural developmentalists view moral development as an orderly progression through a number of stages occurring as a result of interaction between the person and the environment. In addition, they differentiate between content and structure. Specific beliefs, thoughts, and values represent the content of thought, while the structure is reflected in the person's pattern of moral reasoning.

Among the significant contributions of Kohlberg's work is the identification of a culturally universal six-stage sequence of moral development. A stage in this sequence refers to the underlying structure of reasoning and is an approach to moral problem solving. Classifying the six stages into three levels, Kohlberg described moral growth as moving from an egocentric to a societal to a universal perspective of distinguishing right from wrong. At the first level, known as the preconventional level, people adopt an egocentric perspective in their approach to moral problems, and in solving moral conflicts they give primary consideration to the self. At this level, the individual does not comprehend yet the impact of social rules and norms on moral responsibility. At the second level, known as the conventional level, people approach moral conflict through the eyes of their group or society as a whole; what is right is defined by the norms of one's reference group or society. Finally, at the third level, known as the postconventional level, people recognize universal values such as justice, equality, life, and truthfulness that are not associated with a particular society. Moral decisions are based upon self-chosen ethical principles aside from society's norms and rules. Thus, moral development is inferred from one's stage of moral reasoning, and sport studies grounded in Kohlberg's theory have typically examined moral reasoning as an indicator of moral development.

Norma Haan

Haan (1978, 1983), also a structural developmentalist, has focused on how people believe they should deal with moral conflicts in daily life. Moral balance, moral dialogue, and moral levels are the three basic concepts of Haan's model. *Moral balance* refers to an interpersonal state where all parties are in agreement regarding each other's rights and obligations. When people disagree about respective rights and obligations, they are in moral imbalance, in which case the parties involved try to restore moral balance using *moral dialogue*. The most common form of moral dialogue is verbal negotiation. However, any form of communication, verbal or nonverbal, can be considered moral dialogue as long as its aim is to maintain or restore moral balance (see Bredemeier & Shields, 1993).

Haan distinguished five levels in the development of moral maturity. Each level reflects a different understanding of the way one reasons about moral conflicts and attempts to achieve moral balance. In levels 1 and 2, the assimilation phase, people believe that the moral balances should give preference to the needs of the self. They have an egocentric view of morality, not because they are selfish, but because they are unable to clearly understand the needs and desires of others. Levels 3 and 4 comprise the accommodation phase, in which people seek to give more than they receive; thus priority is given to the needs of others. Finally, at level 5, the equilibration phase of moral development, people pay equal attention to the needs and interests of all parties involved in a moral conflict. Thus, similar to Kohlberg's approach, Haan views one's level of moral reasoning as the indicator of moral growth, and sport studies grounded on Haan's theory have typically measured athletes' moral reasoning as an indicator of moral development.

James Rest

Rest (1983, 1984) has taken a different approach to moral development from those of Kohlberg and Haan. Rest argued that we need to focus on understanding and explaining *moral action*, because that is what ultimately matters. According to Rest, at least four major processes are implicated in each moral action, and a number of factors influence each process. The four processes are as follows:

1. Interpreting the situation by recognizing the possible courses of action and how different actions would influence the welfare of all parties involved.

2. Forming a moral judgment about the right thing to do, which involves both moral judgment and moral reasoning (judgment being the person's decision about what ought to be done and reasoning being the criteria the person uses to form a moral judgment).

3. Deciding what one intends to do by selecting among competing values.

4. Executing and implementing what one intends to do, that is, actual behavior.

Rest proposed that the four processes are dynamic, interact with each other, and are influenced by a number of factors. For example, the process of making a moral decision is influenced by motivational factors and social norms, while actual behavior is affected by fatigue or distraction as well as factors that physically prevent someone from carrying out a plan of action. Because of the interactive nature of the four processes, factors proposed to act primarily on one process also indirectly influence the others. Due to the large number of factors influencing the four processes, prediction of moral behavior is an extremely difficult task (Rest, 1984), and deficiency in any of these processes can result in failure to behave morally.

Rest's model of morality is inclusive because it attempts to account for all processes that influence moral action. Moral development is viewed as gaining competence in all these processes. In Rest's view, moral reasoning reflects only one aspect of moral development and, together with moral judgment, addresses process 2 of the model. Although this is an important part, alone it does not tell us the full story about morality. Thus, all processes of morality are important to our understanding of moral action. Sport studies using Rest's model have typically examined judgment, reason, intention, and behavior as indices of moral functioning.

David Shields and Brenda Bredemeier

Drawing upon theory and research on moral development, Shields and Bredemeier (1995) applied Rest's (1984) model to the physical activity domain. They have suggested that (a) the same four processes are implicated in any moral action in sport, (b) failure to behave morally is the result of deficiencies in any of these processes, and (c) a number of variables can influence each process. Similar to Rest, Shields and Bredemeier suggest that although certain variables are assumed to be more or less related to each process, these variables are not exclusively related to one process. They may primarily influence one process, but they can also act on the remaining processes.

Three sets of variables are proposed to influence each process: contextual factors, personal competencies, and ego processes. *Contextual factors* involve social-environment variables such as the goal structure (e.g., whether the context emphasizes competition or cooperation) and the moral atmosphere (e.g., the prevailing group norms or what the team as a whole views as moral behavior). *Personal competencies* involve cognitive and affective competencies that make moral action possible. Role taking and perspective taking, moral reasoning, motivational orientation, self-regulation, and social problem-solving skills are some of the competencies proposed to influence the four processes. Finally, *ego processes* are distinguished into coping processes, which enable people to think clearly and coordinate their feelings and ideals, and defending processes, which are used to distort reality for the sake of maintaining a positive sense of self. Examples of ego processes are empathy and the ability to focus attention. Thus, a number of variables have been proposed to influence each process. For a full description of the model, see Shields and Bredemeier (1995).

Morality Research in Sport

The vast majority of morality research conducted in sport has been guided by Kohlberg's, Haan's, and Rest's theories. These theorists differ in how they define moral development and behavior, and these differences are reflected in the way morality in sport has been operationalized and measured. Consequently, empirical research in sport grounded on Kohlberg's and Haan's theories has examined moral reasoning as an indicator of moral development, while studies using Rest's model have investigated multiple components of morality including judgment, intention, and behavior. Sport studies have also investigated other variables that are relevant to morality. For example, some studies have examined judgments about the legitimacy of injurious acts and aggressive tendencies as variables reflecting low levels of morality, while other work has investigated attitudes and orientations of sportsmanship, concepts not emanating from a morality theory per se but nonetheless relevant to morality in sport. In this section, research examining the effects of the type

of sport on moral variables is discussed, followed by studies investigating the influence of the social context on sport morality. The section concludes with a review of studies investigating personal influences on moral variables in sport.

Sport Type

Although not directly concerned with the effects of participation in different types of sport, initial research identified significant differences in moral development among basketball players, swimmers, and nonathletes. Using Kohlberg's theory and measures of general moral maturity, early work (Bredemeier & Shields, 1984; Hall, 1981) found that college basketball players reasoned at a less mature level than college norms. Subsequent work (Bredemeier & Shields, 1986a) using Haan's theory and dilemmas set in contexts of sport and daily life reported that college basketball players demonstrated less mature moral reasoning than nonathletes in response to both life and sport moral dilemmas and less mature moral reasoning than swimmers in response to sport dilemmas. Swimmers' life and sport scores on moral reasoning did not differ significantly from those of nonathletes (Bredemeier & Shields, 1986a).

These findings indicate that the type of sport one is involved in has implications for one's level of moral reasoning. Basketball and swimming differ on at least two accounts: (a) the level of physical contact inherent in each sport (swimming involves no contact whereas basketball involves medium contact) and (b) the degree to which winning depends upon one or more people (swimming is an individual sport whereas basketball is a team sport). A few studies have examined the effect of these variables on morality, and it is to these studies that we now turn.

Level of Physical Contact

Studies examining the effect of the level of physical contact on moral variables have typically made comparisons between athletes who participate in noncontact, contact, and collision sports. The labels *low, medium,* and *high contact* have also been used to refer to the respective categories. Low or noncontact sports are those that involve no contact, such as swimming, baseball, track and field, and volleyball. In medium-contact or contact sports, when contact occurs, it is incidental. Basketball, soccer, and field hockey fall within this category. Finally, high-contact or collision sports are those in which contact is an implicit aspect of goal-directed behavior (Silva, 1983). Examples of these sports are American football, ice hockey, and rugby.

The effect of contact level on moral reasoning and aggressive tendencies in summer sport-camp participants has been examined by Bredemeier and colleagues

Sport can cultivate and develop moral reasoning or moral values.

(Bredemeier, Weiss, Shields, & Cooper, 1986). Children responded to dilemmas that assessed moral reasoning in sport and daily life, completed a paper-and-pencil measure of aggression tendencies, and reported the number of seasons they had participated in low-, medium-, and high-contact sports. Boys' involvement in high-contact sports and girls' involvement in medium-contact sports (the highest level of contact in which girls were involved) were associated with lower levels of moral reasoning and greater tendencies to aggress in sport and daily life.

Level of contact has also been examined in relation to judgments about the legitimacy of aggressive acts. Silva (1983) presented male and female college students with 12 slides illustrating rule-violating behaviors in baseball, basketball, American football, ice hockey, and soccer. Participants were asked to indicate how acceptable it would be for them to exhibit the displayed behaviors at some point during a game. The higher the contact level of sport male students had participated in, the more likely they were to judge rule-violating behaviors as legitimate. Among females, those who

had not participated in sport and those who had participated in collision sports or a combination of sports reported slightly higher levels of legitimacy judgments. Similar findings were revealed in a study with summer sport-camp participants (Bredemeier, Weiss, Shields, & Cooper, 1987). Among boys—but not girls—extensive involvement in high-contact sports was associated with judgments that intentionally injurious acts are legitimate.

Two studies have used scenarios describing rule-violating behaviors to investigate the effects of contact level on legitimacy judgments. Conroy, Silva, Newcomer, Walker, and Johnson (2001) presented children and adolescents ranging from 8 to 19 years in age with descriptions of 10 sport situations portraying aggressive, rule-violating behaviors in a variety of sports and asked them to indicate whether they consider those acts as legitimate. The more seasons that children had participated in medium-contact sports, the more likely they were to view rule-violating behaviors as legitimate. Interestingly, males tended to view aggressive behaviors as increasingly more legitimate after the age of 12. Tucker and Parks (2001) also found that college athletes participating in high-contact sports were significantly more accepting of the aggressive behaviors described in the scenarios than were participants in medium-contact sports.

These findings clearly indicate that the contact level of the sports people participate in has some influence on moral variables, including moral reasoning, aggressive tendencies, and judgments of what is acceptable behavior within the sport context. It has been argued that sports involving higher levels of contact allow rough play, thereby encouraging aggressive tendencies. These sports may actually impede moral growth because of their informal combat mentality, which discourages altruistic interaction and encourages a negative view of others (Bredemeier et al., 1986). This state of affairs is not compatible with the more advanced levels of moral development, which are marked by concern for other people, altruistic motivation, and a view of others as basically good moral beings. Thus, the level of contact of the sport one participates in appears to have an influence on participants' moral functioning.

Individual Versus Team Sport

An alternative way of classifying sport is whether one participates in individual versus team sports. Vallerand, Deshaies, and Cuerrier (1997) investigated the effect of participation in individual versus team sports on moral intention. The individual sports included badminton, gymnastics, swimming, and track and field, while team sports were volleyball, basketball, and ice hockey. Athletes were presented with two hypothetical scenarios involving a moral issue: informing an official of one's undeserved outcome and lending equipment to a fellow competitor who was one of the favorites in an important meet. Following each scenario, participants were asked to indicate how they would behave in that situation. Team-sport athletes were less likely to indicate the intention to act morally than individual-sport athletes.

The authors argued that because team-sport athletes are subjected to intragroup influences from their teammates and coach, they are likely to feel pressured to conform and to help the team reach the goal of winning. In contrast, individual-sport athletes are less likely to feel pressure from others to engage in unsportsmanlike conduct. They spend much more time on their own and have to rely on their own standards when they face moral conflicts. However, this is merely speculation, as the pressure to win that athletes may feel from their teammates and the coach was not examined in this study. This pressure depends on the prevailing values of the team, which may or may not condone unsportsmanlike conduct.

Finally, although no comparison was made between individual and team sports, Kavussanu and Ntoumanis (2003) reported a significant relationship between extent of participation in team sports and three indices of moral functioning based on Rest's model. Specifically, in a study with university athletes participating in soccer, field hockey, basketball, or rugby, it was found that the more seasons athletes had participated in their sport, the lower the level of moral functioning they reported as reflected in their judgment, intention, and behavior.

The findings of these studies suggest that sport type has implications for athletes' moral functioning. However, to date, research has not clarified the degree to which the level of contact versus the individual–team sport distinction is responsible for the low levels of morality observed in some athletes. These variables have been confounded in past research. For example, basketball is a medium-contact sport, but it is also a team sport. Swimming is both a noncontact and an individual sport. In the only study investigating the distinction between individual and team sport (Vallerand et al., 1997), the individual sports examined were also low-contact sports, while in the team-sport category, a combination of low-contact (i.e., volleyball), medium-contact (i.e., basketball), and high-contact (i.e., ice hockey) sports were included. Research has yet to clarify which of the two is the crucial variable. The level of contact matters because differences have consistently been identified among varied levels of contact. But the distinction between individual and team sport may also affect morality within the sport context. It is also possible that those two dimensions interact with each other, making the situation even more complex.

Social Context

Sport does not occur in a social vacuum. The social context in which sport takes place can exert a powerful influence on participants' moral functioning. The social context involves the people directly or indirectly associated with the sport experience. Three aspects of the social context have received research attention and are reviewed in this section: the moral atmosphere of the team, the athletes' perceptions of significant others in their social environment, and the motivational climate of the team.

Moral Atmosphere

The concept of moral atmosphere was originally described by Kohlberg and associates (Higgins, Power, & Kohlberg, 1984; Kohlberg & Higgins, 1987; Power, Higgins, & Kohlberg, 1989), who investigated school and prison environments to determine the influence of the group norms of these settings on moral reasoning and behavior. As a result of interaction among group members, groups develop their own culture and a shared understanding of what constitutes appropriate behavior. These shared group norms define the moral atmosphere of a group. Moral atmosphere therefore involves a set of collective norms regarding moral action on the part of group members (Power et al., 1989).

Moral atmosphere is an aspect of Kohlberg's work that is particularly applicable to sport settings. For example, in a soccer or basketball team certain philosophies are developed regarding appropriate behavior in that context. These philosophies are developed over time and are partly the outcome of characteristics of the coach and team members. Teammates' perceptions of their peers' choices in situations that give rise to moral conflict are also part of the moral atmosphere. These collective norms are presumed to influence moral decision making and subsequent behavior within the athletic context (Shields & Bredemeier, 1995).

To date, several studies have investigated moral atmosphere in relation to various aspects of morality in sport. Initial research focused on moral action, operationally defined as self-described likelihood to aggress against an opponent. Stephens and Bredemeier (1996) presented young female football (soccer) players with an aggression scenario featuring a hypothetical protagonist who was faced with the decision of tackling an opponent from behind, thereby risking injuring her. Athletes were asked to imagine themselves in this situation and indicate how likely they would be to tackle from behind. Moral atmosphere was assessed based on athletes' perceptions of the number of teammates willing to engage in the behavior and of the coach's characteristics, namely goal orientation. When athletes perceived that a large number of their teammates would engage in the described behavior and that the coach emphasized ego-oriented goals focusing on normative success, they indicated greater likelihood to behave aggressively. Similarly, in two other studies, athletes' perceptions of their team's proaggressive norms were the main predictor of reported likelihood to aggress for boys and girls in coed soccer leagues (Stephens, 2000) and for female basketball players participating in summer skill camps (Stephens, 2001).

Moral atmosphere has also been examined in relation to multiple components of morality based on Rest's model, namely moral judgment, intention, and behavior. In the first study to examine this issue (Kavussanu & Rameswaran, 2000), interscholastic hockey players responded to scenarios describing unsportsmanlike behaviors likely to occur during a hockey game, such as pushing, risking injury, and deliberately injuring an opposing player. Based on past research (Shields et al., 1995), two aspects of the moral atmosphere were examined: the atmosphere created by the coach and the atmosphere created by the teammates. When athletes perceived their coach as encouraging the described behaviors and a large number of teammates as willing to engage in the behaviors, they were more likely to judge the behaviors as appropriate, to report the intention to engage in the behaviors, and to engage in the behaviors at a greater frequency. Similar findings were reported in two other studies that employed similar methodology and involved American college basketball players (Kavussanu, Roberts, & Ntoumanis, 2002) and British adolescent male soccer players (Kavussanu & Spray, 2006). Thus, moral atmosphere of the team appears to have a profound influence on athletes' moral functioning.

The findings of the studies conducted so far are unequivocal in suggesting that the context within which moral behaviors are performed is critical. It appears that the roots of unsportsmanlike conduct encountered in the sport domain may reside within one's own athletic team. Many inappropriate actions occurring in the sport realm may be the result of certain social norms that become predominant in each team over time, thereby reinforcing unsportsmanlike conduct. Eliminating such behaviors from sport may not be easy because they become part of the norms of behavior. Nevertheless, interventions that educate coaches and athletes about the important role they play in maintaining the integrity of the sport institution may be promising (Kavussanu et al., 2002).

Significant Others

In addition to the moral atmosphere of the team, the wider social environment plays an important role in moral action. Stuart and Ebbeck (1995) examined multiple components of morality based on Rest's model. Young basketball players were presented with basketball-specific moral dilemmas that described behaviors such as injuring another player to prevent a basket, cursing an opposing player, and pushing an opposing player when the referees are not looking. Judgment, reason (defined as the importance athletes place on various reasons in deciding whether to engage in these behaviors), intention, and behavior were assessed across the dilemmas. Participants were also asked about their perceptions of how their mother, father, coach, and teammates viewed the behaviors. When athletes perceived that significant others in their social environment approved of the behaviors, they judged those actions as appropriate and indicated the intention to engage in them. In addition, older children who perceived that significant others in their environment approved the behaviors described in the dilemmas gave less mature reasons for making a moral decision and were rated by coaches as engaging in the behaviors more frequently.

In a related study, Vallerand and colleagues (1992) presented 1,056 athletes with two hypothetical situations portraying moral conflict and asked the athletes to indicate whether they would engage in the described behaviors. The situations were criticizing an official for making a bad call that cost the athlete the event and informing the official of one's undeserved outcome that, if told, would cost the athlete the event. Athletes' perceptions of what significant others thought the athlete should do in these situations were assessed. Significant others included father, mother, teammates, friends, coach, and physical education teacher. In addition, athletes' perceptions of what most people who are important to them thought the athletes should do (subjective norms) and their attitudes toward the behavior were assessed. The authors showed that attitudes and subjective norms had significant direct effects on moral intention. Perceptions of significant others' views regarding moral action also influenced intention through attitudes and subjective norms.

The findings of these studies (Stuart & Ebbeck, 1995; Vallerand et al., 1992) underscore the importance of the social environment in determining moral action. It has been suggested that through interaction with significant others such as parents, teachers, coaches, and peers, people learn appropriate behavioral conduct and over time develop relevant beliefs (Vallerand et al., 1992) that influence moral behavioral intention. Although moral inclination may reside in the social environment, it is one's perceptions of the social environment rather than the actual views of significant others that determine the person's attitudes and subjective norms toward moral behaviors. The individual therefore plays an active role in the potential influence of significant others.

Motivational Climate

Another factor proposed to influence moral functioning in sport is the contextual goal structure, that is, whether the context within which behavior occurs is competitive, noncompetitive, or cooperative (Shields & Bredemeier, 1995), referred to as *motivational climate*. As highlighted in part III of this volume, the motivational climate of a context involves the achievement goals emphasized and the values conveyed to the participants by significant others such as teachers, parents, and coaches (Ames, 1992; Duda, 1993; Roberts, Treasure, & Kavussanu, 1997). Those significant others who structure the achievement situation determine important features of the context such as the criteria for success, evaluation procedures, and distribution of rewards. A performance motivational climate is salient when success is defined in normative terms, the top athletes typically receive recognition, and the emphasis is on how one's ability compares to that of others. This type of climate is also referred to as an *ego-involving climate*. In contrast, a mastery motivational climate is predominant when success is defined as skill mastery and individual improvement, the focus is on skill development and embracement of one's potential, and all athletes have an important role. The term *task-involving climate* is also used to refer to this type of climate.

It has been suggested (Anderman, Griesinger, & Westerfield, 1998; Bredemeier, 1999) that the two types of motivational climate are differentially related to moral variables; a few studies have investigated motivational climate in relation to these variables. In their study with college basketball players, Kavussanu et al. (2002) found no significant relationship between perceptions of a performance motivational climate and indices of moral functioning. In contrast, Ommundsen, Roberts, Lemyre, and Treasure (2003) reported that footballers (soccer players) who perceived a motivational climate that was high in performance and low in mastery were more likely to engage in amoral behavior than footballers who reported any other combination of perceptions. In addition, those athletes who perceived a climate high in mastery and low in performance reported more mature reasons for their judgment resolving the moral dilemma. Miller, Roberts, and Ommundsen (2003) also found that adolescent male football (soccer) players who perceived a high mastery climate in their team also reported higher scores on four sportsmanship orientations (e.g., respect for commitment to sport, social conventions, opponent, and rules and officials) than did those athletes who perceived a low mastery climate. In addition, athletes who perceived a high performance climate reported lower respect for social conventions and rules and officials than those perceiving a low performance climate. Thus, the motivational climate that athletes perceive to be predominant in their team has some implications for their moral functioning.

Personal Influences in Sport

There is no doubt that the characteristics of the sport context may exert a major influence on moral variables. When studies investigating moral issues in sport have included both contextual and personal variables, the strongest predictor that typically emerges is the moral atmosphere of the team (e.g., Stephens, 2000, 2001; Stephens & Bredemeier, 1996). Thus, the social context of sport appears to be crucial. However, other significant influences on moral functioning in sport emanate from the person. Two major personal influences have been investigated, namely motivational orientation and gender.

Motivation

The concept of motivation refers to the forces that initiate, direct, and sustain behavior (Roberts, 1984, 2001). Motivation has a prominent place in the literature on moral behavior. Moral development theorists generally agree that moral behavior is motivated behavior (e.g., Blasi, 1980; Kohlberg, 1984; Rest, 1984). Rest (1984), for example, proposed that one factor influencing moral behavior is one's motives, which are assumed to act on the decision-making process. Kohlberg (1984) has also underscored the influence of motives on whether people will behave in a way that is congruent with their moral judgment. He implies that when one's motives are not congruent with one's moral judgment, a discrepancy between moral thought and action is likely to occur. Thus, motivation is considered an important moderator of moral action. The role of motivation on moral functioning in sport has been examined using two theoretical perspectives: achievement goal theory (Nicholls, 1989) and self-determination theory (Deci & Ryan, 1985).

Achievement Goals and Morality in Sport   The theory that has generated the bulk of the work dealing with motivational and moral issues in sport is achievement goal theory. The main premise of this theory is that the driving force of individuals in achievement situations is the demonstration of competence. However, perceptions of competence are predicted to vary as a function of one's goal perspective (Nicholls, 1989). Two major goal perspectives are assumed to operate in achievement contexts such as sport: a task goal orientation and an ego goal orientation (see chapter 9). Task-oriented individuals tend to use self-referenced criteria to judge competence and feel successful when they have achieved learning or mastery of the task. In contrast, ego-oriented individuals tend to use other-referenced criteria to define success and judge competence, and feel successful when they have outperformed others. The primary means through which the ego-oriented athlete demonstrates competence is winning.

Achievement goals have implications for morality within the sport context. Because athletes who are predominantly ego oriented feel successful when they demonstrate superiority over others, they are more likely to engage in rule violations and cheating if they think these behaviors might facilitate their goal. In contrast, the task-oriented individual's motivational goal is doing one's best and fulfilling one's potential. Because competence is judged with respect to self-referenced criteria, cheating and aggressing against others to demonstrate competence in the normative sense is irrelevant. Task-oriented athletes want to play by the rules because only a fair competition can provide a true test of their competence.

Research stemming from achievement goal theory has examined achievement goals in relation to a variety of moral variables, including judgments about the legitimacy of injurious acts, indices of moral functioning, reported likelihood to aggress against an opponent, moral reasoning, and sportsmanship. In the first study investigating morality in sport from the perspective of achievement goal theory, Duda and colleagues (1991) presented interscholastic basketball players with six scenarios depicting aggressive acts in basketball. Following each scenario, participants were asked if the behavior was OK (legitimate) if it was necessary in order to win the game. Athletes high in ego orientation believed that injuring opponents so that they missed a game or were out for the season and nonphysically intimidating the opponent were legitimate acts. Similar findings were reported in two studies with elite male ice-hockey players (Dunn & Causgrove-Dunn, 1999) and intercollegiate female basketball players (Kavussanu & Roberts, 2001). In both studies, ego orientation corresponded to the view that intentionally injurious acts in sport are legitimate. No relationship emerged between task orientation and legitimacy judgments in any of the studies described in this paragraph.

A few studies have investigated achievement goals in relation to Rest's (1983, 1984) model by examining three components of the model: judgment, intention, and behavior. Specifically, Kavussanu and Roberts (2001) presented American college basketball players with scenarios describing unsportsmanlike behaviors likely to occur during a basketball game, such as faking an injury, risking injury to an opposing player, or intentionally injuring an opponent to take that player out of the game. The higher the ego orientation, the more likely the athlete was to judge the described behaviors as appropriate and to report the intention to engage in the

behaviors. Similar findings were reported in a second study with a sample of high school Singaporean hockey players (Kavussanu & Rameswaran, 2000). Finally, in a study using British college athletes participating in basketball, football (soccer), hockey, and rugby (Kavussanu & Ntoumanis, 2003), ego orientation corresponded to low levels of moral functioning whereas task orientation had small but significant effects, suggesting a weak link between the two constructs.

Tod and Hodge (2001) employed a qualitative methodology to examine the relationship between achievement goals and moral reasoning in adult male Rugby Union players. Individuals who were high in ego orientation appeared to use lower levels of moral reasoning, expressing little concern for the welfare of the other players and being more egocentric in their thinking. In contrast, those players who were high in task orientation employed more mature levels of moral reasoning, and were more concerned about the welfare of others and with playing fairly rather than winning at all costs.

Finally, research has identified a link between achievement goals and sportsmanship. Early work examining attitudes toward sportsmanship as well as unsportsmanlike attitudes (Duda et al., 1991) found that ego orientation corresponded to approval of unsportsmanlike play or cheating among interscholastic basketball players. In more recent work, task orientation has been identified as a significant positive predictor of three sportsmanship orientations, namely respect for social conventions, respect for rules and officials, and personal commitment to participation, whereas ego orientation has emerged as a negative predictor of respect for rules and officials (Dunn & Causgrove-Dunn, 1999). Similar findings have been reported in a study with male youth soccer players (Lemyre, Roberts, & Ommundsen, 2002). However, studies using young female soccer players (Stephens & Bredemeier, 1996); athletes playing in coed, all-girls, or all-boys soccer leagues (Stephens, 2000); and female adolescent athletes enrolled in basketball summer camps (Stephens, 2001) found no significant relationship between players' goal orientation and reported likelihood to aggress against an opponent.

Overall, the findings of these studies highlight the importance of motivational goal orientation, particularly ego orientation, on athletes' moral functioning within the sport context. Thus, athletes whose primary focus is demonstrating competence in the normative sense by outperforming others also operate in overall lower levels of moral functioning as indicated by a number of measures: They tend to view intentionally injurious sport acts as justified; employ less mature moral reasoning; display lower levels of moral judgment, intention, and behavior within the sport context; and express unsportsmanlike attitudes and orientations. It is possible that striving to accomplish primarily ego-oriented goals has the potential to deter individuals from achieving moral maturity. Indeed, a prerequisite for advancing to higher levels of moral development is one's ability to equally consider the needs of all parties involved in a moral conflict as well as one's concern with the welfare of others (Shields & Bredemeier, 1995). The excessive focus on the self and the preoccupation with winning and demonstrating superiority over others that characterize ego-oriented athletes may not be compatible with accomplishing progress in the moral arena (Kavussanu & Roberts, 2001).

Although the link between ego orientation and moral variables has been established, the role of task orientation is less clear, as this goal has not been consistently associated with moral variables (e.g., Dunn & Causgrove-Dunn, 1999; Kavussanu & Roberts, 2001; Stephens & Bredemeier, 1996). This is especially true when judgments about the legitimacy of intentionally injurious acts have been examined, or when moral functioning has been measured using scenarios portraying inappropriate action likely to occur during a game and asking players to indicate their judgment, intention, and behavior in relation to those scenarios. However, task orientation has consistently emerged as a positive predictor of various dimensions of sportsmanship. The manner in which moral variables are measured might explain the inconsistent findings. For example, the sportsmanship dimensions that have been linked to task orientation involve respect for rules and officials, respect for social conventions such as shaking hands, and respect for personal commitment to participation in sport. Task orientation reflects one's tendency to use self-referenced criteria to define success and judge competence. It is reasonable to expect that task-oriented individuals would show more respect for rules and officials and be concerned with fair play, because only when playing by the rules can they truly test their competence. In addition, respect for personal commitment to participation in sport resembles task orientation; some of the items assessing this dimension are similar to the items assessing task orientation (e.g., give maximum effort, think about how to improve).

Motivation As a Mediating Variable   Although identifying factors associated with moral variables is important, it is also important to move beyond description and start examining the processes that operate in the context of sport. For example, why does participation in sport lead some athletes to operate at lower levels of moral functioning? If sport per se is neither moral nor immoral (Shields & Bredemeier, 1995), what are the variables that mediate the relationship between sport participation and moral functioning? This was one of the issues examined in the Kavussanu and Ntoumanis (2003) study discussed earlier. This study examined whether ego orientation mediates the relationship between extent of sport involvement and athletes' moral functioning as indicated by judgment, intention, and behavior. Sport involvement was assessed by the number of seasons athletes had participated in their respective sport. Using structural equation modeling the authors examined the path between sport experience and moral functioning in the presence and absence of ego orientation. The path was .22 and significant in the absence of ego orientation, but when ego orientation was introduced in the model the path was reduced to .11 and became nonsignificant, indicating that ego orientation partially mediates the relationship between extent of sport involvement and moral functioning.

This finding is important because, together with past research (e.g., Bredemeier, Weiss, Shields, & Cooper, 1986), it points to factors that are key to the relationship between sport participation and morality. Extensive involvement in competitive sport is associated with high ego orientation (see also White & Duda, 1994), and this variable in turn has the potential to influence moral functioning in the sport context. Thus, research grounded in achievement goal theory has provided some insight into the motivational processes that operate in the sport realm and are associated with various aspects of morality.

Self-Determined Motivation and Morality in Sport   Self-determination theory (Deci & Ryan, 1985) distinguishes among different types of motivation that lie on a continuum reflecting varying degrees of self-determination. On the higher end of the continuum lie motivated actions that are self-determined, that is, actions endorsed by one's sense of self and engaged in volitionally (Deci & Ryan, 1991). The self-determination continuum is postulated to run from high to low levels of self-determination as one moves from intrinsic motivation to extrinsic motivation to amotivation. Intrinsic motivation refers to doing an activity for its own sake in the absence of extrinsic rewards or incentives, such as playing basketball out of pure enjoyment. Extrinsic motivation involves doing the activity for some extrinsic reward or incentive such as money or prestige. Different forms of extrinsic motivation have also been identified based on the degree to which the extrinsically motivated behavior is self-determined. Finally, amotivation refers to the absence of motivation for pursuing an activity. An index of self-determination can be computed based on the level of each type of motivation the individual possesses. Obviously, the higher one is on the self-determination continuum, the greater one's self-determined motivation.

Different types of motivation reflect different reasons for participating in sport. It has been suggested (Vallerand & Losier, 1994) that the reasons people participate in sport have implications for the way they play the game. For instance, athletes who are more intrinsically motivated and participate in sport for the pure enjoyment they derive from the activity are more likely to be concerned with fair play. In contrast, athletes who participate in sport primarily for extrinsic reasons such as to receive external recognition, awards, or prestige are more likely to bend the rules and engage in unsportsmanlike action if they think these behaviors will facilitate extrinsic gains.

To date, only one study has examined the role of motivation on morality in sport from the perspective of self-determination theory. Specifically, Vallerand and Losier (1994) administered questionnaires measuring self-determined motivation and sportsmanship to adolescent male elite ice-hockey players 2 weeks into the season and then 5 months later at the end of the season. Using a cross-lag correlational design, the authors found that over this 5-month period, self-determined motivation had a greater influence on sportsmanship than sportsmanship had on self-determined motivation. Thus, the findings of this study suggest that playing hockey for primarily self-determined reasons may lead one to display higher levels of sportsmanship.

Gender

A consistent finding in sport psychology literature concerns differences between males and females on moral variables. For example, gender differences have emerged in studies examining athletes' general moral maturity as well as moral reasoning in response to life and sport moral dilemmas. Specifically, female basketball players displayed higher levels of general moral maturity than males (Bredemeier & Shields, 1984; Hall, 1981), college and high school female basketball players reasoned at a more mature level than males in response to sport dilemmas, and high school females reasoned at a more mature level than males in response to life dilemmas (Bredemeier & Shields, 1986a).

Gender differences have been identified in work using diverse samples and methodologies to examine the effects of participation in different types of sport on legitimacy judgments. In this work, undergraduate males perceived the rule-breaking behaviors depicted on slides as more legitimate than did females (Silva, 1983). Similarly, adolescent male athletes indicated greater perceptions of legitimacy judgments than did their female counterparts in response to scenarios describing injurious behaviors (Conroy et al., 2001).

Finally, boys participating in a summer camp accepted more acts as legitimate than did girls and reported significantly greater tendencies toward aggression (Bredemeier et al., 1987).

Gender differences have also been revealed in samples involving more elite athletes. Specifically, in a study with adolescent interscholastic basketball players, male athletes were significantly more likely than females to approve unsportsmanlike play (Duda et al., 1991). Other work using intercollegiate basketball players (Kavussanu & Roberts, 2001) has also reported gender differences. In this study, females expressed significantly greater disapproval of aggressive acts than did males and reported higher levels of moral functioning as reflected in their moral judgments, intentions, and behaviors. Similar findings have been revealed in high school Singaporean field-hockey players (Kavussanu & Rameswaran, 2000) and British university athletes participating in basketball, soccer, rugby, and field hockey (Kavussanu & Ntoumanis, 2003).

Bredemeier and Shields (1986b) have attempted to explain the gender differences that consistently appear in research examining morality in sport. Specifically, these researchers have suggested that the egocentric aspects of competitive interaction may be embraced more by males than females because sport traditionally has been a male domain (Oglesby, 1978) and expression and acceptance of physical aggression is viewed as more consistent with the male gender role (Weiss & Bredemeier, 1990). Thus, gender differences appear consistent with the culture of male and female sport.

Future Research

Empirical work in the sport domain has revealed interesting findings regarding factors that influence morality in sport. However, many questions remain. For example, do differences in moral reasoning between athletes and nonathletes exist in other types of sports and other competitive levels besides college basketball? More sports need to be explored before we generalize current findings. What is the influence on morality of extensive involvement in sports that involve different levels of interaction among participants? For instance, coactive sports such as rowing offer much less opportunity for interaction among team members than highly interactive sports such as basketball or soccer. The degree of interaction between members of the team may influence moral variables.

Research is needed to identify aspects of the sport experience that are related to the processes involved in moral thought and action. For example, the level of task and social cohesion or the leadership style of the coach may facilitate or impede moral growth. An autocratic coaching style has been linked to perceptions of peer aggression in baseball and softball (Shields et al., 1995), while perceptions of team norms supporting cheating and aggression have been associated with a performance motivational climate in basketball (Kavussanu et al., 2002). Future work should determine the influence of the coach's goal orientation, philosophy, and coaching style on athletes' moral functioning. In particular, whether coaches are more autocratic rather than democratic and more ego rather than task oriented might be related to the moral judgments and behaviors of athletes and to the team's perception of the moral atmosphere.

Other factors relevant to the wider social environment need to be investigated in relation to morality. For example, it is worth noting that even though it is generally agreed that the mass media play a major role in shaping individuals' attitudes and behaviors, very little empirical evidence exists to verify the extent and nature of the media's influence on athletes' moral attitudes and behaviors. Finally, researchers need to move toward a holistic examination of morality, considering multiple components, their interrelationships, and the factors that influence them. We need to simultaneously consider the influence of both personal and environmental factors and unravel the relative influence of these variables on athletes' moral functioning.

Practical Implications

The work examining moral issues in sport to date has considerably enhanced our understanding of athletes' moral functioning. The knowledge gained through this research has several implications for practice. First, as preliminary evidence suggests, extensive participation in team, medium-contact, and high-contact sports is associated with low levels of moral functioning. Although more research is needed to replicate and explain these findings, coaches of these sports need to be aware of the findings, pay particular attention to athletes' moral behavior, and make every attempt to promote moral behavior and discourage unsportsmanlike conduct.

Second, findings from several studies suggest that the most important influence on morality in sport may be the moral atmosphere of the team, that is, the predominant team norms regarding acceptable behavior in the sport context. A moral atmosphere that condones unsportsmanlike conduct has been associated with low levels of moral functioning in several studies. These findings highlight the vital role coaches can play in promoting moral behavior in sport. For example, coaches could engage the whole team in discussions about the importance of moral action, and they could offer positive reinforcement for such conduct and impose sanctions for negative behaviors toward teammates and opponents. Coaches could also build moral dilemmas into their motor skills curriculum by creating situations involving moral conflicts such as taking unfair advantages, cheating, or intentionally injuring opponents and then encouraging moral dialogue in response to these situations. These types of interventions have been implemented in past work in the physical activity context and have been shown to be efficacious (e.g., Bredemeier, Weiss, Shields, & Shewchuk, 1986; Romance, Weiss, & Bockoven, 1986).

Finally, the motivational climate of the team, which is created primarily by the coaches, and the athletes' motivational goal orientations have also been linked to various aspects of morality in sport. Specifically, mastery (task-involving) climate and task orientation have been associated with some dimensions of sportsmanship, whereas performance (ego-involving) climate and ego orientation have been negatively linked to a variety of moral variables. Coaches therefore could direct athletes' attention to fulfilling their potential and doing their best as opposed to focusing on winning at all costs. By creating a climate where every player is valued and has an important role, coaches could have an impact on athletes' moral functioning.

Summary

Moral issues in sport have received increased research attention in recent years. Most empirical work has been grounded on Kohlberg's, Haan's, and Rest's theories and examined moral reasoning, but other variables relevant to morality such as aggressive tendencies, judgments about the legitimacy of injurious acts, and sportsmanship also have been examined. Kohlberg and Haan viewed moral reasoning as an indicator of moral development, while Rest focused on the processes underlying moral behavior. Shields and Bredemeier (1995) applied Rest's model to the sport domain and identified three sets of variables that influence moral action in sport.

Empirical research in sport has identified several factors associated with the sport context as influencing athletes' moral functioning. Participation in medium-contact sports, high-contact sports, and some team sports has been linked to certain aspects of morality, such as moral reasoning, aggressive tendencies, judgments that intentionally injurious acts are legitimate, and moral intention. Three significant social influences have been linked to moral variables, namely the moral atmosphere of the team, significant others, and the motivational climate. Specifically, perceptions of a team atmosphere that condones inappropriate action have been associated with reported likelihood to aggress against an opponent and with lower levels of moral functioning; perceptions that significant others approve inappropriate action have been linked to lower moral intention and behavior; perceptions of a mastery team climate have been associated with sportsmanship; and perceived performance climate has been linked to low levels of moral functioning.

The major personal factor that has the potential to influence moral functioning in sport is motivation as reflected in an athlete's goal orientation. Ego orientation has been associated with several variables such as judgments that intentionally injurious acts are legitimate; low levels of moral functioning as reflected in athletes' reports of judgment, intention, and behavior; low levels of moral reasoning; and unsportsmanlike attitudes and orientations. Task orientation has been associated

with sportsmanship orientations and, in work using qualitative methodology, with higher levels of moral reasoning. In addition, research has identified a positive relationship between self-determined motivation and sportsmanship. Gender differences have also consistently emerged in moral research in sport with females displaying higher levels of morality than males.

Future research is necessary to identify aspects of the sport experience that are related to the processes involved in moral thought and action and to investigate other factors relevant to the wider social environment in relation to morality. Finally, there are many practical implications of research on morality, particularly for coaches; findings thus far highlight the vital role coaches can play in promoting moral behavior in sport.

DISCUSSION QUESTIONS

1. What are the major theories that have spawned morality research in sport?
2. How does participation in different types of sport influence athletes' moral functioning?
3. Which aspects of the social context influence morality in sport?
4. What is the influence of motivation on athletes' moral functioning?
5. Imagine that you are the coach of a youth sport team. One of your athletes repeatedly breaks the rules. Based on empirical research on morality in sport, what steps would you take to correct this athlete's behavior?

chapter 20

Cross-Cultural Issues in Sport Psychology Research

Gangyan Si, PhD, and Hing-chu Lee, PhD

Learning Objectives

On completion of this chapter, the reader should have

1. understanding of the historical evolution of cross-cultural psychology, particularly as it pertains to the sport context;
2. knowledge of definitions that describe important concepts such as culture, race, and ethnicity;
3. ability to discuss two popular frameworks, individualism–collectivism and ecoculturalism, often used in cross-cultural psychology in sport;
4. understanding of the three main goals of cross-cultural research and the manner in which they relate to studies of relationship dynamics in sport;
5. awareness of methodological issues and of the four-stage conceptual framework in designing cross-cultural studies in sport; and
6. awareness of potential cross-cultural research directions in areas of interpersonal relationships and group dynamics.

AP Photo/Greg Baker

Television viewers from all over the world might have been amazed at the different reactions of the coaches of the two teams at the 2004 Olympic women's volleyball final. The Russian coach, nicknamed "the Roaring Lion" by the Chinese, appeared angry and frustrated with the performance of his team and was physically and verbally expressive of his emotions. His team gathered around him on the sideline, looking somewhat tense and uneasy. The Chinese coach, on the other hand, appeared calm and collected and talked to his team in an even voice with occasional hand gestures and smiles. It was an extremely close contest, but the Chinese team won a hard-earned gold medal for the first time in 20 years.

We all behave in a way that we think is natural and appropriate. We are all different because we come from different socioeconomic and cultural backgrounds. We are different because we have different resources at our disposal and different beliefs and values, yet we may be more similar than we think. Perhaps if the Russian coach had watched a video playback of his behavior, he might have thought, "If I had been gentler or more relaxed with my team, the team might have played differently."

Cross-cultural psychology does not attempt to change people's behaviors. Rather, it aims to study the similarities and differences of psychological processes in human behaviors in various cultural contexts in an attempt to discover psychological universals (Berry, Poortinga, Segall, & Dasen, 2002). The approach of this chapter consists of two positions. The first is that we need to consider *cultural contexts* in understanding human psychological processes, and the second is that we need to do this *comparatively* across cultures. Both positions are necessary and intertwined. Both the cultural and the comparative elements define cross-cultural psychology. In this chapter, we review the developments of cross-cultural research in psychology and in sport psychology more specifically, focusing on theories, methodological concerns, implications for practice, and future research directions.

Historical Overview of Cross-Cultural Psychology in Sport

Cross-cultural psychology in sport stems from the broader field of cross-cultural psychology, which is a relatively new field that has descended from general psychology. In addition, cross-cultural psychology has links with diverse disciplines such as anthropology, physiology, sociology, history, and political science. Although there is no conclusive evidence, it is believed that ancient philosophers were aware of human diversity and social differences in human behavior. After the relatively stagnant Middle Ages, changes in scientific interest in diversity started to emerge. The most radical changes in human thought on diversity probably occurred during the Enlightenment, between the 17th and 19th centuries. By the beginning of the 20th century, the interest in comparative human and social sciences was still growing. Anthropologists, psychologists, and other social scientists offered different theories to explain cross-cultural human behavior. In due course, research changed from being heavily speculative to relying on empirical evidence.

With the publication of the *Journal of Cross-Cultural Psychology* in 1970, cross-cultural psychology was informally established. In 1972, the International Association for Cross-Cultural Psychology and the Society for Cross-Cultural Research were established. By the 1980s, a major handbook was published in cross-cultural psychology by Triandis and Lambert (1980). More recent developments include the publication of a new edition of the *Handbook of Cross-Cultural Psychology: Research and Applications* (Berry et al., 2002) and a number of textbooks in cross-cultural psychology (e.g., Brislin, 1993; Lonner & Malpass, 1994; Segall, Dasen, Berry, & Poortinga, 1990) and cross-cultural social psychology (e.g., Matsumoto, 1994; Smith & Bond, 1998; Triandis, 1994). The growth of cross-cultural research in this area of study is encouraging (e.g., Bond et al., in press; Leung & Bond, 2004; Leung et al., 2002). To date, cross-cultural psychology has become an established and truly international discipline, with researchers representing cultures from all over the world.

Despite significant development in the general field of cross-cultural psychology and increasing research activity in recent years, there has been relatively little interest among sport psychologists in pursuing cross-cultural studies. In their survey of papers published by the *Journal of Sport Psychology* from 1979 to 1987, Duda and Allison (1990) found that over 96% of the empirical papers did not report the racial or ethnic composition of their participants. As for theoretical papers, there is little or no attempt to consider the ways in which race and ethnicity affect psychological processes and behavior. The authors went on to cite studies that suggest the influence of culture on variations in motor development (Malina, 1988) and sport performance (Coakley, 1986; Samson & Yerles, 1988). They concluded by encouraging sport psychologists to conduct more cross-cultural studies in order to determine the meaning and motivation of the physical domain among different cultural groups and to predict the theoretical and practical benefits of these cross-cultural analyses in sport psychology.

Partly in response to Duda and Allison's (1990) calls for cross-cultural research, psychologists have somewhat increased their output in relevant studies. In addition, two developments are worthy of note. In 1997, the *International Journal of Sport Psychology* created a section for cross-cultural research studies in sport. Moreover, in 2001 at the 10th World Congress of Sport Psychology in Skiathos, Greece, we presented a keynote speech titled, "East Meets West—Indigenous and Cross-Cultural Analysis of Sport and Exercise Psychology."

Basic Definitions

To study cross-cultural issues in sport, it is important to understand the meaning of common terms like *culture, race,* and *ethnicity* and to be able to identify the subtle differences between them.

Culture

Human beings possess few genetically based mechanisms that control our behaviors in predetermined ways. Instead, our learning capacity enables us to adapt to and modify our behaviors and environment. Such capacity is subsequently transmitted to future generations and falls under the term *culture.* Cuber (1968) views culture as the "changing pattern of learned behavior and the products of learned behavior (including attitudes, values, knowledge, and material objects) that are shared by and transmitted among members of the society" (p. 76).

Many definitions of culture are for scientists or for laypeople. Whereas for laypeople the term *culture* tends to connote refinement, good taste, and social etiquette, social scientists use the term in a nonevaluative sense. Culture can be classified as material and nonmaterial. *Material culture* explores the relationship between artifacts and social relations. It consists of the forms and meanings of objects, images, and environments in everyday life. In the context of sport, material culture includes tangible objects such as balls, rackets, uniforms, skis, scoreboards, and the like. Many of these physical artifacts are products of technology. A captivating example of material culture in sport is the stadium, especially multimillion-dollar sport places such as the SkyDome in Toronto and the Georgia Dome in Atlanta. These architectural creations have symbolic significance (e.g., a symbol of unity and glory) well beyond their usefulness.

Nonmaterial culture, or subjective culture, on the other hand, consists of intangibles. Common nonmaterial cultural elements include attitudes, beliefs, language, values, and norms. Subjective culture is defined as the characteristic way in which people perceive their social environment (Triandis, 1973). The nature of sport in terms of its organization, values, goals, functions, and structure provides revealing clues about a society. Ries-

man and Denney (1951), for example, suggested that the transition of rugby into American football was consistent with the dominant American ethos. The early 1940s was a time when the civilian heroes of the previous era were replaced by those with military connections. Glenn Davis and Felix "Doc" Blanchard, football stars at West Point, were catapulted to fame. Then the 1950s and 1960s saw football emerge as a source of admiration, with the highly complex organization, specialization, and division of labor in the game coinciding with the key characteristics of the highly industrialized American society (Smith, 1973). Hence, it is reasonable to argue that sport provides a means for expressing the core values of a society (Edwards, 1973).

Taking the previous definitions into consideration, for the purposes of this chapter culture is viewed as both material and nonmaterial and is mostly learned. We define it as a set of attitudes, behaviors, symbols, and contextual variables (e.g., political, social, historical, ecological, and biological) shared by a group of people and usually transmitted from one generation to another (Shiraev & Levy, 2001).

Race and Ethnicity

Race is defined by some researchers (e.g., Rushton, 1995) as groups of people distinguished by similar and genetically transmitted physical characteristics. For example, whereas narrow nasal passages mark Caucasians, distinct cheekbones identify Mongoloids. Other experts, however, suggest that race is a social construct (e.g., Brace, 1995); in other words, all racial differences are a product of social assignment and reflect only the differences between arbitrarily established categories. Dole (1995) went so far as to recommend abandoning the term *race* altogether and suggest instead using terms such as *continental origin* (e.g., African) or *anthropological designation* (e.g., Caucasian) to describe large categories of people. Despite the controversy over the usefulness of the term, *race* is still considered an important element of people's identification in countries with a large number of minorities.

The term *ethnicity* suggests a person's cultural heritage and the shared experiences of people having a common ancestral origin, language, traditions, and often religion and geographic territory.

Popular Frameworks for Cross-Cultural Psychology

In this section, we provide an overview of individualism and collectivism as well as ecoculturalism as cultural frameworks for understanding cross-cultural psychology research. Within these frameworks, researchers develop research questions and measurement instruments to study the effects of culture on sport.

Individualism and Collectivism (I-C)

In the past few decades, the idea of comparing societies on the basis of cultural dichotomies has increased in popularity, in large part because of the highly influential work of Hofstede (1980). Hofstede's work was important because it organized cultural differences into overarching patterns, which facilitated comparative research and launched a rapidly expanding body of cultural and cross-cultural research in the ensuing years. In general, researchers conceptualize individualism as the opposite of collectivism (e.g., Hui, 1988), especially when contrasting European American and East Asian cultural frames (e.g., Chan, 1994; Yamaguchi, 1994).

The core element of *individualism* is the assumption that individuals are independent of one another. Hofstede (1980) defined individualism as a focus on rights above duties, a concern for oneself and one's immediate family, an emphasis on personal autonomy and self-fulfillment, and the basing of one's identity on one's personal accomplishments. *Collectivism*, on the other hand, is interpreted as behavior based on concerns for others and group harmony as well as care for traditions and values. The core element is the assumption that groups bind and mutually obligate individuals.

The individualism–collectivism (I-C) dimension is perhaps one of the most widely researched areas in cross-cultural psychology, with its greatest strength being its theoretical parsimony. Hofstede's (1980, 1983) pioneering research is an example in this area. His studies systematically mapped 53 countries on four dimensions, one of which is I-C. Hofstede's model organized cultural differences into overarching patterns, which facilitated comparative research and stimulated a rapidly expanding body of cultural and cross-cultural research. However, the I-C framework has been subjected to much criticism in recent years. The main objection is the overly broad and diffuse ways in which researchers define and assess the construct and their apparent willingness to accept any cross-cultural differences as evidence of I-C processes.

For example, Voronov and Singer (2002) argued that the I-C research is characterized largely by insufficient conceptual clarity and a lack of systematic data. They questioned the wisdom of presenting whole societies or explaining research findings in black-and-white terms, thus glossing over subtle differences of a given social entity. Fijneman, Willemsen, and Poortinga (1996) also challenged the oversimplification in the traditional understanding of the I-C framework. Moreover, national examples of I-C may vary: American collectivism is different from Asian collectivism and from Latino collectivism. Take sport in Mexico as a hypothetical example; Mexican athletes desire to maintain balanced relationships with their teammates and other athletes outside their team, "but at the same time they remain competitive against each other in indirect ways for the pursuit of personal goals." In other words, for the Mexican athletes, the appearance of confrontation avoidance may be accompanied by the hidden pursuit of personal goals. The Asian form of collectivism, on the other hand, puts pressure on individuals to avoid disagreements with others, because in the Asian cultures a concern about harmony with and happiness of others (especially the elders and superiors) is seen as more important than one's own personal comfort (Barnlund, 1989). Thus, for example, in a Japanese soccer team, close and harmonious relationships are emphasized more than anything else among team members so that they can win matches on the field.

Sport psychology has not used the I-C framework extensively; therefore, future research may do well to refocus attention on the core elements of individualism (independence and uniqueness) and collectivism (duty to in-group and internationally, maintaining harmony), allowing them to be accurately operationalized, assessed, and manipulated. It is only under such conditions that social scientists can evaluate the usefulness of the I-C framework.

Ecoculturalism

The ecocultural framework is a comprehensive multidisciplinary approach guided by the premise that individuals cannot be separated from their environmental context. People constantly exchange messages with the environment, thus transforming the environment and themselves. Human beings are not passive and influenced by the environment, but are dynamic and interact with and change the environment. In other words, the interactions are reciprocal (Goodnow, 1990). For example, coaches train and influence their athletes, and at the same time, their athletes train and influence them.

According to this framework, the human environment is a part of a larger cultural system. Both the environment and the individual are seen as open and interchanging systems. For example, in sport, each athlete's development takes place within a particular developmental niche that can be viewed as a combination of settings: First, the physical and social settings in which the athlete lives and trains (e.g., staff, available

Honor for the sport or country: Swedish versus Russian ice-hockey players. People who are members of the same race may still differ in their competition goals due to ecological and cultural differences.

equipment, services); second, the collection of customary practices (e.g., roles, rules, norms) that convey messages to and from the athlete and coach; and finally, the coach's and athlete's beliefs and expectations about each other. These three types of settings mediate the individual athlete's (and coach's) development within the larger culture.

The ecocultural model in cross-cultural psychology was recently elaborated by Berry et al. (2002). They identified four major factors that influence the individual. These factors are *ecological* (i.e., the natural setting in which humans and the environment interact; includes economic activity, diet, climate, and population density); *biological* (i.e., genetic transmission); *cultural* (i.e., cultural transmission); and *acculturational* (i.e., the modification of the culture, a group, or an individual as a result of contact with a different culture). Through these factors, people adjust to existing realities and acquire roles as members of a specific culture. When these factors are identified and taken into consideration, we may be able to explain how and why people differ from one another and why they are the same. Despite the usefulness of the ecocultural framework, it remains a conceptual scheme rather than a theoretical model with a concrete hypothesis open to empirical scrutiny.

Goals of Cross-Cultural Research

Embedded in the definitions and frameworks discussed in the previous section are a set of goals that cross-cultural psychology should aim to accomplish. Specifically, Berry et al. (2002) proposed three main goals, all of which are presented here with cross-cultural examples to illustrate the main points.

The first goal is to test the generality and validity of existing psychology knowledge and theories in other cultural contexts (Berry et al., 2002). For instance, we may wish to study coach leadership behaviors in Canada and Korea using the multidimensional model of leadership (Chelladurai & Saleh, 1980; see also chapter 5) as a guide to this investigation. Such an investigation may aim to explore (a) when the model is applicable to other cultures besides Canada and (b) whether the generated results suggest similarities in coach leadership behaviors between the two distinct cultural groups. An assessment of only the similarities of particular human behaviors in different cultures is insufficient, however.

Berry et al. (2002) have proposed a second goal for cross-cultural psychology, namely, to look for differences in human behaviors that are attributable to the cultural context. Using the same example, if the results obtained suggested that Korean and Canadian coaches differ, we should try to interpret and subsequently explore these findings in terms of the specific cultural context in which Korean coaches operate (e.g., a coach leadership style unique to Korean culture).

The third goal is to "attempt to assemble and integrate into a broadly based psychology, the results obtained when pursuing the first two goals, and to generate a more nearly universal psychology that will be valid for a broader range of cultures" (Berry et al., 2002, p. 4). Using the previous example on coach leadership, an extension of the study that includes a representative sample of cultures could yield data relating to psychological processes in coach leadership behaviors common to different cultures. In this way, the presumptive goal of psychology to achieve integration or universal status can be brought one step closer (Bond & Smith, 1996).

Methodological Issues

Research in psychology is dominated by Western industrialized societies (Pawlik & Rosenzweig, 2000). This state of affairs extends to cross-cultural psychology and cross-cultural studies in sport. Content analysis of the *Journal of Cross-Cultural Psychology* since 1970 (Ongel & Smith, 1994) and the *Journal of Exercise & Sport Psychology* reveals that North American theories and authors predominate (Duda & Allison, 1990). This Western domination highlights the need for cross-cultural researchers in sport to be especially attentive to methodology. Central to these concerns is the analysis of equivalence in measurements and in concepts and constructs for which the measures (mostly developed in the West) are supposed to test.

Cross-cultural organizational research has been making great strides in both output and quality control. Borrowing from the methodologies applied in organizational research (Schaffe & Riordan, 2003), we proposed the following four-stage framework for addressing methodology issues in cross-cultural studies in sport (figure 20.1).

Stage 1: Development of the Research Question

The development of the research question has important implications for the design and measurement of a study. Two issues are relevant: Researchers must decide whether to establish an emic or etic perspective, and they must determine the way in which culture is treated. The terms *emic* and *etic* were coined by Pike (1967) in analogy with phonetics and phonemics. Berry (1969) subsequently summarized Pike's comments on

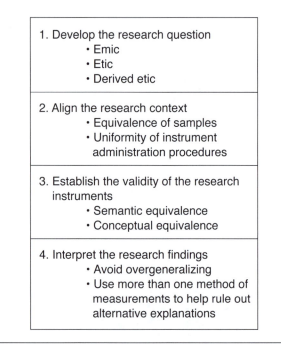

Figure 20.1 Four-stage conceptual framework for designing cross-cultural studies in sport.

the emic–etic distinction as it applies in cross-cultural psychology.

The emic approach focuses on examining a construct from within a specific culture and understanding the construct as the people from within that culture understand it (Gudykunst, 1997). Much of the research based in the United States, for example, is emic in that it examines issues as they apply to North Americans. An important factor for researchers to consider when using an emic approach is that shared frames of references may not exist across cultures (Ronen & Shenkar, 1988). Since this approach studies behavior from within a single culture, the emphasis is on understanding insiders' viewpoints and their thinking patterns within a particular setting (Weick, 1979). Thus, the unique features of a particular culture are incorporated into the theory, hypotheses, measurement, and analyses, and generalizability across cultures may be limited.

While the emic approach captures important aspects of the particular culture under study, the etic approach employs broader comparative analyses of two or more cultures. Specifically, etic cross-cultural research involves developing an understanding of a construct by explicitly comparing it across cultures using predetermined characteristics. In this way, measurement criteria in an etic approach are often viewed as common absolutes that can be applied across cultures (Berry, 1979), and key constructs are usually applied to all cultural samples in the same way. A major problem with this perspective is the tendency to make cross-cultural comparisons without fully taking into account relevant culture-specific emic factors. This failure to consider emic factors, along with the assumption that key constructs exist equally across all cultures, has been labeled *imposed etics* (Berry, 1990).

As a better way to make cross-cultural comparisons in sport, we suggest a *derived etic approach.* For example, suppose we want to compare coach–athlete relationships in Britain and China. Rather than identifying the nature of coach–athlete relationships in Britain (emic A) only and simply applying the theory (see, e.g., Jowett & Ntoumanis, 2004) to China (emic B), which would be an imposed etic, a derived etic approach requires researchers to first attain emic knowledge on coach–athlete relationships in both Britain and China. This allows researchers to put aside their cultural biases and to become familiar with the relevant cultural differences in each setting. It may then be possible to make cross-cultural links between the emic aspects of coach–athlete relationships in Britain and China. Only when there are observed commonalities can cross-cultural comparisons appropriately be made.

Another important issue in the development of research questions is determining how culture is operationally defined. Although country may be an appropriate indicator of culture and many researchers have used the terms *cross-cultural* and *cross-national* interchangeably (Chelladurai, Imamura, Yamaguchi, Oinuma, & Miyauchi, 1988; Leung & Bond, 2004) for the sake of convenience, using it as the sole operational definition of culture is problematic except when the population of a country is homogeneous.

Stage 2: Alignment of Research Context

The alignment of contexts refers to establishing congruence between the different cultures being studied. Several aspects of the research contexts must be considered when designing cross-cultural studies: Researchers should address the equivalence of their samples across contexts and the uniformity of their instrument administration procedures.

An important concern with respect to contextual alignment is whether cross-cultural samples are equivalent on dimensions other than those under examination. Researchers need to minimize the effects of sample differences that are not relevant to the main purpose of their studies. For instance, in designing a cross-cultural study on career transitions of elite athletes in Germany, Japan, and Korea, the cultural samples would need to be equivalent in at least these characteristics: level of achievement, duration of the athletic career, gender, and age.

Three strategies for sample selection have been proposed (Van de Vijver & Leung, 1997). One strategy is availability or *convenience sampling* in which the researcher chooses a sample by chance or because of the researcher's professional or personal contacts in the country in which the samples are selected. A second type of sampling is called *systematic sampling* or theory-guided sampling. The researcher selects nations or ethnic samples according to a theory or theoretical assumptions. Researchers who want to study causal attribution in sport in different cultures might choose countries that are considered individualist (e.g., Germany) and collectivist (e.g., China) for ready comparisons (Si, Rethorst, & Willimczik, 1995). A third sampling strategy is *random sampling* in which a large sample is randomly chosen; that is, any country or group has an equal chance of being selected in the research sample. This is a most reliable, but difficult to achieve, method to design a representative sample. Apart from broad sample selection strategies, specific concerns such as the size of the sample and familiarity of respondents with the measurement instruments and the general testing procedure need to be addressed.

Another concern related to contextual alignment is whether the administration of surveys is consistent across research settings. For example, in completing a measurement scale, participants in all cultures should be given equivalent instructions in an equivalent setting using equivalent methods (e.g., oral, written, or online). Cross-cultural researchers need to establish equivalence in their data collection procedures and to maintain rapport with respondents from different cultural backgrounds.

Stage 3: Validity of Research Instruments

A major problem in cross-cultural research is that many studies fail to take into full account critical measurement concerns (Sinha, 1996). Most of the tests and instruments for data collection in non-Western cultures have been developed in Western countries and there is a problem of equivalence and comparability. In this section, two types of equivalence are reviewed: semantic equivalence and conceptual equivalence.

To achieve *semantic equivalence,* the researcher has to make sure that different versions of a self-report instrument used cross-culturally fully account for linguistic differences among the samples. A common practice is to employ independent back-translation following the original translation from the target language. If inconsistencies are found, items can be reworded or, if necessary, eliminated. If the original wording is reproduced more or less precisely, the item is retained.

In validating a measure in cross-cultural research, researchers must also be concerned with conceptual equivalence. *Conceptual equivalence* refers to the degree to which members of different cultures use a common frame of reference when responding to items on a survey instrument (Riordan & Vandenberg, 1994).

For example, if we study motivational climate (mastery versus performance; Duda, 1993) among white, African, and Asian athletes and we believe that certain types of motivational climate are more strongly related to certain types of goal orientations (task versus ego), we should make sure that the items reflecting these climates and orientations carry the same meaning to all groups and are good indices of motivational climates and goal orientations for all the groups. Then we can say with some confidence that the questionnaire is of acceptable conceptual equivalence.

In addition, researchers can use correlational techniques to examine the interrelationships among the items of an instrument in various cultures. Factor analysis is usually used to investigate such correlational patterns. An exploratory factor analysis in each cultural sample will then produce factors common to all samples (Berry et al., 2002). Such factors will increase the researchers' confidence in the conceptual equivalence of their instrument for all cultural samples.

A related problem is the tendency for certain cultural groups to differ in their response sets (Triandis, 1994). Differences in response sets and bias across samples may very well be due to inherent cultural differences. In Asian cultures, for example, a tendency to respond neutrally to items might be related to cultural norms dictating modesty and cautious responses, whereas in Western culture, a tendency to use extreme responses may be related to norms that endorse individual expressiveness. Thus, researchers may do well to include a direct measure of socially desirable response tendency in a cross-cultural study to check for response bias in participants' answers.

Stage 4: Interpretation of Research Findings

Several challenges are related to the interpretation of cross-cultural research findings. Statistically significant differences in the mean scores between two countries may not reflect true differences in the constructs supposedly measured because the difference increases with the sample size as well as with the magnitude of the bias effect. In addition, interpretation of statistically significant differences as meaningful is problematic. To resolve this, researchers may do well to also report the effect size and proportion of the total variance accounted for by it (Cohen, 1988). In general, researchers do formulate conclusions about groups of people based on certain findings of cross-cultural comparisons that highlight differences that are prominent or salient. These conclusions may be prone to overgeneralizations reflecting artifacts of the research design (e.g., sampling).

In cross-cultural research, it is difficult to rule out all plausible alternative explanations. This is due to the nonrandom allocation of respondents and the lack of experimental control over cultural conditions that are considered independent variables. The effect of a postulated cultural factor is typically inferred post hoc on the basis of ethnographic descriptions, and researchers need to be aware of this when interpreting their findings.

One way open to eliminate the effects of irrelevant variables is statistical analysis (e.g., analysis of covariance or regression techniques). However, this is a poor alternative to proper experimental control (Cook & Campbell, 1979). Another way to rule out plausible alternative interpretations is to use more than one method of measurement. An example of this is a study by Marsh, Asci, and Tomas (2002). They used multitrait-multimethod analyses to demonstrate cross-cultural support for the convergent and discriminant validity of the Physical Self-Description Questionnaire (PSDQ) and the Physical Self-Perception Profile (PSPP) commonly used in sport settings (see chapter 12).

Future Research

As a starting point, we propose the implementation of a three-step framework to guide researchers in designing cross-cultural research in the context of sport. The framework includes

1. determining a particular area or phenomenon to investigate (e.g., group cohesion) using relevant theory,

2. deciding on a clear cultural framework (e.g., individualism–collectivism), and

3. formulating testable hypotheses within the theoretical framework by highlighting the sociocultural context in which the phenomenon is explored.

Let us use the example of group cohesion to illustrate the steps. In this case, we want to find out the relationship between group cohesion (task and social) and performance in football (soccer) in a cross-cultural study. First, we use an established group cohesion theory (Carron, Widmeyer, & Brawley, 1985; see also chapter 7) to guide our study. Second, we use a clearly defined individualism–collectivism dimension as our cultural framework. Third, we test the following hypotheses: (1) Athletes in a collectivist culture (i.e., China) value social cohesion (versus task cohesion) more than those in an individualist culture (i.e., United States); (2) task cohesion is strongly correlated with performance (Cox, 2002) in American athletes but social cohesion is not; (3) social cohesion is more highly correlated with performance among Chinese athletes than among American athletes; (4) the sociocultural variable of goal of sport achievement is a mediator in the group cohesion–performance relationship. This is followed by a collection of data from Chinese and American samples to test the hypotheses. The findings will enable us to draw conclusions on the relationship between group cohesion and performance in a cross-cultural context.

We recently reviewed the state of cross-cultural research in sport and exercise psychology from 1988 to 2004. Our review was based on 33 papers selected from the following eight journals: *International Journal of Sport and Exercise Psychology*, *Journal of Sport & Exercise Psychology*, *The Sport Psychologist*, *Research Quarterly for Exercise and Sport*, *Journal of Cross-Cultural Psychology*, *Journal of Sport Behavior*, *Perceptual and Motor Skills*, and *Journal of Comparative Physical Education and Sport*.

Our review has yielded numerous findings that can be used to accelerate and extend research endeavors in cross-cultural research, including the following. (1) The majority of the cross-cultural studies were empirical studies, using country as a proxy for culture (79%). (2) Areas studied included achievement motivation (Kim, Williams, & Gill, 2003), leadership styles (Chelladurai et al., 1988), the self (e.g., Marsh et al., 2002), and coach–athlete relationships (Jowett & Ntoumanis, 2003, 2004). (3) The studies exhibited nonequivalence of sample size and characteristics in comparisons of several cultural groups (e.g., Hale, James, & Stambulova, 1999). (4) The majority used quantitative methods of survey by questionnaire (94%), without any discussion of the items' conceptual equivalence when used in a different cultural context.

Researchers need to focus on areas that are likely to benefit from understanding of their cross-cultural underpinnings, such as coach leadership, team cohesion, motivational climates, self-perception, and morality. To take morality as an example, the research questions could include the following: Does participation in sport enhance character development? Does culture mediate the relationship between development of character and moral reasoning? A well-designed cross-cultural study can help us understand which cultural variables are responsible. Similarly, the roles played by the uniquely Chinese sport of tai chi (a sport that is characterized by slow, even, fluid motions and that emphasizes humans in harmony with nature) and the Western sport of track and field athletics (a sport that stresses the importance of humans' independence and ability to compete with and even overcome nature) in the development of moral reasoning and character can also be compared meaningfully in a cross-cultural study.

The growing interest in developing indigenous psychologies in non-Western countries in the 1990s comes as a reaction to Western dominance in psychology (Berry et al., 2002). It also represents a desire on the part of non-Western psychologists to address the limitations and criticisms of current cross-cultural research and their inability to comprehend all cultures of the world. What are indigenous psychologies? The plural form is used here because each cultural population needs to develop its own psychology. Enriquez (1990) and Kim (1990) define indigenous psychology as a system of psychological thought and practice that is rooted in a particular cultural tradition. Ho (1998) explains that indigenous psychology is characterized by the use of conceptions and methodologies associated exclusively with the cultural group under investigation.

The efforts and cooperation of some Western and non-Western researchers have brought about the emergence of indigenous psychologies for Asian cultures (Bond, 1986, 1996; Ko & Yang, 1991; Si, Chung, & Liu, 2003; Yang, 1999; Yang & Ho, 1988). Kim and Berry's (1993) text, *Indigenous Psychologies: Research and Experience in Cultural Context*, takes a step further and includes indigenous psychology studies from different parts of the world. The emphasis is on examining a particular sociocultural context and then drawing insights from it for a psychology that is rooted in that context. Such a direction may appeal to some sport psychology researchers.

Finally, given the global nature and dynamics of cultural diversity within sport (as exemplified by the Olympic Games and international competitions), it is important to consider strategies that can capture this diversity. One strategy is conducting cross-indigenous comparisons in different areas of sport psychology. Such comparisons not only highlight the differences in the sporting behaviors, motivations, and thought patterns of people from different cultural backgrounds, they can also discover their similarities. Using the derived etic approach, cross-cultural research in sport can truly contribute to the realization of the ultimate goal for psychology.

Practical Implications

This chapter has discussed the importance of quality cross-cultural research in sport. The findings of cross-cultural studies can have major implications for practice. Cross-cultural findings highlight not only the differences but also the similarities of particular sporting behaviors in dyadic and group relationships (e.g., team cohesion, coach–athlete and peer relationships) among various cultural groups under investigation. For example, if a cross-cultural study suggests an orthogonal (i.e., independent) relationship between ego and task orientation in goal achievement among athletes of one culture but a significant correlation between the same two variables among athletes of another culture, then appropriate interventions can be developed for each of these two groups by way of providing suitable and adaptive motivational sporting environments.

Moreover, if the results of another cross-cultural study indicate that athletes of different cultural groups prefer democratic versus autocratic but socially supportive coach leadership styles, applied sport psychologists can use this information to match actual coach leadership with the athletes' preferred coaching styles in an effort to create an environment that is more likely to maximize athletes' performance and satisfaction. This matching may prove crucial because more and more coaches from other countries are being hired to train athletes of different cultures; for example, Chinese coaches are working with elite athletes in European countries and Taiwanese athletes are working in tennis and track and field in the United States. Finally, knowledge relevant to supporting retired athletes in an individualist culture versus in a collectivist culture can enable us to make appropriate, timely, and integrated plans to prepare athletes for successful career transition.

All in all, we have pointed out the role that culture plays and how it can affect dyadic and group relationships in practical terms. This knowledge will increase sport psychology practitioners' sensitivity and effectiveness in their consultation work with athletes and coaches who come from different cultural backgrounds. The same knowledge can also increase sport administrators' and coaches' awareness as they make policy decisions regarding the training and long-term welfare of athletes. In this way, all parties benefit.

Summary

Cross-cultural psychology research requires an understanding of what constitutes this type of research, definitions of key terms, and popular frameworks. Culture, race, and ethnicity are commonly used terms, and although they have sometimes been used interchangeably, there are subtle differences among them. Two popular frameworks of cross-cultural studies are individualism-collectivism (I–C) and ecoculturalism. Although the I–C framework has been much criticized in recent years, the ecoculturalism approach has not been used extensively in psychology and especially in sport psychology.

The three basic goals of research in cross-cultural psychology are assessment of the similarities of human behaviors in different cultural contexts, assessment of the differences in human behaviors attributable to the cultural context, and exploration of human behaviors common to most cultural groups. The study of dyadic relationships and group dynamics in sport, when placed in proper sociocultural contexts, not only enables researchers to discover differences in sporting behaviors among cultural groups but also similarities.

Methodological concerns for cross-cultural research center on the issue of equivalence in measurements and psychological constructs when applied to people of different cultures. A literature review of cross-cultural studies in sport from 1988 to 2004 suggests that cross-cultural research is still in its infancy despite the increase in the number of papers published, and it also suggests that there have been some methodological problems. In this chapter, we propose a four-stage conceptual framework to help researchers become aware of methodological challenges and to guide them in conducting quality cross-cultural research in sport. Carrying out this research is paramount because the generated findings of cross-cultural studies can have vital practical implications for athletes, coaches, psychologists, technical-support staff, and sport administrators. Thus, research and practice are meaningfully linked together.

DISCUSSION QUESTIONS

1. What are the goals of cross-cultural studies in sport? Provide examples to illustrate main points.

2. Discuss the development of cross-cultural research in general psychology and in sport in particular.

3. What is central to the methodological concerns of cross-cultural research in sport psychology, and what steps do researchers need to take to ensure the quality of their studies?

4. Define *indigenous psychology* and discuss its relationship with cross-cultural psychology.

5. Which area in sport psychology do you think is the most promising for cross-cultural research and why?

6. Discuss the practical implications of findings of cross-cultural work on either coach–athlete relationships or achievement goal orientations in sport.

afterword

The endpiece to a text represents a chance to reflect, to look back on what has been achieved and, perhaps, what else could have been said. Normally this reflection is restricted to the contents of the book itself. However, on this occasion I thought it would be interesting to widen the scope of the endeavor, to use this opportunity to consider the recent history of sport psychology as manifest in this excellent collection of writings and to muse on any advances that may have been made. In particular, I was interested to evaluate where sport psychology currently stands in relation to the broad expanse of work described under the label of social psychology.

In assessing the advances made over recent years, two historical benchmarks came to mind. The first was Albert Carron's book, *Social Psychology of Sport* (Mouvement, 1980). His book was divided into five sections (Introduction, The Athlete, The Coach, The Team, The Spectator). Beyond the introductory chapter, the remaining eight chapters were The Athlete, Personality and the Athletes, Psychological Motivation and Athletic Performance, The Nature and Dynamics of Leadership, Coach–Athlete Interaction, The Group, Dynamics in Task Performing Groups, and Social Facilitation. This earlier text was very successful in reviewing material available at that time, but the sparsity of primary research in the 1970s as compared with the present day is immediately obvious, along with huge advances in both methods and theory.

Moving forward to the 1990s, Deirdre Scully and I put together a book specifically for psychologists called *Psychology in Sport* (Taylor & Francis, 1994), a text that presented the state of play in sport and exercise psychology framed within categories of knowledge as recognizable to the discipline as a whole. In the chapter dealing with the social psychology of sport, we set out to not only identify those areas of work that psychologists of any sort would be familiar with but also highlight the areas of investigation that we felt had been ignored or underinvestigated. At the end of the chapter we commented,

> Now the mood is shifting and, in common with social psychology as a whole, sport psychology is beginning to become more critical and self-reflective in recognition of the complexity of the social world. Sport psychologists are now

willing to recognise the need to develop research methodologies and theoretical frameworks which can cope with a higher level of sophistication (p.127).

Having spent time reflecting on the contributions to *Social Psychology in Sport* set against these earlier efforts, I firmly believe that the years have been more than kind. Not only have earlier expectations of progress been met, they have been exceeded in a way that would have seemed improbable even 10 years ago. As one unexpected consequence, I think it is now a much more daunting task to try to summarize the extant literature on the social psychology in sport settings in one volume, but this text has gone a long way toward achieving that goal and should be commended for both its breadth and its depth.

Without doubt, the applied focus of most of the research remains center stage. However, this focus does not detract from but actually enhances the significant theoretical contributions that so many of the chapters are able to make. Nowhere is this more apparent than in part I (relationships in sport), part II (coach leadership and group dynamics), and part III (motivational climate), where the level of scrutiny afforded to the role of coaches and their relationships with others, from so many varied yet complementary perspectives, is extraordinary. There were signs in the early 1990s that traditional barriers were being surmounted as sport psychologists strove to explore the subtleties of social behavior and experience in sport, but widespread evidence was hard to find. The present collection shows there is now more consistent testimony to the growing maturity of the subdiscipline. The range of methodologies that underpin the research on social influence and especially coach behavior is most impressive and invigorating, with qualitative and quantitative techniques combining to produce a solid foundation of knowledge.

Using these and other parts of the text as a guide, it would not be stretching a point to say that in certain fields, cutting-edge research on social behavior is now being carried out in sport settings above all others. I believe this work has great potential to enrich wider debates around the contingencies of leadership, interpersonal relationships, and social influence in many other contexts, and perhaps this is the next stage of development that now awaits exploitation.

To take a further example from the present volume, while general research on intragroup dynamics and processes has tended to stagnate somewhat within social psychology as a whole since the 1970s, in this volume we see novel and stimulating accounts of many aspects of small-group behavior (see, e.g., chapters on team cohesion, audience effects, and efficacy beliefs in groups). These accounts should now be made to resonate loudly and confidently across social psychology as a whole. In the present volume, this work is set squarely in the context of sport teams, but the implications for small groups well beyond the world of sport are enormous and are as yet untapped. The potential carryover to small-group dynamics in work settings should be immediately obvious to even the casual reader and it would seem remiss not to go the extra mile and generalize to other life domains.

At the risk of stretching a point, I would argue it may not be impudent to suggest that we may now have reached payback time. Sport psychology research has progressed to a stage where sport psychologists should legitimately feel empowered to go forth and educate the wider social psychological community, confident that their level of understanding is impressive and the research base is sufficiently robust to withstand the severest challenge from those who may still be inclined to look askance at this newcomer on the block.

In one domain this level of sophistication has long been apparent. Many of the contributions in part III confirm the minute level of scrutiny that now characterizes work on participation motivation, especially research associated with achievement goal theory and goal orientations. Without question this work is impressive in its level of detail, but at the same time when reading through the chapters that addressed this literature I was reminded of another comment from our earlier chapter in *Psychology in Sport:*

> To search for sovereign, grandiose theories with which to tie all loose ends together is to follow a false trail to enlightenment. This search goes against the grain of modern social psychology where multiple perspectives and the judicious employment of mini-theories and the development of multifaceted process models appear to be the order of the day (p. 128).

Without a shadow of a doubt, achievement goal theory goes a long way toward understanding aspects of motivation in sport, especially those relating to contextual influences on individual and collective goal orientations. However, perhaps it should be seen as only one of a number of complementary perspectives that in combination may help untie the tricky Gordian knot of participation motivation, and maybe there is a need to be rather less blinkered to alternative yet complementary perspectives that may progress our understanding.

As to the identity of those researching in this area, this book is also revealing of a more liberal or tolerant approach to methodological pluralism that has not always characterized sport psychology, and again this must engender optimism for the future. To explain, it is over 100 years since Norman Triplett first established the irrefutable fact that social psychology and sport psychology go together like the proverbial horse and carriage. It does not take great insight to confirm the truism that sport invariably involves social interaction and that sport and exercise are integral to our social lives, past and present, whether as participants, administrators, or spectators. Therefore, to think of one without the other is well nigh impossible. Despite these cold facts the number of sport psychologists who would define themselves as social psychologists or vice versa remains negligible.

In the 1890s, presumably Triplett did not give a second thought as to whether he should be identified as a sport psychologist or a social psychologist; he simply carried on with his work. In the process he developed a model of good practice in terms of action research, moving from observation to archival work and finally to a series of experimental studies that have stood the test of time remarkably well. Ironically, in keeping with one of social psychology's contemporary research priorities (social identity and intergroup behavior), latter-day psychologists are now far more preoccupied with social categorization and labeling, and it is unfortunate that so often these labels have not facilitated but instead have hindered the advancement of science.

This book is particularly refreshing because often it casts asunder these arbitrary assignations and makes explicit what have often been hidden links between the two subdisciplines. In the process it reveals an interesting landscape of activity, some of which is obvious and commonsensical, some more challenging to accepted wisdom. This is wholly in keeping with social psychology and its investigations of the human social condition.

The reasons for the ebb and flow of interest in particular topics becomes a topic of interest in its own right. In a book of this nature you would not expect to find all angles covered, and they are not. Traditionally those who have an interest in the social psychology in sport settings have tended to focus their attention in particular directions, and these hot spots continue to shine through in the text. At the same time there are interesting new fields that have developed rapidly over recent years, and it is encouraging to see the number of authors who are publishing in these areas, some old and revered, others new and, I would predict, soon to be revered.

Speaking personally, I encountered sport psychology fairly early in my academic career, having studied social psychology in the 1970s at Loughborough University and having lectured in social psychology since 1980 at Queen's University, Belfast. My first impression of sport psychology in the mid-1980s was of a subdiscipline that I knew precious little about, one that was immediately interesting and inspiring but that was partial and sustained by a small number of key players. As a team, it would have been characterized as star studded but with little else to bring in off the bench.

I was delighted to see from this book that some of the stars of sport psychology are still shining as brightly as ever, but what is equally impressive is the range of new talent that has appeared on the scene, building on existing strengths and also having the confidence to range ever wider across social psychology as a whole. The eclectic style of many of the newer contributors is refreshing and must serve as a huge compliment to the teaching of sport psychology in both sport science and psychology departments over recent years. Where previously there would have been gaping holes in terms of accumulated knowledge, now there appears to be a mentality that not only recognizes any field of psychology as having the potential for harvesting but that can also evaluate just what those fields may have to contribute.

As a consequence, I detect that there is no longer quite such a sense of isolation from general psychological business. Quite naturally, sport psychology still only presents an element of social psychology and there are tracts of business that remain untouched, but this is probably now through choice rather than ignorance. As one example, the vast social-psychological literature on social identity and intergroup behavior continues to attract relatively little attention within sport psychology, as is revealed in the contents of this volume. Personally, this has always struck me as anomalous. On the one hand, sport almost invariably involves making aspects of identity salient and in stage-managing intergroup conflict between teams, nations, or whomever, yet the sport literature seems only to concern itself with limited considerations such as spectators or fans and rarely players or athletes.

More generally, the varied field of social cognition continues to dominate social psychology, bringing it ever closer to cognitive psychology in an attempt to interpret processes of social representation. However, this preeminence does not entirely manifest itself in sport psychology's current priorities. Reflecting this trend, it is interesting how few chapters deal with social cognition's normal business, including heuristics and social construction, or how previous interest in topics such as causal attribution has now waned.

This observation is offered as a comment on current priorities, which, it may be fair to say, overall continue to place a higher priority on social behavior as manifest in performance related to sport and exercise than on social experience per se.

Some sections of the book that significantly depart from this trend come from parts IV and V. From the writings of James, Cooley, Mead, and Goffman through to the present day, social psychologists have continued to discuss the multifaceted nature of the self in social-psychological context. Topics have ranged across constructs including self-awareness, self-regulation, self-concept, self-schema, and self-esteem, with an increasing focus on cross-cultural concern. In truth, no strong consensus has ever emerged, nor is it likely to, around many of these constructs and, quite correctly, in the present volume these intriguing debates continue to be represented. The chapters brought together in part V are interesting not only in their diversity but also in the challenging way in which they address the notion of self in the context of sport. The insight that they bring and, more importantly, the opportunities that they open for future work, are immense and intriguing.

To end, I would argue that this book and its many and varied contributions will help mark the coming of age of sport psychology as related to the social world. With this in mind, one final comment from *Psychology in Sport* would seem germane. Reflecting on the need to recognize that greater sophistication was required to address the complexities of social behavior and experience, we wrote:

> Whether this recognition will act as a spur to future generations of sport psychologists, or as a discouragement, only time will tell (p. 128).

Judging by the contents of this book, time has told that the challenge has been met head on. Sport psychology has matured to a point where it can confidently announce that it has a great many interesting things to say not only to the world of sport but also to the wider psychological community. As a sign of this maturity it would be encouraging to see ever more sport psychologists making their mark within social-psychological circles, for example by regularly presenting at social psychology conferences and by publishing in related social journals. In time, perhaps the gesture will be reciprocated, but it is certain that the work is too significant to remain the sole preserve of sport. To use a sporting analogy, while a good team can play well at home, a great team can play even better away. Now may be the time to hit the road!

John Kremer, PhD
Queen's University, Belfast

references

Foreword

Martens, R. (1975). *Social psychology and physical activity*. New York: Harper & Row.

Chapter 1

Adios Becks? (2003). Retrieved September 16, 2003, from www.channel4.com/news/2003/04/week _3/24_beck. html.

Barnett, N.P., Smoll, F.L., & Smith, R.E. (1992). Effects of enhancing coach–athlete relationships on youth sport attrition. *The Sport Psychologist, 6*, 111-127.

Berscheid, E., & Reis, H.T. (1998). Interpersonal attraction and close relationships. In D. Gilbert, S. Fiske, G. Lindzey, & E. Aronson (Eds.), *Handbook of social psychology* (4th ed., pp. 193-281). New York: McGraw-Hill.

Berscheid, E., Snyder, M., & Omoto, A.M. (1989). Issues in studying close relationships: Conceptualising and measuring closeness. In C. Hendric (Ed.), *Close relationships* (pp. 63- 91). Newbury Park, CA: Sage.

Bradbury, T.N. (2002). Invited program overview: Research on relationships as a prelude of action. *Journal of Social and Personal Relationships, 19*, 571-600.

Burke, M. (2001). Obeying until it hurts: Coach–athlete relationships. *Journal of the Philosophy of Sport, 28*, 227-240.

Chelladurai, P. (1990). Leadership in sport: A review. *International Journal of Sport Psychology, 21*, 328-354.

Conroy, D.E., & Coatsworth, J.D. (2004). The effects of coach training on fear of failure in youth swimmers: A latent growth curve analysis from a randomized, controlled trial. *Applied Developmental Psychology, 25*, 193-214.

Jordan, J., Kaplan, A., Miller, J.B., Stiver, I.P., & Surrey, J. (1991). Women's growth in connection: *Writings from the Stone Center.* New York: Guilford Press.

Jowett, S. (2003). When the honeymoon is over: A case study of a coach–athlete dyad in crisis. *The Sport Psychologist, 17*, 444-460.

Jowett, S. (2005). On enhancing and repairing the coach–athlete relationship. In S. Jowett & M. Jones (Eds.), *The psychology of coaching* (pp. 14-26). Leicester: British Psychological Society.

Jowett, S., & Chaundy, V. (2004). An investigation into the impact of coach leadership and coach–athlete relationship on group cohesion. *Group Dynamics: Theory, Research and Practice, 8,* 302-311.

Jowett, S., & Clark-Carter, D. (in press). Perceptions of empathic accuracy and assumed similarity in the coach–athlete relationship. *British Journal of Social Psychology.*

Jowett, S., & Cockerill, I.M. (2002). Incompatibility in the coach–athlete relationship. In I.M. Cockerill (Ed.), *Solutions in sport psychology* (pp. 16-31). London: Thomson Learning.

Jowett, S., & Cockerill, I.M. (2003). Olympic medallists' perspective of the athlete–coach relationship. *Psychology of Sport and Exercise, 4,* 313-331.

Jowett, S., & Meek, G.A. (2000). The coach–athlete relationship in married couples: An exploratory content analysis. *The Sport Psychologist, 14,* 157-175.

Jowett, S., & Ntoumanis, N. (2004). The Coach-Athlete Relationship Questionnaire (CART-Q): Development and initial validation. *Scandinavian Journal of Medicine and Science in Sports, 14,* 245-257.

Jowett, S., Paull, G., & Pensgaard, A.M. (2005). Coach–athlete relationship. In J. Taylor & G.S. Wilson, A*pplying sport psychology: Four perspectives* (pp. 153-170). Champaign, IL: Human Kinetics.

Jowett, S., & Timson-Katchis, M. (2005). Social networks in the sport context: The influences of parents on the coach–athlete relationship. *The Sport Psychologist, 19,* 267-287.

Kelley, H.H., & Thibaut, J.W. (1978). *Interpersonal relations: A theory of interdependence.* Canada: Wiley.

Kenny, D.A. (1995). Relationships science in the 21st century. *Journal of Social Personal Relationships, 12,* 597-600.

Kiesler, D.J. (1983). The 1982 interpersonal circle: A taxonomy for complementarity in human transactions. *Psychological Review, 90,* 185-214.

Kiesler, D.J. (1997). *Contemporary interpersonal theory research and personality, psychopathology, and psychotherapy.* New York: Wiley.

LaVoi, N.M. (2004, September). Dimensions of closeness and conflict in the coach–athlete relationship. Paper presented at the meeting of the Association for the Advancement of Applied Sport Psychology, Minneapolis, MN.

Mageau, G.A., & Vallerand, R.J. (2003). The coach–athlete relationship: A motivational model. *Journal of Sport Sciences, 21,* 883-904.

Miller, P.S., & Kerr, G.A. (2002). Conceptualising excellence: Past, present, and future. *Journal of Applied Sport Psychology, 14,* 140-153.

Miller, J.B., & Stiver, I.P. (1997). *The healing connection: How women form relationships in therapy and in life.* Boston, MA: Beacon Press.

Montgomery, B.M., & Baxter, L.A. (1998). Dialogism and relational dialectics. In B.M. Montgomery & L.A. Baxter (Eds.), *Dialectical approaches to studying personal relationships* (pp. 155-184). London: Erlbaum.

Muehlhoff, T.M., & Wood, J.T. (2002). Speaking of marital communication: The marriage between theory and practice. *Journal of Social and Personal Relationships, 19,* 613-620.

Newcomb, T.M. (1953). An approach to the study of communicative acts. *Psychological Review, 60,* 393-404.

Nielsen, J.T. (2001). The forbidden zone: Intimacy, sexual relations, and misconduct in the relationship between coaches and athletes. *International Review for the Sociology of Sport, 36,* 165-182.

Ogilvie, B.C. (1995). Consultation concerns when working with "best" athletes. In K.P. Henschen & W.F. Straub (Eds.), *Sport psychology: An analysis of athlete behavior* (3rd ed., pp. 287-302). Longmeadow, MA: Mouvement.

Olga Korbut—the gymnast, her coach, her rival and the president [television broadcast]. (2001). Retrieved September 16, 2003, from http://news.bbc.co.uk/sport1/hi/other_sports/1512051.stm. London: BBC Two.

Olympiou, A., Jowett, S., & Duda, J. (2005). The psychological interface between motivational climate and coach–athlete relationships. Manuscript under review.

Poczwardowski, A. (1997). *Athletes and coaches: An exploration of their relationship and its meaning.* Unpublished doctoral dissertation, University of Utah, Salt Lake City.

Poczwardowski, A., Barott, J.E., & Henschen, K.P. (2000, October 19). *The influence of team dynamics on the interpersonal relationships of female gymnasts and their coaches: A qualitative perspective.* Paper presented at AAASP 15th Annual Convention, Nashville, Tennessee.

Poczwardowski, A., Barott, J.E., & Jowett, S. (2006). Diversifying approaches to research on athlete-coach relationship. *Psychology of Sport and Exercise, 7,* 125-142.

Poczwardowski, A., Barott, J.E., & Peregoy, J.J. (2002). The athlete and coach: Their relationship and its meaning. Methodological concerns and research process. *International Journal of Sport Psychology, 33(1),* 98-115.

Poczwardowski, A., Henschen, K.P., & Barott, J. (1998, August 13). *Relationship issues in sports: A challenge for applied sport psychology at the threshold of the Third Millennium.* Paper presented at 24th International Congress on Applied Psychology, San Francisco.

Poczwardowski, A., Henschen, K.P., & Barott, J.E. (2001, October 4). *Phases and stages in athlete-coach relationship: A qualitative exploration of a female college gymnastics team.* Paper presented at AAASP 16th Annual Convention, Orlando, Florida.

Poczwardowski, A., Henschen, K.P., & Barott, J.E. (2002). The athlete and coach: Their relationship and its meaning. Results of an interpretive study. *International Journal of Sport Psychology, 33,* 116-140.

Reis, H.T. (2002). Action matters, but relationship science is basic. *Journal of Social and Personal Relationships, 19,* 601-612.

Rosenblatt, P.C. (1977). Needed research on commitment in marriage. In G. Levinger & H.L. Rausch (Eds.), *Close relationships: Perspectives on the meaning of intimacy* (pp. 73-86). Amherst, MA: University of Massachusetts Press.

Ruane, M.E. (2004, July 4). Coach is the force behind gold medal dreams. *Washington Post.* Retrieved November 8, 2004, from http://washingtonpost.com.

Smith, E.R. (2000). Research design. In H.T. Reis & C.M. Judd (Eds.), *Handbook of research methods in social and personality psychology* (pp. 17-39). New York: Cambridge University Press.

Smoll, F.L., & Smith, R.E. (1989). Leadership behaviors in sport: A theoretical model and research paradigm. *Journal of Applied Social Psychology, 19,* 1522-1551.

Waterman, A.S. (1993). Two conceptions of happiness: Contrasts of personal expressiveness (eudaimonia) and hedonic enjoyment. *Journal of Personality and Social Psychology, 64,* 678-691.

Wylleman, P. (2000). Interpersonal relationships in sport: Uncharted territory in sport psychology research. *International Journal of Sport Psychology, 31,* 555-572.

Chapter 2

Adie, J., & Jowett, S. (2006). Coach–athlete relationships and achievement goals. Manuscript under review.

Bowlby, J. (1969/1982). *Attachment and loss: Vol. 1. Attachment* (2nd ed.). New York: Basic Books.

Burke, M. (2001). Obeying until it hurts: Coach-athlete relationships. *Journal of the Philosophy of Sport, 28,* 227-240.

Drewe, S.B. (2002). The coach-athlete relationship: How close is too close? *Journal of Philosophy of Sport, 29,* 174-181.

Gilbert, W.D. & Trudel, P. (2004). Role of the coach: how model youth team coaches frame their roles. *The Sport Psychologist, 18,* 21-43.

Harter, S. (1999). *The construction of the self: A developmental perspective.* New York: Guilford Press.

Jowett, S. (2002). *The coach-athlete relationship questionnaire and dyad maps manual* (Research Monograph No. 1). Staffordshire, UK: Staffordshire University.

Jowett, S. (2003). When the honeymoon is over: A case study of a coach–athlete relationship in crisis. *The Sport Psychologist, 17,* 444-460.

Jowett, S. (2005). On repairing and enhancing the coach–athlete relationship. In S. Jowett & M. Jones (Eds.), *The psychology of coaching* (pp. 14-26). Leicester: British Psychological Society.

Jowett, S. (2006). Interpersonal and structural features of Greek coach–athlete dyads performing in individual sports. *Journal of Applied Sport Psychology, 18,* 69-81.

Jowett, S., & Carpenter, P. (2004, October). *Coaches' and athletes' perceptions of rules in the coach-athlete relationship.* Poster session presented at the Annual Conference of the Association of the Advancement of Applied Sport Psychology, MN.

Jowett, S., & Chaundy, V. (2004). An investigation into the impact of coach leadership and coach-athlete relationship on group cohesion. *Group Dynamics: Theory, Research and Practice, 8,* 302-311.

Jowett, S., & Cockerill, I.M. (2002). Incompatibility in the coach–athlete relationship. In I.M. Cockerill (Ed.), *Solutions in sport psychology* (pp. 16-31). London: Thomson Learning.

Jowett, S., & Cockerill, I.M. (2003). Olympic medallists' perspective of the athlete–coach relationship. *Psychology of Sport and Exercise, 4,* 313-331.

Jowett, S., & Clark-Carter, D. (in press). Perceptions of empathic accuracy and assumed similarity in the coach–athlete relationship. *British Journal of Social Psychology.*

Jowett, S., & Don Carolis, G. (2003, July). *The coach–athlete relationship and perceived satisfaction in team sports.* In R. Stelter (Ed.), XIth European Congress of Sport Psychology Proceedings (pp. 83-84). Copenhagen, Denmark: Det Samfundsvidenskabelige Fakultets.

Jowett, S., & Frost, T.C. (in press). Race and ethnicity in the all male coach–athlete relationship: Black footballers' narratives. *International Journal of Sport and Exercise Psychology.*

Jowett, S., & Meek, G.A (2000a). The coach–athlete relationship in married couples: An exploratory content analysis. *The Sport Psychologist, 14,* 157-175.

Jowett, S. & Meek, G. (2000b, May). *Outgrowing the family coach–athlete relationship: A case study.* Oral presentation at the International Conference on Sport Psychology organized by the Centre of Sports Science and Halmstad University, Sweden.

Jowett, S., & Ntoumanis, N. (2004). The Coach-Athlete Relationship Questionnaire (CART-Q): Development and initial validation. *Scandinavian Journal of Medicine and Science in Sports, 14,* 245-257.

Jowett, S., Paull, G., & Pensgaard, A.M. (2005). Coach–athlete relationship. In J. Taylor & G.S. Wilson, *Applying Sport Psychology: Four Perspectives* (pp. 153-170). Champaign, IL: Human Kinetics.

Jowett, S., & Timson-Katchis, M. (2005). Social networks in the sport context: The influences of parents on the coach–athlete relationship. *The Sport Psychologist, 19,* 267-289.

Jowett, S., Timson-Katchis, M., & Adams, R. (2005, March). *Too close for comfort: Narratives of the parent/coach–child/athlete relationship.* Symposium conducted at the Annual Conference of the British Psychological Society, Manchester, UK.

Kelley, H.H. (1979). *Personal relationships.* New Jersey: Erlbaum.

Kelley, H.H., & Thibaut, J.W. (1978). *Interpersonal relations: A theory of interdependence.* Canada: Wiley.

Neale, P.E., & Tutko, T.A. (1975). *Coaching girls and women: Psychological perspectives.* Boston: Allyn & Bacon.

Olympiou, A., Jowett, S., & Duda, J. (2006). The psychological interface between motivational climate and coach–athlete relationships. Manuscript under review.

Philippe, R.A. & Seiler, R. (2006). Closeness, co-orientation and complementarity in all male coach–athlete relationships: What male swimmers say about their male coaches. *Psychology of Sport and Exercise, 7,* 159-172

Rusbult, C.E., & Arriaga, X.B. (2000). Interdependence in personal relationships. In W. Ickes & S. Duck, *The social psychology of personal relationships* (pp. 79-108). Chichester, UK: Wiley.

Rusbult, C.E., Kumashiro, M., Coolsen, M.K., & Kirchner, J.L. (2004). Interdependence, closeness, and relationships. In D.J. Mashek, & A. Aron (Eds.), *Handbook of closeness and intimacy* (pp. 137-161). London: Erbaum.

Thibaut, J.W., & Kelley, H.H. (1959). *The social psychology of groups.* New York: Wiley.

Tomlinson, A. (1997). Male coach/female athlete relations: Gender and power relations in competitive sport. *Journal of Sport and Social Issues, 21,* 134-155.

Yambor, J. (1995). Effective communication. In K.P. Henschen (Ed.), *Sport psychology: An analysis of athlete behaviour* (pp. 383-391). Longmeadow, MA: Mouvement.

Yukelson, D.P. (2001). Communicating effectively. In J.M. Williams (Ed.), *Sport psychology: Peak performance to personal growth* (4th ed., pp. 135-149). Palo Alto, CA: Mayfield.

Chapter 3

Allen, J.B., & Howe, B.L. (1998). Player ability, coach feedback, and female adolescent athletes' perceived competence and satisfaction. *Journal of Sport & Exercise Psychology, 20,* 280-299.

Armour, N. (2001). On her own, Kwan takes gold gamble. Retrieved January 03, 2005 from www.press-enterprise.com/newsarchive/2001/10/24/1003900012.html.

Bateson, G. (1972). *Steps to an ecology of the mind.* New York: Ballantine.

Baxter, L.A. (1988). A dialectical perspective on communication strategies in relationship development. In S. Duck (Ed.), *Handbook of personal relationships: Theory, research and interventions* (pp. 257-273). Chichester, UK: Wiley.

Baxter, L.A., & Montgomery, B.M. (1998). A guide to dialectical approaches to studying personal relationships. In B.M. Montgomery & L.A. Baxter (Eds.), *Dialectical approaches to studying personal relationships* (pp. 1-16). Mahwah, NJ: Erlbaum.

Berscheid, E. (2001, April). *Relationships as developmental contexts: The biological, cognitive, and socio-emotional significance of dyadic processes.* Response presented at the meeting of the Society for Research on Child Development, Minneapolis, MN.

Bloom, G. (2002). Coaching demands and responsibilities of expert coaches. In J.M. Silva and D.E. Stevens (Eds.), *Psychological foundations of sport* (pp. 438-465). Boston: Allyn and Bacon.

Blumer, H. (1969). *Symbolic interactionism: Perspective and method.* Englewood, Cliffs, NJ: Prentice-Hall.

Canary, D.J., & Cupach, W.R. (1988). Relational and episodic characteristics associated with conflict tactics. *Journal of Social and Personal Relationships, 5,* 305-325.

Canary, D.J., Cupach, W.R., & Serpe, R.T. (2001). A competence-based approach to examining interpersonal conflict. *Communication Research, 28(1),* 79-104.

Chelladurai, P. (1984). Discrepancy between preferences and perceptions of leadership behavior and satisfaction of athletes in varying sports. *Journal of Sport Psychology, 6,* 27-41.

Chelladurai, P., & Riemer, H.A. (1992). Measurement of leadership in sport. In J. Duda (Ed.) *Advances in measurement in sport psychology* (pp. 227-253). Morgantown, WV: Fitness Information Technologies.

Chelladurai, P., & Saleh, S.D. (1980). Dimensions of leader behavior in sports: Development of a leadership scale. *Journal of Sport Psychology, 2,* 34-45.

Chelladurai, P., & Saleh, S.D. (1978). Preferred leadership in sports. *Canadian Journal of Applied Sport Sciences, 3,* 85 90.

Collins, W.A., & Laursen, B. (1992). Conflict and relationship during adolescence. In W. Hartup and C. Shantz (Eds.), *Conflict in child and adolescent development* (pp. 216-241). New York: Cambridge University Press.

Connelly, D., & Rotella, R.J. (1991). The social psychology of assertive communication: Issues in teaching assertiveness skills to athletes. *The Sport Psychologist, 5,* 73-87.

Côté, J., Salmela, J.H., Trudel, P., Baria, A., & Russell, S.J. (1995). The coaching model: A grounded assessment of expert gymnastic coaches' knowledge. *Journal of Sport & Exercise Psychology, 17,* 1-17.

Côté, J., & Sedgewick, W.A. (2003). Effective behaviors or expert rowing coaches: A qualitative investigation of Canadian athletes and coaches. *International Sport Journal, 7(1),* 62-77.

Covey, S.R. (1989). *The seven habits of highly effective people.* New York: Simon & Schuster.

Crick, N.R, & Rose, A.J. (2000). Toward a gender-balanced approach to the study of social-emotional development: A look at relational aggression. In K.E. Schlonick & P.H. Miller (Eds.), *Toward a feminist developmental psychology* (pp. 153-168). Florence, KY: Taylor & Francis.

Crocker, P.R (1990). Facial and verbal congruency: Effects on perceived verbal and emotional coaching feedback. *Canadian Journal of Sport Sciences, 15(1),* 17-22

Cross, S.E., & Madson, L. (1997). Models of the self: Self-construals and gender. *Psychological Bulletin, 122(1),* 5-37

Dale, G.A., & Wrisberg, C.A. (1996). The use of a performance profiling technique in a team setting: Getting the athletes and coach on the same page. *The Sport Psychologist, 10,* 261-277.

Deci, E.L., & Ryan, R.M. (1985). *Intrinsic motivation and self-determination in human behavior.* New York: Plenum.

Deci, E.L., & Ryan, R.M. (2000). The "what" and "why" of goal pursuits: Human needs and the self determination theory of behavior. *Psychological Inquiry, 11,* 227-268.

Delia, J.G., O'Keefe, B.J., & O'Keefe, D.J. (1982). The constructivist approach to communication. In F.E.X. Dance (Ed.), *Human communication theory* (pp. 147-191). New York: Harper and Row.

Deutsch, M. (1973). Conflicts: productive and destructive. In F.E. Jandt (Ed.), *Conflict resolution through communication.* New York: Harper & Row.

DeVito, J.A. (1986). *The interpersonal communication book* (4th ed.). New York: Harper & Row.

Eagly, A.H., Wood, W., & Diekman, A.B. (2000). Social role theory of sex differences and similarities: A current appraisal. In T. Eckes & H.M. Trautner (Eds.), *The developmental social psychology of gender* (pp. 123-174). Mahwah, NJ: Erlbaum.

ESPN.com. (2004, November 18). Johnson's time in Tampa appears to be over. Retrieved January 10, 2005, from http://sports.espn.go.com/nfl/news/story?id=1664796.

Fletcher, J.K. (1999). *Disappearing acts: Gender, power, and relational practice at work.* Cambridge, MA: MIT Press.

Gottman, J.M. (1994). An agenda for marital therapy. In L.S. Greenberg, & S.M. Johnson (Eds.), *The heart of the matter: Perspectives on emotion in marital therapy* (pp. 256-293). Philadelphia: Brunner/Mazel.

Gouran, D.S., Weithoff, W.E., & Doelger, J.A. (1994). *Mastering communication* (2nd ed.). Boston: Allyn and Bacon.

Greenleaf, C., Gould, D., & Dieffenbach, K. (2001). Factors influencing Olympic performance: Interviews with Atlanta and Nagano U.S. Olympians. *Journal of Applied Sport Psychology, 13,* 154-184.

Hargie, C.T.C., & Tourish, D. (1997). Relational communication. In O.D.W. Hargie (Ed.), *The handbook of communication skills* (2nd ed., pp. 359-382). New York: Routledge.

Hartup, W.W. (2001, April). *Relational antipathies.* Paper presented at the meeting of the Peer Pre-Conference, Society of Research on Child Development, Minneapolis, MN.

Hartup, W.W., & Laursen, B. (1993). Conflict and context in peer relations. In C.H. Hart (Ed.), *Children on playgrounds: Research perspectives and applications* (pp. 44-84). Albany, NY: State University of New York Press.

Heitler, S. (2001). Combined individual/marital therapy: A conflict resolution framework and ethical considerations. *Journal of Psychotherapy Integration, 11(3),* 349-383.

Horn, T.S. (2002). Leadership effectiveness in the sport domain. In T.S. Horn (Ed.), *Advances in sport psychology* (2nd ed., pp. 181-200). Champaign, IL: Human Kinetics.

Jehn, K.A. (1995). A multimethod examination of the benefits and determinants of intragroup conflict. *Administrative Science Quarterly, 40,* 256-282.

Jehn, K. 1997. A qualitative analysis of conflict types and dimensions in organizational groups. *Administrative Science Quarterly 42(3).*

Jehn, K.A., Northcraft, G.B., & Neale, M.A. (1999). Why differences make a difference: A field study of diversity, conflict, and performance in workgroups, *Administrative Science Quarterly, 44,* 741-763.

Jordan, J.V. (1995). *Transforming disconnection* (Working Paper No. 75). Wellesley, MA: Stone Center.

Jordan, J.V. (1997). *The healing connection.* Boston: Beacon Press.

Jordan, J.V., Kaplan, A.G., Miller, J.B., Stiver, I.P., & Surrey, J.L. (1991). Women's growth in connection: *Writings from the Stone Center.* New York: Guilford Press.

Jowett, S. (2003). When the honeymoon is over: A case study of a coach–athlete dyad in crisis. *The Sport Psychologist, 17,* 446-462.

Jowett, S., & Carpenter, P. (2004, September). *Coaches' and athletes' perceptions of rules in the coach–athlete relationship.* Poster presented at the meeting of the Association for the Advancement of Applied Sport Psychology, Minneapolis, MN.

Jowett, S., & Cockerill, I.M. (2002). Incompatibility in the coach–athlete relationship. In I.M. Cockerill (Ed.), *Solutions in sport psychology* (pp. 16-31). London: Thomson Learning.

Jowett, S., & Cockerill, I.M. (2003). Olympic medalists' perspective of the athlete–coach relationship. *Psychology of Sport and Exercise, 4,* 313-331.

Jowett, S., & Ntoumanis, N. (2004). The Coach–Athlete Relationship Questionnaire (CART-Q): Development and initial validation. *Scandinavian Journal of Medicine and Science in Sports, 14,* 245-257.

Laursen, B., & Bukowski, W.M. (1997). A developmental guide to the organization of close relationship. *International Journal of Behavior Development, 21,* 747-770.

LaVoi, N.M. (2004, September). *Dimensions of closeness and conflict in the coach–athlete relationship.* Paper presented at the meeting of the Association for the Advancement of Applied Sport Psychology, Minneapolis, MN.

Liang, B., Tracy, A., Taylor, C., Williams, L.M., Jordan, J.V., & Miller, J.B. (2002). The relational health indices: A study of women's relationships. Women's Quarterly, 26, 25-35.

Lyle, J. (2002). *Sports coach concepts: A framework for coaches' behaviour.* New York: Routledge.

Mageau, G.A., & Vallerand, R.J. (2003). The coach–athlete relationship: A motivational model. *Journal of Sport Sciences, 21,* 883-904.

Martens, R. (1987). *Coaches guide to sport psychology.* Champaign, IL: Human Kinetics.

Mehrabian, A. (1968). Communication without words. *Psychology Today, 2,* 53-55.

Miller, J.B. (1976). *Toward a new psychology of women.* Boston: Beacon Press.

Miller, J.B., & Stiver, I.P. (1997). *The healing connection: How women form relationships in therapy and in life.* Boston, MA: Beacon Press.

Montgomery, B. (1988). Overview. In S. Duck (Ed.), *Handbook of personal relationships: Theory, research and interventions* (pp. 233-238). Chichester, UK: Wiley.

Poczwardowski, A., Barott, J.E., & Henschen, K.P. (2002). The athlete and coach: Their relationship and its meaning. *International Journal of Sport Psychology, 33,* 116-140.

Poczwardowski, A., Barott, J.E., & Jowett, S. (2006). Diversifying approaches to research on athlete-coach relationships. *Psychology of Sport and Exercise, 7(2),* 125-142.

Potrac, P., Brewer, C., Jones, R., Armour, K., & Hoff, J. (2000). Toward a holistic understanding of the coaching process. *Quest, 52,* 186-199.

Portrac, P., Jones, R.L., & Armour, K.M, (2002). It's about getting respect: The coaching behaviors of an expert English soccer coach. *Sport, Education and Society, 7,* 183-202.

Rahim, M. (2002). Toward a theory of managing organizational conflict. *International Journal of Conflict Management 13(3),* 206-235.

Rahim, M., & Bonoma, T.V. (1979). Managing organizational conflict: A model for diagnosis and intervention. *Psychological Reports, 44,* 1323-1344.

Reis, H.T., Capobianco, A., & Tsai, F. (2002). Finding the person in personal relationships. *Journal of Personality, 70,* 813-850.

Reis, H.T., Collins, W.A., & Berscheid, E. (2000). The relationship context of human behavior and development. *Psychological Bulletin, 126,* 844-872.

Riemer, H.A., & Chelladurai, P. (1995). Leadership and satisfaction in athletics. *Journal of Sport & Exercise Psychology, 17,* 276-293.

Roloff, M.E. (1987). Communication and conflict. In C.R. Berger & S.H. Chaffee (Eds.), *Handbook of communication science* (pp. 484-534). Newbury Park, CA: Sage.

Ryan, R., & Deci, E. (2001). On happiness and human potentials: A review of research on hedonic and eudaimonic well-being. *Annual Review of Psychology, 52,* 141-166.

Singer, R.N., Hausenblaus, H.A., Janelle, C.M. (2001). *Handbook of sport psychology* (2nd ed.). New York: Wiley

Slack, T. (1997). *Understanding sport organizations: The application of organization theory.* Champaign, IL: Human Kinetics.

Smith, R.E., Smoll, R.L., & Hunt, E.B. (1977). A system for the behavioral assessment of athletic coaches. *Research Quarterly, 48,* 401-407.

Starkes, J.L., Helsen, W., & Jack, R. (2001). Expert performance in sport. In R.N. Singer, H.A. Hausenblas, & C.M. Janelle (Eds.), *Handbook of sport psychology* (2nd ed., pp. 174-201). New York: Wiley.

Steinberg, L. (1990). Interdependency in the family: Autonomy, conflict and harmony in the parent–adolescent relationship. In S. Feldman & G. Elliot (Eds.), *At the threshold: The developing adolescent* (pp. 255-276). Cambridge, MA: Harvard University Press.

Sternberg, R. (1998). Abilities are forms of developing expertise. *Educational Researcher, 3,* 22-35.

Sternberg, R.J. (1999). Intelligence as developing expertise. *Contemporary Educational Psychology, 24(4),* 359-375.

Vealey, R.S. (2005). *Coaching for the inner edge.* Morgantown, WV: Fitness Information Technologies.

Vogel-Bauer, S. (2003). Maintaining family relationships. In D.J. Canary & M. Dainton (Eds.), *Maintaining relationships through communication* (pp. 31-49). Mahwah, NJ: Erlbaum.

Waltman, M.S. (Spring, 2002). Developments in constructivist work in communication students, psychology, and education: Introduction to the special section on constructivism. *American Communication Journal, 5(3).*

Weinberg, R., & Gould, D. (2003). Communication. In R. Weinberg & D. Gould (Eds.) *Foundations of Sport and Exercise Psychology* (3rd ed, pp. 220-237). Champaign, IL: Human Kinetics.

Williams, J.M. (ed.). (2006). *Applied Sport Psychology* (5th ed.). Mountain View, CA: Mayfield.

Wilmot, W.W., & Hocker, J.L. (1998). *Interpersonal conflict* (5th ed.). New York: McGraw-Hill.

Wooden, J. & Jaimeson, S. (1997). *Wooden: A lifetime of observations and reflections on and off the court.* Chicago, IL: Contemporary Books.

Zadra, D. (2005). Dan Zadra quotes. Retrieved January 05, 2005, from www.quotationspage.com/quotes/Dan_Zadra.

Chapter 4

Adler, P.A., Kless, S.J., & Adler, P. (1992). Socialization to gender roles: Popularity among elementary school boys and girls. *Sociology of Education, 65,* 169-187.

Ainsworth, M.D.S. (1967). *Infancy in Uganda: Infant care and the growth of love.* Baltimore: Johns Hopkins Press.

Ainsworth, M.D.S., Blehar, M.C., Waters, E., & Wall, S. (1978). *Patterns of attachment: A psychological study of the strange situation.* Hillsdale, NJ: Erlbaum.

Allen, J.B. (2003). Social motivation in youth sport. *Journal of Sport & Exercise Psychology, 25,* 551-567.

Bandura, A. (1986). *Social foundations of thought and action: A social cognitive theory.* Englewood Cliffs, NJ: Prentice Hall.

Berndt, T.J. (2004). Friendship and the three A's (aggression, Adjustment, and attachment). *Journal of Experimental Child Psychology, 88,* 1-4.

Berndt, T.J., & Ladd, G.W. (Eds.). (1989). *Peer relationships in child development.* New York: Wiley.

Bigelow, B.J., Lewko, J.H., & Salhani, L. (1989). Sport-involved children's friendship expectations. *Journal of Sport & Exercise Psychology, 11,* 152-160.

Bowlby, J. (1973). *Attachment and loss. Vol. 2: Separation: Anxiety and anger.* New York: Basic Books.

Bowlby, J. (1982). *Attachment and loss. Vol. 1: Attachment* (2nd ed.). New York: Basic Books.

Brawley, L.R. (1993). The practicality of using social psychological theories for exercise and health research and intervention. *Journal of Applied Sport Psychology, 5,* 99-115.

Brown, B.A., Frankel, B.G., & Fennell, M.P. (1989). Hugs or shrugs: Parental and peer influence on continuity of involvement in sport by female adolescents. *Sex Roles, 20,* 397-412.

Brustad, R.J., Babkes, M.L., & Smith, A.L. (2001). Youth in sport: Psychological considerations. In R.N. Singer, H.A. Hausenblas, & C.M. Janelle (Eds.), *Handbook of sport psychology* (2nd ed., pp. 604-635). New York: Wiley.

Brustad, R.J., & Partridge, J.A. (2002). Parental and peer influence on children's psychosocial development through sport. In F.L. Smoll & R.E. Smith (Eds.), *Children and youth in sport: A biopsychosocial perspective* (2nd ed., pp. 187-210). Dubuque, IA: Kendall/Hunt.

Buchanan, H.T., Blankenbaker, J., & Cotten, D. (1976). Academic and athletic ability as popularity factors in elementary school children. *Research Quarterly, 47,* 320-325.

Buhrmann, H.G., & Bratton, R.D. (1977). Athletic participation and status of Alberta high school girls. *International Review of Sport Sociology, 12,* 57-69.

Bukowski, W.M., & Hoza, B. (1989). Popularity and friendship: Issues in theory, measurement, and outcome. In T.J. Berndt & G.W. Ladd (Eds.), *Peer relationships in child development* (pp. 15-45). New York: Wiley.

Bukowski, W.M., Hoza, B., & Boivin, M. (1993). Popularity, friendship, and emotional adjustment during early adolescence. In B. Laursen (Ed.), *Close friendships in adolescence* (pp. 23-37). San Francisco: Jossey-Bass.

Chase, M.A., & Dummer, G.M. (1992). The role of sports as a social status determinant for children. *Research Quarterly for Exercise and Sport, 63,* 418-424.

Coakley, J., & White, A. (1992). Making decisions: Gender and sport participation among British adolescents. *Sociology of Sport Journal, 9,* 20-35.

Cotterell, J. (1996). *Social networks and social influences in adolescence.* London: Routledge.

Crick, N.R., & Nelson, D.A. (2002). Relational and physical victimization within friendships: Nobody told me there'd be friends like these. *Journal of Abnormal Child Psychology, 30,* 599-607.

Eitzen, D.S. (1975). Athletics in the status system of male adolescents: A replication of Coleman's "The adolescent society." *Adolescence, 10,* 267-276.

Escartí, A., Roberts, G.C., Cervelló, E.M., & Guzmán, J.F. (1999). Adolescent goal orientations and the perception of criteria of success used by significant others. *International Journal of Sport Psychology, 30,* 309-324.

Evans, J., & Roberts, G.C. (1987). Physical competence and the development of children's peer relations. *Quest, 39,* 23-35.

Ewing, M.E., & Seefeldt, V. (1996). Patterns of participation and attrition in American agency-sponsored youth sports. In F.L. Smoll & R.E. Smith (Eds.), *Children and youth in sport: A biopsychosocial perspective* (pp. 31-45). Madison, WI: Brown & Benchmark.

Feltz, D.L. (1978). Athletics in the status system of female adolescents. *Review of Sport and Leisure, 3,* 98-108.

Fox, K.R. (2002). Self-perceptions and sport behavior. In T.S. Horn (Ed.), *Advances in sport psychology* (2nd ed., pp. 83-99). Champaign, IL: Human Kinetics.

Furman, W. (1993). Theory is not a four-letter word: Needed directions in the study of adolescent friendships. In B. Laursen (Ed.), *Close friendships in adolescence* (pp. 89-103). San Francisco: Jossey-Bass.

Furman, W. (1996). The measurement of friendship perceptions: Conceptual and methodological issues. In W.M. Bukowski, A.F. Newcomb, & W.W. Hartup (Eds.), *The company they keep: Friendship in childhood and adolescence* (pp. 41-65). New York: Cambridge University Press.

Gauze, C., Bukowski, W.M., Aquan-Assee, J., & Sippola, L.K. (1996). Interactions between family environment and friendship and associations with self-perceived well-being during early adolescence. *Child Development, 67,* 2201-2216.

Gifford-Smith, M.E., & Brownell, C.A. (2003). Childhood peer relationships: Social acceptance, friendships, and peer networks. *Journal of School Psychology, 41,* 235-284.

Haan, N. (1978). Two moralities in action contexts: Relationship to thought, ego regulation, and development. *Journal of Personality and Social Psychology, 36,* 286-305.

Hartup, W.W. (1996). The company they keep: Friendships and their developmental significance. *Child Development, 67,* 1-13.

Horn, T.S. (2004). Developmental perspectives on self-perceptions in children and adolescents. In M.R. Weiss (Ed.), *Developmental sport and exercise psychology: A lifespan perspective* (pp. 101-143). Morgantown, WV: Fitness Information Technology.

Horn, T.S., & Amorose, A.J. (1998). Sources of competence information. In J.L. Duda (Ed.), *Advances in sport and exercise psychology measurement* (pp. 49-63). Morgantown, WV: Fitness Information Technology.

Kane, M.J. (1988). The female athletic role as a status determinant within the social systems of high school adolescents. *Adolescence, 23,* 253-264.

Kerns, K.A. (1996). Individual differences in friendship quality: Links to child–mother attachment. In W.M. Bukowski, A.F. Newcomb, & W.W. Hartup (Eds.), *The company they keep: Friendship in childhood and adolescence* (pp. 137-157). New York: Cambridge University Press.

Kohlberg, L. (1969). Stage and sequence: The cognitive-developmental approach to socialization. In D. Goslin (Ed.), *Handbook of socialization theory and research* (pp. 347-480). Chicago: Rand McNally.

Kunesh, M.A., Hasbrook, C.A., & Lewthwaite, R. (1992). Physical activity socialization: Peer interactions and affective responses among a sample of sixth grade girls. *Sociology of Sport Journal, 9,* 385-396.

Maassen, G.H., van der Linden, J.L., Goossens, F.A., & Bokhorst, J. (2000). A ratings-based approach to two-dimensional sociometric status determination. In A.H.N. Cillessen & W.M. Bukowski (Eds.), *Recent advances in the measurement of acceptance and rejection in the peer system* (pp. 55-73). San Francisco: Jossey-Bass.

Martin, J.J., & Smith, K. (2002). Friendship quality in youth disability sport: Perceptions of a best friend. *Adapted Physical Activity Quarterly, 19,* 472-482.

Mugno, D.A., & Feltz, D.L. (1985). The social learning of aggression in youth football in the United States. *Canadian Journal of Applied Sport Sciences, 10,* 26-35.

Parke, R.D., & O'Neil, R. (1999). Social relationships across contexts: Family-peer linkages. In W.A. Collins & B. Laursen (Eds.), *Relationships as developmental contexts: The Minnesota symposia on child psychology* (Vol. 30, pp. 211-239). Mahwah, NJ: Erlbaum.

Parker, J.G., & Asher, S.R. (1993). Friendship and friendship quality in middle childhood: Links with peer group acceptance and feelings of loneliness and social dissatisfaction. *Developmental Psychology, 29,* 611-621.

Passer, M.W., & Wilson, B.J. (2002). Motivational, emotional, and cognitive determinants of children's age-readiness for competition. In F.L. Smoll & R.E. Smith (Eds.), *Children and youth in sport: A biopsychosocial perspective* (pp. 83-103). Dubuque, IA: Kendall/Hunt.

Patrick, H., Ryan, A.M., Alfeld-Liro, C., Fredricks, J.A., Hruda, L.Z., & Eccles, J.S. (1999). Adolescents' commitment to developing talent: The role of peers in continuing motivation for sports and the arts. *Journal of Youth and Adolescence, 28,* 741-763.

Piaget, J. (1965). *The moral judgment of the child.* Glencoe, IL: Free Press.

Rubin, K.H., Bukowski, W., & Parker, J.G. (1998). Peer interactions, relationships, and groups. In N. Eisenberg (Ed.), *Handbook of child psychology* (5th ed., Vol. 3, pp. 619-700). New York: Wiley.

Scanlan, T.K., Stein, G.L., & Ravizza, K. (1989). An in-depth study of former elite figure skaters: II. Sources of enjoyment. *Journal of Sport & Exercise Psychology, 11,* 65-83.

Schneider, B.H., Atkinson, L., & Tardif, C. (2001). Child–parent attachment and children's peer relations: A quantitative review. *Developmental Psychology, 37,* 86-100.

Shantz, C.U., & Hartup, W.W. (Eds.). (1992). *Conflict in child and adolescent development.* New York: Cambridge University Press.

Sheridan, S.M., Buhs, E.S., & Warnes, E.D. (2003). Childhood peer relationships in context. *Journal of School Psychology, 41,* 285-292.

Shields, D.L.L., & Bredemeier, B.J.L. (1995). *Character development and physical activity.* Champaign, IL: Human Kinetics.

Smith, A.L. (1999). Perceptions of peer relationships and physical activity participation in early adolescence. *Journal of Sport & Exercise Psychology, 21,* 329-350.

Smith, A.L. (2003). Peer relationships in physical activity contexts: A road less traveled in youth sport and exercise psychology research. *Psychology of Sport and Exercise, 4,* 25-39.

Smith, M.D. (1974). Significant others' influence on the assaultive behavior of young hockey players. *International Review of Sport Sociology, 3,* 45-56.

Stephens, D.E. (2001). Predictors of aggressive tendencies in girls' basketball: An examination of beginning and advanced participants in a summer skills camp. *Research Quarterly for Exercise and Sport, 72,* 257-266.

Stuart, M.E., & Ebbeck, V. (1995). The influence of perceived social approval on moral development in youth sport. *Pediatric Exercise Science, 7,* 270-280.

Stuntz, C.P., & Weiss, M.R. (2003). Influence of social goal orientations and peers on unsportsmanlike play. *Research Quarterly for Exercise and Sport, 74,* 421-435.

Sullivan, H.S. (1953). *The interpersonal theory of psychiatry.* New York: Norton.

Treasure, D.C. (2001). Enhancing young people's motivation in youth sport: An achievement goal approach. In G.C. Roberts (Ed.), *Advances in motivation in sport and exercise* (pp. 79-100). Champaign, IL: Human Kinetics.

Ullrich-French, S., & Smith, A.L. (2006). Perceptions of relationships with parents and peers in youth sport: Independent and combined prediction of motivational outcomes. *Psychology of Sport and Exercise, 7,* 193-214.

Weimer, B.L., Kerns, K.A., & Oldenburg, C.M. (2004). Adolescents' interactions with a best friend: Associations with attachment style. *Journal of Experimental Child Psychology, 88,* 102-120.

Weiss, M.R., & Duncan, S.C. (1992). The relationship between physical competence and peer acceptance in the context of children's sports participation. *Journal of Sport & Exercise Psychology, 14,* 177-191.

Weiss, M.R., & Ferrer-Caja, E. (2002). Motivational orientations and sport behavior. In T.S. Horn (Ed.), *Advances in sport psychology* (2nd ed., pp. 101-183). Champaign, IL: Human Kinetics.

Weiss, M.R., & Petlichkoff, L.M. (1989). Children's motivation for participation in and withdrawal from sport: Identifying the missing links. *Pediatric Exercise Science, 1,* 195-211.

Weiss, M.R., & Raedeke, T.D. (2004). Developmental sport and exercise psychology: Research status on youth and directions toward a lifespan perspective. In M.R. Weiss (Ed.), *Developmental sport and exercise psychology: A lifespan perspective* (pp. 1-26). Morgantown, WV: Fitness Information Technology.

Weiss, M.R., & Smith, A.L. (1999). Quality of youth sport friendships: Measurement development and validation. *Journal of Sport & Exercise Psychology, 21,* 145-166.

Weiss, M.R., & Smith, A.L. (2002a). Friendship quality in youth sport: Relationship to age, gender, and motivation variables. *Journal of Sport & Exercise Psychology, 24,* 420-437.

Weiss, M.R., & Smith, A.L. (2002b). Moral development in sport and physical activity: Theory, research, and intervention. In T.S. Horn (Ed.), *Advances in sport psychology* (2nd ed., pp. 243-280). Champaign, IL: Human Kinetics.

Weiss, M.R., Smith, A.L., & Theeboom, M. (1996). "That's what friends are for": Children's and teenagers' perceptions of peer relationships in the sport domain. *Journal of Sport & Exercise Psychology, 18,* 347-379.

Weiss, M.R., & Stuntz, C.P. (2004). A little friendly competition: Peer relationships and psychosocial development in youth sport and physical activity contexts. In M.R. Weiss (Ed.), *Developmental sport and exercise psychology: A lifespan perspective* (pp. 165-196). Morgantown, WV: Fitness Information Technology.

Williams, J.M., & White, K.A. (1983). Adolescent status systems for males and females at three age levels. *Adolescence, 18,* 381-389.

Wylleman, P., De Knop, P., Ewing, M.E., & Cumming, S.P. (2000). Transitions in youth sport: A developmental perspective on parental involvement. In D. Lavallee & P. Wylleman (Eds.), *Career transitions in sport: International perspectives* (pp. 143-160). Morgantown, WV: Fitness Information Technology.

Youniss, J. (1980). *Parents and peers in social development.* Chicago: University of Chicago Press.

Zarbatany, L., Ghesquiere, K., & Mohr, K. (1992). A context perspective on early adolescents' friendship expectations. *Journal of Early Adolescence, 12,* 111-126.

Zimmermann, P. (2004). Attachment representations and characteristics of friendship relations during adolescence. *Journal of Experimental Child Psychology, 88,* 83-101.

Chapter 5

Bales, R.F., & Slater, P. (1955). Role differentiation in small decision-making groups. In P. Parsons and R.F. Bales (Eds.), *Family, socialization, and interaction process* (pp. 259-306). Glencoe, IL: Free Press.

Ball, J.R., & Carron, A.V. (1976). The influence of team cohesion and participation motivation upon performance success in intercollegiate ice hockey. *Canadian Journal of Applied Sport Sciences, 1,* 271-275.

Barrow, J.C. (1977). The variables of leadership: A review and conceptual framework. *Academy of Management Review, 2,* 231-251.

Bass, B.M. (1985). *Leadership and performance beyond expectations.* New York: Free Press.

Bass, B.M., & Aviolo, B.J. (1990). *Transformational leadership development: Manual for the Multifactor Leadership Questionnaire.* Palo Alto, CA: Consulting Psychologist Press.

Bauer, T.N. & Green, S.G. (1996). Development of leader-member exchange: A longitudinal test. *Academy of Management Journal, 39,* 1538-1567.

Berger-Gross, V. (1982). Difference score measures of social perceptions revisited: A comparison of alternatives. *Organizational Behavior and Human Performance, 29,* 279-285.

Berger-Gross, V. & Kraut, A.I. (1984). "Great expectations": A no-conflict explanation of role conflict. *Journal of Applied Psychology, 69,* 261-271.

Bryman, A. (1992). *Charisma and leadership in organization.* London: Sage.

Burns, J. (1978). *Leadership.* Mew York: Harper & Row.

Campbell, D.T. & Stanley, J.C. (1963). *Experimental and quasi-experimental designs for research.* Boston: Houghton Mifflin.

Chelladurai, P. (1978). *A contingency model of leadership in athletics.* Unpublished doctoral dissertation, University of Waterloo, Canada.

Chelladurai, P. (1984). Discrepancy between preferences and perceptions of leadership behavior and satisfaction of athletes in varying sports. *Journal of Sport Psychology, 6,* 27-41.

Chelladurai, P. (1990). Leadership in sports: A review. *International Journal of Sport Psychology, 21,* 328-354.

Chelladurai, P. (1993). Leadership. In R.N. Singer, M. Murphey, & L.K. Tennant (Eds.), *Handbook on research on sport psychology* (pp. 647-671). New York: MacMillan.

Chelladurai, P. (2001). *Managing organization for sport and physical activity: A systems perspective.* Scottsdale, AZ: Holcomb-Hathaway.

Chelladurai, P., & Carron, A.V. (1978). *Leadership.* Ottawa: Canadian Association for Health, Physical Education and Recreation.

Chelladurai, P., & Carron, A.V. (1981). Task characteristics and individual differences, and their relationship to preferred leadership in sports. In G.C. Roberts & D.M. Landers (Eds.), *Psychology of motor behavior and sport-1980* (p. 87). Champaign, IL: Human Kinetics.

Chelladurai, P. & Carron, A.V. (1983). Athletic maturity and preferred leadership. *Journal of Sport Psychology, 5,* 371-380.

Chelladurai, P., Imamura, H., Yamaguchi, Y., Oinuma, Y., Miyauchi, T. (1988). Sport leadership in a cross-national setting: The case of Japanese and Canadian university athletes. *Journal of Sport & Exercise Psychology, 10,* 374-389.

Chelladurai, P., Malloy, D., Imamura, H., & Yamaguchi, Y. (1987). A cross-cultural study of preferred leadership in sports. *Canadian Journal of Sport Sciences, 12,* 106-110.

Chelladurai, P., & Riemer, H.A. (1997). A classification of facets of athlete satisfaction. *Journal of Sport Management, 11,* 133-159.

Chelladurai, P., & Riemer, H.A. (1998). Measurement of leadership in sports. In J. Duda (Ed.), *Advances in sport and exercise psychology measurement* (pp. 227-256). Morgantown, WV: Fitness Information Technology.

Chelladurai, P., & Saleh, S.D. (1978). Preferred leadership in sports. *Canadian Journal of Applied Sport Sciences, 3,* 85-92.

Chelladurai, P., & Saleh, S.D. (1980). Dimensions of leader behavior in sports: Development of a leadership scale. *Journal of Sport Psychology, 2,* 34-45.

Chemers, M.M. (1997). *An integrative theory of leadership.* Mahwah, NJ: Erlbaum.

Child, J., & Tayeb, M. (1983). Theoretical perspectives in cross-national research. *International Studies of Management and Organizations, 12(4),* 23-70.

Conger, J.A. (1989). *The charismatic leader: Behind the mystic of exceptional leadership.* San Francisco: Jossey-Bass.

Cronbach, L. (1958). Proposals leading to analytic treatment of social perception scores. In R. Tagiuri & L. Petrullo (Eds.), *Person perception and interpersonal behavior.* (pp. 353-379) Palo Alto, CA: Stanford University Press.

Doherty, A. (1997). The effect of leader characteristics on the perceived transformation/transactional leadership and impact of interuniversity athletic administrators. *Journal of Sport Management, 11*, 275-285.

Doherty, A., & Danylchuk, K. (1996). Transformational and transactional leadership in interuniversity athletics management. *Journal of Sport Management, 10*, 292-310.

Dwyer, J.M., & Fischer, D.G. (1990). Wrestler's perceptions of coaches' leadership as predictors of satisfaction with leadership. *Perceptual & Motor Skills, 71*, 511-517.

Erle, F.J. (1981). *Leadership in competitive and recreational sport.* Unpublished master's thesis, University of Western Ontario, London, Canada.

Evans, M.G. (1970). The effects of supervisory behaviour on the path-goal relationship. *Organizational Behavior & Human Performance, 5(3)*, 277-298.

Fayerweather, J. (1959). The executive overseas. Syracuse, NY: Syracuse University Press.

Fiedler, F.E. (1967). *A theory of leadership effectiveness.* New York: McGraw-Hill.

Gabriel, L., & Brooks, D. (1986, October). *An investigation of the leadership behavior of selected NAIA and NJCAA women's tennis coaches.* Paper presented at the Annual Meeting of the North American Society for the Sociology of Sport, Las Vegas.

Garland, D.J., & Barry, J.R. (1988). The effects of personality and perceived leader behavior on performance in collegiate football. *Psychological Record, 38*, 237-247.

George, T. (1993, September 8). Victory to Redskins, but credit to Petitbon. *The New York Times,* B18.

Gordon, S. (1986). *Behavioral correlates of coaching effectiveness.* Unpublished doctoral dissertation, University of Alberta, Canada.

Halpin, A.W., & Winer, B.J. (1957). A factorial study of the leader behavior description. In R.M. Stogdill & A.E. Coons (Eds.), *Leader behavior: Its description and measurement* (pp. 39-51). Columbus: Ohio State University.

Helgeson, V.S., & Lepore, S.J. (1997). Men's adjustment to prostate cancer: The role of agency and unmitigated agency. *Sex Roles, 37(3/4)*, 251-267.

Hemphill, J.K. (1950). Leader behavior description. Columbus: Ohio State University.

Hemphill, J.K., & Coons, A.E. (1957). Development of the leader behavior description questionnaire. In R.M. Stogdill & A.E. Coons (Eds.), *Leader behavior: Its description and measurement (pp. 6-38).* Columbus: Ohio State University.

Hersey, P. & Blanchard, K. (1969). Life cycle theory of leadership. *Training & Development Journal, 23(5)*, 26-34.

Horne, T., & Carron, A.V. (1985). Compatibility in coach–athlete relationships. *Journal of Sport Psychology, 7*, 137-149.

House, R.J. (1971). A path-goal theory of leader effectiveness. *Administrative Science Quarterly, 16*, 321-338.

House, R.J., & Dressler, G. (1974). A path-goal theory of leadership. In J.G. Hunt & L.L. Larson (Eds.), *Contingency approaches to leadership* (pp. 29-55). Carbondale, IL: Southern Illinois University Press.

Huang, J.M., Chen, S., Chen, C.W., & Chiu, T.C. (2003). A study of perceived leadership styles, preferred leadership styles, and team cohesion of high school basketball teams in East Taiwan. *Missouri Journal of Health, Physical Education, Recreation & Dance, 13*, 38-46.

Jambor, E.A., & Zhang, J. (1997). Investigating leadership, gender, and coaching level using the Revised Leadership for Sport Scale. *Journal of Sport Behavior, 20*, 313-321.

Johns, G. (1981). Difference score measures of organizational behavior variables: A critique. *Organizational Behavior and Human Performance, 27*, 443-463.

Kahn, R.L. (1951). An analysis of supervisory practices and components of morale. In H Guetzkow (Ed.), *Groups, leadership and men: Research in human relations.* (pp. 86-89) Oxford, England: Carnegie Press.

Kang, B. (2003). *A comparison of preferred coaching leadership behaviors in selected sports by United States and Korean collegiate athletes.* Unpublished master's thesis, Ball State University.

Katz, D., & Kahn, R.L. (1951). Human organization and worker motivation. In L.R. Tripp (Ed.), *Industrial productivity.* (pp. 146-171) Madison, WI: Industrial Relations Research Association.

Kellerman, B. (1984). *Leadership: Multidisciplinary perspectives.* Englewood Cliffs, N.J.: Prentice-Hall.

Kim, B-H., Lee, H-K., & Lee, J-Y. (1990). *A study on the coaches' leadership behavior in sports.* Unpublished manuscript. Korea Sport Science Institute, Seoul.

Kuhnert, K.W., & Lewis, P. (1987). Transactional and transformation leadership: A constructive/developmental analysis. *Academy of Management Journal, 12*, 648-657.

Lam, T.C. (1996). *A comparison of the leadership behavior of winning and losing high school basketball coaches.* Unpublished master's thesis, Springfield College, MA.

Lewin, K., Lippet, R., & White, R.K. (1939). Patterns of aggressive behavior in experimentally created social climates. *Journal of Social Psychology, 10*, 271-301.

Lippet, R., & White, R.K. (1943). The social climate in children's groups. In R.G. Baker, J.S. Kounin, & H.F. Wright (Eds.), *Child behavior and development.* (pp. 485-508). New York: McGraw-Hill.

McCreary, D.R., & Korabik, K. (2000). Examining the relationships between the socially desirable and undesirable aspects of agency and communion. *Sex Roles, 43*, 637-651.

McMillin, C.J. (1990). *The relationship of athlete self-perceptions and athlete perceptions of leader behaviors to athlete satisfaction.* Unpublished doctoral dissertation, University of Virginia.

Nesselroade, J.R. (1994). Exploratory factor analysis with latent variables and the study of processes of development and change. In A. von Eye & C. Clogg (Eds.), *Latent variables analysis* (pp. 131-154). Thousand Oaks, CA: Sage.

Nieva, V., & Gutek, B. (1981). *Women and work: A psychological perspective.* New York: Praeger.

Osborn, R.N., & Hunt, J.G. (1975). An adaptive-reactive theory of leadership: The role of macro variables in leadership research. In J.G. Hunt & L.L. Larson (Eds.), *Leadership frontiers* (pp. 27-44). Kent, OH: Kent State University.

Pascale, R.T. (1978). Communication and decision making across cultures: Japanese and American comparisons. *Administrative Science Quarterly, 23*, 91-110.

Peele, S. (1981). Reductionism in the psychology of the eighties. *American Psychologist, 36*, 807-818.

Pizzi, J. (2002). *Measuring leadership styles and success of college basketball coaches.* Unpublished master's thesis, Springfield College, MA.

Posner, B. & Brodsky, B. (1992). A leadership development instrument for college students. *Journal of College Student Development, 33,* 231 – 238.

Riemer, H.A., & Chelladurai, P. (1995). Leadership and satisfaction in athletics. *Journal of Sport & Exercise Psychology, 17,* 276-293.

Riemer, H.A., & Chelladurai, P. (1998). Development of the athlete satisfaction questionnaire. *Journal of Sport & Exercise Psychology, 20(2),* 127-156.

Riemer, H.A., & Chelladurai, P. (2001). Satisfaction and commitment of Canadian university athletes: The effects of gender and tenure. *AVANTE, 7,* 1-13.

Riemer, H.A., & Toon, K. (2001). Leadership and satisfaction in tennis: Examination of congruence, gender and ability. *Research Quarterly for Exercise & Sport, 72,* 243-256.

Robinson, T.T., & Carron, A.V. (1982). Personal and situational factors associated with dropping out versus maintaining participation in competitive sport. *Journal of Sport Psychology, 4,* 364-378.

Ross, I.C., & Zander, A. (1957). Need satisfactions and employee turnover. *Personnel Psychology, 10,* 327-338.

Sashkin, M. (1988). The visionary leader. In J.A. Conger & R.N. Kanungo (Eds.), *Charismatic leadership: The elusive factor in organizational effectiveness* (pp. 122-160). San Francisco: Jossey-Bass.

Schliesman, E.S. (1987). Relationship between the congruence of preferred and actual leader behavior and subordinate satisfaction with leadership. *Journal of Sport Behavior, 10(3),* 157-166.

Schliesman, E.S., Beitel, P.A., & DeSensi, J.T. (1994). *Athlete and coach gender, leader behavior, and follower satisfaction in sport.* Unpublished manuscript, University of Tennessee, Knoxville, TN.

Serpa, S. (1990). *Research work on sport leadership in Portugal.* Unpublished manuscript, Lisbon Technical University, Portugal.

Serpa, S., Pataco, V., & Santos, F. (1991). Leadership patterns in handball international competition. *International Journal of Sport Psychology, 22,* 78-89.

Smith, R.E., Smoll, F.L., & Curtis, B. (1979). Coach effectiveness training: A cognitive-behavioral approach to enhancing relationship skills in youth sport coaches. *Journal of Sport Psychology, 1,* 59-75.

Smoll, F.L., Smith, R.E., Curtis, B., & Hunt, E. (1978). Toward a mediational model of coach–player relationships. *Research Quarterly, 49,* 528-541.

Spence, J.T., & Helmreich, R.L. (1978). *Masculinity and femininity: Their psychological dimensions, correlates, and antecedents.* Austin: University of Texas Press.

Spence, J., Helmreich, R., & Holahan, C. (1979). Negative and positive components of masculinity and femininity and their relationships to self-reports of neurotic and acting out behaviors. *Journal of Personality and Social Psychology, 37,* 1673-1682.

Summers, R.J. (1983). *A study of leadership in a sport setting.* Unpublished master's thesis, University of Waterloo, Canada.

Terry, P.C. (1984). The coaching preferences of elite athletes competing at Universiade '83. *Canadian Journal of Applied Sport Sciences, 9,* 201-208.

Terry, P.C., & Howe, B.L. (1984). The coaching preferences of athletes. *The Canadian Journal of Applied Sport Sciences, 9,* 188-193.

Trow, D.B. (1957). Anatomy and job satisfaction in task-oriented groups. *Journal of Abnormal & Social Psychology, 54,* 204-209.

Tsutsumi, T. (2000). *Players' and coaches' perceptions about leadership styles of successful women's basketball coaches.* Unpublished manuscript, Ball State University.

Vallerand, R.J., & Ratelle, C.F. (2002). Intrinsic and extrinsic motivation: A hierarchical model. In E.L. Deci & R.M. Ryan (Eds.), *Handbook of Self-Determination Research* (pp. 37-63). Rochester, NY: University of Rochester Press.

Vroom, V.H. (1959). *Some personality determinants of the effects of participation.* Englewood Cliffs, NJ: Prentice Hall.

Vroom, V.H. (1964). *Work and motivation.* New York: Wiley.

Wang, Y.T. (1997). *A comparison of the coach leadership behavior preferred by male and female track and field athletes.* Unpublished master's thesis, Springfield College, MA.

Weese, W.J. (1994). A leadership discussion with Dr. Bernard Bass. *Journal of Sport Management, 8,* 177-189.

Weiss, M.R., & Friedrichs, W.D. (1986). The influence of leader behaviors, coach attributes, and institutional variables on performance and satisfaction of collegiate basketball teams. *Journal of Sport Psychology, 8,* 332-346.

Yammarino, F.J., Dubinsky, A.J., Comer, L.B., & Jolson, M.A. (1997). Women and transformational and contingent reward leadership: A multiple levels of analysis perspective. *Academy of Management Journal, 40,* 205-222.

Yukl, G. (1971). Toward a behavioral theory of leadership. *Organizational Behavior and Human Performance, 6,* 414-440.

Zeller, R.A., & Carmines, E.G. (1980). *Measurement in the social sciences.* New York: Cambridge University Press.

Zhang, J., Jensen, B.E., & Mann, B.L. (1996). Modification and revision of the leadership scale for sport. *Journal of Sport Behavior, 20(1),* 105-122.

Chapter 6

Bales, R. F., & Slater, P. (1955). Role differentiation in small decision-making groups. In P. Parson & R.F. Bales (Eds.), *Family, socialization, and interaction process* (pp. 259-306). Glencoe, IL: Free Press.

Bandura, A. (1986). *Social foundations of thought and action: A social-cognitive theory.* Englewood Cliffs, NJ: Prentice Hall.

Barnett, N.P., Smoll, F.L., & Smith, R.E. (1992). Effects of enhancing coach–athlete relationships on youth sport attrition. *Sport Psychologist, 6,* 111-127.

Baron, R.M., & Kenny, D.A. (1986). The moderator-mediator variable in psychological research: Conceptual, strategic, and statistical considerations. *Journal of Personality and Social Psychology, 51, 1173-*1182.

Bem, D.J. (1983). Constructing a theory of the triple typology: Some (second) thoughts on nomothetic and idiographic approaches to personality. *Journal of Personality, 51,* 566-577.

Campbell, J.P. (1977). The cutting edge of leadership: An overview. In J.G. Hunt & L.L. Larson (Eds.), *Leadership: The cutting edge* (pp. 221-234). Carbondale, IL: Southern Illinois University Press.

Carmichael, B.D. (2002). *Children's perceptions of coaching style and their association with perceived competence, self-esteem, and anxiety.* Unpublished doctoral dissertation, California School of Professional Psychology, Berkeley/Almeda.

Chaumeton, N.R., & Duda, J.L. (1988). Is it how you play the game or whether you win or lose? The effect of competitive level and situation on coaching behaviors. *Journal of Sport Behavior, 11,* 157-173.

Chelladurai, P. (1984). Discrepancy between preferences and perceptions of leadership behavior and satisfaction of athletes in varying sports. *Journal of Sport Psychology, 6,* 27-41.

Chelladurai, P., & Carron, A.V. (1983). Athletic maturity and preferred leadership. *Journal of Sport Psychology, 5,* 371-380.

Coppel, D.B. (1979, April). *Children's reactions to recreational versus competitive emphases in youth sport programs.* Paper presented at the meeting of the Western Psychological Association, San Diego.

Curtis, B., Smith, R.E., & Smoll, F.L. (1979). Scrutinizing the skipper: A study of leadership behaviors in the dugout. *Journal of Applied Psychology, 64,* 391-400.

Dittes, J. (1959). Attractiveness of a group as a function of self-esteem and acceptance by group. *Journal of Abnormal and Social Psychology, 59,* 77-82.

Dweck, C.S. (1975). The role of expectations and attributions in the alleviation of learned helplessness. *Journal of Personality and Social Psychology, 31,* 674-685.

Dweck, C.S. (1999). *Self-theories and goals: Their role in motivation, personality, and development.* Philadelphia: Taylor & Francis.

Duda, J.L., & Hall, H.K. (2001). Achievement goal theory in sport: Recent extensions and future directions. In R. Singer, H. Hausenblas, & C. Janelle (Eds.), *Handbook of sport psychology* (2nd ed., pp. 417-443). New York: Wiley.

Eagly, A.H., & Johnson, B.T. (1990). Gender and leadership style: A meta-analysis. *Psychological Bulletin, 108,* 233-256.

Edwards, W. (1962). Subjective probabilities inferred from decisions. *Psychological Review, 69,* 109-135.

Elliott, A.J., & Church, M.A. (1997). A hierarchical model of approach and avoidance achievement motivation. *Journal of Educational Psychology, 72,* 218-232.

Ewing, M.E., Seefeldt, V.D., & Brown, T.P. (1996). Role of organized sport in the education and health of American children and youth. In A. Poinsett (Ed.), *The role of sports in youth development* (pp. 1-157). New York: Carnegie Corporation.

Feltz, D. (1978). Athletics in the status system of female adolescents. *Review of Sport and Leisure, 3,* 98-108.

Fiedler, F.E. (1967). *A theory of leadership effectiveness.* New York: McGraw-Hill.

Fishbein, M., & Ajzen, I. (1975). *Belief, Attitude, intention and behavior: An introduction to theory and research.* Reading, MA: Addison-Wesley.

Gould, D. (1984). Psychosocial development and children's sports. In J.R. Thomas (Ed.), *Motor development during preschool and elementary years* (pp. 212-235). Minneapolis, MN: Burgess.

Gould, D. (1987). Understanding attrition in children's sport. In D. Gould & M.R. Weiss (Eds.), *Advances in pediatric sport sciences* (pp. 61-85). Champaign, IL: Human Kinetics.

Graen, G., & Schiermann, W. (1978). Leader member agreement: A vertical dyad linkage approach. *Journal of Applied Psychology, 63,* 206-212.

Greendorfer, S.L., Lewko, J.H., & Rosengren, K.S. (2002). Family and gender-based influences in sport socialization of children and adolescents. In F.L. Smoll & R.E. Smith (Eds.), *Children and youth in sport: A biopsychosocial perspective* (pp. 153-186). Dubuque, IA: Kendall/Hunt.

Hersey, P., & Blanchard, K.H. (1977). *Management of organizational behavior* (3rd ed.). Englewood Cliffs, NJ: Prentice Hall.

Horn, T.S. (1985). Coaches' feedback and changes in children's perceptions of their physical competence. *Journal of Educational Psychology, 77,* 174-186.

Horn, T.S., & Hasbrook, C. (1984). Informational components influencing children's perceptions of their physical competence. In M.R. Weiss & D. Gould (Eds.), *Sport for children and youths* (pp. 81-88). Champaign, IL: Human Kinetics.

Jones, D.F., Housman, L.D., & Kornspan, A.S. (1997). Interactive decision making and behavior of experienced and inexperienced basketball coaches during practices. *Journal of Teaching in Physical Education, 16,* 454-468.

Komaki, J.L. (1986). Toward effective supervision: An operant analysis and comparison of managers at work. *Journal of Applied Psychology, 71,* 270-279.

Komaki, J.L., Zlotnick, S., & Jensen, M. (1986). Development of an operant-based taxonomy and observational index of supervisory behavior. *Journal of Applied Psychology, 71,* 260-269.

Krane, V., Eklund, R., & McDermott, M. (1991). Collaborative action research and behavioral coaching intervention: A case study. In W.K. Simpson, A. LeUnes, & J.S. Picou (Eds.), *The applied research in coaching and athletics annual, 1991* (pp. 119-147). Boston, MA: American Press.

Lennox, R.D., & Wolfe, R.N. (1984). Revision of the self-monitoring scale. *Journal of Personality and Social Psychology, 46,* 1349-1364.

Martens, R. (1977). *Sport Competition Anxiety Test.* Champaign, IL: Human Kinetics.

Martens, R. (1997). *Successful coaching* (2nd ed.). Champaign, IL: Human Kinetics.

Martens, R., & Gould, D. (1979). Why do adults volunteer to coach children's sports? In G.C. Roberts & K.M. Newell (Eds.), *Psychology of motor behavior and sport, 1978* (pp. 79-89). Champaign, IL: Human Kinetics.

McArdle, S., & Duda, J.K. (2002). Implications of the motivational climate in youth sports. In F.L. Smoll & R.E. Smith (Eds.), *Children and youth in sport: A biopsychosocial perspective* (2nd ed., pp. 409-434). Dubuque, IA: Kendall/Hunt.

Mischel, W., & Shoda, Y. (1995). A cognitive-affective system theory of personality: Reconceptualizing situations, dispositions, dynamics, and invariance in personality structure. *Psychological Review, 102,* 246-268.

Mischel, W., Shoda, Y., & Smith, R.E. (2004). *Introduction to personality: Toward an integration* (7th ed.). New York: Wiley.

Mitchell, T., & Biglan, A. (1971). Instrumentality theories. *Psychological Bulletin, 76,* 432-454.

Myers, D.G. (2005). *Social psychology* (8th ed.). Boston: McGraw-Hill.

Osborn, R.N., & Vicars, W.M. (1976). Sex stereotypes: An artifact in leader behavior and subordinate satisfaction analysis. *Academy of Management Journal, 19,* 439-449.

Rejeski, W., Darracott, C., & Hutslar, S. (1979). Pygmalion in youth sport: A field study. *Journal of Sport Psychology, 1,* 311-319.

Rise, J., Thompson, M., & Verplanken, B. (2003). Measuring implementation intentions in the context of the theory of planned behavior. *Scandinavian Journal of Psychology, 44,* 87-95.

Roberts, G.C., Treasure, D.C., & Kavussanu, M. (1997). Motivation in physical activity contexts: An achievement goal perspective. In M.L. Maehr & P.R. Pintrich (Eds.), *Advances in motivation and achievement* (Vol. 10, pp. 413-447). Greenwich, CT: JAI.

Scanlan, T.K. (2002). Social evaluation and the competition process: A developmental perspective. In F.L. Smoll & R.E. Smith (Eds.), *Children and youth in sports: A biopsychosocial perspective* (2nd ed., pp. 393-408). Dubuque, IA: Kendall/Hunt.

Scanlan, T.K., & Lewthwaite, R. (1984). Social psychological aspects of competition for male youth sport participants: I. Predictors of competitive stress. *Journal of Sport Psychology, 6,* 208-226.

Scanlan, T.K., & Passer, M.W. (1978). Factors related to competitive stress among male youth sports participants. *Medicine and Science in Sports, 10,* 103-108.

Scanlan, T.K., & Passer, M.W. (1979). Sources of competitive stress in young female athletes. *Journal of Sport Psychology, 1,* 151-159.

Shoda, Y., & LeeTiernan, S. (2002). What remains invariant? Finding order within a person's thoughts, feelings, and behaviors across situations. In D. Cervone & W. Mischel (Eds.), *Advances in personality science* (pp. 241-270). New York: Guilford.

Smith, R.E. (1999). The sport psychologist as scientist-practitioner: Reciprocal relations linking theory, research, and intervention. In R. Lidor & M. Bar-Eli (Eds.), *Sport psychology: Linking theory and practice* (pp. 15-34). Champaign, IL: Human Kinetics.

Smith, R.E. (2006). Understanding sport behavior: A cognitive-afective processing systems approach. *Journal of Applied Sport Psychology, 18,* 1-27.

Smith, R.E., & Smoll, F.L. (1983). [Sex differences in player perceptions and valence ratings of youth sport coaching behaviors]. Unpublished raw data.

Smith, R.E., & Smoll, F.L. (1990). Self-esteem and children's reactions to youth sport coaching behaviors: A field study of self-enhancement processes. *Developmental Psychology, 26,* 987-993.

Smith, R.E., & Smoll, F.L. (1997). Coach-mediated team building in youth sports. *Journal of Applied Sport Psychology, 9,* 114-132.

Smith, R.E., & Smoll, F.L. (2002). *Way to go, coach! A scientifically-proven approach to coaching effectiveness* (2nd ed.). Portola Valley, CA: Warde.

Smith, R.E., Smoll, F.L., & Barnett, N.P. (1995). Reduction of children's sport performance anxiety through social support and stress-reduction training for coaches. *Journal of Applied Developmental Psychology, 16,* 125-142.

Smith, R.E., Smoll, F.L., & Cumming, S.P. (2004). [Situationally-defined behavioral signatures in youth sport coaches]. Unpublished raw data.

Smith, R.E., Smoll, F.L., Cumming, S.P., & Grossbach, J.R. (2006). Measurement of multidimensional sport performance anxiety in children and adults: The sport anxiety scale-2. Manuscript submitted for publication.

Smith, R.E., Smoll, F.L., & Curtis, B. (1978). Coaching behaviors in Little League Baseball. In F.L. Smoll & R.E. Smith (Eds.), *Psychological perspectives in youth sports* (pp. 173-201). Washington, D.C.: Hemisphere.

Smith, R.E., Smoll, F.L., & Curtis, B. (1979). Coach effectiveness training: A cognitive-behavioral approach to enhancing relationship skills in youth sport coaches. *Journal of Sport Psychology, 1,* 59-75.

Smith, R.E., Smoll, F.L., & Hunt, E.B. (1977). A system for the behavioral assessment of athletic coaches. *Research Quarterly, 48,* 401-407.

Smith, R.E., Smoll, F.L., & Schutz, R.W. (1990). Measurement and correlates of sport-specific cognitive and somatic trait anxiety: The Sport Anxiety Scale. *Anxiety Research, 2,* 263-280.

Smith, R.E., Zane, N.W.S., Smoll, F.L., & Coppel, D.B. (1983). Behavioral assessment in youth sports: Coaching behaviors and children's attitudes. *Medicine and Science in Sports and Exercise, 15,* 208-214.

Smoll, F.L., & Smith, R.E. (1984). Leadership research in youth sports. In J.M. Silva & R.S. Weinberg (Eds.), *Psychological foundations of sport* (pp. 371-386). Champaign, IL: Human Kinetics.

Smoll, F.L., & Smith, R.E. (1989). Leadership behaviors in sport: A theoretical model and research paradigm. *Journal of Applied Social Psychology, 19,* 1522-1551.

Smoll, F.L., & Smith, R.E. (2005). *Coaches who never lose: Making sure athletes win, no matter what the score* (2nd ed.). Palo Alto, CA: Warde.

Smoll, F.L., & Smith, R.E. (2006). Development and implementation of a coach-training program: Cognitive-behavioral principles and techniques. In J.M. Williams (Ed.), *Applied sport psychology: Personal growth to peak performance* (5th ed., pp. 458-480). New York: McGraw-Hill.

Smoll, F.L., Smith, R.E., Barnett, N.P., & Everett, J.J. (1993). Enhancement of children's self-esteem through social support training for youth sport coaches. *Journal of Applied Psychology, 78,* 602-610.

Smoll, F.L., Smith, R.E., Curtis, B., & Hunt, E. (1978). Toward a mediational model of coach-player relationships. *Research Quarterly, 49,* 528-541.

Snyder, M., & Gangestad, S. (1986). On the nature of self-monitoring: Matters of assessment, matters of validity. *Journal of Personality and Social Psychology, 51,* 125-139.

Spielberger, C.D. (1966). Theory and research on anxiety. In C.D. Spielberger (Ed.), *Anxiety and behavior* (pp. 3-20). New York: Academic Press.

Stogdill, R.M. (1972). Group productivity, drive, and cohesiveness. *Organizational Behavior and Human Performance, 8,* 26-43.

Swann, W.B., Jr., Griffin, J.J., Predmore, S.C., & Gaines, B. (1987). The cognitive-affective crossfire: When self-consistency confronts self-enhancement. *Journal of Personality and Social Psychology, 54,* 881-889.

Tesser, A., & Campbell, J. (1983). Self-definition and self-evaluation maintenance. In J. Suls & A.G. Greenwald (Eds.), *Psychological perspectives on the self* (Vol. 2, pp. 1-32). Hillsdale, NJ: Erlbaum.

Triandis, H.C. (1977). *Interpersonal behavior.* Monterey, CA: Brooks/Cole.

Vroom, V.H. (1964). *Work and motivation.* New York: Wiley.

White, M.A. (1975). Natural rates of teacher approval and disapproval in the classroom. *Journal of Applied Behavior Analysis, 8,* 367-372.

Williams, J.M., Jerome, G., Kenow, L.J., Rogers, T., Sartain, T.A., & Darland, G. (2003). Factor structure of the Coaching Behavior Questionnaire and its relationship to athlete variables. The *The Sport Psychologist, 7,* 16-34.

Wylie, R.C. (1978). *The self-concept. Vol. 2: Theory and research on selected topics.* Lincoln, NE: University of Nebraska Press.

Zelli, A., & Dodge, K.A. (1999). Personality development from the bottom up. In D. Cervone & Y. Shoda (Eds.), *The coherence of personality: Social-cognitive bases of personality consistency, variability, and organization* (pp. 94-126). New York: Guilford Press.

Chapter 7

Bollen, K.A., & Hoyle, R. (1990). Perceived cohesion: A conceptual and empirical examination. *Social Forces, 69,* 479-504.

Brawley, L.R., Carron, A.V., & Widmeyer, W.N. (1987). Assessing the cohesion of teams: Validity of the group environment questionnaire. *Journal of Sport Psychology, 9,* 275-294.

Brawley, L.R., Carron, A.V., & Widmeyer, W.N. (1988). Exploring the relationship between cohesion and group resistance to disruption. *Journal of Sport & Exercise Psychology, 10,* 199-213.

Brawley, L.R., Carron, A.V., & Widmeyer, W.N. (1993). The influence of the group and its cohesiveness on perceptions of group-related variables. *Journal of Sport & Exercise Psychology, 15,* 245-260.

Bray, C.D., & Whaley, D.E. (2001). Team cohesion, effort, and objective individual performance of high school basketball players. *The Sport Psychologist, 15,* 260-275.

Butler, R.J., & Hardy, L. (1992). The performance profile: Theory and application. *The Sport Psychologist, 6,* 253-264.

Carron, A.V., Brawley, L.R., & Widmeyer, W.N. (1998). The measurement of cohesiveness in sport groups. In J.L. Duda (Ed.), *Advances in sport and exercise psychology measurement* (pp. 213-226). Morgantown, WV: Fitness Information Technology.

Carron, A.V., & Chelladurai, P. (1981). The dynamics of group cohesion in sport. *Journal of Sport Psychology, 3,* 123-139.

Carron, A.V., Colman, M.M., Wheeler, J., & Stevens, D. (2002). Cohesion and performance in sport: A meta-analysis. *Journal of Sport & Exercise Psychology, 24,* 168-188.

Carron, A.V., Hausenblas, H.A., & Eys, M.A. (2005). *Group dynamics in sport* (3rd. ed.). Morgantown: Fitness Information Technology.

Carron, A.V., & Hausenblas, H.A. (1998). *Group dynamics in sport* (2nd ed.). Morgantown: Fitness Information Technology, Inc.

Carron, A.V., Prapavessis, H., & Grove, J.R. (1994). Group effects and self-handicapping. *Journal of Sport & Exercise Psychology, 16,* 246-258.

Carron, A.V., & Widmeyer, W.N. (1996). *Team building in sport and exercise.* Workshop presented at the Association for the Advancement of Applied Sport Psychology, Williamsburg, VA.

Carron, A.V., Widmeyer, W.N., & Brawley, L.R. (1985). The development of an instrument to assess cohesion in sport teams: The group environment questionnaire. *Journal of Sport Psychology, 7,* 244-266.

Carron, A.V., Widmeyer, W.N., & Brawley, L.R. (1988). Group cohesion and individual adherence to physical activity. *Journal of Sport & Exercise Psychology, 10,* 119-126.

Cohen, J. (1969). Statistical power analysis for the behavioral sciences. New York: Academic Press.

Cohen, J. (1992). A power primer. *Psychological Bulletin, 112,* 155-159.

Donnelly, K.D., Carron, A.V., & Chelladurai, P. (1978). *Group cohesion and sport.* Ottawa: CAHPER Sociology of Sport Monograph Series.

Eys, M.A., & Carron, A.V. (2001). Role ambiguity, task cohesion, and task self-efficacy. *Small Group Research, 32,* 356-373.

Eys, M.A., Hardy, J., Carron, A.V., & Beauchamp, M.R. (2003). The relationship between task cohesion and competitive state anxiety. *Journal of Sport & Exercise Psychology, 25,* 66-76.

Gammage, K.L., Carron, A.V., & Estabrooks, P.A. (2001). Team cohesion and individual productivity: The influence of the norm for productivity and the identifiability of individual effort. *Small Group Research, 32,* 3-18.

Golembiewski, R. (1962). The small group. Chicago: University of Chicago Press. Hardy, J., Eys, M.A., & Carron, A.V. (2005). Exploring the potential disadvantages of high task cohesion in sport teams. *Small Group Research, 36,* 166-189

Granito, V.J., & Rainey, D.W. (1988). Differences in cohesion between high school and college football teams and starters and nonstarters. *Perceptual and Motor Skills, 66,* 471-477.

Gruber, J.J., & Gray, G.R. (1982). Response to forces influencing cohesion as a function of player status and level of male varsity basketball competition. *Research Quarterly for Sport and Exercise, 53,* 27-36.

Hausenblas, H.A., & Carron, A.V. (1996). Group cohesion and self-handicapping in female and male athletes. *Journal of Sport & Exercise Psychology, 18,* 132-143.

Jones, E.E., & Berglas, S. (1978). Control of attributions about the self through self-handicapping strategies: The appeal of alcohol and the role of underachievement. *Personality and Social Psychology Bulletin, 4,* 200-206.

Jowett, S., & Chaundy, V. (2004). An investigation into the impact of coach leadership and coach–athlete relationship on group cohesion. *Group Dynamics: Theory, Research and Practice, 8,* 302–311.

Kahn, R.L., Wolfe, D.M., Quinn, R.P., Snoek, J.D., & Rosenthal, R.A. (1964). *Organizational stress: Studies in role conflict and ambiguity.* New York: McGraw-Hill.

Kozub, S.A. (1993). *Exploring the relationships among coaching behavior, team cohesion, and player leadership.* Unpublished doctoral dissertation, University of Houston, TX.

Kozub, S.A., & McDonnell, J.F. (2000). Exploring the relationship between cohesion and collective efficacy in rugby teams. *Journal of Sport Behavior, 23,* 120-129.

Landers, D.M., & Lüschen, G. (1974). Team performance outcome and cohesiveness of competitive co-acting groups. *International Review of Sport Sociology, 9,* 57-69.

Lee, H. K., Kim, B. H., & Lim, B. J. (1993). The influence of structural characteristics on team success in sport groups. *Korean Journal of Sport Science, 5,* 138-154.

Locke, E.A., Shaw, K.N., Saari, L.M., & Latham, G.P. (1981). Goal setting and task performance: 1969-1980. *Psychological Bulletin, 90,* 125-152.

Lott, A.J., & Lott, B.D. (1965). Group cohesiveness as interpersonal attraction: A review of relationships with antecedent and consequent variables. *Psychological Bulletin, 64,* 259-309.

Mariotti, J. (2004, August 18). Dream team, fans deserve each other. *Chicago Sun-Times.* Retrieved August, 18, 2004, from www.suntimes.com/output/mariotti/cst-spt-jay18.html.

McKnight, P., Williams, J.M., & Widmeyer, W.N. (1991, October). *The effects of cohesion and identifiability on reducing the likelihood of social loafing.* Paper presented at the Association for the Advancement of Applied Sport Psychology Annual Conference, Savannah, GA.

Mills, T.M. (1984). *The sociology of small groups* (2nd ed.). Englewood Cliffs, NJ: Prentice Hall.

Munroe, K., Terry, P., & Carron, A. (2002). Cohesion and teamwork. In B. Hale & D. Collins (Eds.), *Rugby Tough* (pp. 137-154). Champaign, IL: Human Kinetics.

Orlick, T. (1986). *Psyching for sport.* Champaign, IL: Human Kinetics.

Paskevich, D.M. (1995). *Conceptual and measurement factors of collective efficacy in its relationship to cohesion and performance outcome.* Unpublished doctoral dissertation, University of Waterloo, Canada.

Paskevich, D.M., Brawley, L.R., Dorsch, L.R., & Widmeyer, W.N. (1995). Implications of individual and group level analyses applied to the study of collective efficacy and cohesion [Abstract]. *Journal of Applied Sport Psychology, 7,* S95.

Peterson, R. (2004, June 14). Party of five. Retrieved August 13, 2004, from www.nba.com/finals2004/blog.html.

Prapavessis, H., & Carron, A.V. (1996). The effect of group cohesion on competitive state anxiety. *Journal of Sport & Exercise Psychology, 18,* 64-74.

Prapavessis, H., & Carron, A.V. (1997). Sacrifice, cohesion, and conformity to norms in sport teams. *Group Dynamics, 1,* 231-240.

Prapavessis, H., Carron, A.V., & Spink, K.S. (1997). Team building in sport. *International Journal of Sport Psychology, 27,* 269-285.

Robinson, T.T. & Carron, A.V. (1982). Personal and situational factors associated with dropping out versus maintaining

participation in competitive sport. *Journal of Sport Psychology, 4,* 364-378. Spink, K.S. (1990). Cohesion and collective efficacy of volleyball teams. *Journal of Sport & Exercise Psychology, 12,* 301-311.

Stevens, D. (2002). Building the effective team. In J.M. Silva & D.E. Stevens (Eds.), *Psychological Foundations of Sport* (pp. 306-327). Boston: Allyn & Bacon.

Szreter, A. (2004, July 4). Greeks upset the odds again. Retrieved August 13, 2004, from www.euro2004.com/tournament/matches/round=1623/match=1059194/Report=rw.html.

Terry, P.C., Carron, A.V., Pink, M.J., Lane, A.M., Jones, G.J.W., & Hall, M.P. (2001). Perceptions of group cohesion and mood in sport teams. *Group Dynamics: Theory, Research, and Practice, 4,* 244-253.

Terry, P.C., Keohane, L., & Lane, H.J. (1996). Development and validation of a shortened version of the Profile of Mood States suitable for use with young athletes. *Journal of Sports Sciences, 14,* 49.

Voight, M., & Callaghan, J. (2001). A team-building intervention program: Application and evaluation with two university soccer teams. *Journal of Sport Behavior, 24,* 420-431.

Westre, K. R., & Weiss, M. R. (1991). The relationship between perceived coaching behaviors and group cohesion in high school football teams. *The Sport Psychologist, 5,* 41-54.

Widmeyer, W. N., Brawley, L. R., & Carron, A. V. (1990). The effects of group size in sport. *Journal of Sport & Exercise Psychology, 12,* 177-190.

Widmeyer, W.N., & DuCharme, K. (1997). Team building through team goal setting. *Journal of Applied Sport Psychology, 9,* 97-113.

Williams, P. (1997). *The magic of teamwork: Proven principles for building a winning team.* Nashville, TN: Thomas Nelson.

Yukelson, D. (1993). Communicating effectively. In J.M. Williams (Ed.), *Applied sport psychology: Personal growth to peak performance* (pp. 122-136). Palo Alto, CA: Mayfield.

Yukelson, D. (1997). Principles of effective team building interventions in sport: A direct services approach at Penn State University. *Journal of Applied Sport Psychology, 9,* 73-96.

Zaccaro, S.J., Blair, V., Peterson, C., & Zazanis, M. (1995). Collective efficacy. In J. Maddux (Ed.), *Self-efficacy, Adaptation, and adjustment* (pp. 305-328). New York: Plenum.

Chapter 8

Agnew, G.A., & Carron, A.V. (1994). Crowd effects and the home advantage. *International Journal of Sport Psychology, 25,* 53-62.

Aiello, J.R., & Douthitt, E.A. (2001). Social facilitation from Triplett to electronic performance monitoring. *Group Dynamics: Theory Research and Practice, 5,* 163-180.

Allport, F.H. (1920). The influence of the group upon association and thought. *Journal of Experimental Psychology, 3,* 159-182.

Andrisani, J. (2002). *Think like Tiger: An analysis of Tiger Woods' mental game.* New York: Penguin Putnam.

Baumeister, R.F. (1984). Choking under pressure: Self-consciousness and paradoxical effects of incentives on skillful performance. *Journal of Personality and Social Psychology, 46,* 610-620.

Baumeister, R.F. (1995). Disputing the effects of championship pressures and home audiences. *Journal of Personality and Social Psychology, 68,* 644-648.

Baumeister, R.F., & Cairns, K.J. (1992). Repression and self-presentation: When audiences interfere with self-deceptive strategies. *Journal of Personality and Social Psychology, 62,* 851-862.

Baumeister, R.F., & Steinhilber, A. (1984). Paradoxical effects of supportive audiences on performance under pressure: The home field disadvantage in sports championships. *Journal of Personality and Social Psychology, 47,* 85-93.

Blascovich, J., & Mendes, W.B. (2000). Challenge and threat appraisals: The role of affective cues. In J. Forgas (Ed.), *Feeling and thinking: The role of affect in social cognition* (pp. 59-82). Cambridge, UK: Cambridge University Press.

Blascovich, J., Mendes, W.B., Hunter, S.B., & Salomon, K. (1999). Social "facilitation" as challenge and threat. *Journal of Personality and Social Psychology, 77,* 68-77.

Bray, S.R., Jones, M.V., & Owen, S. (2002). The influence of competition location on athletes' psychological states. *Journal of Sport Behavior, 25,* 231-242.

Bray, S.R., & Martin, K.A. (2003). The influence of competition location on individual sport athletes' performance and psychological states. *Psychology of Sport and Exercise, 4,* 117-123.

Bray, S.R., & Widmeyer, W.N. (1995, September). *Athletes' perceptions of a home advantage in women's basketball.* Paper presented at the meeting of the Association for the Advancement of Applied Sport Psychology, New Orleans.

Bray, S.R., & Widmeyer, W.N. (2000). Athletes' perceptions of the home advantage: An investigation of perceived causal factors. *Journal of Sport Behavior, 23,* 1-10.

Bull, S.J., Albinson, J.G., & Shambrook, C.J. (1996). *The mental game plan: Getting psyched for sport.* Eastbourne, UK: Sports Dynamics.

Butler, R.J. (1996). *Sports psychology in action.* Oxford: Butterworth-Heinemann.

Butler, J.L., & Baumeister, R.F. (1998). The trouble with friendly faces: Skilled performance with a supportive audience. *Journal of Personality and Social Psychology, 75,* 1213-1230.

Clarke, S.R., & Norman, J.M. (1995). Home advantage of individual clubs in English soccer. *Statistician, 44,* 509-521.

Cohn, P.J., Rotella, R.J., & Lloyd, J.W. (1990). Effects of a cognitive-behavioural intervention on the preshot routine and performance in golf. *The Sport Psychologist, 4,* 33-47.

Collins, D., Jones, B., Fairweather, M., Doolan, S., & Priestley, N. (2001). Examining anxiety associated changes in movement patterns. *International Journal of Sport Psychology, 31,* 223-242.

Cottrell, N.B., Wack, D.L., Sekerak, G.J., & Rittle, R.H. (1968). Social facilitation of dominant responses by the presence of an audience and the mere presence of others. *Journal of Personality and Social Psychology, 9,* 245-250.

Courneya, K.S., & Carron, A.V. (1992). The home advantage in sport competitions: A literature review. *Journal of Sport & Exercise Psychology, 14,* 28-39.

Dashiell, J.F. (1930). An experimental analysis of some group effects. *Journal of Abnormal and Social Psychology, 25,* 190-199.

Dowie, J. (1982). Why Spain should win the World Cup. *New Scientist, 94,* 693-695.

Duffy, L.J., & Hinwood, D.P. (1997). Home field advantage: Does anxiety contribute? *Perceptual and Motor Skills, 84,* 283-286.

Easterbrook, J.A. (1959). The effect of emotion on cue utilization and the organization of behavior. *Psychological Review, 66,* 183-201.

Eysenck, M.W. (1992). *Anxiety: The cognitive perspective.* Hove, UK: Erlbaum.

Forsyth, D.R. (1999). *Group dynamics* (3rd ed.). Pacific Grove, CA: Brooks/Cole.

Goldberg, A.S. (1998). *Sports slump busting: 10 steps to mental toughness and peak performance.* Champaign, IL: Human Kinetics.

Greer, D.L. (1983). Spectator booing and the home advantage: A study of social influence in the basketball arena. *Social Psychology Quarterly, 46,* 252-261.

Hardy, J., Gammage, K., & Hall, C. (2001). A descriptive study of athlete self-talk. *The Sport Psychologist, 15,* 306-318.

Hardy, L., Jones, G., & Gould, D. (1996). *Understanding psychological preparation for sport: Theory and practice of elite performers.* Chichester, UK: Wiley.

Hockey, G.R.J., & Hamilton, P. (1983). The cognitive patterning of stress states. In G.R.J. Hockey (Ed.), *Stress and fatigue in human performance* (pp. 331-362). Chichester, UK: Wiley.

Jenas urges the fans to stick by Souness. (2005, February 7). *Newcastle Chronicle & Journal Ltd, 3.*

Jones, G. (1993). The role of performance profiling in cognitive behavioral interventions in sport. *The Sport Psychologist, 7,* 160-172.

Jones, M.V., Bray, S.R., & Bolton, L. (2001). Do cricket umpires favour the home team? Officiating bias in English club cricket. *Perceptual and Motor Skills, 93,* 359-362.

Jones, M.V., Mace, R.D., Bray, S.R., MacRae, A., & Stockbridge, C. (2002). The impact of motivational imagery on the emotional state and self-efficacy levels of novice climbers. *Journal of Sport Behavior, 25,* 57-73.

Jurkovac, T. (1985). *Collegiate basketball players' perceptions of the home advantage.* Unpublished master's thesis, Bowling Green State University, Bowling Green, OH.

Kerr, J.H., & Vanschaik, P. (1995). Effects of game venue and outcome on psychological mood states in rugby. *Personality and Individual Differences, 19,* 407-410.

Laird, D.A. (1923). Changes in motor control under the influence of razzing. *Journal of Experimental Psychology, 6,* 236-246.

Lavallee, D., Kremer, J., Moran, A., & Williams, M. (2004). *Sport psychology: Contemporary themes.* London: Palgrave.

Law, J., Masters, R.S.W., Bray, S.R., Eves, F., & Bardswell, I. (2003). Motor performance as a function of audience affability and metaknowledge. *Journal of Sport & Exercise Psychology, 25,* 484-500.

Malmo, R.B. (1959). Activation: A neuropsychological dimension. *Psychological Review, 66,* 367-386.

Martin, K.A., Moritz, S.E., & Hall, C.R. (1999). Imagery use in sport: A literature review and applied model. *The Sport Psychologist, 13,* 245-268.

Maynard, I.W., Hemmings, B., & Warwick-Evans, L. (1995). The effects of a somatic intervention strategy on competitive state anxiety and performance in semiprofessional soccer players. *The Sport Psychologist, 9,* 51-64.

McEnroe, J., & Kaplan, J. (2002). *Serious*. London: Little Brown.

Michaels, J.W., Blommel, J.M., Brocato, R.M., Linkous, R.A., & Rowe, J.S. (1982). Social facilitation and inhibition in a natural setting. *Replications in Social Psychology, 2,* 21-24.

Moore, J.C., & Brylinsky, J.A. (1993). Spectator effect on team performance in college basketball. *Journal of Sport Behavior, 16,* 77-84.

Moran, A.P. (1996). *The psychology of concentration in sports performers: A cognitive analysis*. East Sussex, UK: Psychology Press.

Moran, A.P. (2004). *Sport and exercise psychology: A critical introduction*. Hove, UK: Routledge.

Moran, A., Byrne, A., & McGlade, N. (2002). The effects of anxiety and strategic planning on visual search behavior. *Journal of Sports Sciences, 20,* 225-236.

Mullen, B., Bryant, B., & Driskell, J.E. (1997). Presence of others and arousal: An integration. *Group Dynamics, 1,* 52-64.

Neave, N., & Wolfson, S. (2003). Testosterone, territoriality, and the 'home advantage.' *Physiology and Behavior, 78,* 269-275.

Nevill, A.M., Balmer, N.J., & Williams, A.M. (2002). The influence of crowd noise and experience upon refereeing decisions in football. *Psychology of Sport and Exercise, 2,* 261-272.

Nevill, A.M., & Holder, R.L. (1999). Home advantage in sport: An overview of studies on the advantage of playing at home. *Sports Medicine, 28,* 221-236.

Nevill, A.M., Newell, S.M., and Gale, S. (1996). Factors associated with home advantage in English and Scottish soccer matches. *Journal of Sports Sciences, 14,* 181-186.

Noteboom, J.T., Barnholt, K.R., & Enoka, R.M. (2001). Activation of the arousal response and impairment of performance increase with anxiety and stressor intensity. *Journal of Applied Physiology, 91,* 2093-2101.

Noteboom, J.T., Fleshner, M., & Enoka, R.M. (2001). Activation of the arousal response can impair performance on a simple motor task. *Journal of Applied Physiology, 91,* 821-831.

Oxendine, J.B. (1970). Emotional arousal and motor performance. *Quest, 13,* 23-32.

Parfitt, C.G., Jones, J.G., & Hardy, L. (1990). Multidimensional anxiety and performance. In J.G. Jones and L. Hardy (Eds.), *Stress and performance in sport* (pp. 43-80). Chichester, UK: Wiley.

Parfitt, G., Hardy, L., & Pates, J. (1995). Somatic anxiety and physiological arousal: Their effects upon a high anaerobic, low memory demand task. *International Journal of Sport Psychology, 26,* 196-213.

Pollard, R. (1986). Home advantage in soccer: A retrospective analysis. *Journal of Sports Sciences, 4,* 237-248.

Prapavessis, H., Grove, J.R., McNair, P.J., & Cable, N.T. (1992). Self-regulation training, state anxiety, and sport performance: A psychophysiological case study. *The Sport Psychologist, 6,* 213-229.

Salminen, S. (1993). The effect of the audience on the home advantage. *Perceptual and Motor Skills, 76,* 1123-1128.

Schlenker, B.R., Phillips, S.T., Boniecki, K.A., & Schlenker, D.R. (1995). Championship pressures: Choking or triumphing in one's own territory? *Journal of Personality and Social Psychology, 68,* 632-641.

Schlenker, B.R., Weigold, M.F., & Hallam, J.R. (1990). Self-serving attributions in social context: Effects of self-esteem and social pressure. *Journal of Personality and Social Psychology, 58,* 855-863.

Schwartz, B., & Barsky, S.F. (1977). The home advantage. *Social Forces, 55,* 641-661.

Spence, K.W. (1956). *Behavior theory and conditioning*. New Haven, CT: Yale University Press.

Strauss, B. (2002a). Social facilitation in motor tasks: A review of research and theory. *Psychology of Sport and Exercise, 3,* 237-256.

Strauss, B. (2002b). The impact of supportive spectator behavior on performance in team sports. *International Journal of Sport Psychology, 33,* 372-390.

Taylor, S.E., & Brown, J.D. (1988). Illusion and well-being: A social psychological perspective on mental health. *Psychological Bulletin, 103,* 193-210.

Terry, P.C., Walrond, N., & Carron, A.V. (1998). The influence of game location on athletes' psychological states. *Journal of Science and Medicine in Sport, 1,* 29-37.

Thirer, J., & Rampey, M. (1979). Effects of abusive spectator behavior on the performance of home and visiting intercollegiate basketball teams. *Perceptual and Motor Skills, 48,* 1047-1053.

Thuot, S.M., Kavouras, S.A., & Kenefick, R.W. (1998). Effect of perceived ability, game location, and state anxiety on basketball performance. *Journal of Sport Behavior, 21,* 311-321.

Tice, D.M. (1992). Self-concept change and self-presentation: The looking glass self is also a magnifying glass. *Journal of Personality and Social Psychology, 63,* 435-451.

Travis, L.E. (1925). The effect of a small audience upon eye–hand coordination. *Journal of Abnormal and Social Psychology, 20,* 142-146.

Triplett, N. (1898). The dynamogenic factors in pacemaking and competition. *American Journal of Psychology, 9,* 505-523.

Wankel, L. (1984). Audience effects in sport. In J.M. Silva & R.S. Weinberg (Eds.), *Psychological foundations of sport* (pp. 293-314). Champaign, IL: Human Kinetics.

Williams, J.M., & Andersen, M.B. (1998). Psychosocial antecedents of sport injury: Review and critique of the stress and injury model. *Journal of Applied Sport Psychology, 10,* 5-25.

Williams, J.M., & Harris, D.V. (2001). Relaxing and energizing techniques for regulation of arousal. In J.M. Williams (Ed.), *Applied sport psychology: Personal growth to peak performance* (4th ed., pp. 229-246). Mountain View, CA: Mayfield.

Wright, E.F., Jackson, W., Christie, S.D., McGuire, G.R., & Wright, R.D. (1991). The home course disadvantage in golf championships: Further evidence for the undermining effect of supportive audiences on performance under pressure. *Journal of Sport Behavior, 14,* 51-60.

Wright, E.F., Voyer, D., Wright, R.D., & Roney, C. (1995). Supporting audiences and performance under pressure: The home-ice disadvantage in hockey championships. *Journal of Sport Behavior, 18,* 21-28.

Zajonc, R.B. (1965). Social facilitation. *Science, 149,* 269-74.

Zajonc, R.B. (1980). Compresence. In P.B. Paulus (Ed.), *Psychology of group influence* (pp. 35-60). Hillsdale, NJ: Erlbaum.

Chapter 9

Ames, C. (1992a). Classrooms, goal structures, and student motivation. *Journal of Educational Psychology, 84,* 261-274.

Ames, C. (1992b). Achievement goals, motivational climate, and motivational processes. In G.C. Roberts (Ed.), Motivation in sport and exercise (pp. 161-176). Champaign, IL: Human Kinetics.

Ames, C., & Archer, J. (1988). Achievement goals in the classroom: Students' learning strategies and motivation processes. *Journal of Educational Psychology, 80,* 260-267.

Balaguer, I., Castillo, I., & Duda, J.L. (2003). Interrelaciones entre el clima motivacional y la cohesión en futbolistas cadetes [Intercorrelations beweeen motivational climate and cohesion in football players]. *EduPsykhé, 2(2),* 243-258.

Balaguer, I., Crespo, M., & Duda, J.L. (1996). The relationship of motivational climate and athletes' goal orientations to perceived/preferred leadership style. *Journal of Sport & Exercise Psychology, 18,* S13.

Balaguer, I., Duda, J.L., Atienza, F.L., & Mayo, C. (2002). Situational and dispositional goals as predictors of perceptions on individual and team improvement, satisfaction and coach ratings among elite female handball teams. *Psychology of Sport and Exercise, 3,* 293-308.

Balaguer, I., Duda, J.L., & Crespo, M. (1999). Motivational climate and goal orientations as predictors of perceptions of improvement, satisfaction, and coach ratings among tennis players. *Scandinavian Journal of Medicine and Science in Sports, 9,* 381-388.

Balaguer, I., Duda, J.L., & Mayo, C. (1997). The relationship of goal orientations and the perceived motivational climate to coaches' leadership style in competitive handball. In R. Lidor & M. Bar-Eli (Eds.), *Innovations in sport psychology: Linking theory and practice. Proceedings of the IX World Congress in Sport Psychology: Part I* (pp. 94-96). Netanya, Israel: Ministry of Education, Culture, and Sport.

Bloom, G.A., Crumpton, R., & Anderson, J.E. (1999). A systematic observation study of the teaching behaviors of an expert basketball coach. *The Sport Psychologist, 13,* 157-170.

Bloom, G.A., Durand-Bush, N., & Salmela, J.H. (1997). Pre- and postcompetition routines of expert coaches of team sports. *The Sport Psychologist, 11,* 127-141.

Boixados, M., Cruz, J., Torregrosa, M., & Valiente, L. (2004). Relationships among motivational climate, satisfaction, perceived ability, and fair play attitudes in young soccer players. *Journal of Applied Sport Psychology, 16,* 301-317.

Burton, D., & Martens, R. (1986). Pinned by their own goals: An exploratory investigation into why kids drop out of wrestling. *Journal of Sport Psychology, 8,* 183-197.

Carpenter, P., & Morgan, K. (1999). Motivational climate, personal goal perspectives, and cognitive and affective responses in physical education classes. *European Journal of Physical Education, 4,* 31-44.

Chi, L., & Duda, J.L. (1995). Multi-group confirmatory factor análisis of the Task and Ego Orientation in Sport Questionnaire. *Research Quarterly for Exercise and Sport, 66,* 91-98.

Christodoulidis, T., Papaioannou, A., & Digelidis, N. (2001). A year-long intervention to change motivational climate and attitudes toward exercise in Greek senior high school. *European Journal of Sport Science, 1.* Available online at www.humankinetics.com/ejss/content/toc.cfm.

Côté, J., Salmela, J.H., & Russell, S. (1995). The knowledge of high-performance gymnastic coaches: methodological framework. *The Sport Psychologist, 9,* 65-75.

Cury, F., Da Fonseca, D., Rufo, M., & Sarrazin, P. (2002). Perceptions of competence, implicit theory of ability, perception of motivational climate, and achievement goals: A test of the trichotomous conceptualization of the endorsement of achievement motivation in the physical education setting. *Perception and Motor Skills, 95,* 233-244.

Deci, E.L. & Ryan, R.M. (1985). *Intrinsic motivation and self-determination in human behavior.* New York: Plenum Press.

Duda, J.L. (2001). Goal perspectives research in sport: Pushing the boundaries and clarifying some misunderstandings. In G.C. Roberts (Ed.), *Advances in motivation in sport and exercise* (pp. 129-182). Champaign, IL: Human Kinetics.

Duda, J.L., Balaguer, I., & Moreno, Y., & Crespo, M. (2001). *The relationship of the motivational climate and goal orientations to burnout among junior elite tennis players.* Paper presented at the meetings of AAASP, Orlando, FL.

Duda, J.L., Benardot, D., & Kim, M-S. (2004). *The relationship of the motivational climate to psychological and energy balance correlates of eating disorders in female gymnasts.* Unpublished manuscript.

Duda, J.L., & Hall, H. (2001). Achievement goal theory in sport: Recent extensions and future directions. In R. Singer, H. Hausenblas, & C., Janelle (Eds.), *Handbook of sport psychology,* (2nd ed., pp. 417-443). New York: Wiley.

Duda, J.L., & Hom, H. (1993). Interdependencies between the perceived and self-reported goal orientations of young athletes and their parents. *Pediatric Exercise Science, 5,* 234-241.

Duda, J.L., Newton, M.L., & Yin, Z. (1999). Variation in perceptions of the motivational climate and its predictors. In V. Hosek, P. Tilinger, & L. Bilek (Eds.), *Psychology of sport and exercise: Enhancing the quality of life—Proceedings of the 10th European Congress of Sport Psychology (FEPSAC)* (pp. 167-169). Prague: Charles University Press.

Duda, J.L., & Pensgaard, A.M. (2002). Enhancing the quantity and quality of motivation: The promotion of task involvement in a junior level football team. In I. Cockerill (Ed.), *Solutions in sport psychology* (pp. 49-57). London: Thomson.

Duda, J.L., & Whitehead, J. (1998). Measurement of goal perspectives in the physical domain. In J. Duda (Ed.), *Advances in sport and exercise psychology measurement* (pp. 21-48). Morgantown, WV: Fitness Information Technology.

Dweck, C.S. (1986). Motivational processes affecting learning. *American Psychologist, 41,* 1040-1048.

Dweck, C.S. (1999). *Self-theories: Their role in motivation, personality, and development.* Philadelphia: Psychology Press.

Dweck, C.S., & Leggett, E.L. (1988). A social-cognitive approach to personality and motivation. *Psychological Review, 95,* 256-273.

Ebbeck, V., & Becker, S.L. (1994). Psychosocial predictors of goal orientations in youth soccer. *Research Quarterly for Exercise and Sport, 65,* 355-362.

Elliot, A.J. (1997). Integrating the "classic" and "contemporary" approaches to achievement motivation: A hierarchical model of approach and avoidance achievement motivation. In M.L. Maehr & P.R. Pintrich (Eds.), *Advances in motivation and achievement* (Vol.10, pp. 143-179). Greenwich, CT: JAI Press.

Elliot, A.J. (1999). Approach and avoidance motivation and achievement goals. *Educational Psychologist, 34,* 169-189.

Elliot, A.J., & Conroy, D.E. (2005). Beyond the dichotomous model of achievement goals in sport and exercise psychology. *Sport and Exercise Psychology Review, 1,* 17-25.

Elliot, A.J., & McGregor, H.A. (2001). A 2×2 achievement goal framework. *Journal of Personality and Social Psychology, 80,* 501-519.

Epstein, J. (1989). Family structures and student motivation: A developmental perspective. In C. Ames & R. Ames (Eds.), *Research on motivation in education* (Vol.3, pp. 259-295). New York: Academic Press.

Gano-Overway, L., Guivernau, M., Magyar, M., Waldron, J.J., & Ewing, M.E. (2005). Achievement goal perspectives, perceptions of the motivational climate, and sportspersonship: Individual and team effects. *Psychology of Sport and Exercise, 6,* 233-250.

Gardner, D.E. (1998). *The relationship between perceived coaching behaviors, team cohesion, and team motivational climates among Division I athletes.* Unpublished doctoral dissertation, Boston University.

Gernigon, C., d'Arripe-Longueville, F., Delignieres, D., & Ninot, G. (2004). A dynamical systems perspective on goal involvement states in sport. *Journal of Sport & Exercise Psychology, 26,* 572-596.

Guivernau, M., & Duda, J.L. (1998) Norms for aggression/cheating, goal orientations, beliefs, perceived motivational climate, and athletic aggression: Potential gender differences. *Journal of Applied Sport Psychology, 10,* 5132.

Harwood, C., & Swain, A. (1998). Antecedents of pre-competition achievement goals in elite junior tennis players. *Journal of Sport Sciences, 16,* 357-371.

Harwood, C., Hardy, L., & Swain, A. (2000). Achievement goals in sport: A critique of conceptual and measurement issues. *Journal of Sport & Exercise Psychology, 22,* 235-255.

Horn, T.S. (1985). Coaches' feedback and changes in children's perceptions of their physical competence. *Journal of Educational Psychology, 77,* 174-186.

Jackson, P. (1995). *Sacred hoops: Spiritual issues of a hardwood warrior.* New York: Hyperion Books.

Janssen, J., & Dale, G.A. (2002). *The seven secrets of successful coaches.* Tucson, AZ: Winning the Mental Game.

Kavussanu, M., & Roberts, G.C. (1996). Motivation in physical activity contexts: The relationship of perceived motivational climate to intrinsic motivation and self-efficacy. *Journal of Sport & Exercise Psychology, 18,* 254-280.

Kim, M.S, & Duda, J.L. (1998). Achievement goals, motivational climate, and occurrence of and responses to psychological difficulties and performance debilitation among Korean athletes. *Journal of Sport & Exercise Psychology, 20 (Suppl.),* S124.

Kimiecik, J. & Gould, D. (1987). Coaching psychology: The case of James "Doc" Counsilman. *The Sport Psychologist, 1,* 350-358

Kuczka, K.K., & Treasure, D.C. (2005). Self-handicapping in competitive sport: Influence of the motivational climate, self-efficacy, and perceived importance. *Psychology of Sport and Exercise, 6,* 539-550.

Miller, B.W., Roberts, G.C., & Ommundsen, Y. (2005). Effect of perceived motivational climate on moral functioning, team moral atmosphere perceptions, and the legitimacy of intentionally injurious acts among competitive youth football players. *Psychology of Sport and Exercise, 6,* 461-477.

Morgan, K., & Carpenter, P.J. (2002). Effects of manipulating the motivational climate in physical education lessons. *European Journal of Physical Education, 8,* 209-232.

Morgan, K., Sproule, J., Weigand, D., & Carpenter, P. (2005). A computer-based observational assessment of the teaching behaviors that influence motivational climate in physical education. *Physical Education and Sport Pedagogy, 10,* 113-135.

Newton, M.L., & Duda, J.L. (1999). The interaction of motivational climate, dispositional goal orientation and perceived ability in predicting indices of motivation. *International Journal of Sport Psychology, 29,* 1-20.

Newton, M.L., Duda, J.L., & Yin, Z. (2000). Examination of the psychometric properties of the Perceived Motivational Climate in Sport Questionnaire-2 in a sample of female athletes. *Journal of Sport Sciences, 18(4),* 275-290.

Nicholls, J.G. (1984). Achievement motivation: Conceptions of ability, subjective experience, task choice, and performance. *Psychological Review, 91,* 328-346.

Nicholls, J.G. (1989). *The competitive ethos and democratic education.* Cambridge, MA: Harvard University Press.

Ntoumanis, N., & Biddle, S.J.H. (1998). The relationship between competitive anxiety, Achievement goals, and motivational climates. *Research Quarterly for Exercise and Sport, 69,* 176-187.

Ntoumanis, N., & Biddle, S.J.H. (1999). A review of motivational climate in physical activity. *Journal of Sport Sciences, 17,* 643-665.

Olympiou, A., Jowett, S., & Duda, J.L. (2005, August). *Contextual factors and optimal functioning in the team sport context: The mediating role of needs satisfaction.* 11th World Congress of Sport Psychology. Sydney, Australia.

Ommundsen, Y., Roberts, G.C., Kavussanu, M. (1998). Perceived motivational climate and cognitive and affective correlates among Norwegian athletes. *Journal of Sports Sciences, 16,* 153-164.

Ommundsen, Y., Roberts, G.C., Lemyre, P.N., & Treasure, D. (2003). Perceived motivational climate in male youth soccer: Relations to social-moral functioning, sportspersonship and team norm perceptions. *Psychology of Sport and Exercise, 25,* 397-413.

Ommundsen, Y., Roberts, G., Lemyre, P.N., & Miller, B.W. (2005). Peer relationships in adolescent competitive soccer: Associations to perceived motivational climate, Achievement goals and perfectionism. *Journal of Sports Sciences, 23,* 977-989.

Papaioannou, A. (1994). Development of a questionnaire to measure achievement orientations in physical education. *Research Quarterly for Exercise and Sport, 65,* 11-20.

Papaioannou, A., & Kouli, O. (1999). The effect of task structure, perceived motivational climate and goal orientations on students' task involvement and anxiety. *Journal of Applied Sport Psychology, 11,* 51-71.

Papaioannou, A., Marsh, H.W., & Theodorakis, Y. (2004). A multi-level approach to motivational climate in physical education and sport settings: An individual or a group level construct? *Journal of Sport & Exercise Psychology, 26,* 90-118.

Pensgaard, A.M., & Duda, J.L. (2004). Relationship of situational and dispositional goals to coach ratings, perceived stressors and performance among Olympic Athletes. Manuscript under review.

Pensgaard, A.M., & Roberts, G.C. (2002). Elite athletes' experiences of the motivational climate: The coach matters. *Scandinavian Journal of Medicine & Science in Sports, 12(1),* 54-59.

Reinboth, M., & Duda, J.L. (2004). Relationship of the perceived motivational climate and perceptions of ability to psychological and physical well-being in team sports. *The Sport Psychologist, 18,* 237-251.

Reinboth, M., & Duda, J.L. (2006). Perceived motivational climate, need satisfaction and indices of well-being in team sports: A longitudinal perspective. *Psychology of Sport and Exercise, 7,* 269-286.

Reinboth, M., Duda, J.L., Ntoumanis, N. (2004). Dimensions of coaching behavior, need satisfaction, and the psychological and physical welfare of young athletes. *Motivation and Emotion, 28,* 297-313.

Roberts, G.C. (1992). Motivation in sport: Conceptual constraints and convergence. In G.C. Roberts (Ed.), *Motivation in sport and exercise* (pp. 3-29). Champaign, IL: Human Kinetics.

Roberts, G.C. (2001). Understanding the dynamics of motivation in physical activity: The influence of achievement goals on motivational processes. In G.C. Roberts (Ed.), A*dvances in sport and exercise* motivation (pp. 1-50). Champaign, IL: Human Kinetics.

Ryan, R., & Deci, E. (2000). Self-determination theory and the facilitation of intrinsic motivation, social development, and well being. *American Psychologist, 55,* 68-78.

Ryska, T.A., Yin, Z., & Boyd, M. (1999). The role of dispositional goal orientation and team climate on situational self-handicapping among young athletes. *Journal of Sport Behavior, 22,* 410-425.

Sarrazin, P., Vallerand, R., Guillet, E. Pelletier, L., & Cury, F. (2002). Motivation and dropout in female handballers: A 21-month prospective study. *European Journal of Social Psychology, 32(3),* 395-418.

Scanlan, T.K. and Lewthwaite, R. (1986). Social psychological aspects of competition for male youth sport participants: IV. Predictor of enjoyment. *Journal of Sports Psychology, 9,* 25-35.

Scanlan, T.K., & Passer, M.W (1979) Sources of competitive stress in young female athletes. *Journal of Sport Psychology, 1,* 151-159.

Seifriz, J., Duda, J.L., & Chi, L. (1992). The relationship of perceived motivational climate to intrinsic motivation and beliefs about success in basketball. *Journal of Sport & Exercise Psychology, 14,* 375-391.

Sinclair, D.A., & Vealey, R.S. (1989). Effects of coaches' expectations and feedback on the self-perceptions of athletes. *Journal of Sport Behavior, 12,* 77-91.

Sluis, M., Kiukkonen, J., Jaakola, T., Kokkonan, J. Saarelainen, S., Piirainen, U., & Pakkala, P. (1999). Observation of physical education teacher feedback from the motivational climate perspective. In V. Hosek, P. Tilinger, & L. Bilek (Eds.), *Psychology of sport and exercise: Enhancing quality of life—Proceedings of the 10th European Congress of Sport Psychology-FEPSAC, part II* (pp. 166-168). Prague: Charles University Press.

Smith, A., Balaguer, I., and Duda, J.L. (in press). Goal orientation profile differences on perceptions of the motivational climate, perceptions of peer relationships, and motivation-related responses of youth athletes. *Journal of Sports Sciences.*

Smith, R.E., & Smoll, F.L. (2005). Assessing psychosocial outcomes in coach training programs. In D. Hackfort, J. Duda, & R. Lidor (Eds.), *Handbook of applied sport and exercise psychology* (pp. 293-316). Morgantown, WV: Fitness Technology.

Smith, R.E., Smoll, F.L., & Hunt, E.B. (1977). A system for the behavioral assessment of athletic coaches. *Research Quarterly, 48,* 401-407.

Smith, R.E., Zane, N.S., Smoll, F.L., & Coppel, D.B. (1983). Behavioral assessment in youth sports: Coaching behaviors and children's attitudes. *Medicine and Science in Sports and Exercise, 15,* 208-214.

Smith, S.L., Fry, M.D., Ethington, C.A., & Li, Y. (2005). The effect of female athletes' perceptions of their coaches' behaviors on their perceptions of the motivational climate. *Journal of Applied Sport Psychology, 17,* 170-177.

Standage, M., Duda, J.L., & Pensgaard, A.M. (2005). The effect of competitive outcome and the motivational climate on the psychological well-being of individuals engaged in a coordination task. *Motivation and Emotion, 29,* 41-68.

Theeboom, M., De Knop, P., & Weiss, M.R. (1995). Motivational climate, psychological responses, and motor skill development in children's sport: A field-based intervention study. *Journal of Sport & Exercise Psychology, 17,* 294-311.

Treasure, D.C. (1993). *A social-cognitive approach to understanding children's achievement behavior, cognitions, and affect in competitive sport.* Unpublished doctoral dissertation, University of Illinois at Urbana-Champaign.

Treasure, D.C., Duda, J.L., Hall, H.K., Roberts, G.C., Ames, C., & Maehr, M.L. (2001). Clarifying misconceptions and misrepresentations in achievement goal research in sport: A response to Harwood, Hardy, and Swain. *Journal of Sport & Exercise Psychology, 23,* 317-329.

Treasure, D.C., & Roberts, G.C. (1998). Relationship between female adolescents' achievement goal orientations, perceptions of the motivational climate, beliefs about success and sources of satisfaction in basketball. *International Journal of Sport Psychology, 29,* 211-230.

Vallerand, R.J. (2001). A hierarchical model of intrinsic and extrinsic motivation in sport and exercise. In G.C. Roberts (Ed.), A*dvances in sport and exercise motivation* (pp. 263-319). Champaign, IL: Human Kinetics.

Vazou, S., Ntoumanis, N., & Duda, J.L. (2005). Peer motivational climate in youth sport: A qualitative inquiry. *Psychology of Sport & Exercise, 6,* 497-516.

Vazou, S., Ntoumanis, N., & Duda, J.L. (2006). Predicting young athletes' motivational indices as a function of their perceptions of the coach- and peer-created climate. *Psychology of Sport and Exercise, 7,* 215-234.

Walling, M.D., Duda, J.L., & Chi, L. (1993). The Perceived Motivational Climate in Sport Questionnaire: Construct and predictive validity. *Journal of Sport & Exercise Psychology, 15,* 172-183.

Weigand, D.A., & Burton, S. (2005). Manipulating achievement motivation in physical education by manipulating the motivational climate. *European Journal of Sport Sciences, 2.* Available online at www.humankinetics.com/ejss/content/toc.cfm.

Weigand, D.A., Carr, S., Petherick, C., & Taylor, A. (2001). Motivational climate in sport and physical education: The role of significant others. *European Journal of Sport Sciences, 1,* Available online at www.humankinetics.com/ejss/content/toc.cfm.

White, S.A. (1996). Goal orientation and perceptions of the motivational climate initiated by parents. *Pediatric Exercise Science, 8,* 122-129.

White, S.A., Duda, J.L., & Hart, S. (1992). An exploratory examination of the Parent-Initiated Motivational Climate Questionnaire. *Perceptual and Motor Skills, 75,* 875-880.

Williams, L. (1998). Contextual influences and goal perspectives among female youth sport participants. *Research Quarterly for Exercise and Sport, 69,* 47-57.

Wooden, J., & Jamison, S. (2005). *Wooden on leadership.* New York: McGraw-Hill.

Chapter 10

Ames, C. (1984). Competitive, cooperative, and individualistic goal structures: A motivational analysis. In R. Ames & C. Ames (Eds.), *Research on motivation in education: Student motivation* (Vol. 3, pp. 177-207). New York: Academic Press.

Ames, C. (1992). Achievement goals, motivational climate, and motivational processes. In G.C. Roberts (Ed.), *Motivation in sport and exercise* (pp. 161-176). Champaign, IL: Human Kinetics.

Ames, C., & Archer, J. (1987). Mothers' beliefs about the role of ability and effort in school learning. *Journal of Educational Psychology, 79,* 409-414.

Babkes, M.L., & Weiss, M.R. (1999). Parental influence on children's cognitive and affective response to competitive soccer participation. *Pediatric Exercise Science, 11,* 44-62.

Baumrind, D. (1991). Effective parenting during the adolescent transition. In P.A. Cowan & M Hetherington (Eds.), *Family transitions* (pp. 111-164). Hillsdale, NJ: Erlbaum.

Belsky, J. (1998). Prental influence and children's well-being: Limits of and new directions for understanding. In A. Booth & A.C. Crouter (Eds.), *Men in families* (pp. 279-293). Mahwah, NJ: Erlbaum.

Biddle, S., Curry, F., Goudas, M., Sarrazin, P., Famose, J.P., & Durand, M. (1995). Development of scales to measure perceived physical education class climate: A cross-national project. *British Journal of Educational Psychology, 65,* 341-358.

Brody, G.H., Flor, D.L., & Gibson, N.M. (1999). Linking maternal efficacy beliefs, developmental goals, parenting practices, and child competence in rural, single-parent, African American families. *Child Development, 70,* 1197-1208.

Brustad, R.J. (1993). Who will go out and play? Parental and psychological influences on children's attraction to physical activity. *Pediatric Exercise Science, 5,* 210-223.

Carr, S., & Weigand, D.A. (2001). Parental, peer, teacher and sporting hero influence on the goal orientations of children in physical education. *European Physical Education Review, 7,* 305-328.

Carr, S., Weigand, D.A., & Hussey, W. (1999). The relative influence of parents, teachers and peers on children's and adolescents' achievement and intrinsic motivation and perceived competence in PE. *Journal of Sport Pedagogy, 5,* 28-51.

Cauce, A.M., Felner, R.D., & Primavera, J. (1982). Social support in high-risk adolescents: Structural components and adaptive impact. *American Journal of Community Psychology, 10,* 417-428.

Connell, J.P., Spencer, M.B., & Aber, J.L. (1994). Educational risk and resilience in African-American youth: Context, self, Action, and outcomes in school. *Child Development, 65,* 493-506.

Dweck, C. (1999). Self-theories: *Their role in motivation, personality, and development.* Philadelphia: Psychological Press.

Dweck, C.S., & Leggett, E.L. (1988). A social-cognitive approach to motivation and personality. *Psychological Review, 95,* 256-272.

Dweck, C.S., & Lennon, C. (2001, April). *Person vs. process focused parenting: Impact on achievement motivation.* Paper presented at the meeting of the Society for Research in Child Development, Minneapolis, MN.

Duda, J.L. (2001). Achievement goal research in sport: Pushing the boundaries and clarifying some misunderstandings. In G.C. Roberts (Ed.), *Advances in motivational sport and exercise* (pp. 129-182). Champaign, IL: Human Kinetics.

Duda, J.L., & Hom, H.L. (1993). Interdependencies between the perceived and self-reported goal orientations of adolescents and their parents. *Pediatric Exercise Science, 5,* 234-241.

Duda, J.L., & Nicholls, J.G. (1992). Dimensions of achievement motivation in schoolwork and sport. *Journal of Educational Psychology, 84,* 290-299.

Duda, J.L., & Whitehead, J. (1998). Measurement of goal perspectives in the physical domain. In J.L. Duda (Ed.), *Advances in sport and exercise psychology measurement* (pp. 21-48). Morgantown, WV: Fitness Information Technology.

Ebbeck, V., & Becker, S.L. (1994). Psychosocial predictors of goal orientations in youth soccer. *Research Quarterly for Exercise and Sport, 65,* 355-362.

Eccles, J.S. (1993). School and family effects on the ontogeny of children's interests, self-perceptions, and activity choice. In Jacobs (Ed.), *Nebraska symposium on motivation, 1992: Developmental perspectives on motivation* (pp. 145-208) Lincoln, NE: University of Nebraska Press.

Eccles, J., Adler, T.F., Futterman, R., Goff, S.B., Kaczala, C.M., Meece, J.L., et al. (1983). Expectancies, values, and academic behaviors. In J.T. Spence (Ed.), *Achievement and achievement motivation* (pp. 75-146). San Francisco: W.H. Freeman.

Eccles, J.S., & Harold, R.D. (1991). Gender differences in sport involvement: Applying the Eccles expectancy-value model. *Journal of Applied Sport Psychology, 3,* 7-35.

Eccles, J.S., Jacobs, J., & Harold, R.D. (1990). Gender-role stereotypes, expectancy effects, and parents' role in the socialization of gender differences in self-perceptions and skill acquisition. *Journal of Social Issues, 45,* 183-201.

Eccles, J.S., Wigfield, A., Harold, R., & Blumenfeld, P. (1993). Age and gender differences in children's self- and task perceptions during elementary school. *Child Development, 64,* 830-847.

Elliott, A.J., & Church, M.A. (1997). A hierarchical model of approach and avoidance achievement motivation. *Journal of Personality and Social Psychology, 72,* 218-232.

Epstein, J. (1989). Family structures and student motivation: A developmental perspective. In R. Ames & C. Ames (Eds.), *Research on motivation in education* (Vol. 3, pp. 259-295). New York: Academic Press.

Escartí, A., Roberts, G.C., Cervelló, E.M., & Guzmán, J.F. (1999). Adolescent goal orientations and the perception of criteria of success used by significant others. *International Journal of Sports Psychology, 30,* 309-324.

Felner, R.D., Aber, M.S., Primavera, J., & Cauce, A.M. (1985). Adaptation and vulnerability in high-risk adolescents: An examination of environmental mediators. *American Journal of Community Psychology, 13,* 365-379.

Fox, K.R., Goudas, M., Biddle, S., Duda, J.L., & Armstrong, N. (1994). Children's task and ego profiles in sport. *British Journal of Educational Psychology, 64,* 253-261.

Fry, M., & Duda, J.L. (1997). Children's understanding of effort and ability in the physical and academic domains. *Research Quarterly for Exercise and Sport, 68,* 331-334.

Galper, A., Wigfield, A., & Seefeldt, C. (1997). Head start parents' beliefs about their children's abilities, task values, and performance on different activities. *Child Development, 68,* 897-907.

Ginsberg, G.S., & Bronstein, P. (1993). Family factors related to children's intrinsic/extrinsic motivational orientations and academic performance. *Child Development, 64,* 1461-1474.

Givvin, K.B. (2001). Goal orientations of adolescents, coaches, and parents: Is there a convergence of beliefs? *Journal of Early Adolescence, 21,* 228-248.

Gottfried, A.E., Fleming, J.S., & Gottfried, A.W. (1998). Role of cognitively simulating home environments in children's academic intrinsic motivation: A longitudinal study. *Child Development, 69,* 1448-1460.

Guest, S.M., & White, S.A. (2001). A cross-situational investigation of goal orientations and perceived motivational climate in a physical education class and an organized sport setting. *International Sports Journal, 1,* 1-17.

Halle, T.G., Kurtz-Cortes, B., & Mahoney, J.L. (1997). Family influences on school achievement in low-income African American children. *Journal of Educational Psychology, 89,* 527-537.

Harter, S. (1978). Effectance motivation reconsidered. *Human Development, 21,* 34-64.

Harwood, C., & Hardy, A. (1999, June). Achievement goals in sport: A critique of conceptual and measurement issues. In *Proceedings of the 10th European Congress of Sport Psychology* (pp. 241-243). Prague: Charles University Press.

Harwood, C., Hardy, A., & Swain, A. (2000). Achievement goals in sport: A critique of conceptual and measurement issues. *Journal of Sport & Exercise Psychology, 22,* 235-255.

Heyman, G.D., & Dweck, C.S. (1998). Children's thinking about traits: Implications for judgments of the self and others. *Child Development, 69,* 391-403.

Heyman, G.D., Dweck, C.S., & Cain, K. (1992). Young children's vulnerability to self-blame and helplessness. *Child Development, 63,* 401-415.

Hokoda, A., & Fincham, F.D. (1995). Origins of children's helpless and mastery achievement patterns in the family. *Journal of Educational Psychology, 87,* 375-385.

Kimiecik, J.C., Horn, T.S., and Shurin, C.S. (1996). Relationship among children's beliefs, perceptions of their parents' beliefs, and moderate-to-vigorous physical activity. *Research Quarterly for Exercise and Sport, 67,* 324-336.

Maehr, M.L. (1984). Meaning and motivation: Toward a theory of personal investment. In R. Ames & C. Ames (Eds.), *Research on motivation in education: Student motivation* (pp. 115-144). New York: Academic Press.

Meece, J.L. (1997). Child and adolescent development for educators. New York: McGraw-Hill

Newton, M., & Duda, J.L. (1993). The Perceived Motivational Climate in Sport Questionnaire-2: Construct and predictive validity. *Journal of Sport & Exercise Psychology, 15* (Suppl.), S59.

Nicholls, J.G. (1989). *The competitive ethos and democratic education.* Cambridge, MA: Harvard University Press.

Nicholls, J.G. (1992). The general and the specific in the development and expression of achievement motivation. In G.C. Roberts (Ed.), *Advances in motivational sport and exercise* (pp. 31-56). Champaign, IL: Human Kinetics.

Ntoumanis, N., & Biddle, S.J.H. (1999). A review of the motivational climate in physical activity. *Journal of Sports Sciences, 17,* 643-665.

Papaioannou, A. (1994). Development of a questionnaire to measure achievement orientation in physical education. *Research Quarterly for Exercise and Sport, 65,* 11-20.

Papaioannou, A. (1995). Differential perceptual and motivational patterns when different goals are adopted. *Journal of Sport & Exercise Psychology, 17,* 18-34.

Pintrich, P.R., & Schunck, D.H. (1996). *Motivation in education: Theory, research, and applications.* Englewood Cliffs, NJ: Prentice Hall.

Rathunde, K. (1996). Family context and talented adolescents' optimal experience in school-related activities. *Journal of Research on Adolescence, 6,* 605-628.

Roberts, G.C. (2001). Understanding the dynamics of motivation in physical activity: The influence of achievement goals on motivational processes. In G.C. Roberts (Ed.), *Advances in motivational sport and exercise* (pp. 6-18). Champaign, IL: Human Kinetics.

Roberts, G.C., Treasure, D.C., & Balague, G. (1998). Achievement goals in sport: The development and validation of the Perceptions of Success Questionnaire. *Journal of Sports Sciences, 16,* 337-347.

Roberts, G.C., Treasure, D.C., & Hall, H. (1994). Parental goal orientation and beliefs about the competitive sport experience of their children. *Journal of Applied Sport Psychology, 24,* 631-645.

Roberts, G.C., Treasure, D.C., & Kavusaanu, M. (1996). Orthogonality of achievement goals and its relationship to beliefs about the causes of success and satisfaction in sport. *The Sport Psychologist, 10,* 398-404.

Ryan, R.M. (1993). Agency and organization: Intrinsic motivation, Autonomy and the self in psychological development. In J. Jacobs (Ed.), *Nebraska symposium on motivation: Developmental perspectives on motivation* (Vol. 40, pp. 1-56). Lincoln, NE: University of Nebraska Press.

Smiley, P.A., Coulson, S.L., & Van Ocker, J.C. (2000, April). *Beliefs about learning in mothers and fathers of preschoolers.* Paper presented at the meeting of the American Educational Psychological Association, New Orleans.

Tamis-LeMonda, C.S., & Cabrera, N. (1999). *Perspectives on father involvement: Research and policy* (Social Policy Report, Vol. 13). Ann Arbor, MI. Society for Research in Child Development.

Wentzel, K.R. (1998). Social support and adjustment in middle school: The role of parents, teachers and peers. *Journal of Educational Psychology, 90,* 202-209.

Wentzel, K.R. (1999). Social-motivational processes and interpersonal relationships: Implications for understanding students' academic success. *Journal of Educational Psychology, 91,* 76-97

White, S.A. (1996). Goal orientation and perceptions of the motivational climate initiated by parents. *Pediatric Exercise Science, 8,* 122-129.

White, S.A. (1998). Adolescent goal orientation profiles, perceptions of the parent-initiated motivational climate, and competitive trait anxiety. *The Sport Psychologist, 12,* 16-32.

White, S.A., & Duda, J.L. (1993, June). *The relationship between goal orientation and parent-initiated motivational climate among children learning a physical skill.* Paper presented at the meeting of the International Society for Sport Psychology, Lisbon, Portugal.

White, S.A., Duda, J.L., & Hart, S. (1992). An exploratory examination of the parent-initiated motivational climate questionnaire. *Perceptual and Motor Skills, 75,* 875-880.

White, S.A., Kavussanu, M., & Guest, S.M. (1998). Goal orientations and perceptions of the motivational climate created by significant others. *European Journal of Physical Education, 3,* 212-228.

White, S.A., Kavussanu, M., Tank, K.M., & Wingate, J.M. (2004). Perceived parental beliefs about the causes of success in sport: Relationship to athletes' achievement goals and personal beliefs. *Scandinavian Journal of Medicine Science and Sport, 14,* 57-66.

White, S.A., & Morgan, J.Q. (1996, May). Structuring the environment for maximum motivation in physical conditioning for colleyball: Part 2 for parents. *Performance Conditioning for Volleyball,* p. 42.

Wigfield, A., & Eccles, J.S. (2002). *Development of achievement motivation.* San Diego: Academic Press.

Chapter 11

Allen, J.B. (2003). Social motivation in youth sport. *Journal of Sport & Exercise Psychology, 25,* 551-567.

Ames, C. (1992). Classrooms: Goals, structures, and student motivation. *Journal of Educational Psychology, 84,* 261-271.

Ames, C., & Archer, J. (1988). Achievement goals in the classroom: Student's learning strategies and motivation processes. *Journal of Educational Psychology, 80,* 260-267.

Balaguer, I., Duda, J.L., Atienza, F.L., & Mayo, C. (2002). Situational and dispositional goals as predictors of perceptions of individual and team improvement, satisfaction and coach ratings among elite female handball teams. *Psychology of Sport and Exercise, 3,* 293-308.

Biddle, S., Cury, F., Goudas, M., Sarrazin, P., Famose, J.P., & Durand, M. (1995). Development of scales to measure perceived physical education class climate: A cross-national project. *British Journal of Educational Psychology, 65,* 341-358.

Brustad, R.J., Babkes, M.L., & Smith, A.L. (2001). Youth in sport: Psychological considerations. In R.N. Singer, H.A. Hausenblas, & C.M., Janelle (Eds.), *Handbook of sport psychology* (pp. 604-635). New York: Wiley.

Brustad, R.J., & Partridge, J.A. (2002). Parental and peer influence on children's psychological development through sport. In F.L. Smoll & R.E. Smith (Eds.), *Children and youth in sport: A bio-psychosocial perspective* (pp. 187-209). Dubuque, IA: Kendall/Hunt.

Carpenter, P.J. (1995). Modification and extension of the Sport Commitment Model. *Journal of Sport & Exercise Psychology, 17,* S37.

Carr, S., Weigand, D.A., & Hussey, W. (1999). The relative influence of parents, teachers, and peers on children and adolescents' achievement and intrinsic motivation and perceived competence in physical education. *Journal of Sport Pedagogy, 5,* 28-51.

Carr, S., Weigand, D.A., & Jones, J. (2000). The relative influence of parents, peers and sporting heroes on goal orientations of children and adolescents in sport. *Journal of Sport Pedagogy, 6,* 34-55.

Cobb, N.J. (1994). *Adolescence: Continuity, change, and diversity.* Mountain View, CA: Mayfield.

Deci, E., & Ryan, R. (1985). *Intrinsic motivation and self-determination in human behavior.* New York: Plenum.

Duda, J.L. (2001). Achievement goal research in sport: Pushing the boundaries and understanding some misunderstandings. In G.C. Roberts, (Ed.), *Advances in motivation in sport and exercise* (pp. 129-182). Champaign, IL: Human Kinetics.

Duda, J.L., & Hall, H. (2001). Achievement goal theory in sport: Recent extensions and future directions. In R.N. Singer, H.A. Hausenblas, & C.M., Janelle (Eds.), *Handbook of sport psychology* (pp. 417-443). New York: Wiley.

Duda, J.L., & Ntoumanis, N. (2005). After-school sport for children: Implications of a task-involving motivational climate. In J.L. Mahoney, R. Larson, & J. Eccles (Eds.), *Organized activities as contexts of development: Extracurricular activities, After-school and community programs* (pp. 311-330). Mahwah, NJ: Erlbaum.

Fabrigar, L.R., Wegener, D.T., MacCallum, R.C., & Strahan, E.J. (1999). Evaluating the use of exploratory factor analysis in psychological research. *Psychological Methods, 4,* 272-299.

Goudas, M. (1998). Motivational climate and intrinsic motivation of young basketball players. *Perceptual and Motor Skills, 86,* 323-327.

Heck, R.H. (2001). Multilevel modeling with SEM. In G.A. Marcoulides & R.E. Schumacker (Eds.), *New developments and techniques in structural equation modeling* (pp. 89-127). Mahwah, NJ: Erlbaum.

Horn, T.S., & Amorose, A.J. (1998). Sources of competence information. In J.L. Duda (Ed.), *Advances in sport and exercise psychology measurement* (pp. 49-63). Morgantown, WV: Fitness Information Technology.

Horn, T.S., & Weiss, M.R. (1991). A developmental analysis of children's self-ability judgments in the physical domain. *Pediatric Exercise Science, 3,* 310-326.

Kavussanu, M., & Roberts, G.C. (1996). Motivation in physical activity contexts: The relationship of perceived motivational climate to intrinsic motivation and self-efficacy. *Journal of Sport & Exercise Psychology, 18,* 264-280.

Lewko, J.H. & Greendorfer, S.L. (1988). Family influences in sport socialization of children and adolescents. In F.L. Smoll, R.A. Magill, & M.J. Ash (Eds.), *Children in sport* (3rd ed., pp. 287-300). Champaign, IL: Human Kinetics.

Magyar, T.M., & Feltz, D.L. (2003). The influence of dispositional and situational tendencies on adolescent girls' sport confidence sources. *Psychology of Sport and Exercise, 4,* 175-190.

McAuley, E., Duncan, T., & Tammen, V.V. (1989). Psychometric properties of the intrinsic motivation inventory in a competitive sport setting: A confirmatory factor analysis. *Research Quarterly for Exercise and Sport, 60,* 48-58.

Newton, M., & Duda, J.L. (1999). The interaction of motivational climate, dispositional goal orientations, and perceived ability in predicting indices of motivation. *International Journal of Sport Psychology, 30,* 63-82.

Newton, M., Duda, J.L., & Yin, Z. (2000). Examination of the psychometric properties of the Perceived Motivational Climate in Sport Questionnaire-2 in a sample of female athletes. *Journal of Sports Sciences, 18,* 275-290.

Nicholls, J.G. (1989). *The competitive ethos and democratic education.* Cambridge, MA: Harvard University Press.

Ntoumanis, N. (2001). A self-determination approach to the understanding of motivation in physical education. *British Journal of Educational Psychology, 71,* 225-242.

Ntoumanis, N., & Biddle, S. (1999). A review of motivational climate in physical activity. *Journal of Sports Sciences, 17,* 643-665.

Ntoumanis, N., & Vazou, S. (2005). Peer motivational climate in youth sport: Measurement development. *Journal of Sport & Exercise Psychology, 27,* 432-455.

Papaioannou, A., & Kouli, O. (1999). The effect of task structure, perceived motivational climate and goal orientations on students' task involvement and anxiety. *Journal of Applied Sport Psychology, 11,* 51-71.

Papaioannou, A., Marsh, H.W., & Theodorakis, Y. (2004). A multilevel approach to motivational climate in physical education and sport settings: An individual or a group level construct? *Journal of Sport & Exercise Psychology, 26,* 90-118.

Reinboth, M., & Duda, J.L. (2004). Relationship of the perceived motivational climate and perceptions of ability to psychological and physical well-being in team sports. *The Sport Psychologist, 18, 237-251.

Sarrazin, P., Guillet, E., & Cury, F. (2001). The effect of coach's task- and ego- involving climate on the changes in perceived competence, relatedness, and autonomy among girl handballers. *European Journal of Sport Science, 1(4).* Retrieved April, 17, 2002, from www.humankinetics.com/ejss/content.

Scanlan, T.K., Simons, J.P., Carpenter, P.J., Schmidt, G.W., & Keeler, B. (1993). The sport commitment model: Measurement development for the youth-sport domain. *Journal of Sport & Exercise Psychology, 15,* 16-38.

Seifriz, J.J., Duda, J.L., & Chi, L. (1992). The relationship of perceived motivational climate to intrinsic motivation and beliefs about success in basketball. *Journal of Sport & Exercise Psychology, 14,* 375-391.

Smith, A.L. (1999). Perceptions of peer relationships and physical activity participation in early adolescence. *Journal of Sport & Exercise Psychology, 21,* 329-350.

Smith, A.L. (2003). Peer relationships in physical activity contexts: A road less traveled in youth sport and exercise psychology research. *Psychology of Sport and Exercise, 4,* 25-39.

Smith, R.E., Smoll, F.L., & Schutz, R.W. (1990). Measurement and correlates of sport-specific cognitive and somatic trait anxiety: The Sport Anxiety Scale. *Anxiety Research, 2,* 263-280.

Solmon, M.A. (1996). Impact of motivational climate on students' behaviors and perceptions in a physical education setting. *Journal of Educational Psychology, 88,* 731-738.

Sonstroem, R.J. (1997). The physical self-esteem: A mediator of exercise and self-esteem. In K.R. Fox (Ed.), *The physical self: From motivation to well-being* (pp. 3-26). Champaign, IL: Human Kinetics.

Standage, M., Duda, J.L., & Ntoumanis, N. (2003a). A model of contextual motivation in physical education: Employing constructs from self-determination and achievement goal theories to predict physical activity intentions. *Journal of Education Psychology, 95,* 97-110.

Standage, M., Duda, J.L., & Ntoumanis, N. (2003b). Predicting motivational regulations in physical education: The interplay between dispositional goal orientations, motivational climate and perceived competence. *Journal of Sports Sciences, 21,* 631-647.

Theeboom, M., DeKnop, P., & Weiss, M.R. (1995). Motivational climate, psychological response, and motor skill development in children's sport: A field-based intervention study. *Journal of Sport & Exercise Psychology, 17,* 294-311.

Treasure, D.C. (2001). Enhancing young people's motivation in youth sport: An achievement goal approach. In G.C. Roberts (Ed.), A*dvances in motivation in sport and exercise* (pp. 79-100). Champaign, IL: Human Kinetics.

Treasure, D.C., & Roberts, G.C. (1998). Relationship between female adolescents' achievement goal orientations, perceptions of the motivational climate, belief about success and sources of satisfaction in basketball. *International Journal of Sport Psychology, 29,* 211-230.

Vazou, S. (2004). *Peer motivational climate in youth sport.* Unpublished doctoral dissertation, University of Birmingham, UK.

Vazou, S., Ntoumanis, N., & Duda, J.L. (2005). Peer motivational climate in youth sport: A qualitative inquiry. *Psychology of Sport & Exercise, 6,* 497-516.

Vazou, S., Ntoumanis, N., & Duda, J.L. (2006). Predicting young athletes' motivational indices as a function of their perceptions of the coach- and peer-created climate. *Psychology of Sport & Exercise, 7,* 215-233.

Weinberg, R.S., & Gould, D. (2003). *Foundations of sport and exercise psychology* (3rd ed.). Champaign, IL: Human Kinetics.

Weiss, M.R., & Petlichkoff, L.M. (1989). Children's motivation for participation in and withdrawal from sport: Identifying the missing links. *Pediatric Exercise Sciences, 1,* 195-211.

Weiss, M.R., & Smith, A.L. (2002). Friendship quality in youth sport: Relationship to age, gender, and motivation variables. *Journal of Sport & Exercise Psychology, 24,* 420-437.

Weiss, M.R., & Stuntz, C.P. (2004). A little friendly competition: Peer relationships and psychosocial development in youth sport and physical activity contexts. In M.R. Weiss (Ed.), *Developmental sport and exercise psychology: A lifespan perspective* (pp. 165-196). Morgantown, WV: Fitness Information Technology.

Weiss, M.R., & Williams, L. (2004). The why of youth sport involvement: A developmental perspective on motivational processes. In M.R. Weiss (Ed.), *Developmental sport and exercise psychology: A lifespan perspective* (pp. 223-268). Morgantown, WV: Fitness Information Technology.

White, S.A. (1996). Goal orientation and perceptions of the motivational climate initiated by parents. *Pediatric Exercise Science, 8,* 122-129.

White, S.A., Kavussanu, M., & Guest, S.M. (1998). Goal orientations and perceptions of the motivational climate created by significant others. *European Journal of Physical Education, 3,* 212-228.

Whitehead, J.R. (1995). A study of children's physical self-perceptions using an adapted physical self-perception profile questionnaire. *Pediatric Exercise Science, 7,* 132-151.

Yoo, J. (2003). Motivational climate and perceived competence in anxiety and tennis performance. *Perceptual and Motor Skills, 96,* 403-413.

Chapter 12

Bandura, A. (1986). *Social foundations of thought and action: A social cognitive theory.* Englewood Cliffs, NJ: Prentice Hall.

Bong, M., & Clark, R.E. (1999). Comparison between self-concept and self-efficacy in academic motivation research. *Educational Psychologist, 34,* 139-153.

Byrne, B.M. (1984). The general/academic self-concept nomological network: A review of construct validation research. *Review of Educational Research, 54,* 427-456.

Calsyn, R.J., & Kenny, D.A. (1977). Self-concept of ability and perceived evaluation of others: Cause or effect of academic achievement? *Journal of Educational Psychology, 69,* 136-145.

Fleishman, F.A. (1964). *The structure and measurement of physical fitness.* Englewood Cliffs, NJ: Prentice Hall.

Fox, K.R. & Corbin, C.B. (1989). The Physical Self-Perception Profile: Development and preliminary validation. *Journal of Sport & Exercise Psychology, 11,* 408-430.

Gill, D.L., Dzewaltowski, D.A., & Deeter, T.E. (1988). The relationship of competitiveness and achievement orientation to participation in sport and nonsport activities. *Journal of Sport & Exercise Psychology, 10,* 139-150.

Hattie, J. (1992). *Self-concept.* Hillsdale, NJ: Erlbaum.

James, W. (1890/1963). *The principles of psychology.* New York: Holt, Rinehart and Winston.

Marsh, H.W. (1988). Multitrait-multimethod analyses. In J.P. Keeves (Ed.), *Educational research methodology, measurement and evaluation: An international handbook* (pp. 570-580). Oxford: Pergamon Press.

Marsh, H.W. (1989). Age and sex effects in multiple dimensions of self-concept: Preadolescence to adulthood. *Journal of Educational Psychology, 81,* 417-430.

Marsh, H.W. (1990). A multidimensional, hierarchical self-concept: Theoretical and empirical justification. *Educational Psychology Review, 2,* 77-171.

Marsh, H.W. (1993a). Academic self-concept: Theory measurement and research. In J. Suls (Ed.), *Psychological perspectives on the self* (Vol. 4, pp. 59-98). Hillsdale, NJ: Erlbaum.

Marsh, H.W. (1993b). The multidimensional structure of physical fitness: Invariance over gender and age. *Research Quarterly for Exercise and Sport, 64,* 256-273.

Marsh, H.W. (1993c). Physical fitness self concept: Relations to field and technical indicators of physical fitness for boys and girls aged 9-15. *Journal of Sports & Exercise Psychology, 15,* 184-206.

Marsh, H.W. (1994). Sport motivation orientations: Beware of the jingle-jangle fallacies. *Journal of Sport & Exercise Psychology, 16,* 365-380.

Marsh, H.W. (1996a). Construct validity of Physical Self-Description Questionnaire responses: Relations to external criteria. *Journal of Sport & Exercise Psychology, 18(2),* 111-131.

Marsh, H.W. (1996b). Physical Self-Description Questionnaire: Stability and discriminant validity. *Research Quarterly for Exercise and Sport, 67,* 249-264.

Marsh, H.W. (1997). The measurement of physical self-concept: A construct validation approach. In K. Fox (Ed.), *The physical self-concept: From motivation to well-being* (pp. 27-58). Champaign, IL: Human Kinetics.

Marsh, H.W. (1998). Age and gender effects in physical self-concepts for adolescent elite-athletes and non-athletes: A multi-cohort-multi-occasion design. *Journal of Sport & Exercise Psychology, 20(3),* 237-259.

Marsh, H.W. (1999). Cognitive discrepancy models: Actual, ideal, potential, and future self-perspectives of body image. *Social Cognition, 17,* 46-75.

Marsh, H.W. (2002). A multidimensional physical self-concept: A construct validity approach to theory, measurement, and research. *Psychology: The Journal of the Hellenic Psychological Society, 9,* 459-493.

Marsh, H.W., Asci, F.H., Tomas-Marco, I. (2002). Multitrait-multimethod analyses of two physical self-concept instruments: A cross-cultural perspective. *Journal of Sports & Exercise Psychology, 24,* 99-119.

Marsh, H.W., Byrne, B.M., & Yeung, A.S. (1999). Causal ordering of academic self-concept and achievement: Reanalysis of a pioneering study and revised recommendations. *Educational Psychologist, 34,* 155-167.

Marsh, H.W., Chanal, J.P., Sarrazin, P.G., & Bois, J.E. (in press). Self-belief does make a difference: A reciprocal effects model of the causal ordering of physical self-concept and gymnastics performance. *Journal of Sport Sciences.*

Marsh, H.W., & Craven, R. (1997). Academic self-concept: Beyond the dustbowl. In G. Phye (Ed.), *Handbook of classroom assessment: Learning, Achievement, and adjustment* (pp. 131-198). Orlando, FL: Academic Press.

Marsh, H.W., & Hattie, J. (1996). Theoretical perspectives on the structure of self-concept. In B.A. Bracken (Ed.), *Handbook of self-concept* (pp. 38-90). New York: Wiley.

Marsh, H.W., Hau, K.T., Sung, R.Y.T., Yu, C.W. (2005). *Childhood obesity, gender, Actual–ideal body image discrepancies, and physical self-concept in Hong Kong children: Cultural differences in the value of moderation.* Sydney: University of Western Sydney.

Marsh, H.W., Hey, J., Johnson, S., & Perry, C. (1997). Elite Athlete Self-Description Questionnaire: Hierarchical confirmatory factor analysis of responses by two distinct groups of elite athletes. *International Journal of Sport Psychology, 28,* 237-258.

Marsh, H.W., Hey, J., Roche, L.A., & Perry, C. (1997). The structure of physical self-concept: Elite athletes and physical education students. *Journal of Educational Psychology, 89,* 369-380.

Marsh, H.W. & Jackson, S.A. (1986). Multidimensional self-concepts, masculinity and femininity as a function of women's involvement in athletics. *Sex Roles, 15,* 391-416.

Marsh, H.W., Papaioannou, A., & Theodorakis, Y. (in press). Causal ordering of physical self-concept and exercise behavior: Reciprocal effects model and the influence of physical education teachers. *Health Psychology.*

Marsh, H.W., & Peart, N. (1988). Competitive and cooperative physical fitness training programs for girls: Effects on physical fitness and on multidimensional self-concepts. *Journal of Sport & Exercise Psychology, 10,* 390-407.

Marsh, H.W., & Perry, C. (2005). Does a positive self-concept contribute to winning gold medals in elite swimming? The causal ordering of elite athlete self-concept and championship performances. *Journal of Sport & Exercise Psychology, 27,* 71-91.

Marsh, H.W., Perry, C., Horsely, C., & Roche, L.A. (1995). Multidimensional self-concepts of elite athletes: How do they differ from the general population? *Sport and Exercise Psychology, 17,* 70-83.

Marsh, H.W., & Richards, G. (1988). The Outward Bound bridging course for low achieving high-school males: Effect on academic achievement and multidimensional self-concepts. *Australian Journal of Psychology, 40,* 281-298.

Marsh, H.W., Richards, G., & Barnes, J. (1986a). Multidimensional self-concepts: A long-term follow-up of the effect of participation in an Outward Bound program. *Personality and Social Psychology Bulletin, 12,* 475-492.

Marsh, H.W., Richards, G., & Barnes, J. (1986b). Multidimensional self-concepts: The effect of participation in an Outward Bound program. *Journal of Personality and Social Psychology, 45,* 173-187.

Marsh, H.W., Richards, G.E., Johnson, S., Roche, L., & Tremayne, P. (1994). Physical Self-Description Questionnaire: Psychometric properties and a multitrait-multimethod analysis of relations to existing instruments. *Sport and Exercise Psychology, 16,* 270-305.

Marsh, H.W., & Roche, L.A. (1996). Predicting self-esteem from perceptions of actual and ideal ratings of body fatness—is there only one ideal supermodel? *Research Quarterly for Exercise and Sport, 67,* 13-23.

Marsh, H.W., & Shavelson, R.J. (1985). *Self-concept: Its multifaceted, hierarchical structure. Educational Psychologist, 20,* 107-125.

Marsh, H.W., Tomas, I., & Asci, F.H. (2002). Cross-cultural validity of the Physical Self-Description Questionnaire: Comparison of factor structures in Australia, Spain, and Turkey. *Research Quarterly for Exercise and Sport, 73(3),* 257-270.

Marsh, H.W., Walker, R., & Debus, R. (1991). Subject-specific components of academic self-concept and self-efficacy. *Contemporary Educational Psychology, 16,* 331-345.

Marsh, H.W., & Yeung, A.S. (1997). Coursework selection: The effects of academic self-concept and achievement. *American Educational Research Journal, 34,* 691-720.

O'Mara, A.J., Marsh H.W., Craven, R.G., & Debus, R. (in press). Do self-concept interventions make a difference? A synergistic blend of construct validation and meta-analysis. *Educational Psychologist.*

Richards, G.E. (1988). *Physical Self-Concept Scale.* Sydney: Australian Outward Bound Foundation.

Seligman, M.E.P., & Csikszentmihalyi, M. (2000). Positive psychology: An introduction. *American Psychologist, 55,* 5-14.

Shavelson, R.J., Hubner, J.J., & Stanton, G.C. (1976). Validation of construct interpretations. *Review of Educational Research, 46,* 407-441.

Sonstroem, R.J. (1978). Physical estimation and attraction scales: Rationale and research. *Medicine and Science in Sport, 10,* 97-102.

Valentine, J.C., DuBois, D.L., & Cooper, H. (2004). The relations between self-beliefs and academic achievement: A systematic review. *Educational Psychologist, 39,* 111-133.

Vallerand, R.J., Blanchard, C., Mageau, G.A., Koestner, R., Ratelle, C., Leonard, M., Gagne, M., & Marsolais, J. (2003). Les passions de l'ame: On obsessive and harmonious passion. *Journal of Personality and Social Psychology, 85,* 756-767.

Wylie, R.C. (1979). *The self-concept* (Vol. 2). Lincoln, NE: University of Nebraska Press.

Wylie, R.C. (1989). *Measures of self-concept.* Lincoln, NE: University of Nebraska Press.

Chapter 13

Ames, C. (1992). Achievement goals, motivational climates, and motivational processes. In G.C. Roberts (Ed), *Motivation in sport and exercise* (pp. 161-176). Champaign, IL: Human Kinetics.

Avolio, B.J., Bass, B.M., & Jung, D.I. (1999). Reexamining the components of transformational and transactional leadership using the multifactor leadership questionnaire. *Journal of Occupational and Organizational Psychology, 72,* 441-462.

Bandura, A. (1977). Self-efficacy: Toward a unifying theory of behavioral change. *Psychological Review, 84,* 191-215.

Bandura, A. (1986). *Social foundations of thought and action: A social cognitive theory.* Englewood Cliffs, NJ: Prentice Hall.

Bandura, A. (1997). *Self-efficacy: The exercise of control.* New York: W.H. Freeman & Company.

Bandura, A. (1999). Social cognitive theory of personality. In D. Cervone & Y. Shoda (Eds.), *The coherence of personality: Social-cognitive bases of consistency, variability, and organization* (pp. 105-241). New York: Guilford.

Bandura, A. (2000). Exercise of human agency through collective efficacy. *Current Directions in Psychological Science, 9,* 75-78.

Bass, B.M., & Avolio, B.J. (1994). *Improving organizational effectiveness through transformational leadership.* Thousand Oaks, CA: Sage.

Beauchamp, M.R., & Bray, S.R. (2001). Role ambiguity and role conflict within interdependent teams. *Small Group Research, 32,* 133-157.

Beauchamp, M.R., Bray, S.R., & Albinson, J.G. (2002). Precompetition imagery, self-efficacy and performance in collegiate golfers. *Journal of Sports Sciences, 20,* 697-705.

Beauchamp, M.R., Bray, S.R., Eys, M.A., & Carron, A.V. (2002). Role ambiguity, role efficacy, and role performance: Multidimensional and mediational relationships within interdependent sport teams. *Group Dynamics: Theory, Research, and Practice, 6,* 229-242.

Beauchamp, M.R., Bray, S.R., Fielding, A., & Eys, M.A. (2005). A multilevel investigation of the relationship between role ambiguity and role efficacy in sport. *Psychology of Sport and Exercise, 6,* 289-302.

Beauchamp, M.R., Welch, A.S., & Hulley, A.J. (in press). Transformational and transactional leadership and exercise-related self-efficacy: An exploratory study. *Journal of Health Psychology.*

Beauchamp, M.R., & Whinton, L.C. (2005). Self-efficacy and other-efficacy in dyadic performance: Riding as one in equestrian eventing. *Journal of Sport & Exercise Psychology, 27,* 245-252.

Biddle, B.J., & Thomas, E.J. (1966). *Role theory: Concepts and research.* New York: Wiley.

Bray, S.R. (2004). Collective efficacy, group goals, and group performance of a muscular endurance task. *Small Group Research, 35,* 230-238.

Bray, S.R., Balaguer, I., & Duda, J.L. (2004). The relationship of task self-efficacy and role efficacy beliefs to role performance in Spanish youth soccer. *Journal of Sports Sciences, 22,* 429-437.

Bray, S.R., & Brawley, L.R. (2002). Role efficacy, role clarity, and role performance effectiveness. *Small Group Research, 33,* 233-253.

Bray, S.R., Brawley, L.R., & Carron, A.V. (2002). Efficacy for interdependent role functions: Evidence from the sport domain. *Small Group Research, 33,* 644-666.

Bray, S.R., Gyurcsik, N.C., Culos-Reed, S.N., Dawson, K.A., & Martin, K.A. (2001). An exploratory investigation of the relationship between proxy efficacy, self-efficacy and exercise attendance. *Journal of Health Psychology, 6,* 425-434.

Bray, S.R., Gyurcsik, N.C., Martin-Ginis, K.A., & Culos-Reed, S.N. (2004). The proxy efficacy exercise questionnaire: Development of an instrument to assess female exercisers' proxy efficacy beliefs in structured group exercise classes. *Journal of Sport & Exercise Psychology, 26,* 442-456.

Caprara, G.V., Barbaranelli, C., Borgogni, L., Petitta, L., Rubinacci, A. (2003). Teachers', school staff's and parents' efficacy beliefs as determinants of attitudes toward school. *European Journal of Psychology of Education, 18,* 15-31.

Caprara, G.V., Barbaranelli, C., Borgogni, L., & Steca, P. (2003). Efficacy beliefs as determinants of teachers' job satisfaction. *Journal of Educational Psychology, 95,* 821-832.

Carron, A.V., & Hausenblas, H. (1998). *Group dynamics in sport* (2nd ed). Morgantown, WV: Fitness Information Technology.

Chan, D. (1998). Functional relations among constructs in the same content domain at different levels of analysis: A typology of composition models. *Journal of Applied Psychology, 83,* 234-246.

Chase, M.A., Lirgg, C.D., & Feltz, D.F. (1997). Do coaches' efficacy expectations for their team predict team performance? *The Sport Psychologist, 11,* 8-23.

Chelladurai, P., & Riemer H.A. (1998). Measurement of leadership in sport. In J.L. Duda (Ed.), *Advances in sport and exercise psychology measurement* (pp. 227-253). Morgantown, WV: Fitness Information Technology.

Chemers, M.M., Watson C.B., & May, S. (2000). Dispositional affect and leadership effectiveness: A comparison of self-esteem, optimism, and efficacy. *Personality and Social Psychology Bulletin, 26,* 267-231.

Chen, G., & Bliese, P.D. (2002). The role of different levels of leadership in predicting self- and collective efficacy: Evidence for discontinuity. *Journal of Applied Psychology, 87,* 549-556.

Cleary, M. (2004, September 8). Robinson determined to make suit fit. *The Telegraph,* p. S2.

Cleary, M. (2004, November 25). Black keeps Jonny on the ball. *The Telegraph,* p. S5.

Cracknell, J. (2004, December 1). There's nobody else I would rather have in my boat than the big fella. *The Telegraph,* p. S5.

Crocker, J., & Luhtanen, R. (1990). Collective self-esteem and in-group bias. *Journal of Personality and Social Psychology, 58,* 60-67.

Denham, C.H., & Michael, J.J. (1981). Teacher sense of efficacy: A definition of the construct and a model for further research. *Educational Research Quarterly, 5,* 39-63.

Dowrick, P.W. (1999). A review of self-modeling and related interventions. *Applied and Preventive Psychology, 8,* 23-39.

Duhatschek, E. (2002, February 15). Waiting game is about to end. *The Globe and Mail* [city of publication], p. O6.

Escartí, A., & Guzmán, J. (1999). Effects of feedback on self-efficacy, performance and choice in an athletic task. *Journal of Applied Sport Psychology, 11,* 83-96.

Feltz, D.L. (1992). Understanding motivation in sport: A self-efficacy perspective. In G.C. Roberts (Ed.), *Motivation in sport and exercise* (pp. 107-128). Champaign, IL: Human Kinetics.

Feltz, D.L., & Chase, M.A. (1998). The measurement of self-efficacy and confidence in sport. In J.L. Duda (Ed.), *Advances in sport and exercise psychology measurement* (pp. 65-80). Morgantown, WV: Fitness Information Technology.

Feltz, D.L., Chase, M.A., Moritz, S.E., & Sullivan, P.J. (1999). A conceptual model of coaching efficacy: Preliminary investigation and instrument development. *Journal of Educational Psychology, 91,* 765-776.

Feltz, D.L., & Lirgg, C.D. (1998). Perceived team and player efficacy in hockey. *Journal of Applied Psychology, 83,* 557-564.

Feltz, D.L., & Lirgg, C.D. (2001). Self-efficacy beliefs of athletes, teams, and coaches. In R.N. Singer, H.A. Hausenblas, & C.M. Janelle (Eds.), *Handbook of sport psychology* (2nd ed., pp. 340-361). New York: Wiley.

Forsyth, D.R. (1999). *Group dynamics* (3rd ed.). Belmont, CA: Wadsworth.

Gibson, C.B. (1999). Do they do what they believe they can? Group efficacy and group effectiveness across tasks and cultures. *Academy of Management Journal, 42,* 138-152.

Gibson, C.B., Randel, A.E., & Earley, P.C. (2000). Understanding group efficacy: An empirical test of multiple assessment methods. *Group and Organization Management, 25,* 67-97.

Greenlees, I.A., Nunn, R.L., Graydon, J.K., & Maynard, I.W. (1999). The relationship between collective efficacy and precompetitive affect in rugby players: Testing Bandura's model of collective efficacy. *Perceptual Motor Skills, 89,* 431-440.

Halliwell, W. (1990). Providing sport psychology consultant services in professional hockey. *The Sport Psychologist, 4,* 369-377.

Hayward, P. (2001, June 25). Sampras back on centre stage. *The Telegraph,* p. 61.

Heuzé, J.P., Raimbault, N., & Fontayne, P. (2004). Collective efficacy as a mediator of the cohesion-performance relationship in professional basketball teams. *Journal of Sport & Exercise Psychology, 26,* S91.

Hodges, L., & Carron, A.V. (1992). Collective efficacy and team performance. *International Journal of Sport Psychology, 23,* 48-59.

Hoyt, C.L., Murphy, S.E., Halverson, S.K., & Watson, C.B. (2003). Group leadership: Efficacy and effectiveness. *Group Dynamics: Theory, Research, and Practice, 7,* 259-274.

Jex, S.M., & Bliese, P.D. (1999). Efficacy beliefs as a moderator of the impact of work-related stressors: A multilevel study. *Journal of Applied Psychology, 84,* 349-361.

Jung, D.I., & Sosik, J.J. (2002). Transformational leadership in work groups: The role of empowerment, cohesiveness, and collective efficacy on perceived group performance. *Small Group Research, 33,* 313-336.

Kahn, R.L., Wolfe, D.M., Quinn, R.P., Snoek, J.D., & Rosenthal, R.A. (1964). *Organizational stress: Studies in role conflict and ambiguity.* New York: Wiley.

Kane, T.D., Marks, M.A., Zaccaro, S.J., & Blair, V. (1996). Self-efficacy, personal goals, and wrestlers' self-regulation. *Journal of Sport & Exercise Psychology, 18,* 36-48.

Kent, A., & Sullivan, P.J. (2003). Coaching efficacy as a predictor of university coaches' commitment. *International Sports Journal, 7,* 78-88.

Lent, R.W., & Lopez, F.G. (2002). Cognitive ties that bind: A tripartite view of efficacy beliefs in growth-promoting relationships. *Journal of Social and Clinical Psychology, 21,* 256-286.

Lindsley, D.H., Brass, D.J., & Thomas, J.B. (1995). Efficacy-performance spirals: A multilevel perspective. *Academy of Management Review, 20,* 645-678.

Mabry, E.A., & Barnes, R.E. (1980). *The dynamics of small group communication.* Englewood Cliffs, NJ: Prentice Hall.

Mair, L. (2004, November 17). Confidence in Casey. *The Telegraph,* p. S2.

Magyar, T.M., Feltz, D.L., & Simpson, I.P. (2004). Individual and crew level determinants of collective efficacy in rowing. *Journal of Sport & Exercise Psychology, 26,* 136-153.

Malete, L., & Feltz, D.L. (2000). The effect of a coaching education program on coaching efficacy. *The Sport Psychologist, 14,* 410-417.

McAuley, E., Duncan, T.E., & McElroy, M. (1989). Self-efficacy cognitions and causal attributions for children's motor performance: An exploratory investigation. *Journal of Genetic Psychology, 150,* 65-73.

McAuley, E., Talbot, H., & Martinez, S. (1999). Manipulating self-efficacy in the exercise environment in women: Influences on affective responses. *Health Psychology, 18,* 288-294.

McCullagh, P., & Weiss, M.R. (2001). Modeling: Considerations for motor skill performance and psychological responses. In R.N. Singer, H.A. Hausenblas, & C.M. Janelle (Eds.), *Handbook of sport psychology* (2nd ed., pp. 205-238). New York: Wiley.

Milne, M.I., Hall, C., & Forwell, L. (2004). The predictive relationships between self-efficacy, imagery use, and rehabilitation adherence. *Journal of Sport & Exercise Psychology, 26,* S137.

Moritz, S.E., Feltz, D.L., Fahrbach, K.R., & Mack, D.E. (2000). The relation of self efficacy measures to sport performance: A meta-analytic review. *Research Quarterly for Exercise and Sport, 71,* 280-294.

Moritz, S.E., & Watson, C.B. (1998). Levels of analysis issues in group psychology: Using efficacy as an example of a multilevel model. *Group Dynamics: Theory, Research, and Practice, 2,* 285-298.

Myers, N.D., Feltz, D.L., & Short, S.E. (2004). Collective efficacy and team performance: A longitudinal study of collegiate football teams. *Group Dynamics: Theory, Research, & Practice, 8,* 126-138.

Myers, N.D., Payment, C.A., & Feltz, D.L. (2004). Reciprocal relationships between collective efficacy and team performance in women's ice hockey. *Group Dynamics: Theory, Research, and Practice, 8,* 182-195.

Myers, N.D., Vargas-Tonsing, T.M., & Feltz, D.L. (2005). Coaching efficacy in intercollegiate coaches: Sources, coaching behavior, and team variables. *Psychology of Sport and Exercise, 6,* 129-143.

Myers, N., Wolfe, E., & Feltz, D. (2004). An evaluation of the psychometric properties of the Coaching Efficacy Scale (CES) for American coaches. *Journal of Sport & Exercise Psychology, 26,* S141.

Paskevich, D.M., Brawley, L.R., Dorsch, K.D., & Widmeyer, W.N. (1999). Relationship between collective efficacy and team cohesion: Conceptual and measurement issues. *Group Dynamics: Theory, Research, and Practice, 3,* 210-222.

Prussia, G.E., & Kinicki, A.J. (1996). A motivational investigation of group effectiveness using social-cognitive theory. *Journal of Applied Psychology, 81,* 187-198.

Salas, E., Dickinson, T., Converse, S.A., & Tannenbaum, S.I. (1992). Toward an understanding of team performance and training. In R.W. Swezey & E. Salas (Eds.), *Teams: Their training and performance* (pp. 3-29). Norwood, NJ: Ablex.

Seefeldt, V., & Brown, E.W. (1990). *Program for athletic coaches education.* Carmel, IN: Benchmark Press.

Shaw, M.E., & Costanzo, P.R. (1982). *Theories of social psychology* (2nd ed). New York: McGraw-Hill.

Shea, G.P., & Guzzo, R.A. (1987). Groups as human resources. In K.M. Rowland & G.P. Ferris (Eds.), *Research in personnel and human resources* (Vol. 5, pp. 323-356). Greenwich, CT: JAI Press.

Shea, C.M., & Howell, J.M. (2000). Efficacy-performance spirals: An empirical test. *Journal of Management, 26,* 791-812.

Sherif, M., & Sherif, C.W. (1953). *Groups in harmony and tension.* New York: Harper & Row.

Sherif, M., & Sherif, C.W. (1969). *Social psychology.* New York: Harper & Row.

Swift, E.M. (1996, October 7). The good old days: What Mark Messier and Wayne Gretzky hope to recapture in New York. *Sports Illustrated, 85,* 54-60.

Treasure, D.C., Monson, J., & Lox, C.L. (1996). Relationship between self-efficacy, wrestling performance, and affect prior to competition. *The Sport Psychologist, 10,* 73-83.

Vealey, R.S., Hayashi, S.W., Garner-Holman G., & Giacobbi, P. (1998). Sources of sport confidence: Conceptualization and instrument development. *Journal of Sport & Exercise Psychology, 20,* 54-80.

Watson, C.B., Chemers, M.M., & Preiser, N. (2001). Collective efficacy: A multilevel analysis. *Personality and Social Psychology Bulletin, 27,* 1057-1068.

Zaccaro, S.J., Blair, V., Peterson, C. & Zazanis, M. (1995). Collective efficacy. In J.E. Maddux (Ed.), *Self-efficacy, Adaptation, and adjustment* (pp. 305-330). New York: Plenum Press.

Chapter 14

Anderson, N.H. (1981). *Foundations of information integration theory.* New York: Academic Press.

Ansorge, C.J., Scheer, J.K., Laub, J., & Howard, J. (1978). Bias in judging women's gymnastics induced by expectations of within team order. *Research Quarterly, 49,* 399-405.

Argyle, M. (1994). *The psychology of interpersonal behaviour* (5th ed.). London: Penguin.

Barnes, J. (1999). *John Barnes: The autobiography.* London: Headline Books.

Beck, A.T. (1976). *Cognitive therapy and the emotional disorders.* Madison, CT: International Universities Press.

Bodenhausen, G.V., Macrae, C.N., & Sherman, J.W. (1999). On the dialectics of discrimination: Dual processes in social stereotyping. In S. Chaiken & Y. Trope (Eds.), *Dual process theories in social psychology* (pp. 271-290). New York: Guilford.

Bull, S.J., Albinson, J.G., & Shambrook, C.J. (1996). *The mental game plan: Getting psyched for sport.* Morgantown, WV: Fitness Information Technology.

Chapman, L.J., & Chapman, J.P. (1967). Genesis of popular but erroneous diagnostic observations. *Journal of Abnormal Psychology, 72,* 193-204.

Chapman, L.J., & Chapman, J.P. (1969). Illusory correlation as an obstacle to the use of valid psychodiagnostic signs. *Journal of Abnormal Psychology, 74,* 271-280.

Christie, L. (1996). *To be honest with you.* London: Penguin.

Cohen, C.E. (1981). Goal schemata in person perception: Making sense from the stream of behaviour. In N. Cantor & J. Kihlstrom (Eds.), *Personality, cognition and social behaviour* (pp. 45-68). New Jersey: Erlbaum.

Darley, J.M., & Gross, R.H. (1983). A hypothesis-confirming bias in labelling effects. *Journal of Personality & Social Psychology, 44,* 20-33.

Dijker, A.J.M. (1987). Emotional reactions to ethnic minorities. *European Journal of Social Psychology, 17,* 305-325.

Eyal, N., Bar-Eli, M., Tenenbaum, G., & Pie, J.S. (1995). Manipulated outcome expectations and competitive performance in motor tasks with gradually increasing difficulty. *The Sport Psychologist, 9,* 188-200.

Eysenck, M.W. (1992). *Anxiety: The cognitive approach.* Hove, UK: Erlbaum.

Feltz, D.L., & Reissinger, C.A. (1990). Effects of in vivo emotive imagery and performance feedback on self-efficacy and muscular endurance. *Journal of Sport & Exercise Psychology, 12,* 132-143.

Findlay, L.C., & Ste-Marie, D.M. (2004). A reputation bias in figure skating. *Journal of Sport & Exercise Psychology, 26,* 154-166.

Fiske, S.T., Lin, M., & Neuberg, S.L. (1999). The continuum model: Ten years later. In S. Chaiken & Y. Trope (Eds.), *Dual process theories in social psychology* (pp. 231-254) New York: Guilford.

Fiske, S.T., & Neuberg, S.L. (1990). A continuum of impression formation, from category-based to individuating processes: Influences of information and motivation on attention and interpretation. In M.P. Zanna (Ed.), *Advances in experimental social psychology* (Vol. 23, pp. 1-74). New York: Academic Press.

Fiske, S.T., Neuberg, S.L., Beattie, A.E., & Milberg, S.J. (1987). Category-based and attribute-based reactions to others: Some informational conditions of stereotyping and individuating processes. *Journal of Experimental Social Psychology, 23,* 399-427.

Fiske, S.T., & Taylor, S.E. (1991). Social cognition. Reading, MA: Addison-Wesley.

Frank, M.G., & Gilovich, T. (1988). The dark side of self- and social perception: Black uniforms and aggression in professional sports. *Journal of Personality & Social Psychology, 54,* 74-85.

Greenlees, I.A., Bradley, A., Holder, T.P., & Thelwell, R.C. (2005). The impact of two forms of opponents' nonverbal communication on impression formation and outcome expectations. *Psychology of Sport & Exercise.*

Greenlees, I., Buscombe, R., Thelwell, R., Holder, T., & Rimmer, M. (2005). *Impact of opponents' clothing and body language on impression formation and outcome expectations.* Manuscript submitted for publication.

Hackfort, D. & Schlattmann, A. (2002). Self-presentation training for top athletes. *International Journal of Sport Psychology, 33,* 61-71.

Hashtroudi, S., Mutter, S.A., Cole, E.A., & Green, S.K. (1984). Schema-consistent and schema-inconsistent information: Processing demands. *Personality & Social Psychology Bulletin, 97,* 363-386.

Horn, T.S. (1984). Expectancy effects in the interscholastic athletic setting: Methodological considerations. *Journal of Sport Psychology, 1,* 60-76.

Horn, T.S., & Lox, C. (1993). The self-fulfilling prophecy theory: When coaches' expectations become reality. In J.M. Williams (Ed.), *Applied sport psychology: Personal growth to peak performance* (pp. 68-81). Mountain View, CA: Mayfield.

Janelle, C.M., Singer, R.M., & Williams, A.M. (1999). External distraction and attentional narrowing: Visual search evidence. *Journal of Sport & Exercise Psychology, 21,* 70-91.

Jones, E.E. (1996). *Interpersonal perception.* New York: Freeman.

Jones, M.V., Paull, G.C. and Erskine, J. (2002). The impact of a team's aggressive reputation on the decisions of association football referees. *Journal of Sports Sciences, 20,* 991-1000.

Kahneman, D. (1973). *Attention and effort.* Englewood Cliffs, NJ: Prentice Hall.

Knapp, M.L. (1978). *Nonverbal communication in human interaction.* New York: Holt, Rhinehart & Winston.

Langer, E. (1975). The illusion of control. *Journal of Personality & Social Psychology, 32,* 311-328.

Lazarus, R. (2000). How emotions influence performance in competitive sports. *The Sport Psychologist, 14,* 229-252.

Loehr, J.E. (1990). *Mental toughness training for sports: Achieving athletic excellence.* Lexington: Stephen Green Press.

Macrae, C.N. (2000). Social cognition: Thinking categorically about others. *Annual Review of Psychology, 51,* 93-120.

Macrae, C.N., Bodenhausen, G.V., Milne, A.B., & Jetten, J. (1994). Out of mind but back in sight: Stereotypes on the rebound. *Journal of Personality & Social Psychology, 67,* 808-817.

Miki, H., Tsuchiya, H., & Nishino, A. (1993). Influence of expectancy of opponents' competence upon information processing of their discrete attributes. *Perceptual & Motor Skills, 77,* 987-993.

Miller, D.T. & Turnbull, W. (1986). Expectancies and interpersonal processes. *Annual Review of Psychology, 37,* 233-256.

Nadler, A., Fisher, J.D., & Streufert, S. (1974). The donor's dilemma: Recipients' reactions to aid from friend or foe. *Journal of Applied Social Psychology, 4,* 275-285.

Olson, J.M., Roese, N.J., & Zanna, M.P. (1996). Expectancies. In E.T. Higgins & A.W. Kruglanski (Eds.), *Social psychology: Handbook of basic principles* (pp. 211-237). New York: Guilford.

Pendry, L.F., & Macrae, C.N. (1996). What the disinterested perceiver overlooks: Goal directed social categorization. *Personality & Social Psychology Bulletin, 22,* 249-256.

Plessner, H. (1999). Expectation biases in gymnastics judging. *Journal of Sport & Exercise Psychology, 21,* 131-144.

Prapavessis, H., Grove, J.R., & Eklund, R.C. (2004). Self-presentational issues in competition and sport. *Journal of Applied Sport Psychology, 16,* 19-40.

Redgrave, S., & Townsend, N. (2000). *A golden age.* London: BBC Worldwide.

Rejeski, W., Darracott, C., & Hutslar, S. (1979). Pygmalion in youth sport: A field study. *Journal of Sport Psychology, 1,* 311-319.

Rimmer, M., Greenlees, I.A., Graydon, J.K. & Buscombe, R. (2004). *A qualitative examination of the role of interpersonal perception in tennis competition.* Manuscript submitted for publication.

Rosenthal, R., & Jacobsen, L. (1968). *Pygmalion in the classroom: Teacher expectations and pupils' intellectual development.* New York: Holt, Rhinehart & Winston.

Ruscher, J.B., & Fiske, S.T. (1990). Interpersonal competition can cause individuating processes. *Journal of Personality & Social Psychology, 58,* 832-843.

Ruscher, J.B., Fiske, S.T., Miki, H., & Van Manen, S. (1991). Individuating processes in competition: Interpersonal versus intergroup. *Personality & Social Psychology Bulletin, 17,* 595-605.

Sadalla, E.K., Linder, D.E., Jenkins, B.A. (1988). Sport preference: A self-presentational analysis. *Journal of Sport & Exercise Psychology, 10,* 214-222.

Scheer, J.K. (1973). Effect of placement in the order of competition on scores of Nebraska high school students. *Research Quarterly, 44,* 79-85.

Scheer, J.K., & Ansgorge, C.J. (1975). Effects of naturally induced judges' expectations on the ratings of physical performances. *Research Quarterly, 46,* 463-470.

Scheer, J.K., Ansgorge, C.J., & Howard, J. (1983). Judging bias induced by viewing contrived videotapes: A function of selected psychological variables. *Journal of Sport Psychology, 5,* 427-437.

Sinclair, D.A., & Vealey, R.S. (1989). Effects of coaches' expectations and feedback on the self-perceptions of athletes. *Journal of Sport Behavior, 12,* 77-91.

Snyder, M. (1984). When belief creates reality. *Advances in Experimental Social Psychology, 18,* 247-305.

Snyder, M., Tanke, E.D., & Berscheid, E. (1977). Social perception and interpersonal behavior: On the self-fulfilling nature of social stereotypes. *Journal of Personality & Social Psychology, 35,* 656-666.

Solomon, G.B., Golden, A.J., Ciapponi, T.M., & Martin, A.D. (1998). Coach expectations and differential feedback: Perceptual flexibility revisited. *Journal of Sport Behavior, 21,* 298-310.

Solomon, G.B., & Kosmitzki, C. (1996). Perceptual flexibility and differential feedback among intercollegiate basketball coaches. *Journal of Sport Behavior, 19,* 163-177.

Solomon, G.B., Striegel, D.A., Eliot, J.F., Heon, S.N., & Maas, J.L. (1996). The self-fulfilling prophecy in college basketball: Implications for effective coaching. *Journal of Applied Sport Psychology, 8,* 44-59.

Solomon, G.B., Wiegardt, P.A., Yusuf, F.R., Kosmitzki, C., Williams, J., Stevens, C.E., & Wayda, V.K. (1996). Expectancies and ethnicity: The self-fulfilling prophecy in college basketball. *Journal of Sport & Exercise Psychology, 18,* 83-88.

Stone, J., Perry, Z.W., & Darley, J.M. (1997). White men can't jump: Evidence for the perceptual confirmation of racial stereotypes following a basketball game. *Basic and Applied Social Psychology, 19,* 291-306.

Warr, P.B., & Knapper, C. (1968). *The perception of people and events.* London: Wiley.

Weinberg, R.S. (1988). *The mental advantage: Developing your psychological skills in tennis.* Champaign, IL: Leisure Press.

Weinberg, R., Gould, D., & Jackson, A. (1979). Expectations and performance: An empirical test of Bandura's self-efficacy theory. *Journal of Sport Psychology, 3,* 345-354.

Williams, A.M., & Elliott, D. (1999). Anxiety, expertise and visual search strategy in karate. *Journal of Sport & Exercise Psychology, 21,* 362-375.

Woodman, T., & Hardy, L. (2003). The relative impact of cognitive anxiety and self-confidence on sport performance: A meta-analysis. *Journal of Sport Sciences, 13,* 443-457.

Wyer, N.A., Sherman, J.W., & Stroessner, S.J. (1998). The spontaneous suppression of racial stereotypes. *Social Cognition, 16,* 340-352.

Zadney, J., & Gerard, H.B. (1974). Attributed intentions and informational selectivity. *Journal of Experimental Social Psychology, 10,* 34-52.

Chapter 15

Bailis, D.S. (2001). Benefits of self-handicapping in sport: A field study of university athletes. *Canadian Journal of Behavioral Sciences, 33,* 213-223.

Berglas, S., & Jones, E.E. (1978). Drug choice as a self-handicapping strategy in response to noncontingent success. *Journal of Personality and Social Psychology, 36,* 405-417.

Carron, A.V., Burke, S.M., & Prapavessis, H. (2004). Self-presentation and group influence. *Journal of Applied Sport Psychology, 16,* 41-58.

Carron, A.V., Prapavessis, H., & Grove, J.R. (1994). Group effects and self-handicapping. *Journal of Sport & Exercise Psychology, 16,* 246-257.

Cooley, D. (2004). An investigation of the assumptions of self-handicapping: Youth responses to evaluative threat in the physical domain. Unpublished doctoral thesis, Victoria University of Technology, Australia.

Crant, J.M. (1996). Doing more harm than good: When impression management is likely to evoke a negative response. *Journal of Applied Social Psychology, 26,* 1454-1471.

Deppe, R.K., & Harackiewicz, J.M. (1996). Self-handicapping and intrinsic motivation: Buffering intrinsic motivation from the threat of failure. *Journal of Personality & Social Psychology, 70,* 868-876.

Feick, D.L., & Rhodewalt, F. (1997). The double-edged sword of self-handicapping: Discounting, Augmentation, and the protection and enhancement of self-esteem. *Motivation & Emotion, 21,* 147-163.

Ferrari, J.R., & Tice, D.M. (2000). Procrastination as a self-handicap for men and women: A task-avoidance strategy in a laboratory setting. *Journal of Research in Personality, 34,* 73-83.

Goffman, E. (1959). *The presentation of self in everyday life.* New York: Doubleday.

Gould, R., Brounstein, P.J., & Sigall, H. (1977). Attributing ability to an opponent: Public aggrandizement and private denigration. *Social Psychology Quarterly, 40,* 254-261.

Harris, R.N., & Snyder, C.R. (1986). The role of uncertain self-esteem in self-handicapping. *Journal of Personality & Social Psychology, 51,* 451-458.

Hausenblas, H., & Carron, A.V. (1996). Group cohesion and self-handicapping in female and male athletes. *Journal of Sport & Exercise Psychology, 18,* 132-143.

Heider, H. (1958). *The psychology of interpersonal relations.* New York: Wiley.

Higgins, R.L. (1990). Self-handicapping: Historical roots and contemporary branches. In R.L. Higgins, C.R. Snyder, & S. Berglas (Eds.), *Self-handicapping: The paradox that isn't* (pp. 1-35). New York: Plenum Press.

Higgins, R.L., & Harris, R.N. (1988). Strategic "alcohol" use: Drinking to self-handicap. *Journal of Social and Clinical Psychology, 6,* 191-202.

Higgins, R.L., & Snyder, C.R. (1990). Self-handicapping from a Heiderian perspective: Taking stock of "bonds." In R.L. Higgins, C.R. Snyder, & S. Berglas (Eds.), *Self-handicapping: The paradox that isn't* (pp. 239-273). New York: Plenum Press.

Hirt, E.R., Deppe, R.K., & Gordon, L.J. (1991). Self-reported versus behavioral self-handicapping: Empirical evidence for a theoretical distinction. *Journal of Personality & Social Psychology, 61,* 981-991.

Hirt, E.R., McCrea, S.M., & Kimble, C.E. (2000). Public self-focus and sex differences in behavioral self-handicapping: Does increasing self-threat still make it "just a man's game?" *Personality & Social Psychology Bulletin, 26,* 1131-1141.

Hobden, K., & Pliner, P. (1995). Self-handicapping and dimensions of perfectionism: Self-presentation vs. self-protection. *Journal of Research in Personality, 29,* 461-474.

Jones, E.E., & Berglas, S. (1978). Control of attributions about the self through self-handicapping strategies: The appeal of alcohol and the role of underachievement. *Personality & Social Psychology Bulletin, 4,* 200-206.

Jones, E.E., & Rhodewalt, F. (1982). *The Self-Handicapping Scale.* Unpublished manuscript, Princeton University.

Kelly, H.H. (1971). *Attribution in social interaction.* New York: General Learning Press.

Knee, C.R., & Zuckerman, M. (1998). A nondefensive personality: Autonomy and control as moderators of defensive coping and self-handicapping. *Journal of Research in Personality, 32,* 115-130.

Kolditz, T.A., & Arkin, R.M. (1982). An impression management interpretation of the self-handicapping strategy. *Journal of Personality & Social Psychology, 43,* 492-502.

Kuczka, K., & Treasure, D.C. (2002). Self-handicapping in competitive sport: Influence of the motivational climate and perceived ability. *Journal of Sport & Exercise Science, 24,* S82.

Leary, M.R. (1992). Self-presentation processes in exercise and sport. *Journal of Sport & Exercise Psychology, 14,* 339-351.

Leary, M.R., & Kowalski, R.M. (1990). Impression management: A literature review and two component model. *Psychological Bulletin, 107,* 34-47.

Leary, M.R., & Shepperd, J.A. (1986). Behavioral self-handicapping vs. self-reported handicaps: A conceptual note. *Journal of Personality and Social Psychology, 51,* 1265-1268.

Leary, M.R., Tchivdijian, L.R., & Kraxberger, B.E. (1994). Self-presentation can be hazardous to your health: Impression management and health risk. *Health Psychology, 13,* 461-470.

Levesque, M.J., Lowe, C.A., & Mendenhall, C. (2001). Self-handicapping as a method of self-presentation: An analysis of costs and benefits. *Current Research in Social Psychology, 6,* 221-237.

Luginbuhl, J., & Palmer, R. (1991). Impression management aspects of self-handicapping: Positive and negative affect. *Personality and Social Psychology Bulletin, 17,* 655-662.

Maddison, R., Prapavessis, H., & Fletcher, R. (in preparation). Scale development of a sport-specific Self-Handicapping Scale.

Martens, R. (1977). *Sport Competition Anxiety Test.* Champaign, IL: Human Kinetics.

Martens, R., Vealy, R.S., & Burton, D. (1990). *Competitive anxiety in sport.* Champaign, IL: Human Kinetics.

Martin, K.A., & Brawley, L.R. (1996). Self-presentational motive, self-esteem, and self-handicapping in sport. *Journal of Sport & Exercise Psychology, 18,* S56.

Martin, K.A., & Brawley, L.R. (1999). Is the Self-Handicapping Scale reliable outside of academic achievement settings? *Personality and Individual Differences, 27,* 901-911.

Martin, K.A. & Brawley, L.R. (2002). Self-handicapping in physical achievement settings: The contributions of self-esteem and self-efficacy. *Self and Identity, 1,* 337-351.

McCrea, S.M., & Hirt, E.R. (2001). The role of ability judgments in self-handicapping. *Personality & Social Psychology Bulletin, 27,* 1378-1389.

Midgley, C., Arunkumar, R., & Urdan, T.C. (1996). "If I don't do well tomorrow, there's a reason": Predictors of adolescents' use of academic self-handicapping strategies. *Journal of Educational Psychology, 88,* 423-434.

Newman, L.S., & Wada, R.F. (1997). When stakes are higher: Self-esteem instability and self-handicapping. *Journal of Social Behavior and Personality, 12,* 217-233.

Ommundsen, Y. (2001). Self-handicapping strategies in physical education classes: The influence of implicit theories of the nature of ability and achievement goal orientations. *Psychology of Sport and Exercise, 2,* 139-156.

Prapavessis, H., & Grove, J.R. (1994). Personality variables as antecedents of precompetitive mood state temporal patterning. *International Journal of Sport Psychology, 25,* 347-365.

Prapavessis, H., & Grove, J.R. (1998). Self-handicapping and self-esteem. *Journal of Applied Sport Psychology, 10,* 175-184.

Prapavessis, H., Grove, J.R., & Eklund, R.C. (2004). Self-presentational issues in competition and sport. *Journal of Applied Sport Psychology, 16,* 19-40.

Prapavessis, H., Grove, J.R., Maddison, R., & Zillmann, N. (2003). Self-handicapping tendencies, coping, and anxiety responses among athletes. *Psychology of Sport & Exercise, 4,* 357-375.

Rhodewalt, F. (1990). Self-handicappers: Individual differences in the preference for anticipatory, self-protective acts. In R.L. Higgins, C.R. Snyder, & S. Berglas (Eds.), *Self-handicapping: The paradox that isn't* (pp. 69-106). New York: Plenum Press.

Rhodewalt, F. (1994). Conceptions of ability, Achievement goals, and individual differences in self-handicapping behavior: On the application of implicit theories. *Journal of Personality, 62,* 67-85.

Rhodewalt, F., & Fairfield, M. (1991). Claimed self-handicaps and the self-handicapper: The relation of reduction in intended effort to performance. *Journal of Research in Personality, 25,* 402-417.

Rhodewalt, F., Morf, C., Hazlett, S., & Fairfield, M. (1991). Self-handicapping: The role of discounting and augmentation in the preservation of self-esteem. *Journal of Personality & Social Psychology, 61,* 122-131.

Rhodewalt, F., Saltzman, A.T., & Wittmer, J. (1984). Self-handicapping among competitive athletes: The role of practice in self-esteem protection. *Basic & Applied Social Psychology, 5,* 197-209.

Rhodewalt, F., Sanbonmatsu, D.M., Tschanz, B., Feick, D.L., & Waller, A. (1995). Self-handicapping and interpersonal trade-offs: The effects of claimed self-handicaps on observer's performance evaluations and feedback. *Personality and Social Psychology Bulletin, 21,* 1042-1050.

Ross, S.R., Canada, K.E., & Rausch, M.K. (2002). Self-handicapping and the five factor model of personality: Mediation between neuroticism and conscientiousness. *Personality and Individual Differences, 32,* 1173-1184.

Ryska, T.A. (2002). Effects of situational self-handicapping and state self-confidence on the physical performance of young participants. *Psychological Record, 52,* 461-478.

Ryska, T.A., Yin, Z., & Boyd, M. (1999). The role of dispositional goal orientation and team climate on situational self-handicapping among young athletes. *Journal of Sport Behavior, 22,* 410-425.

Ryska, T.A., Yin, Z., & Cooley, D. (1998). Effects of trait and situational self-handicapping on competitive anxiety among athletes. *Current Psychology: Developmental, Learning, Personality, Social, 17,* 48-56.

Sanna, L.J., & Mark, M.M. (1995). Self-handicapping, expected evaluation, and performance: Accentuating the positive and attenuating the negative. *Organizational Behavior and Human Decision Processes, 64,* 84-102.

Self, E.A. (1990). Situational influences on self-handicapping. In R.-L. Higgins, C.R. Snyder, & S. Berglas (Eds.), *Self-handicapping: The paradox that isn't* (pp. 37-68). New York: Plenum Press.

Shepperd, J.A., & Arkin, R.M. (1991). Behavioral other-enhancement: Strategically obscuring the link between performance and evaluation. *Journal of Personality & Social Psychology, 60,* 79-88.

Shepperd, J.A., & Arkin, R.M. (1989). Self-handicapping: The moderating roles of public self-consciousness and task importance. *Personality and Social Psychology Bulletin, 15,* 252-265.

Shepperd, J.A., & Arkin, R.M. (1991). Behavioral other-enhancement: Strategically obscuring the link between performance and evaluation. *Journal of Personality & Social Psychology, 60,* 79-88.

Shields, C.A., Paskevich, D.M., & Brawley, L.R. (2003). Self-handicapping in structured and unstructured exercise: Toward a measurable construct. *Journal of Sport & Exercise Psychology, 25,* 267-283.

Smith, T.W., Snyder, C.R., & Handelsman, M.M. (1982). On the self-serving function of an academic wooden leg: Test anxiety as a self-handicapping strategy. *Journal of Personality and Social Psychology, 42,* 314-321.

Smith, T.W., Snyder, C.R., & Perkins, S.C. (1983). The self-serving function of hypochondriacal complaints: Physical symptoms as self-handicapping strategies. *Journal of Personality & Social Psychology, 44,* 787-797.

Snyder, C.R. (1990). Self-handicapping processes and sequelae: On the taking of a psychological dive. In R.L. Higgins, C.R. Snyder, & S. Berglas (Eds.), *Self-handicapping: The paradox that isn't* (pp. 107-150). New York: Plenum Press.

Snyder, C.R., Augelli, R.W., Ingram, R.E., & Smith, T.W. (1985). On the self-serving function of social anxiety: Shyness as a self-handicapping strategy. *Journal of Personality and Social Psychology, 48,* 970-980.

Snyder, C.R., & Higgins, R.L. (1988). Excuses: Their effective role in the negotiation of reality. *Psychological Bulletin, 104,* 23-45.

Strube, M.J. (1986). An analysis of the Self-Handicapping Scale. *Basic and Applied Social Psychology, 7,* 211-224.

Thill, E.E., & Curry, F. (2000). Learning to play golf under different goal conditions: Their effects on irrelevant thoughts and on subsequent control strategies. *European Journal of Social Psychology, 30,* 101-122.

Thompson, T., & Richardson, A. (2001). Self-handicapping status, claimed self-handicaps, and reduced practice effort following success and failure feedback. *British Journal of Educational Psychology, 71,* 151-170.

Tice, D.M. (1991). Esteem protection or enhancement? Self-handicapping motives and attributions differ by trait self-esteem. *Journal of Personality & Social Psychology, 60,* 711-725.

Tice, D.M. (1993). The social motivations of people with low self-esteem. In R.F. Baumeister (Ed.), *Self-esteem: The puzzle of low self-regard* (pp. 37-53). New York: Plenum Press.

Tice, D.M., & Baumeister, R.F. (1990). Self-esteem, self-handicapping, and self-presentation: The strategy of inadequate practice. *Journal of Personality, 58,* 443-464.

Vallerand, R.J., Pelletier, L.G., & Gagne, F. (1991). On the multidimensional versus unidimensional perspectives of self-esteem: A test using the group-comparison approach. *Social Behavior and Personality, 19,* 121-132.

Chapter 16

Bandura, A. (1997). *Self-efficacy: The exercise of control.* New York: Freeman.

Bianco, T. (2001). Social support and recovery from sport injury: Elite skiers share their experiences. *Research Quarterly for Exercise and Sport, 72,* 376-388.

Bianco, T., & Eklund, R.C. (2001). Conceptual considerations for social support research in sport and exercise settings: The case of sport injury. *Journal of Sport & Exercise Psychology, 23,* 85-107.

Brewer, B.W. (2001). Psychology of sport injury rehabilitation. In R.N. Singer, H.A. Hausenblas, & C.M. Janelle (Eds.), *Handbook of sport psychology* (2nd ed., pp. 787-809). New York: Wiley.

Brookings, J.B., & Bolton, B. (1988). Confirmatory factor analysis of the Interpersonal Support Evaluation List. *American Journal of Community Psychology, 16,* 137-147.

Chelladurai, P. (1993). Leadership. In R.N. Singer, M. Murphey, & L.K. Tennant (Eds.), *Handbook of research on sport psychology* (pp. 647-671). New York: Macmillan.

Chelladurai, P., & Saleh, S.D. (1978). Preferred leadership in sports. *Canadian Journal of Applied Sport Sciences, 3,* 85-92.

Chelladurai, P., & Saleh, S.D. (1980). Dimensions of leader behaviour in sports: Development of a leadership scale. *Journal of Sport Psychology, 2,* 34-45.

Cohen, S. (1988). Psychosocial models of the role of social support in the etiology of physical disease. *Health Psychology, 7,* 269-297.

Cohen, S. (1992). Stress, social support and disorder. In H.O.F. Veiel & U. Baumann (Eds.), *The meaning and measurement of social support* (pp. 109-124). New York: Hemisphere.

Cohen, S., Gottlieb, B.H., & Underwood, L.G. (2000). Social support and health. In S. Cohen, L.G. Underwood, & B.H. Gottlieb (Eds.), *Social support measurement and intervention: A guide for health and social scientists* (pp. 3-25). New York: Oxford University Press.

Cohen, S., Mermelstein, R., Kamarck, T., & Hoberman, H. (1985). Measuring the functional components of social support. In I.G. Sarason & B.R. Sarason (Eds.), *Social support: Theory, research, and applications* (pp. 73-94). Dordrecht: Martinus Nijhoff.

Cohen, S., & Syme, S.L. (1985). *Social support and health.* New York: Academic Press.

Cohen, S., Underwood, L.G., & Gottlieb, B.H. (2000). *Social support measurement and intervention: A guide for health and social scientists.* New York: Oxford University Press.

Cohen, S., & Wills, T.A. (1985). Stress, social support and the buffering hypothesis. *Psychological Bulletin, 98,* 310-357.

Coriell, M., & Cohen, S. (1995). Concordance in the face of a stressful event: When do members of a dyad agree that one person supported the other? *Journal of Personality and Social Psychology, 69,* 289-299.

Cox, T. (1978). *Stress.* London: MacMillan.

Crocker, P.R.E. (1992). Managing stress by competitive athletes: Ways of coping. *International Journal of Sport Psychology, 23,* 161-175.

Cutrona, C.E., & Russell, D.W. (1990). Type of social support and specific stress: Toward a theory of optimal matching. In B.R. Sarason, I.G. Sarason, & G.R. Pierce (Eds.), *Social support: An interactional view* (pp. 319-366). New York: Wiley.

Dakof, G.A., Taylor, S.E. (1990). Victims' perceptions of social support: What is helpful from whom? *Journal of Personality and Social Psychology, 58,* 80-89.

Dunkel-Schetter, C., & Bennett, T.L. (1990). Differentiating the cognitive and behavioral aspects of social support. In B.R. Sarason, I.G. Sarason, & G.R. Pierce (Eds.), *Social support: An interactional view* (pp. 267-296). New York: Wiley.

Gottlieb, B.H. (1992). Quandaries in translating support concepts to intervention. In H.O.F. Veiel & U. Baumann (Eds.), *The meaning and measurement of social support* (pp. 293-309). New York: Hemisphere.

Gould, D., Jackson, S.A., & Finch, L.M. (1993). Life at the top: The experiences of U.S. national champion figure skaters. *The Sport Psychologist, 7,* 354-374.

Gould, D., Tuffey, S., Udry, E., & Loehr, J. (1996). Burnout in competitive junior tennis players: II: Qualitative analysis. *The Sport Psychologist, 10,* 341-366.

Hardy, C.J., Burke, K.L., & Crace, R.K. (1999). Social support and injury: A framework for social support-based interventions with injured athletes. In D. Pargman (Ed.), *Psychological bases of sport injuries* (2nd ed., pp. 175-198). Morgantown, WV: Fitness Information Technology.

Hardy, C.J., & Crace, R.K. (1991). Social support within sport. *Sport Psychology Training Bulletin, 3,* 1-8.

Hardy, L., & Jones, G. (1994). Current issues and future directions for performance-related research in sport psychology. *Journal of Sports Sciences, 12,* 61-92.

Hardy, L., Jones, G., & Gould, D. (1996). *Understanding psychological preparation for sport: Theory and practice of elite performers.* Chichester, UK: Wiley.

Harris, T.O. (1992). Some reflections on the process of social support and nature of unsupportive behaviors. In H.O.F. Veiel & U. Baumann (Eds.), *The meaning and measurement of social support* (pp. 171-190). New York: Hemisphere.

Heitzmann, C.A., & Kaplan R.M. (1988). Assessment of methods for measuring social support. *Health Psychology, 7,* 75-109.

Helgeson, V.S. (1993). Two important distinctions in social support: Kind of support and perceived versus received. *Journal of Applied Social Psychology, 23,* 825-845.

House, J.S., & Kahn, R.L. (1985). Measures and concepts of social support. In S. Cohen & S.L. Syme (Eds.), *Social support and health* (pp. 83-108). New York: Academic Press.

Jaccard, J., Turrisi, R., & Wan, C.K. (1990). *Interaction effects in multiple regression* (Quantitative Applications in the Social Sciences No. 72). Newbury Park, CA: Sage.

Johnston, L.H., & Carroll, D. (1998). The provision of social support to injured athletes: A qualitative analysis. *Journal of Sport Rehabilitation, 7,* 267-284.

Lakey, B., & Cohen, S. (2000). Social support theory and measurement. In S. Cohen, L.G. Underwood, & B.H. Gottlieb (Eds.), *Social support measurement and intervention: A guide for health and social scientists* (pp. 29-52). New York: Oxford University Press.

Lakey, B., McCabe, K.M., Fisicaro, S.A., & Drew, J.B. (1996). Environmental and personal determinants of support perceptions: Three generalizability studies. *Journal of Personality and Social Psychology, 70,* 1270-1280.

Lazarus, R.S. (1966). *Psychological stress and coping process.* New York: McGraw-Hill.

Lazarus, R.S., & Folkman, S. (1984). *Stress appraisal and coping.* New York: Springer.

Lehman, D.R., Ellard, J.H., & Wortman, C.B. (1986). Social support for the bereaved: Recipients' and providers' perspectives on what is helpful. *Journal of Consulting and Clinical Psychology, 54,* 438-446.

Madden, C.C., Kirkby, R.J., & McDonald, D. (1989). Coping styles of competitive middle distance runners. *International Journal of Sport Psychology, 20,* 287-296.

Martin, R., Davis, G.M., Baron, R.S., Suls, J., & Blanchard, E.B. (1994). Specificity in social support: Perceptions of helpful and unhelpful provider behaviours among irritable bowel syndrome, headache, and cancer patients. *Health Psychology, 13,* 432-439.

Rees, T., & Hardy, L. (2000). An investigation of the social support experiences of high-level sports performers. *The Sport Psychologist, 14,* 327-347.

Rees, T., & Hardy, L. (2004). Matching social support with stressors: Effects on factors underlying performance in tennis. *Psychology of Sport and Exercise, 5,* 319-337.

Rees, T., Hardy, L., & Freeman, P. (in press). Stressors, social support and effects upon performance in golf. *Journal of Sports Sciences.*

Rees, T., Hardy, L., Ingledew, D.K., & Evans, L. (2000). Examination of the validity of the social support survey in confirmatory factor analysis. *Research Quarterly for Exercise and Sport, 71,* 322-330.

Rees, T., Ingledew, D.K., & Hardy, L. (1999). Social support dimensions and components of performance in tennis. *Journal of Sports Sciences, 17,* 421-429.

Rees, T., Smith, B., & Sparkes, A. (2003). The influence of social support on the lived experiences of spinal cord injured sportsmen. *The Sport Psychologist, 17,* 135-156.

Reis, H.T., & Collins, N. (2000). Measuring relationship properties and interactions relevant to social support. In S. Cohen, L.G. Underwood, & B.H. Gottlieb (Eds.), *Social support measurement and intervention: A guide for health and social scientists* (pp. 136-192). New York: Oxford University Press.

Richman, J.M., Hardy, C.J., Rosenfeld, L.B., & Callanan R.A.E. (1989). Strategies for enhancing social support networks in sport: A brainstorming experience. *Journal of Applied Sport Psychology, 1,* 150-159.

Richman, J.M., Rosenfeld, L.B., & Hardy, C.J. (1993). The Social Support Survey: A validation of a clinical measure of the social support process. *Research on Social Work Practice, 3,* 288-311.

Rook, K.S. (1992). Detrimental aspect of social relationships: Taking stock of an emerging literature. In H.O.F. Veiel & U. Baumann (Eds.), *The meaning and measurement of social support* (pp. 157-169). New York: Hemisphere.

Rosenfeld, L.B., & Richman, J.M. (1997). Developing effective social support: Team building and the social support process. *Journal of Applied Sport Psychology, 9,* 133-153.

Sarason, B.R., Sarason, I.G., & Pierce, G.R. (1990a). *Social support: An interactional view.* New York: Wiley.

Sarason, B.R., Sarason, I.G., & Pierce, G.R. (1990b). Traditional views of social support and their impact on assessment. In B.R. Sarason, I.G. Sarason & G.R. Pierce (Eds.), *Social support: An interactional view* (pp. 9-25). New York: Wiley.

Sarason, B.R., Shearin, E.N., Pierce, G.R., & Sarason, I.G. (1987). Interrelations of social support measures: Theoretical and practical implications. *Journal of Personality and Social Psychology, 52,* 813-832.

Sarason, I.G., Sarason, B.R., & Pierce, G.R. (1990). Social support, personality and performance. *Journal of Applied Sport Psychology, 2,* 117-127.

Shumaker, S.A., & Brownell, A. (1984). Toward a theory of social support: Closing conceptual gaps. *Journal of Social Issues, 40,* 11-36.

Sparkes, A. (2002). *Telling tales in sport and physical activity: A qualitative journey.* Champaign, IL: Human Kinetics.

Thoits, P.A. (1995). Stress, coping, and social support processes: Where are we? What next? *Journal of Health and Social Behavior (Extra Issue),* 53-79.

Uchino, B.N., Cacioppo, J.T., & Kiecolt-Glaser, J.K. (1996). The relationship between social support and physiological processes: A review with emphasis on underlying mechanisms and implications for health. *Psychological Bulletin, 119,* 488-531.

Udry, E. (1996). Social support: Exploring its role in the context of athletic injuries. *Journal of Sport Rehabilitation, 5,* 151-163.

Udry, E., Gould, D., Bridges, D., & Tuffey, S. (1997). People helping people? Examining the social ties of athletes coping with burnout and injury stress. *Journal of Sport & Exercise Psychology, 19,* 368-395.

Vaux, A. (1992). Assessment of social support. In H.O.F. Veiel & U. Baumann (Eds.), *The meaning and measurement of social support* (pp. 193-216). New York: Hemisphere.

Veiel, H.O.F., & Baumann, U. (1992a). The many meanings of social support. In H.O.F. Veiel & U. Baumann (Eds.), *The meaning and measurement of social support* (pp. 1-9). New York: Hemisphere.

Veiel, H.O.F., & Baumann, U. (1992b). Comments on concepts and methods. In H.O.F. Veiel & U. Baumann (Eds.), *The meaning and measurement of social support* (pp. 313-319). New York: Hemisphere.

Veiel, H.O.F., & Baumann, U. (1992c). *The meaning and measurement of social support.* New York: Hemisphere.

Warwick, R., Joseph, S., Cordle, C., & Ashworth, P. (2004). Social support for women with chronic pelvic pain: What is helpful from whom. *Psychology and Health, 19,* 117-134.

Weiss, M.R., & Friedrichs, W.D. (1986). The influence of leader behaviours, coach attributes, and institutional variables on performance and satisfaction of collegiate basketball teams. *Journal of Sport Psychology, 8,* 332-346.

Westre, K., & Weiss, M. (1991). The relationship between perceived coaching behaviors and group cohesion in high school football teams. *The Sport Psychologist, 5,* 41-54.

Wethington, E., & Kessler, R.C. (1986). Perceived support, received support and adjustment to stressful life events. *Journal of Health and Social Behavior, 27,* 78-89.

Williams, J.M. (2001). In R.N. Singer, H.A. Hausenblas, & C.M. Janelle (Eds.), *Handbook of sport psychology* (2nd ed., pp. 766-786). New York: Wiley.

Wills, T.A., & Shinar, O. (2000). Measuring perceived and received social support. In S. Cohen, L.G. Underwood, & B.H. Gottlieb (Eds.), *Social support measurement and intervention: A guide for health and social scientists* (pp. 86-135). New York: Oxford University Press.

Woodman, T., & Hardy, L. (2001). Stress and anxiety. In R.N. Singer, H.A. Hausenblas, & C.M. Janelle (Eds.), *Handbook of sport psychology* (2nd ed., pp. 290-318). New York: Wiley.

Chapter 17

American Sport Education Program (ASEP). (1994). Sport-parent. Champaign, IL: Human Kinetics.

Australian Sports Commission. (2003). How do elite athletes develop? A look through the 'rear-view mirror': A preliminary report from the National Athlete Development Survey. Canberra, Australia: Australian Sports Commission.

Baxter-Jones, A.D.G., & Maffulli, N. (2003). Parental influence on sport participation in elite young athletes. Journal of Sports Medicine and Physical Fitness, 43, 250-255.

Beamish, R. (1992). Towards a socio-cultural profile of Canada's high performance athletes. International Review for the Sociology of Sport, 27, 279-292.

Bloom, B.S. (Ed.). (1985). Developing talent in young people. New York: Ballantine.

Bona, I. (1998). Soziale netzwerke ehemaliger jugendlicher leistungssportler [Social network of retired elite youth athletes]. In R. Selier, G. Anders, and P. Irlinger (Eds.), Das leben nach dem spitzensport. 37. Magglinger Symposium vom 21.-23. Mai 1998—La vie après le sport de haut niveau. [Life after an elite athletic career. 37th Magglingen Symposium 21-23 May 1998] (pp. 2221-231). Magglingen, Switzerland: BASPO.

Brustad, R.J. (1988). Affective outcomes in competitive youth sport: The influence of intrapersonal and socialization factors. Journal of Sport & Exercise Psychology, 10, 307-321.

Brustad, R.J., Babkes, M.L., & Smith, A.L. (2001). Youth in sport: Psychological considerations. In R.N. Singer, H.E. Hausenblas, & C.M. Janelle (Eds.), Handbook of sport psychology (pp. 604-635). New York: Wiley.

Bussmann, G., & Alfermann, D. (1994). Drop-out and the female athlete: A study with track-and-field athletes. In D. Hackforth (Ed.), Psycho-social issues and interventions in elite sport (pp. 89-128). Frankfurt: Lang.

Carlson, R. (1988). The socialization of elite tennis players in Sweden: An analysis of the players' backgrounds and development. Sociology of Sport Journal, 5, 241-256.

Carpenter, P.J., & Kieran, G. (1997). A retrospective study of adolescent track and field athletes' commitment. Journal of Applied Sport Psychology, 9, S75.

Carron, G. (2004). Topsport: Solidair of solitair? Een exploratieve studie naar het carrière-einde van Vlaamse ex-Olympische atleten [Elite sport: Solidarity or solitary? An explorative study into the career end of Flemish former Olympic athletes]. Unpublished master's thesis, Vrije Universiteit Brussel.

Cecič-Erpič, S., Wylleman, P., & Zupančič, M. (2004). Characteristics of the sports career termination and adaptation to post-career transitions in perspective. Psychology of Sport and Exercise, 5, 45-60.

Conzelmann, A., Gabler, H., & Nagel, S. (2001). Hochleistungssport: Persönlicher gewinn oder Verlust. Lebensläufe von Olympioniken [Elite level sport: Personal success or loss. Life of Olympians]. Tübingen: Attempto.

Coppel, D.B. (1995). Relationship issues in sport: A marital therapy model. In S.M. Murphy (Ed.), Sport psychology interventions (pp. 193-204). Champaign, IL: Human Kinetics.

Côté, J. (1999). The influence of the family in the development of talent in sport. The Sport Psychologist, 13, 395-417.

Csikszentmihalyi, M., Rathunde, K., & Whalen, S. (1993). Talented teenagers: The roots of success and failure. New York: Cambridge University Press.

De Knop, P., De Bosscher, V., & Leblicq, S. (2004). Onderzoek naar het topsportklimaat in Vlaanderen [Reseach into the elite sports climate in Flanders]. Brussels: Vrije Universitiet Brussel.

De Knop, P., Wylleman, P., Theeboom, M., De Martelaer, K., Van Puymbroeck, L., & Wittock, H. (1994). Youth-friendly sport clubs: Developing an effective youth sport policy. Brussels: VUBpress.

De Knop, P., Wylleman, P., Van Hoecke, J., & Bollaert, L. (1999). Sports management: A European approach to the management of the combination of academics and elite-level sport. In S. Bailey (Ed.), Perspectives. Vol. 1: School sport and competition (pp. 49-62). Oxford: Meyer & Meyer Sport.

Donnelly, P. (1993). Problems associated with youth involvement in high-performance sport. In B.R. Cahill and A.J. Pearl (Eds.), Intensive participation in children's sports (pp. 95-126). Champaign, IL: Human Kinetics.

Duffy, P., Lyons, D., Moran, A., Warrington, G., & MacManus, C. (2001). Factors promoting and inhibiting the success of high performance players and athletes in Ireland. Limerick, Ireland: University of Limerick.

Durand-Bush, N., & Salmela, J. (2002). The development and maintenance of expert athletic performance. Journal of Applied Sport Psychology, 14, 154-171.

Durand-Bush, N., Salmela, J., & Thompson, K.A. (2004). Le role joué par les parents dans le développement et le maintien de la peformance athlétique experte [The role played by parents in the development and maintenance of expert athletic performance]. STAPS, 64, 15-38.

Erikson, E.H. (1963). Childhood and society. New York: Stonton.

Ewing, M., Hedstrom, R.A., & Wiesner, A.R. (2004). Perception de l'engagement des parents dans la pratique du tennis de leur enfant [Perceptions of parental involvement in their children's tennis]. STAPS, 64, 53-70.

Fredericks, J.A., & Eccles, J.S. (2004). Parental influences in youth involvement in sports. In M.Weiss (Ed.), Developmental sport and exercise psychology: A lifespan perspective (pp. 145-164). Morgantown, WV: Fitness Information Technology.

Gibbons, T. (Ed.). (2002). The path to excellence: A comprehensive view of development of U.S. Olympians who competed from 1984-1998. Initial report: Results of the talent identification and development questionnaire to U.S. Olympians. Colorado Springs, CO: United States Olympic Committee.

Gould, D., Dieffenbach, K., & Moffett, A. (2002). Psychological characteristics and their development in Olympic champions. Journal of Applied Sport Psychology, 14, 172-204.

Gould, D., Guinan, D., Greenleaf, C., Medbery, R., & Peterson, K. (1999). Factors affecting Olympic performance: Perceptions of athletes and coaches from more and less successful teams. The Sport Psychologist, 13, 371-394.

Greendorfer, S.L, & Blinde, E.M. (1985). "Retirement" from intercollegiate sport: Theoretical and empirical considerations. Sociology of Sport Journal, 2, 101-110.

Greendorfer, S.L. (1977). Role of socializing agents in female sports involvement. Research Quarterly, 48, 304-309.

Greendorfer, S.L. (1992). Sports socialization. In T.S. Horn (Ed.), Advances in sport psychology (pp. 201-218). Champaign, IL: Human Kinetics.

Greendorfer, S.L., Lewko, J.H., & Rosengren, K.S. (1996). Family and gender-based influences in sport socialization of children and adolescents. In F.L. Smoll & R.E. Smith (Eds.), Children and youth in sport: A biopsychosocial perspective (pp. 89-111). Dubuque, IA: Brown & Benchmark.

Haerle, R.K. (1975). Career patterns and career contingencies of professional baseball players: An occupational analysis. In D.W. Ball & J.W. Loy (Eds.), Sport and social order (pp. 461-519). Reading, MA: Addison-Wesley.

Hallden, O. (1965). The adjustment of athletes after retiring from sport. In F. Antonelli (Ed.), Proceedings of the 1st International Congress of Sport Psychology (pp. 730-733). Rome: International Society of Sport Psychology.

Harwood, C., & Swain, A. (2002). The development and activation of achievement goals within tennis: II. A player, parent, and coach intervention. The Sport Psychologist, 16, 111-137.

Havighurst, R.J. (1973). History of developmental psychology: Socialization and personality development through the life span. In P.B. Baltes & K.W. Schaie (Eds.), Life-span developmental psychology: Personality and socialization (pp. 3-24). New York: Academic Press.

Hellstedt, J.C. (1987). The coach/parent/athlete relationship. The Sport Psychologist, 1, 151-160.

Hellstedt, J.C. (1990). Early adolescent perceptions of parental pressure in the sport environment. Journal of Sport Behavior, 13, 135-144.

Hellstedt, J.C. (1995). Invisible players: A family systems model. In S.M. Murphy (Ed.), Sport psychology interventions (pp. 117-146). Champaign, IL: Human Kinetics.

Holt, N.L. (2001). Psychosocial characteristics of elite adolescent athletes: An initial exploration. Journal of Sport & Exercise Psychology, 23 (Suppl.), S28.

Holt, N.L., & Morley, D. (2004). Gender differences in psychosocial factors associated with athletic success during childhood. The Sport Psychologist, 18, 138-153.

Howie, L. (2004). The official FA guide for football parents. London: Hodder & Stoughton.

Jowett, S., & Meek, G.A. (2000). The coach–athlete relationship in married couples: An exploratory content analysis. The Sport Psychologist, 14, 157-175.

Kay, T. (2000). Sporting excellence: A family affair? European Physical Education Review, 6, 151-169.

Kerr, G., & Dacyshyn, A. (2000). The retirement experiences of elite, female gymnasts. Journal of Applied Sport Psychology, 12, 115-133.

Koukouris, K. (1991). Disengagement of advanced and elite Greek male athletes from organized competitive sport. International Review for the Sociology of Sport, 26, 289-306.

Lavallee, D., & Wylleman, P. (Eds.). (2000). Career transitions in sport: International perspectives. Morgantown, WV: Fitness Information Technology.

Lavallee, D., Gordon, S., & Grove, J.R. (1997). Retirement from sport and the loss of athletic identity. Journal of Loss and Interpersonal Loss, 2, 129-147.

Leonard, W.M., II. (1996). The odds of transiting from one level of sports participation to another. Sociology of Sport Journal, 13, 288-299.

Marriott, L., & Nilsson, P. (2003). Golf parent for the future. Phoenix: Vision 54.

Mihovilovic, M. (1968). The status of former sportsmen. International Review of Sport Sociology, 3, 73-93.

Monsaas, J. (1985). Learning to be a world-class tennis player. In B. Bloom (Ed.), Developing talent in young people (pp. 211-269). New York: Ballantine Books.

Naul, R. (1994). The elite athlete career: Sport pedagogy must counsel social and professional problems in life development. In D. Hackfort (Ed.), Psycho-social issues and interventions in elite sport (pp. 237-258). Frankfurt: Lang.

North, J., & Lavallee, D. (2004). An investigation of potential users of career transition services in the United Kingdom. Psychology of Sport and Exercise, 5, 77-84.

Olympic News (December, 1994). De 61 aanbevelingen en conclusies van het IOC Conges [The 61 recommendations and conclusions of the IOC Congress], 11-12.

Petitpas, A.J., Champagne, D., Chartrand, J., Danish, S., & Murphy, S. (1997). Athlete's guide to career planning: Keys to success from the playing field to professional life. Champaign, IL: Human Kinetics.

Petitpas, A., Brewer, B.W., & Van Raalte, J.L. (1996). Transitions of the student-athlete: Theoretical, empirical, and practical perspectives. In E.F. Etzel, A.P. Ferrante, & J.W. Pinkney (Eds.), Counseling college student-athletes: Issues and interventions (pp. 137-156). Morgantown, WV: Fitness Information Technology.

Piaget, J. (1971). Biology and knowledge: An essay on the relations between organic regulations and cognitive processes. Chicago: University of Chicago Press.

Power, T.G., & Woolger, C. (1994). Parenting practices and age-group swimming: A correlational study. Research Quarterly for Exercise and Sport, 65, 59-66.

Rea, T. (2003). An examination of the normative transitions experienced by professional football players in academy setting. Unpublished master's dissertation, Loughborough University.

Rees, T., & Hardy, L. (2000). An investigation of the social support experiences of high-level sports performers. The Sport Psychologist, 14, 327-347.

Rice, P.F. (1998). Human development: A life-span approach. Upper Saddle River, NJ: Prentice Hall.

Rimbaut, T. (2004). Career transition from junior to senior athlete in lifesaving. Unpublished master's dissertation, KULeuven, Belgium.

Robertson-Wilson, J., & Côté, J. (2002). The role of parents in children's hockey participation. Calgary, Alberta: Canadian Hockey Association.

Rotella, R.J., & Bunker, L.K. (1987). Parenting your superstar. Champaign, IL: Leisure Press.

Scanlan, T.K. (1988). Social evaluation and the competition process: A developmental Perspective. In F.L. Smoll, R.A. Magill, & M.J. Ash (Eds.), Children in sport (pp. 135-148). Champaign, IL: Human Kinetics.

Scanlan, T.K., & Lewthwaite, R. (1986). Social psychological aspects of competition for male youth sport participants IV: Predictors of enjoyment. Journal of Sport Psychology, 8, 25-35.

Seiler, R., Schmid, J., & Schilling, G. (1998). Accès aux carriers postsportives en Suise [Access to a career following an athletic career]. In R. Selier, G. Anders, and P. Irlinger (Eds.), Das leben nach dem spitzensport. 37. Magglinger Symposium vom 21.-23. 37e symposium de Macolin du 21 au 23 mai 1998 [Life after an elite athletic career. 37th Magglingen Symposium 21-23 May 1998] (pp. 113-123). Magglingen, Switzerland: BASPO.

Smith, A.L. (2003). Perceptions of peer relationships in physical activity contexts: A road less travelled in youth sport and exercise psychology research. Psychology of Sport and Exercise, 4, 25-39.

Smith, R.E., & Smoll, F.L. (1996). The coach as focus of research and intervention in youth sports. In F.L. Smoll & R.E. Smith (Eds.), Children and youth in sport: A biopsychosocial perspective (pp. 125-141). Dubuque, IA: McGraw-Hill.

Stambulova, N.B. (1994). Developmental sports career investigations in Russia: A post-perestroika analysis. The Sport Psychologist, 8, 221-237.

Stambulova, N.B. (1995). Sports career satisfaction of Russian athletes. In R. Vanfraechem-Raway and Y. Vanden Auweele (Eds.), IXth European Congress on Sport Psychology, Part I (pp. 526-532). Brussels: ATM.

Stambulova, N.B. (2000). Athlete's crises: A developmental perspective. International Journal of Sport Psychology, 31, 584-601.

Stambulova, N.B. (2004, August). First competition as a career transition. Paper presented at the 2004 Pre-Olympic Congress, Thessaloniki, Greece.

Stein, G.L., Raedeke, T.D., & Glenn, S.D. (1999). Children's perceptions of parent sport involvement: It's not how much, but to what degree that's important. Journal of Sport Behavior, 22, 591-601.

Stephan, Y., Bilard, J., Ninot, G., & Delignières, D. (2003). Repercussions of transition out of elite sport on subjective well-being: A one-year study. Journal of Applied Sport Psychology, 15, 354-371.

Stevenson, C.L. (1990). The athletic career: Some contingencies of sport specialization. Journal of Sport Behavior, 13, 103-113.

Talent Identification and Development Taskforce. (2003). Linking promise to the podium: Talent identification and development in New Zealand. Wellington, New Zealand: New Zealand Academy of Sport.

Van Rossum, J.H.A. (1995). Talent in sport: Significant others in the career of top-level Dutch athletes. In M.W. Katzko & F.J. Mönks (Eds.), Nurturing talent: Individual needs and social ability (pp. 43-57). Assen, the Netherlands: Van Gorcum.

Van Rossum, J.H.A., & Van der Loo, H. (1997). Gifted athletes and complexity of family structure: A condition for talent development? High Ability Studies, 8, 19-30.

Van Yperen, N. (1995). Interpersonal stress, performance level, and parental support: A longitudinal study among highly skilled young soccer players. The Sport Psychologist, 9, 225-241.

Vanden Auweele, Y., De Martelaer, K., Rzewnicki, R., De Knop, P., & Wylleman, P. (2004). Parents and coaches: A help or a harm? Affective outcomes for children in sport. In Y. Vanden Auweele (Ed.), Ethics in youth sport. Analyses and recommendations (pp. 179-194). Tielt, Belgium: LannooCampus.

Vanden Auweele, Y., Van Mele, V., & Wylleman, P. (1994). La relation entraîneur-athlète [The coach–athlete relationship]. Enfance, 2-3, 187-202.

Verdet, M.C., Lévêque, M., & Wylleman, P. (2001, June). Gymnasts, parents, and coaches' interpersonal relationships. Paper presented at the Xth World Congress of Sport Psychology, Skiathos, Greece.

Verdet, M.C., Wylleman, P., & Lévêque, M. (2003, July). Transcultural validation of the Sport Interpersonal Relationship Questionnaire: A French version. Paper presented at the XIth European Congress of Sport Psychology, Copenhagen.

Weiss, M.R., & Fretwell, S. (2003). The parent-coach phenomenon in youth sport: Perspectives from the child, teammates, and parent-coach. Journal of Sport & Exercise Psychology, 25 (Suppl.), S138.

Weiss, M.R., & Stuntz, C.P. (2004). A little friendly competition: Peer relationships and psychosocial development in youth sport and physical activity contexts. In M. Weiss (Ed.), Developmental sport and exercise psychology: A lifespan perspective (pp. 165-196). Morgantown, WV: Fitness Information Technology.

Weiss, M.R., & Williams, L. (2004). The why of youth sport involvement: A developmental perspective on motivational processes. In M. Weiss (Ed.), Developmental sport and exercise psychology: A lifespan perspective (pp. 223-268). Morgantown, WV: Fitness Information Technology.

Weiss, M.R., Smith, A.L., & Theeboom, M. (1996). "That's what friends are for": Childrens' and teenagers' perceptions of peer relationships in the sport domain. Journal of Sport & Exercise Psychology, 18, 347-379.

Würth, S., Lee, M.J., & Alfermann, D. (2004). Parental involvement and athletes' career in youth sport. Psychology of Sport and Exercise, 5, 21-33.

Wylleman, P. (2000). Interpersonal relationships in sport: Uncharted territory. International Journal of Sport Psychology, 31, 1-18.

Wylleman, P. (Ed.). (2001). Evaluatie van de opzet en de werking van de topsportscholen in Vlaanderen. Globaal rapport [Evaluation of the aim and functioning of the topsportschools in Flanders: Global report]. Brussels: Interuniversitair Onderzoekscentrum voor Sportbeleid.

Wylleman, P., & De Knop, P. (1998). Athletes' interpersonal perceptions of the "parent-coach" in competitive sport. Journal of Applied Sport Psychology, 10 (Suppl.), S165.

Wylleman, P., & Lavallee, D. (2004), A developmental perspective on transitions faced by athletes. In M. Weiss (Ed.), Developmental sport and exercise psychology: A lifespan perspective (pp. 507-527). Morgantown, WV: Fitness Information Technology.

Wylleman, P., & Parker, R. (2004). Lifestyle management for elite athletes: A European perspective. In E. De Boever (Ed.), Book of abstracts of the 12th European Congress on Sport Management (p. 263). Ghent: Publicatiefonds voor Lichamelijke Opvoeding.

Wylleman, P., De Knop, P., & Sillen, D. (August, 1998). Former Olympic athletes' perceptions of retirement from high-level sport. Paper presented at the 24th International Congress of Applied Psychology, San Francisco.

Wylleman, P., De Knop, P., & Van Kerckhoven, C. (2000, October). The development of the athlete family as perceived by talented swimmers and their parents. Paper presented at the AAASP Conference, Nashville, TN.

Wylleman, P., De Knop, P., Ewing, M., & S. Cumming (2000). Transitions in youth sport: A developmental perspective on parental involvement. In D. Lavallee & P. Wylleman (Eds.), Career transitions in sport: International perspectives (pp. 143-160). Morgantown, WV: Fitness Information Technology.

Wylleman, P., De Knop, P., Menkehorst, H., Theeboom, M., & Annerel, J. (1993). Career termination and social integration among elite athletes. In S. Serpa, J. Alves, V. Ferreira, & A. Paula-Brito (Eds.), Proceedings of the VIII World Congress of Sport Psychology (pp. 902-906). Lisbon: International Society of Sport Psychology.

Wylleman, P., De Knop, P., Sloore, H., Vanden Auweele, Y., & Ewing, M. (2003). Talented athletes' perceptions of the athlete-coach-parents relationships. Kinesiologia Slovenica, 2, 59-69.

Wylleman, P., Lavallee, D., & Theeboom, M. (2004). Successful athletic careers. In C. Spielberger (Ed.), Encyclopedia of Applied Psychology (pp. 511-518). San Diego: Elsevier Ltd.

Wylleman, P., Vanden Auweele, Y., De Knop, P., Sloore, H., & De Martelaer, K. (1995). Elite young athletes, parents and coaches: Relationships in competitive sports. In F.J. Ring (Ed.), The 1st Bath Sports Medicine Conference (pp. 124-133). Bath, UK: Centre for Continuing Education.

Wylleman, P., Verdet, M-C., Lévèque, M., De Knop, P., & Huts, K. (2004). Athlètes de haut niveau, transitions scolaires et rôle des parents [Elite level athletes, Academic transitions, and role of parents]. STAPS, 64, 71-87.

Chapter 18

Aron, A., Aron, E. N., & Smollan, D. (1992). Inclusion of other in the self scale and the structure of interpersonal closeness. Journal of Personality and Social Psychology, 63, 596-612.

Bouchard, C., Shephard, R.J., & Stephens, T. (1994). Physical activity, fitness, and health: International proceedings and consensus statement. Champaign, IL: Human Kinetics.

Bandura, A. (1986). Social foundations of thought and action: A social cognitive theory. Englewood Cliffs, NJ: Prentice Hall.

Bradley, B. (2000). The values of the game. New York: Broadway Books.

Brewer, B.W., Van Raalte, J.L., & Linder, D.E. (1993). Athletic identity: Hercules' muscles or Achilles' heel? International Journal of Sport Psychology, 24, 237-254.

Carmac, M.A., & Martens, R. (1979). Measuring commitment to running: A survey of runners' attitudes and mental states. Journal of Sport Psychology, 1, 25-42.

Csikszentmihalyi, M., Rathunde, K., & Whalen, S. (1993). Talented teenagers: The roots of success and failure. New York: Cambridge.

Deci, E.L., Eghrari, H., Patrick, B.C., & Leone, D.R. (1994). Facilitating internalization: The self-determination perspective. Journal of Personality, 62, 119-142.

Deci, E.L., & Ryan, R.M. (1985). Intrinsic motivation and self-determination in human behavior. New York: Plenum.

Deci, E.L., & Ryan, R.M. (1994). Promoting self-determined education. Scandinavian Journal of Educational Research, 38, 3-14.

Deci, E.L., & Ryan, R.M. (2000). The "what" and "why" of goal pursuits: Human needs and the self-determination of behavior. Psychological Inquiry, 11, 227-268.

Elliot, A.J. (1997). Integrating the "classic" and "contemporary" approaches to achievement motivation: A hierarchical model of approach and avoidance achievement motivation. In M.L. Maehr & P.R. Pintrinch (Eds.), Advances in motivation and achievement (Vol. 10, pp. 143-179). Greenwhich, CT: JAI Press.

Elliot, A.J., & Church, M.A. (1997). A hierarchical model of approach and avoidance achievement motivation. Journal of Personality and Social Psychology, 72, 218-232.

Elliot, A.J., & Harackiewicz, J.M. (1996). Approach and avoidance achievement goals and intrinsic motivation: A mediational analysis. Journal of Personality and Social Psychology, 70, 968-980.

Emmons, R.A. (1999). The psychology of ultimate concerns: Motivation and spirituality in personality. New York: Guilford.

Ericsson, K.A., & Charness, N. (1994). Expert performance: Its structure and acquisition. American Psychologist, 49, 71-76.

Frederickson, B.L., & Joiner, T. (2002). Positive emotions trigger upward spirals toward emotional well-being. Psychological Science, 13, 172-175.

Frijda, N.H., Mesquita, B., Sonnemans, J., & Van Goozen, S. (1991). The duration of affective phenomena or emotions, sentiments and passions. In K.T. Strongman (Ed.), International review of studies on emotion (Vol. 1, pp. 187-225). New York: Wiley.

Glasser, W. (1976). Positive addiction. New York: Harper & Row.

Grolnick, W.S., & Ryan, R.M. (1989). Parent styles associated with children's self-regulation and competence in school. Journal of Educational Psychology, 81, 143-154.

Guay, F., Mageau, G.A., & Vallerand, R.J. (2003). On the hierarchical structure of intrinsic and extrinsic motivational processes: A test of top-down, bottom-up, reciprocal, and horizontal effects. Personality and Social Psychology Bulletin, 29, 992-1004.

Hatfield, E., & Sprecher, S. (1986). Measuring passionate love in intimate relationships. Journal of Adolescence, 9, 383-410.

Hausenblas, H.A., & Symons Downs, D. (2002). Exercise dependence: A systematic review. Psychology of Sport and Exercise, 3, 89-123.

Houlfort, N., Koestner, R., Vallerand, R.J., & Blanchard, C.B. (2006). Passion at work: A look at psychological adjustment. Unpublished manuscript, McGill University.

Kenyon, G.S., & McPherson, B.D. (1973). Becoming involved in physical actiity and sport: A process of socialization. In

G.L. Rarick (Ed.), *Physical activity: Human growth and development* (pp. 303-332). New York: Academic Press.

Koeske, G.F. & Kelly, T. (1995). The impact of overinvolvement on burnout and job satisfaction. *American Journal of Orthopsychiatry, 65,* 282-292.

Koestner, R., & Losier, G.F. (2002). Distinguishing three ways of being highly motivated: A closer look at introjection, identification, and intrinsic motivation. In E.L. Deci & R.M. Ryan (Eds.), *Handbook of self-determination research* (pp. 101-121). Rochester, NY: University of Rochester Press.

Koestner, R., Losier, G.F., Vallerand, R.J., & Carducci, D. (1996). Identified and introjected forms of political internalization: Extending self-determination theory. *Journal of Personality and Social Psychology, 70,* 1025-1036.

Mageau, G.A., Vallerand, R.J., Koestner, R., & Charest, J. (2006). On the development of passion. Unpublished manuscript. Université de Montréal.

Mageau, G.A., Vallerand, R.J., Rousseau, F.L., Ratelle, C.F., & Provencher, P.J. (2005). Passion and gambling: Investigating the divergent affective and cognitive consequences of gambling. *Journal of Applied Social Psychology, 35,* 100-118.

Morgan, W.P. (1979). Negative addiction in runners. *Physician and Sports Medicine, 7,* 57-77.

Raedeke, T.D., Granzyk, T.L., & Warren, A. (2000). Why coaches experience burnout: A commitment perspective. *Journal of Sport & Exercise Psychology, 22,* 85-105.

Ratelle, C.F., Vallerand, R.J., Mageau, G.A., Rousseau, F.L., & Provencher, P. (2004). When passion leads to problematic outcomes: A look at gambling. *Journal of Gambling Studies, 20,* 105-119.

Rip, B., Fortin, S., & Vallerand, R.J. (2006). The relationship between passion and injury in dance students. *Journal of Dance Medicine & Science.*

Rony, J-A. (1990). *Les passions (The passions).* Paris: Presses universitaires de France.

Rousseau, F.L., & Vallerand, R.J. (2006). An examination of the relationship among passion, Affect, and subjective well-being in seniors. Manuscript submitted for publication.

Rousseau, F.L., Vallerand, R.J., Ratelle, C.F., Mageau, G.A., & Provencher, P.J. (2002). Passion and gambling: Validation of the Gambling Passion Scale (GPS). *Journal of Gambling Studies, 18,* 45-66.

Ryan, R.M. (1995). The integration of behavioral regulation within life domains. *Journal of Personality, 63,* 397-429.

Ryan, R.M., & Deci, E.L. (2000). Self-determination theory and the facilitation of intrinsic motivation, social development, and well-being. *American Psychologist, 55,* 68-78.

Sachs, M.L. (1981). Running addiction. In M.H. Sacks & M.L. Sachs (Eds.), *Psychology of running* (pp. 116-126). Champaign, IL: Human Kinetics.

Séguin-Lévesque, C., Laliberté, M.L., Pelletier, L.G., Vallerand, R.J., & Blanchard, C. (2003). Harmonious and obsessive passions for the Internet: Their associations with couples' relationships. *Journal of Applied Social Psychology, 33,* 197-221.

Sheldon, K.M. (2002). The self-concordance model of healthy goal-striving: When personal goals correctly represent the person. In E.L. Deci & R.M. Ryan (Eds.), *Handbook of self-determination research* (pp. 65-86). Rochester, NY: University of Rochester Press.

Sheldon, K.M., & Kasser, T. (1995). Coherence and congruence: Two aspects of personality integration. *Journal of Personality and Social Psychology, 68,* 531-543.

Squires, R.L., & Kagan, D.M. (1985). Personality correlates of disordered eating. International *Journal of Eating Disorders, 4,* 80-85.

Starkes, J.L., Deakin, J.M., Allard, F., Hodges, N.J., & Hayes, A. (1996). Deliberate practice in sports: What is it anyway? In K.A. Ericsson (Ed.), *The road to excellence: The acquisition of expert performance in the arts and sciences, sports, and games* (pp. 81-106). Mahwah, NJ: Erlbaum.

Sternberg, R.J. (1986). A triangular theory of love. *Psychological Review, 93,* 119-135.

Vallerand, R.J. (1997). Toward a hierarchical model of intrinsic and extrinsic motivation. *Advances in Experimental and Social Psychology, 29,* 271-360.

Vallerand, R.J. (2001). A hierarchical model of intrinsic and extrinsic motivation in sport and exercise. In G. Roberts (Ed.), *Advances in motivation in sport and exercise* (pp. 263-319). Champaign, IL: Human Kinetics.

Vallerand, R.J., & Blanchard, C. (2000). The study of emotions in sport and exercise: Historical, definitional, and conceptual perspectives. In Y. Hanin (Ed.), *Emotions in sports* (pp. 3-37). Champaign, IL: Human Kinetics.

Vallerand, R.J., Blanchard, C.M., Mageau, G.A., Koestner, R., Ratelle, C., Léonard, M., Gagné, M., & Marsolais, J. (2003). Les passions de l'âme: On obsessive and harmonious passion. *Journal of Personality and Social Psychology, 85,* 756-767.

Vallerand, R.J., Fortier, M.S., & Guay, F. (1997). Self-determination and persistence in a real-life setting: Toward a motivational model of high-school dropout. *Journal of Personality and Social Psychology, 72,* 1161-1176.

Vallerand, R.J., & Houlfort, N. (2003). Passion at work: Toward a new conceptualization. In D. Skarlicki, S. Gilliland, & D. Steiner (Eds.), *Research in Social Issues in Management* (Vol. 3, pp. 195-204). Greenwich, CT: Information Age.

Vallerand, R.J., Mageau, G.A., Demers, M.-A., Elliot, A.J., Dumais, A., & Rousseau, F.L. (2005). Passion and performance attainment in sport. Unpublished manuscript. University of Quebec at Montreal.

Vallerand, R.J. & Reid, G. (1984). On the causal effects of perceived competence on intrinsic motivation: A test of cognitive evaluation theory. *Journal of Sport Psychology, 6,* 94-102.

Vallerand, R.J., & Reid, G. (1988). On the relative effects of positive and negative verbal feedback on males' and females' intrinsic motivation. *Canadian Journal of Behavioural Sciences, 20,* 239-250.

Vallerand, R.J., & Rousseau, F.L. (2001). Intrinsic and extrinsic motivation in sport and exercise: A review using the hierarchical model of intrinsic and extrinsic motivation. In R. Singer, H. Hausenblas, & C. Janelle (Eds.), *Handbook of Sport Psychology* (2nd ed., pp. 389-416). New York: Wiley.

Vallerand, R.J., Grouzet, F.M.E., Dumais, A., Grenier, S. & Blanchard, C.M. (in press). Passion in sport: A look at determinants and affective experiences. *Journal of Sport and Exercise Psychology.*

Vallerand, R.J., Salvy, S.-J., Mageau, G.A., Elliot, A.J., Denis, P.L., Grouzet, F.M.E., & Blanchard, C.M. (in press). On the role of passion in performance. *Journal of Personality.*

Chapter 19

Ames, C. (1992). Achievement goals, motivational climate, and motivational processes. In G.C. Roberts (Ed.), *Motivation in sport and exercise* (pp. 161-176). Champaign, IL: Human Kinetics.

Anderman, E.M., Griesinger, T., and Westerfield, G. (1998). Motivation and cheating during adolescence. *Journal of Educational Psychology, 90,* 84-93.

Blasi, A. (1980). Bridging moral cognition and moral action: A critical review of the literature. *Psychological Bulletin, 88,* 1-45.

Bredemeier, B.J. (1985). Moral reasoning and the perceived legitimacy of intentionally injurious sport acts. *Journal of Sport Psychology, 7,* 110-124.

Bredemeier, B.J. (1994). Children's moral reasoning and their assertive, Aggressive, and submissive tendencies in sport and daily life. *Journal of Sport and Exercise Psychology, 16,* 1-14.

Bredemeier, B.J.L. (1999). Character in action: Promoting moral behavior in sport. In R. Lidor & M. Bar Eli (Eds.), *Innovations in sport psychology: Linking theory and practice* (pp. 247-260). Morgantown WV: Fitness Information Technology.

Bredemeier, B.J., & Shields, D.L. (1984). The utility of moral stage analysis in the investigation of athletic aggression. *Sociology of Sport Journal, 1,* 138-149.

Bredemeier, B.J., & Shields, D.L. (1986a). Moral growth among athletes and nonathletes: A comparative analysis. *Journal of Genetic Psychology, 147,* 7-18.

Bredemeier, B.J., & Shields, D.L. (1986b). Game reasoning and interactional morality. *Journal of Genetic Psychology, 147,* 257-275.

Bredemeier, B.J., & Shields, D.L. (1993). Moral psychology in the context of sport: In R. Singer, M. Murphey, & L.L. Tennant (Eds.), *Handbook of research in sport psychology* (pp. 587-599). New York: MacMillan.

Bredemeier, B.J., Weiss, M.R., Shields, D.L., & Cooper, B. (1986). The relationship of sport involvement with children's moral reasoning and aggression tendencies. *Journal of Sport Psychology, 8,* 304-318.

Bredemeier, B.J., Weiss, M.R., Shields, D.L., & Cooper, B. (1987). The relationship between children's legitimacy judgments and their moral reasoning, Aggression tendencies, and sport involvement. *Sociology of Sport Journal, 4,* 48-60.

Bredemeier, B.J., Weiss, M.R., Shields, D.L., & Shewchuk, R.M. (1986). Promoting moral growth in a summer sport camp: The implementation of theoretically grounded instructional strategies. *Journal of Moral Education, 15,* 212-220.

Conroy, D.E., Silva, J.M., Newcomer, R.R., Walker, B.W., & Johnson, M.S. (2001). Personal and participatory socializers of the perceived legitimacy of aggressive behavior in sport. *Aggressive Behavior, 27,* 405-418.

Deci, E.L., & Ryan, R.M. (1985). *Intrinsic motivation and self determination in human behavior.* New York: Plenum Press. Deci, E.L., & Ryan, R.M. (1991). A motivational approach to self: Integration in personality. In R. Dienstbier (Ed.), *Nebraska Symposium on Motivation: Vol. 38, Perspectives on motivation* (pp. 237-288). Lincoln, NE: University of Nebraska Press.

Duda, J.L. (1993). A social cognitive approach to the study of motivation in sport. In R.N. Singer, M. Murphey, & L.K. Tennant (Eds.), *Handbook on research in sport psychology* (pp. 421-436). New York: MacMillan.

Duda, J.L., Olson, L.K., & Templin, T.J. (1991). The relationship of task and ego orientation to sportsmanship attitudes and the perceived legitimacy of injurious acts. *Research Quarterly for Exercise and Sport, 62,* 79-87.

Dunn, J.G.H., & Causgrove-Dunn, J.C. (1999). Goal orientations, perceptions of aggression, and sportspersonship in elite male youth ice hockey players. *The Sport Psychologist, 13,* 183-200.

Haan, N. (1978). Two moralities in action contexts: Relationship to thought, ego regulation, and development. *Journal of Personality and Social Psychology, 32,* 255-270.

Haan, N. (1983). An interactional morality of everyday life. In N. Haan, R. Bellah, P. Rabinow, & W. Sallivan (Eds.), *Social science as moral inquiry* (218-250). New York: Columbia University Press.

Hall, E.R. (1981). *Moral development levels of athletes in sport specific and general social situations.* Unpublished doctoral dissertation, Texas Woman's University, Denton, Texas.

Higgins, A., Power, C., & Kohlberg, L. (1984). The relationships of moral judgment to judgments of responsibility. In W. Kurtinez & J. Gewirtz (Eds.), *Morality, moral behavior, and moral development* (pp. 74-106). New York: Wiley.

Kavussanu, M., & Ntoumanis, N. (2003). Participation in sport and moral functioning: Does ego orientation mediate their relationship? *Journal of Sport and Exercise Psychology, 25,* 1-18.

Kavussanu, M., & Rameswaran, R. (2000). *The relationship between goal orientations and moral functioning in hockey players.* Paper presented at the Sport Psychology Conference in the New Millennium, Halmstad, Sweden.

Kavussanu, M., & Roberts, G.C. (2001). Moral functioning in sport: An achievement goal perspective. *Journal of Sport and Exercise Psychology, 23,* 37-54.

Kavussanu, M., Roberts, G.C., & Ntoumanis, N. (2002). Contextual influences on moral functioning of college basketball players. *The Sport Psychologist, 16,* 347-367.

Kavussanu, M., & Spray, C.M. (2006). Contextual influences on moral functioning of male youth footballers. *The Sport Psychologist, 20,* 1-23.

Kohlberg, L. (1969). Stage and sequences: The cognitive developmental approach to socialization. In D.A. Goslin (Ed.), *Handbook of socialization theory and research* (pp. 347-380). Chicago: Rand McNally.

Kohlberg, L. (1971). Stages of moral development as a basis of moral education. In M. Beck, B.S. Crittenden, & E.V. Sullivan (Eds.), *Moral education: Interdisciplinary approaches* (pp. 23-92). Toronto: University of Toronto Press.

Kohlberg, L. (1984). *Essays on moral development. Vol. 2: The psychology of moral development.* San Francisco: Harper & Row.

Kohlberg, L., & Higgins, A. (1987). School democracy and social interaction. In W. Kurtines & J. Gewirtz (Eds.), *Moral development through social interaction* (pp. 102-128). New York: Wiley.

Lemyre, P.N., Roberts, G.C., & Ommundsen, Y. (2002). Achievement goal orientations, perceived ability, and sportspersonship in youth soccer. *Journal of Applied Sport Psychology, 14,* 120-136.

Miller, B., Roberts, G.C., & Ommundsen, Y. (2003). Effect of motivational climate on sportspersonship among competitive male and female football players. *Scandinavian Journal of Medicine and Science in Sports, 13,* 1-14.

Nicholls, J.G. (1989). *The competitive ethos and democratic education.* Cambridge: Harvard University Press.

Oglesby, C. (1978). The masculinity-femininity game: Called on account of! In C. Oglesby (Ed.), *Women and sport: From myth to reality.* Philadelphia: Lea & Febiger.

Ommundsen, Y., Roberts, G.C., Lemyre, P.N., & Treasure, D.C. (2003). Perceived motivational climate in male youth soccer: Relations to social–moral functioning, sportspersonship and team norm perceptions. *Psychology of Sport and Exercise, 4,* 397-413.

Power, C., Higgins, A., & Kohlberg, L.A. (1989). *Lawrence Kohlberg's approach to moral education.* New York: Columbia University Press.

Rest, J.R. (1983). Morality. In J., Flavell & E. Markman (Eds.), *Handbook of child psychology. Vol. 3: Cognitive development* (pp. 556-629). New York: Wiley.

Rest, J.R. (1984). The major components of morality. In W. Kurtines & J. Gewirtz (Eds.), *Morality, moral behavior, and moral development* (pp. 356-429). New York: Wiley.

Roberts, G.C. (1984). *Achievement motivation in children's sport. In J.G. Nicholls (Ed.) Advances in motivation and achievement. Vol. 3. The development of achievement motivation* (pp. 251-281). Greenwich, CT: JAI Press.

Roberts, G.C. (2001). Understanding the dynamics of motivation in physical activity: the influence of achievement goals on motivational processes. In *Advances in Motivation in Sport and Exercise* (edited by G.C. Roberts), pp. 1-50. Champaign, IL: Human Kinetics.

Roberts, G.C., Treasure, D.C. & Kavussanu, M. (1997). Motivation in physical activity contexts: An achievement goal perspective. In P. Pintrich & M. Maehr (Eds.), *Advances in Motivation and Achievement (Vol. 10).* Stamford, CT: JAI Press, pp. 413-447.

Romance, T.J., Weiss, M.R., & Bockoven, J. (1986). A program to promote moral development through elementary physical education. *Journal of Teaching in Physical Education, 5,* 126-136.

Shields, D.L., & Bredemeier, B.J.L. (1995). *Character development and physical activity.* Champaign, IL: Human Kinetics.

Shields, D.L., & Bredemeier B.J.L. (2001). Moral development and behavior in sport. In R.N. Singer, H.A. Hausenblas, & C.M. Janelle (Eds.), *Handbook of sport psychology* (pp. 585-603). New York: Wiley.

Shields, D.L., Bredemeier, B., Gardner, D., & Bostrom, A. (1995). Leadership, cohesion, and team norms regarding cheating and aggression. *Sociology of Sport Journal, 12,* 324-336.

Silva, J.M. (1983). The perceived legitimacy of rule violating behaviour in sport. Journal of Sport Psychology, 5, 438-448.

Stephens, D.E. (2000). Predictors of likelihood to aggress in youth soccer: An examination of coed and all-girls teams. *Journal of Sport Behavior, 23,* 311-325.

Stephens, D.E. (2001). Predictors of aggressive tendencies in girls' basketball: An examination of beginning and advanced participants in a summer skills camp. *Research Quarterly for Exercise and Sport, 72,* 257-266.

Stephens, D.E., & Bredemeier, B.J.L. (1996). Moral atmosphere and judgments about aggression in girls' soccer: Relationships among moral and motivational variables. *Journal of Sport and Exercise Psychology, 18,* 158-173.

Stuart, M., & Ebbeck, V. (1995). The influence of perceived social approval on moral development in youth sport. Pediatric Exercise Science, 7, 270-280.

Tod, D., and Hodge, K. (2001). Moral reasoning and achievement motivation in sport: A qualitative inquiry. *Journal of Sport Behavior, 23,* 307-327.

Tucker, L.W., & Parks, J.B. (2001). Effects of gender and sport type on intercollegiate athletes' perceptions of the legitimacy of aggressive behaviors in sport. *Sociology of Sport Journal, 18,* 403-413.

Vallerand, R.J., Briere, N.M., Blanchard, C., & Provencher, P. (1997). Development and validation of the multidimensional sportspersonship orientations scale. *Journal of Sport and Exercise Psychology, 16,* 126-140.

Vallerand, R.J., Deshaies, P., & Cuerrier, J.P. (1997). On the effects of the social context on behavioral intentions of sportsmanship. *International Journal of Sport Psychology, 28,* 126-140.

Vallerand, R.J., Deshaies, P., Cuerrier, J.P., Pelletier, L.G., & Mongeau, C. (1992). Ajzen and Fishbein's theory of reasoned action as applied to moral behavior: A confirmatory analysis. *Journal of Personality and Social Psychology, 62(1),* 98-109.

Vallerand, R.J., & Losier, G.F. (1994). Self-determined motivation and sportsmanship orientations: An assessment of their temporal relationship. *Journal of Sport and Exercise Psychology, 16,* 229-245.

Weiss, M.R., & Bredemeier, B.J. (1990). Moral development in sport. In K.B. Pandolf & J.O. Holloszy (Eds.), *Exercise and Sport Science Reviews, 18,* 331-378.

Weiss, M.R., & Smith, A.L. (2002). Moral development in sport and physical activity: Theory, research, and intervention. In T.S. Horn (Ed.), *Advances in Sport Psychology* (pp. 243-280). Champaign: Human Kinetics.

White, S.A., & Duda, J.L. (1994). The relationship of gender, level of sport involvement, and participation motivation to task and ego orientation. *International Journal of Sport Psychology, 25,* 4-18.

Chapter 20

Barnlund, (1989). *Communicative styles of Japanese and Americans: Images and realities.* Belmont, CA: Wadsworth.

Berry, J.W. (1969). On cross-cultural comparability. *International Journal of Psychology, 4,* 119-128.

Berry, J.W. (1979). A cultural ecology of social behavior. In L. Berkowitz (Ed.), *Advances in experimental social psychology* (Vol. 12, pp. 177-206). New York: Academic Press.

Berry, J.W. (1990). The role of psychology in ethnic studies. *Canadian Ethnic Studies, 22,* 8-21.

Berry, J.W., Poortinga, Y.H., Segall, M.H., & Dasen, P.R. (2002). *Cross-cultural psychology: Research and applications* (2nd ed.). New York: Cambridge University Press.

Bond, M.H. (Ed.). (1986). *The psychology of the Chinese people.* Hong Kong: Oxford University Press (China).

Bond, M.H. (Ed.). (1996). *The handbook of Chinese psychology.* Hong Kong: Oxford University Press (China).

Bond, M.H., Leung, K., Au, A., Tong, K.K., Reimel de Carrasquel, S., Murakami, F. et al. (in press). Culture-level dimensions of social axioms and their correlates across 41 cultures. *Journal of Cross-Cultural Psychology.*

Bond, R., & Smith, P.B. (1996). Culture and conformity: A meta-analysis of studies using Asch's line judgment task. *Psychological Bulletin, 119,* 111-137.

Brace, C.L. (1995). Race and political correctness. *American Psychologist, 50(8),* 725-726.

Brislin, R.W. (1993). *Understanding culture's influence on behavior.* Fort Worth, TX: Harcourt, Brace, Jovanovich.

Carron, A., Widmeyer, W., & Brawley, L. (1985). The development of an instrument to assess cohesion in sport teams: The Group Environment Questionnaire. *Journal of Sport Psychology, 7,* 244-267.

Chan, D.K. (1994). COLINDEX: A refinement of three collectivism measures. In U. Kim, H.C. Triandis, D. Kagitchbasi, S. Choi, & G. Yoon (Eds.), *Individualism and collectivism: Theory, method, and applications* (pp. 200-210). Thousand Oaks, CA: Sage.

Chelladurai, P., Imamura, H., Yamaguchi, Y., Oinuma, Y., & Miyauchi, T. (1988). Sport leadership in a cross-national setting: The case of Japanese and Canadian university athletes. *Journal of Sport & Exercise Psychology, 10,* 374-389.

Chelladurai, P., & Saleh, S.D. (1980). Dimensions of leader behavior in sports: Development of a leadership scale. *Journal of Sport Psychology, 2,* 34-35.

Coakley, J. (1986). *Sport in society: Issues and controversies* (3rd ed.). St. Louis: C.V. Mosby.

Cohen, J. (1988). *Statistical power analysis for the behavioral sciences* (2nd ed.). Hillsdale, NJ: Erlbaum.

Cook, T.D., & Campbell, D.T. (1979). *Quasi-experimentation: Design and analysis issues for field settings.* Chicago: Rand McNally.

Cox, R.H. (2002). *Sport psychology: Concepts and application* (5th ed.). New York: McGraw-Hill.

Cuber, J.F. (1968). *Sociology.* East Norwalk, CT: Appleton-Century-Crofts.

Dole, A. (1995). Why not drop race as a term? *American Psychologist, 50,* 40.

Duda, J.L. (1993). Goals: A social cognitive approach to the study of achievement motivation in sport. In R.N. Singer, M. Murphey, & L.K. Tennant (Eds.), *Handbook of research on sport psychology* (pp. 421-436). New York: Macmillan.

Duda, J.L., & Allison, M.T. (1990). Cross-cultural analysis in exercise and sport psychology: A void in the field. *Journal of Sport and Exercise Psychology, 12,* 114-131.

Edwards, H. (1973). *Sociology of sport.* Homewood, IL: Dorsey Press.

Enriquez, V.G. (Ed.). (1990). *Indigenous psychology.* Quezon City: Psychology Research and Training House.

Fijneman, Y.A., Willemsen, M.E., & Poortinga, Y.H. (1996). Individualism-collectivism: An empirical study of a conceptual issue. *Journal of Cross-Cultural Psychology, 27,* 381-402.

Goodnow, J.J. (1990). The socialization of cognition: What's involved? In J.W. Stigler, R.A. Shweder, & G. Herdt (Eds.), *Cultural psychology: Essays on comparative human behavior* (pp. 259-286). Cambridge: Cambridge University Press.

Gudykunst, W.B. (1997). Cultural variability in communication. *Communication Research, 24(4),* 327-348.

Hale, B.D., James, B., & Stambulova, N. (1999). Determining the dimensionality of athletic identity: A Herculean cross-cultural undertaking. *International Journal of Sport Psychology, 30,* 83-100.

Ho, D. (1998). Indigenous psychologies: Asian perspectives. *Journal of Cross-Cultural Psychology, 29,* 88-103.

Hofstede, G. (1980). *Culture's consequences.* Beverly Hills, CA: Sage.

Hofstede, G. (1983). Dimensions of national cultures in fifty countries and three regions. In J.B. Deregowski, S. Dziurawiec, & R.C. Annis (Eds.), *Expiscations in cross-cultural psychology* (pp. 335-355). Lisse: Swets & Zeitlinger.

Hui, C.H. (1988). Measurement of individualism-collectivism. *Journal of Research in Personality, 22,* 17-36.

Jowett, S., & Ntoumanis, N. (2003). The Greek Coach–Athlete Relationship Questionnaire (GrCART-Q): Scale construction and validation. *International Journal of Sport Psychology, 34,* 101-124.

Jowett, S., & Ntoumanis, N. (2004). The Coach–Athlete Relationship Questionnaire (CART-Q): Development and initial validation. *Scandinavian Journal of Medicine & Science in Sport, 14,* 245-257.

Kim, B.J., Williams, L., & Gill, D. (2003). A cross-cultural study of achievement orientation and intrinsic motivation in young USA and Korean athletes. *International Journal of Sport Psychology, 34,* 168-184.

Kim, U. (1990). Indigenous psychology: Science and applications. In R. Brislin (Ed.), *Applied cross-cultural psychology* (pp. 142-160). Newbury Park, CA: Sage.

Kim, Y., & Berry, J.W. (Eds.). (1993). *Indigenous psychologies: Research and experiences in cultural context.* Newbury Park, CA: Sage.

Ko, H.S.R., & Yang, C.F. (Eds.). (1991). *The Chinese and the Chinese mind.* Taipei: Yuan Liu.

Leung, K., & Bond, M.H. (2004). Social axioms: A model for social beliefs in multicultural perspective. In M.P. Zanna (Ed.), *Advances in experimental social psychology* (Vol. 36, pp. 119-197). New York: Academic Press.

Leung, K., Bond, M.H., Reimel de Carrasquel, S., Munoz, C., Hernandez, M., Murakami, F., et al. (2002). Social axioms: The search for universal dimensions of general beliefs about how the world functions. *Journal of Cross-Cultural Psychology, 33,* 286-302.

Lonner, W.J. & Malpass, R. (Eds.). (1994). Psychology and culture. Boston: Allyn & Bacon.

Malina, R. (1988). Racial/ethnic variations in motor development and performance of American children. *Canadian Journal of Sport Sciences, 13,* 136-143.

Marsh, H.W., Asci, F.H., & Tomas, I.M. (2002). Multitrait-multimethod analyses of two physical self-concept instruments: A cross-cultural perspective. *Journal of Sport & Exercise Psychology, 24,* 99-119.

Matsumoto, D. (1994). *People: Psychology from a cultural perspective.* Pacific Grove, CA: Brooks/Cole.

Ongel, U., & Smith, P.B. (1994). Who are we and where are we going? JCCP approaches its 100th issue. *Journal of Cross-Cultural Psychology, 25,* 25-53.

Pawlik, K., & Rosenzweig, M. (Eds.). (2000). *International handbook of psychology.* London: Sage.

Pike, K.L. (1967). *Language in relation to a unified theory of the structure of human behavior.* The Hague, the Netherlands: Mouton.

Riesman, D., & Denney, R. (1951). Football in America: A study of cultural diffusion. *American Quarterly, 3,* 309-319.

Riordan, C.M., & Vandenberg, R.J. (1994). A central question in cross-cultural research: Do employees of different cultures interpret work-related measures in an equivalent manner? *Journal of Management, 20,* 643-671.

Ronen, S., & Shenkar, O. (1988). Clustering variables: The application of nonmetric multivariate analysis techniques in comparative management research. *International Studies of Management & Organization, 18(2),* 72-87.

Rushton, J.P. (1995). Sex and race differences in cranial capacity from International Labor Office data. *Intelligence, 19,* 281-294.

Samson, J., & Yerles, M. (1988). Racial differences in sport performance. *Canadian Journal of Sport Sciences, 13,* 109-116.

Schaffe, B.S., & Riordan, C.M. (2003). A review of cross-cultural methodologies for organizational research: A best-practices approach. *Organizational Research Methods, 6,* 169-216.

Segall, M.H., Dasen, P.R., Berry, J.W., & Poortinga, Y.H. (1990). *Human behavior in global perspective: An introduction to cross-cultural psychology.* New York: Pergamon.

Shiraev, E., & Levy, D. (2001). *Introduction to cross-cultural psychology: Crtical thinking and contemporary applications.* Boston: Allyn & Bacon.

Si, G.Y., Chung, P.K., & Liu, H. (2003). Development and test of Social- & Individual-Oriented Sport Achievement Motivation Scale. *Journal of Wuhan Institute of Physical Education, 37,* 136-140.

Si, G.Y., Rethorst, S., & Willimczik, K. (1995). Causal attribution perception in sports achievement: A cross-cultural study on attributional concepts in Germany and China. *Journal of Cross-Cultural Psychology, 26,* 537-553.

Sinha, D. (1996). Cross-cultural psychology: The Asian scenario. In J. Pandy, D. Sinha, & D.P.S. Bhawuk (Eds.), *Asian contributions to cross-cultural psychology* (pp. 20-41). New Delhi: Sage.

Smith, G. (1973). The sport hero: An endangered species. *Quest, 19,* 59-70.

Smith, P.B., & Bond, M.H. (1998). *Social psychology across cultures* (2nd ed.). Hemel Hempstead: Harvester/Wheatsheaf.

Triandis, H.C. (1973). Subjective culture and economic development. *International Journal of Psychology, 8,* 163-180.

Triandis, H.C. (1994). *Culture and social behavior.* New York: McGraw Hill.

Triandis, H.C., & Lambert, W.W. (Eds.). (1980). *Handbook of cross-cultural psychology. Vol. 1: Perspectives.* Boston: Allyn & Bacon.

Van de Vijver, R.J.R., & Leung, K. (1997). Methods and data analysis of comparative research. In J.W. Berry, Y.H. Poortinga, & J. Pandey (Eds.), *Theory and method: Vol. I of Handbook of cross-cultural psychology* (2nd ed., pp. 257-300). Boston, MA: Allyn & Bacon.

Voronov, M., & Singer, J.A. (2002). The myth of individualism-collectivism: A critical review. *Journal of Social Psychology, 142,* 461-480.

Weick, K.E. (1979). *The social psychology of organizing.* Reading, MA: Addison-Wesley.

Yamaguchi, S. (1994). Collectivism among the Japanese: A perspective from the self. In U. Kim, H.C. Triandis, C. Kagitcibasi, S.H. Choi, & G. Yoon (Eds.), *Individualism and collectivism: Theory, method, and applications* (pp. 175-188). Thousand Oaks, CA: Sage.

Yang, K.S. (1999). Toward an indigenous Chinese psychology: A selected review of methodological, theoretical, and empirical accomplishments. *Chinese Journal of Psychology, 41,* 181-211.

Yang, K.S., & Ho, D.Y.F. (1988). The role of yuan in Chinese social life: A conceptual and empirical analysis. In A.C. Paranjpe, D.Y.F. Ho, & R.W. Rieber (Eds.), *Asian contributions to psychology* (pp. 163-181). New York: Praeger.

index

Note: The italicized *f* and *t* following page numbers refer to figures and tables, respectively.

about the editors

Sophia Jowett, PhD, is a senior lecturer in sport and exercise psychology at Loughborough University. She received her PhD from the University of Exeter in 2001. Her main research revolves around the affective, cognitive, and behavioral aspects of interpersonal relationships in sport. Her research has been supported by the Economic and Social Research Council, the British Academy, the Nuffield Foundation, the Hellenic Olympic Committee, and the Hellenic Ministry of Culture and Sport. Dr. Jowett has published in peer-reviewed journals, including the *British Journal of Social Psychology, Journal of Applied Sport Psychology, The Sport Psychologist, International Journal of Sport Psychology, Scandinavian Journal of Medicine Sciences and Sports*, and *Group Dynamics: Theory, Research, and Practice.* She has presented her work at national and international conferences and has authored chapters in edited books. She has recently coedited a special issue on interpersonal relationships in *Psychology of Sport and Exercise* and a monograph on psychology of sport coaching for the British Psychological Society. She is an accredited sport psychologist of the British Association of Sport and Exercise Sciences and served as a sport psychology consultant of the 2004 Greek Olympic team. Sophia and her husband Peter, have two daughters, Christina and Phillippa.

David Lavallee, PhD, is a reader in sport and exercise psychology at Loughborough University. His educational qualifications include a master's degree in psychology from Harvard University and a PhD in sport and exercise psychology from the University of Western Australia. He is also an associate fellow and chartered psychologist of the British Psychological Society. Dr. Lavallee has published more than 100 scholarly publications in academic and professional outlets, including two edited books, one authored book, 18 book chapters, and numerous peer-reviewed journal articles. He has also edited special issues of *The Psychologist, Journal of Personal and Interpersonal Loss,* and *Psychology of Sport and Exercise* and two monographs. He currently serves as editor of *Sport and Exercise Psychology Review,* associate editor of *The Psychologist,* and digest editor for the *Journal of Sport & Exercise Psychology.* David and his wife, Ruth, have two sons, Joseph and Noah.

about the contributors

Isabel Balaguer, PhD, is an associate professor of psychology at the University of Valencia, Spain. She teaches graduate and undergraduate courses in social psychology and the social-psychological aspects of sport and exercise. In terms of research interests, Isabel has focused on the antecedents and consequences of coach behaviors and the psychosocial predictors of positive youth development and lifestyles in teenagers.

Mark R. Beauchamp, PhD, is an assistant professor in the School of Human Kinetics at the University of British Columbia. He received his PhD in 2002 from the University of Birmingham, United Kingdom. His research focuses on the social psychology of groups within sport and exercise settings, with a particular interest in communication processes, role perceptions, and motivation. Mark has published in a wide range of sport and social psychology journals, including the *Journal of Sport & Exercise Psychology*, *The Sport Psychologist*, *Journal of Applied Social Psychology*, *Small Group Research*, and *Group Dynamics: Theory, Research, and Practice*. His current research is funded by a Nuffield Foundation Social Sciences Grant. Mark has also worked in a consulting capacity with athletes from a range of sports, including amateur, professional, and international competitors. He is married to Karrie and has a young son, Benjamin. In his spare time Mark enjoys traveling, skiing, keeping fit, and recently ran his first London Marathon.

Steven R. Bray, PhD, is currently an assistant professor in the Department of Kinesiology at McMaster University in Hamilton, Canada. His research interests focus on social-psychological and group dynamics in sport, exercise, and rehabilitation contexts. He has published numerous articles examining the home advantage in ice hockey, basketball, cricket, baseball, soccer, and alpine ski racing.

Shauna M. Burke is a PhD candidate in the health sciences at the University of Western Ontario. Her primary research interest is group dynamics in sport and exercise. Shauna has presented her research at several national and international scientific and professional conferences, and she is currently a Canadian regional student representative for the Association for the Advancement of Applied Sport Psychology.

Albert V. Carron, EdD, is a professor at the University of Western Ontario and has been an author or coauthor of 14 books and monographs, 30 chapters in edited texts, and 125 refereed publications. He is a fellow in the American Academy of Kinesiology and Physical Education, the Association for the Advancement of Applied Sport Psychology, and the Canadian Psychomotor Learning and Sport Psychology Association. He is a past president of the Canadian Association for Sport Sciences and a former member of the board of directors of the Sports Medicine Council of Canada. In 1998, Carron was a corecipient of the International Council of Sport Science and Physical Education's Sport Science Award of the International Olympic Committee President. Currently, Carron is a member of the editorial board of *Journal of Sport & Exercise Psychology*, *International Journal of Sport Psychology*, and *Small Group Research*.

Saša Cecič-Erpič, PhD, is an assistant professor of developmental psychology in the faculty of sport at Ljubljana University. Her research interests fit broadly into the area of developmental and sport psychology. She has published several articles and a scientific monograph on sport career transitions, focusing on both sport and developmental aspects. She is an editor in chief of *Kinesiologia Slovenia*. Besides teaching, she works as an applied sport psychologist with elite and young athletes in Slovenia.

Paul De Knop, PhD, is a professor of sports sociology and sports management at the Vrije Universiteit Brussel and has also been appointed to the professorial chair of Social, Policy-Oriented and Didactical Aspects of Sport and Physical Education at the Universiteit Tilburg (the Netherlands). He is also head of the Department of Top Level Sport and Studies at the Vrije Universiteit Brussel, chairman of the board of the Flemish sport administrative body (Bloso), and acting advisor to the Flemish minister of sport. Dr. De Knop has been an author or coauthor of 32 books, 108 chapters in books, 88 publications in international journals, and 179 publications in national journals.

Joan L. Duda, PhD, is a professor of sports psychology in the School of Sport and Exercise Sciences at the University of Birmingham, United Kingdom. She is past president of the Association for the Advancement of Applied Sport Psychology; has been a member of the executive boards of the North American Society for the Psychology of Sport and Physical Activity, the Sport Psychology Academy, Division 47 of the American Psychological Association, and the International Society for Sport Psychology; and is currently on the scientific committee of the European Congress of Sport Science. She was editor of the *Journal of Applied Sport Psychology* and is on the editorial board of several other leading journals in the field. A fellow of the Association for the Advancement of Applied Sport Psychology and the American Academy of Kinesiology and Physical Education, Dr. Duda has authored over 170 publications on motivation in the physical domain and the psychological aspects of sport and exercise behavior. She is certified as a mental skills consultant by the Association for the Advancement of Applied Sport Psychology and is accredited as a sport psychology consultant by the British Association for Sport and Exercise Sciences.

Mark A. Eys, PhD, is an assistant professor of sport psychology in the School of Human Kinetics at Laurentian University in Sudbury, Ontario. His area of interest is group dynamics in sport and physical activity. Current research interests include role ambiguity and acceptance in sport and exercise groups, the measurement and correlates of cohesion, and social influences in exercise.

Iain Greenlees, PhD, teaches undergraduate and postgraduate courses in social psychology of sport in the School of Sport, Exercise, and Health Sciences at University College Chichester, United Kingdom. His research interests include impression formation in sport, collective efficacy, and team-referent attributions. Dr. Greenlees is coeditor of the book *Concentration Skills Training in Sport* (British Psychological Society, 2003) with Aidan Moran. He is a British Association of Sport and Exercise Sciences accredited sport psychologist and works with the English Golf Union to develop mental skills in junior golfers.

Marc V. Jones, PhD, is currently a reader in sport and exercise psychology at Staffordshire University, United Kingdom. Marc completed an undergraduate degree in applied psychology at Cardiff University and a PhD examining the role of emotion in sport performance at Newman College, United Kingdom. His main areas of research include the impact of emotions on sport performance and understanding how emotional control can be developed in athletes. As a sport psychology consultant, Marc has worked with a number of athletes across a range of sports, ages, and abilities. He is accredited by the British Association of Sport and Exercise Sciences for providing sport psychology support and is a chartered psychologist with the British Psychological Society.

Maria Kavussanu, PhD, completed a first degree at the University of Athens, Greece, an MS at the University of North Carolina at Greensboro, and a PhD at the University of Illinois at Urbana-Champaign. She has specialized in sport and exercise psychology. After working as a lecturer at Illinois State University and Loughborough University, United Kingdom, Maria moved to the University of Birmingham in 2002, where she took up her present post as a lecturer in the School of Sport and Exercise Sciences. Maria was the recipient of the North American Society for the Psychology of Sport and Physical Activity student research award in sport psychology in 1995 and 1996, and received the fourth prize in the poster competition of the European College of Sports Science in 1998. Maria's research interests are motivation and moral functioning in physical activity contexts, and her work has been supported by research grants from the Universities of Illinois, Loughborough, and Birmingham. She has published her research in several peer-reviewed journals, including the *Journal of Sport & Exercise Psychology, The Sport Psychologist,* and the *Journal of Cross-Cultural Psychology,* and has made numerous presentations at meetings of professional organizations in Europe and the United States.

John Kremer, PhD, is a half-time reader in the School of Psychology at the Queen's University of Belfast, where he has lectured in applied psychology since 1980. He combines his academic interest in sport and exercise psychology with consultancy work with a wide range of sport and governing bodies, including soccer, netball, Gaelic football, squash, athletics, gymnastics, darts, cycling, bowls, sailing, motor sports, cricket, rugby, badminton, tennis, snooker, weightlifting, and golf. His 12 books include *Sport Psychology: Contemporary Themes* (Palgrave, 2003), *Psychology in Sport* (Taylor & Francis, 1994), and *Young People's Involvement in Sport* (Routledge, 1998). He has also edited special sport psychology issues of both the *Irish Journal of Psychology* and *The Psychologist.*

Nicole M. LaVoi, PhD, is director of sports programming with the Center for Ethics and Education at the University of Notre Dame, where she also teaches in the psychology department. Her interdisciplinary expertise spans developmental, moral, and social psychological issues of sport. She examines the relational dynamics of teaching and learning, focusing on dimensions of quality (e.g., authenticity, empowerment, closeness) and conflict in the coach–athlete relationship and under what conditions sport produces engaged citizens and develops character. She bridges the research–praxis gap by developing coaching education curricula that help coaches expand relational competence and create a nurturing climate that increases the likelihood of self-determined motivation, moral behavior, mutual growth, and well-being within sport contexts.

Hing-chu Lee, PhD, was a faculty member in the psychology department at the University of Hong Kong for 6 years before joining the Hong Kong Sports Institute as their sport psychologist. She provides consultation and on-field support to elite athletes in triathlon, rowing, fencing, and squash. Her research interests include stress and coping in competitions, psychology of injury, motor learning, and technique correction.

Ralph Maddison, PhD, completed his PhD in sport and exercise psychology from the University of Auckland in 2004. Ralph has research interests in sport and exercise psychology, in particular self-presentation issues, the association between psychological factors and injury, and the psychology of exercise in clinical populations. He is currently a postdoctoral research fellow with the National Institute of Public and Mental Health, Auckland University of Technology.

Herbert W. Marsh, PhD, is professor of education at Oxford University and was the founding director of the SELF (Self-Concept Enhancement and Learning Facilitation) Research Centre at the University of Western Sydney. He is the author of internationally recognized psychological tests that measure self-concept, motivation, and university students' evaluations of teaching effectiveness. He has published more than 250 articles in international journals, 22 chapters, 8 monographs, and 250 conference papers. He is widely recognized as one of the most productive researchers in sport, educational, developmental, and social psychology, and is a highly cited researcher on the ISI's list of the "world's most cited and influential scientific authors." He has reviewed articles for more than 50 journals and has been on the editorial boards of 10 international journals, including the *Journal of Sport & Exercise Psychology, International Journal of Sport Psychology,* and *International Journal of Sport and Exercise Psychology.* His major research interests include self-concept and motivational constructs, evaluations of teaching effectiveness, developmental psychology, quantitative analysis, sport psychology, peer review, gender differences, peer support, and antibullying interventions.

Paule Miquelon, PhD, received her PhD in social psychology at the Université du Québec à Montréal. She completed her MS in leisure sciences at the Université du Québec à Trois-Rivières, during which she studied the relationship between group motivation and team performance. Her main research area is human motivation, with a special interest in health psychology. She is particularly interested in the relationship between personal goals self-concordance and psychological well-being and physical health.

Nikos Ntoumanis, PhD, is a senior lecturer in sport and exercise psychology in the School of Sport and Exercise Sciences at the University of Birmingham, United Kingdom. He graduated from the University of Athens in Greece with a BEd in physical education and sports science in 1993. He then moved to the United Kingdom to complete his MS in sports science at Loughborough University (1995) and his PhD in medical sciences at the University of Exeter (1999). One of his PhD studies received the third prize in the Young Investigators competition at the second annual congress of the European College of Sport Science. Ntoumanis is on the editorial board of four sport psychology journals and has over 40 refereed journal articles in the areas of motivation, anxiety, and coping. He is also a chartered psychologist with the British Psychological Society and a British Association of Sport and Exercise Sciences accredited researcher for sport and exercise psychology.

Artur Poczwardowski, PhD, has teaching, research, and consulting activities that center on applied sport psychology. Courses he has taught include psychosocial aspects of sport, interpersonal dynamics in sport, group dynamics in sport, applied sport psychology, motor learning and control, and qualitative research methods. His research focuses on delivery of sport psychology services, coach–athlete relationships, and coping strategies of elite performers. He has over 20 publications and 40 professional presentations on the national and international levels to his credit. For over a decade, he has consulted with athletes and teams in a number of sports (e.g., judo, soccer, golf, track and field, air-pistol shooting, speed skating). At the elite level, he worked with the Polish national judo team (1992 Olympics) and St. Lawrence University division I women's hockey team (United States). Poczwardowski received his PhD in exercise and sport science with specialization in psychosocial aspects of sport from the University of Utah, a master's degree from the University of Physical Education in Gdansk, Poland (physical education and coaching), and a master's degree from Gdansk University, Poland (psychology).

Harry Prapavessis, PhD, is a senior lecturer in the Department of Sport and Exercise Science at the University of Auckland. He received his PhD from the University of Western Australia in 1992. His research fits within the broad area of social and behavioral science and medicine. His research program has focused on four major areas: exercise and health, rehabilitation psychology, group dynamics, and self-presentational issues in exercise and sport.

Tim Rees, PhD, is a lecturer in sport psychology and statistics at the University of Exeter, United Kingdom. He studied for his BA at the University of Wales, Bangor, and remained there to complete his PhD, for which he received the prestigious University of Wales scholarship. His research interests focus upon the impact of social support and attributions on factors underpinning sport performance. Dr. Rees has published in various international peer-reviewed journals, including *Journal of Applied Sport Psychology* and *Research Quarterly for Exercise and Sport.* He has also presented papers at conferences in Europe and the United States and has appeared on national radio and television. As a British Association of Sport and Exercise Sciences accredited sport psychologist, he has worked with various national and international performers in sports such as association football (soccer), rugby, ice dance, and high-board diving.

Harold A. Riemer, PhD, is an associate professor in the faculty of kinesiology and health studies at the University of Regina in Canada. He received his PhD from the Ohio State University in 1995. His research interests fit into the area of organizational behavior in sport-related contexts. His current work focuses on leadership in sport organizations, athlete satisfaction, volunteerism in sport-related contexts, and attitudes toward bodychecking in youth hockey. In his spare time, Riemer enjoys curling and spending time with his three young children in the outdoors canoeing, hiking, fishing, and hunting.

Gangyan Si, PhD, is the head sport psychologist at Hong Kong Sports Institute and is also a professor in the Department of Sport Psychology at Wuhan Institute of Physical Education, China. His current work is mainly involved with mental training and consultation for elite athletes in Hong Kong and mainland China. He travels with athletes for major international competitions, including the Asian Games, world championships, and the Olympic Games. His research interests include competitive sport psychology and social psychology in sport.

Alan L. Smith, PhD, is an associate professor of sport and exercise psychology at Purdue University (Indiana). He also holds an adjunct appointment with the Department of Psychological Sciences and codirects Boilermaker Sport and Performance Psychology Services at Purdue University. His primary research interests pertain to the link between social relationships and motivational processes in sport and physical activity. He is particularly interested in youth peer relationships and the interactive contribution of social agents (e.g., peers and parents) to youth sport and physical activity

motivation. Smith is a fellow of the research consortium of the American Alliance for Health, Physical Education, Recreation and Dance; a member of the editorial board of the *Journal of Sport & Exercise Psychology;* and a certified consultant for the Association for the Advancement of Applied Sport Psychology. He is past chair of the Sport Psychology Academy of the National Association for Sport and Physical Education. In his spare time, Dr. Smith enjoys playing with his two young children, running and other fitness activities, and fantasizing about having additional spare time.

Ronald E. Smith, PhD, is professor of psychology and director of clinical psychology training at the University of Washington. His major research interests are personality; the study of anxiety, stress, and coping; and performance-enhancement research and interventions. He has done extensive work in youth sport, researching the effects of coaching behaviors on child athletes and developing and evaluating intervention programs for coaches and parents, and he has also done considerable consultation in college and professional sport. He is a past president of the Association for the Advancement of Applied Sport Psychology. Dr. Smith has served as head of the social psychology and personality area and as codirector of the clinical sport psychology graduate training program at Washington. He has published more than 150 scientific articles and book chapters, and he has authored or coauthored 23 books on introductory psychology, personality, stress and stress management, sport psychology, and human performance enhancement.

Frank L. Smoll, PhD, is professor of psychology at the University of Washington. He teaches courses in sport psychology, and his administrative duties include serving as human subjects coordinator and codirector of the sport psychology graduate training program. Dr. Smoll's research focuses on coaching behaviors in youth sport and on the psychological effects of competition on children and adolescents. He has authored more than 110 scientific articles and book chapters, and he is coauthor or editor of 15 books and manuals. Dr. Smoll has made over 100 presentations at scientific and professional conferences. His professional honors include election to fellow status in the following organizations: American Psychological Association, American Academy of Kinesiology, and Association for the Advancement of Applied Sport Psychology (AAASP). He was the recipient of the AAASP's 2002 Distinguished Professional Practice Award. With respect to professional services, Dr. Smoll has been an officer for several associations, and he has organized and participated in many sport psychology symposia. He is a certified sport consultant (AAASP) and has been actively involved with local and national youth sport organizations.

Robert J. Vallerand, PhD, is a professor of psychology and director of the laboratoire de recherche sur le comportement social in the Department of Psychology at Université du Québec à Montréal. He has written or edited four books and more than 150 articles and book chapters, mainly in the area of motivation, and has presented a number of invited addresses in several countries. He has also been awarded numerous research grants. He has served as president of the Quebec Society for Research in Psychology and chair of both the social psychology and the sport psychology sections of the Canadian Psychological Association. He has also served as associate editor of *The Canadian Journal of Behavioural Sciences* and as an editorial board member of several journals, including the *Journal of Personality and Social Psychology, Personality and Social Psychology Bulletin, Motivation and Emotion, Journal of Exercise and Sport Psychology, Psychology of Sport and Exercise,* and *International Journal of Sport and Exercise Psychology.* Dr. Vallerand's current research interests focus on the hierarchical model of intrinsic and extrinsic motivation as well as on a new conceptualization of passion toward activities. He has supervised 15 doctoral students, most of whom are now in academia. He is a fellow of the Canadian Psychological Association and an elected member of the Society of Experimental Social Psychology. Dr. Vallerand also received the Sport Science Award from the International Olympic Committee.

Spiridoula Vazou, PhD, completed her doctoral degree in 2004 at the University of Birmingham (thesis: *Peer Motivational Climate in Youth Sport).* She graduated from the University of Athens in Greece with a BEd in physical education and sports science in 1997. She also holds an MS in sports psychology and motor behavior (2001) from the same university. Her research interests are focused on motivational aspects of youth sport as well as the effects of exercise on psychological functioning. She was a competitive swimmer for over 10 years and for the last 9 years has been an active aerobics instructor. Dr. Vazou was recently employed by the School of Education at the University of Crete, Greece.

Marie-Christine Verdet, PhD, is a senior lecturer in sport psychology and physical education at the Université d'Orléans. Her general area of interest is interpersonal relationships in physical education and sport. Her doctoral research has focused on the perceptions of interpersonal relationships within the athletic triangle of elite young gymnasts. A former competitive gymnast herself, she has been a gymnastics coach and a teacher in primary school for 15 years.

Sally A. White, PhD, is dean and professor in the College of Education at Lehigh University, a nationally ranked graduate college in Bethlehem, Pennsylvania. She has facilitated the development of the college's first research center focused on promoting research to practice and has expanded the international program in the Middle East, South America, and Europe. Before Lehigh, Dr. White was a senior consultant with RWD Technologies in Columbia, Maryland, finding innovative e-Learning solutions for Fortune 100 companies. Her career in higher education spans 16 years, and she has served as dean of the graduate school and associate vice president for research at Towson University and held administrative and teaching positions at Illinois State University and the University of New Hampshire. Dr. White is an accomplished scholar who studies achievement motivation in various contexts, including sport, exercise, and academia. She is widely published, has secured federal and foundation grants, and has been honored with teaching and national research awards. She has worked closely with USA Volleyball, chaired a national sport commission, and has been a sport psychology consultant for the U.S. Olympic Committee. She won an early career professional award from AAHPERD and was chosen to attend the Harvard MLE program in 2003. Dr. White is an avid golfer; enjoys flying airplanes; and is involved in music and the arts, including opera, theatre, and ballet.

Paul Wylleman, PhD, is an associate professor of sport psychology as well as a coordinator of the Department of Top Level Sport and Study at the Vrije Universiteit Brussel, where he acts as tutor and counselor to elite student-athletes. He is also a mental consultant to the Belgian Olympic and Interfederal Committee as well as to a number of elite athletes and national teams in tennis, swimming, track and field, golf, figure skating, and judo. He currently serves as secretary-general of the European Federation of Sport Psychology (FEPSAC) and as acting coordinator of the European Forum for Applied Sports Psychologists in Top-Sport (FAST) and FEPSAC's Special Interest Group on Career Transitions. He serves on the editorial board of *Psychology of Sport and Exercise* and *The Sport Psychologist.* His publications include 8 authored, co-authored, and edited books, 22 chapters, 19 peer-reviewed articles, and more than 40 publications in national journals on interpersonal relationships, career development, and lifestyle management of talented and elite athletes, as well as on the role of the applied sport psychologist.

You'll find
other outstanding
sport psychology resources at

www.HumanKinetics.com

In the U.S. call

1-800-747-4457

Australia..08 8277 1555
Canada...1-800-465-7301
Europe...+44 (0) 113 255 5665
New Zealand.....................................0064 9 448 1207

HUMAN KINETICS
The Information Leader in Physical Activity
P.O. Box 5076 • Champaign, IL 61825-5076 USA